Graham Freudenberg grew up in Brisbane during the Second World War. A journalist by profession, he worked closely with leaders of the Australian Labor Party as adviser and speechwriter, including two prime ministers and three premiers of New South Wales from 1961 to 2005. His father served with the First AIF on Gallipoli.

By the same author:

A Certain Grandeur – Gough Whitlam in Politics
Cause for Power – Official History of the New South Wales Labor Party
A Figure of Speech – A Political Memoir

GRAHAM FREUDENBERG

Churchill
and
Australia

MACMILLAN
Pan Macmillan Australia

. Imperial measurements have been used in this book as they were in documents
and letters from the two world wars.

1 inch	25.4 millimetres	1 centimetre	0.394 inches
1 foot	30.5 centimetres	1 metre	3.28 feet
1 yard	0.914 metres	1 metre	1.09 yards
1 mile	1.61 kilometres	1 kilometre	0.621 miles
1 acre	0.405 hectares	1 hectare	2.47 acres

First published 2008 in Macmillan by Pan Macmillan Australia Pty Limited
This Macmillan edition published 2009 by Pan Macmillan Australia Pty Limited
1 Market Street, Sydney

National Library of Australia
Cataloguing-in-Publication data:

Freudenberg, Graham (Norman Graham), 1934–
Churchill and Australia/Graham Freudenberg.

978 1 4050 3944 4 (pbk.)

Churchill, Winston, Sir, 1874–1965.
Great Britain – Politics and government – 20th century.
Great Britain – Foreign relations – Australia.
Australia – Foreign relations – Great Britain.

940.5322

Typeset by Midland Typesetters, Australia
Printed in Australia by McPherson's Printing Group

Papers used by Pan Macmillan Australia Pty Ltd are natural, recyclable products made from
wood grown in sustainable forests. The manufacturing processes conform to the environmental
regulations of the country of origin.

Contents

Author's preface

This story is set on the stage of the British Empire. I belong to the last Australian generation that grew up under the Empire as both a going concern and a focus for allegiance. Mine was also the last Australian generation that, in adolescence, took being British for granted; and many of us attached equal weight to the definitions inscribed on the Australian passport after 1948: 'Australian citizen – British subject'. As children during the Second World War, we listened to broadcasts by King George VI with reverence, and by Winston Churchill with awe. The background crackle and short-wave surge of the wireless, like the low roar of a distant ocean, added drama to the miracle of hearing London calling. I saw Winston Churchill in the flesh, in the House of Commons in 1956, the year of the Suez crisis, the sunset of the British Empire.

From 1907 to 1955, Churchill's conflicts with Australia were about his concept of the Empire and Australia's role in it. The sections of this book that deal with his disputes with the wartime governments under Menzies and Fadden and, most severely, with the Curtin Labor Government in 1942, are partly a reply to the one-sided accounts in Volumes III and IV of Churchill's war memoirs. It is proper that I should declare my long association with the Australian Labor Party, and my admiration of John Curtin. Yet for my generation, nothing can remotely outweigh the intense conviction that, except for Winston Churchill, the doctrines and practices of Hitler's Germany would have prevailed in Europe and far beyond, protracted, in Churchill's words, by 'the lights of a perverted science'; and that the British Empire, including Australia, would have been enrolled as an accomplice in Hitler's crimes.

Acknowledgements

Carol Summerhayes' indispensable contribution to this work crowns a collaboration that spans forty years. Her creative talents and expertise have enabled me to keep up the pleasant fiction that I write it all by myself in hand. Tom Kusano provided an orderly lifestyle in which I was able to do the work. Phil Davis kept me on track in developing the themes of this story. Les Carlyon, who has set new standards for Australian historiography, and the incomparable Barry Jones, were generous and perceptive in reading the early manuscript, as were Roger Holdich and Gordon Murphy. Dr David Clune gave invaluable help from the resources of the New South Wales Parliamentary Library. Through Alex Mitchell I made the public commitment to this task, which my publisher at Pan Macmillan, Tom Gilliatt, encouraged and enhanced at every stage. I thank my editors, Sybil Nolan and Brianne Tunnicliffe, for their sympathetic understanding. Continuing encouragement came from my friends of my own generation, the Churchie Class of '51, John Biggs, David Cohen, John Godfrey, John Greenwood, Barrie Hayne, Jack Hutchinson and Ian Macfarlane, my brother Rex, and Evan Williams. The inspiration of Andrew Smart kept me in touch with the new generation. I thank Laurie McNeice for her guidance on matters Canadian. I owe the debt of a lifetime to Gough Whitlam who, apart from everything else, taught me the first lesson of a would-be historian: 'Go to the documents'.

Prologue

'The Prime Minister is in a belligerent mood,' Winston Churchill's doctor, Sir Charles Wilson, wrote in his diary for 9 January 1942. A month after Pearl Harbor, Churchill was taking a break in Florida from momentous talks with President Franklin Roosevelt at the White House. Together, Churchill and Roosevelt had forged the Grand Alliance against Germany and Japan. They had agreed to 'Beat Hitler First'; the war against Japan would be 'a holding operation'. Wilson recorded:

> He told us that he had sent a stiff telegram to Curtin, the Prime Minister of Australia. The situation was making Australia jumpy about invasion. Curtin was not satisfied with the air position. He had renewed his representations to London in blunt terms. The P.M. fulminated in his reply. London had not made a fuss when it was bombed. Why should Australia? At one moment he took the line that Curtin and his [Labor] government did not represent the people of Australia. At another that the Australians came of bad stock.

Not for the first or last time, Australia seemed to bring out the worst in Winston Churchill. Often enough to form a discernible pattern,

Australia was on the wrong side of the very qualities – his strength of will, singleness of purpose, his refusal to 'give way, in things great or small, large or petty', the power of his imagination to set grim reality at defiance, his mastery of the English language – that made Winston Churchill, as the philosopher Isaiah Berlin described him, 'the saviour of his country, the largest human being of his time'. His total self-belief and his urge for action had their stubborn, reckless, and spiteful aspect. Australia often seemed to bring out that darker side.

Churchill's commanding importance to Australia rests on the fact that the British Empire was central to Australian history for the five decades he strode the imperial stage, the years between the inauguration of the Commonwealth of Australia in 1901 and the Cold War. The theme of the first part of this book is Churchill's belief in the Empire as proof of Britain's greatness. The theme of the second part is that, for all his love of the Empire, Churchill was obliged to accept its decline, if not its fall, as the price of defeating Hitler's Germany.

Churchill's involvement with Australia, unparalleled by any other British leader, covered and influenced every stage of our transition from a dependent colony of the British Empire to a dependent ally of the United States. From beginning to end, his primary interest in Australia lay in its capacity to contribute to Britain's military strength, on which he believed everything else depended. Australia mostly accepted this view. But when the supreme crisis of the war against Japan forced the Australian leadership to look to the United States, Churchill reacted angrily. A relationship which began with the boyish enthusiasm of the Boer War days sank into bitterness and recrimination.

Churchill's jibe about 'bad stock', aimed presumably at Australia's convict origins – or possibly its Irish element – may be forgiven as the exasperation of an embattled and exhausted Titan. Wilson (later Lord Moran) noted in his diary: 'I did not worry about the Australians. I knew that he had been persuaded to tone down the cable before it was sent. Besides, he liked them as men and respected them as fighting soldiers.' Nevertheless, Churchill's use of the word 'stock' carries a special significance. In any story about Australia and the British Empire, the prevailing assumptions about white superiority are always in the background. In the age of empire, words such as stock, breed, blood, and race were used casually, complacently, and interchangeably by Victorians and Edwardians such as Churchill. To be proud of the British Empire was to be proud of the British race. After Churchill had taken part in the British army's last cavalry charge in 1898, at Omdurman in the Sudan, and had shot and killed a couple of the ten thousand Dervishes slaughtered there, the young lieutenant wrote to an army friend in India: 'My faith in our race and our blood was much strengthened.'

At the turn of the century, in the year that saw the death of Queen Victoria and the birth of the Commonwealth of Australia, the sense of white superiority was deemed thoroughly compatible with enlightened liberal and radical views. Ideas of racial superiority were integral to the prevailing doctrines of imperialism and nationalism. The vocabulary of race permeated public discourse in the most advanced democracies. The Australian Labor Party, from its birth ten years before, was pre-eminently the party of White Australia. The poet of the Empire, Rudyard Kipling, urged the United States to take up 'the white man's burden' of bringing civilisation to the unbleached peoples of the world – 'half devil and half child'. In his will establishing the Rhodes Scholarships, Cecil Rhodes wrote in 1899: 'I contend that we are the finest race in the world and that the more of the world we inhabit the better it is for the human race. Just fancy those parts that are at present inhabited by the most despicable of human beings, what an alteration there would be in them if they were brought under Anglo-Saxon influence.'

Churchill was more specific. 'I do not admit,' he said in 1937, 'that a great wrong has been done to the Red Indians of America, or the black people of Australia. I do not admit that a wrong has been done to these people by the fact that a stronger race, a higher grade of race, a more worldly-wise race, to put it that way, has come in and taken their place.' The context of these remarks makes reading them all the more sombre today. Churchill was appearing before an inquiry into Jewish immigration into Palestine. He referred to the 'dog in the manger attitude' of the Palestinians, and the superiority of Jewish settlers. Meanwhile, the United States, Australia, and other countries of like mind were severely limiting the entry of Jewish refugees fleeing Hitler's doctrines of racial purity and the Aryan master race. Churchill confessed to Charles Wilson in 1943: 'When you learn to think of a race as inferior beings, it is difficult to get rid of that way of thinking. When I was a subaltern the Indian did not seem to me equal to the white man.' Yet he could use the same thoughts to inspire. The peoples of the British Empire, he told the Canadian Parliament in December, 1941, 'do not seek the lands or wealth of any country, but they are a tough and hardy lot. We have not journeyed all this way across the centuries, across the oceans, across the mountains, across the prairies, because we are made of sugar candy!'

Churchill gloried in the rich diversity of the Empire that his 'famous island race' had created. So did most Australians. To many of them it was proof of a racial superiority endorsed by divine providence. But what mattered most to Australians was not the diversity of empire but the homogeneity, their sameness with the people of Britain and between themselves. There was always this basic difference: when Australians thought about the Empire, they were trying to define a place for Australia within it; for Churchill, it was not so much the British Empire, but Britain's Empire.

When Churchill spoke about the Australians' 'bad stock', he was echoing their deepest fears about themselves. Our convict origins were only one element in our anxieties. From the 1870s, when the Australian-born began to outnumber those arrived from the British Isles, colonial orators and observers began to worry that conditions in Australia, including its remarkable prosperity, urban concentration, and warm climate, might produce moral, mental, and physical degeneration. These fears were by no means allayed by the condescension of English grandees like Lord Beauchamp who, before taking up the governorship of New South Wales in 1899, cabled greetings to his future subjects, adapting a verse by Rudyard Kipling:

Your birthstain have you turned to good
Forcing strong wills perverse to steadfastness.

4

The first flush of the tropics in your blood
And at your feet success.

No event in Australian history is more closely associated with Churchill, with praise or blame, than the Gallipoli campaign of 1915. It gained its immediate power as a national legend because it proved that the British race in the Antipodes had not degenerated. In an almost theological sense, Australian Britons had been born again in the baptism of fire at Anzac Cove. Andrew Barton 'Banjo' Paterson, who in 1900 became the first noteworthy Australian of Churchill's acquaintance when they were war correspondents together in South Africa, wrote:

The mettle that a race can show,
Is proved with shot and steel,
And now we know what nations know
And feel what nations feel.

The tensions between Churchill and Australian leaders, from Alfred Deakin to John Curtin, reflected Australians' mixed feelings about their place in the British Empire, divided between nationalism and imperialism, and between Empire loyalties and the desire for a more independent Australia. Most of the Australian leaders in themselves embodied these tensions: Deakin, Australia's second Prime Minister, described himself as 'an independent Australian Briton'. Churchill's ambivalence about Australia was a mirror-image of Australia's own ambivalence about itself.

For the Australians, the ultimate purpose of the Empire was to protect 'White Australia', itself a project of empire. British sea power had made White Australia a viable policy. For Australians, belonging to an Empire composed so largely of non-whites was a source of anxiety as well as pride and identity. In grudging deference to imperial opinion in London, the first Commonwealth Parliament diluted its restrictive immigration laws, replacing absolute colour bans with a language test deemed by Whitehall to be less offensive to the King's 'coloured' subjects. The small minority of Australian republicans argued that Britain's responsibilities and Whitehall's favouritism towards the 'nigger empire', as the nationalist and republican writers in the Sydney *Bulletin* called it, conflicted with its duty to protect White Australia. Inevitably, White Australia ceased to be official Australian policy when the British Empire ceased to be.

Robert Rhodes James, whose admiration for Churchill never got the better of his objectivity, wrote in *Churchill: A Study in Failure 1900–1939*:

> In his view the Empire was a possession that gave to Britain a world position and prestige that she would not otherwise have enjoyed, and whose absolute retention was essential . . . Churchill's interest in Imperial matters had never been one of the major themes of his political career. He accepted the British Empire; he believed deeply in its continuance and in its civilizing mission; any diminution of its power and authority dismayed him. The concept of the Commonwealth as a world entity did not attract Churchill.

There was a conceptual gap at the heart of Churchill's failure to engage wholeheartedly with Australia. Robert Menzies, heading his first Australian administration, complained to Cabinet in June 1941: 'Churchill has no conception of the British dominions as separate entities.' This was the problem. It was the source of disputes and misunderstandings between them for nearly half a century. From his tussles with Alfred Deakin at the Colonial Conference in 1907 to his brutal confrontation with John Curtin in 1942, Churchill's matchless gift – his imagination – failed him when it came to understanding why Australians should want to assert any sense of separate identity. He was the more impatient with the Australians because, more than any other part of the Empire they insisted on their essential Britishness – except perhaps for the New Zealanders, who even so were proud to acknowledge the Maori contribution in both world wars.

During Churchill's glory years from 1940 to 1945, George VI's private secretary, Sir Alan Lascelles, had unique opportunities to observe Churchill's relations with the dominions and their prime ministers. His verdict, confided to his diary in October, 1943, was that 'Winston is incurably colonial-minded'. Revising his diaries in his old age, Lascelles noted in 1967: 'By this I meant that Winston tended to think of the self-governing Dominions as Victorian colonies. I don't think he had ever absorbed the 1931 Statute of Westminster' – the formal recognition of Dominion equality. Lascelles then thought fit to record a story which he admitted 'was probably untrue but well founded'. He wrote: 'At the time of the Coronation in 1953 when it was suggested to him that he should participate in the Naval Review on board the ship allotted to the other Commonwealth Prime Ministers, he was reported to have protested indignantly: "What – am I to go round the British Navy with all that poor white trash?"' By 1953, Menzies, back in power for the second time, was the very doyen of the 'poor white trash'. At Churchill's funeral in 1965, from the crypt of St Paul's Cathedral in London, Menzies would speak to the world in praise of Churchill, on behalf of the Commonwealth of Nations.

WHEN CHURCHILL SAID that he had not become the King's First Minister in order to preside over the liquidation of the British Empire – a shot across the bows, aimed at President Roosevelt's support for Indian independence – he imagined Queen Victoria's Empire with India of the Raj the jewel in the crown. At the time, however, Churchill's priority was not saving the British Empire, but using the Empire to save Britain and defeat Hitler. His love of the British Empire boiled down to his love of England. Unless one accepts that, there can be no true understanding of what Winston Churchill did on behalf of the British Empire or his ultimate sacrifice of the Empire's greatness in order that his England might survive. It is not, perhaps, too far-fetched to imagine that the idea of a greater English-speaking union appealed to him in large measure because its common bond would be the language of England, and that Shakespeare would triumph where he had failed.

1

'Our account with the Boers'

1900

'The great Winston Churchill rode through the town of Johannesburg on a bicycle in the night,' Banjo Paterson wrote in the *Sydney Morning Herald*. As early as June, 1900, Paterson, balladeer and war correspondent with the Australian soldiers fighting for the British Empire in South Africa, could take it for granted that readers in Australia would be familiar with 'the great Winston Churchill', and interested in his exploits. On this occasion, the British capture of Johannesburg, Paterson informed them that Lieutenant Churchill had told him 'the Dutch were leaving Johannesburg wholesale, the English scouts were in the town, and some Dutch were capturing English, while other English were capturing Dutch – in fact, [it was] a regular pandemonium'.

Churchill was then twenty-five. For the next half century he was seldom out of the Australian newspapers. Both Paterson and Churchill had gone to South Africa as war correspondents in search of adventure and fame. For Paterson, a Sydney solicitor turned poet and journalist ten years Churchill's senior, such hopes were incidental to his main job of reporting the deeds of the colonial Australian contingents helping to suppress the independence of the Dutch-descended

Boer farmers and their republics, the Transvaal and the Orange Free State. For Churchill, the adventure and fame were central to his limitless ambitions.

'This correspondent job is nothing to me,' Churchill told Paterson, 'but I mean to get into Parliament through it'. In his account of his South African experiences, published in 1935, Paterson recalled the young Churchill saying: 'They wouldn't listen to me when I put up for parliament because they had never heard of me.'

Now, he said, 'I am going to plaster the *Morning Post* with cables about our correspondent, Mr Winston Churchill, driving an armoured train, or pointing out to Lord Roberts [the British commander-in-chief] where the enemy is. When I go up for parliament again, I'll fly in.'

The young Churchill, Paterson wrote, 'was the most curious combination of ability and swagger. The Army could neither understand nor like him; for when it came to getting anywhere or securing any job, he made his own rules.'

The Boer War in South Africa was the last of Queen Victoria's seventy 'little wars' of empire. It was also the final act in the scramble for Africa by which the European powers – Britain, France, Germany, Belgium, Italy, Spain, and Portugal – carved up the Dark Continent in pursuit of their civilising mission. With exquisite irony, the last war in the European grab for black Africa was fought against two white Christian republics. Britain had occupied the Dutch colony around Cape Town in 1806. Rejecting British authority and the edict outlawing slavery in the Empire in 1834, several thousand Dutch farmers, the Boers, trekked north and set up republics across the Orange and Vaal rivers. Following their victory at the battle of Majuba Hill in 1881, they received grudging recognition from the imperial government, but five years later, the discovery of gold on the Rand revived London's determination to assert its control.

A rush of mainly British immigrants, including about a thousand from Australia, flooded into the Boer lands. The British High Commissioner at the Cape, Alfred Milner, backed to the hilt by the

British Secretary of State for the Colonies, Joseph Chamberlain, demanded a range of electoral, tax, and legal concessions for the so-called Outlanders. President Paul Kruger and the Boer governments, noisily supported by Kaiser Wilhelm II of Germany, rejected the British demands. Kruger's intransigence provided the excuse for a regime change by a war which the British Government was determined to have. In twenty-first-century parlance, it was decidedly 'a war of choice'.

In 1897, Winston Churchill, a 22-year-old cavalry subaltern serving in India and Afghanistan, wrote a newspaper article which he entitled 'Our Account with the Boers':

> Imperial aid must redress the wrongs of the Outlanders. Imperial troops must curb the insolence of the Boers . . . If it be unscrupulous for the people of Great Britain to defend their most vital interests, to extend their protection to their fellow countrymen in distress and to maintain the integrity of their Empire, 'unscrupulousness' is a word we shall have to face. Sooner or later, in a righteous cause or a picked quarrel, with the approval of Europe or in the teeth of Germany, for the sake of our Empire, for the sake of our honour, for the sake of the race, we must fight the Boers.

'A picked quarrel' it was to be, and, not for the last time, Australians, from their outpost of empire, entered an imperial war almost completely indifferent to, and ignorant of, the character, motives, and abilities of their enemy. Banjo Paterson perhaps had reservations. Soon after his arrival in November, 1899, he interviewed Olive Schreiner, South African author of the classic *Story of an African Farm*. One of Paterson's earliest despatches to Sydney, dated 21 January 1900, contained a sympathetic report of his interview:

> 'You Australians and New Zealanders and Canadians,' she said, 'I cannot understand why you come here light-heartedly to shoot down other colonists of whom you know nothing – it is terrible. Such fine men too – fine fellows . . .

'The English Tommy Atkins goes where he is sent – he fights because he is ordered; but you people – you are all volunteers! Why have you come?

'You say that England was at war, and you wished to show the world that when the Mother Country got into a war, the colonies were prepared to take their place beside her. Yes, but you ought to ask, you ought to make inquiries before you come over! You Australians do not understand. This is a capitalists' war. They want to get control of the Rand and the mines.'

Fifteen years before, the man destined to become Australia's first Prime Minister had given the definitive Australian answer to the kind of questions that Olive Schreiner put to Banjo Paterson. The orator was Edmund Barton, then Speaker of the New South Wales Legislative Assembly. At issue was the colony's offer to send a volunteer contingent to campaign with the British army in the Sudan, following the news of the killing of General George Gordon at the hands of Islamic fundamentalists at Khartoum. 'If England's quarrels are not to be ours, when are our quarrels to be hers?' Barton told a 'Monster' public meeting. 'Is the good old country always to be succouring us and not to expect succour from us? Let it be known, not only to the people of Australia, but to the whole world, that we belong to the greatest Empire that ever the sun has risen on.'

Australia was fighting for the Empire at the hour of its birth as a nation. The Boer War coincided with the final stages of the creation of the Commonwealth of Australia, and the exciting prospect of a war competed for interest with referendum campaigns for a federal constitution. In June and July, 1899, first Queensland, then New South Wales and Victoria, offered troops in expectation that Britain would soon move to settle accounts with the Boers. News of the outbreak of war reached Australia on 11 October and, by the end of the month, the SS *Medic* sailed from Melbourne with a Victorian contingent, picking up contingents from Tasmania, South Australia, and Western Australia on the way to Cape Town. Banjo Paterson sailed from Sydney with the First Australian Horse contingent, on 28 October. These remarkable feats of mobilisation were sped by fears among the volunteers that the fun would all be over by Christmas.

As things turned out, the Boer War fell into three phases: British reverses, under the command of General Sir Redvers Buller in the first months; next, British victories under the commander-in-chief, Lord Roberts of Kandahar, convincing the public in Britain and Australia that the war had been won – 'mission accomplished' as it were; and then, the long guerrilla war waged by Sir Herbert Kitchener with 'methods of barbarism', in the words of the British Liberal Leader, Sir Henry Campbell-Bannerman. These methods saw the first use of the term 'concentration camp' – the separation of Boer women and children from their husbands and sons and fathers, all of whom were deemed to be insurgents.

The Boer War helped define the relationship between Britain and Australia, and Churchill's role in it, for the next forty years. In Australia, opposition to the war was invariably couched in terms of loyalty to the Empire, just as opposition to Australia's involvement in the war in Vietnam sixty-five years later, and to the invasion of Iraq, over a century after the Boer War, had to be stated in terms of loyalty to the American alliance. William Holman, a future Labor Premier of New South Wales, said in that colony's Legislative Assembly on 10 October 1899:

> I am loyal to the Empire. I happen to have been born in England and come of as solid and patriotic English stock as Mr Barton and Mr Cook. But I see, with emotions of shame and indignation which I can hardly express, the name and reputation of that Empire being dragged in the dust at the behest of a little gang of swindling speculators on the Rand. We know that this affair is no movement of the Empire at all.

Barton had been primed to make an interjection: 'Would the honourable gentleman mind telling us one thing – whether he wants the Boers to win or the British?' Holman: 'I am not alarmed at any question of that sort. Whilst my country is fighting in a just cause, I hope I shall be as ready to support its claims as any other member. But as I believe from the bottom of my heart that this is the most iniquitous, most immoral war ever waged with any race, I hope that England may be defeated.' Shock and horror!

Inevitably, the contradictions inherent in a war waged by an empire in the name of democracy accumulated. The right to vote, which the British Government claimed was being denied to British subjects in Johannesburg, was not available to the majority of British subjects in Britain itself. But the origins of the war became irrelevant. In March, 1900, when Roberts' army, including units from New South Wales and Queensland, had occupied Bloemfontein, the capital of the Orange Free State, the war correspondents gave a celebratory dinner. Churchill had taken part in the march on Bloemfontein; but his name does not appear among the signatures on Paterson's souvenir menu. Next to Paterson's own name is the signature of Rudyard Kipling, the poet of the Empire. Paterson's dispatch to the *Herald* records: 'Kipling speaks very humorously, and made a great hit by proposing an unexpected toast, the health of Paul Kruger. He said that Kruger had done more to knit the Empire together than any man that ever lived. He had been consistent throughout in his refusal to budge an inch from his position and he had enabled us to make a white man's country of South Africa.'

For the Australians in South Africa, the war had another dimension. Their motivation was not only to show solidarity with Britain but to show that their British 'stock' had not deteriorated. We might be different, and that was a good thing, but we had not degenerated. In his ballad *With French to Kimberley*, Banjo Paterson wrote:

And in the front the Lancers that New South Wales had sent
With easy stride across the plain their long, lean Walers went
Unknown, untried, those squadrons were, but proudly out they drew
Beside the English regiments that fought at Waterloo.

At the same time, Paterson wanted to emphasise the distinctiveness of the new breed of Australians. He wrote about these 'long-legged young fellows, brown and hard-faced, and all with the alert wide-awake look that distinguishes the Australian soldier from the more stolid English Tommy'.

Churchill's first despatch to the *Morning Post* reported his earliest encounter with Australian soldiers, even before he reached Cape Town. A mounted squadron, the New South Wales Lancers, had gone to England in 1897 for Queen Victoria's sixtieth Jubilee, and stayed on for training at Aldershot. They volunteered to serve in South Africa as soon as the war broke out. In his first letter datelined 'RMS *Dunottar Castle* at sea, 26 October 1899', Churchill wrote:

On the 23rd we sighted a sail – or rather the smoke of another steamer. As the comparatively speedy *Dunottar Castle* overtook the stranger, everybody's interest was aroused. Under the scrutiny of many brand-new telescopes and field glasses – for all wanted to see as much of a war as possible – she developed as the *Nineveh*, hired transport carrying the Australian Lancers to the Cape. The Lancers crowded the bulwarks and rigging of the *Nineveh* and one of them waggled a flag violently. An officer on our ship replied with a pocket-handkerchief. The Australians asked questions: 'Is Sir Redvers Buller on board?' The answer 'Yes' was signalled back, and immediately the Lancers gave three tremendous cheers, waving their broad-brimmed hats and gesticulating with energy while the steam siren emitted a frantic whoop of salutation. She signalled again: 'What won the Cesarewitch?'

Thus Winston Churchill was the first writer to witness and record the oldest tradition of the Australian soldier overseas. If it had been a fortnight later, the New South Wales Lancers would have asked not the result of the latest big horse race in England, but 'What won the Melbourne Cup?'.

Churchill's springboard to Empire-wide fame was his 'great escape' from the Boers. He spent his twenty-fifth birthday, 30 November 1899, in prison in Pretoria, the Transvaal capital, after he was seized by the Boers from the wreckage of an armoured train. 'I am 25 today,' he wrote. 'It is terrible to think how little time remains.' He escaped a fortnight later, and avoided recapture by 'my strange luck or the favour of heaven – which you will', when he chanced upon the residence of a British mine manager, one John Howard, who told him: 'Thank God you have come here. It is the only house for twenty miles where you would not have been handed over, but we are all British here, and we will see you through.' Churchill made sure that his escape made news around the Empire, a bright episode during 'Black Week' in December and the gloomy first phase of the war.

The Australian units in South Africa were mixed into the British army, so it is not surprising that Churchill's despatches contained few specific references to their deeds. He paid tribute, however, to their part in the capture of Pretoria, the Boer capital, in June, 1900:

> Colonel de L'Isle's Corps of mounted infantry, composed mainly of Australians, made a much shorter circuit, reaching the level ground before the cavalry espied a Boer Maxim retreating towards the town. To this they immediately gave chase, and the strong Waler horses were urged to their utmost speed. The appearance of this clattering swarm of horsemen must have been formidable to those below. But we who watched from the heights saw what Ian Hamilton [commanding the campaign], who was in high spirits, described as 'a charge of infuriated mice' streaming across the brown veldt, so great are the distances in modern war.

General Sir Ian Hamilton would command some of the 'infuriated mice', and their brothers or sons, among the Anzacs at Gallipoli fifteen years later.

By the time, thirty-four years later, that Paterson wrote a long pen-portrait of Churchill for his South African memoir, Churchill's career was a study in failure. He had indeed been 'pretty well everything' – President of the Board of Trade, Home Secretary, First Lord of the Admiralty, Secretary of State for War, Secretary of State for the Colonies, and Chancellor of the Exchequer. His ferocious opposition to Indian self-government had meant his exclusion from the all-party national government formed in the crisis of the Great Depression. He had not yet begun his crusade against Hitler, who had come to power in Germany in 1933. These were gloomy years for Churchill although, chirpy as ever, he insisted on being introduced to Don Bradman at London's Victoria Station in April 1934. But Paterson must have believed that he was writing about a man of yesterday, a great has-been, when he wrote of the Churchill he had met in 1900:

> With his great social influence, his aggressiveness, and undoubted ability, he was a man to be feared if not liked. He would even take a fall out of General French: and that, for a correspondent, was about equal to earning the VC twice over.
>
> One day, when something had gone wrong and Johnnie French was in a particularly bad temper, Churchill said to me: 'Come along up to HQ. I am going to give French a turn. He was very rude to me last time we met.'
>
> On that particular day I would as soon have faced a Hyrcanian tiger, and said so. But Churchill insisted: 'General,' he said, 'I want to ask whether I am to report today's operations as a success or a failure?'
>
> French (choking down a few appropriate words that he would have liked to say): 'Well, Churchill, that depends on how you look at it.'
>
> Churchill: 'I am afraid that my point of view would not carry much weight, Sir. What I want to know is, whether from *your* point of view, the affair was a success or a failure?'
>
> French (very dignified): 'If you apply to Major Haig, he will let you see the official report. Good morning.'

Paterson concluded: 'It was a victory for the Press, but one felt that a few such victories would mean annihilation.' General Sir John French would become commander-in-chief of the British Expeditionary Force in France in 1914. He was present at the meeting of the British War Council in January, 1915, that approved Churchill's Gallipoli venture. Haig would replace French as commander-in-chief in France in 1916, become the architect of the bloodbaths of the Somme and Passchendaele, and gain credit from the Australian successes in France in 1918.

Between October, 1899, and June, 1902, more than sixteen thousand troops and sixteen thousand horses – the 'Walers' mentioned by Paterson and Churchill – sailed to South Africa from Australia. Five hundred men died of wounds or disease. About two thirds of the Australian forces were despatched under the authority of the six colonial governments, before Federation on 1 January 1901. Most units bore titles with a distinctively Australian flavour, such as 'First Australian Horse' (from New South Wales), 'Bushmen', 'Citizen Bushmen', or 'Imperial Bushmen'. After Federation, they were formed as companies of the Australian Commonwealth Horse. The units from Australia were attached to larger British forces under British command. Lord Roberts gratified Australian sentiment with his testimonial: 'All the colonials did extremely well. They were very intelligent and they had what I wanted our men to have, more individuality. They could find their way about the country far better than the British cavalry men could do.' With contingents from Canada and New Zealand as well as Australia, the Empire put 450,000 men in the field, against 90,000 Boers at most.

Churchill returned to England in July, 1900. Paterson stayed until the following September. The war had passed its glamorous days, but the impression Churchill had made on Paterson never left him. He concluded his 1934 profile:

> Churchill had such a strong personality that even in those early days, the army were prepared to bet that he would either get into jail or become Prime Minister. He had done some soldiering; but he had an uncanny knack of antagonising his superior and inferior officers. As he said himself: 'I could see nothing in soldiering except looking after the horses' backs [Churchill actually said 'looking at horses' arses' but this was deemed too vulgar for Australian readers in 1934] and the men's mess-tins in barracks. There's not enough wars to make soldiering worthwhile.' The soldiers tried to retaliate by stirring him up in their own crude way. Once, when he went as a subaltern in charge of some expedition, they sent him a wire: 'Don't make a bigger fool of yourself than you can help.' But trying to get through the hide of the pachydermatous Churchill with a telegram was like shooting 'old man rhinossyhoss' with paper darts.

Exactly as he told Banjo Paterson he would, Churchill made the most of his South African adventures. Although he was the grandson of an English duke and an American millionaire, he inherited no fortune of his own; throughout his career, he depended on his earnings from his books, journalism, and lectures to keep up his lavish lifestyle. His escape from the Boers provided the centrepiece for a lecture tour of the United States and Canada during the last six weeks of 1900. He was already famous enough to have his first lecture in New York chaired by Mark Twain, who introduced him by saying: 'Mr Churchill by his father is an Englishman, by his mother he is an American, no doubt a blend that makes the perfect man.' No doubt the American author was ready to overlook any embellishments in Churchill's story. After all, on a visit to Australia in 1895, Twain had been delighted to find Australian history 'full of beautiful lies – and all of them true'.

Churchill found the New Yorkers 'distressingly pro-Boer'. But the statesman already in him sought a deeper purpose for the war. As early as March, 1900, he had declared: 'A generous and forgiving policy must be followed . . . Peace and happiness can only come to South Africa through the fusion and concord of the Dutch and British races, who must forever live side by side under the supremacy of Britain.' Barely six years later, when he was only thirty-one, and already helping to run the Empire, Churchill was able to match his words with deeds, although the generous concessions he helped achieve for the vanquished Boers were to mean generations of oppression for the blacks of South Africa. As for the Australians, Banjo Paterson probably expressed the feelings of most of them:

They came to prove to all the earth that kinship conquers space
And those who fight the British Isles must fight the British race.

2

'I am a glow-worm'
1901–07

Australia's help to Britain in punishing the Boers gave Churchill a resounding imperial theme for his maiden speech in the House of Commons. He was an instant success in the theatre in which he was to star for the next fifty-five years. Churchill acknowledged that the House heard him with 'kindness and patience, not on my own account, but because of a certain splendid memory' – his father, Lord Randolph Churchill, whose rashness, arrogance, and lack of judgement had destroyed a brilliant political career. The maverick in the father might have been detected in the unfashionable defiance of the son: 'If I were a Boer fighting in the field – and if I were a Boer, I hope I should be fighting in the field . . .' It was, he said, on both sides 'a war of duty'. He recommended to 'any honourable members feeling unhappy about the state of affairs in South Africa' a recipe from which he 'derived much exhilaration':

Let them look to the other great dependencies and colonies of the British Empire and see what the effect of the war has been there. Whatever we have lost in doubtful friends in Cape Colony, we have gained ten times, or perhaps twenty times, over in Canada and Australia, where the

19

people – down to the humblest farmer in the most distant provinces – have, by their effective participation in the conflict, been able to realise, as they could never realise before, that they belong to the Empire, and that the Empire belongs to them.

Churchill delivered his maiden speech seven weeks after the Commonwealth of Australia had been proclaimed on 1 January 1901, three weeks before the death of Queen Victoria on 22 January. In the timing of her death, the old Queen (she was eighty-one, and had been on the throne for sixty-three years) gave a superb example of the maxim of France's Henri Quatre that punctuality is the politeness of kings. A month earlier, and the Australian celebrations would have been utterly spoilt! By her gracious departure, Victoria gave the Empire a new reign for a new nation and a new century. Royal thoughtfulness can go no further. One of her last important duties – on 9 July 1900 – had been to give her royal assent to the Act of the British Parliament establishing the Commonwealth of Australia. The Act embodied the Constitution hammered out in Sydney, Melbourne, and Adelaide at conventions between 1891 and 1898, and then adopted by the people voting in the referendums of 1898 and 1899. Australia became the first nation to be created under a Constitution adopted at the ballot-box. Introducing the bill on 14 May 1900, the Secretary of State for the Colonies, Joseph Chamberlain, told the House of Commons that federation was good for Australia, and 'whatever is good for Australia is good for the whole British Empire'.

In the wake of the Boer War, imperial sentiment enjoyed a resurgence in federated Australia. The sanctification of Queen Victoria's birthday, 24 May, re-named Empire Day in 1904, was another high point for the imperial idea. A voice for Australian nationalism, the Brisbane *Worker*, saw Empire Day as an official endorsement of 'a lickspittle reverence for the Empire and its hereditary monarchs to be infused into the sensitive blood of the State school children'. *The Worker* deplored 'the slobbering adulation of the deceased Queen'. The Labor Party Objective, 'the cultivation of an Australian sentiment based on the development in Australia of an enlightened and self-reliant community', would never be achieved 'while a spirit of grovelling Imperialism and queen-worship is inculcated in our schools,' the labour newspaper said.

Churchill had wasted no time making good his boast to Banjo Paterson that he would use his South African fame to enter the House of Commons. But it was no 'fly-in'. He just scraped in at Oldham on the pro-war, pro-government tide of Britain's first 'khaki election' in October, 1900. He campaigned as a supporter of the Conservative Prime Minister, Lord Salisbury. Churchill lashed his Liberal opponents as 'prigs, prudes and faddists', and described the British Liberal Party as 'hiding from the public view like a toad in a hole, but when it stands forth in all its hideousness we Tories will have to hew the filthy object limb from limb'.

Within three years, he was proclaiming: 'I hate the Tories. I am an English Liberal.' It would be easy to write down Churchill's decision to change parties in 1904 as mere ambition, cynicism, and opportunism. He defected to the British Liberal Party when its fortunes were dramatically on the rise, and abandoned it when the party was in irretrievable decline two decades later. He is alleged to have said: 'To rat once is easy; to re-rat takes ingenuity.' Nevertheless, he genuinely believed that he was fighting to uphold Free Trade, the policy which since the repeal of the Corn Laws in 1846 had made Britain and its Empire the greatest power in the world.

Since the 1870s, Britain had lost its pre-eminence as the workshop of the world. By the turn of the century, in the face of growing competition from the newly unified German Empire and the United States post bellum, British manufacturers were calling for tariff protection. Increasingly, advocates of protectionism in Britain and Australia coupled it with the notion of 'imperial preference'. They wanted to create an Empire Common Market – tariff barriers against the world, free trade within the Empire. Churchill summed up their arguments contemptuously and concisely: 'We are told that the colonies will leave us unless Canadian loyalty is purchased at two shillings a quarter of wheat and Australian allegiance at a penny a pound of wool.'

In Australia, tariff protection for its infant industries was becoming the settled national policy. In Britain, the battle lines between Free Trade and Protection were drawn by the same hand that had made the Boer War – Joseph Chamberlain's, the Secretary of State for the Colonies. In the 1880s, Chamberlain had split the British Liberal Party by his opposition to Home Rule for Ireland, and doomed it to two decades of impotence. Now he was to perform much the same service for the British Conservative Party. Both times, he claimed he was doing it to preserve the strength and unity of the British Empire. Chamberlain split the Conservative Party, destroyed the Balfour Conservative Government, and built for Churchill a golden bridge on which he would cross the floor of the House of Commons in 1904, and reach the ministerial bench of a Liberal government by the end of 1905.

Churchill's ambivalence towards Australia may well have begun with the great Free Trade versus Protection row in Britain. With his tendency to seek base motives in those with whom he disagreed, he detested all Protectionists, colonial or imperial. He was convinced that protection fostered corruption and that it was the product of parochial greed and parish-pump politics. He drew his examples from the United States, and the corrupt corporate power of its late–nineteenth century Gilded Age. We now choose to forget that throughout the long ascendancy of the American Republican Party after the Civil War, the United States was among the most protectionist nations on earth; and in the era of globalisation, we ignore that American economic strength was built on protection. Churchill flatly denied Chamberlain's claim that protection would unite the Empire. 'I do not want a self-contained Empire,' he wrote to a Tory Free Trader from Birmingham in May, 1903. 'The almost insuperable difficulties of framing any scheme which would satisfy all the Colonies and the certainty of future bickerings and hagglings are alone enough to discourage any but an old man in a hurry. It is far more sensible to try to get the Colonies gradually to adopt our free trade system than that we should try their vicious policy of protection.'

In Australia, the foremost advocate of what Churchill called the 'vicious policy of protection' was Alfred Deakin, who succeeded Edmund Barton as Prime Minister in September, 1903. Deakin and Churchill were both firm Empire loyalists. Yet, as noted, there was a fundamental difference in their concepts. While Churchill thought of Britain's Empire, Deakin thought of a Briton's empire. This most eloquent and idealistic of the Federation founders never found any conflict between his twin loyalties, Australia and the British Empire. His nationalism and his imperialism went hand in hand.

The momentum in the 1890s towards the federation of the six Australian colonies had coincided with the growth of the idea of imperial federation, either through colonial representation in the House of Commons, or through a permanent Imperial Council of Ministers. The advocates of imperial federation took it for granted that such representation would be limited to the white-settler colonies. They never spelt out the place that India, the jewel in the imperial Crown, might have in their grand design. Chamberlain's advocacy of imperial protectionism gave the imperial federation movement a fresh impetus. But this new momentum was brought to a shuddering halt by the Conservative disarray which Chamberlain had caused.

Racked by dissension over imperial policy, the Balfour Tory Government resigned in December, 1905. Elections in January, 1906, gave the Liberals a three-to-one majority with Labour and Irish Nationalist support. The new Liberal Prime Minister, Sir Henry Campbell-Bannerman, offered Churchill the junior post of Parliamentary Under-Secretary for the Colonies. Churchill was delighted. His boss at the Colonial Office, Lord Elgin, a former viceroy of India, would sit in the House of Lords; Churchill would be the spokesman of Empire in the place that mattered, the House of Commons. The historian of the Elgin–Churchill partnership, Ronald Hyams, wrote:

Churchill at the Colonial Office presents a curious combination of magisterial statesman and mischievous school boy. The Pitt in him jostled with the Puck in him. He was just as capable of producing a rash and unrealistic suggestion as he was of producing a reasonable and statesmanlike one . . . Contemporaries agreed that his basic weakness was that phrases mastered him, rather than he them.

A lifelong friend and observer, Leo Amery, once said: 'Churchill's patriotism was always for England, not for the Empire or Commonwealth.' Churchill's conduct at the Colonial Office reflected that patriotism; his love of Empire was love for the power and prestige of England, and England's good name. He upheld the principle of self-government for the settler colonies because he believed that the parliamentary system was the outstanding English contribution to the theory and practice of human government.

Churchill's zeal for England's good name showed to advantage in a largely ignored aspect of his career: his personal battles for justice for obscure individuals in the Crown colonies. In a dozen cases, he fought the bureaucrats in the Colonial Office – and sometimes his chief, Lord Elgin – to secure the rights of low-ranking officials whom he believed had been unfairly dismissed, demoted, or otherwise discriminated against. He demanded that Zulu chiefs 'taken in rebellion' be treated with sympathy and dignity. He castigated Natal's treatment of its blacks as 'hooliganism'. In many ways, Churchill never presented a more engaging figure than during the two years he spent as Parliamentary Under-Secretary for the Colonies. Of himself at this time, he said: 'We are all worms; but I do believe that I am a glow-worm.'

For the Tories he had deserted, Churchill remained an object of hatred and derision. For some, their hostility was enduring and hereditary. In 1907, Joe Chamberlain's son Neville campaigning on behalf of his stroke-afflicted father, told a Birmingham audience: 'The Colonial Office is represented in the House of Commons by a bumptious youth who thinks he can harangue these great self-governing states as if they were a parcel of schoolboys and he, forsooth, their schoolmaster (applause). The sooner Mr Winston Churchill is sent as an ambassador to Timbuctoo, the better it would be for the country and the Empire (applause).' Neville Chamberlain was only five years older than the bumptious youth; Churchill would replace him as Prime Minister in May, 1940.

Churchill had his first opportunity to 'harangue the great self-governing states' in person at the Colonial Conference of 1907. He grabbed it with glee. The conference found the British Liberal Government in full enjoyment of its huge majority. In Australia, by contrast, Deakin's Liberal Protectionists had narrowly survived the third federal election in December, 1906, governing with the support of the Australian Labor Party, led by Chris Watson, who had briefly formed a minority government in 1904. Not for the last time, Churchill was to act on the assumption that Australian prime ministers were mainly motivated by their political difficulties at home. Nevertheless, Deakin went to London with high hopes for his imperial objectives, which he believed would 'provide a fulcrum from which our world empire may be moved to a realisation of the vast powers it possesses within itself that can and ought to be diligently and deliberately employed for its own development'.

Although only fifty-one, Deakin was entitled to feel that he was the elder statesman at the Colonial Conference. As Victoria's Colonial Secretary, he had attended the first of them in 1887, held in conjunction with Queen Victoria's fiftieth jubilee, when Churchill, aged twelve, had sent a flurry of letters to his mother begging to be allowed to come to London, to see the Queen's Procession and the other attraction that year, Buffalo Bill.

Churchill angered Deakin even before the conference began. In doing so, he showed his poor understanding of the nature and purpose of the Australian Federation. As the first Attorney-General and the second Prime Minister of Australia, Deakin had to ward off repeated attempts by state premiers to assert their sovereignty against the new Commonwealth. The wrangles centred on the question of access to the British Government: could the states communicate directly with London through the governors? Or was the Australian government through the Governor-General the sole channel? The question was not finally and formally laid to rest until 1986, when the Australia Acts terminated all residual links between the states and the United Kingdom. But Churchill, inexperienced and impetuous, chose to barge into this domestic dispute.

It is not hard to imagine Deakin's dismay when he learnt that Churchill was supporting the state premiers, who wanted to attend the London conference in their own right. He would have been even more dismayed had he known that Edward VII also thought that the Australian states should be separately represented, and had told Lord Elgin so. To Deakin, this was a nullification of everything federated Australia stood for. He had not dedicated ten years of his life to the battle for federation so that six state premiers could swan around Britain and sit at the high table of Empire.

Churchill bombarded Lord Elgin with letters and memoranda to push the pretensions of the Australian states. He lectured his chief: 'I had always hoped that the creation of the Commonwealth meant the addition of a new strand to the ties which joined Australia to the Mother Country, that the parts might reinforce the combination, and the combination fortify the parts. [By excluding the state premiers] we now decide that it shall mean, not an addition, but the substitution of one weak strand for six solid ones which have been cut.' With a self-confidence in his own opinions that never deserted him, Churchill informed Lord Elgin: 'The hold of the State prime ministers upon their people is much more real and intimate than that of the Federal premier upon the loosely-knit and sullenly united Confederation over which he presides.' Lord Elgin and common-sense prevailed over the Churchillian blitz and the royal hint. The state premiers remained unbidden to the imperial feast.

Deakin's political judgement was even more astray than Churchill's. Deakin came to London with grand designs for imperial reorganisation and imperial trade. He wanted an Imperial Council to give the white dominions a greater say in the counsels of Empire. He wanted a permanent imperial secretariat in London. He wanted a system of imperial trade preference. In a sense he was a prophet of the coming British Commonwealth of Nations. He fore-shadowed the imperial trade preference which developed after the First World War, and was formally established at the Imperial Conference in Ottawa in 1932. It lasted until Britain sought to enter the European Common Market in the 1960s, not long before Churchill's death. Essentially, Deakin was pushing the Chamberlain line, yet Chamberlain was a spent force, and the Conservative Party was now a disunited, rudderless opposition. His political misjudgement was the more surprising in that this archetypal Australian liberal, in sympathy with the British Liberals on every domestic issue except protectionism, was so adroit and sensitive a politician at home, the master manipulator of the game, in which, as he put it, there were 'three elevens in the field' – his own Liberal Protectionists, the 'anti-socialist' Free Traders, and the Australian Labor Party – until Deakin arranged the Fusion against Labor in 1909.

Deakin failed to see the obvious: that protection, even if dressed up as imperial preference, had become as divisive a party issue in Britain as it had been in Australia where, until the rise of the Australian Labor Party, protection versus free trade had defined the party contest. Deakin failed to see that the British Liberals, now the Government of the United Kingdom with a huge majority, would view his campaign as interference in their domestic affairs. Churchill was the last man likely to let such impudence pass unchallenged. The ninth Lord Elgin, whose grandfather had stolen the Parthenon Marbles, and who sat, serene and secure, in the House of Lords, could perhaps afford a benevolent detachment. Churchill, the aristocratic adventurer, could not. The Conservative convert needed to prove his Liberal credentials, and Deakin gave him the perfect opportunity.

As well, Deakin was invading Churchill's turf, the Colonial Office. No junior minister was ever less overawed by his departmental officials than Churchill; but no junior minister was less likely to let go unchallenged criticism from outside. With his open challenge to Colonial Office authority, Deakin was bound to collide with Under-Secretary Churchill, throughout his career the personification of the territorial imperative.

In practical terms, Deakin wanted to move dominion affairs from 14 Downing Street to 10 Downing Street, from the Colonial Office to the Prime Minister. For Deakin, the Colonial Office was the symbol of Australian servitude. It not only had a record of arrogance and incompetence; it had retarded the end of transportation and the convict system, resisted self-government, appointed unsuitable governors, and supported unpopular ones. After the grant of self-government to the Australian colonies in 1856, the Colonial Office had punished governors who sided with elected governments in the battle for supremacy between the Lower and Upper Houses of the colonial parliaments. Its ineptitude and inertia had allowed the Germans to seize the northern half of New Guinea, and the French to set up a detestable penal colony on New Caledonia. It had smiled on New South Wales politicians who stood for free trade and spurned Victorian politicians who supported protection. It treated correspondence, protests and petitions from the colonies with disdainful negligence. As long as the Colonial Office was responsible for British–Australian relations, Australia would remain a congerie of colonies, not a true and equal partner in the Empire. That, at any rate, was how Deakin saw it.

When Deakin saw that the grander parts of his design – such as his proposal for an Imperial Council of Ministers – were dead in the water, he held the more tenaciously to his proposal for a permanent secretariat serving as a direct link between the British Prime Minister and the dominion prime ministers. He wanted this body to be under the personal control of the Prime Minister, not the Secretary of State for the Colonies. In pushing this proposal, Deakin showed scant awareness of realities or personalities in Downing Street. He reckoned without Churchill's energy and Campbell-Bannerman's lethargy. The last thing any British Prime Minister ever wanted was direct responsibility for imperial management, least of all the easy-going, ageing, and ailing Campbell-Bannerman. In any case, the Prime Minister of the United Kingdom did not run a department as such; his handful of clerks and messengers came by virtue of his office as First Lord of the Treasury; his power derived from the King's commission and chairmanship of the Cabinet. A secretariat of prying experts and busy officials would have been an anomalous nuisance, not to say un-English. It was not the British way of doing things. Lord Elgin had already decided to hand Deakin a sop by way of setting up a separate dominions section within the Colonial Office. He specifically asked Campbell-Bannerman not to announce this in his opening address to the conference – he would do it himself as a seeming concession to Deakin's demands. For his part, Churchill had not become the Parliamentary Under-Secretary of State for the Colonies in order to preside over the emasculation of the Colonial Office.

Even Deakin's personality, the 'Affable Alfred' who charmed his fellow Australians for a generation, seemed to grate with the grandees of Westminster. Lord Elgin confided to the Governor-General of Australia, Lord Northcote, that Deakin's 'extraordinary eloquence sometimes led to points being obscured in exuberance'. The Secretary of State for India, John Morley, thought Deakin a tiresome windbag. With the ineffable condescension of generations of English statesmen towards Australian politicians, Morley wrote to a friend: 'Our robust young Colonials are apt to be frightful bores, and if you had been condemned to eat twenty meals day after day in their company, and to hear Deakin yarn away by the hour, I believe you would be as heartily glad to see their backs as I am.'

Churchill at least didn't mind the dinners. Rather, he seemed to think they were the point of the whole business. His friend from Harrow schooldays, Leo Amery, an ardent imperialist, recorded 'an hour and a half of hammer and tongs talk with Churchill' on the eve of the conference. 'His own idea seemed to be that the colonial Prime Ministers should be given a good time and sent away all banqueted but empty-handed.' As to Deakin's demand for more consultation, Amery noted in his diary: 'I found Churchill strongly opposed to any idea of consulting the Colonies on foreign affairs, seeing no point in doing so until they were military powers whose alliance could be of any real value to us.' Churchill adopted this approach for the next forty years.

Deakin had hoped that the Prime Minister of Canada, Sir Wilfrid Laurier, would be his chief ally in his battles with the Colonial Office. He was to be disappointed. Laurier, an eighth-generation Canadian of French lineage, had been Prime Minister since 1896. He had spoken very much in Deakinite terms about the unity of the Empire family at the Colonial Conferences of 1897 and 1902, but by 1907 had become sceptical about the usefulness of a more formal organisation, not least because of growing anti-imperial sentiment in his home base of Quebec. Years later, Laurier delivered himself of a magisterial survey of his conference experiences: 'The Australians for the most part were a disappointment, distinctly inferior to the Afrikaners [Generals Louis Botha and Jan Smuts]. Perhaps it was their remoteness, perhaps their racial unity, that gave them a parochial insularity, a lack of perspective in world affairs.' Barton, who had represented Australia at the 1902 conference, was 'the ablest, but lethargic', Laurier said. 'Deakin was a very likeable man, of brilliant endowments, a splendid orator, with much fire and force. He was open minded to new ideas; perhaps too much so, as he seemed unable to hold any steady course.'

In his own diary, Deakin blamed Churchill for 'a bold manoeuvre' which frustrated his London campaign. Deakin's biographer John La Nauze accuses Churchill of 'kidnapping Laurier'. Deakin put it less violently. In a letter to the leading imperial publicist of the time, Richard Jebb, he wrote that he 'was authorised to offer Laurier the leadership if he would undertake to adopt a fighting policy'; but that Churchill intercepted Laurier en route to Downing Street. Deakin told Jebb: 'He was taken from another station, I believe by W. Churchill, to Downing Street where he had a private interview and accepted their offers before meeting us.'

Kidnapped by Churchill or not, Sir Wilfrid Laurier was not a man to be manipulated or duchessed. It was absurd of Deakin to think otherwise, but loss of perspective is an occupational hazard for Australian politicians travelling overseas. By 1911, when he wrote his letter to Jebb, Deakin's superb faculties were at the beginning of their slow sad decline. Two years before his death in October, 1919, he scribbled in his diary: 'Life has ended – in truth, in fact and in judgement. No one can know, not even myself at my best can learn what once I was capable of doing or did. My memory is but a little fiction, a chance return of the pitiful and withering memorial of A. D. Such is my miserable end.' This was a long way from the Deakin of 1907; but his recollections in 1911 show the depth of his resentment at what he remembered as Churchill's act of sabotage.

Deakin had only himself to blame for his disappointments. His efforts in London were misjudged and mistimed. He was not only running against the British Liberal Government, but against the tide of opinion in Australia itself. There, he was dependent on the support of the Labor Party, and the Labor Party, loyal as it was to the Empire, was strongly opposed to imperial federation. Labor's attitude reflected majority opinion in Australia – and the tug-of-war between Australian nationalism and imperial sentiment.

Churchill attended on most of the fifteen sitting days of the Colonial Conference between 15 April and 14 May, and spoke whenever the spirit moved him. The debate on imperial organisation extended over four days. No wonder Elgin complained that the conference disrupted the normal business of governing the Empire. The pettifogging level into which the debate descended is conveyed in the following exchange on the third day of the conference. The discussion was about the wording of the resolution on 'consultation between the self-governing colonies and the British Government'.

MR DEAKIN: Are they all dominions? 'Dominion' is a technical title. In Canada the word 'Dominion' includes the subordinate Provinces, just as the word 'Commonwealth' with us includes the States.

MR CHURCHILL: But in the plural, 'Dominions', it is quite different.

MR DEAKIN: I suggest you should bring in the words 'local government' to put it beyond doubt, but I am not particular about it – you might have both expressions.

LORD ELGIN: It stands thus: 'That upon matters of importance requiring consultation in common, either in this country . . .'

MR DEAKIN: What does 'consultation in common' mean?

MR CHURCHILL: It means consultation in general.

MR DEAKIN: It is sufficient to say 'representatives of the Dominions and the Mother Country'.

MR CHURCHILL: Good.

The mountain laboured and brought forth a mouse, Deakin later admitted. From now on, the conference would be called 'Imperial' instead of 'Colonial'; it would be held regularly at five-year intervals;

and there would be a dominions department within the Colonial Office; the Prime Minister of the United Kingdom, rather than the Secretary of State for the Colonies, would be ex officio chairman of the Imperial Conference. They all congratulated themselves that this was in the best British tradition: British institutions grew from precedent to precedent, not by formal rules and new-fangled theories. That sort of thing was for the Americans.

Churchill held his fire on the less controversial and, to him, less interesting items on the agenda: judicial appeals, uniformity of trademarks and patents, company law, naturalisation, development of Empire communications, and emigration. No doubt to a sympathetic audience, Deakin explained at length the history and practice of Australia's immigration laws, the first major legislation of the Commonwealth Parliament: 'We will have a White Australia, cost what it may. We are anxious to let everyone know it.'

Although official custodian of a quarter of the world's population in Africa, Asia and the West Indies, Churchill let all that pass without comment. As he wrote after a safari around his East African domains later in the year: 'The right of the white colonies to forbid the entry of large numbers of Asiatics and to preserve themselves from the racial chaos and economic disturbance inseparable from such immigration cannot be denied.' He hoped, however, that the right would be exercised 'with prudence'.

He kept his powder dry for the major debate of the conference, on imperial trade preference. Deakin canvassed the protectionist arguments with which he had converted audiences around Australia; but with its huge free trade mandate, the British Government was immovable. Asquith, soon to be Prime Minister, said that Protection was a 'fetish'. Deakin interjected: 'There was once a fetish of Protection in England'.

MR ASQUITH: I do not ask you to agree with me any more than you ask me to agree with you.

MR DEAKIN: English Protection 60 years ago was a fetish and nothing else.

MR ASQUITH: People then did not think so. It is just the difference

when times move. It may be in time you will persuade the
people of Great Britain that Free Trade is a fetish.

MR DEAKIN: We think it is so now.

MR ASQUITH: Go and persuade the people of that. If you can
persuade them, we will have another Colonial Conference, and
we will see what happens. We may be a set of absolute
lunatics, wandering in the twilight and darkness – fiscal
twilight – and the time may come when we shall have a rude
awakening.

Churchill then rose to pour scorn on Deakin and his arguments
about protection and the unity of the Empire. The reality was, he
said, that any system of preference would mean taxes on food and
basic raw materials like wool – 'taxes that would have to be
included in every Budget in every successive year in the House of
Commons':

> I cannot conceive any process better calculated to create an anti-colonial
> party in this country, than this process of subjecting to the scrutiny of
> the House of Commons year by year, through the agency of taxation,
> the profit and loss, so to speak, in its narrow financial aspect, of the
> relations of Great Britain and her Dominions and dependencies.

The result would be, Churchill said, 'to expose the fabric of the
Empire to a wrench and shock it had never before received'. The
Australian Prime Minister could not let that pass:

MR DEAKIN: Most of your propositions seem incontestable to
you, but our experience refutes many of them.

MR CHURCHILL: In that respect, Mr Deakin, I enjoy the same
advantage of conviction as you enjoy yourself.

Churchill concluded the most passionate speech of the fifteen-day
conference: 'I do not doubt that in the future, when Imperial unifica-
tion has been carried to a stage which it has not now reached, and
will not, perhaps, in our time attain, people in that more fortunate

age will look back to the Conference of 1907 as a date in the history of the British Empire when one grand wrong turn was successfully avoided.'

The 'wrong turn' was avoided not by Churchill's eloquence but by the British Government's veto. The Colonial Conference reaffirmed the resolution of its 1902 predecessor 'recognising that the principle of preferential trade between the United Kingdom and His Majesty's Dominions beyond the seas would stimulate and facilitate mutual commercial intercourse and would, by promoting the development of the resources and industries of the several parts, strengthen the Empire'. The dominions 'respectfully urge on His Majesty's Government the expediency of granting in the United Kingdom preferential treatment to the products and manufactures of the Colonies'. For its part, His Majesty's Government 'was unable to give its assent'. And that was the end of that. The resolution, debated during three days by the most powerful speakers in the Empire, was a nullity. Free trade had triumphed, at least in Britain, while the dominions and colonies were left to pursue their 'vicious' protectionist policies more or less at will.

Churchill declared his own victory, denying the colonials any crumb of comfort. In a speech in Edinburgh four days after the conference had rambled to its close, he said:

> The Government have banged the door upon Imperial taxation of food. Yes, they have banged it, barred it, and bolted it. It is a good stout door of British oak, the largest Liberal, Radical and Labour majority ever seen in the House of Commons have their backs firmly against it. The Liberal Party stands like a rock between the hard-working masses, and all who would exploit their food supply and squeeze some shameful little profit out of the scanty pittance of the weak and poor. Popular or unpopular, in office or in opposition, that is the line on which we fight. We shall not concede one inch. We shall not give one farthing preference on a single peppercorn.

In the British Budget Speech of 1927, the Chancellor of the Exchequer in the Conservative Government announced tariff preferences for Australian dried fruits, wines, tobacco, and sugar. That Chancellor of the Exchequer was none other than Winston Churchill.

DEAKIN AND CHURCHILL had a parting spat just before the conference closed. Deakin poured out his long-standing grievances with the Colonial Office over the administration of the New Hebrides – 'a vexed question', as Deakin said, which had soured Australian relations with Britain and France since 1887. Made without warning, Deakin's charge against Churchill was the most serious one parliamentarian can make against another – that Churchill had misled parliament. He gave Churchill no notice that he would be raising the issue, and may have set out deliberately to embarrass him in front of the assembled prime ministers. The previous February, answering a question in the House of Commons alleging that Australian trade policy was harming British settlers in the New Hebrides, Churchill had begun his reply: 'I accept the facts in the first part of the honourable member's question.' According to Deakin, that meant that Churchill was endorsing the allegations, 'to Australia's great detriment'. Mr Churchill, he said, 'was wrong then and the statement you are now making is wrong again'. The wrangle continued for fifteen pointless minutes, until Churchill brought it to an end by saying: 'I very much regret that I have to leave for Manchester almost immediately.' Acknowledging delays and errors in official exchanges, Churchill exited with a flourish: 'True, Mr Deakin, distance is one of the most difficult facts we have to deal with, in the British Empire.'

Churchill's encounter with Deakin at the 1907 Colonial Conference coloured his attitude towards Australian politicians for the rest of his life. Deakin had made the mistake of appearing to play party politics in the heart and home of the Empire, appealing to British public opinion over the heads of the elected British Government. Churchill knew about Deakin's difficulties back in Australia, and wrongly assumed that Deakin's campaign was calculated to shore up his political support there. Churchill never got this notion out of his head, and his conviction that Australian leaders who stood up to him were driven by domestic politics was to strain his relations with Australia to breaking point thirty-five years later. Perhaps it was true, as Sir Charles Wilson was to write in his diary, that by 1942 Churchill had come to 'like the Australians as men'. But they got off to a poor start with him in London in 1907.

3

'Commence hostilities . . .'
1907–14

Churchill's prejudice against Australia and its Prime Minister was fed by the haughty disdain of the Colonial Office. His senior official adviser, Bertram Cox, was especially contemptuous. After Deakin returned home, there was another dispute over the Anglo–French Agreement on the New Hebrides. Cox told Churchill: 'The Australians, who have never had to face any diplomatic difficulty, seem to think that we can treat France as if she were a Tonga or a Samoa.' Dealing with France needed 'courteous people able to work with the French', Cox told Churchill, 'and I doubt if any Australian will fulfil these requirements'. Following further protests from Deakin in August, 1907, Churchill instructed his private secretary, Edward Marsh, who was to devote much of his career to Churchill's service: 'Compose a soothing but serious and unyielding reply, leading to a conclusion of this correspondence.'

'Mr Deakin's hatred of Great Britain colours all his views and from all I hear he will be out of office before long,' Cox had advised Churchill. It was, of course, absurd to speak of Deakin's hatred of Britain; and, in fact, he was to survive in office until November, 1908, when the Labor Party, then led by Andrew Fisher, withdrew its support; Deakin in turn withdrew his support from Fisher in May, 1909, to form his third government, a coalition of Protectionists and Free Traders. By this manoeuvre, Deakin established the two-party system of Labor and anti-Labor, which has been the powerhouse of Australian parliamentary democracy ever since.

Under-Secretary Churchill had one last shot at Prime Minister Deakin. There were raised eyebrows at Downing Street and the Admiralty when they learnt that, in January, 1908, Deakin had sounded out the US Consul in Melbourne to include Australia in the Pacific itinerary of President Theodore Roosevelt's Great White Fleet in its proposed voyage around the world later in the year. Deakin then asked the Colonial Office: Would His Majesty's Government make the formal request to the United States, on behalf of the government and people of Australia? Churchill and his officials saw Deakin's initiative as disloyalty. 'It ought to be discouraged from every point of view', Churchill grumbled.

'I hardly understand your want of sympathy with the visit of the U.S. Fleet,' Deakin complained to his friend, Churchill's old school fellow, Leo Amery. Amery, a journalist and writer, was a leading advocate of imperial federation, and thus Deakin's ally against Churchill, but even he detected a whiff of disloyalty about inviting the Americans to Australia. 'It has nothing to do with our national development but everything to do with our racial sympathies,' Deakin protested. 'If we can help to balance the pro-German and anti-British prejudices of the United States, we should have done good work for the Empire.' America had nothing to gain by a quarrel with the Mother Country, Deakin told Amery. 'The closer the alliance between us, the better, for though I am fully alive to the many objectionable features of their political life, after all they are nearest to us in blood and in social, religious and even political developments.'

Despite Churchill's objections, the British Government grudgingly endorsed the Australian invitation. The Great White Fleet duly sailed into Sydney Harbour on 20 August 1908, to a rapturous welcome from 650,000 people lining the foreshores and streets, the largest crowd to assemble in Sydney until the visit of Queen

Elizabeth II forty-six years later, when Churchill was her first Prime Minister.

The London rumblings over the American visit reflected imperial irritation with Australia's yearning for a navy of its own. In his speech of welcome to the US Fleet in August, 1908, Deakin used the opportunity to promote Australian naval aspirations:

> But for the British Navy there would be no Australia. That does not mean that Australia should sit still under the shelter of the British Navy – those who say we should sit still are not worthy of the name of Briton. We can add to the squadron in these seas from our own blood and intelligence something that will launch us on the beginning of a naval career, and may in time create a force which shall rank among the defences of the Empire.

Deakin and his Labor opposite number, Fisher, have the chief claim to be the political fathers of the Royal Australian Navy. Both leaders rode on a tide of national sentiment – strongest in the Labor Party, the most defence-minded of the parties of the time, with an Australian navy and compulsory military training among the chief planks of its platform. Bipartisanship on the White Australia policy and the navy question gave continuity to the volatile early years of Federation.

The British Admiralty opposed Australia's ambitions. They wanted Australia to continue and increase its annual subsidy (in 1904, £200,000 in a naval budget of £20 million), in return for keeping a Royal Navy squadron in the Pacific. As the First Lord of the Admiralty, Lord Tweedmouth, had put it at the 1907 Colonial Conference: 'There is one sea, there is one Empire, and there is one Navy.'

The decisive event for the creation of an Australian navy was a special conference on Imperial defence, in London in July, 1909. The conference gave the go-ahead, while reaffirming the basic Admiralty principle of 'concentration of the main fleets of the Empire at the point of greatest danger'. Deakin's Defence Minister, Joseph Cook, asked the House of Representatives to approve the new scheme on 24 November 1909:

Our tutelary stages are past, our time of maturity is here. Let us hope that with it has come a deepening and increasing conviction of the immensity of the debt which we owe to the Mother Country, for sheltering us while we grew. In passing this motion, we shall enter what has been called the great Sea League of the Empire, and the wardenship of the Pacific will be allotted to us, as the worthiest and most adequate contribution to the defence of the Empire that the highest naval authorities can devise.

The birth of the Royal Australian Navy coincided with a resurgence of the naval arms race between Britain and Germany. Joe Cook declared: 'This is also our response to the fevered war preparations which various nations are making.'

THREE DAYS BEFORE the sixteen battleships of President Theodore Roosevelt's Great White Fleet sailed into Sydney Harbour, and six years to the month before the outbreak of the First World War, Winston Churchill delivered a speech as remarkable as any of his career. Churchill is not usually thought of as a pacifist, much less an advocate for the international solidarity of the workers of the world. Yet in an address to the coalminers of Swansea, on 17 August 1908, Churchill used arguments brimming with warmth for both causes. To the applause of the Welsh miners, Churchill called for peace and cooperation with the Imperial Germany of Kaiser Wilhelm. 'I think it is greatly to be deprecated,' he said, 'that persons should try to spread the belief in this country that war between Great Britain and Germany is inevitable.'

'The alarmists have no ground whatever for their panic or fear.' Britain was an island, he said, 'and no Government which is in power in this country in the near future, or likely to be in power, will depart in any degree from the naval policy which shall secure us effectively from outside invasion'. There was 'no collision of primary interests – big, important interests – between Great Britain and Germany in any quarter of the globe'. The Germans were 'among our very best customers and, if anything were to happen to them, I don't know what we should do for a market.'

'Destruction of a most appalling and idiotic character' would be the only result of war, Churchill told the Welsh miners. 'It is never worthwhile fighting for the sake of trade. In a month of fighting you would destroy more wealth than the successful trade of five years would produce if everyone worked twelve hours a day.' Churchill revealed a broader vision of the Empire's future than he had ever acknowledged before and, at least in regard to India, than he would ever concede again:

> We are told there are colonies which could be seized by Germany. Why, gentlemen, nothing will alter the destiny of great communities like Canada, Australia, South Africa and India. They are pruning their own path and their own destiny, and that destiny will not be altered in the future as a result of any struggle between European powers.

Churchill then raised his argument against war into a clarion call for the unity of the workers of the world:

> Are we all such sheep? Is democracy in the 20th century so powerless to effect its will? Are we all become such puppets and marionettes to be wire-pulled against our interests into such hideous convulsions? I have a high and prevailing faith in the essential goodness of great people. I believe that working classes all over the world are recognising they have common interests and not divergent interests. I believe that what is called the international solidarity of labour has an immense boon to confer upon all the peoples of the world.

This speech is a striking example of Churchill's capacity to grow and change. At Swansea, he was adding new ideas to the theme he had sounded in the House of Commons on 12 May 1901, when he said that 'a European war can end only in the ruin of the vanquished and the scarcely less fatal commercial dislocation and exhaustion of the conquerors'. Then, he had warned the House and the world: 'Democracy is more vindictive than cabinets . . . The wars of peoples will be more terrible than those of kings.' Unfortunately for mankind, he was more prescient about democracy's wars than the power of workers' solidarity to prevent them. Nevertheless, that Winston Churchill could make such a speech in 1908 speaks volumes about the kind of world men and women of goodwill believed possible and achievable in the years before the madness of the First World War wrecked everything.

Churchill's new situation may have exercised its sunny influence in broadening his outlook. As his son and official biographer, Randolph Churchill, notes, the Swansea speech was made on the day he announced his engagement to Clementine Hozier, a true English Liberal, and a lifelong influence for moderation on her impetuous husband. Churchill concluded his most endearing book, *My Early Life*, with the words: 'I married and lived happily ever after.'

Perhaps an even sunnier influence on Churchill was his promotion to Cabinet rank. At the end of March, 1908, Campbell-Bannerman was persuaded by his doctors to resign. His anointed successor, Henry Herbert Asquith, had gone to Biarritz to 'kiss hands', King Edward not being about to break his holiday for anything so trivial as a change of Prime Minister. From there, on 6 April, Asquith offered Churchill the job of President of the Board of Trade, in place of Lloyd George. In turn, Lloyd George took Asquith's place as Chancellor of the Exchequer. Churchill was thirty-three when he joined the supreme council of the Empire as a full Cabinet member.

For the next six years, in Australia and Britain alike, the naval question dominated the imperial defence debate. In accord with his new-found credo, 'I am an English Liberal', Churchill pursued the Gladstone formula: 'Peace, retrenchment, reform'. Churchill never did things by halves. So he joined enthusiastically with Lloyd George in his campaign to resist the demands of the Royal Navy for its program of Dreadnoughts, the new model of super-battleship. Their argument was simple: big new spending was needed for reforms such as old age pensions; growth in other spending must be curtailed, and the Royal Navy must play its part. The Admiralty was demanding six new Dreadnoughts a year to meet the German naval challenge. Economisers like Lloyd George and Churchill argued for no more than four. As Churchill later said: 'We compromised on eight.'

In September, 1911, in a brief pause between the Asquith Government's constitutional struggle with the House of Lords and the renewal of the ancient battle over Irish Home Rule, Asquith appointed Churchill First Lord of the Admiralty – the civilian chief of the Empire's mighty navy. Churchill at the Admiralty was a man transformed. Forgotten was his campaign to curb the navy's expansion; consigned to merciful oblivion his jibe at the traditions of the Royal Navy: 'What are these traditions? Rum, sodomy and the lash.' Forgotten, too, was his Swansea optimism about the good people and good faith of Germany, and the benign effect of public opinion there. His son, Randolph, dates Churchill's change of mind to the Agadir crisis of 1911, when Kaiser Wilhelm engaged in a little gunboat diplomacy on the English model by sending the *Panther* to annoy the French in Morocco. Churchill himself described his epiphany during his first inspection of the fleet at Portsmouth, realising that on these ships, 'so vast in themselves, yet so small, so easily lost to sight on the surface of the waters . . . floated the might, majesty, and dominion of the British Empire'. What, he conjectured, would happen if somehow this fleet were to be lost?:

> The British Empire would dissolve like a dream; each isolated community struggling forward by itself; the central power of union broken; mighty provinces, whole empires in themselves, drifting hopelessly out of control, and falling prey to strangers; and Europe after one sudden convulsion passing into the iron grip and rule of the Teuton and of all that the Teutonic system meant. There would only be left far off across the Atlantic unarmed, unready, and as yet uninstructed America to maintain, single-handed, law and freedom any more.

From the moment he became First Lord of the Admiralty, Churchill swallowed whole the Admiralty doctrine that the only thing that really mattered was the strength and concentration of the Home

Fleet in the North Sea, a fleet able to blockade and starve Germany, and destroy the German navy in one big, decisive battle.

Churchill's conduct at the Admiralty amply confirmed the Australians in the wisdom of their decision to buy, build and run a navy of their own. In 1909, the Fisher Labor Government had ordered the building of three destroyers in Britain, and later that year the Deakin Government had ordered the battle cruiser *Australia*. On 9 February 1910, at the Govan shipyards in Scotland, Margot Asquith, wife of the British Prime Minister, launched the first of the destroyers with a bottle of Australian wine and the words: 'First born of the Commonwealth Navy, I name you *Parramatta*. God bless you and those who sail you, and may you uphold the glorious traditions of the British Navy in the Dominions over the sea.' On 4 October 1913, the Royal Australian Navy squadron – HMAS *Australia*, a battle cruiser of 18,800 tons, with eight 12-inch and sixteen 4-inch guns, the light cruisers *Melbourne*, *Sydney*, and *Encounter*, and the destroyers *Parramatta*, *Warrego*, and *Yarra* – made its ceremonial entry into Sydney Harbour.

The First Lord of the Admiralty signalled his congratulations. He had also approved, in July, 1913, the transfer of all Royal Navy establishments in Australia to Commonwealth ownership and control, including Admiralty House, now the Sydney residence of the Governor-General of Australia. Churchill was always a great innovator. As First Lord of the Admiralty, he became the first British minister to communicate with an Australian government directly, ignoring protocol and bypassing official 'channels', instead of through the Secretary of State for the Colonies and the Governor-General. In August, 1912, the Colonial Secretary, Lewis Harcourt, and the Governor-General, Lord Denman, complained about Churchill's improprieties; he promised Asquith to mend his ways – and went his own way as usual, treating the Australian navy as an extension of his own.

Churchill nailed his colours to the Admiralty mast when he tried to prevent HMAS *Australia* leaving the Atlantic for the Pacific, to take its place as the flagship of the Australian navy. Under Churchill's rule, 'Britain's power in the Pacific has been stripped of its gunfire strength', one Australian journalist wrote. These were the words of the young and ambitious Keith Murdoch, in an article published in the radical magazine *Lone Hand* to coincide with the arrival of Australia's new navy in Sydney Harbour:

> Strip it of its bombast. Silence the band. Subdue the millineried speakers and the pomp. And what do you get? The elemental sound, the boom of a gun. And that sound may be the beginning of security for the homes of Australia . . . Australia's task in becoming the guardian of white civilisation in the Pacific is fraught with many possibilities.

'The Englishman,' Murdoch wrote, 'has as little appreciation of the Australian's nationalism as the Australian has of the European's heritage – the ever present sense of racial hatred and racial danger.' The 'racial hatred and racial danger' to which he referred in 1913 was not White Australia's fear of the 'Yellow Peril', but the seething European hatreds – the French for the Germans, the Germans for the Slavs, the Balkan peoples for one another, and the danger this cauldron of fear and hate meant for Britain. In May, 1914, Colonel Edward M. House, President Woodrow Wilson's grey eminence, visited the capitals of Europe. He reported back: 'The situation is extraordinary. It is jingoism run stark mad. Unless someone acting for you can bring about a different understanding, there is some day to be an awful catastrophe. No one in Europe can do it. There is too much hatred, too many jealousies.'

In one of those grim jokes by which history mocks posterity, the 'Yellow Peril' phrase was coined by Germany's Wilhelm II, as a call for the unity of Christian Europe against the threat to its civilisation from heathen Asia. It was the first time since the Crusades that the head of a modern empire had invoked the doctrine of the 'clash of civilisations'. The Yellow Peril manifested itself in the Boxer Rebellion in China in 1900. Australia sent the gunboat *Protector*, pride of the Victorian navy, to join British, German, Russian, American, and Japanese forces in putting down the rebellion, saving the tottering Manchu throne, and tightening the West's grip on China's trade.

By 1913, however, the Australians were much more worried about Japan than China. Japan had won a stunning victory over the Russian Fleet at the Battle of Tsushima in 1905. The Sydney *Bulletin*, the strident voice of Australian nationalism, declared that 'if Australia isn't ready to fight for its White Australia policy, and if Britain doesn't care to take up the question, which, as the greatest nigger power on earth, it can hardly do with any enthusiasm, then there is an end to White Australia, with its glories and its dreams and its unique opportunities'. Noting that Japan had become a world power through its program of modernisation since 1865, the *Bulletin* predicted: 'A time is liable to come when Japan will cheerfully risk two million soldiers in the conquest of Australia – and they are no poor specimens in the military line. Now that Britain has abandoned the job of policing the seas and has been driven to gather its fleet closely round its own coasts, the chance [for Japan] to fight for the possession of Australia may not be so very remote after all.'

Churchill's attitude to Japan and the Pacific became the focus for Australian anxieties. On 17 March 1914, he addressed the House of Commons on the Naval Estimates. It was a rehearsal of assurances he would give to Australia almost to the eve of Pearl Harbor. First, he denied that he had breached the 1909 agreements with Australia, or that he had stripped the Pacific of British firepower. True, he acknowledged, 'we are keeping the new battle cruisers at Home', but the ships still in the Pacific were 'quite sufficient for the work they will have to do'. In any case, 'the Alliance with Japan has now been renewed up to 1921, with the full concurrence of the Overseas Dominions'. This was a Churchillian gloss; the dominions had nothing to do with it at all, and had not been remotely consulted. Nevertheless, Churchill continued, there was now a bond of self-interest between Japan and Britain, and, 'quite apart from the good sense and moderation for which the Japanese Government have become renowned', this bond of mutual interest was 'the true and effective protection for the safety of Australia and New Zealand, and this bond depends entirely on the maintenance of British naval supremacy'.

Churchill asserted the Admiralty doctrine of naval concentration in home waters more emphatically than any of his predecessors: 'If the British Fleet were defeated in the North Sea, all the dangers which it now wards off from the Australasian Dominions would be let loose. If the victorious European Power desired any territorial expansion or naval status in the Pacific, there would be no forces which Australia and New Zealand could command which could effectively prevent it.' He made a prophecy:

> If Japan chose to indulge in ambitions of empire or colonisation in the Southern Pacific, she would be no loser as far as the European situation was concerned. But we should have lost at a stroke the means of both making our friendship serviceable and our hostility effective. There are no means by which, in the next ten or twelve years, Australia and New Zealand can expect to maintain themselves single-handed. If the power of Great Britain were shattered on the sea, the only course of the five million of white men in the Pacific would be to seek the protection of the United States.

Churchill praised New Zealand ('ever in the vanguard of Empire'), which was footing the bill for a Dreadnought in home waters. That was the way to do things, Churchill said: 'Two or three Australian and New Zealand Dreadnoughts, if brought into line in the decisive theatre, might turn the scale and make victory not merely certain but complete. The same two or three Dreadnoughts in Australian waters would be useless the day after the defeat of the British Navy in home waters. Their existence would only serve to prolong the agony without altering the course of events, just as surely as if they had been sunk in the battle.' However, Churchill haughtily conceded, 'the Dominions are perfectly free. The matter rests entirely in their hands, and the Admiralty's responsibility ceases when the facts have been placed plainly before Ministers and those to whom they are responsible.'

Churchill concluded with a thought all the more irritating for the Australians because it showed that he understood perfectly well the nature of the Australian aspiration on which he was pouring such an oceanful of cold water. 'The Dominions want to have their own ships, under their own control, cruising in their own waters and based on their own ports,' he acknowledged, with scorn and sympathy in equal doses. 'They want to have something they can see, and touch, and take pride in, with feelings of ownership and control.' Then, as if giving up on the Australians as incorrigible, he concluded: 'These feelings, although unrecognised by military truth, are natural. They are real facts which will govern events.' For his part, he would do his duty to 'uphold and proclaim the broad principles of unity in command, unity in strategic conception, and of concentration in the decisive theatre and for decisive events.' In short, the Australians could jump in the Pacific lake.

To the Australians, the shocking implication of Churchill's speech was that their security depended on the goodwill of Japan. The *Melbourne Punch* fumed that 'the first dignitary of the Imperial shipping department' had shown how little he understood 'Australia's attitude towards our discoloured neighbours' in Asia and the Pacific. 'The First Lord would probably be amazed if he heard that Australians were insulted at the idea of their depending on Japan, or any other yellow, brown, pink, black or blue race, for any measure of protection whatever . . .' Australians understood the position because 'we have only to look over our back fence to see it grinning at us'. By contrast, said Mr Punch, 'John Bull and his First Lord are away at the other end of creation'. To them, 'the Japanese menace is as absurd as if someone cried out against the possibility of a fly-speck falling on an elephant and breaking its neck. To offer us Japanese protection is very like telling Mary's little lamb – Have no fear, small and tender sheep, you are excellently provided for. We have set the wolf to watch over you!'

Australia's official response was more measured but all the more pointed because Australian anger was bipartisan. Although both parties jockeyed for the credit of creating the Australian navy, it was, as Labor's Andrew Fisher had said in May, 1908, 'a matter of national policy, absolutely above any party question'. Deakin had retreated to the backbenches after a heavy electoral defeat at the hands of Labor in 1910; Fisher was again Leader of the Opposition, narrowly defeated in the elections at the end of May, 1913. Joseph

Cook, ex-miner, ex-Labor founder, ex-Free Trade leader, was Prime Minister. His Minister for Defence, Senator Edward Davis Millen, replied to Churchill point by point, on behalf of a united Parliament, and the people of Australia.

'The pages of history are strewn with the wreckage of fruitless alliances,' Millen told an *Age* reporter. Then, drawing himself up to his full 5 feet 4 inches: 'Australia will not be deflected from her course by the pronouncement of the First Lord of the Admiralty.' Mr Churchill had given 'an interpretation of the effect of the Anglo-Japanese Alliance which is not accepted in Australia'.

Senator Millen charged Churchill with breach of faith. He was echoing the charge the Australians had made against the British Government down the decades, against its attempts in the 1840s to resume convict transportation, and its tardiness against French and German incursions into the Pacific in the 1880s:

> Mr Churchill's statement involves the definite non-fulfilment by the Admiralty of obligations undertaken by the 1909 Agreement. It involves the destruction of the basis on which the Royal Australian Navy was organised, and as a result of which the Australian people committed themselves to the expenditure of several millions of public money . . .
>
> Mr Churchill's statement means the abandonment of those features of the Royal Australian Navy which, in 1909, were regarded by the Admiralty as most essential, especially his expression of opinion that battle cruisers are not needed in the Pacific and should be sent to Home waters.

Churchill, Millen said, was effectively 'replacing a definite inter-Imperial cooperative policy with an uncoordinated, ephemeral scheme possessing neither permanence, nor clear aim and function. He had ignored all the other considerations so important from the wider Imperial point of view, and on which the Admiralty had laid so much stress in 1909.' All this – 'a vital departure in many important respects from a policy agreed upon between the Dominions and the Imperial Government' – had been announced by Churchill 'without any previous consultation with, or even preliminary notification to, the governments of the Dominions'. For its part, Millen declared, 'Australia is irrevocably pledged to, and will pursue with determination and consistency, the policy on which she embarked on the advice of the Imperial Government five years ago'. The complaint about lack of consultation would be a constant theme in Anglo–Australian relations for the next thirty years, especially whenever Churchill was involved.

The Australians would have been even more outraged and frightened had they realised the lengths to which Churchill was pushing the doctrine of naval concentration in home waters. They could, perhaps, have understood that the mounting tension between Britain and Germany required more power in the North Atlantic than the South Pacific, but they could hardly have believed that Churchill would urge the withdrawal of the Royal Navy from the Mediterranean – Australia's lifeline to the heart of the Empire. Yet that is precisely what he was doing.

Churchill was deeply influenced by Lord Fisher, the dynamic, eccentric former First Sea Lord (1904–10), a relentless advocate of concentrated sea power. 'Jacky' Fisher had created the Dreadnought, the super-battleship, immediately making every other big ship in the Royal Navy obsolete and starting a new naval arms race with Germany, one of the key factors leading to the First World War. He had begun the reduction of the China and North Pacific squadrons as far back as 1904. He was forever feuding with his fellow admirals, implacable in the pursuit of his endless vendettas. In 1914, Churchill was to persuade the septuagenarian Fisher to return as First Sea Lord, the operational chief of the Royal Navy. In Fisher's own view, their relationship was more a love affair than a partnership; and like many love affairs, it had its courtship, its honeymoon, its squabbles, its reconciliations, and, ultimately, its irretrievable breakdown. He bombarded Churchill with letters in his highly idiosyncratic style, sometimes verging on the hysterical, signing off, 'Yours till Hell freezes over'. This improbable event was to take place on the waters of the Dardanelles and the shores of Gallipoli in 1915.

In May, 1912, Churchill wrote to his Cabinet colleague, Richard Burdon Haldane, the War Secretary who had modernised the British army: 'We cannot possibly hold the Mediterranean or guarantee any of our interests there until we have obtained a decision in the North Sea. It would be very foolish to lose England in safeguarding Egypt. If we win the big battle in the decisive theatre, we can put everything else straight afterwards. If we lose it, there will not be any afterwards.'

In vain did Lord Kitchener, the overlord of Egypt, protest that 'Egypt was the front line of the Empire'. Egypt had been occupied, although not annexed, by Britain since 1882. For the next forty years, Britain and Australia were to treat Egypt as part of the British Empire and their strategic backyard. Kitchener argued that weakening the Mediterranean fleet would mean the 'loss of Egypt, Cyprus and Malta, and the erosion of British power in India, China and Australasia'. But Churchill was not to be moved. Unknown to the British public and the Australian Government, Churchill began to withdraw his battleships from the Mediterranean. Four came home, and four were left at Gibraltar, available to sail north or east according to circumstances. Churchill promised Asquith, who sided with Kitchener, that by 1916 Britain would have enough new capital ships to re-enter the Mediterranean in the style to which the Empire had become accustomed. In September, 1912, the French Admiralty announced that six battleships of the French Atlantic Fleet, stationed at Brest, would transfer to the Mediterranean. Churchill insisted that this was not a swap, and that it did not involve any British obligation to defend the French Atlantic coast. But the consequences were to be immense.

When the British Foreign Secretary, Sir Edward Grey, rose in the House of Commons at 3.00 p.m. on 3 August 1914 to explain why Britain was about to serve an ultimatum upon the German Empire, he opened by denying that there was any secret arrangement with France. Nevertheless, he said, Britain was bound to France, if not by obligation, then by honour and interest. He revealed Churchill's arrangement by which the French Fleet had been transferred to the Mediterranean, leaving 'the northern and western coasts of France absolutely undefended'. Britain had made no commitment to defend those coasts but, Grey said: 'My own feeling is that if a foreign fleet, engaged in a war which France had not sought and in which she had not been the aggressor, came down the English Channel and bombarded and battered the unprotected coasts of France, we could not stand aside and see the thing going on practically within sight of our eyes, with our arms folded, looking on dispassionately, doing nothing.' Hansard records that at the words 'could not stand aside', the House erupted in cheers. When it is remembered that Britain claimed that moral obligations to Belgium and France were the basis of its decision to go to war against Germany, Churchill's share of responsibility becomes clear.

In the bitter record of human folly, there is nothing so heart-breaking as reading the chronology, step by fatal step, of Europe's plunge into war, between the assassination of the Archduke Ferdinand, heir to the throne of the ramshackle Austro–Hungarian Empire, at Sarajevo on 28 June 1914, and the outbreak of war in the first week of August, 1914. None of the main actors comes out well, yet none was particularly wicked by standards set later in the twentieth century. The Kaiser, for instance, makes a most unsatisfactory villain. Many, most culpably the Austrian ministers and generals, wanted war, to punish Serbia for its suspected involvement in the assassination; but none wanted the war they got. Yet there was such an irresistible momentum towards a war of some sort – the war they all thought would be over by Christmas – that war there had to be. Europe sleep-walked its way to ruin.

Fear ruled. Fear of war was overwhelmed by fear of not going to war. The rulers in Vienna were afraid of appearing weak in the face of Serbia's restless ambition to build a great Slav state on the ruins of the Austro–Hungarian Empire. Emboldened by a virtual blank cheque from Germany, Austria served an impossible ultimatum on Serbia on 23 July, then declared war on 28 July, when a full month had elapsed since the assassination, and much of the world, not least Britain and Australia, was hoping that yet another Balkan crisis was passing. Next day, Tsarist Russia, fearing the loss of its prestige as protector of the Southern Slavs, mobilised against Austria. Germany, conjuring up fears of a revived Russia and a vengeful France, gave Russia twelve hours to revoke its mobilisation. The Russians, fearful of German might, rejected the demand. On 1 August, Germany declared war on Russia. France, Russia's treaty ally, mobilised. The relentless logistics of mobilisation and railway timetables overtook the power of politicians and soldiers to control events.

The German High Command presented the Kaiser with the only war plan it had ready for a war on two fronts with Russia and France – the Schlieffen Plan, which involved the invasion of Belgium for a sweep around to Paris. On 3 August, Germany declared war on France and demanded passage for its armies through Belgium.

Britain, meanwhile, confronted its traditional fear – domination of the Continent and the English Channel ports by a single power. The British Liberal Government, fearful of finding Britain isolated, and fearful that the Conservative Party could form a pro-war government if Britain failed to support France and Belgium, invoked the 1839 Treaty guaranteeing Belgian neutrality – the 'scrap of paper' in the words of the German Chancellor Bethmann-Holweg – and declared war on Germany on 4 August. Honour, so-called, as well as fear, worked its chemistry in this dreadful brew: Germany's debt of honour to Austria, Russia's to Serbia, France's to Russia, Belgium's to its own fragile nationhood, and Britain's to France and Belgium. Serbia begged Austria for 'chivalrous understanding'. They all cried chivalry on the way to the Calvary they were imposing upon their millions.

Britain's decision for war rested with five men – Prime Minister Asquith, the Foreign Secretary, Sir Edward Grey, the Chancellor of the Exchequer, Lloyd George, and, to the extent they represented the pro-war hardliners, Churchill and the leader of the Tory Opposition, Andrew Bonar Law. Once they had decided for war, their task was to impose their view on the groups from which they derived their power – first the Cabinet, then their parties, then the Parliament, and ultimately the public. That was why Germany's invasion of Belgium was so important to them: it was the great selling-point. The British Empire went to war not so much because Germany invaded Belgium, but because the German invasion of Belgium united the British Liberal Party behind the tiny group of men who had decided that it was in the imperial and national interest to go to war.

'The wars of peoples will be more terrible than those of kings,' Churchill had foretold in 1901. He saw that kings who fought for honour and prestige or territory were likely to be more flexible than politicians who must justify themselves before an electorate. Nationalism, imperialism, and industrialism created the conditions for this conflict; but when all is said and done, the Great War was so terrible and long because the peoples of Europe allowed it. There would be, at the top, stupidity, vainglory, blunders, and crimes aplenty; there would be mutinies, most dangerously in the French army, and war-weariness, industrial strikes, and civil unrest among all the belligerents, including Australia. But the fundamental resolve to continue the war until victory hardly ever faltered, almost to the end. This was, perhaps, even more true in the democracies than in the autocracies. The first of the warring nations to sue for peace was the most autocratic, Russia of the Tsars; after the last Tsar abdicated, the revolutionary government of Alexander Kerensky vowed to continue the war, and did so until Lenin's coup of October, 1917. When there were leadership changes in Britain and France, they came about because Lloyd George and Georges Clemenceau pledged even more resolute efforts to win the war. In Australia, the defeat of the conscription referendum was followed by a resounding electoral victory for W. M. Hughes and the win-the-war party. By 1917, the higher the death toll, the harder it became for leaders and peoples alike to contemplate any end to the sacrifice short of total victory. And it became the necessary sustaining belief of the soldiers themselves. The Canadian war poet, John McRae, claimed to speak for the war dead when urging his fellow countrymen to fight to the end: 'If ye break faith with us now, we shall not sleep, though poppies grow in Flanders fields.'

In London, Churchill was at fever pitch. He felt his hour had come; he was still only thirty-nine. The Liberal Government had been bogged down in the latest crisis of the Irish saga, with senior army officers in Ulster threatening mutiny over Home Rule. In the last week of July, the British Cabinet turned away, almost with relief, to the European crisis. Prime Minister Asquith wrote to his confidante, the 27-year-old daughter of a peer, Venetia Stanley: 'Winston is all for this way of escape from Irish troubles, and when things looked rather better last night, he exclaimed moodily that it looked after all as if we were in for a "bloody peace".' Asquith seemed to treat his correspondence with his platonic lover as a substitute for Cabinet minutes. At the first Cabinet meeting of the war, he wrote to her: 'Winston dashed into the room radiant, his face bright, his manner keen and told us – one word pouring out on the other – how he was going to send telegrams to the Mediterranean, the North Sea and God knows where! You could see he was a really happy man. I wondered if this was the state of mind to be in, at the opening of such a fearful war as this.' Asquith concluded: 'For about a quarter of an hour he poured forth a ceaseless cataract of invective and appeal, and I much regretted that there was no shorthand writer within hearing, as some of his unpremeditated phrases were quite priceless.'

Churchill himself sometimes felt twinges of guilt about his enthusiasm for war. As Britain lurched towards conflagration, he confessed to his wife at the end of July that he was 'geared up and happy'. He wrote to Clementine: 'Is it not horrible to be built like that? I pray to God to forgive me for such fearful moods of levity.' Six months later, in a week of fateful decisions about Gallipoli, he told Asquith's daughter, Violet Bonham Carter: 'I think a curse should rest on me because I am so happy. I know this war is smashing and shattering the lives of thousands every moment – and yet – I cannot help it. I love every second I live.'

In *The World Crisis*, Churchill wrote of the hour when Sir Edward Grey spoke of 'the lamps going out all over Europe':

It was 11 o'clock at night – 12 by German time – when the ultimatum expired. The windows of the Admiralty were thrown wide open in the warm night air. Under the roof from which Nelson had received his orders were gathered a small group of Admirals and Captains and a cluster of clerks, pencil in hand, waiting. Along the Mall from the direction of the Palace the sound of an immense concourse singing 'God Save the King' floated in. On this deep wave there broke the chimes of Big Ben; and as the first stroke of the hour boomed out, a rustle of movement swept across the room. The war telegram, which meant 'Commence hostilities against Germany', was flashed to the ships and establishments under the White Ensign all over the world. I walked across the Horse Guards Parade to the Cabinet room and reported to the Prime Minister and the Ministers who were assembled there that the deed was done.

4

'Australia will be there'
August–November, 1914

From the moment he sent the signal 'Commence hostilities against Germany', Winston Churchill became ruler of the Royal Australian Navy. Australia was automatically at war, declared in the name of George V 'of the United Kingdom of Great Britain and Ireland and of the British Dominions beyond the Seas, Defender of the Faith, Emperor of India'. In the terms of its 1909 agreement, the Australian Government handed over its navy to the British Admiralty as soon as the declaration was made. So, from the start of the Great War, Churchill acquired the habit of treating Australian forces as an extension of British arms, taking their orders direct from London. He was never able to break the habit.

Churchill's flurry of signals to the Empire's naval outposts had alerted the Australian Government to the emergency even before the official communication to the Governor-General, Sir Ronald Munro Ferguson, arrived via the Colonial Office. As a result, the chief of the RAN, Admiral Sir George Patey, was the best informed authority in Australia about the rush of events, and he alerted his army counterpart, General William Bridges. This was particularly useful, given the electioneering preoccupations of the Australian Ministry.

Australia was in the middle of a federal election campaign. The Liberal Prime Minister, Joseph Cook, spoke at an election meeting at Colac, Victoria, on 1 August 1914: 'I hope that the negotiations going on will result in peace in that troubled theatre. But if it is to be war, if the Armageddon is to come, you and I shall be in it. We are ready to do our very best with and for the rest of the Empire in defending our interests in any part of the world.' At Horsham, Victoria, the Leader of the Opposition, Andrew Fisher, said: 'Turn your eyes to the European situation, and give the kindliest of feeling towards the Mother Country at this time. Should the worst happen after everything has been done that honour will permit, we Australians will help and defend her to our last man and our last shilling.'

In Sydney, Labor's little dynamo, Fisher's deputy, Billy Hughes, declared: 'For the time being I leave all things to the one side that can in any way savour of party. Whatever needs to be done to defend the interests of the Commonwealth and of the Empire must be done.' Cook was an English coalminer, Fisher a Scottish coalminer, and Hughes a London-born Welshman, a schoolteacher and jack-of-all-trades; but they expressed the overwhelming sentiment of Australians, wherever born. Hughes even suggested that the federal election should be cancelled. 'I know that is illegal and unconstitutional,' he conceded, but such trivialities could be set aside by an Act of the Imperial Parliament in London. Typically, he made his offer without consulting his leader, and it was probably inspired as much by partisanship as by patriotism. In the days before opinion polls, Cook's Liberals were fairly confident of being returned. That was why Cook had taken the unprecedented step of asking the Governor-General for a double dissolution of both Houses of Parliament – the House of Representatives where he had a small majority, and the Senate where Labor had a majority. But on 5 September, Labor was elected comfortably (42 to 32, with one pro-Labor independent in the House of Representatives; and 30 to 6 in the Senate). The Labor Party seemed set for a long period of strong, united government.

The coincidence of the federal election with the outbreak of the war made Australia unique. In reality, its government, much less its people, had no say about going to war. But given the pledges of the party leaders, it is fair to say that Australian voters gave their mandate for war at the polls in 1914.

The young nation was in surprisingly good shape to organise a mobilisation, despite its lack of a military establishment and tradition. The Englishman who had contributed most to this state of readiness was Lord Kitchener of Khartoum, now coopted as Churchill's Cabinet colleague, as Secretary of State for War. The Australian Government had asked Kitchener to visit in 1910, to recommend ways of implementing its scheme of compulsory military training – another bipartisan defence measure introduced by Labor at the urging of Billy Hughes. As a result of Kitchener's report, Australia entered the war with a cadre of junior officers and a core of some eighty thousand trainees. They provided the backbone of the first volunteers for the proposed expeditionary force. Its name – the Australian Imperial Force – defined its dual identity.

Volunteers flocked to recruiting stations around the continent. *The Age* sought the meaning of it all when it reported the procession of five thousand men, the first units of the newly named Australian Imperial Force, down Collins Street, Melbourne, 'their bayonets gleaming in the fitful sunshine' of an early spring day:

> The immensely significant and important thing about yesterday's demonstration was that every man who took part in it was a volunteer. No military despatch had driven him to war. From many parts of Victoria, from the public schools and the State schools, from the cities and back blocks, from the homes of comparative luxury and the homes of poverty, these men had volunteered. In the march-past yesterday all distinctions were blotted out. They were all Australians; Britons by blood and descent, by sentiment and tradition. But yet – Australians.

If the five thousand were typical of the AIF as a whole, probably one in five was British-born; but from the beginning, three key elements of the Anzac legend were established: volunteerism, egalitarianism and Australian nationalism within the British Empire. 'Mateship' was a later construct, drawing upon traditions of unionism among shearers, miners, and wharf labourers in the 1890s.

On war's eve, the Prime Minister had held a Cabinet meeting in Melbourne, called in the representatives of the army and navy, offered to send 'a force of 20,000 men of any suggested composition to any destination desired by the Home Government', and formally placed the navy in the hands of the British Admiralty. Churchill thus became the master of a fleet whose independent existence he had deplored. He rushed to make full use of it, on 6 August sending Australia the first of countless instructions he issued in the course of two world wars:

> If your Ministers desire and feel themselves able to seize German wireless stations at Yap, the Marshall Islands, Nauru or Pleasant Island and New Guinea, we should feel that this was a great and urgent Imperial service. You will, however, realise that any territory now occupied must be at the disposal of the Imperial Government for purposes of an ultimate settlement at conclusion of the war.

The Australian Defence Minister, Senator Millen, was disappointed. The Minister and the Australian Naval Board wanted its navy, especially its flagship, *Australia*, to go on a search and destroy mission in the Pacific against a German squadron under the command of Admiral Graf von Spee. The seizure of German wireless stations seemed a sideshow. The Government knew, however, that it had no real choice in the matter, and replied that 'they would willingly render the required service, provided that the German fleet in the Pacific is considered the first objective'.

Melbourne laid claim to firing the first shot of the war anywhere in the Empire. On 5 August, a couple of hours after the official declaration, the German merchant ship *Pfalz* attempted to leave Port Phillip Bay, but was stopped by a shot across its bows from the artillery at Fort Nepean on the Mornington Peninsula. On 19 August, the Australian Government sent an expeditionary force under Colonel William Holmes for preliminary training on Palm Island in north Queensland, en route to seize the German settlement at

Rabaul. The capture of the German wireless station on New Britain cost six Australian lives, the first of sixty thousand. On 14 September, the navy incurred its first loss: the submarine *AE1* disappeared without trace somewhere off Rabaul, the fate of its thirty-five officers and crew forever unknown. The following day, Colonel Holmes accepted the German surrender. The Union Jack flew over Rabaul, thirty years after Alfred Deakin had urged the British Government to add New Guinea to the British Empire.

From the Admiralty in London, Churchill monitored with approval and intense interest the operations to seize German possessions in the Pacific. Von Spee's flotilla, with its cruisers *Scharnhorst* and *Gneisenau*, disappeared in the vastness of the Pacific. As Churchill wrote: 'He had only to hide and to strike'. But the German admiral was left isolated by the seizure of all German outposts in the Pacific by the Australians, New Zealanders, and Japanese, and was forced to flee into the South Atlantic in an attempt to reach home. His destruction at the Battle of the Falklands on 2 December 1914, a saga of naval gallantry on both sides, gave Churchill the most notable sea success of his term at the Admiralty. The German light cruiser, *Emden*, meanwhile, entered the Indian Ocean, its track traced only by the wreckage of British and French shipping in the Bay of Bengal.

The Australian sailors were not happy with Churchill. They were puzzled and resentful that the most powerful ship in the Pacific, HMAS *Australia*, had not been put to better use in hunting and destroying the German raiders. In 1926, the official Australian naval historian Arthur Jose wrote that the Australian commanders had been unfairly accused 'of having dragged a big battle-cruiser about the Pacific on minor expeditions, and then detained her from her proper work of chasing the German ships until they were run down by more enterprising commanders'. The orders came from Whitehall, he insisted. Jose did not name Churchill but sailors, of course, understood exactly whom he was criticising. *Australia* was ordered to leave the Pacific, and arrived at Plymouth 'shortly after midnight' on 28 January 1915. At last Churchill had the Australian flagship where he had always wanted her – with the Home Fleet.

Surveying the situation of the RAN as it existed in early 1915, Jose grumbled about Churchill's naval dispositions:

> The Australian Squadron was by now scattered over the seven seas. The *Australia* was in the North Sea and the two fast light cruisers in the North Atlantic. The *Encounter* patrolled the Pacific from Fiji eastwards and northwards. One submarine was lost; the other at work in the Eastern Mediterranean. Even the old *Pioneer*, after months of patrol off the Western Australian coast, had been called away to aid in the capture of German East Africa. The *Una* was busy in the occupied islands. Only the three destroyers on the Queensland coast were left to remind Australians that they had ever had a navy of their own.

Von Spee's flight from the Pacific had relieved the immediate anxieties of the New Zealand Government about the safety of their troops crossing the Tasman to join the Australian convoy then assembling in King George's Sound, Western Australia – their destination still undecided, but eagerly assumed to be France via England. The new Labor Government proceeded apace with the plans of its predecessor. Its eagerness to fulfil Australia's obligation was tempered only by its anxieties over the safety of the convoys. Jose wrote:

> Andrew Fisher himself was a man of extreme caution, and he was intensely anxious not only to give the Empire all possible help, but to prevent any occurrence that might harmfully affect the nerves or zeal of Australians. He had conjured up a picture of thirty thousand young untried men afloat, of enemy cruisers dashing in to sink them, of Australia, unused to war, shocked and angered. At so early a stage, he felt, the sinking of a transport from preventable causes might push Australia practically out of the war for many months.

Churchill responded sympathetically to Australian concerns. 'Although the Admiralty adheres to its view that the dispatch of transport from New Zealand and Australian ports to point of concentration at Fremantle [W.A.] is an operation free from undue risk,' he cabled to the Governor-General, Munro Ferguson, 'in view of anxiety felt by your Ministers and Government, they propose to send *Minotaur* and *Ibuki* to Wellington to fetch New Zealand convoy and escort it westward along Australian coast, picking up the Australian transports on way and bringing the whole to their destination.' Churchill did not specify the destination, because it was still undecided.

For a civilian chief with no naval experience, Churchill's hands-on approach was astonishing and unprecedented. The intensity of his interference in day-to-day operations is shown in his daily instructions to the Admiralty. On 1 October he wrote:

> Now that *Scharnhorst* and *Gneisenau* have been located in the Society Islands there is no need for *Melbourne* and *Sydney* to remain in Australasian waters. *Sydney* should immediately be ordered to join *Hampshire*, *Yarmouth* and *Chikuma* in the *Emden* hunt, and *Melbourne* should come there with the Australasian convoy . . . What is the use of *Psyche*, *Pyramus* and *Philomel* in New Zealand waters after the convoy has started? There is nothing but the *Scharnhorst* and *Gneisenau* to be considered, and they are sufficiently dealt with by (1) *Australia, Montcalm*; (2) First Japanese Squadron; (3) Second Japanese Squadron.

Churchill, whose naval experience was limited to summer cruising in the Mediterranean on the Admiralty yacht, HMS *Enchantress*, told the heirs of Drake and Nelson: 'I propose, therefore, that these three ships should accompany the Australian and New Zealand convoys home to India waters, and should then join up with the seven cruisers which will then be under *Hampshire* in hunting *Emden*.' Then on 15 October he ordered: '*Sydney* should escort Australians and thereafter hunt *Emden*.' 'This shot,' he was to claim in his memoirs, 'went home.'

The Japanese squadrons fulfilled the hopes for cooperation expressed by Churchill in his speech of March, 1914, which had caused such alarm in Australia. Although it was not bound to do so under the Anglo–Japanese alliance, Japan had eagerly declared war against Germany; in Churchill's phrase, with 'an attitude of fierce menace'. Tokyo demanded the surrender forthwith of the German naval base at Tsingtao, assumed naval responsibility for the Northern Pacific, and sent the battle cruiser *Ibuki* to protect the Australian convoy across the Indian Ocean.

While the convoy was assembling, Churchill sent Australia an unwelcome proposal. With the convoy's ultimate destination still undetermined, General Botha, the old Boer leader, now Prime Minister of the Union of South Africa which Churchill had helped nurse into existence in 1910, asked London for help in putting down a new Boer rebellion. The rebels, remembering the Kaiser's support in their fight against Britain, were threatening to link up with the German colony in East Africa. Churchill thought the Australians could stop off at Cape Town, mop up the rebellion, and then continue on to Britain and France. The Australian Government reluctantly agreed to this diversion; but before the convoy sailed, Botha signalled that he no longer needed help. So the Australians sailed away and nobody knew where they were headed.

At 6.45 a.m. on 1 November, the liner SS *Orvieto*, carrying General William Bridges and the Australian staff officers, led the troop transports out of the heads of King George's Sound. Charles Bean, the official war historian, described a naval departure as unique and unlikely as the arrival of the First Fleet at Sydney Harbour 126 years earlier with its seven hundred convicts:

> The 26 Australian transports formed up first, in three divisions in line ahead (or, as the Army would say, in single file). The 10 New Zealand ships in two similar divisions followed, and the warships escorted. Two days later two Western Australian transports met the fleet at sea. Then with the British cruiser *Minotaur* five miles ahead, the *Ibuki* and *Melbourne* four miles out on either beam, and the *Sydney* far astern, the 38 transports headed for Suez *en route* to England.

Or so they all thought.

The *Emden* continued to ravage shipping in the Indian Ocean as the Australasian convoy steamed towards Colombo. In *The World*

Crisis, Churchill takes the credit for the decision to include HMAS *Sydney* in the escort:

> The reader will remember for what purpose the *Sydney* and *Melbourne* had been attached to the great Australian convoy which was now crossing the Indian Ocean. On the 8th [November] the *Sydney*, cruising ahead of the convoy, took in a message from the wireless station at Cocos Island that a strange ship was entering the Bay. Thereafter silence from Cocos Island. Thereupon the large cruiser *Ibuki* increased her speed, displayed the war flag of Japan and demanded permission from the British officer in command of the convoy to pursue and attack the enemy. But the convoy could not divest itself of this powerful protection and the coveted task was accorded to the *Sydney*. At 9 o'clock she sighted the *Emden* and the first sea fight in the history of the Australian Navy began. It could have only one ending. In a hundred minutes the *Emden* was stranded, a flaming mass of twisted metal, and the whole of the Indian Ocean was absolutely safe and free.

Churchill was enthused not only by the event itself but by his exaggerated sense of his own part in placing *Sydney* at the decisive point. He was, however, nothing like as imaginative as Sir Henry Newbolt, the self-appointed 'poet laureate' of the Royal Navy, who wrote of the Australian naval gunners at the Cocos Islands:

> Their hearts were hot, and, as they shot,
> They sang like kangaroos.

The destruction of the *Emden* inspired other poets as well. W. W. 'Skipper' Francis, a Welsh vocalist on an Australian tour when war broke out, was moved to write 'Australia will be there', an immensely popular song, the sheet music of which ran into ninety-five editions by November, 1916. The second verse proclaimed:

> You've heard about the *Emden* that was cruising all around
> It was sinking British shipping where e'er it could be found,

Till one fine summer morning, Australia's answer came;
The good ship *Sydney* hove in sight, and put the foe to shame.

The refrain, as popular in the Second World War as the First, called upon Australians to:

Rally round the banner of your country,
Take the field with brothers o'er the foam,
On land or sea, wherever you may be,
Keep your eye on Germany,
But England, home and beauty have no cause to fear,
Should auld acquaintance be forgot?
No! No! No! No! No!
Australia will be there,
Australia will be there.

Churchill took justifiable pride in the navy's convoy work. Its main task had been to carry the British Expeditionary Force to Belgium and France across the English Channel. In the first four months of the war 'not a ship was sunk, not a man was drowned'. He wrote in *The World Crisis*: 'One after another the German cruisers and commerce destroyers were blocked in and hunted down. The great convoys arrived. The Expeditions were safely landed. Ocean after ocean became clear.' The Australasian convoy from New Zealand to Egypt was the longest voyage in military history.

The Australian convoy had reached Aden by the time the British Government at last decided where its troops should be put ashore. The delay proved a blessing. The Canadian Expeditionary Force, also twenty thousand strong, had suffered badly through lack of adequate facilities at their training camp on Salisbury Plain. The Australian representative at the War Office in London, Colonel Harry Chauvel, was dismayed at the damage these conditions did to Canadian morale. He was convinced that the Australians would fare even worse in the English winter. Chauvel placed his concerns before the Australian High Commissioner in London, Sir George Reid, former Premier of New South Wales 1894–99 and Prime Minister of

Australia 1904–05. Reid, every considerable inch the politician and patriot, held the same fears, and dared to put them to Lord Kitchener, now Secretary of State for War. The Kitchener of 1914 overawed every member of Cabinet, even Churchill. Although he had played a key role in creating the Australian army, Kitchener was not overly impressed by Australian progress in the martial arts. He granted, however, that the raw material, properly trained, could be 'made equal, if not superior to, any army in the world'. Sir George Reid's urgings probably came as a relief to Kitchener as he pondered what to do with twenty thousand half-trained Australians. They would complete their training in Egypt, Kitchener decided; and what Lord Kitchener decided was law. Churchill had delivered the Australian Imperial Force safely to Egypt. The question was: Where would they go now? Churchill was to provide an epic answer.

5

'An excess of imagination'
December, 1914–January, 1915

'So, through a Churchill's excess of imagination, a layman's ignorance of artillery and the fatal power of a young enthusiasm to
overwhelm older and slower brains, the tragedy of Gallipoli was
born.' Thus wrote Charles Bean in *The Story of Anzac*, the first
volume of his monumental work on the First AIF, published in 1921.
Bean's accusation hurt Churchill badly and permanently. It has
remained a leading text for all accounts of the Gallipoli campaign
ever since.

Churchill saw at once how much Bean would damage his reputation. He was swift and severe in his response in *The World Crisis*,
published in 1923: 'It is my hope that the Australian people, towards
whom I have always felt a solemn responsibility, will not rest content
with so crude, so inaccurate, so incomplete and so prejudiced a
judgement, but will study the facts themselves.' Bean's assessment is
neither crude nor ignorant. It is no less accurate than any other
account of Gallipoli, including Churchill's own. Bean's prejudices
were not especially against Churchill or the British leaders, but overwhelmingly on the side of his fellow countrymen who fought and
died on Gallipoli.

Bean's version took hold for several reasons: it was the first account published as official history; it was the key conclusion of a fine writer and reporter who had shared, from beginning to end, the hardships of men whose sacrifices he believed had been squandered; and it reinforced earlier assessments of Churchill. Even at Gallipoli itself, Churchill's reputation for grandstanding and recklessness was well known. Colonel John Monash wrote from Gallipoli to his wife, Vic, in Melbourne during the lead-up to the costly failure of the Suvla Bay operation in August, 1915: 'We have dropped the Churchill way of rushing in before we are ready, and hardly knowing what we are going to do next, in favour of the Kitchener way of making careful and complete preparations on lines which just can't go wrong.'

Lloyd George wrote an assessment of Gallipoli which runs largely counter to Bean's. As a close ally of Churchill, he was no impartial judge, and it was in his self-interest to praise Churchill and damn Asquith and Kitchener. He wrote in his war memoirs, in 1933:

The Dardanelles failure was due not so much to Mr Churchill's precipitancy as to Lord Kitchener's and Mr Asquith's procrastination. Mr Churchill's part in that unfortunate enterprise had been worked out by him with the most meticulous care to the last particular, and nothing had been overlooked or neglected as far as the Naval operations were concerned. The fatal delays and mishandlings had all been in the other branch of the Service. It is true that the conception of a one-sided naval operation without simultaneous military action was due to Mr Churchill's impetuosity, but both the Prime Minister and Lord Kitchener were equally convinced that it was the right course to pursue.

Such contradictory assessments show the difficulty, if not the impossibility, of making a final judgement on Churchill's role in the Dardanelles campaign, in its conception and its execution. Bean, however, makes important points which help us understand the criticism Churchill faced over Gallipoli for the rest of his career. Bean's three charges, against Churchill's imagination, his enthusiasm, and his ignorance, were to surface again and again, not only about

Gallipoli, but also about his exercise of the supreme power during the Second World War.

'WHO IS TO HOLD Constantinople?' Napoleon had once asked. 'That is the crux of the problem.' Is it any wonder that a proposal to seize Constantinople would fire Churchill's mind, memory, and imagination? Here he was, this direct descendant of the Duke of Marlborough who had set the Sun King, Louis XIV of France, at defiance, in charge of the mightiest navy the world had seen, the sword and shield of the greatest empire the world had known. Now he was empowered to act in the vast theatre where Achilles and Hector had fought; where Xerxes had crossed to Europe, and Alexander had crossed to Asia; where Caesar and Pompey, Antony and Octavius, had struggled for the mastery of Rome; where the heirs of Constantine had sustained the brilliant civilisation of the Eastern Empire for a thousand years against the degeneracy of dynasties, the fanaticism of sectarians, the scourge of the plague, the greed of Crusaders and the anathema of popes, until Constantinople in 1453 fell to the heirs of Mohammed. Twice, in 1529 and 1683, the Ottoman Turks had marched from Constantinople to the gates of Vienna, the bulwark of Christendom. In Churchill's own lifetime, Disraeli had gone to Berlin in 1878 to meet Bismarck and keep Russia out of Constantinople, and had brought back 'peace with honour'; it was to get the Turks out of Constantinople, and out of Europe 'bag and baggage', that Gladstone had made a political comeback just when Queen Victoria was hoping that she had got rid of 'that madman'. Now the whirligig of time had placed Churchill in a position to settle a 500-year-old question once and for all.

Churchill was enthralled by the possibilities: not only the fall of Constantinople, but with it the entry of Greece on the Allies' side, Russia relieved in the south, Bulgaria kept neutral, Serbia rescued, the Balkans aflame against Austria, and Germany threatened with war on three fronts. This is what Charles Bean condemned as 'a Churchill's excess of imagination'. But was it excessive? Did Asquith and Kitchener think so? Did Bean himself believe it before the Gallipoli campaign ended in defeat?

Whose were the older and slower brains Churchill overpowered? Heading Bean's list were Asquith and Kitchener. The Prime Minister and the Secretary for War, Bean wrote, were regarded by the British people 'as the two pillars of the British Government, great men standing aloof with a certain grand imperiousness to the violent changes of war'; but 'between these two minds, both possessing stability, there was a third, unceasingly active and almost boyishly impetuous', namely Winston Churchill.

Asquith was now sixty-two. Lloyd George, the man who replaced him as Prime Minister at the end of 1916, wrote: 'He won his way to the Premiership entirely by superb talent and parliamentary achievement. No Prime Minister in history – with the notable exceptions of Gladstone and Disraeli – possessed a better mental equipment for a political career.' Yet Lloyd George condemned Asquith for 'his inability to face facts except under pressure'.

No Prime Minister ever observed a Cabinet colleague's foibles, excesses, and enthusiasms more closely than Asquith did Churchill's. He assessed Churchill with cool, cruel precision: 'Winston, whom most people would call ugly, but whose eyes, when he is really interested, have the glow of genius'. Asquith sometimes wrote two or three letters a day to Venetia Stanley; they were vastly indiscreet, full of shrewd judgements, intimacies, and State secrets, written while presiding over the War Council at 10 Downing Street – perhaps the ultimate example of power as autoerotic aphrodisiac. Only in this intimate correspondence did Asquith abandon the discretion and caution innate in a politician whose best known dictum was 'Wait and see'.

Kitchener might be said to have had a slow brain. That was part of his strength, as his more brilliant colleagues perceived it: the source of his steady, mature judgement, force of character, and unrivalled military knowledge. The trust he inspired made the 1914 recruiting poster 'Your Country needs YOU' perhaps the most powerful advertisement ever published, his haunting eyes and accusing finger beckoning a million young volunteers into the trenches of France and Flanders. Asquith's wife, Margot, stated in her forthright way: 'Kitchener is not a great man but he is a great poster.' If there was one thing Kitchener distrusted more than civilians and politicians, it was imagination, and Churchill's imagination most of all. The impudent young subaltern had publicly criticised his conduct of the Sudan war in 1898, particularly his desecration of the tomb of the Mahdi, the Muslim holy man who had declared a jihad against Britain and General Gordon in 1885, and whose skull Kitchener had considered making into an ashtray before having it thrown into the Nile.

Kitchener's changes of mind over the Dardanelles campaign must be seen in the context of his strategy for winning the war. He saw from the outset that it would be a long conflict, and would be won by 'the last million British soldiers'. That, he believed, would be in the third year at the earliest. Accordingly, his policy was to raise and train his new armies, nursing his forces for a last grand entrance in 1917. He was not a rigid 'westerner' in the sense of refusing to engage in any operation away from the western front in France and Belgium. All his training and experience in India, Egypt, South Africa, and not least in Australia in 1910, made him deeply aware of Britain's imperial reach and responsibilities. Nevertheless he believed in husbanding his resources for the supreme effort against Germany. 'Unfortunately,' he conceded in August, 1915, 'we have to make war as we must, not as we should like to.'

Bean also faulted Churchill's 'young enthusiasm', which certainly existed in overflowing abundance; the seas and oceans guarded by the Royal Navy were not enough to contain it. Churchill had rushed to Belgium to take personal command of the desperate defence of Antwerp, ordering the Royal Naval Division about as if it was his private army. On 5 October he sent Asquith 'what must surely rank as one of the most extraordinary communications ever made by a British Cabinet Minister to his leader', in the apt words of the military historian Michael Howard. 'I am willing to resign my office and undertake command of relieving and defensive forces assigned to Antwerp in conjunction with the Belgian Army,' the First Lord of the Admiralty telegraphed to London amidst the chaos and havoc of the German bombardment, 'provided that I am given necessary military rank and authority, and full powers of a commander of a detached force in the field.' Asquith recorded that the Olympian gods of the Cabinet greeted the proposal with 'Homeric laughter'. When Churchill returned to London after the fall of Antwerp, Asquith told him that 'he could not be spared from the Admiralty, but he scoffs at that'. Churchill's 'mouth was watering at the sight and sound of Kitchener's new armies'. Asquith told Venetia Stanley that Churchill had cried: 'Are these glittering commands to be entrusted to dug-out trash bred on the obsolete tactics of twenty-five years ago, mediocrities who have led a sheltered life mouldering in military routine?'

Bean's most specific charge against Churchill was his 'layman's ignorance of artillery': that he overestimated the power of naval guns to destroy the forts guarding the Straits. In *The World Crisis*, Churchill complained that this view had been popularised 'in thousands of newspaper articles and recorded in many so-called histories'. He gave his own sarcastic version of the criticism: 'Mr Churchill, having seen the German heavy howitzers smash the Antwerp forts, being ignorant of the distinction between a howitzer and a gun, and overlooking the difference between firing ashore and afloat, thought that the naval guns would simply smash the Dardanelles forts. Although the highly competent Admiralty experts pointed out these obvious facts, the politicians so bewitched them that they were reduced to supine or servile acquiescence in a scheme which they knew was based upon a series of monstrous technical fallacies.' Bean portrayed Churchill waving the magic wand of his enthusiasm and eloquence over not only the admirals, but Kitchener himself: 'Churchill's alluring vision of the power of the naval gun, which had enticed the great soldier into the undertaking, had proved false. It was a case either of a great military expedition or of a withdrawal. Kitchener replied that, if large military operations on the Peninsula were necessary, they must be carried through.' Yet Bean's own account shows that Gallipoli defies such simplification; this great human tragedy cannot be reduced to a mistake about technology.

In the end, Gallipoli was a political test of the British Prime Minister and his colleagues' conduct of the war. Asquith was a superb political chief who had presided over one of the great reform governments in history. His mistake in 1914 was to believe that the methods of subtle persuasion and steady perseverance, by which he had outwitted the Tories in their last-ditch resistance against reform of the House of Lords and Home Rule for Ireland, would serve just as well in the supreme crisis of a tremendous war. It was not until November, 1914, that he established a ten-man War Council. As will be seen, it proved hardly more effective than the 24-man Cabinet. The War Council included the departmental chiefs of the army and navy, who were always unsure of their role and their rights, even to speak, much less decide. Balfour, the former conservative Prime Minister, represented the Tories. The Council's decisions were seldom recorded, printed, or circulated, or even communicated to the rest of the Cabinet. The group met when Asquith felt like it; in the critical weeks of the Gallipoli campaign, from late March to mid-May, it did not meet at all. At point after point, the failures at Gallipoli were the failures of Asquith to lead and coordinate. On the eve of Gallipoli, Sir John Maxwell, the general of the British forces in Egypt, where the Australians were waiting to embark for Gallipoli, cried in despair: 'Who is coordinating and directing this great combine?' Or, to use one of Churchill's favourite expressions: 'Who is in charge of the clattering train?'

Asquith was the cleverest British Prime Minister of the twentieth century. Kitchener was hailed as the greatest British soldier since the Duke of Wellington, and Lord Fisher as the greatest British seaman since Nelson. Churchill became the greatest wartime Prime Minister in British history. Between them they produced Gallipoli.

'ARE THERE NOT other alternatives than sending new armies to chew barbed wire in Flanders?' Churchill wrote to Asquith on 29 December 1914. 'Further, cannot the power of the Navy be brought more directly to bear upon the enemy? If it is impossible or unduly costly to pierce the German lines on existing fronts, ought we not, as new forces come to hand, to engage him on new frontiers, and enable the Russians to do so too?' In these questions, and Churchill's search for answers to them, lay the genesis of Gallipoli.

By December, 1914, the western front was deadlocked. From the English Channel through Belgium and France to the frontiers of neutral Switzerland, the armies of Belgium, Britain, and France faced the Germans across more than four hundred miles of trenches and fortifications, in lines that hardly changed in the next four years of mutual slaughter, of which the bloodbaths of Verdun, the Somme, and Passchendaele are only the most notorious. On the eastern front, the German army had annihilated more than a million Russians in the battles of Tannenberg (23–31 August 1914) and the Masurian Lakes (5–13 September 1914). As Churchill wrote in *The World Crisis*: '. . . the three salient facts of the war situation at the beginning of 1915 were: first, the deadlock in France, the main and central theatre; secondly, the urgent need of relieving that deadlock before Russia was overwhelmed; and thirdly, the possibility of relieving it by great amphibious and political-strategic operations on either flank.'

In his letter to Asquith, Churchill did not specify an attack on Germany's eastern ally, Turkey, as a possible flanking operation, although he had canvassed the possibilities in the East from the moment Turkey entered the war. The War Council's minutes of 25 November 1914 record: 'Mr Churchill suggested that the ideal method of defending Egypt was by an attack on the Gallipoli Peninsula. This, if successful, would give us control of the Dardanelles and we could dictate terms at Constantinople. This, however, was a very difficult operation requiring a large force.' At that stage, Churchill was thinking mainly in terms of an action in the Baltic Sea. He was supported in this idea by his executive head, Admiral Fisher. Churchill had brought Fisher out of retirement in September, and reinstalled him as First Sea Lord in place of Prince Louis of Battenberg, hounded out by the London press because of his German background which, except for his birthplace in Germany, was much the same as the entire British Royal Family's. When George V changed the family name to Windsor, Battenberg changed his to

Mountbatten. These name changes prompted Kaiser Wilhelm to make a rare joke: 'I am looking forward to the next performance of Shakespeare's *Merry Wives of Saxe-Coburg-Gotha.*'

Churchill himself had made decisions that helped bring Turkey into the war on Germany's side. Since 1909, the Ottoman Empire, the nineteenth-century 'sick man of Europe', had been run, and to some extent revived, by the 'Young Turks', a junta of army officers and Turkish nationalists, organised as the Committee for Union and Progress (CUP), ruling through a parliament behind the traditional façade of a sultan and grand vizier. Its most colourful leader, Enver Pasha, was pro-German, but like most of his CUP colleagues wanted to stay neutral until a likely winner emerged. On 26 July 1914, as war clouds gathered over Europe, Churchill ordered the seizure of two battle cruisers being completed for the Turkish navy in British shipyards. 'These ships are vital to us,' he claimed. The effect in Constantinople was electrifying. The ships had been bought and already paid for, largely by public subscription; thousands of Turkish women had donated their rings and jewellery. Turkish crews were already in Britain to sail the cruisers home. The German Government skilfully exploited Turkish outrage against Britain when the cruisers *Goeben* and *Breslau* made good their escape from the Mediterranean, where British naval supremacy had been weakened by Churchill's policy of 'home waters concentration'. When they reached the Golden Horn, the German Government offered the ships to the Turkish navy, explicitly to replace the vessels Churchill had commandeered. The German officers and crews donned the Turkish red fez, but otherwise celebrated their escapade as a German victory over the mighty British navy. The Turkish tilt towards Germany became a steep roll.

To be fair to Churchill, these dramatic events were taking place while Enver, as Turkish Minister for War, was already negotiating an alliance with Germany. Enver accepted a German proposal to place General Otto Liman von Sanders, who had been reorganising the Turkish army since 1913, in command of Turkish forces defending Constantinople and the Gallipoli Peninsula. The British Cabinet, in particular Lloyd George and the Foreign Secretary, Sir Edward Grey, underestimated the Turks, and were far keener to seek allies among former Ottoman conquests such as Greece, Romania, and Bulgaria, than to keep Turkey neutral. If it came to war, they were convinced that this ramshackle empire, its twenty million divided between Turks, Arabs, Armenians, Egyptians, Syrians, Lebanese, Palestinians, Kurds, Greeks, Jews, Copts, and other varieties of Christians, would be a pushover. British contempt for Turkey pervaded all its dealings. At the end of October, with Enver's connivance, the German ships shelled Russian ports and ships in the Black Sea. Britain, France, and Russia declared war on the Ottoman Empire on 1 November 1914.

Enver, against the advice of Liman von Sanders, who regarded him as a buffoon, began his war with two campaigns – both disasters. One was against the British in Egypt, to seize the Suez Canal; his ragtag force was easily repulsed, confirming British opinion about Turkish incompetence. He took personal command of ninety thousand ill-trained men in a campaign against Russia in the Caucasus region. Headstrong, egotistical, and incompetent, Enver achieved some early success only because of Russia's overwhelming preoccupation with its fronts against the Germans and the Austrians. These initial setbacks impelled the Russians to request British assistance, to ease the pressure until Russia's manpower, Russia's distances, and Russia's winter could do their work with Enver, as they had once with Napoleon, and would with Hitler.

On the last day of 1914, the commander-in-chief of the Russian army, the Grand Duke Nicholas, the Tsar's uncle, sent a message to London: Would it be possible for Lord Kitchener to arrange for a demonstration of some kind against the Turks, and thus ease the position of the Russians? In particular, the Grand Duke wanted to know, could something be done in the Dardanelles to threaten the Turks at their capital, Constantinople? Kitchener at once passed the request on to the First Lord of the Admiralty. Churchill's response led, step by step, to Gallipoli.

THE DARDANELLES STRAIT, which divides and bridges Europe and Asia, is sixty-four kilometres long, and runs north-east from the

Aegean Sea to the Sea of Marmara. On the northern shore of the Marmara, at the mouth of the Bosporus, stands the city known variously over its 2600 years of recorded existence as Byzantium, Constantinople, Stamboul, and – currently – Istanbul. The Dardanelles spans almost four kilometres at its mouth in the Aegean Sea, widening to more than six kilometres, then contracting gradually to the Narrows, about a kilometre and a half wide. The tongue of land that thrusts into the Aegean from the European side is known in English as the Gallipoli Peninsula. Some eighty kilometres long, and nineteen kilometres at its widest point, its westward shores are mostly narrow beaches with jagged cliffs behind. Along its spine run ridges of hills and plateaux less than three hundred metres high.

Churchill had sailed through the Dardanelles on a private cruise in September, 1910. Did he notice that at the Narrows the gun-range was only eight hundred yards? It had long been navy orthodoxy that ships alone could not force their way through the strait because of the strong fortifications on both the Gallipoli and the Asia Minor sides. In fact, as recently as 1911 Churchill himself had circulated a Cabinet minute endorsing the navy's view of the impossibility of forcing the Dardanelles. 'Nobody would expose a modern fleet to such a peril,' he wrote. That did not deter him from ordering the Royal Navy to bombard the outer fortifications at the entrance to the strait as soon as Turkey joined the war. This pointless operation had two effects: it confirmed Churchill's opinion of Turkish vulnerability, and it put the Turks on alert. They immediately began to strengthen the defences along the strait, and to reinforce the Gallipoli Peninsula.

Most serious of all, the Turks and their German advisers accelerated the laying of mines in the strait. This was the real beginning of the Gallipoli disaster – the key reason for the navy's failure to force the straits, and the need for an army to capture the forts from landside. Robert Rhodes James wrote: 'The British, both in London and at the Dardanelles, persisted in treating the forcing of the Dardanelles in terms of knocking out the main established batteries at the Narrows.' This was a fact, James wrote, 'never fully grasped by the British, and which has not been understood by some historians of the campaign'. One historian who did understand it clearly is the Australian, Les Carlyon. In his brilliant account, *Gallipoli*, Carlyon posed the perfect catch-22: 'And the riddle goes like this: the navy couldn't get in close enough to destroy the forts and batteries until the mines had been cleared; the mines couldn't be cleared because the forts and batteries kept firing on the minesweepers.'

At first, Kitchener poured cold water on prospects for helping Russia. After a brief conversation with Churchill on 2 January 1915, he sent a telegram to Petrograd (St Petersburg): 'Please assure the Grand Duke that steps will be taken to make a demonstration against the Turks. It is, however, to be feared that any action we can devise and carry out will be unlikely to seriously affect numbers of enemy in the Caucasus, nor cause their withdrawal.' On the same day, he wrote to Churchill summing up their conversation, saying: 'The only place that a demonstration might have some effect in stopping reinforcements going East would be the Dardanelles. Particularly if, as the Grand Duke says, reports could be spread at the same time that Constantinople was threatened.' Kitchener made it clear, however, that he was thinking solely in terms of a naval demonstration. 'We have no troops to land anywhere,' he wrote to Churchill. 'We shall not be ready for anything big for some months.'

Next day, Churchill sent off a fateful telegram to the commander of the Adriatic Squadron on patrol in the Eastern Mediterranean, Vice-Admiral Sir Sackville Carden: 'Do you consider the forcing of the Dardanelles by ships alone a practical operation? It is assumed older battleships fitted with mine-bumpers would be used, preceded by colliers or other merchant craft as mine-bumpers and sweepers. Importance of results would justify severe loss. Let me know your views.' With these forty-eight words, Churchill opened his Dardanelles campaign.

Admiral Carden responded in less than two days, on 5 January cabling Churchill from his flagship, HMS *Inflexible*: 'With reference to your telegram of 3rd instant, I do not consider Dardanelles can be rushed. They might be forced by extended operations with large number of ships.' A layman might be excused for thinking that nothing could be more tentative, more equivocal, than Carden's no–yes–maybe message. Churchill thought otherwise. He read it out that same afternoon to the War Council where 'it was heard with extreme interest', he claimed. He then returned to the Admiralty, and discussed Carden's message with two admirals, Sir Henry Oliver, the Chief of the Naval Staff, and the chief of the Admiralty War Group, Sir Henry Jackson – but, significantly, not with Lord Fisher, whose support was indispensable. On 6 January, Churchill cabled to Carden: 'Your view is agreed with by high authorities here. Please telegraph in detail what you think could be done by extended operations, what force would be needed, and how you consider it should be used.'

Winston Churchill famously coined the phrase 'terminological inexactitude'. Another favourite expression of his was 'being economical with the truth'. In this cable correspondence and in his use of Carden's answers, he demonstrated both. Admiral Carden's first response on 5 January had been a bob-each-way affair if ever there was one. Yet this is what Churchill read into it: 'Its significance lay in the fact that it offered a prospect of influencing the Eastern situation in a decisive manner without opening a new military commitment on a large scale; and further it afforded an effective means of helping the Grand Duke without wasting the Dardanelles possibilities upon nothing more than a demonstration.' Where is any of this to be found in Carden's brief answer? At the Dardanelles Commission, appointed in 1916 to inquire into the whole disaster, Carden himself claimed that all he meant by his telegram was 'that it *might* be done'.

Churchill's assertion that Carden's view was 'agreed with by high authorities' was utterly misleading. The vice-admiral, then aged fifty-eight, was known throughout the navy for his caution and deference to rank. With those five words, Churchill was placing immense but subtle pressure on him at his most vulnerable points. It must have been inconceivable to Carden that Fisher, the First Sea Lord, the 'high authority' who counted most, had not been properly consulted, and had not approved. Fisher, in fact, blew hot and cold – tempestuously so – about the Dardanelles project. But on one thing he was adamant and consistent throughout: it could not and should not be done by the navy alone.

Acting in the belief that he was under definite orders from his naval superiors in London, Carden instructed his officers on board *Inflexible* to draw up a plan. They sent a detailed plan of four hundred words to the Admiralty on 11 January. They would need twelve battleships, four of them fitted with mine-bumpers, sixteen destroyers, twelve minesweepers, and six submarines. Frequent reconnaissance by sea planes would be indispensable. They envisaged the destruction of the forts and batteries in four gradual stages, destroying the forts piecemeal – the difference between 'rushing' and 'forcing' the straits. Depending 'on the morale of the enemy under bombardment' and weather conditions, Carden said, they 'might do it all in a month about'.

Churchill placed this plan before the War Council on 13 January 1915. Most of the meeting was taken up by Sir John French, commander-in-chief on the western front, who argued long and hard for a new offensive to break the stalemate in France. The Council Secretary, Sir Maurice Hankey, recorded:

> At this point events took a dramatic turn, for Churchill suddenly revealed his well-kept secret of a naval attack on the Dardanelles! The idea caught on at once. The whole atmosphere changed. Fatigue was forgotten. The War Council turned eagerly from a dreary vista of a 'slogging match' on the Western Front to brighter prospects, as they seemed, in the Mediterranean. The Navy, in whom everyone had implicit confidence and whose opportunities so far had been few and far between, was to come into the front line. Even French with his enormous preoccupations caught something of the general enthusiasm. Churchill unfolded his plans with the skill that might be expected of him, lucidly but quietly and without exaggerated optimism.

Lord Fisher later gave a more colourful version of Churchill's performance, but to the same effect, at the Dardanelles Commission of Inquiry: 'He was beautiful. He has got the brain of Moses and the voice of Aaron. He could talk a bird out of a tree, and they were all carried away with him. I was not, myself.' Yet, at this vital meeting, Fisher said nothing. 'It was none of my business to kick the shins of the First Lord of the Admiralty under the table,' he told the inquiry. 'He was my chief and it was silence or resignation.' His silence was taken for assent. Everybody around the Cabinet table assumed that Churchill was speaking for a united and eager Admiralty. In fact, he had not discussed his proposal or Carden's response with the Board of Admiralty, his constitutional advisers. Nor had the naval experts of his Admiralty War Group seen Carden's response before Churchill presented it to the Council. Churchill won the War Council's approval because he played fast and loose with the facts.

Churchill not only failed to consult properly with his expert advisers; he concealed from the War Council the true nature of such advice as he did receive. In saying that he had the support of 'high authorities', he relied mainly on the advice of Admiral Sir Henry Jackson. Jackson told the Dardanelles inquiry that he had only supported the first stage of the plan – the bombarding of the outer forts. If that was successful the next stage could be tried; if unsuccessful, the whole thing could be called off. Further, in a memo to Churchill dated 5 January, Jackson had seriously questioned the worth of the naval operation itself. Even if the fleet got through and Constantinople surrendered, Jackson wrote, 'It could not be occupied and held without troops and would probably result in indiscriminate massacres'. At the inquiry, he claimed that he had always maintained that it would be 'a very mad thing to go into the Sea of Marmara without troops holding the Gallipoli Peninsula'. Churchill never brought Jackson's serious reservations to the notice of the War Council or before any other authority. Terms like 'suppressed' and 'duped' spring readily to mind regarding his conduct.

After Churchill had spoken, 'Asquith was seen to be writing'. This time it was not a letter to Venetia Stanley. Rather, it was his conclusions about that day's deliberations: a final decision on the western front offensive was to be postponed until February, and 'the Admiralty should also prepare for a naval expedition in February to bombard and take the Gallipoli Peninsula, with Constantinople as its object'.

Asquith had given Churchill all he needed to plunge onwards. He telegraphed Carden on 14 January: 'Your scheme was laid by the First Sea Lord and myself before the Cabinet War Council yesterday and was approved in principle.' Technically true; but, like his other messages, it was calculated to impress Carden with a false sense of Cabinet and Admiralty unanimity. It was a deliberate gloss. 'We entirely agree with your plan of methodical, piecemeal reduction of forts as Germans did at Antwerp,' Churchill signalled. 'Continue to perfect your plan.' The reference to Antwerp carried Churchill's conviction that modern artillery had revolutionised warfare and had rendered obsolete previous views, including his own, about the impregnability of the Dardanelles' fortifications. This was what Charles Bean meant by 'a layman's ignorance of modern artillery'.

Churchill took it upon himself to inform the French Government of the proposal on 18 January. The French agreed to send a naval squadron to serve under Carden. On 20 January, he instructed the Admiralty to order Carden to have his force ready to open fire on the Dardanelles fortifications not later than 15 February. That deadline, he said, was dictated 'by urgent political considerations'. This setting of political imperatives upon military decisions was to become the hallmark of the Churchillian way of waging war – the approach that a quarter of a century later would determine the fate of Australian forces in North Africa, Syria, Greece, Crete, Malaya, Singapore, and Burma.

Carden may well have wondered what he had got himself into by his ambiguous response of 5 January; from this time on, his health began to give way. Fisher became increasingly uneasy at Churchill's frenetic activity. The First Sea Lord now had two basic objections: without an army of at least 200,000, the operation was foredoomed, and the navy's margin against the German High Fleet was too small to be risked on peripheral operations in the Eastern Mediterranean. To keep Fisher more or less on board, Churchill stressed two points: that the naval attack could be called off at any stage; and, as only older battleships were involved, their loss would not weaken the navy's all-important strength against the Germans in the North Sea. Fisher retorted that even the loss of old ships meant the loss of irreplaceable young men. Yet, despite his objections, he agreed to strengthen Carden's force by sending out his special pride and joy, the *Queen Elizabeth*, the most powerful warship afloat, and the finest product of Churchill's momentous decision in 1912 to convert the Royal Navy from coal to oil.

Fisher waited a week before putting his objections in writing. In a memo to Churchill, he pressed for the return to home waters of the destroyers at the Dardanelles. Australia's remaining submarine, *AE2*, had just reached the Aegean. Fisher wanted it brought to the North Sea. He told Churchill: 'It would be inexcusable to waste her on the Turks.' Churchill ignored Fisher's demand. *AE2* stayed in the Aegean, and navigated the strait on 25 April, at the same time as the landings on Gallipoli, becoming the first British vessel to reach the Sea of Marmara. The submarines were the only British vessels of the entire campaign to make it through the Dardanelles. *AE2* was sunk there on 30 April. Its crew became Turkish prisoners of war. Of all Churchill's grand vision of the fleet sailing in triumph to Constantinople, a lonely Australian submarine came closest to fulfilling it.

Lord Fisher's anxieties turned into panic when the German High Fleet ventured into the North Sea and scarpered back after losing the battleship *Blucher* in the Battle of the Dogger Bank on 23 January. Although hailed in the London press as a 'glorious victory', it served only to sharpen Fisher's demands for the concentration of British naval power in home waters. He told Churchill: 'It might easily have been a disaster. Had we lost the *Lion*, [badly damaged in the battle] victory would have turned into a defeat.' On 28 January Fisher resigned, in letters to Asquith and Churchill. To both he said that the Dardanelles bombardment could 'only be justified on naval grounds by military cooperation, which would compensate for the loss in ships and irreplaceable officers and men'. He wrote: 'The British Empire ceases if our Grand Fleet ceases. No risks can be taken.'

Prime Minister Asquith bestirred himself. He summoned Fisher and Churchill to meet him at 10 Downing Street twenty minutes before that day's War Council meeting. After hearing both sides, Asquith said that he agreed with Churchill: the 13 January decision must stand. The trio then descended from Asquith's study to the Cabinet room. Fisher, inwardly fuming, threatened to walk out when the Dardanelles came up for discussion. He interjected: 'I understood that this question would not be raised today. The Prime Minister is well aware of my views.' As he stalked out, Kitchener jumped up, took him aside to a window, and told him: 'You are the only dissentient. The Prime Minister has decided. It is your duty to your country to carry on.' Fisher sat down and sulked. No more was heard of his resignation, at least for the time being.

Far better for the fate of Gallipoli, and everybody involved in the campaign, had Asquith accepted Lord Fisher's resignation then and there. The shock would have forced a fundamental and no doubt agonising reappraisal of the whole venture, before decisions became irreversible. It would have concentrated minds wonderfully. It would have dispelled the complacency by which Asquith, Grey, Lloyd George, and Balfour, the Opposition's representative on the War Council, had accepted Churchill's proposal. It would have forced them to think hard about exactly what it was that he had proposed and they had approved. It would have obliged Kitchener to take a definite stand one way or another. Perhaps most importantly at that stage of the game, it would have alerted Admiral Carden and his colleagues on the spot about the true state of things in Whitehall, and the disarray of opinion at the Admiralty, which made a mockery of Churchill's claim that he was merely passing on the opinion of 'high authorities'.

Alternatively, if Asquith, Kitchener, and Churchill believed that Fisher was indispensable, they should have locked him into a pledge to abide by Council decisions, on the very conditions he had set in his letter of resignation: that he would support the venture 'if accompanied by military cooperation on such a scale as will permanently hold the Dardanelles Forts'. Yet even when these conditions were met, or intended to be met, by a series of War Council decisions in the following weeks, Fisher continued his campaign of denigration and sabotage until, with his actual resignation in May, he destroyed himself and Churchill – and the Liberal Government to boot.

Admittedly, it was almost impossible to lock Jacky Fisher into anything. His mood swings belong to the study of psychology rather than naval strategy. One week he was saying: 'I'll go through the straits tomorrow.' Next week, he was writing to Churchill: 'You are just simply eaten up with the Dardanelles and can't think of anything else! Damn the Dardanelles! They'll be our grave.' But this volatility should surely have warned Asquith and Churchill either to pin him down, once and for all, to one agreed line – or to get rid of him.

Asquith's motives were purely political. He was obsessed with maintaining a superficial Cabinet unity, and he believed it could not survive Fisher's resignation. He dreaded what the London press and the Tories would make of it. Churchill's motives were personal. He still admired Fisher, and believed that he could charm and chivvy him along as he had so often in the past. Fisher himself feared Churchill's power to mesmerise him and deliberately avoided face-to-face encounters as much as possible. 'He out-argues me,' he told friends. Towards Asquith, Churchill was increasingly disillusioned but still deferential. Early in February, he wrote a stiff letter to the Prime Minister pleading for action in the Balkans to save Serbia from being crushed by the Austrian armies: 'Surely in your position you cannot be content to sit as a judge pronouncing on events *after* they have taken place.' On second thoughts, he sent his letter minus this deadly accurate assessment of Asquith's performance. Churchill had hit the nail on the head, but baulked at driving it home.

When it had all ended in disaster, Churchill attempted a breath-taking reversal of responsibility – it was all Fisher's fault. Speaking in the House of Commons after his resignation in 1915, he asserted that Fisher could and should have vetoed the whole thing. 'If the First Sea Lord had not approved the operations,' Churchill told the House, 'if he had believed they were unlikely to take the course that was expected of them, if he thought they would lead to undue losses, *it was his duty to refuse consent*. No one could have prevailed against such a refusal. The operation would never have begun.'

6

'Only dig, dig, dig'
February–May, 1915

'Are the Australians good enough for an important operation of war?' Prime Minister Asquith wanted to know at the War Council on 16 February, 1915. 'Quite good enough if a cruise to the Sea of Marmara is all that is contemplated,' Lord Kitchener replied. Kitchener personified the way in which the Dardanelles project transmuted, by fits and starts, from a naval demonstration to large naval exercise, then to a combined naval–military operation, then to a predominantly military campaign, drifting to disaster; and he expressed the off-handedness with which the Australians and New Zealanders were sent to Gallipoli.

Churchill never shared Kitchener's cavalier attitude towards the Anzacs. From the time he delivered the first contingents to Egypt, he envisaged a role for them very different from either a 'cruise to the Marmara' or 'chewing barbed wire in Flanders'. More than a month before he learnt of the Russian plea for relief, he spoke at the War Council about the need for wide-ranging military action against Turkey. This idea led him to cancel Kitchener's order that the transports which had carried the AIF to Egypt should be dispersed; Churchill kept them ready at Alexandria Harbour. As he saw it, 'The arrival of the Anzacs in Egypt created the nucleus of an army needed to attack the heart of the Turkish Empire.'

They had been training for three months in Egypt. The main Australian camp was at Mena near Cairo. According to Churchill, 'The Australian battalions trampled the crisp sand of the Egyptian desert in tireless evolutions.' According to the British major general, Alexander Godley, in charge of the New Zealand Expeditionary Force, the Australians 'crammed Cairo full every night, and never seem to make any attempt to go home at the time they should'. Unlike his exemplary New Zealanders, the Australians 'really painted Cairo red', Godley told his wife – although they were better behaved 'now that their money is running out and Christmas is over'. Their pay was six shillings a day, two shillings more than the British 'Tommy' received. They saw the Sphinx and clambered up the Great Pyramid, some scratching their names, like the soldiers of Alexander the Great, Julius Caesar, and Napoleon Bonaparte before them. My father, Norman Henry Freudenberg, with the 2nd Light Horse from Queensland, recorded in his journal a visit to the Great Mosque of Cairo, noting 'the chandelier donated by Napoleon' in 1798. Some could afford to go further afield, like Lieutenant-Colonel John Monash, who organised an excursion to the ruins of Memphis. He had a poor opinion of the locals, expressing to his wife opinions held by Australians of all ranks: 'My principal impression was of a yelling, screaming crowd of dirty, smelly Arabs, donkey-boys, Bedouins, Dragomans, donkeys, camels and mules, whirling along in a pandemonium of confusion, noise, shouting and muddled arrangements.' Perhaps it was this sort of activity which earned them back home the sardonic title of 'six bob a day tourists'. That was before Gallipoli.

The story of the Anzacs and Gallipoli begins formally on 16 February 1915. Churchill called it 'The Day of Resolve'. On that day, the Cabinet War Council in London took the crucial decision which turned the enterprise into a joint navy–army campaign: the Anzacs in Egypt were to be 'available in case of necessity' to support the naval attack on the Dardanelles. They were to assemble on the Greek island of Lemnos, about one hundred kilometres west of the entrance to the Dardanelles. They would be joined by the Royal Naval Division, which Churchill had created, and the 29th Division – the last fully-trained division of the old regular army not yet committed to France. 'You get through,' Kitchener told Churchill, 'and I will find the men.'

Three days later, Kitchener reneged. It was the very day the fleet opened fire on the outer forts of the Dardanelles. Kitchener informed the War Council on 19 February that in view of Russian reverses in East Prussia and the hard fighting in France, it was too risky to send his prized 29th Division to the Mediterranean; the thirty thousand Australian and New Zealand troops in Egypt were enough for the job. Churchill protested: 'The Australians and New Zealanders could not be called first-rate troops at present, and they require a stiffening of regulars.' Kitchener remained unmoved. 'I felt at that moment in an intense way a foreboding of disaster,' Churchill wrote in *The World Crisis*. 'I urged the Prime Minister to make his authority effective and to insist upon the despatch of the 29th Division to Lemnos or Alexandria.' Asquith squibbed it. He told Churchill, 'Nothing more can be done. I've done my best to persuade Kitchener. I can't overrule him or face his resignation on a question like this.'

Churchill had given Admiral Carden all that he had asked for – and more. On 19 February, Carden's fleet opened its campaign by bombarding the outer forts guarding the entrance to the Strait. First reports claimed success, but in the days that followed, it became clear that Turkish defences were far stronger than anticipated. Churchill, however, was jubilant on hearing a report from the American Ambassador to Turkey that Constantinople was in a state of panic, and that the Sultan was packing up to leave. In London, the Foreign Secretary, Sir Edward Grey, claimed that news of the Allied action had strengthened pro-British attitudes in Greece and throughout the Balkans. Perhaps after all, the key pieces in Churchill's grand design were falling into place.

Such was the euphoria in London at the Fleet's apparent early success that Churchill drew up the terms of surrender: 'Should we get through the Dardanelles, as is now likely, we cannot be content with anything less than the surrender of everything Turkish in Europe,' he wrote to Sir Edward Grey on 28 February, 'but remember Constantinople is only the means to an end – and the only end is the march of the Balkan States against the Central Powers.' In short, from Constantinople to Vienna and Berlin!

Asquith's daughter, Violet, recorded about these days: 'I was sitting with Clemmie at the Admiralty when Winston came in in a state of wild excitement and joy. Winston totted up our combined forces: we now had the Anzac Army Corps on the spot, the Royal Naval Division on the way, the French division, the promise of three Greek divisions and the Russian Army Corps at Batoum.' The Greeks and Russians never materialised. 'The 29th Division was still in the balance,' Churchill had told her, 'but Turkey, encircled by a host of enemies, was doomed, the German flank was turned, the Balkans for once united and on our side, the war shortened perhaps by years' and, she concluded, 'Winston's vision and persistence vindicated'.

Reality began to take over. Day by day, it became clearer that naval action alone would not be enough, and that ultimate success would require substantial support from the army. On 26 February, Churchill told the War Council: 'With proper military and naval cooperation and with the forces which are available, we can make certain of taking Constantinople by the end of March.' If the 29th Division and the promised French and Russian brigades, with possible Greek contingents, were added to the thirty thousand Anzacs, he calculated, the force available could be as high as 115,000 – all without detriment to the battles then raging on the western front. Next day, Churchill placed a formal demand before Asquith and Kitchener:

> I must now put on record my opinion that the military force provided viz. two Australian divisions supported by nine naval battalions and the French division, is not large enough for the work it may have to do; and that the absence of any British regular troops [i.e. the 29th Division] will, if fighting occurs, expose the naval battalions and the Australians to undue risk.

Even if the Navy succeed unaided in forcing the passage, the weakness of the military force may compel us to forgo a large part of the advantages which would otherwise follow.

At the very least, these two paragraphs, and the date on which they were presented to the War Council – 27 February, the day the naval bombardment was temporarily suspended – exonerate Churchill from the charge made by Charles Bean and Lloyd George, among others, that he persisted impetuously with a one-sided naval operation, and from the other charge that he was to blame for inadequate army support. It certainly exonerates Churchill from any accusation that he was careless about the Anzacs and the burdens they would be called upon to bear.

At the end of the War Council meeting on 27 February, Asquith explained the whole situation to Venetia Stanley, setting out for her benefit all its political, strategic and diplomatic ramifications:

We are all agreed (except K) that the naval adventure in the Dardanelles should be backed up by a strong military force. I say 'except K' but he quite agrees in principle. Only he is very sticky about sending out there the 29th Division, which is the best one we have left at home. He is rather perturbed by the strategic situation both in the East and West, and wants to have something in hand, in case the Germans are so far successful against Russia for the moment, as to be able to despatch westwards a huge army – perhaps of a million – to try and force through Joffre and French's lines . . .

One must take a lot of risks in war, and I am strongly of opinion that the chance of forcing the Dardanelles, and occupying Constantinople and cutting Turkey in half, and arousing on our side the whole Balkan peninsula, presents such a unique opportunity that we ought to hazard a lot elsewhere rather than forgo it.

Churchill went all out to convince Kitchener. At the next War Council, Asquith wrote, 'Winston was at his worst, noisy, rhetorical, tactless – or full. K, I think on the whole rightly, insisted on keeping his 29th Division at home, free to go either to the Dardanelles or to

France.' But Kitchener's vacillation was at last about to end. He was waiting for firsthand information from his man-on-the-spot, General Sir William Riddell Birdwood, hand-picked by Kitchener to command the Australian Imperial Force in Egypt.

Birdwood was then 49. He had served on Kitchener's staff in South Africa and India, and regarded him as 'the greatest influence on my life'. He was to form a first-class relationship with the officers and men of the AIF, leading them throughout the Gallipoli campaign, and then in France until May, 1918, when he handed over command of the Anzac Corps to Sir John Monash, retaining administrative control of the AIF until the end of the war. When elevated to the peerage in 1938, he took the title of Baron Birdwood of Anzac.

Kitchener ordered Birdwood to go aboard Carden's flagship and assess his prospects. As for the Anzacs, Kitchener told him, they were 'intended not so much for operation on the Gallipoli Peninsula as operations in the neighbourhood of Constantinople'. On 5 March, after three days with Carden, Birdwood cabled Kitchener: 'I am very doubtful if the Navy can force the passage unassisted.'

Those twelve words from the soldier on the spot did more to energise Kitchener than three weeks of Churchillian eloquence and bluster: the army would have to support the fleet in full strength. On 10 March, Kitchener announced that the situation in France was 'now sufficiently secure to justify the despatch of the 29th Division to the Mediterranean'. On the same day, he decided to send General Sir Ian Hamilton to command what he called the Constantinople Expeditionary Force; it would total seventy thousand troops. In a brief interview at Horse Guards, whence for two hundred years scores of generals had been despatched to defend the Empire, Kitchener told Hamilton: 'We are sending a military force to support the Fleet now at the Dardanelles, and you are to have command.' Next day, farewelled by Churchill, but without proper plans, maps, or staff, Hamilton left London by train for Marseilles, to be taken by sea to the seat of war. Kitchener's parting words rang in his ears: 'If the Fleet gets through, Constantinople will fall of itself and you will have won not a battle but the war.'

Another decisive factor in forming the new campaign strategy was a revised assessment from Sir Henry Jackson at the Admiralty. In all his presentations and his misrepresentations, Churchill had relied heavily on Jackson's highly qualified support for action by the Royal Navy alone. Now, in a minute dated 11 March, Jackson said: 'The position has considerably changed recently; there are now ample forces ready at short notice for cooperation [with the navy] if necessary, and I suggest the time has arrived to make use of them . . . I suggest the Vice-Admiral be asked if he considers the time has now arrived to make use of military forces to occupy the Gallipoli Peninsula, and clear away the enemy artillery on that side – an operation he would support with his squadrons.' Thus, just when Kitchener was making up his mind to send his 29th Division and Ian Hamilton to Gallipoli, the Admiralty 'high authorities' were recasting the entire enterprise. Since the Anzacs were at that time the only 'ample forces ready at short notice', their role had suddenly been placed at centrestage.

At sixty-two, Sir Ian Hamilton was the very model of a modern British general – elegant, intellectual, cultivated, brave, and generous. One of the best assets he took to Gallipoli was a keen insight into the character of the Australians who would form one third of his command. Like Birdwood, and unlike the vast majority of British officers, he liked Anzacs, and tried to understand them. He had come a long way from the amused witness of the 'infuriated mice' at Pretoria in 1900. As Inspector-General of Overseas Forces, he had been invited by the Australian Government to report on the progress of Australia's compulsory training scheme. He had delivered his report on 24 April 1914 – a year and a day before the landings at Gallipoli. Hamilton found that the chief defects of the Australian scheme were the short period of recruit training – equivalent to sixteen days, of which only eight were spent in camp – and the centralisation of administrative and financial control at Victoria Barracks, Melbourne. This, he warned, could lead to 'loss of the spirit of initiative', an 'increasing unwillingness on the part of officers to act on their own responsibility', and 'finally, the most fruitful cause of disaster in time of war – namely, the collapse of the officer, trained for many years to be frightened to death of a sixpence when he is suddenly called upon to decide a matter in which thousands of pounds may be involved'.

Hamilton was enthusiastic about Australia's fighting potential. 'The best assets of the Australian land forces at the present stage of development,' he reported, 'are to be found in the national soldier-like spirit; in the intelligence, and in the wiry, athletic frames of the bulk of the rank and file.' On the matter of discipline, a prime source of friction between the British and the Australians throughout the war, Hamilton wrote: 'I freely confess that my recollections of South Africa, coupled with the assurances of numerous Australian friends, had caused me to feel sceptical regarding the quality of the discipline I should find regulating the ranks of the army. But, if I came here prepared to ban, I can only say now – I was mistaken.' Hamilton stated:

> The Australian soldier is very amenable to discipline. That a contrary impression should be so prevalent is due to the following facts:
> (1) There are not yet competent commanders enough to go round;
> (2) Manifestation of any feeling, but more especially of feelings of respect, are discountenanced under the unwritten Australian code of conduct;
> (3) The private soldier does not clearly understand that what an officer *is*, is one thing, and that what he *stands for* is another and, militarily speaking, the significant thing.

Ian Hamilton never changed his mind on this; the Australians on Gallipoli, once they had found competent commanders of their own, never gave him cause to change it.

Churchill cabled Carden on 15 March: 'You must concert any military operations on a large scale which you consider necessary with General Hamilton when he arrives on Tuesday night. Meanwhile we are asking the War Office to send the rest of the two Australian divisions to Mudros Bay at once.' This would make fifty-nine thousand men available, and a further eighteen thousand from the 29th British division arriving early in April, Churchill told Carden.

This was his last message to the hapless vice-admiral, for there was a sudden change of command. Carden finally buckled under the pressure from Churchill pushing one way, Fisher the other. In his last days in charge, he locked himself in the lavatory of his cabin, communicating with his officers by means of notes passed under the door, until the doctors ordered a complete rest. Churchill signalled to his second-in-command, Rear Admiral John de Robeck, to take charge. Hamilton arrived on the eve of the day of decision at the Dardanelles.

The main achievement of Churchill's naval action so far had been to destroy any element of surprise. When the bombardment had opened on 19 February, the Turks had two divisions on the Gallipoli Peninsula. By March they had four. The fortifications had all been strengthened; mobile howitzers had been brought down from Constantinople, with German gunnery experts to help man them. Worst of all, the bad weather which had delayed the fleet's operations had provided a cover for the laying of new mines in the strait. By March, there were ten lines of them in the ten miles leading to the Narrows.

Churchill had telegraphed Carden on 11 March – the day after Kitchener's big mind-change: 'We suggest for your consideration that a point has now been reached when it is necessary to overwhelm the forts of the Narrows at decisive range by bringing to bear upon them the fire of the greatest number of guns, great and small.' Churchill was more peremptory on 14 March, after receiving top-secret naval intelligence that the Turkish forts were desperately low on ammunition: 'The operation should now be pressed forward methodically and resolutely by night and day.' This time even Fisher was enthusiastic: 'By God, I'll go through tomorrow. We shall probably lose six ships, but I'm going through.' The new commander, de Robeck, complied. Nobody could have imagined it then, least of all Churchill himself – but it was the last time a direction from Churchill was to have a decisive impact on the Gallipoli campaign. The day of decision and disaster for his navy – 18 March 1915 – was to be the day that began Churchill's eclipse.

It dawned a sparkling spring morning on the Aegean. The most powerful fleet the Dardanelles had ever seen in its long history entered the strait in all its might and majesty. In the first line sailed *Queen Elizabeth, Agamemnon, Lord Nelson, Inflexible, Triumph*, and *Prince George*; behind them the French battleships *Suffren, Bouvet, Charlemagne*, and *Gaulois*, alongside *Cornwallis* and *Canopus*; the reserves brought up the rear, *Vengeance, Irresistible, Albion, Ocean, Swiftsure*, and *Majestic*. Churchill later described a scene of 'terrible magnificence':

> The mighty ships wheeling, manoeuvring and firing their guns, great and small, amid fountains of water, the forts in clouds of dust and smoke pierced by enormous flashes; the roar of the cannonade reverberating back from the hills on each side of the Straits, both shores alive with the discharges of field guns; the attendant destroyers, the picket-boats darting hither and thither on their perilous service – all displayed under shining skies and upon calm blue water, combined to make an impression of inconceivable majesty and crisis.

Within two hours the forts had been silenced and the minesweepers were ordered to enter the strait. Suddenly, *Bouvet* exploded and sank with the loss of six hundred men. Soon after, *Inflexible* also struck the same minefield, a newly laid, undetected line running parallel with the Asian shore; then *Irresistible*, then *Ocean*, both sinking later that night after their crews had been rescued by the destroyers. De Robeck called off the action about 5.00 p.m. The fleet retired, never to return.

On 22 March, Hamilton and Birdwood conferred with Admiral de Robeck on board his flagship, *Queen Elizabeth*. They informed London that they had agreed there would be no further attack by the navy alone; the forts would have to be taken from behind; and this would have to be done by landing Hamilton's army on the Gallipoli Peninsula. Churchill was stunned. He penned a long telegram, denying that the losses of 18 March justified abandoning the naval effort, and urging a renewal of the sea attack as soon as possible. Fisher flatly refused to send it, telling Churchill: 'What more could we want? The Army is going to do it. They ought to have done it all along.'

Churchill rushed to 10 Downing Street and showed his draft telegram to Asquith: 'I found him in hearty agreement with it.' But Asquith refused to act. Churchill wrote in *The World Crisis*: 'Looking back, one can see now that this was the moment for the Prime Minister to intervene and make his view effective.' Some chance! 'The Admirals had definitely stuck their toes in,' Churchill wrote. 'I was therefore compelled under extreme duress to abandon the intention of sending direct orders to Admiral de Robeck to renew the attack.' Churchill was no longer the master. From that moment, the Royal Navy fell into a secondary role, providing transport, convoys, reconnaissance, logistical support, and covering fire for the multitude of military movements which led to Anzac Cove. Churchill was to become hardly more than a bystander, at most a cheerleader, as the Anzacs prepared for their part in the largest amphibious operation in history, until the Allied landings in Sicily in 1943 and Normandy in 1944.

Churchill was becoming isolated. Fisher would not pass on his orders to the fleet. Kitchener avoided talking to him. Asquith, in his letters to Venetia, mocked him. The War Council, Churchill's best forum, did not meet between 19 March and 14 May. All the forces now assembling in Mudros Harbour on Lemnos were there on Churchill's initiative: he had delivered the Anzacs to Egypt; he had prevailed on Kitchener to despatch the 29th Division; he had personally ordered his Royal Naval Division to the Mediterranean; he had appealed to French ambitions in the Near East, to persuade them to divert a division from the defence of the sacred soil of France. But at some seventy-five thousand, those troops totalled only half the number Churchill believed necessary to take the forts and let the fleet through. Now the fleet had withdrawn and, against his emphatic wishes, cast the whole burden on Hamilton's forces.

Churchill could perhaps console himself with the thought that Hamilton would have been his own choice for the Gallipoli command. The pair had formed something of a mutual admiration society from their times together in India and South Africa. Of a paper Churchill had written in August, 1911, predicting with uncanny accuracy a war with Germany in August or September, 1914, and what would happen in France in the first forty days, Hamilton wrote: 'A masterly paper. All the way down you hit the nail bang on the head as if you were a historian recapitulating rather than a statesman risking prophecy.' And Churchill had written of Hamilton: 'His mind is built upon a big scale, being broad and strong, capable of thinking in army corps and if necessary in continents, and working always with serene smoothness undisturbed alike by responsibility or danger.'

But now even Hamilton had cut himself off from Churchill. Before leaving London, he had promised Kitchener that he would not contact Churchill direct. On the same day that he had his sea meeting with de Robeck, Hamilton wrote in his diary words that must surely send a chill of anger to the heart of any Australian who reads them today:

> The sailors say special craft are being built back home for possible landing on the Baltic coast. Each lighter can carry 500 men and has bulletproof bulwarks. They call them 'beetles'. Landing from these would be child's play. Winston would lend us some. But how do I get a cable to Winston? If it falls into the hand of Fisher it fails. The sailors tell me he is obsessed by the North Sea and the Baltic and grudges us every rope's end or halfpennyworth of tar. Rotten luck to have cut myself off from wiring to Winston. Still, I see no way out of it. With K. as jealous as a tiger, what can I do? The sailors won't cable themselves. Frightened of Fisher. So I've asked K. for the beetles myself.

Such was the code of gentlemen among those who ran the British Empire in 1915. The 'beetles' duly arrived – in August!

Hamilton's concept was simplicity itself. 'In my mind,' he recalled in his *Gallipoli Diary* in 1924, 'the crux was to get my army ashore. Once ashore I could hardly think that in the long run Great Britain and France could not defeat Turkey; the problem as it presented itself to us was how to get the troops ashore.' In the long run, Britain and France did defeat Turkey and the Ottoman Empire. In the short

run, they left forty-five thousand British, Indians, French, Australians, and New Zealanders dead on Gallipoli. Hamilton's remark
reflects the attitude that had pervaded British thinking from the day
of conception to the day of execution: contempt for the Turks. In his
general order before sailing from Alexandria, Hamilton had sur-
mised that the Turks would offer stout resistance, but that once
beaten off, 'they would turn on their German masters'. After that it
would be a pushover or, perhaps, in the language of an American
general to the President of the United States ninety years later, a
'cake-walk'.

The general and his staff ignored a number of factors: the element
of surprise had been utterly lost; Liman von Sanders had reinforced
the defence to eighty thousand men or more, and had marshalled
them skilfully at the key points on the high ground along the peninsula; the savage terrain mocked the idea that, once a foothold was
gained, it would be easy to push inland and across the peninsula; and,
above all, that the Turks, famous for their stubbornness in defence,
were fighting on and for their own soil. Despite his faith in British
power, Hamilton was denied the full support of the Empire's greatest
resource, its navy. In Churchill's cry of despair, 'a wall of crystal,
utterly immovable, began to tower up in the Narrows, and against
this wall of inhibition no weapon could be employed'. The No principle had become established, Churchill wrote: 'I could never lift the
No that had descended, and soon I myself was to succumb.'

Hamilton's plan provided for two main landings and two feints.
The British 29th Division would make five landings on beaches at
Cape Helles, the peninsula's southern tip; their objective would be
the Achi Baba Ridge. The Anzacs would land at Gaba Tepe, a small
promontory on the west coast further north; their objective would
be Chunuk Bair heights on the Sari Bair Ridge. Whoever possessed
these heights would dominate the peninsula. Diversionary landings
would be made by the French Division on the Asia Minor coast at
Kumkale, opposite Cape Helles, and by the Royal Naval Division at
the Bulair Isthmus in the north of the peninsula. On the morning of
Sunday, 25 April, all these landings were made more or less according to plan. After that, nothing went according to plan.

Churchill's clear and vivid account of the Anzac landing echoes in style the description of another historic amphibious campaign, the account by Julius Caesar of his more successful invasion of Britain in 55 BC, which Churchill had struggled to translate as a thirteen-year-old:

It had been intended to land the Australian and New Zealand Army Corps near Gaba Tepe with the purpose of striking across the neck of the Peninsula towards Maidos [a town overlooking the strait]. In contrast to the landings of the 29th Division at Helles, this all-important descent was to take place before dawn and without artillery preparation. It was hoped that while the Turkish forces were involved at the end of the Peninsula with the 29th Division, the Anzacs would make great headway in its most vulnerable part. The arrangements provided for successive landings from boats and launches, aided by destroyers, of 1500 men at a time. A rugged and difficult spot half a mile north of Gaba Tepe, unlikely to be elaborately defended, was chosen for the landing. In the dark, the long lines of boats missed their direction and actually reached the coast a mile further to the north, entering a small bay steeply overhung by cliffs till then called Ari Burnu, but in future Anzac Cove. This accident led the attack to a point quite unexpected by the defenders. The actual landing was made with little loss and the foot of the cliffs proved in practice well sheltered from artillery fire. On the other hand, it carried the Australian advance away from the broad depression from Gapa Tepe to Maidos into the tangled and confused underfeatures and deep ravines radiating in all directions from the mountain of Sari Bair.

Doubtless keen to give the Royal Navy due credit for its role, and point to the imperial character of the operation, Churchill continued:

As the flotilla approached the shore, a scattered fire from the Turkish pickets rang out; but the Australians leaping from the boats into the water or on to the beach scrambled up the cliffs and rocks driving the Turks before them in the dim but growing light of dawn. The destroyers were close at hand with another 2500 men and, in scarcely half an hour, upwards of 4000 men had been landed. The skirmish developing constantly into an action rolled inland towards the sunrise, and by daylight considerable progress had been made. By half-past seven, 8000 men in all had been landed. In spite of rifle and artillery fire which steadily increased against the Beach, by 2 o'clock the whole infantry of the leading Australian division, 12,000 strong, and two batteries of Indian mounted artillery, were ashore occupying a semi-circular position of considerable extent. The 2nd Division, including a New Zealand brigade, followed, and within a period of twenty-four hours in all 20,000 men and a small proportion of artillery were effectively landed.

In fact, the achievement compounded the problem – twenty thousand men with equipment and stores crammed on a beach about a kilometre long and a hundred metres wide were not a source of strength but a logistical nightmare. Churchill, of course, knew no more about the topography of Gallipoli or the terrain behind Ari Burnu, the northern part of Anzac Cove, than any of the Anzacs who landed there. No more did Hamilton, or the Anzac commanders, Birdwood, Bridges, and Godley. Their great misfortune was to be confronted by a Turkish commander who knew a lot about it, and how to defend it – Lieutenant-Colonel Mustafa Kemal. The man known to history as Kemal Ataturk, 'Father of the Turks', was to rebuild the debris of the Ottoman Empire into the modern Republic of Turkey. During the Balkan Wars of 1912 and 1913, Kemal had been in charge of the Turkish defence of the Gallipoli Peninsula. With the insight of a born general, he had been convinced of two facts: that a sea-borne attack on Gallipoli would come at two points, Cape Helles and Gaba Tepe; and that the key to the defence of the peninsula was 'to hold the ridges – the rugged vertebrae of the peninsula – and oblige the enemy to storm them once he had landed'. On the very eve of Anzac, he had ordered three of his battalions on an exercise in the direction of Chunuk Bair – the objective Hamilton had set for the Anzacs. Alerted by the naval bombardment before dawn on 25 April, he mustered another ten battalions with the call: 'I do not order you to attack, I order you to die.'

'The long-limbed athletic Anzacs thrust inland in all directions with fierce ardour,' wrote Churchill. 'They now came into contact with extremely well-handled and bravely led troops and momentarily increasing artillery fire. In the deep gullies, among the rocks and scrub, many small bloody fights were fought to the end. Quarter was neither asked nor given; parties of Australians cut off were killed to the last man; no prisoners wounded or unwounded were taken by the Turk.'

If it is asserted that the birth of Australian nationhood occurred with the landing at Anzac Cove, then it was nearly aborted within twenty-four hours of the landing. Ian Hamilton saved it. General Hamilton had witnessed the first landings from *Queen Elizabeth*. Passing Anzac Cove on the way to Helles, he saw the Australians of the 3rd Brigade 'all the way from the Southern Cross for love of the old country and of liberty. Wave after wave of little ants press up and disappear. We lose sight of them as they lie down. Bravo!' About sixteen hours later, Hamilton was appalled to receive a despairing message from Birdwood. At 10.00 p.m. Bridges and Godley, in charge of the landing, had asked Birdwood to come ashore from his headquarters on board HMS *Queen* for an urgent conference. As a result of their discussions, Birdwood sent a hurried message to Hamilton: 'Both my divisional generals and brigadiers have represented to me that they fear their men are thoroughly demoralised by shrapnel fire to which they have been subjected all day after exhaustive and gallant work in the morning.' He said he feared a fiasco in the morning, and said ominously: 'If we are to re-embark, it must be at once.' Birdwood's message implied more than it said directly: there was no express request for evacuation. Like so many Gallipoli documents, there is always a loophole for posterity. But when this one reached the *Queen Elizabeth* about 2.00 a.m. on 26 April, Hamilton saw at once the horrendous implications, not only for his entire campaign, but for the Anzacs in the eye of history.

Without fuss or fury, Hamilton sat down and wrote to Birdwood: 'Your news is indeed serious. But there is nothing for it but to dig yourselves right in and stick it out. It would take at least two days to re-embark you.' He encouraged Birdwood by telling him (correctly) that the Australian submarine *AE2* had got through the Narrows that day and (incorrectly) that the 29th Division at Helles would be 'advancing tomorrow to relieve the pressure on you . . .' He appealed to Birdwood: 'Make a personal appeal to your men and Godley's to make a supreme effort to hold their ground.' Then, in a postscript which has justly become part of the Anzac Legend, Hamilton wrote:

> You have got through the difficult business. Now you only have to dig, dig, dig, until you are safe.

Australians at home could not know how close the Anzac landing had come to ignominy. In fact, they knew nothing about it at all for days. Early reports, via the London press, were meagre and misleading. On 29 April, the Australian Prime Minister, Andrew Fisher, had to admit to the Parliament in Melbourne that he did not know where the Australian forces were or what they were doing. He had, Fisher said, just received a cablegram from the Secretary of State for the Colonies offering 'His Majesty's warmest congratulations on the splendid gallantry and magnificent achievement of your contingent in the successful progress of the operations at the Dardanelles'. Apart from that, said Fisher, 'We cannot say what part of the Australian Forces has been sent and what has not.' The despatch by Charles Bean, the Australian official war correspondent, was delayed by military censorship and bureaucracy. The first full report, published in Australian papers on 8 May, nearly a fortnight after the landings, was the work of the British correspondent Ellis Ashmead-Bartlett, a flamboyant adventurer with influential connections and a zest for life and love. His biographer, the distinguished Australian journalist Fred Brenchley, described him as 'the journalist who sparked the Gallipoli legend'. Certainly, Ashmead-Bartlett's account, later expanded into books and lectures in Britain and Australia, laid the foundation. His despatch said: 'There has been no finer feat in this war than this sudden landing in the dark and the storming of the heights and, above all, the holding on whilst reinforcements were landed. These raw colonial troops in these desperate hours proved worthy to fight side by side with the heroes of Mons, the Aisne, Ypres and Neuve Chapelle.' John Monash later complained in a letter to his wife that Australian readers had a 'total lack of perspective' about Gallipoli, because of the prominence given to 'the first mad rush ashore'.

It was not until 12 May that Prime Minister Fisher had enough information to make a formal statement in the House of Representatives. His speech, devoid of any account of the landings or their purpose, was largely a reading of congratulatory messages, from George V, the Prime Minister of Canada, the Governor of New Zealand, and the First Lord of the Admiralty. Churchill's message, dated 30 April, noted that 'the Fleet is filled with intense admiration at the feat of arms accomplished by the Army'. Fisher concluded by reading a message, dated 11 May, from Ian Hamilton:

> May I, speaking out of a full heart, be permitted to say how gloriously the Australian and New Zealand Contingent have upheld the finest traditions of our race during the struggle still in progress, at first with audacity and dash, since then with sleepless valour and untiring resource they have already created for their countries an imperishable record of military virtue.

On behalf of the Opposition, Joe Cook said: 'The news made our pulses thrill. It verified our belief that our brave boys were willing to stand alongside the seasoned troops of the Motherland.'

Except in Australia, the Gallipoli landings quickly passed from centrestage. Whatever its significance for Australia April, 1915, was full of portent for a new and terrible age. Across the English Channel, on 22 April, Sir John French launched the Second Battle of Ypres which, in a month's fighting, cost the British Expeditionary Force in Flanders nearly sixty thousand casualties, and set the template for the Somme and Passchendaele. In response the Germans let loose the first gas attack of the war. In the dominion stakes, Canada beat Australia by a day in the race for first blooding, with the engagement of the Canadian Expeditionary Force at Ypres, with heavy losses. German Zeppelins appeared in the skies above

England. At sea, Germany unleashed its U-boats in unrestricted submarine warfare; American outrage over the sinking of the passenger liner RMS *Lusitania* on 7 May persuaded the Kaiser to rescind the order – for the time being. And then there was the matter of the Armenians. For all the bravery and sacrifice of its soldiers on Gallipoli, the regime in Constantinople chose that moment to commit the characteristic crime of the twentieth century – genocide. Starting in April, they began the massacre of not less than a million Armenians during 1915. A quarter of a century later, an Austrian then serving in the ranks of the German army in France would justify the Final Solution with the comment: 'Who remembers the Armenians?'

On the same day as the speeches about Anzac in the House of Representatives in Melbourne, a Turkish torpedo sank the HMS *Goliath* near the entrance to the Dardanelles. The explosion aboard the battleship ignited a chain of self-destruction in London which sank the First Lord of the Admiralty. With the Anzacs and the British, at Helles, struggling to hold their beachheads, the loss of *Goliath* convinced Lord Fisher that the Dardanelles campaign was doomed, and that his fleet there was in deadly peril. As he now saw it, Winston Churchill was to blame for the whole fiasco, yet Churchill still persisted, obstinately urging de Robeck on to another frontal attack. Fisher had had enough. He insisted that his pride and joy, HMS *Queen Elizabeth*, be brought home out of harm's way. After a fierce row, Churchill backed away.

Now it was Kitchener's turn for a tantrum. Churchill and Fisher were breaking faith with the army, he shouted at Churchill, during the War Council meeting of 14 May – the first in six weeks. The order to bring *Queen Elizabeth* home stood; but, to mollify Kitchener, Churchill proposed to send some lesser ships and more submarines to de Robeck as replacements. When Fisher saw Churchill's draft of the new order, he finally cracked. He sent Churchill another resignation. He wrote: 'I am off to Scotland at once so as to avoid all questionings.' A search found him holed up in a room at the Charing Cross Hotel, a few hundred yards from the Admiralty. Asquith ordered Fisher to return to his post 'in the King's name'.

Amid all this brawling over Gallipoli, Asquith and Kitchener – and the Liberal Government as a whole – faced a first-class political crisis. As the fighting on the Ypres salient stalled, Sir John French leaked to the London *Times* a story blaming a shortage of shells for the bloody failure at the Battle of Loos. For the first time, the mighty Lord Kitchener became a press target. The Tory Leader, Bonar Law, a dour Scottish-Canadian of impeccable integrity and reliable mediocrity, declared an end to the political truce that had prevailed uneasily since the outbreak of war. Asquith realised that he could not face the House of Commons with two scandals on his hands – the shell shortage and Fisher's resignation. Spurred on by Lloyd George, he entered negotiations for a coalition with Bonar Law. Law made a condition: Churchill must go. Asquith had no intention of putting up a fight, least of all on behalf of Winston Churchill. In any case, the fight had gone out of the Prime Minister himself. He had just received a letter from Venetia Stanley informing him that she intended to marry Edwin Montagu, the Chancellor of the Duchy of Lancaster, a minister without portfolio, and the lowest-ranking member of Cabinet. On 17 May, Churchill breezed into the Prime Minister's room in the House of Commons, ready with a fighting speech to defend the government and a list of names for a new Board of the Admiralty, post-Fisher. Asquith greeted him with the news of the impending coalition and the query: 'What are we to do for you?' Over the next week, Asquith reconstructed his Cabinet as a coalition of Liberals, Conservatives, and one Labour representative. The great British Liberal Party never again formed a government in its own right. Asquith solved the problem of what to do for Churchill with deft malice: he dropped Montagu and put Churchill in his place as Chancellor of the Duchy of Lancaster.

To the end of his life, Churchill maintained that the dither and delay which had marked Asquith and Kitchener's handling of Gallipoli in these critical weeks had caused its failure. He argued that two divisions could have occupied the Gallipoli Peninsula as early as February 'with little fighting'. These two divisions would, of course, have been the Anzacs. As each month passed, the number of divisions available always fell short of the number needed. Churchill wrote in *The World Crisis*: 'The paralysis of the Executive during the formation of the coalition in May delayed for six weeks the arrival of the British reinforcements and enabled the Turks to double the strength of their Army.' The result, he wrote, 'was a combination of evil happenings extraordinary among the hazards of war'.

7

'The last and finest crusade'
May–November, 1915

The Gallipoli campaign was lost in London in May 1915. The political crisis was the work of generals and admirals as much as politicians; but it undermined the political support on which any chance of military success at Gallipoli depended. Asquith's early enthusiasm evaporated. Because his expressions of that enthusiasm had been limited to the War Council and his letters to Venetia Stanley, everybody else assumed that his treatment of Churchill meant that he had withdrawn his support. Kitchener, rendered vulnerable by the shells scandal, wrapped himself in a cocoon of majestic silence. Hamilton was reluctant to press Kitchener too hard for the arms and men he needed, for fear of making life even more difficult for his embattled hero. Fisher bombarded his former colleagues with hysterical letters denouncing Churchill and the madness of Gallipoli. Lloyd George, created Minister for Munitions to fix the shell shortage, still favoured action in the East, in the Balkans or Palestine or Mesopotamia, but distanced himself from Churchill and Gallipoli. Balfour, Churchill's first and firmest supporter in the War Council in January, and his replacement as First Lord of the Admiralty, had grown weary of the whole business.

The admirals at the Dardanelles lost their nerve when they lost Churchill and his driving force.

Churchill was down but not yet out. Asquith kept him on the War Council; but his very advocacy now became counterproductive. The hostility of the Tories guaranteed their contempt for his views and rejection of his advice. The Tory entry into the Cabinet signalled a victory for the hard-line westerners such as Sir Douglas Haig and the Chief of the Imperial General Staff, Sir William Robertson. Before the year was out, Haig would replace Sir John French as commander-in-chief on the western front, and begin to apply the deadly calculus of attrition.

Asquith had shown all his old political mastery in forming the coalition. By persuading Bonar Law to accept the second-rank post of Secretary of State for the Colonies, Asquith achieved his main objective of keeping the key levers in Liberal hands. In a sense, it was a triumph for parliamentary government-as-usual. But Asquith's smart political footwork only confirmed the assessment that Lloyd George had made to the newspaper proprietor, Sir George Riddell, two months earlier: 'Asquith lacks initiative and takes no steps to control or hold together the public departments, each of which goes its own way without criticism. This is all very well in time of peace, but during a great war the Prime Minister should direct and overlook the whole machine.' Lloyd George was to try to adopt his own formula, with only partial success, when he deposed Asquith in December, 1916. When Churchill became Prime Minister in May, 1940, he was to adopt it thoroughly, controlling all the levers by making himself Minister of Defence.

After the reconstruction of his government, Asquith officially changed the name of the War Council to the Dardanelles Committee (not to be confused with the Dardanelles Commission of Inquiry, appointed later to whitewash the fiasco). At first glance, the new name might suggest that he was upgrading the status of the Gallipoli campaign. In reality, it meant a shift of war-making power from the politicians to the generals, who took the hint that Downing Street was opting out of the direction of the main game on the western front. It was as if the circus-master of the Greatest

Show on Earth suddenly declared that his main concern was Sideshow Alley.

On his last day on duty at the Admiralty, Churchill received news that a German submarine had torpedoed HMS *Triumph* off Gaba Tepe. The Anzacs watched in horror as the battleship sank with the loss of two hundred men. Among the awe-stricken watchers on the Anzac shore was my father, who had arrived with the 2nd Light Horse in time to act as a stretcher-bearer in the fierce Anzac attacks and Turkish counterattacks throughout May. As the fighting continued, both sides declared a twelve-hour truce to enable them to bury their three thousand dead. The symbolism of it all was immense: Lord Fisher's fears about the vulnerability of the fleet were vindicated; the stalemate on the Gallipoli Peninsula had become, literally, entrenched. A different kind of symbolism occurred on the other side of the world. The day of the burial truce, 24 May, was also Empire Day; in schools throughout Australia, the name of Anzac was invoked to identify and glorify Australia's new place in the annals of the British Empire.

Churchill hid his true feelings about Asquith's betrayal. Fifty-four years later, Clementine Churchill told his biographer Martin Gilbert: 'The Dardanelles haunted him for the rest of his life. He always believed in it. When he left the Admiralty, he thought he was finished. I thought he would never get over the Dardanelles. I thought he would die of grief.'

Churchill never behaved, at least in public, like a man dying of grief. On 5 June, he journeyed to Dundee to report to his constituents on the dramatic turn of events. He expressed unqualified support for the new Coalition and undaunted faith in success at Gallipoli: 'Beyond those few miles of ridge and scrub on which our soldiers, our French comrades, our gallant Australians and our New Zealand fellow-subjects are now battling, lie the downfall of a hostile empire, the destruction of an enemy's fleet and army, the fall of a world-famous capital, and probably the accession of powerful allies.' In terms reminiscent of the recipe for exhilaration he had given in his maiden speech fourteen years before, he reached a tremendous Churchillian peroration:

The loyalty of our Dominions and Colonies vindicates our civilisation, and the hate of our enemies proves the effectiveness of our warfare. Yet I would advise you from time to time, when you are anxious or depressed, to dwell a little on the colour and light of the terrible war picture now presented to us. See Australia and New Zealand smiting down, in the last and finest crusade, the combined barbarism of Prussia and of Turkey. See General Louis Botha holding South Africa for the King. See Canada defending to the death the last few miles of shattered Belgium. Look further, and, across the smoke and carnage of the immense battlefield, look forward to the vision of a united British Empire on the calm background of a liberated Europe.

Four days after Churchill's Dundee speech, Asquith put Gallipoli on the agenda of the full Cabinet for the first time. 'A very hot discussion arose on the general principle of whether the Dardanelles enterprise should be persevered with, or whether we should "cut our loss" and come away,' Churchill wrote, in a 1915 version of the 2005 taunt of 'cut and run'. In Churchill's view: 'From the moment of the formation of the coalition, power was dispersed and counsels were divided, and every military decision had to be carried by the same sort of process of tact, temporising and exhaustion which occurs over a clause in a keenly contested Bill in the House of Commons in time of peace.' However, the new Cabinet agreed to Kitchener's proposal to send three of his 'New Army' divisions to Gallipoli. It was the first time that the British Cabinet had made a definite decision on anything to do with Gallipoli.

Kitchener's reinforcements (including, at last, the 'beetles' wanted in March), enabled Ian Hamilton to plan his August offensive, in which the Anzacs were slated to play the key role. Once again their goal was to capture the heights of Sari Bair – the same objective they had been set on 25 April. This time, the big push forward was to be flanked and strengthened by a new landing with divisions fresh from England, at Suvla Bay, a few miles north of Anzac Cove. Churchill was to write: 'The long and varied annals of the British Army contain no more heart-breaking episode than the Battle of Suvla Bay. The greatness of the prize in view, the narrowness by which it was missed, the extremes of valiant skill and of incompetence, of effort and inertia, which were equally presented, the malevolent fortune which played about the field, are features not easily to be matched in our history.' The British failure at Suvla Bay was the genesis of another enduring element in the Anzac legend: that Australian courage and lives were squandered by the reckless, uncaring incompetence of British officers.

The stuff of legend was evident in abundance during these terrible August days. At Lone Pine, in fierce hand to hand fighting to dislodge the Turks from a few acres known to the Turks as the Ridge of Blood, the Australians won seven Victoria Crosses. The New Zealanders lost eighteen hundred men on the crest of Chunuk Bair. The four suicidal charges straight into Turkish machine-gun fire at the Nek inspired, more than sixty years later, the Australian film *Gallipoli*, which created an indelible version of the campaign and its meaning for a new Australian generation.

Ellis Ashmead-Bartlett wrote a glowing account of the fight in a despatch dated 19 August. Published in the London *Times* on 3 September (such were the delays caused by Hamilton's rigid censorship), it said: 'The Anzac Corps fought like lions and accomplished a feat of arms in climbing those heights almost without a parallel, but all fell through, by the failure of a corps to make good its position on the Anafarta Hills further north and thus clinch the enemy's shell-fire.' This was a veiled reference to the unforgivable tardiness with which the British general, Sir Frederick Stopford, followed up his unopposed landing at Suvla Bay, allowing the Turks to bring up all the men and guns they needed to wreck the whole operation. Stopford, sixty-one, owed his appointment entirely to his seniority in the army list; he had never commanded in battle of any kind. Ashmead-Bartlett continued his mission to establish the Anzac legend: 'It was a contest of giants in a giant's country, and if one point stands out more than another, it is the marvellous courage, tenacity and reckless courage shown by the Australians and New Zealanders.'

The British correspondent's admiration for the Anzacs was deep, genuine, and abiding. But his real opinion of Suvla Bay was expressed in a secret letter he wrote to Asquith, dated 8 September: 'Our last great effort to achieve some definite success against the Turks was the most ghastly and costly fiasco in our history since the Battle of Bannockburn [against the Scots under Robert the Bruce in 1314].' This letter was potential dynamite. Ashmead-Bartlett had already made a dash to London in May to lay his mounting concerns before his influential friends, but had been thwarted by the political turmoil. Churchill he found 'the perfect picture of a fallen minister, taking great gulps of brandy like some wretch who is strengthening his hand for suicide'. He claimed that Churchill moaned: 'The Navy never fought it out to a finish. They never gave my schemes a fair trial.' He had meetings with Asquith and Kitchener and was staggered by their ignorance about conditions at Gallipoli. He returned to Gallipoli in despair, but determined to get them to see the truth. After Suvla Bay, he could hold back no longer. In his letter to Asquith, he questioned the whole campaign, but focused on Hamilton and his headquarters staff:

> The fundamental evil at the present moment is the absolute lack of confidence amongst all ranks in the Headquarters Staff. The confidence of the Army will never be restored until a really strong man is placed at its head. The lack of a real Chief at the head of the Army destroys its discipline and efficiency all through, and gives full rein to the jealousies and recriminations which ever prevail amongst the divisional leaders. At present the Army is incapable of a further offensive. The splendid Colonial Corps has been almost wiped out. The outlook for the unfortunate troops is deplorable. We do not hold a single commanding position on the Peninsula and at all three points, Helles, Anzac and Suvla Bay, we are everywhere commanded by the enemy's guns.

Ashmead-Bartlett entrusted his explosive letter to a visiting Australian journalist, Keith Murdoch. Murdoch had been defeated by Charles Bean in a ballot conducted among its members by the Australian Journalists' Association for the job of official war correspondent with the AIF. In the small, intimate world of politics and journalism in Melbourne, Murdoch had pursued his urge to cultivate and exploit men of power and influence, a talent inherited and globalised by his son Rupert. In particular, he cultivated the Labor leaders Andrew Fisher and W. M. Hughes. In mid-1915, he had been appointed to head the London office of the United Cable Service. Prime Minister Fisher asked him to stop at Egypt on the way to investigate complaints from the Anzacs that their letters were being lost or delayed. But Fisher also had a more confidential task for Murdoch: Would he undertake certain inquiries in the Mediterranean theatre of war? Prime Minister Fisher told Murdoch that the Australian Government was concerned at the lack of accurate information from London and Egypt, or any information at all from Gallipoli. In short, could the correspondent please help the Australian Government find out what was going on?

Sir Ian Hamilton, the recipient of what he called a 'wheedling letter' from Murdoch, allowed him to come over to Gallipoli from Egypt, under conditions of strict censorship. Murdoch spent less than a week at Anzac, largely in the company of Ashmead-Bartlett. According to Ashmead-Bartlett, Murdoch was 'very alarmed at the state of the army and the prospects of a winter campaign', and feared that unless the truth be known in London, there would be 'a great disaster'; but the thirty-year-old journalist from Melbourne felt 'his word would not carry much weight and begged me to write a letter which he would carry through uncensored, telling the plain truth'. When Murdoch reached Marseilles en route to London, British Intelligence officers, tipped off by one of Ashmead-Bartlett's press rivals, confiscated the letter even though it was addressed to the Prime Minister of the United Kingdom.

In London, Keith Murdoch addressed a letter to Andrew Fisher. 'It is undoubtedly one of the most terrible chapters in our history,' Murdoch told the Australian Prime Minister. 'Your fears have been justified.' He wrote:

I have not military knowledge to be able to say whether the enterprise ever had a chance of succeeding. Certainly there has been a series of disastrous underestimations, and I think our Australian generals are right when they say that, had any of these been luckily so un-English a thing as an overestimation, we should have been through to Constantinople at much less cost than we have paid for our slender perch on the cliffs of the Peninsula.

His lack of military knowledge did not prevent Murdoch from describing Hamilton as a 'failed strategist' and Birdwood as 'a good army corps commander and nothing more', who 'did not have the brain of a great general'.

Murdoch had made the most of Andrew Fisher's letters of introduction to gain entrée into high places in London. He showed his document to Lloyd George, who arranged for him to see the Prime Minister. Then Asquith did an extraordinary thing: he had Murdoch's letter, ostensibly written to the Prime Minister of Australia, printed as a state paper for circulation among members of the British Cabinet. The letter itself was not particularly well argued or accurate; but Asquith's act of printing and circulating it in his own name invested it with prime ministerial authority. For most of the Cabinet, it was the first time they had heard that disaster was impending at Gallipoli.

Events everywhere were conspiring to bring an end to the Gallipoli campaign. Churchill's vaunted dominoes of the Dardanelles were falling – but in the wrong direction. True, Italy had been bribed to desert Germany and Austria, its pre-war Triple Alliance partners; but as the situation on Gallipoli worsened, Bulgaria had joined Germany and Austria in an all-out attack on Serbia. The remnants of the Serbian army escaped by an epic march over the mountains to the coast of Albania. The Russian front seemed to be crumbling. Austria stood astride the Balkans. In the end, the Anzacs and the Allied forces were evacuated from Gallipoli because of fears, not that the Turks might hurl them into the sea, but that the Germans might trap them by land.

By mid-September, the British War Council gave up all thought of reinforcement and turned to the idea of withdrawal. On 23 September, Lloyd George brought up a proposal to move the division at Suvla Bay to Salonika in Greece, as part of an operation to rescue Serbia. Churchill protested that the real aim of the proposal was 'to abandon the Dardanelles'. It would be 'throwing up the sponge', he said. 'It would be very hard to explain, particularly in the case of Australia, a sacrifice which had been incurred with no result.' For his part, he said: 'I will not be a party to abandoning the Dardanelles.'

Nearing the end of the game, Churchill played the Australia card. He elaborated on the Anzac theme in a memorandum sent to every member of the Cabinet on 15 October:

> Australia and New Zealand sent the first armies they have ever raised to fight against Germany in Europe. Without consultation with their Governments or Parliaments, these forces were sent by Lord Kitchener to the Gallipoli Peninsula. A greater mark of confidence in a single man has scarcely ever been shown. By feats of arms and military conduct of the highest order, they have seized and held at a cost of 30,000 men and cruel hardships a position close to the vitals of their enemy, from which, if properly sustained, it is probable that no force can be brought to bear to move them.
>
> Anzac is the greatest word in the history of Australasia. Is it for ever to carry for the future generations of Australians and New Zealanders memories of forlorn heroism and of sacrifices made in vain?

With increasing vehemence and irrelevance, Churchill continued to urge renewal of the naval attack and more troops for one last thrust across the peninsula. His arguments became desperate, verging on despicable: 'I trust that the unreasonable prejudice against the use by us of gas upon the Turks will now cease,' he told his Cabinet colleagues. 'The massacres by the Turks of Armenians,' he wrote on 20 October, 'should surely remove all false sentiment on this point, indulged in, as it is, only at the expense of our own men. Large installations of British gas should be sent out without delay.' Churchill gave an odd twist to concerns expressed by Keith Murdoch that the Anzacs would suffer in the unaccustomed harsh winter of Gallipoli: 'The winter season is frequently marked by south-westerly gales, which would afford a perfect opportunity for the employment of gas by us.'

Kitchener telegraphed to Sir Ian Hamilton on 11 October: 'What is your estimate of the probable loss which would be entailed to our forces if the evacuation of the Gallipoli Peninsula was decided upon and carried out in the most careful manner?' Kitchener made it plain to Hamilton that there was to be no argument about politics or strategy: 'In your reply you need not consider the possible future danger to the Empire which might be thus caused.' Kitchener had Hamilton's answer in twenty-four hours: 'It would not be wise to reckon on getting out of Gallipoli with less loss than half the total force' [50,000 out of 100,000]. Two days later, Kitchener decided to recall Hamilton. In his place he sent General Sir Charles Monro.

'General Monro was an officer of swift decision,' Churchill wrote in *The World Crisis*. 'He came, he saw, he capitulated.' Monro, he said, 'belonged to that school whose supreme conception of Great War strategy was killing Germans. Anything that did not kill Germans was useless. To such minds the capture of Constantinople was an idle trophy.' All this was mightily unfair to a brave and competent general. But within three days of his arrival on 29 October, Monro telegraphed London recommending total evacuation; he thought it might be done with losses of a mere thirty to forty per cent. This, says Churchill, 'fell like a thunderbolt on Lord Kitchener.' He decided to go out and see for himself. Of all the generals he had sent to Gallipoli, Birdwood of the Anzacs was the only one he now trusted. Before he left London, Kitchener cabled Birdwood: 'The more I look at the problem, the less I see my way through, so you had better work out very quietly and secretly a scheme for getting the troops off the Peninsula.'

Westminster politics sealed the fate of the Gallipoli campaign. The crucial moment came on 5 November when Bonar Law wrote to Asquith saying that the position was 'untenable', and to delay a decision until Kitchener's return would be a 'fatal error'. Asquith acted with his usual skill and agility when political survival was at stake. He made the most of Kitchener's absence in Egypt and Gallipoli. He installed himself at the War Office, recalled Sir John French from France, and gave Douglas Haig the command of the western front. The hard-line westerners had won out. To terminate

Gallipoli, Asquith abolished the Dardanelles Committee and reconstituted it as the Cabinet War Committee. On 11 November, he submitted the names of its five members to the King. Lord Kitchener was not among them. Nor was Winston Churchill.

For the first time in his life, Churchill admitted defeat. He sent Asquith his resignation: 'I have a clear conscience which enables me to bear any responsibility for past events with composure. Time will vindicate my administration of the Admiralty and assign me my due share in the vast series of preparations and operations which have secured us the command of the seas.' Asquith accepted it with routine regret and said he felt acutely 'on personal grounds the severance of our long association'. In his resignation speech in the House of Commons on 15 November, Churchill remained defiant and unrepentant:

> All through this year I have offered the same counsel to the Government
> – undertake no operation in the West which is more costly to us in life
> than to the enemy; in the East, take Constantinople; take it by ships if
> you can; take it by soldiers if you must; take it by whatever plan,
> military or naval, commends itself to your military experts, but take it,
> and take it soon, and take it while time remains.

That same day, unknown to Churchill, Kitchener had telegraphed London making his own recommendation for the abandonment of the Gallipoli campaign. But Churchill knew what was coming. The signs were everywhere unmistakable that the venture was coming to its end in defeat and recrimination. Distancing himself from the inevitable, he told the House of Commons:

> The situation is now entirely changed, and I am not called upon to offer
> any advice upon its new aspects. But it seems to me that if there were
> any operations in the history of the world which, having begun, it was
> worthwhile to carry through with the utmost vigour and fury, with a
> consistent flow of reinforcements, and an utter disregard of life, it was
> the operations so daringly and brilliantly begun by Sir Ian Hamilton in
> the immortal landing of the twenty-fifth of April 1915.

Three days later, Major Churchill crossed the Channel to take charge of a platoon of Grenadiers in France; he would soon be given command of a battalion.

WITH CHURCHILL GONE and Kitchener sidelined, the Cabinet War Committee repudiated everything they had worked for. Gallipoli must be evacuated immediately. Birdwood wanted the Anzacs at least to stay; de Robeck was willing to make one last naval effort at the Strait. No, said Asquith, Bonar Law, and Lloyd George; if Anzac was overrun, if the Royal Navy failed again, the Empire would suffer an even worse humiliation than withdrawal would be. For the sake of the prestige of the British Empire, the greatest power in the Islamic world, with its sixty million Moslems in India, Gallipoli must be evacuated lock, stock, and barrel.

The evacuation was the best-planned and most successful operation of the campaign. In spite of Hamilton's prediction of fifty per cent losses, and Monro's more optimistic thirty to forty per cent, there were no casualties from hostile fire. For once, the Turks were surprised. When an Anzac said to his mate, 'I hope they don't hear us going', he meant not the Turks, but the Australian dead. My father, wounded at Lone Pine in August, wrote in his journal when they got back to Alexandria, 'What troubled me more than anything was that we were leaving the graves of our brave comrades in enemy hands and I wondered if they would be looked after and respected.' On the few hectares around Anzac Cove, Cape Helles, and Suvla Bay, and in the waters nearby, the dead of Gallipoli numbered 8719 Australians and 2701 New Zealanders; the British lost 21,255 men, the Indians 1358; French losses were estimated at 10,000. The Turkish defenders admitted to 86,000 killed. Seven years later, Churchill was to invoke the Anzac war dead in the graves on Gallipoli when he and Lloyd George brought the British Empire to the brink of another war with Turkey.

8

'True to the Empire'
January, 1916–March, 1919

From the beginning, the legend of Gallipoli was manipulated to strengthen Australia's bonds of Empire. The political and military imperatives of the time, in both Australia and Britain, demanded it. Some Australians, like Banjo Paterson, tried to celebrate Gallipoli in national terms, as a coming of age of the six federated colonies, where 'the old state jealousies of yore were dead as Pharaoh's sow', and where:

> Our old world diff'rences are dead
> Like weeds beneath the plough
> For English, Scotch and Irish-bred
> They're all Australians now.

Australia's oldest Catholic newspaper, the *Freeman's Journal*, the voice of Irish Australians since 1850, also stressed the nationalist theme. In an editorial to mark the first anniversary of Anzac, the paper said: 'Before the Anzacs astonished the watching nations, our national sentiment was of a flabby and sprawling character. We were Australian in name, and we had a flag, but we had been taught by our politicians not to trust ourselves . . . Anzac Day has changed all that.'

Others tried to blend the national and the imperial sentiment. The servicemen's organisation, the Returned Soldiers and Sailors Imperial League of Australia (RSL), formed in time for the first anniversary commemoration, embraced the double identity of Australia and Empire. The league's declared aims were 'to promote the welfare and increase the worth of returned soldiers as citizens of Australia and the British Empire by endeavouring to preserve and extend the spirit of National Devotion and the faith of Imperial Duty in peace as in war'. One of its founders spoke of the RSL as standing 'for the national life of Australia and the imperial destiny of the British race'.

Most political leaders, however, emphasised Gallipoli's imperial character. The two men who did most to tell Gallipoli as a story of Empire were Winston Churchill and the new Prime Minister of Australia, William Morris Hughes. They had different motives. For Churchill, it was self-justification; for Hughes, self-aggrandisement. They were at one, however, in exploiting Gallipoli for all it was worth in rousing the Empire to even greater effort.

Churchill, as we have seen, invoked the Anzacs in his final plea for a renewed attempt on the Dardanelles Strait by the navy, and one more push across the Gallipoli Peninsula by the army. Thereafter, the Anzacs became central to his justifications for the entire enter- prise. They had played a key role in two of the three operations which, he claimed, had brought the campaign to the very edge of triumph and success. These were the landings at Anzac Cove and Cape Helles on 25 April 1915, and Suvla Bay on 7 August; the other near-success, he claimed, was the naval attack on the Strait on 18 March. All three, he argued, could have been successful if properly executed, reinforced, and followed up. The tragedy of Gallipoli, he maintained, lay neither in the concept nor the losses, but in the squandering of a great idea and a noble sacrifice.

Churchill mounted a vigorous defence at the Dardanelles Commission of Inquiry in the last months of 1916. At one level, the appointment of such an inquiry can be seen as a remarkable affirmation of parliamentary democracy in wartime. It can also be seen as another ploy in Asquith's fight for survival; the stock-in-trade of an embattled politician, to avoid, delay, or bury controversy and criticism. Asquith appointed the 75-year-old Lord Cromer, Queen Victoria's proconsul in Egypt, to head the commission and asked Andrew Fisher, now High Commissioner in London, to represent Australia. The Australian Government allowed him to accept, but only 'as the nominee of the Home Government and not as an official representative of Australia'.

The Australian Government wanted nothing to do with the business. It wanted neither recrimination nor scapegoats, and it regarded the inquiry not only as a distraction from the war effort, but as a detraction from the Anzac achievement. The Australian Minister for Defence, George Pearce, said that the inquiry was a 'blunder and a sign of weakness' on Asquith's part. Sir George Reid, now a member of the House of Commons, took part in the debate to set up the inquiry, and expressed his fear that 'the Empire might be weakened by revelations of incapacity on the part of high Imperial officials'. The closest Andrew Fisher came to admitting his own doubts was when he told his fellow commissioners: 'I am in the unhappy position of having been a Prime Minister of a Dominion which sent men, and we relied upon you knowing better about things than we did and being able to look after things with which you could not entrust us.'

The Commission's interim report in March, 1917, covered only the period to the naval failure in March, 1915. It criticised Churchill for inadequate consultation with his Board of Admiralty, and Asquith for failing to meet the War Council in the crucial weeks between March and May; and it deplored 'the atmosphere of vagueness and want of precision which characterised the War Council's proceedings'. It criticised Kitchener for his procrastination over sending the 29th Division. Kitchener, however, was now truly beyond criticism. He had drowned in the North Sea in June, 1916, when a mine sank the ship taking him on a mission to Russia.

Australia's Andrew Fisher managed to criticise Churchill without naming him. He registered his strong dissent from the report's finding that his namesake, Lord Fisher, should have told the War Council that he disagreed with Churchill over the Dardanelles plan. Andrew Fisher wrote: 'It would seal the fate of responsible government if servants of the State were to share the responsibility of Ministers to Parliament and to the people on matters of public policy. The Minister has command of the opinions and views of all officers of the Department he administers. Good stewardship demands from the Ministers of the Crown frank, fair, full statements of all opinions of trusted, experienced officials to [Cabinet] colleagues.' In other words, Churchill had failed to do his constitutional duty.

In contrast to the Australian Government's calculated indifference, the Australian press seized on the interim report's criticism of Churchill to place the blame entirely on him. The *West Australian* said that while he may have had a 'proposal' to knock Turkey out, he had no real scheme. 'Like a new Joshua, he would sound his trumpet and the walls of Jericho would collapse.' The *Sydney Morning Herald*, foreshadowing Charles Bean's criticism in the official war history, said that Churchill's conduct was 'an example of the rashness of an amateur in risking great issues on the strength of his opinion on highly technical subjects'.

In one of several submissions and personal appearances, Churchill had maintained his confidence in the judgement of history; a confidence doubtless strengthened by his later dictum that the verdict of history would be favourable, 'particularly as I intend to write the history myself':

It will then be understood that the capture of Constantinople and the rallying of the Balkans was the one great and decisive manoeuvre open to the allied armies in 1915. It will then be seen that the ill-supported armies struggling on the Gallipoli Peninsula, whose efforts are now viewed with so much prejudice and repugnance, were in fact within an ace of succeeding in an enterprise which would have abridged the miseries of the World and proved the salvation of our cause. It will then seem incredible that a dozen old ships, half a dozen divisions, or a few hundred thousand shells were allowed to stand between them and success. Contemporaries have condemned the men who tried to force the Dardanelles. History will condemn those who did not aid them.

Nothing in the interim report, or the full report delayed until 1919, ever shook him from this position.

CHURCHILL, NOW PROMOTED to colonel, stayed with his battalion in the trenches in France until the lure of Westminster proved too strong. In March, 1916, he returned on leave to make a powerful speech in the House of Commons, mounting an effective attack on Asquith's conduct of the war. Yet, once again, his impulsiveness got the better of his judgement. To the astonishment of his hearers and readers, he ended by calling for the return of Lord Fisher to the Admiralty! The main beneficiary of this speech was Lloyd George, who more than ever seemed the only man capable of providing Britain with energetic leadership. In December, 1916, Lloyd George manoeuvred Asquith out of the prime ministership. He formed a new coalition minus about one hundred Asquithian Liberals, who sank into sullen support or fitful opposition. He was keen to bring Churchill out of the wilderness, but Conservative hostility was too strong, even for Lloyd George. He was unable to overcome their objections until July, 1917, when he took the plunge and made Churchill Minister for Munitions.

The political changes in Australia ran curiously parallel. W. M. Hughes succeeded Andrew Fisher as Prime Minister of Australia on 27 October 1915. Fisher accepted with relief the chance to become High Commissioner of Australia in London. His cavalier treatment at the hands of the British Government, the lack of information about the role or even the whereabouts of the Australian troops he had committed to the fortunes of war, weighed heavily upon him. Although only fifty-eight, the same age as Hughes, he was in poor health. He recognised his limitations as a wartime leader, the last role he would have chosen for himself. By the end of 1915, he had a pretty clear picture about where Hughes, his second-in-command, was taking the Labor Government and the Labor Party, and he did not like what he saw. Fisher knew that Hughes wanted to impose conscription for military service overseas. He believed that any attempt to impose conscription for the AIF would lead to civil disorder and mass disobedience throughout Australia. As Attorney-General, Hughes had pushed through the draconian War Precautions Acts which curtailed civil liberties in a way not attempted in any of the other dominions, and were hardly less repressive than Britain's own Defence of the Realm Act. German-born Australians, less than one per cent of the population, but still the largest white, non-British segment, were treated as 'the enemy within the gates'. The fact that they had boys at Gallipoli (like my father), or in Flanders (like my uncle Berthold, killed at Messines), brought them scant protection. It must have seemed to Andrew Fisher that Billy Hughes, dynamic in peace, had become demonic in war.

Hughes, as skilful and calculating as any politician Australia has produced, knew exactly what he was doing and exactly what he wanted to achieve. He wanted a powerful voice in the councils of the British Empire; and he convinced himself that only the maximum war effort by Australia could entitle him to such a role. For Hughes, that meant conscription for service in the trenches of the western front. His efforts to achieve it split his party, his government, and his nation. The Great Schism over conscription is pivotal to the story of this book. It impacted on Australia in political, social, and military life like nothing else in our history; and it was to have profound effects on Churchill's relations with Australia twenty-five years later. Australian Labor's rejection of conscription for overseas service distorted both Churchill's attitude towards the Curtin Labor Government and the portrayal of Australia's war effort in the account of the Second World War that Churchill transmitted to posterity.

Hughes began his prime ministership with a grovelling statement of loyalty, not so much to the Empire but to the Imperial Government, as he styled it. He was already preparing the ground for his campaign to introduce conscription, despite his denials to his parliamentary colleagues. On 29 October, two days into his premiership, he had been asked about a reported statement by Ashmead-Bartlett in London, that Gallipoli was a 'costly failure'. Hughes replied:

> I am sorry you have put that question. (Hear, hear.) We have no responsibility of directing the campaign. Our business is only to carry out the instructions of the Imperial Government, and to give it what assistance we can. At all events, we owe the Imperial authorities this duty: to refrain from criticising their actions. (Cheers.) I do not pretend to understand the situation but I do know what the duty of this Government is, and it is to mind its own business, (hear, hear) to provide our quota of men for the Imperial Government, and to see that they are efficiently led, fed and equipped. (Loud cheers.)

The principles thus established – that the British Government alone had the right and responsibility to set Australian troop levels, and that Australia's obligation was to meet those levels without question – became central to the pro-conscriptionist case.

Hughes fired the next shot in his campaign for conscription for service overseas on 15 December 1915, when he sent an official letter to the one million Australian male citizens aged between eighteen and forty-five, requiring them to register all their personal details under new regulations of the War Census Act. He headed his letter 'The Call to Arms':

> Dear Sir – The present state of war imperatively demands that the exercise of the full strength of the Empire and its Allies should be put forth. In this way only can speedy victory be achieved and lasting peace secured . . . Prussian military despotism must be crushed once and for all. To wage this war with less than our full strength is to commit national suicide by slowly bleeding to death . . . Our soldiers have done great things in this war. They have carved for Australia a niche in the Temple of the Immortals. Those who have died fell gloriously, but had the number of our forces been doubled, many brave lives would have been spared, the Australian armies would long ago have been camped in Constantinople, and the world war would have been practically over.

For all his devotion to the cause, not even Churchill put Gallipoli quite as high in world history as Hughes. Churchill only went as far as claiming that success at the Dardanelles might have shortened the war by a year or two. Hughes' letter demanded: 'If willing to enlist now, reply Yes or No. If not willing to enlist, state the reason why, as explicitly as possible.' To many of the recipients, Hughes' letter must have seemed like the official version of the white feather some were receiving anonymously in the post.

In January, 1916, the British coalition government adopted conscription of unmarried men over eighteen. The Liberal conscience was eased somewhat by the argument that the very success of the voluntary system had disrupted war production; the 'best workers', it was argued, were providing the fodder instead of making the cannon. Churchill, his Liberalism receding from the time he became First Lord of the Admiralty, had been a strong advocate of conscription. He was away in France and out of the Cabinet which made the decision. Asquith accepted it reluctantly as another instalment in the price of keeping the coalition together, and himself as Prime Minister. Fifty Liberals voted against the legislation. This breach began the disintegration of the British Liberal Party. Britain's acceptance of conscription had obvious implications for Australia. Once Britain had shown the way, it made it easier for Australian pro-conscriptionists to raise the old cry: 'What will they think in England?'

Hughes was anxious to go there to learn for himself. Just before he sailed, he opened a recruiting campaign in Melbourne on 13 January. If there had been just one more Australian division at Gallipoli, or 'two or three perhaps', he said, 'the Australian armies would now be in Constantinople and the whole fate of the world would have been changed'. A generation later, Churchill himself tried to exploit the myth that the mere presence of an Australian force might save an otherwise disastrous military situation, with Rangoon, of all places, replacing Constantinople as the pivot of history. Hughes signalled in unmistakable terms that he was determined to introduce conscription and that, if need be, he would break up the Labor Party in order to get it. There were those, he said, who 'pretend to speak as the mouthpiece of labour and unionism'. They had taken up 'their foul abode as foul parasites in the vitals of labour'. They sneered at patriotism 'because the very sound of the word cut them to the quick'. 'These men know no nationality, religion or principle and in the name of unionism and labourism I pass them out like devils out of swine.' [Tremendous cheering, according to the *Argus* report of 14 January 1916.] 'These no-conscription people, these peace people who babble about peace, who have a good word for every country except this, let them stand where they will, so long as they stand not with us.' By the extremism of his rhetoric, Hughes had deliberately pushed his Labor colleagues into supine support or implacable opposition.

Hughes reached London, via North America, in March and stayed until July. The British Establishment embraced him. He was made a Privy Councillor. He was invited to attend the War Cabinet, seated on Asquith's right hand. He was given freedom of the city by London, Manchester, Birmingham, York, Sheffield, Cardiff, Bristol, and Edinburgh; Oxford made him a doctor of laws; he walked in solemn procession to the Guildhall, arm-in-arm with the Lord Mayor of London. Keith Murdoch, who had flattered his way into the patronage of the press baron Lord Northcliffe, acted as his public relations officer. Murdoch fed the Australian press with glowing accounts of Hughes' reception at the heart of the Empire. The New Zealand-born cartoonist, David Low, who immortalised Hughes in impish caricature, drew him pounding the Cabinet table at 10 Downing Street, with Asquith saying to Lloyd George: 'David, talk to him in Welsh and pacify him.' He slept at Windsor Castle, earning the ultimate accolade from King George's secretary, Lord Stamfordham, in a private letter to the Australian Governor-General: 'He does not look like a Labour Premier – really at Windsor, in his tights (very well fitting) and generally well-turned out appearance, he might have been a diplomat of no little distinction.' Hughes himself tried on occasion to remind his audiences of his humble background. To the grandees of England at the Mansion House, he said: 'To those of us whose minds are filled with imagination, there is something which fires us in the fact of a representative of Australian labour being received by the majesty of this great city and being crowned with its ancient privileges.'

On the first anniversary of Anzac Day, Hughes hijacked the Gallipoli legend on behalf of imperial Australia. He began a process by which, even in Britain, Gallipoli was to become identified almost completely with Australia and the Anzacs. A commemoration of the first anniversary was held in Westminster Abbey, attended by King George and Queen Mary. The presence of Hughes, and a parade by two thousand soldiers of the AIF through London streets from St Paul's to the Abbey, placed Australia at centrestage, crowding out the memory that four times as many British, Indian, and French troops had fought and died at the Dardanelles. Hughes' speech to a select one thousand at the Hotel Cecil after the Abbey ceremony dominated *The Times*' report of the day's proceedings: 'The Australians and New Zealanders, when they landed in Gallipoli, set the seal upon the manhood of their peoples and flung wide the door that the Canadians had already opened to a new life for the British peoples of the Empire . . . On this day of Anzac one year ago the word "Empire" assumed a new and nobler meaning for us and for the world.'

The first anniversary of the Anzac landing fell on the Tuesday after Easter. That Easter weekend was one of the defining moments of the British Empire, and Australia's relationship to it. The Monday saw the Easter Rising in Dublin. In Sydney, the Labor Party Annual Conference 'solemnly pledged itself to oppose, by all lawful means, conscription of human life for military service abroad'. A British–Indian army of ten thousand, besieged in Kut, east of Baghdad, surrendered to the Turkish army. The humiliating news enraged the House of Commons, which on 26 April passed a bill for universal conscription, ending the exemption of married men, but maintaining exemption for Ireland.

On the backs of the 150,000 Australians already serving the Empire on active service, and the other 150,000 promised by June, Hughes was now proposing full-blooded imperial union. He told a luncheon given by the Empire Parliamentary Association: 'We have the means at our disposal, and we can cement for ever a Federation

– Empire – call it what you will – which will ensure the peace of the world.' The first task, Hughes told another banquet at the Carlton Club, the Tory citadel, was 'the extirpation, root, branch and seed, of German control and influence in British commerce and industry'. Nothing short of a decisive victory would avail, Hughes told the assembled Tories: 'Germany's military power must be utterly crushed. In no other way can the peace of the world be assured. Peace under any other conditions would be only a period of feverish preparation for another and even more fearful struggle.'

On the eve of Hughes' departure for home, the Australian residents of London organised a banquet at the Ritz Hotel for 23 June 1916. Hughes' hagiographer, the Australian journalist W. Farmer Whyte, described it as 'a night of oratory', the speakers including the proprietor of *The Times* and *The Daily Mail*, Lord Northcliffe; the Secretary of State for Foreign Affairs, now Viscount Grey; and Lord Rosebery, Gladstone's successor as Liberal Prime Minister in 1894; with Andrew Fisher in the chair. Hughes' theme was that from now on, there must be new ways of doing the Empire's business. 'It could hardly be denied that, if Britain has a right to compel the Dominions to incur such a tremendous burden of debt as this war could impose, their sovereignty or quasi-sovereignty disappeared.' Under the existing arrangements, the dominions had no voice in the questions of peace and war, and this raised issues 'which must be settled when the war is over'.

Churchill was present, having given up his army command in May. Although not listed to speak, he responded to a request from Fisher. Mr Hughes was quite right, he said: 'Imperial Federation, the organization of trade, relations with Germany after the war – these were all questions in which the Dominions had earned the right to have a say.' But they were all questions which depended upon another transcending question, namely, 'Are we going to win a decisive victory?':

> While we sit here, the fighting line of the British Army, with the Australian and Canadian armies included in it, is holding nearly forty of the finest Divisions of the German Army on its front, and every moment

a stream of killed and wounded is passing from the fighting line to the rear.

The Australians are in contact with the enemy, and what we need above all things is the feeling that behind the fighting line there is a resolute, intense, sagacious driving power which, by every means, social, political, military and naval, will be carrying our cause forward to victory.

It was a broadside against Asquith. Churchill reinforced his real meaning when he said of Hughes: 'Here is a man who has a seeing eye, a dauntless heart and a daring hand. And while we wish him god-speed on his journey home, we regret deeply that, at this critical moment in the history of the Empire and of the war, his counsel and inspiration should be withdrawn from the Mother Country.' Proposing the toast to the chairman, Hughes brought the evening to a close and his audience to its feet: 'No effort must be spared to bring the day of victory nearer. We must waste no time.'

Every one of the speeches that Hughes made in Britain, and in France when he crossed to visit the Australians on the western front, was calculated to boost his case for conscription in Australia. He had put the case in extreme terms which he must have known would be unacceptable to the majority of his Labor colleagues. A split was the inescapable consequence of his rhetoric. No other Allied leader, not even among the embattled French, was calling for total victory in Hughes' uncompromising black and white terms in the early part of 1916. The British Cabinet had not yet defined its war aims beyond the liberation of Belgium and the restoration of Alsace and Lorraine, the provinces lost by France in the Franco-Prussian War in 1871. Otherwise, their aims were hidden in secret treaties with allies like Italy. Hughes was the first leader to speak publicly about destroying Germany's trade and its colonial empire once and for all. Ideals such as the war 'to make the world safe for democracy', or a League of Nations to make the Great War 'the war to end all wars', were still in the womb of time and events, until the collapse of Tzarist Russia and the entry of the United States into the war in 1917. But Hughes struck powerful chords. As more and more politicians took his cue, to orchestrated press applause, the possibility of a negotiated peace receded month by month. The higher the death toll, the harder it became for either side to contemplate anything less than total victory. Millions more would have to die so that the dead so far would not have died in vain.

When Hughes returned to Australia at the end of July, 1916, after an absence of five months, he sidestepped questions on the conscription issue. But his extreme language in Britain had locked him irreversibly into conscription for Australia. He had damned anything less than 'total war'. He had preached a crusade against Germany, even unto the 'extirpation' of its trade and the ruin of its economy. Privately, he had excoriated Asquith's fumbling leadership. Asquith was 'too perfectly civilised' to be a war leader. Pervading every utterance was the call for supreme effort and sacrifice. The conclusion was inescapable: men and ever more men. Hughes deliberately raised British expectations about Australia's contribution to a total war effort. By so completely identifying Australia's interests with Britain, by insisting that every part of the white Empire, however remote, had obligations equal to Britain's, by glorifying Gallipoli as the blood sacrifice of a united, indivisible Empire, he set himself on an irrevocable course towards conscription in Australia. Anything less would have been hypocritical. Whatever his faults, Hughes was no hypocrite.

Billy Hughes and Winston Churchill shared the fatal delusion of many great politicians in trouble with their own parties: that their personal charisma might enable them to appeal to the people over the heads of party politicians, in order to form a new party in their own image. Unlike Churchill, Hughes seemed for a time to succeed, at the price of wrecking the Labor Party and depending on the support of men he had spent most of his life opposing and deriding. Yet, when the mundane realities of the two-party system reasserted themselves after the crisis of war, Hughes' dream evaporated. Churchill had to wait for a quarter of a century and an even greater crisis for a chance to realise his dream, and even he lost office as soon as he tried to translate his personal appeal into votes.

In September, 1916, the British Government requested an

Australian reinforcement of another thirty thousand men to make good the losses of the Somme battles. Hughes used the request to justify his announcement that a referendum would be held on 28 October. The question to be put to the people was: 'Are you in favour of the Government having, in this grave emergency, the same compulsory powers over citizens in regard to requiring their military service, for the term of this War, outside the Commonwealth, as it now has in regard to military service within the Commonwealth?'

For Australians, 'referendum' means a vote on a proposal to change their Constitution; but there was no constitutional requirement for the referendum on conscription. The Australian Parliament had legal power to conscript for overseas service. The referendums of October, 1916, and December, 1917, were in fact mere plebiscites, with no power to bind the Government, the Parliament, or any of its members. If either referendum had been carried, it could have had only a moral influence, as the registered expression of the will of the people. Of itself, it could not change a single parliamentary vote.

Hughes' options, however, were severely limited by the lopsided numbers in the Senate. In the 1914 double dissolution, Labor had won a clean sweep in five of the six states under the first-past-the-post voting system then operating. The party thus had thirty senators to the Liberals' six. This meant that Liberal support for a conscription bill would have been useless, unless thirteen Labor senators could be found to vote for it. This was not beyond the bounds of possibility. After the first referendum was defeated in October, 1916, Hughes walked out of the Caucus calling, 'Let those who support me, follow me'. Thirteen members of the House of Representatives and eleven senators followed him. It is reasonable to suppose that, had the referendum carried, another two senators at least would have joined him on the grounds that the people had spoken. With Liberal support, conscription would have then passed both houses.

Two overriding convictions drove Hughes towards the referendum option. Win or lose, it was the best way to keep his grip on the prime ministership. Even if he broke his Labor Government, he was the only man who could form a coalition, with the support of his own Labor followers and Joe Cook's Liberals. No other parliamentary combination had a hope of surviving. That is exactly what happened after the first referendum was defeated. When he led his 'Nationalist' coalition into a general election in May, 1917, he scored an overwhelming victory over Labor. Secondly, win or lose the referendum, it was the best way to appear to keep the commitments he had made in London. Here was a man, it would be said, prepared to risk everything to keep his word. And so it turned out. In all his subsequent appearances in London, he was hailed as the supreme Empire politician who had put country and Empire above party. The bottom line is that Hughes held the referendums, wrecked the Labor Government, split the Labor Party and divided Australia against itself in order to meet the expectations he had raised in Britain, to live up to his reputation there, and at the same time, to hold onto the prime ministership.

The referendum campaigns split the Labor Party in the most bitter and irreparable way imaginable. However much Hughes may have regretted severing his links with the party he had helped found, he saw new vistas of grandeur and opportunity opening before him. As is usual with defectors, he claimed he had not left his party – his party had left him. Labor had blown out its brains, he said. By the time of the first referendum in October, 1916, every state Labor conference had declared against conscription by big majorities. Hughes made no effort to argue his case within the policy-making councils of the ALP. Instead, he appealed to its members' loyalty to the Empire:

> The great enemy of Australia, of Labor, of liberty, is military despotism, of which Germany is the living embodiment. If we defeat her, the future of Australia – free and white – is assured. If we turn tail and, like cravens, desert the Empire, to whom we owe everything, abandon the Allies who have suffered such awful losses and horrors, and made such great sacrifices – but who still fight gallantly on – if we refuse to reinforce the heroic Anzacs, then, indeed, will fall upon us the doom we deserve, and before the tribunal of nations we shall stand condemned.

In the referendum of 28 October 1916, 1,160,033 voted 'no' and 1,087,557 voted 'yes'. The negative of 72,476, or 3.22 per cent, came from New South Wales, Queensland, and South Australia. The soldiers overseas voted 72,399 'yes', against 58,894 'no' votes, a far smaller majority than the conscriptionists had expected. My father told me forty years later that he had voted 'no' because 'if they didn't want to come, we didn't want them'. But the statistic which dominated both sides of the argument came from the battlefields at the end of August. In the battle of the Somme, the AIF casualties were twenty-three thousand killed or wounded in seven weeks of fighting. Over a year later, Hughes' second attempt at conscription was rejected against the background of even worse slaughter at Passchendaele. The fundamental issue in both referendums was always the reinforcement of the AIF versus a man's right not to be forced to the killing fields of France.

The extremism on both sides changed the language of Australia's political discourse permanently. Australia was no stranger to sectarianism or the politics of patriotism; but never before had either God or the Empire been invoked with such vehemence and divisiveness. Old, half-buried bigotries re-emerged with new virulence. In the aftermath of the Easter Rising of April 1916, with eighty-eight ringleaders sentenced to death by the British Government, and fifteen actually executed, anti-conscriptionism became identified with Irish disloyalty. Hughes had made conscription an unequivocal question of Empire:

> The great issue shines out clear and distinct. We are part of the British Empire; that is, we are one of the family of free British nations that engirdle the earth. While the Empire stands, we and all that we hold dear, the many privileges that self-government has enabled us to secure, the White Australia Policy, are safe. If the Empire falls we fall with it. The Empire is fighting for its life. Britain has asked us to do our share. The question is – are you going to do it?

Thus, the Empire itself became the focus for division. To be against conscription was to be against the Empire. The scuffles of the Boer

War now became fierce brawls and riots. W. A. Holman, who had so passionately opposed the Boer War in 1900, but now as Premier of New South Wales was a passionate pro-conscriptionist, turned on his hecklers at a meeting at Marrickville: 'You curs! It is a shame to think that the men who have volunteered will have to associate with you cowards [that is, as conscripts].' Twelve members of the revolutionary syndicate, the International Workers of the World, were charged with treason and arson. One of their leaders, Peter Larkin, had said at a rally in the Sydney Domain: 'Far better to see Sydney melted to the ground than to see the men of Sydney taken away to be butchered.'

Hughes' conscription campaigns opened an historic fault line in Australian political life. He staked everything on the Empire. He defined four basic principles of Australian patriotism: Australia's existence depended on the Empire; the interests of Australia and its imperial protector were identical; the imperial protector's requirements should be fully supported; and anyone who opposed any of these propositions was inherently disloyal. Now, in deadly earnest, loyalty to Australia was being defined in terms of loyalty to its imperial protector.

'THE EIGHTH OF AUGUST, 1918 was the Black Day of the German Army in the history of the war,' wrote General Ludendorff, victor over the Russians in the east, then commander of the Hindenburg Line in the west. As architect of Germany's March offensive on the western front, he had come within an ace of breaking the Allies. In the process, Ludendorff exhausted the German army. Now, in August, with the Allied strength slowly being replenished by the gradual arrival of the US army, France's Marshal Foch and General Haig were able to launch the decisive counterattack. The German army's Black Day was the AIF's day of highest success. Hughes' failure to conscript notwithstanding, the five divisions of the Australian Army Corps had been moulded into a superb fighting force. Their commander was General John Monash, born in Victoria in 1865, the son of German Jewish migrants. In civil life, he was a successful engineer; his pre-war military training and experience were entirely as a citizen-soldier. The English historian, A. J. P. Taylor, described him as 'the only general of creative originality produced by the First World War'. On the outbreak of war in August, 1914, Monash had written to his American cousin, Leo Monasch: 'It may cause you and your people surprise that I should take up arms in this quarrel, but then, you must not fail to remember that I am Australian born, as are my wife and daughter, that my whole interests and sympathies are British.'

Churchill, back in the British Cabinet as Minister for Munitions since June, 1917, by Lloyd George's grace and favour, still believed the war would drag on into 1919 or even 1920. He remained opposed to major new offensives on the western front until the Americans arrived in full strength. Suddenly, prospects changed dramatically. On the morning of 8 August, the Chief of the General Staff, Sir Henry Wilson, excitedly told the War Cabinet that a new British offensive had begun. Churchill at once flew across to France, to see 'this important moment in Allied fortunes' for himself. He had a personal interest. Wilson had told Cabinet that tanks would play an important part in what came to be called the Battle of Amiens. Ever since his Admiralty days, Churchill had fostered their development and as Minister for Munitions had given their production high priority. He arrived in France that afternoon, as the battle was in full swing. Next day he drove to army headquarters near Amiens for lunch with the commander of the British Fourth Army, Sir Henry Rawlinson.

In a letter to his wife, Clementine, written on 10 August, Churchill said: 'The events which have taken place in the last three days are among the most important that have happened in the war. Up to the present there must be at least 30,000 prisoners on our hands, with several hundred guns.' The Australian Corps of five divisions under Monash, along with the four divisions of the Canadian Corps, provided the main strength of the Fourth Army. He highlighted their role:

> The Australian armoured cars rushed through the moment the front was broken and attacked the headquarters of the transport and everything

they could find in the rear. They have reached the headquarters of an Army Corps and shot four of the staff officers. At another place they found the German troops in a village at their dinner and ran down the whole street firing in through the windows upon them, doing tremendous execution.

Churchill's description may be set against Ludendorff's account of the same operation, which Monash proudly reprinted in his own memoirs:

Early on 8 August, in a dense fog that had been rendered still thicker by artificial means, the British, mainly with Australian and Canadian Divisions and French, attacked between Albert and Moreuil with strong squadrons of tanks, but for the rest with no great superiority. They broke between the Somme and the Luce deep into our front. The Divisions in line allowed themselves to be completely overwhelmed. Divisional Staffs were surprised in their Headquarters by enemy tanks.

Ludendorff makes no mention of any shooting of German officers. Nor does Monash, although he contradicted Ludendorff on one point, noting that 'by tanks he meant our armoured cars, [which made the assault] a feat of daring and resolute performance which deserves to be remembered'.

Churchill, Ludendorff, and Monash agreed on the significance of the Australian contribution to the Battle of Amiens. Monash wrote:

A hole had been driven on a width of nearly twelve miles right through the German defence and had blotted out, at one blow, the whole of the military resources which it had contained. The resources of the Australian Corps had suffered scarcely any impairment as the result of that glorious day. Such small losses as had been incurred were more than counter-balanced by the elation of these volunteer troops at this further demonstration of the moral and physical superiority over the professional soldiers of a militarist enemy nation.

Ludendorff wrote that 'this day, the worst experience I had to go through' had 'made things clear for both Army commands'. He meant, as he was soon to tell the Kaiser, that Germany had lost the war.

Churchill saw to it that the tank and his own part in its development would be given due credit. He wrote to Clementine: 'I am so glad about this great and fine victory of the British Army. It is our victory, won chiefly by our troops under a British commander, and largely through the invincible Tank which British brains have invented and developed.' He grumbled about the undue credit given to the Americans, much as the Australians and Canadians grumbled about their achievements being described as British. He told Clementine that only one American regiment had been involved in the battle: 'Would you believe it – only three American Divisions were in the line at any one moment between Rheims and Soissons. They certainly had a good press. That is one reason why I rejoice that we should have won a great success which no one can take from us.'

This remark contains a clue to Churchill's multitude of inconsistencies: his views always reflected the office he held at any particular time. When he had been Home Secretary, he was all for economy against the navy. When he was head of the Royal Navy, he lost interest in reform. When he was out of office, he urged the British High Command to avoid offensives until the Americans arrived. Had his views prevailed, the British armies might have been spared at least some of the losses of Passchendaele; and Australia would have been spared the unnecessary travail of the second conscription referendum on 20 December 1917, even more bitter and divisive than the first, but with an even larger 'no' majority. Now that he was back in the big game as Minister for Munitions, Churchill had become impatient for British action, and apparently dismissive of the American role. At least he was not as jealous of American success as the British commander-in-chief; Haig had prayed in his diary in 1917: 'Please God, let there be victory before the Americans arrive.'

Early on the morning of 11 August, Churchill visited Monash at his headquarters near Villers-Bretonneux. They discussed 'the state of play' and German morale. Monash complained to his wife that his morning's work, preparing plans for a further advance, was 'much interrupted' by visitors: 'Quite early I had a call from Mr Winston Churchill, Minister for Munitions, and at eleven o'clock, according to arrangements, I received a call from Field Marshal Sir Douglas Haig, who came formally to thank me for the work done. We had scarcely started when still three more motor cars arrived, out of which hopped Monsieur Clemenceau, the Prime Minister of France, Marshal Foch and the French Minister for Finance.' The episode moved Monash to write to his wife: 'This completed the gathering, met literally by chance on the actual battlefield and on a site which will live for ever in Australian history. I suppose that it rarely happens that such a distinguished gathering should so meet under such stirring surrounds, with the guns thundering all around.'

On the day Churchill met Monash, Wilhelm II summoned a meeting of his High Council at Spa in Belgium. Field Marshal Hindenburg told the Kaiser: 'We have nearly reached the limit of our power to resist. The war must be ended.' General Ludendorff, on the verge of the hysteria that marked his conduct in the coming three months, screamed at the All-Highest: 'We are finished.' When he had calmed down, he said: 'Termination of the war must be brought about by diplomacy.' Ludendorff was about to embark on his new career as one of the great unsung villains of the twentieth century – the author of the 'stab in the back' theory to explain Germany's defeat, and a key early supporter of Adolf Hitler.

It would take another three months of fierce fighting before the Armistice of 11 November 1918 brought a twenty-year truce to Europe's civil war. Almost ten million soldiers had died, and another six million were crippled for life. The French and German armies each lost two million. The British army lost 700,000. The American Expeditionary Force lost 105,000. Australia had sent 330,000 soldiers overseas from its population of less than five million; sixty thousand had died. Three famous empires – the Russian, German, and Austro–Hungarian – had fallen, and the Ottoman Empire was on the brink. The British Empire reached its greatest territorial extent as a result of the war, but Britain ended heavily in debt to the United States, now emerging clearly as the world's greatest power.

Churchill had been a major player in the events that transformed Australia and its view of its place in the British Empire. Anzac had become a mantra for Australian imperialists and nationalists alike. But the conscription issue had poisoned the wellsprings of Australian patriotism. The undemanding loyalties of old were replaced by stridency and rancour which infected every level of the Australian political discourse and social intercourse for more than a generation. The divisions created not so much by the Great War itself, but by the conscription issue and Hughes' disruptive tactics, hindered and handicapped the nation's response to all the crises of the interwar years, from the Depression to the collapse of collective security in the face of new threats from Germany and Japan; ultimately, even Australia's ability to decide how to defend itself in the Second World War was compromised.

On 16 December, Churchill addressed the Australia and New Zealand Luncheon Club at the Connaught Rooms in London:

> The war is won. All our dreams have come true. We have reached the end of the long, long trail . . . It fills our hearts with pride and with thankfulness that we have lived in such a time and belong to such a race . . . All over the world, in every country, it is to the British way of doing things that they are looking now.

Churchill summed up his thoughts about the meaning of the Great War for the British Empire:

> Of all the tests of soundness of our institutions, nothing can equal that proof which was given when the great communities, the Dominions of the Crown over the seas, so many thousands of miles from the area of conflict, enjoying absolute freedom, enjoying in all senses an absolute practical independence, under no pressure of any kind, but with a pure, spontaneous feeling obeying no call but that of the blood – when these great Dominions, without a moment's hesitation, entered a quarrel, as to the beginning of which they could not necessarily have been

consulted, and hastened to pour out their blood and treasure, and raise themselves in the struggle of arms to a foremost place.

His triumphalism celebrated a double victory. Lloyd George had cashed in on the Armistice and called Britain's second khaki election. Although not himself advocating 'Hang the Kaiser', Churchill endorsed Lloyd George's pledge to 'squeeze Germany until the pips squeak'. When the votes were counted on 15 December 1918, the Lloyd George coalition had scored an overwhelming victory. In the afterglow, Churchill could hardly have been expected to remind his Australian and New Zealand audience that their 'foremost place' in the Empire would involve a lot of imperial dirty work. The Anzacs quickly found it out for themselves. In March, 1919, Australian Light Horse regiments, including men Churchill had convoyed to war in 1914, had to postpone their return home to put down a rebellion in Egypt, the first stirrings of Arab nationalism in the wake of the collapse of the Ottoman Empire. This aspect of 'the British way of doing things' found no place in the legend of Anzac or Churchill's rhetoric of Empire.

9

'Mr Churchill backslides'
1919–21

Billy Hughes was the only Australian Prime Minister whom Churchill admired. Menzies acquired a nostalgic value as a co-survivor from the Finest Hours of the Second World War, but in the wizened, dyspeptic, irascible Hughes, Churchill recognised a fellow buccaneer. In his writings, he made famous some of the countless Billy Hughes anecdotes. Many appear in *The Aftermath*, Churchill's account of the postwar years, which captures the seething antagonisms among the peacemakers in Paris in 1919.

Australia, New Zealand, Canada, and South Africa ranked as independent nations at the Paris Peace Conference, in recognition of their contribution to victory; but they were expected to keep in step as members of the British Empire Delegation. Hughes had two main aims: to hold on to German New Guinea and uphold White Australia. This brought him into collision with the Japanese. Japan demanded a 'racial equality' clause in the Covenant of the League of Nations, Woodrow Wilson's grand design for world peace. Racial equality? Absolutely unacceptable to Australia, said Hughes. Absolutely fundamental to Japan's dignity, said Baron Makino, Japan's Lord Keeper of the Imperial Privy Seal, who threatened that his country might boycott the League of Nations if its demand was refused. The President of the United States thought they had a good case. Hughes warned Wilson that he would take the issue to the people of the United States, and campaign personally in California where anti-Japanese feeling ran especially high. Wilson backed off.

The pair clashed again when Hughes insisted that Australia would apply its immigration laws to its New Guinea Mandate, and generally treat the territory as a colony by right of conquest. Churchill, no fan of Woodrow Wilson, recorded the encounter with relish:

'And do you mean, Mr Hughes,' said the President, 'that in certain circumstances Australia would place herself in opposition to the opinion of the whole civilised world?' Mr Hughes, who was very deaf, had an instrument like a machine-gun emplaced upon the table by which he heard all he wanted; and to this he replied dryly: 'That's about it, Mr President.'

'This discussion,' Churchill wrote, 'had been very gratifying to M. Clemenceau [the French prime minister], and for the first time he heard the feelings of his heart expressed with unbridled candour. He beamed upon Mr Hughes.' Clemenceau saw Woodrow Wilson's high mindedness as mere hypocrisy. In Paris in 1919, he measured all things and all men by his determination to keep France safe from Germany for at least another generation. Of the Fourteen Points, Wilson's recipe for a world made safe for democracy, Clemenceau commented: 'God Himself only had Ten.'

According to Churchill, Clemenceau referred to the dominion prime ministers as Lloyd George's 'savages' – presumably as in Rousseau's 'noble savage', unspoilt by civilisation. To Hughes, Clemenceau said, according to Churchill: 'Mr 'Ughes, I have 'eard that in early life you were a cannibal.' 'Believe me,' said the Australian, 'that has been greatly exaggerated.'

Japan's rebuff at Paris fed anti-Western feelings in Tokyo. Japanese resentment against Australia ran deep. The denial of their racial equality with the West reinforced their innate sense of racial superiority, against the world. There was at least one standard of equality with Britain, France, and the United States to which Japan could aspire – imperial dominance over China and all East Asia. Such were the consequences of Wilson's surrender to Hughes' grandstanding at Paris, however amusing and even admirable Churchill may have found it.

The fellow-politician among Churchill's biographers, Roy Jenkins, judges that his four years in Lloyd George's coalition government from 1919 to 1922 were 'among the least creditable of Churchill's career'. Certainly in Australia, his reputation suffered badly from his involvement in two issues: Ireland and Russia. His conduct raised serious questions about his judgement and his bellicosity; even the person who loved him best, his wife Clementine, sometimes worried about his sense of justice and humanity. She wrote to him in February 1921: 'Do, my darling, use your influence *now* for some sort of moderation or at any rate justice in Ireland. Put yourself in the place of the Irish. If you were their leader, you would not be cowed by severity, and certainly not by reprisals which fall like the rain from Heaven upon the Just and upon the Unjust. It always makes me unhappy and disappointed when I see you inclined to take for granted that the rough iron-fisted "hunnish" way will prevail.'

Clementine meant the scourge of terror and counter-terror, reprisals and counter-reprisals, which Churchill had helped unleash on Ireland as Lloyd George's Secretary for War. After forty years of broken promises over Home Rule, the postwar Irish leadership now demanded independence for an undivided Ireland. In response to Tory reaction at Westminster and Protestant intransigence in Ulster, they set up their own parliament in Dublin and embraced the Irish Republican Army (IRA). Churchill's answer was to recruit the 'Black and Tans' – a force of eight thousand British army veterans so-called because they wore war-issue khaki uniforms and the black belt of the Royal Irish Constabulary, and who were virtually exempt from army discipline in the name of fighting terror. Thus a new cycle of terror in Ireland began. The tragic consequences were still working their way through Anglo–Irish relations at the end of the twentieth century. Churchill and Lloyd George claimed they were only protecting the Irish from themselves – the standard justification of occupying powers through the ages. If Clementine Churchill feared that her husband's attitudes were 'hunnish', it is, perhaps, small wonder that Churchill's name, and its association with the Black and Tans, became a curse among the Irish and their kin in the United States and Australia for generations.

Churchill's implacable hatred of the communist revolution in Russia, and his determination to 'strangle Bolshevism in its cradle', antagonised the labour movements in both Britain and Australia and further removed him from the liberal mainstream. As Secretary for War, he tried to organise international support for the anti-communist White Russians in the civil war which engulfed Russia. His efforts met insuperable barriers: Lloyd George, still an old Liberal at heart, was sympathetic towards the Russian revolution or his concept of it; Wilson was paralysed – literally after a stroke in the last year of his presidency – by his struggle to bring the United States into the League of Nations against congressional resistance; Clemenceau saw the day when France might once again need Russia against Germany; and the smaller allies like Australia and Canada were only interested in bringing their soldiers home.

Above all, the people of Britain were war-weary. To them, Churchill's crusade against Bolshevism was unthinkable. Besides, Churchill's main job as War Secretary was to demobilise the British army. He achieved this with creditable efficiency and fairness. Cash-strapped Britain suffered imperial overstretch from Ireland to Iraq. Hence Churchill's recourse to cheaper expedients like the Black and Tans in Ireland and the bombing of villages in Iraq. For all his crude rhetoric against Lenin and the communists, to whom he routinely referred as 'hairy-pawed baboons', Churchill had no real strategy for intervention in Russia. Asquith's daughter, Violet Bonham Carter, asked him: 'What is your Russian policy?' Churchill replied: 'Kill the Bolshies. Kiss the Hun.'

'Why waste your energy and your usefulness on this vain fretting over Russia which completely paralyses you for other work?' Lloyd

George asked Churchill at the end of 1919. Their differences over Russia led them to agree that Churchill needed a change of office; his energy and usefulness needed a wider sphere of action. So at the end of 1920, Lloyd George gave Churchill the British Empire – or at least that part of it consigned to the Secretary of State for the Colonies. That part included Australia.

Churchill came to an office, and an empire, transformed since his Under-Secretary days, fourteen years before. Victorious in the greatest war in history, the British Empire seemed to stand at the zenith of its power and glory. The war had set the bounds of the Land of Hope and Glory wider, still yet wider. The German colonies in Africa and the Pacific had fallen into her hands. In theory, these colonies were held by Britain, Australia, and New Zealand in trusteeship for the League of Nations, in accord with Woodrow Wilson's doctrine of eventual self-determination. In practice, they were run like Crown colonies. The Empire's largest acquisitions lay in the Middle East, where Britain laid claim to the Ottoman Empire in Palestine, Transjordan, Arabia, and Mesopotamia.

The white dominions now purported to sit as Britain's equals around the imperial table. Whenever they were in London the Australian and Canadian prime ministers sat in on the Imperial Cabinet. The war had taught them, Hughes maintained, that henceforth there should be a single foreign policy for the whole Empire and the dominion prime ministers had earned an equal share in making it. He was soon to be disillusioned.

When he attended the 1921 Imperial Conference, Hughes was much weaker politically than he had been on his previous visits to London. A new Australian party, the Country Party, formed to give a voice to farmers and soldier-settlers, opportunistically conservative and radical by turns, had made its appearance in national politics in 1919. Towards the end of Hughes' long life and career, he was asked why he had been a member of every Australian party since Federation – the Labor Party, the Nationalist Party, the United Australia Party, the All-For-Australia Party, the Liberal Party – but never the Country Party (today's National Party). He replied: 'Well, brother, you have to draw the line somewhere.' The party's wily leader, Earle

Page, a New South Wales country doctor and surgeon with the Australian Medical Corps in France, distrusted Hughes, not least because of his Labor roots, and was determined to get rid of him. He was working towards the day when he would hold the balance of power between Hughes' Nationals and Labor. Meanwhile, with great reluctance and on strict conditions, he agreed to give the Hughes Government immunity from attack during the Prime Minister's absence in London. Page gave his reasons in Parliament: not only did he not trust Hughes – he didn't trust Churchill. 'When we know that the British Prime Minister, Mr Lloyd George, and Mr Winston Churchill, the present Secretary of State for the Colonies, are capable of the most brilliant improvisation in the quickest possible time, we are dubious lest, in the forthcoming conference, we may be committed by plans made for the defence of the Empire, or by conclusions arrived at, upon which the people of Australia will not be able to go back.'

The Imperial Conference of June–July, 1921 exploded the idea that the Empire could speak with one voice. It showed that Australia and Canada had different priorities and that Britain's priorities differed from those of both Canada and Australia; and for the first time, it showed that Britain's relations with the United States might outweigh its relations with the Dominions. Nevertheless, throughout the proceedings in London, Churchill and Hughes tried to outdo each other in proclaiming the greatness and unity of the British Empire. In the background was always the reality of the emergence of the United States as the world's strongest power.

Like the United States, Japan had done very well out of the war. Like Australia did, it kept the Pacific outposts it seized from Germany. Taking advantage of the turmoil after the collapse of the Manchu Empire, and of Europe's preoccupation with war, Japan served its 'Twenty One Demands' on China, warning the struggling republic that its goal was the same kind of brutal protectorate forced on Korea in 1910. These ambitions were bound to earn Japan the hostility of the United States, whose businessmen and missionaries had anticipated a rich harvest from the American demand for an

'Open Door' to China. From the end of the First World War, Pacific rivalry between the United States and Japan was a key factor in international affairs. In particular, the United States suspected Britain's friendship with Japan, enshrined in the 1902 Anglo–Japanese Treaty. The treaty, revised in 1907 and 1911, was due for renewal in 1921. Its renewal became a major item on the agenda of the Imperial Conference.

The conference in London took the first steps along the road to Pearl Harbor. For the first time, Britain and Australia acknowledged that the Empire's future in East Asia and the Pacific would be dominated by the relations between the United States and Japan. Churchill began to sketch an outline of his career's grand theme: 'an overwhelmingly effective alliance between the British Empire and the United States'. The renewal of the Anglo–Japanese Treaty brought the issue into sharp focus. Hughes summed up the Empire's dilemma: 'How were we to please America without offending Japan, and at the same time, protect the Empire and maintain peace in the Pacific?' The Churchill of 1921 was not nearly as circumspect as Hughes. He told Hughes: 'The danger to be guarded against is the danger from Japan. Getting Japan to protect you against Japan is like drinking salt to slake thirst.'

The irony is delicious. This was the Churchill who had grumbled about Deakin's invitation to the American Fleet in 1908, and who had alarmed the Australians in 1914 by consigning them to the protection of the Imperial Japanese Navy. The Hughes who had told Woodrow Wilson that he was prepared to stand against the opinion of civilisation, rather than accept Japan's proposal for racial equality, was now anxious not to offend Japan. In Churchill's case, his 1921 stance may be seen as a temporary aberration. For the next twenty years he was to downplay any threat from Japan, much as he had done in 1914.

Yet, from different angles, Churchill and Hughes came in 1921 to the same conclusion: the overriding importance of the power and interests of the United States. Hughes put Australia's case in straight-forward terms:

> Would I prefer the renewal of the Anglo-Japanese Treaty to an arrangement which would put an end to the suicidal policy of competing armaments? I say a thousand times No! But no such choice is given me.
>
> What is the substantial alternative to the renewal of the Treaty? The answer is, that there is none. If Australia was asked whether she would prefer America or Japan as an Ally, her choice would be America. But that choice is not offered her.

Canada's Prime Minister, the Conservative Arthur Meighen, argued that American cooperation and friendship must be the overriding consideration. Meighen, Hughes countered, had put the case not for the Empire but for America:

> I am as warm a friend and as resolute a champion of the Union of the English-speaking people as any man. I will yield to none – not even to Mr Meighen – in my desire to bring this about. But I do not mistake the voice of a noisy anti-British faction in America for the sentiment of that great Republic, and I will not believe that we shall advance the cause of the peace of the world, and promote more friendly relations with the United States of America, by a weakly vacillating policy which seeks always the approval of this faction before we dare pursue a policy founded on justice, compatible alike with the welfare of mankind and the greatness of this Empire.

Hughes said that the Imperial Conference had been called to formulate a single policy for every part of the Empire, and concluded: 'I am for the renewal of this Treaty and I am against delay.'

Of the British delegation – which included the Prime Minister, Lloyd George; the Lord President of the Privy Council, Lord Balfour; the Foreign Secretary, Lord Curzon; the Chancellor of the Exchequer, Austen Chamberlain (Joe's son and Neville's half-brother); and the Secretary of State for India, Edwin Montagu – only Churchill spoke against renewal of the Anglo–Japanese Treaty. Yet in the end it was Churchill who had his way.

Churchill broke ranks with his Cabinet colleagues to support Canada. His intervention earned him a rebuke from the proud and prickly Lord Curzon, who sent a note to the Secretary of State for the Colonies accusing him of trespassing on the turf of the Secretary of State for Foreign Affairs. Curzon also scribbled a note to Lloyd George: 'It seems to me entirely wrong that the Colonial Secretary should on an occasion like this express his independent views on a Foreign Office question.' Lloyd George replied: 'I quite agree. I have done my best to stopper his fizzing . . . It is intolerable.' The notes shot around the table. Austen Chamberlain wrote to Curzon sympathetically: 'I think you are right to show Winston that you profoundly resent his constant and persistent interference. I despair of doing anything with him.' Churchill was curt in his reply to Curzon: 'In these great matters we must be allowed to have opinions.'

Lloyd George suddenly found a way to break the impasse. Although he agreed with Hughes, he was certainly not going to break with Canada or Churchill on this issue. The American Embassy in London informed him that the United States would regard renewal of the treaty with Japan as a hostile act. Through the British Embassy in Washington, Lloyd George encouraged the Harding Administration to propose a conference, to be attended by Britain, the United States, France, China, and Japan, to discuss the whole future of the Pacific. He let it be known that such a conference would supersede any renewal of the Anglo–Japanese Treaty. The fumbling, scandal-prone Harding Administration responded promptly. Before the dominion prime ministers left London, President Harding's invitation to a conference in Washington duly arrived. For the British, Australians, and Canadians, the President's invitation came as a face-saver. They adjourned the debate on the treaty and the debate was never renewed. Nor was the treaty itself.

By the time the prime ministers had dispersed at the end of July, further messages from the US Secretary of State, Charles Evan Hughes, clarified Washington's intentions: the conference would discuss the future naval strengths of the United States, Britain, and Japan as part of a US-backed move towards general disarmament. The Japanese reluctantly accepted the Washington Conference as a substitute for negotiations on the renewal of the treaty. The Anglo–Japanese Treaty was lost, but the façade of Empire solidarity had been saved.

With face saved all round, except perhaps among pro-British elements in Tokyo, Hughes was never disposed to criticise Churchill for his part in scuttling the Anglo–Japanese alliance. He was, however, taken aback when Churchill dropped a wet blanket over the future of imperial communications. Hughes outlined to the conference delegates a grand vision for a chain of wireless stations stretching throughout the Empire. 'The unity of the Empire depends upon an Empire consciousness,' he said. 'This can be developed only by disseminating more and more Empire news through the vast Commonwealth of Nations.' The means were at hand, he said. 'It is the wireless. But while other countries are active, the Empire does nothing to use this new and wonderful discovery.' There was no direct inter-empire wireless service, Hughes said, and all Britain had done so far was to build a station at Oxford, and consider a link as far as Cairo. Now, to the Australian's amazement, Churchill talked down Hughes' grand scheme. He counselled caution, prudence and patience. 'We must bear in mind,' Churchill said, 'that a great wave of exhaustion has swept through the world after the fighting.' The Empire, he said, 'needed a period of repose to gather its strength'. It would be a mistake to propose very large or drastic actions for 'immense schemes and a huge expenditure of public money'.

'Mr Churchill Backslides' – such was the heading Hughes gave to this episode in his book about the Empire, *The Splendid Adventure*: 'Members of the Conference listened to all this astounded, hardly able to believe their ears. Wonders would never cease, for they had lived to hear Mr Churchill advocate a policy of repose. Mars advocating peace, the head of the Soviet denouncing the Third International, would not have surprised them more. All these soothing reactionary lullabies from Winston Spencer Churchill!' In the end the conference set up a committee under Churchill's chairmanship to examine various schemes for improved Empire communications. Hughes was bitterly disappointed: 'We who expected to fly on the wings of light were offered a limping camel.' When Hughes wrote this in 1929, nobody could foresee the day when Churchill would use the wireless as the most powerful instrument for the leadership and inspiration of the Empire in its history.

Hughes summed up Churchill's performance as Colonial Secretary at the 1921 Imperial Conference: 'When Mr Churchill has established himself, it is usually quite impossible to shift him by argument. He is so fertile of expedient and so mercurial, that one can never corner him. He is here, he is there, he is gone, and again he is where he was before.'

10

'All was to end in shame'
1922–23

The 'fertile and mercurial' Mr Churchill nearly took Australia and the British Empire back to war with Turkey. This was the so-called Chanak crisis of September 1922, now almost forgotten amid the welter of twentieth-century horrors, but at the time a turning point for Empire relations and the history of three nations – Turkey, Greece, and Britain. An outcome of continuing conflict over the postwar carve-up of the Ottoman Empire, the crisis exposed the weakness of the League of Nations at its first test, cracked the great wartime partnership between France and Britain, made Kemal Ataturk master of Turkey, led to the dethroning of King Constantine of Greece and the execution of his Prime Minister, ended the Greek dream of a Greater Greece ruling a Christian Constantinople, and drove a million Greek refugees from Asia Minor. It also brought down the Lloyd George Government – and Winston Churchill with it.

There were, in fact, two distinct Chanak crises in September, 1922. The first was the international crisis, resulting from the smashing of the Greek armies and Kemal's drive towards Constantinople through the Neutral Zones occupied by Allied forces. The other Chanak crisis, the political storm in Britain and Australia, was the product of Lloyd George's hubris and Churchill's over-excitement. The first Chanak crisis ended with Kemal in control of Constantinople, his Grand National Assembly ruling all Turkey from Ankara, the sultanate abolished and the Turkish Republican Government negotiating a new peace treaty on equal terms with the Allies at Lausanne. The other Chanak crisis, a purely political one, led to disenchantment with Lloyd George and Churchill in London, Ottawa, and Melbourne, and the dissolution of the Lloyd George coalition.

What we know as the Gallipoli campaign the Turks call the Battle of Cannakale; Cannakale we call 'Chanak'. It is the port at the Narrows on the Asian side of the Dardanelles; the Turks celebrate it as the place where Churchill's fleet was turned back on 18 March 1915. By September, 1922, it was garrisoned by a small British force representing the Allied occupation of Turkey. For a brief and danger-ous moment, it was thrust into world history because Lloyd George and Churchill decided that Chanak was the place where the British Empire must take a stand against the Turkish insurgency.

Australia's place in Churchill's scheme arose directly from the part its troops had played against the Ottoman Empire. After Gallipoli, the Australian Light Horse regiments had remained in Egypt to form the nucleus of the Anzac Mounted Corps, its two divisions providing the fighting edge of the Eastern Expeditionary Force under General Allenby. On 1 October 1918, General Harry Chauvel and his Desert Column accepted the Turks' surrender of the city of Damascus, and took four thousand Turkish prisoners. That month, Enver Pasha and most other leaders of the Young Turks fled to Berlin or Moscow, leaving the Sultan to surrender the Ottoman Empire. The Sultan's envoys signed an armistice on 30 October, on the deck of HMS *Agamemnon*, one of the battle-ships which had led the failed advance into the Dardanelles on 18 March 1915. The *Agamemnon* then led an Allied convoy sixteen miles long through the Sea of Marmara, to anchor in triumph in the Golden Horn before Constantinople. During the next six weeks, two Anzac mounted regiments were assigned a symbolic occupation of the Gallipoli Peninsula until they handed over to Greek and Italian forces.

All told, the British Empire had put a million soldiers in the field against the Ottoman Empire, in three main theatres – Gallipoli, Palestine, and Mesopotamia (Iraq). For all this effort and expense, the eastern campaigns were never more than a sideshow to the main event in France; and there were sideshows within the sideshow, like T. E. Lawrence's so-called Arab Revolt. Yet these sideshows of empire triggered a chain of events which were to reach down directly to the twenty-first century.

Australia's outstanding part in the defeat of the Ottoman Empire deepened its interest in the Middle East. This was to shape Australian strategic thinking for thirty years and beyond. Palestine and Mesopotamia now joined Egypt and Suez as areas of Australia's vital interest. In the first two years of the Second World War, Australian involvement in the Middle East would dominate the relations between Churchill and the dominion.

Despite its war contribution, Australia was given no part in the work of the Paris peacemakers as they carved up the Ottoman Empire. Under the Treaty of Sevres, the most draconian of all the peace treaties, Constantinople was to remain an Allied protectorate indefinitely, until the future of Turkey-in-Europe could be settled, preferably with Turkey out of Europe altogether. Britain received mandates over Palestine, Transjordan, and Mesopotamia until such time as the Arabs were fit to exercise self-determination in accordance with Woodrow Wilson's Fourteen Points. France took Syria, more or less according to the secret arrangements made between France and Britain during the war. Greece, which had joined the Allies in 1917, was given Thrace, the Ottoman foothold in Europe, and Smyrna (Izmir), the rich, largely Greek province on the coast of Anatolia, the Turkish homeland. Turkish nationalists rejected the treaty with fury and contempt. Mustafa Kemal raised the standard of Turkish nationalism and revolt against the sultanate and anybody else who accepted this humiliation at the hands of the Greeks, whom the Turks had once ruled with remorseless brutality, and whose war of independence in 1829 had begun the break-up of the Ottoman

Empire. As Churchill put it in *The Aftermath*, the Greek occupation of Smyrna transformed Kemal from 'a rebel to a warrior prince'. Mustafa Kemal became Kemal Ataturk, Father of the Turks.

Lloyd George loved the Greeks and despised the Turks. He regarded Eleutherios Venizelos, Prime Minister of Greece and liberator of Crete from the Turks, as the greatest Greek statesman since Pericles. As a Welshman, he saw the Greeks as the Celts of the Mediterranean. As a British Liberal, he regarded himself as the heir to Gladstone, destined to complete the Grand Old Man's call to expel the Turks 'bag and baggage from the provinces they have desolated and profaned'. Lloyd George believed, Churchill tells us, that the Greeks represented 'Christian civilisation against Turkish barbarism'. There was an imperial dimension to Lloyd George's emotional philhellenism, summed up by Churchill in *The Aftermath*: 'The Greeks have a strong sense of gratitude, and if we are the staunch friends of Greece at the period of her national expansion, she will become one of the guarantees by which the main intercommunication of the British Empire can be preserved.'

Hughes thought this was all fantasy, and told the 'Welsh Wizard' so. The Australian soldier, said Hughes, had developed a strong preference for the Turk over the Greek. If it came to a choice, the Australian people would not 'spend one shilling or move one man to further the ambitious projects of King Constantine'. Constantine, forced into exile by Venizelos because of his pro-German proclivities during the war, had been recalled to the throne following the improbable death of his son King Alexander from a monkey-bite turned gangrenous. Of the catastrophe caused by Greek policy after the return of Constantine and the ousting of Venizelos, Churchill would write: 'It is perhaps no exaggeration to say that a quarter of a million persons died of this monkey's bite.'

At first, Churchill had objected that Lloyd George was making Britain hostage to Greek ambitions, and making peace with the Islamic world impossible. In March, 1920, he wrote to his leader: 'On this world so torn with strife I dread to see you let loose the Greek armies – for all sakes and certainly for their sakes... I counsel prudence and appeasement.' At that time, appeasement was not a dirty word, even for Churchill. When the Imperial Conference of 1921 was in session, Churchill told the British Prime Minister: 'If the Greeks go off on another half-cock offensive, the last card will have been played and we shall have neither a Turkish peace nor a Greek army.' Turkish sovereignty over Smyrna was 'an indispensable step towards pacification of the Middle East'. Within a year, the counsels of prudence gave way to the passions of Empire. By September, 1922, Churchill had turned a full 180 degrees. His *volte face* was the result not of Greek disasters or Turkish victories, but the threat which these developments offered to Britain's prestige.

The Greek armies recklessly advanced deep into Asia Minor in August, 1922. They were driven back to the sea by September. Kemal's army burnt Smyrna to the ground. British, French, and Italian warships evacuated 250,000 Greek soldiers and civilians. Kemal then turned north towards the Dardanelles and into the Neutral Zone at Chanak, on his way to Gallipoli and Constantinople. Churchill swerved around completely:

> The re-entry of the Turks into Europe, as conquerors untrammelled and untamed, reeking with the blood of helpless Christian populations must, after all that had happened in the war, signalize the worst humiliation of the Allies. All the fruits of successful war, all the laurels for which so many scores of thousands had died on the Gallipoli Peninsula, in the deserts of Palestine and Mesopotamia [Iraq], in the marshes of the Salonika front, in the ships which fed these vast resources, in men, in arms, in treasure which they required; all was to end in shame.

That, at any rate, is how Churchill in 1929 recollected his views as Kemal drove his army towards Constantinople. But Churchill's crony, the Canadian-born press magnate, Lord Beaverbrook, recalled his mood in less lofty terms. At a dinner party during the crisis, 'the debate became bitter in tone', Beaverbrook wrote in his *Decline and Fall of Lloyd George*. 'Churchill talked of the might and honour and prestige of Britain, which he said I, as a foreigner or invader, did not understand, and of how it would be ruined for ever if we did not immediately push a bayonet into the stomach of anyone in arms who contested it.'

On Friday, 15 September, Lloyd George, Churchill, and other members of the Cabinet still in London, met to discuss the crisis. In *The Aftermath*, Churchill presented this gathering as a meeting of the full Cabinet, solemnly deciding that the British Empire must display its might to resist Kemal's 'aggression against Europe'. In fact, Lloyd George and Churchill were making all the running, with Churchill in the lead over the next few days. Just as in 1914, immense decisions of peace and war were made by two or three persons, on the assumption that they could command endorsement from an obedient and deferential electorate. They were to find times had changed, in Britain and its empire.

Lloyd George asked Churchill to draft a telegram to the dominion prime ministers, a task he undertook with zest. Kemal was intent on driving the Allies out of Constantinople, Churchill wrote. The French and Italian governments, he claimed, agreed with the British Government, and these Allies hoped to secure the military participation of Greece, Romania, and Serbia 'in defence of the deep-water line between Europe and Asia' [the Dardanelles Strait]. Proposals were being made, he said, for an international conference in Venice or possibly Paris; meanwhile, it was right to make a show of united force to repel the Turks.

Much of Churchill's draft had thin connection with reality. In particular, France and Italy were at loggerheads with Britain over its handling of the issue, and were already negotiating their own settlement with Kemal. France had already agreed to restore Constantinople, Eastern Thrace, and the Gallipoli Peninsula to Turkish rule. Churchill glossed over all this in the message he wrote for Lloyd George:

Timely precautions are imperative. Grave consequences in India and among other Mohammedan populations for which we are responsible might result from a defeat or from a humiliating exodus of the Allies from Constantinople. I should be glad to know whether the Dominion Governments are willing to associate themselves with our actions and whether they desire to be represented by a contingent. The announcement of an offer from all or any of the Dominions to send a contingent even of moderate size would undoubtedly exercise in itself a most favourable influence on the situation.

For the version sent to Hughes in Australia, Churchill crafted a special appeal: 'Not only does the freedom of the Straits, for which such immense sacrifices were made in the war, involve vital Imperial and world-wide interests,' he wrote, 'but we cannot forget that there are 20,000 British and Anzac graves in the Gallipoli Peninsula and that it would be an abiding source of grief to the Empire if these were to fall into the ruthless hands of the Kemalists.'

Lloyd George approved Churchill's draft without changing a word. It was sent in code to the dominion prime ministers via their governors-general, at around midnight Friday GMT. Over a Saturday lunch, Lloyd George and Churchill decided it was time to put the British public in the picture. Churchill drew up a press release in even more urgent terms, repeating the call to the dead on Gallipoli: 'His Majesty's Government have also communicated with the Dominions, placing them in possession of the facts and inviting them to be represented by contingents in defence of the interests for which they have already made enormous sacrifices and of soil which is hallowed by immortal memories of the Anzacs.'

Churchill's press release was given to the London press on the afternoon of Saturday, 16 September, and flashed around the world. As Churchill later admitted: 'None of the British Ministers had foreseen that the official telegram approved seventeen hours earlier and with at least twelve hours' start would be overtaken and forestalled by newspaper messages.' Thus Churchill conjured up a picture of the Imperial Cabinet sitting in solemn conclave in London, their weighty deliberations too profound for petty details like transmission, deciphering of codes, and differences in time zones. It was a fantasy. Lloyd George and Churchill had cooked it all up between them.

The premature news break, Churchill acknowledged, was 'vexatious to all concerned'. Vexatious was not the word for it, when

Hughes learnt from the Sunday newspapers that the Empire was on the verge of war and that Australia had been called to the colours once more. He was spending the weekend at his retreat at Sassafras, in the hills outside Melbourne. His embarrassment was the worse, because in those days, Melbourne religiously observed the Sabbath, and forbade Sunday newspapers. Hughes' information was relayed by pressmen informed from sinful Sydney. It was 5.00 p.m. on Sunday before the staff of the Governor-General, Lord Forster, had decoded the Lloyd George–Churchill communique, and delivered it by car to Sassafras. Even then, Hughes knew no more than what half the world already knew from the newspapers. The belated communique was the first information on the state of affairs in Turkey that he had received directly from the British Government in six weeks.

Hughes, however, did his Imperial duty. After telephoning the Defence Minister, Senator George Pearce (his only trusted colleague left over from the Labor days), he issued a press statement saying that the Government had decided 'to associate itself with the British Government in whatever action is deemed necessary to ensure the freedom of the Straits, and the sanctity of the Gallipoli Peninsula'. The Government 'would be prepared, if circumstances required, to send a contingent of Australian troops'. The whole matter would be placed before Parliament when it met on Tuesday, 19 September.

Then Hughes shot off a 2000-word protest to London. 'Your telegram came as a bolt from the blue,' he told Lloyd George. 'Even now we have not been told what the action of the Kemalists is that necessitates this decision.' The Australian Government had 'found itself in the most embarrassing position'. It was being asked, Hughes complained, 'not to decide between peace and war, for that issue has already been decided by Britain without consultation'. Britain had 'already decided to go to war, and had then notified the Press that she had asked the Dominions whether they wished to join her'.

'I feel that I ought to speak quite frankly and say that such action gravely imperils the unity of the Empire', Hughes went on:

The Australian people are sick of war. They regard this war, not in defence of vital national interests, as not only a crime but a blunder.

While they recognise fully the importance of the freedom of the Straits and would be angry and aggrieved if the sanctity of the Anzac graves on Gallipoli were violated, they have no sympathy whatsoever with the ambitious projects of King Constantine, whom the Australian soldiers regarded as a pro-German tool. They do not understand why Britain did not consult the Dominions before taking action, and before the situation had developed. They do not understand why the Allies did not long ago restrain the Greeks from such action as it now appears has led up to the present deplorable situation.

Hughes lashed out against the foolish schemes of the Greeks, the inaction of the League of Nations, the 'chariot of French ambitions and intrigues in the Near East', the harshness of the Treaty of Sevres, for which Australia held no responsibility and, worst of all, the lack of consultation with the Dominions. He concluded:

The Empire ought not to be pushed into a war. The Dominions ought not to be asked whether they will associate themselves with Britain after Britain has in effect committed them. And above all, they should not be asked to join in an unjust or unnecessary war. No one can say where this war once begun will end. We are a peace-loving democracy. We have been through a dreadful ordeal in which we hope you and the world will agree we played our part worthily. We are quite ready to fight in our own defence and in that of the Empire. But we must know where we are going. In a good cause we are prepared to venture all; in a bad one, not a single man.

Churchill had a genius for making the best of a bad job. His capacity to believe what he wanted to believe was heroic. As soon as Hughes' qualified support reached London, he announced to the press 'the prompt and generous support of the Dominions'. In fact, only New Zealand and Newfoundland (not federated with Canada until 1949) responded with a definite pledge of assistance. From Ottawa, the Liberal Prime Minister, William Lyon Mackenzie King, said he could do nothing until his parliament assembled, and he made it clear he was in no hurry to bring that about. Churchill's favourite dominion

Prime Minister, Jan Smuts of South Africa, was on safari in Zululand, and out of contact until the crisis was over. Yet Churchill publicly asserted 'the staunchness of the Dominions', and persisted for years in his claim that the attitude of the dominions, 'particularly Australia and New Zealand', had 'prevented the renewal of the war in Europe and enabled all the Allies to escape without utter shame from the consequences of their lamentable and divided policies'. In a personal message to Hughes dated 1 October, Churchill went so far as to describe his response as 'words of electrifying comfort and encouragement'.

Barely a hint of the real dissension reached the public. The Australian Cabinet endorsed Hughes' Sunday statement, but decided that there was no need yet to discuss sending a contingent. When Parliament met on Tuesday, 19 September, the Australian Prime Minister hid his resentment but made his essential points, in a speech of exceptional finesse and subtlety. Every paragraph of Hughes' speech implied a rebuke to Churchill. 'Whilst we are prepared at all times to stand side by side with Great Britain, we cannot view, without despair, the possibilities of a great conflict arising out of the clashing ambitions of Turkey and Greece,' he told the House of Representatives. 'And so we have thought proper to ask that the fullest information should be supplied to us by the British Government. We wish to be informed of the precise position. We want to know what objective the Allies have in view. We declare that ours is limited to the preservation of the Empire. We are ready to associate ourselves with Britain in wanting the status quo at Constantinople, and the inviolability of the Peninsula, which is necessary for the freedom of the Dardanelles, in the Homeric struggle to secure which so many of our soldiers made the supreme sacrifice. Beyond that we have thought it proper to say we ought not to go.'

Australia would not take part in any 'filibustering expedition', Hughes told Parliament. 'Aggression begets counter-aggression, violence begets violence.' Therefore, Hughes said, the Government had instructed the Australian representative at Geneva to bring the matter before the League of Nations. In his protest to Lloyd George, Hughes had complained that 'a Dominion ought not be stampeded by premature press disclosures'. Now, he sought to damp down the public excitement caused by Churchill's press release: 'There are already signs that the nation is being swept off its feet. At present there is no need for one man to offer his services.' Hughes was referring to calls for volunteers by leaders of the Returned Services League in Sydney and Melbourne.

The Labor Leader of the Opposition, Matthew Charlton, focused on Hughes' refusal to make public the messages between London and Melbourne. 'No, they are secret,' Hughes said, when asked to table them. Charlton said: 'The day has arrived when the citizens of Australia, in common with the people of the rest of the world, should know everything that happens in connexion with matters of this importance. There has been too much secret diplomacy throughout the world and it has had much to do with the creation of war.' Charlton's speech was an honourable expression of faith in the League of Nations, disarmament, and democracy. He concluded: 'Let the people of Australia be asked if they approve of sending Australian soldiers abroad at the present time.' Anticipating the reaction to even the mildest divergence from the high imperial line, he noted: 'I may be charged with being a little disloyal but, although I am a native of Australia, my parents hail from England and I have the deepest affection for the Old Land. Nevertheless I realise that the best I or any other public man of Australia can do is to endeavour to safeguard the world against further war.'

The Leader of the Country Party, Page, took the uncomplicated line of a true-blue Empire loyalist: 'It is the settled policy of the British Commonwealth that the Imperial Government determines and carries out foreign policy, and while that is the position, it is Australia's duty to assist the Imperial Government.' Neither Page nor anyone else in the House of Representatives that day would have been remotely aware of Hughes' true feelings. He recorded them in *The Splendid Adventure*, in 1929: 'To say that this savoured of sharp practice and appeared to be a dodge to manoeuvre the Dominions into a position from which there was no retreat is not to put the matter too strongly.'

'Chastened' is an unlikely word to use about Winston Churchill; but Hughes' anger achieved something approaching it. For the rest of the Chanak crisis, Hughes' protest produced an avalanche of cables to the Australian and other dominion prime ministers from the Secretary of State for the Colonies. Now he kept them posted almost daily. In three weeks, they received more information than in the previous three years. Churchill pleaded for their understanding if sometimes press reports anticipated official communications. When it came to Hughes, Churchill applied Disraeli's maxim about flattery and royalty: 'Lay it on with a trowel.' Glossing over the grudging nature of Australian support, Churchill professed to find 'exhilaration and inspiration' in Hughes' public utterances. In another cable, he claimed to have learnt from secret intelligence that the Kemalists had been shaken by Australia's announcement of support: 'Secret communications of the Turks which have fallen into our hands reveal clearly that the threatened action by Australia and New Zealand in the event of war is a serious factor in Turkish calculations.'

Churchill was now effectively running the show; Lloyd George had appointed him chairman of a council of ministers to manage the crisis. On 27 September, Churchill cabled Hughes that Kemal had rejected the British demand to withdraw his troops from the neutral zone. Next day he told Hughes that a revolution in Athens presented 'a new and formidable complication'. As a result, Kemal would be 'more anxious than ever to break through into Europe in order to smash the Greeks before they can reorganise. Events, therefore, seem to me to cause increasing anxiety.' He insisted, however, that at Chanak itself 'we are growing stronger each day'.

On 29 September, Churchill sent the dominion prime ministers bad news: the Turks massing around the British force at Chanak had doubled to 4500 – four times the strength of the British garrison. 'From secret information,' he claimed, 'the Bolsheviks are strongly pressing the Turks into aggressive courses.' He said he had conferred three times that day with his Cabinet colleagues and they had decided to instruct General Charles Harington, commander-in-chief at Constantinople, to serve Kemal with an ultimatum: unless his forces withdrew from the neutral zone around Chanak immediately, 'all the force at our disposal – naval, military and aerial' would open fire.

Even as Churchill was cabling the dominions with news of this ultimatum, others in the British Cabinet were having second thoughts. At a meeting of ministers on 29 September, Lord Curzon, the Foreign Secretary, strongly urged that the ultimatum should be cancelled. Churchill protested that it would appear as if the British were getting 'cold feet'. Kemal had to be taught a lesson that the British could not be 'trampled on and ignored'. Lloyd George ruled that the ultimatum should stand.

As things turned out, war was averted, not because General Harington issued the ultimatum but because he ignored it. Perhaps, to put it more charitably from Churchill's point of view, he kept it in reserve. In a long telegram to his political masters in London on 30 September, General Harington insisted that the judgement of the men on the spot must prevail; that the garrison at Chanak would not be attacked; that he was confident that Kemal would offer negotiations within 'two or three days'; and that 'to launch an avalanche of fire will put a match to the mine here and everywhere else from which there could be no drawing back'. On 1 October, the British Cabinet agreed that Harington 'need not send the ultimatum unless he considered the situation demanded it'. Churchill drafted the Cabinet's reply to Harington. It was a marvel of the art of the dignified back-down:

> You are indeed right in supposing that His Majesty's Government earnestly desire peace. We do not however desire to purchase a few days peace at the price of actively assisting a successful Turkish invasion of Europe. Such a course would deprive us of every vestige of sympathy and respect and particularly in the United Sates. Nor do we believe that repeated concessions and submissions to victorious orientals is the best way to avert war.

Apart from that, Churchill said, General Harington should use his discretion. And he did. Harington and Kemal agreed that fighting was pointless.

Churchill informed the dominion prime ministers on 1 October that Kemal would meet General Harington at Mudanya, a Turkish port on the Sea of Marmara, to discuss the future of the neutral zone. 'In my personal opinion,' he said, 'it is very doubtful whether any solid result will follow from this conference.' He believed Kemal would use the conference simply to win time to mass his forces for an invasion of Europe. Churchill had still not given up on his hopes for an Australian contingent. In a personal message to Hughes, tacked on to his general cable to the other prime ministers, he said: 'The despatch of Australian troops would have a very steadying effect upon opinion in this country which, while thoroughly sound, is naturally puzzled by the complexity of this tangled problem.'

In yet another message to Hughes next day, ('particularly secret and for the exclusive information of your Cabinet'), Churchill said: 'If Mudanya talks break down and Kemal advances on Constantinople, a very terrible situation will arise . . . a rising in Constantinople is almost certain when the Kemalists arrive at the water's edge. Unless the French at the eleventh hour make a loyal effort in the interests of humanity, we shall have to evacuate the British colony and make ourselves secure at Gallipoli. The peril of the Christian population of Constantinople numbering hundreds of thousands will be great. It is melancholy that Europe cannot find thirty or forty thousand men to ward off such a calamity.'

Four days later, the Conservative leader, Bonar Law, came out of retirement to lob a political bomb. 'We cannot act as the policeman of the world,' he wrote in the London *Times*, on 7 October. 'The prevention of war and massacre in Constantinople and the Balkans is not specially a British interest. It is the interest of humanity. The retention also of the freedom of the Straits is not especially a British interest; it is the interest of the world.' If the French were not prepared to support Britain in its stand, Bonar Law said, 'we have no alternative except to imitate the Government of the United States and to restrict our attention to the safeguarding of the more immediate interests of the Empire'.

Bonar Law had retired from Cabinet and leadership of the Conservative wing of the coalition in March, 1921, because of ill health. With most of his fellow conservatives, he had watched with mounting dismay Britain's lurch towards war. Bonar Law was kept well informed about Cabinet proceedings: how Curzon was being sidelined, how Churchill had been determined to have a showdown with Kemal, the progress of the Mudanya truce talks, and how Lloyd George was planning another khaki election against the background of the Chanak crisis.

Churchill was impervious to the implications of Bonar Law's declaration of Tory independence. He cabled Hughes: 'Bonar Law in a timely letter today expresses a very general view.' He was blithely ignoring the fact that it was a repudiation of his handling of the whole affair. Law's real target was Lloyd George and his election plans; Lloyd George and the coalition had served their purposes. The Conservative majority had no intention of giving the Welsh Wizard and his Liberal rump a new lease of life through another khaki election. On 19 October, the Conservatives met at the Carlton Club and voted to withdraw from the coalition. Lloyd George resigned immediately. He never held office again. Bonar Law accepted the King's commission to form an exclusively Conservative government. On the same day, Kemal's representative declared himself Governor of Constantinople on behalf of the Turkish Grand National Assembly. The Sultan fled on board a British battleship. The Chanak crisis was over. So was what was left of the Ottoman Empire.

Once again Churchill faced political ruin. His despair was all the more bitter because he genuinely believed that he had achieved an historic success at Chanak. With the crash of the coalition only a week away, he had claimed vindication in one of his last messages to Hughes:

> Situation is now greatly relieved and we may hope for a peaceful outcome. We have been greatly hampered by the repeated failures of support from our Allies and also by a vicious and fractious party campaign in this country. In spite of all this we have for the time being preserved all the essential interests . . . There is every reason to hope that the war will be kept out of Europe. Meanwhile the Straits and the Gallipoli Peninsula are in complete control and will remain so until

they are handed over to the League of Nations under conditions satisfactory to the British Empire. These results could not have been
achieved with the small amount of force at our disposal, had it not
been known that behind the British troops on the spot stood the united
strength of the Empire.

It was a masterpiece of spin. In reality, the Turks had triumphed
decisively over the British Empire. The Treaty of Lausanne (July,
1923) replaced the hated Treaty of Sevres. With it went the
autonomy which the Allies had promised the Turkish Armenians
and Kurds. There was a 'population swap' of 1.5 million Greeks and
Turks; it would be called 'ethnic cleansing' today. Turkey retained
Constantinople, Eastern Thrace, all of Anatolia including Smyrna,
and also regained control of the Dardanelles and the Gallipoli Peninsula. In October, 1923, Kemal abolished the sultanate, and became
President of the Republic of Turkey, ruling until his death in 1938.
Throughout the Second World War, Churchill was to waste considerable time and resources, Australian troops included, in a futile
effort to bring Turkey into the war on the Allied side.

Churchill's recklessness over Chanak led to some change in the
way the Empire was run. At the Imperial Conferences of 1923 and
1926, Hughes' successor as Prime Minister, Stanley Melbourne
Bruce, joined Canada's Mackenzie King to demand more say for the
dominions. In Prime Minister Baldwin, Law's successor, they found
a sympathetic listener. The principles established in 1926 were
formally embodied in the Statute of Westminster (1931) which
recognised that Britain and the dominions were 'autonomous
communities within the British Empire, equal in status, in no way
subordinate one to another in any aspect of their domestic or
external affairs, though united by a common allegiance to the
Crown', and freely associated as members of the British Commonwealth of Nations. Australia, however, was in no hurry to parade
its independence. The Australian Parliament did not ratify the
statute until 1943, when the Curtin Labor Government had grown
impatient with the domineering ways of Britain's wartime Prime
Minister, Winston Churchill.

To end the sorry tale of Chanak on a grace note: Churchill sowed a seed during the Chanak crisis that has flourished in Australia's collective mind into the twenty-first century: our sense not only of the sanctity of Gallipoli soil, but of our proprietary rights over it. Australian war cemeteries stretch from Flanders and France, across North Africa and South-East Asia to New Guinea, and from Korea to Vietnam. Almost all our war dead lie in foreign fields. But only on Gallipoli does Australia assert its claim to moral ownership of the territory on which its soldiers fought and fell. Churchill put this idea with all his eloquence during the Chanak crisis. Extraordinary in itself, the idea took root and was nurtured by an even more extra-ordinary circumstance: our special claim to the soil which we had invaded was acknowledged and legitimised by the Turks who had successfully defended it, and by no less a personage than Kemal Ataturk himself. It is this convergence of the defining legends of two nations, Australia and Turkey, that makes Gallipoli unique. When Churchill appealed to Australia for a contingent to protect the Anzac graves, he was striking the same chord as Kemal Ataturk who said, in words now inscribed on the wall at the Australian War Memorial in Canberra, and at Gallipoli itself:

Mothers from faraway countries, wipe away your tears
Your sons are now lying in our bosom and are in peace.
After having lost their lives on this land,
They have become our sons as well.

11

'Winston has gone mad'
1924–35

The generations that rightly honour Winston Churchill for his crusade to curb Hitler in the 1930s largely forget his major role in cutting back the Empire's defences in the 1920s. As Chancellor of the Exchequer (1924–29), his particular target was the naval base at Singapore, the keystone of Australian defence policy between the wars. The British Admiralty planned the Singapore base to deter Japan and to defend Australia. The Australians sheltered under these plans to excuse their own unpreparedness. More than anyone else, Churchill delayed and downsized the work at Singapore, ensuring that the base would be neither a deterrent nor a defence. At the height of Churchill's long-running row over Singapore with the navy, Admiral David Beatty, the commander at the Battle of Jutland, now First Sea Lord, wrote to his wife in despair: 'That extraordinary fellow Winston has gone mad. Economically mad, and no sacrifice is too great to achieve what in his short-sightedness is the panacea for all evils – take one shilling off the income tax.'

Churchill's political resurrection as Chancellor of the Exchequer in the Baldwin Conservative Government testifies to his indestructibility. He was in hospital with appendicitis when Lloyd George fell, and lost his seat in parliament at the subsequent election. 'In the twinkling of an eye,' he was to write, 'I found myself without an office, without a seat, without a party, and even without an appendix.' He broke with the Liberals once and for all when they supported a minority Labour Government in 1924. In the British general election at the end of 1924, he returned to parliament as an anti-socialist with Conservative support. Stanley Baldwin, who had succeeded the dying Bonar Law as Conservative leader in 1923, offered Churchill a post in his new government. 'I would like you to be Chancellor,' Baldwin said. For a flash, Churchill thought that Baldwin might be offering the same wooden spoon Asquith had awarded him in May, 1915 – Chancellor of the Duchy of Lancaster. The glorious truth dawned on him when Baldwin asked: 'Will you go to Treasury?' Churchill recalled: 'I should have liked to have answered: "Will the bloody duck swim?" but as it was a formal and important conversation, I replied, "This fulfils my ambition. I still have my father's robe as Chancellor. I shall be proud to serve you in this splendid office."'

Despite Beatty's diagnosis, there was method in Chancellor Churchill's madness. He was in tune with the spirit of the times: the mood was overwhelmingly in favour of peace, disarmament, and the League of Nations. As Secretary for War in 1919, Churchill had initiated the Ten Year Rule. This rule instructed the army, navy and air force to frame their financial estimates on the assumption that 'the British Empire will not be engaged in any great war during the next ten years'. Now, as Chancellor of the Exchequer, he strengthened and lengthened the Ten Year Rule by advancing it automatically by one day every day. It was an invitation to procrastination. In his own defence, he wrote in his war memoirs: 'Up till the time when I left office in 1929 I felt so hopeful that the peace of the world would be maintained that I saw no reason to take any new decision; nor in the event was I proved wrong. War did not break out till the autumn of 1939. Ten years is a long time in this fugitive world.'

Churchill's Ten Year Rule was abolished in 1932 by the national government led by Ramsay Macdonald and Stanley Baldwin, but the damage had been done. The man who knew more about British defence policy than anyone else, Maurice Hankey, for a quarter of a century Secretary of the Imperial Defence Committee, said in a letter to Baldwin in July, 1936:

> The long continuance of this rule had created a state of mind in Government Departments from which recovery was slow. Even when the situation had become menacing, it took some time before Departments as a whole realized that serious expenditure on armaments was to be undertaken. Meanwhile, contractors, kept short of orders for years and years, had perforce been compelled to close shops, leave their machinery to become obsolete and dismiss skilled labour.

Churchill's own Permanent Head at the Treasury, Sir Warren Fisher, was later to be even more critical: 'We converted ourselves to military impotence . . . the Government of 1924 to 1929 had no excuse for further reducing our armed forces to a skeleton . . . This British Government's tragic action formed unfortunately a model for subsequent Governments.'

The major casualty of Churchill's Ten Year Rule was the Singapore Naval Base – Australia's security blanket. When the interned German High Fleet scuttled itself, and sank beneath the dark waters of Scapa Flow, Scotland, in 1919, the British Admiralty focus turned east of Suez towards Asia and the Pacific. The sailors wanted to restore the Royal Navy's traditional role as the guardian of a worldwide empire. Some even wanted to base the Main Fleet in the Far East. At the request of the Australian Government a month after the end of the Great War, Admiral Lord Jellicoe headed a naval mission to Australia. In August, 1919 – the same month Churchill persuaded the British Cabinet to set the Ten Year Rule – Jellicoe answered the Australian Government's key question, 'How large should Australia's navy be?' by saying that 'the problem could not be considered without taking account of Japan as a possible enemy in the future, and deciding on the naval strength necessary in Far Eastern waters, as a counter to Japan's growing navy'. Jellicoe described Singapore as 'undoubtedly the key to the Far East'.

Two years of Admiralty lobbying at the War Office, the Foreign Office, and the Treasury produced a typical compromise in time for the 1921 Imperial Conference. Four days before the conference opened on 20 June, the British Cabinet decided in principle to construct a naval base at Singapore. The Cabinet minute stressed 'the great importance of being in a position to tell the Dominion Governments that we had a Naval Policy'. Thus, the British Government committed itself to a new global defence strategy with all the political expediency and ambiguity characteristic of its attitude for the next twenty years. Throughout its dismal story, the Singapore base carried the marks of its origins – half-hearted and half-baked.

Almost as soon as the decision was made, construction of the base was postponed. The first excuse was the Washington Naval Conference. Originally intended to supersede the Anglo–Japanese alliance, the Washington conference was dressed up as a move towards naval disarmament. Britain, the United States, and Japan agreed on reduced naval strengths in the ratio of 5:5:3. This was a double triumph for American diplomacy. Without firing a shot, the United States Navy achieved parity with the Royal Navy, and a guaranteed superiority over the Imperial Japanese Navy, a fact bitterly resented in Japan. In the terms of the Washington Naval Treaty, the Australian navy was counted as part of the Royal Navy; to help meet the Empire's obligations, its twenty-five ships were reduced to thirteen; on 12 April 1924, the flagship HMAS *Australia* was ceremoniously sunk outside the Heads of Sydney Harbour, which it had entered in splendour in 1913.

From the first, Churchill opposed the Admiralty strategy for the defence of the Empire in the Far East and Australasia. The Singapore Naval Base, 'however desirable as a pillar of Imperial communications', he complained, 'has become a peg on which to hang the whole vast scheme of scientific naval control of Japan . . . We are invited to live, perhaps for a quarter of a century, with our pistol at full-cock and our finger on the trigger.'

Churchill challenged not only the cost of Singapore, but the entire concept. He vehemently contested the Admiralty's assumption about the threat from Japan. He set out his case in a long letter to Baldwin within weeks of taking office. 'A war with Japan! But why should there be a war with Japan?' he asked. 'I do not believe there is the slightest chance of it in our lifetime.' For once, he found himself in agreement with the British Labour Party, which had suspended the Singapore project during the brief Ramsay Macdonald Government of 1924. 'I am convinced that a war with Japan is not a possibility any reasonable Government need take into account,' Churchill told Baldwin. 'The only war it would be worth our while to fight with Japan would be to prevent an invasion of Australia, and that I am certain will never happen in any period, even the most remote, which we or our children need foresee.' Accordingly, said Churchill, the Admiralty 'should be made to recast all their plans and scales and standards on the basis that no naval war against a first class Navy is likely to take place in the next twenty years'. As he told Baldwin: 'Japan is at the other end of the world. She cannot menace our security in any way.' Of course, Australia's problem was that it, too, was at that 'other end of the world'.

Yet Churchill was being consistent. He had taken the same position towards Japan in 1914, to the dismay and anger of the Australians. Then, too, he had placed his confidence in the prudence and wisdom of Imperial Japan. In a memorandum to his Cabinet colleagues on 7 February 1928, he wrote:

> Great as are the injuries which Japan, if she 'ran amok', could inflict upon our trade in the Northern Pacific, lamentable as would be the initial insults which she might offer to the British flag, I submit that it is beyond the power of Japan, in any period which we need now foresee, to take any action which would prevent the whole might of the British Empire being eventually brought to bear upon her. And I believe that this fact, if true, will exercise a dominating influence on the extremely sane and prudent counsels which we have learned over a long period of time to expect from the Japanese Government.

Backed by Baldwin, Churchill won his battle. His Ten Year Rule was applied to Japan and the Pacific; although the Baldwin Government reversed the Labour Government's decision to scrap Singapore, construction proceeded by fits and starts. In the five years of Churchill's chancellorship he allocated less than one-fourteenth of the estimated cost. His economy drive delayed its completion by eight years. When the base was finally completed in a modified form in 1938, the situation in Europe rendered it useless. The Admiralty's concept of 'Main Fleet to Singapore' became an impossibility, and Singapore became not a deterrent to Japan but a temptation.

At the end of Churchill's term as Chancellor, the naval Chief of Staff, Admiral Sir Frederick Field, prepared a paper for the Geneva Disarmament Conference of 1931–32. He assessed the results of Churchill's cost-cutting:

> The number of our capital ships is now so reduced that, should the protection of our interests render it necessary to move our fleet to the East, insufficient vessels of this type would be left in Home Waters to ensure the security of our trade and territory in the event of any dispute arising with a world power.

Yet in his judgements about Japan, Churchill had a strong case. The Japan of 1925 was a loyal member of the League of Nations. The militarism which led it into its Manchurian and Chinese ventures in the 1930s seemed well contained by its reasonable facsimile of a constitutional monarchy and parliamentary system, confirmed that very year by the introduction of universal male suffrage. Above all, in 1925 optimism about the prospects for world peace reached its zenith. In December, Britain, France, Italy, and Belgium signed up with Germany to the Locarno Treaty, by which they each guaranteed their existing borders and forswore force as a means of changing them. If peace could be kept in Europe, why seek new enemies in Asia? But the verbal fireworks between Churchill and the defence planners over Japan blinded both sides to vital questions: What would be the real role and value of Singapore if and when a threat ever materialised? What would be its worth if the situation in Europe nullified the premise and the promise of sending the Royal Navy to Singapore? The failure of successive British and Australian governments to face these questions was the root cause of the catastrophe at Singapore in 1942.

If anything, Churchill was more suspicious of the United States than Japan at this period. He resented America's naval ascendancy over the Empire in the Pacific. Every international agreement on disarmament seemed to end up with the United States stronger. 'We do not wish to put ourselves in the power of the United States,' he warned during an Anglo–American row at another naval conference, in Geneva in July, 1927. 'We cannot tell what they might do, if, at some future date, they were in a position to give us orders about our policy, say, in India, Egypt or Canada, or on any other great matter behind which their electioneering forces were marshalled.'

THE AUSTRALIAN GOVERNMENT had inside information about Churchill's naval battles. Hughes' successor, Stanley Melbourne Bruce, had created a special post for his promising young friend Major Richard Casey, as the Australian Liaison Officer in London. Casey told Bruce in May that the British Cabinet had decided to 'go ahead with Singapore at a normal, reasonable rate of construction'. No decision had been made, however, on 'the defensive armament, whether 9.2 inch or 15 inch guns, or something in between'. Casey wrote that he had been told that when the Cabinet discussed future financing, one unnamed minister 'went so far as to suggest that Australia and New Zealand should take over the whole Singapore Base and run it'.

The British admirals tried to play Australian loyalty against Churchill's intransigence. Casey wrote to Bruce in July, 1925: 'I saw Admiral Field on the subject of the feeling that would be raised in Australia by the failure to lay down any cruisers this year. He was very distressed by the fact that if such an eventuality came about, you would naturally consider yourself "let down".' Casey explained that the whole business was the result of a 'personal struggle' between Churchill and Beatty, the First Sea Lord, with both threatening resignation. Casey said that Beatty 'was very worried about the reaction to the slackening of effort, which would become evident to the Press, however well camouflaged'. In fact, both sides to the argument were busily leaking to the press. Australia was merely a pawn in the game.

Bruce had replaced Hughes as Prime Minister in February, 1923. Like Lloyd George, Hughes had outlived his usefulness to the conservatives. The election for the House of Representatives in December 1922 resulted in twenty-eight Nationalist, fourteen Country Party, and thirty Labor seats. Earle Page refused to join or support any ministry of which Hughes was a member, much less head. Hence the rise of Stanley Bruce, scion of a great Melbourne warehousing family. He was born in Melbourne in 1883, but had spent much of his adult life in England: at Trinity College, Cambridge, reading for the bar at Middle Temple, and then managing the family business. Although he was back in Melbourne when the war broke out, Bruce returned to London as a captain in the British army, and won the Military Cross at Gallipoli. His entry into Australian politics in 1917 was deemed an act of noblesse oblige, for he professed to despise party politics. His backers in the Melbourne establishment had no doubt that he was destined to become Prime Minister. That was why they had put him into Parliament.

The standard version of Bruce as a slavish imitator of the ways of the English gentleman is mere caricature. He sometimes wore spats, and he spoke with a very English plum in his mouth. Towards the end of his life, he claimed that the achievements that gave him most personal satisfaction were his Cambridge blue, his captaincy of the Royal and Ancient Golf Club of St Andrew's, and his fellowship of the Royal Society. There may have been some pleasant affectation in this, like Churchill's pride in his membership of the bricklayers' union. But if Bruce carried himself with an air of effortless superiority, he did so as a privileged Australian and not as a pseudo-Englishman. He believed in the British Empire and the League of Nations as the two great hopes for world peace, and thought that Australia had a constructive part to play as a member of both. His political slogan was 'Men, Money, and Markets' by which he meant British immigration, British investment and imperial trade. Like Hughes, he had been shocked by the breakdown in Imperial communications at the time of the Chanak crisis. He appointed Casey as his listening post in London to prevent a repetition.

Richard Gardiner Casey, DSO, MC, was nine years Bruce's junior, and cast from the same mould. Casey's family means, his Cambridge education, his distinguished war record with the AIF at Gallipoli and in France, and his good looks and charm gave him entrée to London society and the circuit of country house weekends. Through their Trinity College connection, Casey and Bruce were part of a network of influence closed to lesser mortals like Menzies – and even Churchill. As well as keeping up a steady flow of official information, Casey wrote private letters to Bruce once or twice a week, full of the latest London gossip going the rounds of the rich and the famous. His most valuable source, however, was the Secretary to the Cabinet and the Imperial Defence Committee, Sir Maurice Hankey, who gave him office space near his own rooms in Whitehall. Casey's guesswork over the British Cabinet's decisions on Singapore indicates that, for all his courtesy and friendliness, Hankey strictly rationed the information he was prepared to share with the young Australian.

Casey had met Churchill in France in March 1916. After Gallipoli, he had been sent with an advance party of the Anzac Corps to learn about conditions on the western front, and was attached for a week to Churchill's 6th Royal Scots Fusiliers. He found Churchill 'very civil', giving him 'all the help needed' to absorb the 'unusual situation of trench warfare'. He took up his London post in the same month as Churchill became Chancellor. They did not meet socially, but Churchill appears frequently in Casey's letters. Both Bruce and Casey would play key roles in Australia's relations with Churchill during the Second World War, and both ended up as members of the House of Lords. Prime Minister Churchill gave Casey two important imperial appointments – as British Minister of State in Cairo in 1942, and Governor of Bengal in 1943. In 1925, however, Casey shared the usual conservative mistrust of Churchill, and wrote about him to Bruce with detached, even derisive, amusement.

'Winston Churchill finds himself in some difficulty in his effort to reduce expenditure', Casey wrote to Bruce in July, 1925. 'The only real trees worth pruning are the Fighting Services and they fight like wild cats against it. Winston has the name of being a good fighter too, up to a point, but he is said to be liable to break down at the last moment.' Casey told Bruce that Churchill was 'not quite *persona grata*' with the Conservative Party. 'He is regarded by his fellow Ministers as having got rather a bigger plum than he deserved in the Chancellorship. And the Treasury people are not too pleased with his being there. They realise that if they had, say, Austen Chamberlain [Baldwin's Foreign Secretary], he would resign rather than give way on some all-important point, whereas they feel that Winston would protest up to the last and then put the responsibility on the Cabinet, and retain his job.'

Bruce's other man in London was Frank McDougall, a thirty-year-old farmer turned trade lobbyist for the South Australian wine and dried fruits industry. Although he described himself as the Prime Minister's secret service agent, McDougall's correspondence with Bruce was less gossipy than Casey's, less intimate, and more substantial on trade and economic matters. McDougall chronicled Churchill's resistance against tariff protection for the dominions. Baldwin himself was now a convert to imperial preference, and Leo Amery was its champion in Cabinet, as Secretary of State for the Colonies and Dominion Affairs. 'At the present time,' McDougall told Bruce in October, 1925, 'Winston Churchill is the snag.' A year later, he told Bruce: 'There is a general feeling among Members of Parliament who are very keen on Empire Development that the Treasury and its chief, Mr Winston Churchill, are bitterly opposed to any policy of Empire Development which involves expenditure, and that they would infinitely rather pledge the credit of Great Britain to re-establish the currencies of Europe than to spend comparatively small sums or give guarantees to press forward schemes of Empire Development.' The problem was, said McDougall, 'that Churchill carries too many guns for Mr Amery'.

McDougall, however, began to look more kindly on Churchill after his 1927 Budget, in which he introduced a significant measure of preference for Australian wines. This was a real breakthrough for the Australian officer, who now speculated favourably on

Churchill's future. 'There can be no doubt that Winston Churchill is a very ambitious man who desires above everything else to be Prime Minister,' he wrote to Bruce in October 1928:

> So long as the bulk of the Tory Party feel that Churchill is not a man who can safely be trusted on Imperial affairs, just so long it is impossible to imagine that they will agree to his becoming Prime Minister. If, however, Churchill showed a real change of heart and 'brought forth fruits meet for repentance' – in other words, if he really demonstrated in the clearest and most unmistakable way his interest in the British Empire – he would have removed the biggest stumbling block to his eventually succeeding Baldwin as leader of the Party. It is, of course, more than possible that Churchill's known dislike of 'safeguarding' [McDougall's euphemism for imperial protectionism] may render such a development impossible; but there can be no doubt that a change of attitude on his part in regard to the Empire would go a long way to assist his ambition.

Dick Casey had a less rosy view of Churchill's prospects. He thought Churchill was damaging himself by his lifestyle and his associates; he took a particularly dim view of Churchill's crony, the brilliant barrister F. E. Smith, or Lord Birkenhead as he became. He wrote to Bruce: 'They are great diners-out, do themselves very well, are good and entertaining talkers, and have many friends who are on the lookout for ready means of information, particularly those that originate with highly placed servants of the State.'

Birkenhead, who was Secretary of State for India when Churchill was at the Exchequer, had a pernicious but little-noted influence on Churchill's attitude to the burning issue of imperial politics in the interwar years – the future of India. Churchill's early view of eventual independence for India had been resistant, but not rabid. Under his friend's influence, he changed markedly, and by the 1930s he was implacably opposed to any progress towards Indian independence. When Birkenhead died of drink in 1930, Churchill took up the torch of his lost friend with a romantic and irrational fervour.

If Churchill was a voice crying in the wilderness in the 1930s, he placed himself there by his own conduct and misjudgements. When the Baldwin Government was defeated at the British election in May, 1929, and made way for a second minority Labour Government under Ramsay Macdonald, Churchill – then aged fifty-four – was still in the running for the Tory leadership. Richard Casey, reversing his earlier view, predicted Churchill's leadership in his letters to Bruce; Neville Chamberlain was his only serious rival to succeed Baldwin, Casey suggested. Yet, less than two years later, Churchill resigned from the shadow Cabinet, and led a revolt against Baldwin which threatened to split the Conservative Party. Like Joe Chamberlain thirty years before him, he claimed that he was acting in order to save the British Empire.

Churchill was outraged by the notion that India should be granted the dominion status enjoyed by Australia, New Zealand, South Africa, and Canada. Australians did not care much for the idea either; indeed, on this issue, Churchill probably had firmer support in white Australia than in Britain. The new British Labour Government announced a policy of gradual self-government and eventual Dominion status, and Churchill was appalled when Baldwin gave the proposal his support. Churchill convinced himself that his outrage was shared by most Tory MPs and constituencies. He was possibly correct; but he utterly miscalculated Baldwin's appeal to British commonsense. Baldwin isolated Churchill from the conservative mainstream by depicting him as the mouthpiece for the London press barons, Lords Rothermere and Beaverbrook. In a devastating denunciation of the press lords, in words suggested to him by his cousin, Rudyard Kipling, Baldwin said: 'What the proprietorship of these papers is aiming at is power, and power without responsibility – the prerogative of the harlot throughout the ages.'

Churchill accepted that Australia and the other white dominions had earned their new place in the councils of Empire by their war efforts. The fact that the all-volunteer Indian army had fought alongside them at Gallipoli, and in France and the Middle East, didn't seem to count for much. But, Churchill argued, unlike the

182

twenty million in the white dominions, the three hundred million in India were unfit for self-government. The independence movement, led by the All-India Congress, was an unrepresentative elite, he said, which would oppress even further the sixty million Untouchables. He predicted that the religious hatreds between Hindu and Muslim would lead to massacres unparalleled in history.

At the heart of Churchill's passion was his belief that India was essential to Britain's greatness. 'We must hold our own or lose all,' he wrote in one of his scores of highly paid newspaper articles. He predicted that the loss of India would more than double the number of British unemployed, already at three million during the Depression. The movement towards dominion status for India was a symptom of national decline, he claimed. 'The British lion, so fierce and valiant in bygone days, so dauntless and unconquerable through all the agony of Armageddon, can now be chased by rabbits from the field and forests of his former glory.' It was a sign of 'a disease of the will,' he said. 'We are victims of a nervous collapse.'

The rabbit who roused Churchill's particular ire was the Mahatma, Mohandâs Gandhi, the spiritual leader and political master of India's masses. When the Viceroy of India, Lord Irwin – later Lord Halifax, the man who nearly became Prime Minister instead of Churchill in May 1940 – invited Gandhi for tea and talk at Government House, Delhi, in 1931, Churchill delivered himself of his masterpiece of imperial arrogance and racial contempt: 'It is alarming and also nauseating to see Mr Gandhi, a seditious Middle Temple lawyer, now posing as a fakir of a type well known in the East, striding half-naked up the steps of the Viceregal palace, while he is still organising and conducting a defiant campaign of civil disobedience, to parley on equal terms with the representative of the King-Emperor.' It would, of course, be outrageous to suggest that so saintly a person as Gandhi bore a grudge against Churchill in serving notice to 'Quit India' upon the British Empire in 1942, the most dangerous year of the Second World War. Dominion status for India was a 'crazy dream with a terrible awakening', Churchill wrote. 'Already Nehru, his young rival in the Indian Congress, is preparing to supersede [Gandhi] the moment he has squeezed his last drop from the British lemon.'

Churchill's violent reaction against any move towards Indian self-government had lasting consequences, bearing directly on Australia's security. When war came, it raised fears about the imperial loyalty and effectiveness of the great Indian army against Japan. Perhaps most damaging of all was the effect on his relations with President Roosevelt; it was a constant source of irritation in their wartime partnership. Churchill's attitude towards India fed American suspicions that Britain was using them not to defeat Hitler but to save the British Empire. But the immediate effect of Churchill's Indian obsession was to weaken his influence in Britain and Europe. Many who yearned for leadership against fascism baulked at taking their cue from this hopeless reactionary. Only with the passing of the 1935 India Act, which set India on the road to independence, was Churchill able to concentrate his prodigious energies on the pursuit of Adolf Hitler.

12

'The gathering storm'
1935–39

Winston Churchill disappointed Robert Menzies. The 41-year-old Attorney-General of Australia was present in the House of Commons in May, 1935, to observe Churchill in his new role. By then Adolf Hitler, German Chancellor since January, 1933, and the Führer, sole and supreme German commander, since August, 1934, had repudiated the Treaty of Versailles lock, stock, and barrel. Each step in the resistible rise of Hitler had been assisted by the German people in elections or plebiscites. In March, 1935, he revealed his plans for a massive build-up of the German army and air force, exaggerating its extent for maximum effect with his ecstatic listeners. In April, British, French, and Italian representatives met at Stresa in Italy, and 'agreed to oppose by all practicable means any unilateral repudiation of treaties which may endanger the peace of Europe'; they would oppose any move by Hitler to incorporate Austria into the German Reich. This was the so-called Stresa Front. It was as ineffectual as the British leader, Ramsay Macdonald, visibly crumbling in mind and body, and about to hand over the prime ministership to Baldwin; and as hypocritical as Mussolini, about to invade Abyssinia (Ethiopia) and to cast in Italy's lot with

Hitler. The House of Commons debated these developments on 2 May 1935. From the Speaker's Gallery, Menzies noted that 'the temper of the House favoured a real measure of rearmament'. He wrote in his diary: 'Hitler's lies and untimely truculence have gravely shaken the average Englishman's desire to be generous to a former foe.'

Menzies, who worshipped the House of Commons, was particularly keen to hear its star performer. Churchill said that Hitler had now dropped all pretence, and he predicted that Germany would have air superiority of three or four times over Britain by the end of the year. 'It is very dangerous to underrate German efficiency in any military matter,' he said. Although he still believed that the League of Nations could provide the basis for collective security, Britain must now act to 'retrieve the woeful miscalculations of which we are at present the dupes, and of which, unless we take warning in time, we may some day be the victims'.

The first thing that struck Menzies was that Churchill read his speech from a prepared text. He was surprised that this practice was allowed in the mother of parliaments; it would never do for the Australian House of Representatives. Indeed, he thought Churchill's entire performance second-rate: 'His theme is a constant repetition of "I told you so", and first class men usually don't indulge in this luxury. If a first-rater has once said an important thing, he doesn't need to remind people that he's said it.' Menzies wrote in his diary, 'All in all, the idol has feet of clay.'

Later that month, he met Churchill for the first time, at Chartwell, Churchill's country house in Kent. Menzies was the weekend guest of Churchill's neighbour, Maurice Hankey, still secretary of the Imperial Defence Committee; they walked across for tea, to find Churchill 'wallowing in a pool he had built for himself', and were delivered a lecture on the 'parlous state' of Britain's defences. Menzies wrote in his diary: 'My impression is of a remarkable man who lives too well and lacks that philosophical mental self-discipline which prevents a man from going to excesses either of mind or body.' Nevertheless, he conceded, Churchill was 'an arresting person – and I had no delusions of grandeur in his presence'.

This was Menzies' first visit to Britain. A storekeeper's son and scholarship boy from the Victorian country town of Jeparit, and a hugely successful Melbourne barrister, Menzies had transferred from the Victorian Parliament to Canberra in 1934. He was being groomed to succeed Joe Lyons, a former Labor Premier of Tasmania and federal minister, who had defected to head a national coalition after the Scullin Labor Government fell apart under the pressures of the Great Depression. Menzies went to London with Lyons to attend the 1935 Imperial Conference, and to appear for the Commonwealth in important cases before the Privy Council. He approached his pilgrimage like thousands of Australians before and after him, with enthusiasm, reverence, and a certain Australian prickliness, alert for signs of English decadence or condescension, hoping to impress but determined not to be over-impressed. Before his departure in February, he wrote to his Cabinet colleague W. M. Hughes: 'May I add that my highest hope for England is to do nothing that may diminish the reputation which you, in an outstanding fashion, created for us in the old world.'

The high point of Menzies' trip was a speech to the conference of the European Parliamentary Association, chaired by Stanley Baldwin, who had just become Prime Minister for the third and last time. Menzies recorded:

A red letter day. I speak with Baldwin in Westminster Hall; possibly the first Dominion Minister ever to speak on this historic spot . . . A great occasion, and I have for once written out my speech so that I shall not collapse in the presence of the shades of Edmund Burke and Fox and Sheridan. Baldwin speaks magnificently; he has vigour, eloquence, a rich historical imagination and an immense prestige. My heart sinks. He, contrary to the common practice here, does not read his speech, so I put mine on the table and commit myself to the mercy of providence. I think of Mother and Father listening in 12,000 miles away and trust not to dishonour them and get to my feet, and *mirabile dictu*, get away with it.

His address was a hymn of praise to the British parliamentary system, which would endure because 'its roots were deeply set in the history and character of the British people'. The closest he came to any reference to the matters then agitating people like Churchill was his assertion that 'freedom in Britain had been no concession granted either by a mob or by a dictator'. He received, he said, a great ovation, and was deluged with congratulations. 'Even the Duchess of York (sweet creature) has heard of it,' he recorded. *The Times* reported the speech in full, and praised it editorially. *The Sunday Times* went so far as to say: 'Mr Menzies is Australian-born, but he speaks precisely, in the manner of a cultivated Englishman.'

CHURCHILL SEEMED INCORRIGIBLE in his capacity for political self-mutilation. In 1936, just when his warnings about Hitler were beginning to bite, his loyal support of the new king, Edward VIII, who was determined to marry an American divorcee, Mrs Wallis Simpson, seemed proof of Churchill's hopeless judgement. In Australia, his chivalry towards the love-lorn monarch seemed mere self-indulgence. Among the dominion prime ministers, Lyons of Australia, staunch Catholic father of eleven, was Baldwin's firmest supporter in his skilful manoeuvring to force Edward off the throne in favour of his brother, the Duke of York. When the abdication crisis was over, and the newly created Duke of Windsor went into long and bitter exile, Churchill wrote to a friend: 'Baldwin flourishes like the green bay tree. He has risen somewhat like the Phoenix from the pyre upon which the late monarch committed suicide.'

However unkind the verdict of history on the Baldwin and Chamberlain governments, none ever stood higher in the estimation of Australian conservatives. The 1930s were the high point of imperial sentiment in Australia. The sense of Australia's economic and defence dependence on Britain – all underwritten by the superior wisdom of Westminster and Whitehall – permeated the Australian ruling circles, fed by memories of the Great War and fears of Australian vulnerability in the war to come, with Japan as the inevitable enemy, and the Royal Navy based on Singapore the supreme protector. At the political level, Australian defence thinking was crippled by a sense of Australian weakness and absolute reliance on Britain's strength. Soldiers who queried the conventional wisdom were shunned or silenced. The ruling United Australia Party committed itself entirely to the imperial idea and relied utterly on Britain's promises. The Australian Labor Party had never recovered from the trauma of the conscription split; the resultant mixture of anti-imperialism, vague internationalism, and half-hearted pacifism made a mockery of its profession of self-reliance in defence. Its routine denunciations of fascism rang hollow. In essence, the Australian conservative parties had no defence policy except loyalty to the Empire, while the Australian Labor Party had no defence policy upon which it could unite except defence of White Australia. To the extent that Britain's naval power, supposedly projected at Singapore, was still regarded as the guarantee of both the British Empire and White Australia, both sides could unite in professions of loyalty to the Empire, and trust in the government which presided over it in London.

When Lyons went to London for the 1937 Imperial Conference, he spoke for a nation subservient to Britain by choice. 'It is our duty,' he told his prime ministerial peers, 'in the interests of the Empire as a whole, and in the interests of the world at large, to accept wholeheartedly and loyally the grand principles, laid down and followed with so much courage, generosity and wisdom by the United Kingdom.' That meant, Lyons said, 'support without qualification for the declarations which the Government of the United Kingdom has made, to stand solidly behind that Government and to cooperate in the fullest possible measure with the efforts of that Government to secure world appeasement and peace'.

Of all the dominion prime ministers, Lyons was by far the loudest in support of the British policy of appeasement. From the time Neville Chamberlain succeeded Baldwin as Prime Minister in 1937, Lyons was his constant correspondent, giving unswerving support and encouragement. At the Imperial Conference he loyally went along with a British proposal to offer Hitler the British–French condominium in the New Hebrides as a trade-off for good behaviour in Europe. In the weeks of the Munich crisis over Czechoslovakia, from August to October, 1938, consultation between the

British and Australian governments reached a level of closeness which Deakin or Hughes could barely have imagined. For this brief inglorious moment, the old idea that Australia could take an active part in forming a single imperial policy seemed to be becoming a reality. In his address to the Imperial Conference, Lyons could not have chosen words better designed to set him and the Australian Government at odds with Churchill. Churchill's case rested precisely on his refusal to accept that the British Government, as embodied by Baldwin and Chamberlain, was acting with courage, generosity, or wisdom. His public speeches and prolific journalism were all based on that refusal.

Appeasement began as a rational policy, neither craven nor dishonourable. For Chamberlain and his supporters – the over-whelming majority of the Conservative Party, the London press and the British public – appeasement meant trying to redress Germany's grievances in order to preserve the peace of Europe. Its advocates saw it not in terms of surrender but conciliation. Chamberlain summed up his policy right up to the eve of Hitler's invasion of Poland: 'I want to gain time, for I never accept the view that war is inevitable.' Appeasement was not a rejection of war, but of its inevitability. Churchill himself was a selective appeaser in Europe and, towards Japan, an explicit one. He made a distinction between Hitler and the German people. He had always recognised that the humiliation of the Treaty of Versailles would cause un-dying resentment and could see the power and appeal behind Hitler's rantings.

The Treaty of Versailles saddled Germany with the entire guilt for the Great War; hardly anyone in Britain or Australia believed this by the mid-1930s. The war reparations policy, never as draconic as the Germans claimed, was held responsible for the catastrophic inflation of the German mark in the 1920s, and even for the Great Depression itself. But the blame Germany bore, and the economic woes it suffered, all gave Hitler a potent source for his rhetoric of revenge. Worse, they created a climate of acceptance, even legitimacy, for his political and territorial demands. Britain and France suffered a paralysis of conscience. Hitler played not only on the emotions of the German people, but on the sympathies of the war-weary, and by now, war-fearing, people of Britain and France. The industrial Saar province returned to the Fatherland by plebiscite; not a shot was fired when Hitler occupied the Rhineland in March, 1937; even the French had come to accept it as inevitable, sooner or later. With the same despairing resignation to the irresistible, Britain and France accepted the Anschluss, the incorporation of Austria into the German Reich. Hitler rode into Vienna in triumph on 9 April 1938, the local boy making good with a vengeance.

Czechoslovakia was a democratic state and a divided nation, one of the most prosperous remnants of the Austro-Hungarian Empire. The German speakers of the Sudetenland formed nearly a third of Czechoslovakia's ten million people; the Slovaks were of doubtful loyalty to the government in Prague. The Nazi leaders of the Sudeten Germans demanded an act of self-determination according to the main principle of Wilson's Fourteen Points. Hitler and all Europe knew that such a plebiscite would favour joining the German Reich. This was always Hitler's strongest card in the deadly game he proceeded to play, first with Czechoslovakian President Eduard Beneš, and then with Neville Chamberlain.

The Lyons Government of Australia went far beyond passive support for Chamberlain's policy. It stopped short of being pro-Hitler, but it was clearly anti-Czech. Attorney-General Menzies, in particular, stiffened Lyons in urging Chamberlain to take a tough line, not against Hitler but against Beneš. Menzies, on his third visit to London in three years, had journeyed to Berlin soon after the Anschluss. Hitler was now stepping up his demands on Czecho-slovakia. Menzies fell heavily under the influence of the British Ambassador to Germany, Sir Nevile Henderson, arch-appeaser and Hitler apologist. He applauded Henderson's 'frank and even breezy method of putting the British view to the Germans'; in fact, Hender-son was rather better at putting the German view to the British. Menzies' main criticism of Nazi Germany was 'the easy acceptance by the German people of execution without trial, the complete suppression of criticism and a controlled press'. This, he claimed to have told the President of the Reichsbank, Dr Hellmar Schacht, 'would ultimately destroy Germany'. He dismissed Hitler as 'a dreamer, a man of ideas, many of them good ones'.

Menzies viewed Hitler's Germany with a mix of acceptance and disdain: 'The Nazi philosophy has produced a real and disinterested enthusiasm which regards the abandonment of individual liberty with something of the same kind of ecstasy as that with which the medieval monk donned his penitential hair-shirt,' he wrote. In a letter to his brother Frank in Melbourne, he said: 'To people in London, the Germans every now and then seem to be uncivilised butchers, while the Germans in their turn are constantly misled by their belief that anything said by an irresponsible backbencher in the House of Commons is to be taken as a serious pronouncement of British Government policy.' Frank Menzies would have had no difficulty in identifying the 'irresponsible backbencher'. The only one whose voice was ever heard in Melbourne, and whose pronouncements enraged Berlin, was Winston Churchill.

Unlike Churchill, Menzies had no sympathy whatever for the Czechs. He saw them as a nuisance to be borne with impatience. The President of Czechoslovakia, he told brother Frank, 'is regarded in well-informed circles here as being what we would call a fairly greasy fellow, and what the polite British diplomat would call rather tiresome'. Menzies reported to Lyons after his Berlin visit: 'There appears to be a gloomy feeling in the German mind that Beneš, egged on by France, will refuse to do the fair thing.' There must be a 'very firm hand at Prague', he insisted to Lyons, 'otherwise Beneš will continue to bluff at the expense of much more important nations, including our own'. Menzies found room for hope in the recent visit of the new King and Queen to Paris. He told Lyons that the German Foreign Office agreed with his view that 'this dramatic affirmation of the Entente Cordiale should make the French much less nervous and therefore much less liable to do silly things'. He assured Lyons: 'In Berlin, I came to the conclusion that the actual absorption of Sudeten into the German Reich is not in the immediate programme.'

A month to the day on, Hitler instructed the Sudeten Nazi leaders to break off talks with the Czech Government, and on 12 September announced to a Nazi Party rally at Nuremberg that he would 'march for justice' for their oppressed Sudeten brothers. On 15 September, Chamberlain flew to Berchtesgaden, in the Bavarian Alps, for the first of his three meetings with Hitler, and virtually offered him Sudetenland on a plate, as long as Hitler did not actually invade. On 21 September, the British and French governments advised Beneš to accept Hitler's terms. Next day, Beneš refused to preside over his country's dismemberment, and Chamberlain flew again to meet Hitler, this time at Bad Godesberg, in Bonn. Hitler upped the ante, by demanding that the Czechs immediately evacuate Sudetenland. The Czech army, the third strongest in Europe, mobilised. In London, the authorities began to sandbag public buildings, dig trenches in Hyde Park, distribute gas masks, and plan to evacuate the children from the capital. 'How horrible, fantastic, incredible it is that we should be digging trenches and trying on gas masks here, because of a quarrel in a faraway country between people of whom we know nothing,' Chamberlain told the British people in a broadcast on 27 September. Next day, just as he was telling the House of Commons that war seemed inevitable, he was handed a message from Mussolini saying that Hitler had agreed to receive the British Prime Minister and the French Prime Minister, Édouard Daladier, at Munich. The House of Commons erupted into cheers and tears. Churchill slumped in his seat, but then rose to wish Chamberlain 'God speed'. On 30 September, Hitler, Mussolini, Chamberlain, and Daladier transferred Sudetenland to the Third Reich holus bolus. At Chamberlain's request, Hitler signed a hurriedly typed-up note proclaiming their common desire to live in peace and amity for ever. From the window at 10 Downing Street, Chamberlain waved his piece of paper at an euphoric crowd, saying: 'I believe it is peace in our time.' President Roosevelt cabled the British Prime Minister: 'Good man.'

'We have sustained a total and unmitigated defeat,' Churchill told a hostile House of Commons during the debate on 5 October 1938 to approve the Munich Agreement. 'Nonsense,' interjected Lady Nancy Astor, the American-born heiress who had become Britain's first woman MP in 1919. Churchill ploughed on undaunted: 'The utmost the Prime Minister has been able to secure for Czechoslovakia has been that the German dictator, instead of snatching his victuals from the table, has been content to have them served to him course by course.' Churchill summed up the results of Chamberlain's three meetings with Hitler and the Munich Agreement: 'One pound was demanded at the pistol's point. When it was given, two pounds were demanded at the pistol's point. Finally, the dictator consented to take one pound seventeen shillings and sixpence and the rest in promises of goodwill for the future.'

This time there was little of the 'I told you so' which had so irked Menzies in 1935. Churchill's eyes were focused on the grim future: 'What I find unendurable is the sense of our country falling under the power, into the orbit and influence of Nazi Germany, and of our existence becoming dependent upon their goodwill or pleasure.' Although relatively gentle towards Chamberlain's personal efforts for peace, Churchill was brutal in his counter-effort to puncture the euphoria that Munich had produced:

> We are in the presence of a disaster of the first magnitude which has befallen Great Britain and France. Do not let us blind ourselves to that. It must now be accepted that all the countries of Central and Eastern Europe will make the best terms they can with the triumphant Nazi power . . . And do not suppose that this is the end. This is only the beginning of the reckoning. This is only the first sip, the first foretaste of a bitter cup which will be proffered to us year by year, unless by a supreme recovery of moral health and martial vigour, we arise again and take our stand for freedom as in the olden time.

This was the most important of all Churchill's pre-war speeches. As usual, it jarred with the Conservative majority in the House of Commons, but struck deep chords in the country. It became even more important as events unfolded in Europe according to his predictions.

Munich was the basis for Churchill's statement to Roosevelt, years later, that the Second World War should be called the Unnecessary War. He came to believe that, if Britain and France had stood firm, not only would Hitler have been stopped in his tracks, but that the German generals would have got rid of him. This, of course, is counterfactualism of an extreme order, although it has become an article of faith with Churchill cultists of the neo-conservative brand. Twisted into the doctrine of the pre-emptive strike, which Churchill never once urged, the so-called 'Lesson of Munich' has been used to justify wars from Suez in 1956, to Iraq in 2003.

A more convincing counterfactual has been given by John Lukacs, a historian who has done more than any other writer to demonstrate the supreme importance of Churchill's stand against Hitler in May, 1940. In *The Hitler of History*, Lukacs suggests that, even if Britain and France had declared war in September, 1938, they would have done nothing thereafter to help Czechoslovakia, just as they did nothing to help Poland in September, 1939. Honour satisfied, they would then have accepted Hitler's triumph after the short war he always wanted. Hitler himself resented Chamberlain's interference, precisely because it gave him the Sudentenland without war.

The reality of 1938 was, as the English historian A. J. P. Taylor observed: 'The overwhelming majority of ordinary people, according to contemporary estimates, approved of what Chamberlain had done. The governments of the Dominions were equally approving. If war had come in October 1938, South Africa and Eire certainly, Canada probably, would have remained neutral; Australia and New Zealand would have followed the Mother Country with reluctance.' Chamberlain could not have taken a united Britain, or Lyons a willing Australia, into war over Czechoslovakia. The great cause for wonder is not that the people of Britain and Australia did not go to war against Germany in September, 1938, only twenty years after the last terrible war, but that they went to war eleven months later.

'It is the end of the British Empire,' Churchill had muttered to a friend in his London flat, as Chamberlain was flying off for his second meeting with Hitler. The view of official Australia could not have been more different. 'The Czechoslovakian problem is not a question on which war for the British Empire can justifiably be contemplated,' Lyons had told the British Government in August. He maintained that view in close and urgent communications with Chamberlain, by telephone and cable, throughout the crisis. His widow, Dame Enid Lyons, even claimed posthumous credit on his behalf, for initiating the approach to Mussolini. In the Australian Cabinet, only Hughes and Thomas White, Minister for Trade, strongly dissented. White wrote in his diary for 26 September 1938: 'It seems opposed to the traditions of our race. I think we should hang our heads that we did not stand up to the bully of Europe. It may yet mean peace but at what price?' He was especially disappointed by his fellow Anzac, Richard Casey, who had entered parliament in 1931, and was now Lyons' Treasurer: 'One can expect this attitude from Menzies but Casey is inexplicable . . . While Hitler lives, it seems that small countries will be swallowed up and democracy hangs in the balance.'

Otherwise, the main Australian reaction to Munich was relief, but doubts, reflecting Tommy White's sense of shame, soon spread. Churchill's speech was well reported; its warnings about the implications of Munich began to sink in. The *Sydney Morning Herald* editorialised:

> At the best, the Munich pact embodied a solution to the Sudeten problem so violent and so inimical to the long-range interests of the Western democracies as to be acceptable only as an alternative to war. At the worst it involved, in the words of Mr Churchill, 'a disaster of the first magnitude for Britain and France'.

One aspect of the Munich debate in the House of Commons was more important than Churchill's speech for its impact on public opinion in Australia, especially on the Labor side. It was not Churchill, but the leader of the Labour Party, Clement Attlee, who insisted that the House divide against the Government's motion to approve the agreement. Churchill and thirty Conservatives abstained from voting, but the Labour Opposition voted solidly against Munich. This was an historic shift, with British Labour uniting against appeasement and against Hitler. In the months after Munich, British Labour's example was to influence Australian Labor significantly.

* * *

THE AUSTRALIAN LABOR PARTY had received such terrible blows, and inflicted so many on itself, that its mere survival was a marvel. The conscription split had twisted its soul, the Depression had broken its heart, and the legacy of the Russian Revolution in Stalin's Soviet Union had clouded its intellect. In October, 1929, under James Scullin, Labor had won a sweeping victory over the Bruce–Page Government. Barely a week later, Wall Street crashed. Labor's inability to cope with the Depression destroyed its self-confidence. Like the British Labour Party, nothing in its philosophy of parliamentary socialism equipped it to handle such an economic cataclysm, and it split over attempts to cut unemployment and pension payments, and to follow the cost-cutting financial orthodoxy of this pre-Keynesian, pre-New Deal age. The Australian conservatives found their Ramsay Macdonald in Joseph Aloysius Lyons. The new party he helped form, the United Australia Party, in coalition with Page's Country Party, won the 1931 elections, and was returned comfortably in 1934 and 1937. Because the drastic measures which had split the Labor Government had been imposed at the behest of the Bank of England, and because the charismatic egotist who was Labor Premier of New South Wales, John Thomas Lang, had tried to suspend, if not repudiate debt repayments owed to British bond-holders, Labor's loyalty to the Empire once again came under strain and suspicion. It did not help that the debt owed to Britain was partly a result of Australia's war effort.

John Curtin inherited a torn and damaged party when he was elected its parliamentary leader by one vote in October, 1935. He was torn and damaged himself. Ten years younger than Churchill, his experience of life and politics made a striking contrast. Curtin was the son of an Irish police constable and hotel-keeper, born in the Victorian goldfields town of Creswick in 1885, when Churchill's father, the son of a duke, was the coming man in the House of Commons. When Churchill was finishing at Harrow and Sandhurst, Curtin was beginning at Catholic parish schools in rural Victoria and later, in the poorer suburbs of Melbourne. Both educated themselves through omnivorous reading, but Curtin's staple was the socialist literature of the nineteenth century. Churchill boasted that he had taken more out of alcohol than alcohol had taken out of him. Alcohol was Curtin's demon, his struggle against it never completely won. His supporters for the Labor leadership in 1935 had made their effort on his behalf conditional on a pledge to give up the drink. His biographer David Day reveals that between 1935 and the outbreak of war, before he became Prime Minister, he contrived secret binges in Sydney. Churchill had his 'black dog' and Curtin his 'old bogey' – days of deep depression, probably what would now be diagnosed as bipolar disorder. But while Curtin had long periods of self-doubt and insecurity, Churchill never lost faith in himself or his destiny.

While Churchill was leading his battalion in the trenches in France, between his stints as First Lord of the Admiralty and Minister for Munitions, Curtin, who had tried to enlist in 1915 but had been rejected on account of his eyesight, was campaigning against conscription. He was arrested, and spent three days in jail, for allegedly failing to register for military service. For both men journalism provided a livelihood, Churchill commanding record fees in London and New York, Curtin, as a contributor to hard-up socialist and union journals in Melbourne and later, as editor of the *Westralian Worker* in Perth. Each suffered the indignity of losing his seat in parliament in his political prime, but rebounded within three years, Churchill to become Conservative Chancellor of the Exchequer in 1924, Curtin to become leader of the Australian Labor Party in 1935. When Churchill became Prime Minister in 1940, he had held most high offices of state except Foreign Secretary. When Curtin became Prime Minister in 1941, his top administrative job had been secretary/organiser of the Victorian Timber Workers' Union. Both owed their rise to their oratorical powers, but while Churchill honed his skills in Westminster and at the great British assembly places like the Albert Hall and the Manchester Free Trade Hall, Curtin, in a hundred draughty rooms in Melbourne and its suburbs and on the Yarra Bank, preached variations on a single theme: 'Socialism is the only way – it will end war even as it will conquer poverty.'

Labor's failures in the Great War and the Depression severely challenged Curtin's core beliefs. He held the more tenaciously to a single idea: to re-unite the Australian Labor Party. To Curtin, this was an almost sacred duty. All his actions before 1941, his compromises, his silences that so often seemed weakness, the obscurity of his pronouncements clothed in grandiloquent language, must be set against that single aim. It is a paradox that this disillusioned socialist and anti-militarist became Australia's great wartime Prime Minister. But it is an even stranger paradox that the unity he sought for Labor came through his handling of war and defence issues, potentially so explosive for the ALP.

In his first statement as Labor's new leader, Curtin said: 'Our business is to keep Australia aloof from the wars of the world.' In practice, this doctrine rendered irrelevant anything Curtin might say on the international issues of the day: economic sanctions against Italy for its invasion of Abyssinia in 1935, the Spanish Civil War in 1936, Japan's war on China in 1937, Munich. It mocked the lip-service the Labor Party had formerly paid to the idea of collective security through the League of Nations. It was one thing to be inspired by a hatred of war; but the Labor Party's knee-jerk denunciation – almost renunciation – of all war as the product of capitalism and imperialism left it increasingly isolated from progressive and socialist opinion everywhere in the world, especially after the Soviet Union joined the League of Nations in 1934, and called for a 'united front' against Hitler and fascism. On these issues, particularly Spain, Curtin manoeuvred, mentally and morally, between the Catholic right, strongly represented in the parliamentary party, and the anti-fascist, pro-communist left, predominant in the union movement. Speaking as 'one who knew the man', Paul Hasluck wrote: 'His mind sometimes writhed in tortuous struggles with its own honesty and power of reasoning.'

The lesson of Munich, Curtin said, 'was that Australia must keep out of the quarrels of Europe and not dissipate its resources, thereby exposing this country to far worse danger'. It is hard to imagine a stance further removed from Churchill's or, for that matter, Curtin's brothers in the British Labour Party. And such a stance meant overturning Labor's professed allegiance to the League of Nations. Curtin wrote in the *Australian Worker* in November, 1938:

Sadly we must put aside sentimental adherence to those ideals which inspired the birth of the League of Nations and recognise that, in their present economic environment, they have proved incapable of translation into action. Therefore, the Australian Labor Party stands to its policy of non-participation in European wars while ensuring that we shall attain to the maximum of self-reliance in order to repel aggression.

Saving White Australia was the common ground between the parties in the Australian defence debate. In November, 1936, Curtin had told Parliament:

If an Eastern first-class power [he meant of course Japan] sought an abrogation of a basic Australian policy, such as the White Australia Policy, it would most likely do so when Great Britain was involved or threatened to be involved in a European war. Would the British Government dare to authorise the dispatch of any substantial part of the fleet to help Australia?

Like Churchill, and unlike Lyons, Curtin dared to question the credentials of the Empire's rulers. 'The dependence of Australia upon the competence, let alone the readiness, of British statesmen to send forces to our aid is too dangerous a hazard upon which to found Australian defence policy.'

Curtin attempted to develop a defence policy based on self-reliance. Its most positive feature was his call for a stronger air force, echoing Churchill at least in this respect. Otherwise, Labor's defence statements comprised a series of negatives: no participation in any future overseas war; no compulsory military training; no forces, even of volunteers, to be sent overseas; no production of munitions or war materials by private enterprise. As late as June, 1938, the Labor Party reaffirmed all these nay-sayings as its official defence policy.

As with so much else in the world, Munich and its aftermath changed all that. The 15th Federal ALP Conference, held over five days in Canberra in May, 1939, produced a radically new defence policy, soon after Hitler had destroyed what was left of Czechoslovakia. For all its gestures in the direction of Labor tradition, inseparable from any Labor document, it gave Curtin, its principal author, the basis for a realistic response to the deteriorating world situation. The conference declared 'its adherence to the principles of Democracy, and the necessity of defending our free institutions against all forms of attack'. Its first principle was: 'We stand for the maintenance of Australia as an integral part of the British Common-wealth of Nations.' Its second principle was: 'We stand for a policy of complete national security and economic security.' It 'deplored the lack of preparedness for the defence of the country', and declared 'the urgency of speeding up production of necessary equip-ment, munitions, etc. and all things that are required in connection with adequate defence'. Noting the retention of opposition to 'conscription of human life', Paul Hasluck says in his official war history, 'the party had not travelled far'. He is wrong. With all Labor pronouncements, it is a matter of emphasis, and what the parlia-mentary leadership chooses to make of it. However nuanced and ambiguous, the 1939 ALP Conference gave Curtin all he needed to develop a realistic defence policy for Australia.

Churchill was quite literally writing Australian history in the first months of 1939, just when Hitler was rewriting the political geog-raphy of Europe. He was working on the chapters on Australia and New Zealand for his *History of the English-Speaking Peoples*. The manuscript was contracted for delivery by 1940; other matters inter-vened, however, and *The History* was not published until 1956, after his second prime ministership. It would be pleasant to be able to record that the study of Australian history gave Churchill respite from his grim preoccupations. His role, however, was limited to revising a 10,000-word draft from a young Oxford historian, Alan Bullock, who went on to write a seminal work, *Hitler: A Study in Tyranny*. By now, Churchill was becoming a literary industry. The pedestrian nature of the chapter indicates that he did not bother much over Bullock's draft. He did, however, give Bullock and his other amanuenses a general direction:

> In the main, the theme is emerging of the growth of freedom and law, of the rights of the individual, of the subordination of the State to the

fundamental and moral conceptions of an ever-comprehending community. Of these ideas the English-speaking peoples were the authors, then
the trustees, and must now become the armed champions.

'All this, of course, has current application,' Churchill told his
literary co-workers. On 16 March 1939, Hitler gobbled up the
rest of Czechoslovakia. He then turned his attention to Poland.
Wounded by Hitler's breach of faith, and even more by the blow to
his vanity, Chamberlain announced on 17 April that Britain would
guarantee Poland against German aggression. This was the point at
which war became inevitable, unless Chamberlain was willing to
perpetrate another Munich. The destruction of Poland was crucial
to Hitler's planned enslavement of Eastern Europe. Hitler's pressure
point against Poland was the German-populated Free City of Danzig
(Gdansk), established by the League of Nations as a Baltic port for
Poland, connected by the narrow territory running through north
Germany, known as the Polish corridor. 'Danzig at present is the
danger spot,' Chamberlain wrote to his sister in July. 'I doubt if any
solution short of war is practicable at present but if the Dictator
would have a modicum of patience I can imagine that a way could
be found of meeting German claims while safeguarding Poland's
independence and economic security.' Hitler, however, was impatient and contemptuous. 'I saw the English at Munich,' he told his
master propagandist, Dr Joseph Goebbels: 'They are little worms.'

The Australian Government was appalled at the idea of the
British Empire going to war over Danzig. Australia had a new Prime
Minister. Joe Lyons, sick at heart at the prospect of war abroad, and
at division and disloyalty in his Cabinet at home, died on 7 April
1939. Menzies narrowly beat Hughes, now seventy-seven, for the
leadership of the United Australia Party. The interim Prime Minister,
Earle Page, denounced Menzies in the most vitriolic personal attack
ever delivered in the House of Representatives, questioning his
fitness to lead because of his failure to serve in the Great War; Page
then withdrew the Country Party from the coalition government.
After Chamberlain's guarantee to Poland, Menzies continued to
counsel caution, maintained that there were 'two sides to the Polish

question', and expressed hope that the 'Polish problem' could be solved by negotiation.

In London, Chamberlain seemed more anxious to keep Churchill out of his Cabinet than to keep Hitler out of Danzig. In July, there was a press campaign to bring Churchill back into the government. Chamberlain saw it as a 'regular conspiracy', involving the Russian Ambassador, Ivan Maisky, Churchill's son Randolph, and the press barons, Lords Beaverbrook, Camrose, and Rothermere. Opposing this unlikely combination, Stanley Bruce, former Prime Minister of Australia and now its High Commissioner in London, threw his weight on Chamberlain's side against Churchill, eagerly identifying himself and his country with appeasement. 'It is significant that Bruce came to see me and expressed his consternation at the idea,' Chamberlain wrote to his sister. 'It is evident that Australia and South Africa are rather alarmed at the bellicose tone in the country and they think, as I do, that if Winston got into the government, it would not be long before we were at war.'

Yet the war came. And Churchill got back. Hitler, who since 1923 had fanned hatred of the Jews with denunciations of their alleged part in the international communist conspiracy, signed a non-aggression pact with Stalin's Soviet Union on 23 August 1939. The pact included a secret agreement to share in the destruction of Poland. Chamberlain, who had dragged his feet over negotiations for an anti-Nazi agreement with Russia, reaffirmed his Polish guarantee. Stalin's opportunism rendered the guarantee meaningless. It was a measure of Churchill's hatred of Hitlerism that he had been foremost in calling for a 'grand alliance' with Soviet communism. On 1 September, Hitler invaded Poland. For twenty-four hours, Chamberlain wavered, hoping for further negotiations, perhaps even another face-saving initiative from Mussolini or the dominions. In the meantime, he recalled Churchill as First Lord of the Admiralty. On 2 September, the House of Commons rebelled. They refused to stomach another Munich. On 3 September, Chamberlain announced that his ultimatum requiring Hitler to withdraw his forces from Poland had gone unanswered; therefore, Britain was at war with Germany.

13

'Australia is also at war'
1939–40

Menzies announced that Australia was at war an hour after Chamberlain's speech, in a broadcast at 9.15 p.m. EST, on 3 September 1939. His words were less than Churchillian, but well pitched to the Australian mood and the needs of the occasion. 'It is my melancholy duty to inform you officially,' he told his listeners on every radio station throughout Australia, 'that, in consequence of a persistence by Germany in her invasion of Poland, Great Britain has declared war upon her and that, as a result, Australia is also at war. No harder task can fall to the lot of a democratic leader than to make such an announcement.' Menzies gave a detailed account of the events of the past week, concluding: 'Great Britain and France, with the cooperation of the British Dominions, have struggled to avoid this tragedy. They have, as I firmly believe, been patient. They have kept the door of negotiation open. They have given no cause for aggression. But in the result, their efforts have failed and we are, therefore, as a great family of nations, involved in a struggle which we must at all costs win, and which we believe in our hearts we will win.'

The phrase 'as a result, Australia is also at war' is among the best known, most quoted, and least understood words that Menzies uttered in his long career. It has been painted as the supreme example of his 'British to the bootstraps' attitude, like his well-known homage to Elizabeth II in 1963, 'I did but see her passing by, and yet I'll love her till I die', reputed to have brought a blush of embarrassment to the cheeks of the young Queen. It did not strike most Australians like that in 1939.

The fact is that as things stood in September, 1939, Menzies' formula was the best way to take Australia into the war, more or less united. Australians could unite around their loyalty to Britain much more readily than around their hostility to Nazi Germany. Menzies' Sunday broadcast, like his speech to the House of Representatives three days later, was a powerful indictment of Hitler's invasion of Poland; but it was essentially a barrister's brief, thoroughly documented and closely argued. 'This is not a moment for rhetoric,' he said, 'but a moment for quiet thinking, for the calm fortitude which rests not upon the beating of drums but upon the unconquerable spirit of man, created by God in his own image.' On a more earthly level, he did not actually use the words later fastened on him: 'Business as usual', but the thought was there when he said: 'Our staying power, and particularly the staying power of the Mother Country, will be best assisted by keeping our production going, by continuing our avocations and our business as fully as we can; by maintaining employment and, with it, our strength.' This was not a rousing clarion call to arms, but it was a call for unity around a single proposition – that Britain's decision had placed Australia at war, automatically. And it worked.

Curtin, in particular, had reason to be grateful to Menzies for the form in which he chose to declare war. No one knew better how hard-won and fragile any kind of political unity was, in an Australia still scarred by the Great War and the Great Depression, and in the Labor Party most of all. Only the previous weekend, he had exhausted himself in three days of cajoling, pleading, and bargaining in Sydney, at yet another of the so-called 'unity conferences' which often left the Labor Party in New South Wales more divided than before. This time he had achieved considerable success in bringing its factions together, and laying the foundations for future electoral success. Nothing had more potential to reignite divisions, from the Catholic right to the pro-communist left, than the issue of Australia's involvement in another European war.

Menzies, in effect, presented Curtin with a fait accompli, and Curtin accepted it with relief. In his speech in the House of Representatives on 6 September, Curtin used the phrases: 'the fact of war' and 'the reality of war', as if Menzies had announced an act of God or a natural disaster. Neither Curtin nor any of the other Opposition speakers, in the eight hours of a high standard debate, contested Menzies' basic proposition that Australia was at war because Britain was at war. Not one contested his legal view that once the King of England declared war, the whole Empire was at war. Not one argued that Australia should be following the example of Canada, whose Prime Minister, Mackenzie King, had insisted that the declaration of war should be made by resolution of its parliament (which did not meet to do so until 10 September). Nobody mentioned the Statute of Westminster which gave the dominion parliaments the right to make their own decision. Nobody suggested that it was a matter of regret that Australia had not yet ratified it. Nor did anybody raise Labor's chimerical policy during the heyday of pacifism, that any decision to go to war should be made only after a plebiscite. Even Eddie Ward, the Labor 'firebrand from East Sydney', who had the capacity to get under Curtin's and Menzies' skin with bipartisan irritation, and who was to drive Curtin to the point of resignation in 1943, did not object. Curtin probably listened to Ward's speech with mounting trepidation, as he lambasted Chamberlain and Menzies as much as Hitler for allowing things to come to this pass, the inevitable result of imperialism and capitalism. But even Ward accepted the decision and the terms in which Menzies had chosen to announce it. Menzies had effectively got Curtin off the hook.

Curtin read out the statement for which he had gained Caucus approval before the House met:

> In this crisis, facing the reality of war, the Labor Party stands for its platform. That platform is clear. We stand for the maintenance of Australia as an integral part of the British Commonwealth of Nations.

Therefore, the party will do all that is possible to safeguard Australia and, at the same time, having regard to its platform, will do its utmost to maintain the integrity of the British Commonwealth.

Thus the Empire was restored to the heart of Labor's defence policy, even as Curtin restated Labor's opposition to conscription, an expeditionary force, and a national coalition. These reservations did not prevent Hughes from expressing his 'very great pleasure' with Curtin's speech: 'He has left nothing unsaid that we wanted to hear.' Hughes spoke as the Attorney-General and deputy leader in an anti-Labor government; at the beginning of the war twenty-five years earlier, he had been the Attorney-General and deputy leader in a Labor government. As a result of Curtin's speech, said Hughes, 'we face this new and terrible ordeal as a united people'. If this was true, nothing had done more to bring it about than Menzies' retrospectively maligned formula for the declaration of war.

'WINSTON IS BACK.' The Admiralty signal flashed around the Royal Navy; and for the second time in twenty-five years Churchill, as First Lord of the Admiralty, sent the signal: 'Commence hostilities against Germany.' As in 1914, Churchill's order put Australia on war alert ahead of the official notification from the British Government. Churchill bounded into his old office at the Admiralty and looked for the cupboard containing his specially constructed war maps, with pins showing the location of every ship of the Royal Navy; he found the map and the pins exactly as he had left them on the day he was dismissed in May, 1915. Churchill recalled the lines of the Irish poet Thomas Moore:

I feel like one
Who treads alone
Some banquet-hall deserted,
Whose lights are fled,
Whose garlands dead,
And all but he departed.

'And what of the supreme, measureless ordeal in which we were again irrevocably plunged?' Churchill reflected. 'Poland in its agony. France but a pale reflection of her former warlike ardour; the Russian Colossus no longer an ally, not even neutral, possibly to become a foe. Italy no friend. Japan no ally. Would America ever come in again? The British Empire remained intact and gloriously united but ill-prepared, unready.'

Churchill himself bore much responsibility for the unreadiness of the Australian quarter of that Empire. His attitude and actions as First Lord of the Admiralty second time around rendered the Far East even more ill prepared. Repeating 1914 more urgently, he recalled the navy west of Suez. This included most of the Royal Australian Navy which, on 9 November 1939, was once again placed under control of the British Admiralty and its First Lord. He discarded once and for all the navy's inter-war doctrine of 'Main Fleet to Singapore'. The Singapore Naval Base had been opened nine months before Munich, with much fanfare but without any sign of a fleet to use it. In abandoning the Far East, Churchill was merely ratifying the obvious: Singapore could only serve its deterrent and defensive purpose if there were a fleet to send; once the fleet was needed nearer home, the Singapore strategy became impossible and irrelevant. Yet this Singapore strategy had been the whole foundation of Australian defence policy since 1923. Never was an illusion so hard to kill.

Churchill tried hard to hide the new reality from the Australian Government. In their turn, the Australians were willing to be misled. It all depended on Japanese intentions. Churchill's optimism overcame Australian pessimism. His arguments carried more weight than anybody else's, both in Britain and Australia, in deciding the destination of the divisions of the new Australian Imperial Force, the Second AIF. In his early statements, Menzies had left open the raising of a force to go overseas. He was inhibited by five factors: Labor's opposition, divided counsels in his own government, the low level of military preparedness, his reluctance to make a firm commitment as long as there was a possibility of a settlement with Hitler after he had digested Poland, and fears about Japan.

As at September, 1939, Australia had a regular army of about three thousand men, and the militia, the Citizens Military Force of about eighty thousand volunteer reservists, ill equipped and scarcely trained. Lyons, the old Labor man, had always baulked at restoring compulsory military training, which had been abolished by Scullin's Labor Government in 1930, in the first months of the Depression. On 15 September, Menzies announced that 'a force of one division and auxiliary units of 20,000 volunteers would be created for service at home or abroad as circumstances permit'. Again, there was no clarion call to arms: 'It may be that, under some circumstances, Australian forces might be used to garrison some of the Pacific islands, to cooperate with New Zealand, to release British troops at Singapore, or at other ports around the Indian Ocean. Under other circumstances it may be practicable to send Australian forces to Europe.' With a leader as cautious as this, there was no Australian rush to the colours as in 1914. The rumblings about Menzies' lack of drive and leadership began, in the very first weeks of the war.

The big question for Australia was always how to balance its home defence needs and its judgement about Japan's intentions against its eagerness to help Britain in Europe. The Australian Government relied on the British Government's assessments. At the outbreak of war, this was that 'if Japan adopted an attitude of reserve towards the democratic countries, it will be unwise for Australia to send an expeditionary force to Europe, but if Japan was friendly, then Australia could send brigades to Singapore, Burma and India as they became available, or wait until complete divisions could be sent to the main theatre'. The British Government had an obvious interest in downplaying any threat from Japan. And the strongest proponent of such a view was the strongest man in the British Government, Winston Churchill.

In October, the Australian Chiefs of Staff contested the British Government's benign view of Japan. They counselled postponement of the decision until the end of December; if Japan still seemed friendly, AIF units could be sent overseas to continue training and relieve British garrisons; but if Japan seemed hostile by then, no Australian troops should be sent offshore, except as measures of

Australian defence. The Chiefs of Staff position was not far removed from Curtin's.

Churchill then made a crucial intervention. On 17 November, he drew up a memorandum entitled 'Australian Naval Defence (Winter 1939)'. There was no sign, he said, of any hostile action or intent on the part of Japan. As long as the British navy was undefeated, and as long as we held Singapore, no invasion of Australia or New Zealand was possible. Nevertheless, Churchill assured Australia: 'If the choice were presented of defending Australia against a serious attack, or sacrificing British interests in the Mediterranean, our duty to Australia would take precedence.'

Churchill's post-war excuses for his assessment of Japan echo his cop-out for inventing and continuing the Ten Year Rule twenty years before: 'It was my recorded conviction that *in the first year of a world war* Australia and New Zealand would be in no danger whatever in their homeland, and by the end of the first year we might hope to have cleaned up the seas and the oceans'. As a forecast of the first year of the naval war those thoughts proved true. But he never really explained why he had made a promise to Australia that he must have known would be impossible to keep. An authoritative historian of the Singapore base, James Neidpath, writes:

> Mr Churchill never hesitated to reaffirm that promise; he did so, for instance, on 11 August 1940 and as late as 1 December 1941 [a week before Pearl Harbor]. But it was for him, not for the Australians, to judge the moment when that promise should be implemented, and his consistently complacent view of the Japanese menace prevented its implementation until after the Japanese had attacked. His attitude towards the Australasians could be stigmatised as dishonest. But it might be better characterized as somewhat cavalier: he was prepared to take great risks with their security because he trusted an optimistic forecast of Japanese intentions, and because he never really put himself in the Australian position.

Churchill's promise of November, 1939, was decisive in changing Australian priorities from home defence to the Middle East. It gave the final push to a doubtful Menzies and a divided Cabinet. On 24 November, the full Cabinet decided that the 6th Australian Division should go overseas early in 1940, with Egypt or Palestine its most likely destination. Menzies had come to the decision reluctantly, even resentfully. He felt he was being unfairly pressured by the British Government, and knew that Churchill was the driving force in London. 'Am bound to tell you that we do so under protest,' he cabled Dick Casey in London. Casey was now Minister for Supply, and had gone to London for ministerial talks. Menzies complained to him on 21 November: 'We feel that in this matter we have been in effect forced into a course of action which we would not otherwise have adopted.' Menzies also was angered by the shipping arrangements, under Churchill's control: 'We resent being told that shipping is already on its way for the purpose of collecting our troops on 2 January when we were not consulted before the departure of the vessels.' He made sure, however, that no part of his dissatisfaction was allowed to penetrate the facade of imperial unity. 'It is the general feeling of Cabinet,' Menzies told Casey, 'that there has been in this matter a quite perceptible disposition to treat Australia as a Colony and to make insufficient allowance for the fact that it is for the Government to determine whether and when Australian forces shall go out of Australia.' But, like Hughes before him during the Chanak crisis, Menzies gave no hint of his dissatisfaction during the debate in Parliament on Curtin's motion to oppose the despatch of troops overseas.

On 9 January 1940, the 16th Brigade Group of the 6th Australian Division travelled by train from their camp at Ingleburn, west of Sydney, and embarked on four British liners. Next day, they sailed from Sydney Harbour, and joined at sea six transports of the 4th New Zealand Brigade. Churchill had sent the battleship HMS *Ramillies* to help two Australian cruisers, HMAS *Canberra* and the new HMAS *Australia*, to guard the thirteen thousand Anzacs of the second generation. As he instructed the Admiralty: 'The transportation of the Australasian divisions is an historic episode in Imperial history. An accident would be a disaster.'

* * *

211

WHILE THE NEW Anzacs were at sea, Menzies had his first brush with Churchill. What Churchill called the 'twilight war', and the Americans the 'phoney war', dragged on for months without major action in the West. In the East, Stalin, having shared the carcass of Poland with Hitler, invaded Finland. Only Churchill waged active war at sea, most notably at the Battle of the River Plate. But he was determined to carry the war to Hitler on the Continent. He backed proposals to mine the Rhine, firebomb the Black Forest (against the opposition of the Chancellor of the Exchequer, Sir Kingsley Wood, who protested: 'Do you realise that this is private property?') and, most passionately, to stop neutral Sweden from supplying its iron ore to German industry. The hitch was that any action in Scandinavia would violate the neutrality of Norway, whose northern port of Narvik was a vital link in the trade between Sweden and Germany. Churchill proposed to seize Narvik and mine the Norwegian coast. Chamberlain and his Foreign Secretary, Lord Halifax, still harbouring hopes for negotiations with Hitler, tried to dampen Churchill's provocative enthusiasm.

Menzies weighed in on their side against Churchill. When Churchill told the British Cabinet that 'opening up a new theatre in Scandinavia would force Hitler into situations he had not foreseen', Chamberlain read out a telegram from Menzies, urging that no decision be taken 'until the Dominions had an opportunity to express their views'. Menzies said that Churchill's disregard of Norwegian neutrality 'would have a bad effect in other neutral countries and would present arguments to Germany which she would not otherwise have'.

Menzies' argument cut no ice with Churchill. He told Cabinet: 'Small nations must not tie our hands when we are fighting for their rights and freedom.' He steamrolled his Norway scheme through the British Cabinet, whipping on the Admiralty to come up with a plan of action. Hitler was ahead of him. On 5 April, Chamberlain declared: 'Hitler has missed the bus.' On 9 April, Hitler occupied Denmark and invaded Norway. It was all over in a fortnight. The British counterattack, retreat, and withdrawal was marked, in a concentrated form, by the same confusion and humiliation as the

Dardanelles campaign. Churchill prepared himself once again to be the scapegoat for disaster, more deservedly perhaps in 1940 than in 1915.

But this time, there was an amazing reversal of fortune. The House of Commons, for so long Chamberlain's poodle, turned on its master in one of the greatest debates in its history. Lloyd George, in his last star performance, begged Churchill not to allow himself to be 'converted into an air-raid shelter' to protect the Prime Minister. Leo Amery, now an MP, quoted Oliver Cromwell sacking the Long Parliament in 1653, and shouted at Chamberlain: 'You have sat too long here for any good you have been doing. Depart, I say, and let us have done with you. In the name of God, go!' Churchill wound up the debate on 8 May, according to his friend Harold Nicolson, 'demonstrating by the brilliance of his personality that he has really nothing to do with this confused and timid gang'. Support for Chamberlain fell from its normal majority of more than two hundred to eighty. Nicolson, like most of his fellow parliamentarians, failed to realise or chose to ignore Churchill's central responsibility for the Norwegian fiasco. Churchill knew better. After the war, he wrote in a draft for his war memoirs: 'It was a marvel – I really do not know how – I survived and maintained my position in public esteem while all the blame was thrown on poor Mr Chamberlain.'

Next day, 9 May 1940, Churchill met Chamberlain and Lord Halifax at 10 Downing Street. Chamberlain asked him if he would be prepared to serve in a Halifax Government. Churchill claims to have looked at the garden and to have said nothing. Halifax volunteered the thought that it would be difficult to lead a government from the House of Lords. Crucially, the Leader of the British Labour Party, Clement Attlee, informed Chamberlain that Labour would not serve in a national government if he remained Prime Minister. On 10 May 1940, George VI reluctantly accepted Chamberlain's advice to ask Mr Churchill to form a government. 'I felt as if I were walking with destiny, and that all my past life had been but a preparation for this hour and this trial,' Churchill wrote later.

At the very moment Churchill 'kissed hands', Hitler's armies were clattering into Holland and Belgium. It was the end of the phoney war. The *Sitzkreig* gave way to the *Blitzkreig*. Germany's Panzer divisions took barely five weeks to thrust through Northern France to Paris. Two hundred thousand men of the British Expeditionary Force were evacuated from Dunkirk, a deliverance resulting not from a miracle but from a loss of nerve on Hitler's part. France surrendered to Germany on 22 June 1940. Ten days before it all ended in shame and recrimination, the French commander, General Weygand, implored Churchill to send every British fighter plane for 'the decisive point and the decisive moment' in France. Churchill refused: 'This is not the decisive point. This is not the decisive moment. The decisive moment will come when Hitler hurls his *Luftwaffe* against Britain. If we keep command over our own island – that is all I ask – we will win it all back for you.' Churchill was to take much the same attitude to the defence of Australia in 1942.

14

'I can see my way through'
May–September, 1940

One Big Idea took hold of Churchill after the fall of France: to keep Britain fighting until he could bring America into the war. The operative words were *keep fighting*. Every decision, right or wrong, every move, from the daring to the foolish, every important speech, became directed to this overarching aim. It is the key to his war leadership. Its ultimate success is his justification, and upon it rests his enduring reputation. In its pursuit, Churchill was unswerving, ruthless, and devious. Australia embraced his magnificent obsession and gambled heavily against the odds that he would be vindicated. Anger in Australia at some of his methods must be measured, now as then, against the end result.

Australia's place in Churchill's grand design was clear and simple: to place as many troops as possible at his disposal. As long as Australia could make a direct contribution to Britain's ability to fight on, Churchill was lavish in his praise. When it began to look to its own situation, the Churchillian smile became a frown, and when that situation became truly perilous, and the Australian leadership began to ask whether national and imperial interests were identical, the scowl became an angry growl. Yet at no time between the fall of France and Pearl Harbor did an Australian government challenge Churchill's basic concept – to keep Britain fighting until America came into the war. Australia had harder choices to make than any other country whose support Churchill needed: moral and military choices between its contribution to the imperial effort twelve thousand miles away and its security in its own backyard. Churchill made scant attempt to understand Australia's unique difficulties, much less to accommodate them.

In his first speech to the House of Commons as Prime Minister, Churchill summed up his policy and goals in a single word: *victory*. This was his 'nothing to offer but blood, toil, tears and sweat' speech, of 13 May 1940:

> You ask, what is our aim? I can answer in one word: Victory – victory at all costs, victory in spite of all terror; victory, however long and hard the road may be; for without victory there is no survival. Let that be realised: no survival for the British Empire; no survival for all that the British Empire has stood for, no survival for the urge and impulse of the ages, that mankind will move forward towards its goal.

In his first weeks in office, Churchill did not spell out what he meant by victory. He certainly did not foresee, when he made this speech, that France would collapse within six weeks; but at the very least, victory meant that Hitler must disgorge all his gains since Munich. The wider objective, the extirpation of the Nazi regime, was implicit when Churchill proclaimed his policy of waging war 'by sea, land and air, with all our might and with all the strength that God can give us against a monstrous tyranny, never surpassed in the dark, lamentable catalogue of human crime'.

Churchill's oratory made Britain 'standing alone' the most powerful image from the war. But Britain was not alone and Churchill had no intention of standing still. He was determined to go on the offensive, whenever and wherever he could. It was one thing just to keep Britain in the war, but quite another to find a way to fight, and a place to fight, after Hitler had made himself master of Europe. After the Battle of Britain, Churchill was fairly certain that the Führer would not succeed in any attempt at a full-scale invasion; 'Fortress Britain' could be made invulnerable through command of the air and sea. Any British leader other than Churchill might well have settled for that. It was certainly what Hitler himself expected when he extended his various peace feelers in 1940.

Three times Churchill reached points of no return. Between 24 and 28 May 1940, he persuaded his Cabinet to reject a proposal by Lord Halifax that Mussolini be approached to sound out Hitler on peace terms. The Italian dictator was still waiting until he was sure that Germany would win; he declared war on Britain and France on 10 June, twelve days before France fell. Churchill won out when Chamberlain declared against Halifax. The support of the Labour leader, Attlee, and his deputy, Arthur Greenwood, was also critical. Appeasement in Europe was dead and buried.

The second point of no return was Churchill's decision – which he called 'the most unnatural and painful I ever made' – to attack the French fleet at Oran in French Algeria in July, 1940. This was done to prevent the French navy falling into German hands. The French hated Churchill ever after for the deaths of twelve hundred of their sailors under the guns of 'perfidious Albion', their ally only a fortnight earlier. But, as much as anything else, Churchill wanted to show the President and people of the United States that he would stop at nothing in his determination to keep fighting.

The third point of no return was Churchill's response to Hitler's victory speech to the Reichstag on 19 July 1940. In a speech lasting two hours and twenty minutes, Hitler said: 'It almost causes me pain to think that I should have been selected by Fate to deal the final blow to the structure [the British Empire] which these men [Churchill and the British Cabinet] have already set tottering.' Appealing to 'reason and commonsense' he declared, 'I can see no reason why this war must go on'. Three days later, at Churchill's request, Lord Halifax broadcast Britain's rejection of the 'peace offer'. To the extent that he was willing to make peace with Britain in 1940, Hitler wanted to recruit the British Empire as an accomplice in his criminality on a world-wide scale.

Churchill's rejection of this devil's bargain is his eternal greatness, but it is also the basis for revisionist claims that Churchill sacrificed the Empire by fighting on. It is not hard to imagine the sort of empire that might have survived under Hitler's benevolent patronage. In 1937, Hitler had given Lord Halifax his recipe for India: 'Shoot Gandhi, and if that does not suffice to reduce them to submission, shoot a dozen leading members of Congress, and if that does not suffice, shoot 200 and so on until order is established.' This, of course, was the Führer in his more moderate murderousness. The true Hitlerian mode became clear as soon as he had conquered Poland and began to set up the apparatus of mass murder, forced expulsions and enslavement.

Churchill's overriding objective was not the preservation of the British Empire. His purpose was to destroy Hitler and Nazism, and if that meant driving the Empire to exhaustion and penury, he accepted the price. Certainly, he sustained himself by his belief that if Hitler could be beaten in Europe, Britain could retain its hold on its empire. Yet he was never under any illusion that the United States would not emerge from the war immensely superior to Britain in wealth and strength. He consoled himself with the idea of a common future for the English-speaking peoples, with Britain's prestige secured by her sacrifices; but everything was secondary to the defeat and extinction of Nazi Germany. On that there could be no compromise.

Churchill's Big Idea of fighting while waiting for America had taken root even before the French surrender. He sketched its outline in every word of the most famous utterance of all, the peroration of his House of Commons announcement on 4 June 1940 of the evacuation of Dunkirk:

We shall go on to the end, we shall fight in France, we shall fight on the seas and oceans, we shall fight with growing confidence and growing strength in the air, we shall defend our Island, whatever the cost may be, we shall fight on the beaches, we shall fight on the landing grounds, we shall fight in the fields and in the streets, we shall fight in the hills; we shall never surrender, and even if, which I do not for a moment believe, this Island or a large part of it were subjugated and starving, then our Empire beyond the seas, armed and guarded by the British Fleet, would carry on the struggle until, in God's good time, the New World, with all its power and might, steps forth to the rescue and the liberation of the old.

He is reputed to have mumbled as he slumped back on his seat, 'And we shall fight them with bottles which is about all we bloody well have'; but he had in fact outlined a strategy for victory from which he never diverged.

Churchill had a direct line of communication to the United States. Roosevelt himself had initiated their historic correspondence when Churchill was still at the Admiralty. The pair had met briefly in London in July, 1918, when Roosevelt was Assistant Secretary of the US Navy, and Churchill Minister for Munitions. To Roosevelt's chagrin, Churchill could not remember this meeting, and did not pretend to do so. Roosevelt certainly did, and told his Ambassador to the United Kingdom, Joseph P. Kennedy, the defeatist Anglophobe and father of the future President, John F. Kennedy: 'Churchill acted like a stinker at dinner, lording it over us.' Between 1940 and 1945, the leaders' correspondence grew prodigiously, to over one thousand messages from Churchill and about eight hundred from Roosevelt.

In his first prime ministerial letter, dated 15 May 1940, Churchill, signing himself 'Former Naval Person', warned: 'I trust you realise, Mr President, that the voice and force of the United States may count for nothing if they are too long withheld. You may have a completely subjugated, Nazified Europe established with astonishing swiftness and the weight may be more than we can bear.' His first request was that the United States proclaim non-belligerence (instead of neutrality), 'which could mean that you would help us with everything short of actually engaging armed forces'. He sought 'the loan of 40 or 50 older destroyers', as well as several hundred of the latest types of aircraft, anti-aircraft guns and ammunition, iron ore and other materials for which 'we shall go on paying dollars for as long as we can, but I should like to feel reasonably sure that when we can pay no more you will give us the stuff all the same'.

He suggested the visit of a US naval squadron to neutral Ireland and finally: 'I am looking to you to keep that Japanese dog quiet in the Pacific, using Singapore in any way convenient.'

In reply, Roosevelt promised to consider all Churchill's requests, but stressed the need for Congressional and public support in every move he made. He was especially cold about the proposal for the destroyers, saying that it would probably be unwise to make that suggestion to Congress 'at this moment'. Yet from this idea was to grow, by the end of the year, Roosevelt's Lend-Lease Scheme, the most significant American war contribution until Pearl Harbor. As to Japan, Roosevelt merely said: 'As you know, the American fleet is now concentrated at Hawaii where it will remain at least for the time being.'

Churchill hoped to inveigle the American navy to use the Singapore Naval Base to fill the deterrent role which Britain had abdicated. Roosevelt was persistent in his refusal. Singapore symbolised the Empire for Americans, just as it did for the British and the Australians. There was no way, in 1940, that Roosevelt was going to antagonise the isolationist bloc in Congress, the anti-British press, much of the electorate in the Mid-West, and majority opinion among the voters; not when it was a presidential election year, with Roosevelt seeking re-election for an unprecedented third term. Nothing could be better calculated to inflame isolationist opinion than an American show of strength at Singapore, the symbol of British colonialism.

Whatever he said in his great speeches, Churchill never believed that Britain or even the Empire could destroy Hitler alone. He had proclaimed to the House of Commons and the world that his sole policy was 'victory at all costs', and he meant it. But he knew that only the involvement of the United States could bring the real victory he sought. 'I think I can see my way through,' Churchill told his son Randolph, while shaving one morning in June. 'I shall drag in the United States.' The more fighting Britain did, the more aid would be forthcoming from America. The higher the level of US aid and involvement, the greater the chances of drawing America into the fighting.

He skilfully nursed American public opinion, knowing that shows of strength were more effective than pleas of weakness. He was at pains to disclaim the need for American combat troops. In his 'Give us the tools' speech of 9 February 1941, he said: 'We do not need the gallant armies which are forming through the American Union. We do not need them this year, nor next year, nor in any year that I can foresee.' But while he was grateful enough for any American assistance, when he said 'Give us the tools and we will finish the job', he knew that the proposition was mostly bravado. With American aid, Britain might survive indefinitely, but Hitler could be defeated only if the United States entered the war as a full fighting partner.

Churchill held exaggerated hopes that Britain's fighting stamina might inspire resistance in Nazi-controlled Europe, and 'set Europe ablaze'. He invested unrealistic hopes in the traditional blockade by the Royal Navy, and the novel idea of damaging German industry and resolve by aerial bombing. But his overwhelming aim was to impress American opinion and, above all, President Roosevelt with Britain's determination to keep actively fighting. The decisions that affected Australia most in his first eighteen months as Prime Minister all had this driving imperative. These included the campaigns in North Africa, Greece, Crete, and Syria, and, fatefully, his attitude to developments in the Far East. All had an overriding objective: to prod and push America towards war.

WINSTON CHURCHILL'S ROCKLIKE reputation in Australia rests immovably on his performance between the fall of France in June, 1940, and the Battle of Britain a few months later, in August and September. Most of his memorable utterances come from these four momentous months: 'We shall never surrender'; 'their finest hour'; 'never in the field of human conflict was so much owed by so many to so few'. The speeches that he made then have been absorbed into the fabric of the English language and democratic discourse. The American journalist and broadcaster Ed Murrow, reporting from London during the Blitz, said that Churchill mobilised the English language and sent it into battle. There must have been some kind of osmosis at work, for there are many Australians living today who will swear that they remember hearing speeches that were never broadcast or, if transmitted to Australia by short-wave, were heard well after young listeners, including the author, had been sent to bed. The memory, however created, remains indelible. We heard them because we believed we heard them; and we believed Churchill because we wanted to believe him.

On 18 June, just before the fall of France, Churchill told the House of Commons:

> The Battle of Britain is about to begin. Upon this battle depends our own British life, and the long continuity of our institutions and our Empire. The whole fury and might of the enemy must very soon be turned on us. Hitler knows that he will have to break us in this Island or lose the war. If we can stand up to him, all Europe may be free and the life of the world may move forward into broad, sunlit uplands. But if we fail, then the whole world, including the United States, including all that we have known and cared for, will sink into the abyss of a new Dark Age made more sinister, and perhaps more protracted, by the lights of perverted science.
>
> Let us therefore brace ourselves to our duties, and so bear ourselves that, if the British Empire and its Commonwealth last for a thousand years, men will still say: *This* was their finest hour.

The fate of Britain, much more than the future of its Empire, roused the Australians; the galvanising force of Churchill's speeches lay in Britain's peril. In the last weeks of the phoney war, enlistment for the AIF had dwindled to a few hundred a week. In May, 1940, 8000 men were accepted; in June 48,500. In July, the Australian Government suspended army recruitment for six months, partly because of a lack of equipment and training facilities. By August, Australia had enough volunteers for at least six army divisions, twice the number needed for the three divisions authorised by the Australian Cabinet. The RAAF always had thousands more volunteers than it could handle, whether through the Empire Air Training Scheme based in

Canada, or for training at home. There was clear public support for the despatch of the bulk of the AIF to the Middle East. As the official war historian, Gavin Long, would write: 'The people, not the Government, were deciding policy in the field.'

Menzies and Curtin responded to the sea change in the public mood. Less compelling perhaps than Churchill's promised toll of 'blood, toil, tears, and sweat', an 'all-round sacrifice, unremitting toil and unflinching devotion' was Menzies' appeal. He appointed Australia's most powerful businessman, Essington Lewis of BHP, as Director-General of Munitions; and Keith Murdoch, by then Australia's most powerful newspaperman, as Director-General of Information. He introduced stringent national security measures, banning the Communist Party of Australia and, even-handedly, the fascist party, which never really existed in this country, even in hazy daydreams of the more reactionary denizens of the Melbourne Club or the Australian Club in Sydney. Above all, Menzies decided, eligible males would be compulsorily called up for the Citizens Military Force at the rate of 22,000 per quarter, with a target of 250,000 trained and equipped for home defence. New legislation gave the federal government wide powers for the control and direction of the nation's manpower.

Curtin struggled to balance the demands of national unity and party unity. He had already taken a major step towards both by declaring that the Labor Party would reinforce the AIF overseas, effectively refuting Labor's own argument that the despatch of any expeditionary force would be the thin end of the conscription wedge. He was able to do this with minimum fuss in Labor ranks because he made his declaration while fighting a crucial by-election in Victoria. By-elections have had an extraordinary impact on Australian political history, and the poll in Corio in February, 1940, was one of the most consequential of all. The seat, based on Geelong, had been held for the Government by Richard Casey, before Menzies appointed him Australia's Minister to Washington in a major step towards the establishment of an Australian independent diplomatic service. Labor's candidate, John Dedman, a British ex-serviceman who had served on Gallipoli and in India, took the seat from Menzies' United Australia Party, which campaigned under the implausible slogan 'Hitler's eyes are on Corio'.

Churchill's first act as Prime Minister – bringing the British Labour leaders into his Cabinet to create a national government – influenced Australian politics strongly. Following the loss of Corio, Menzies persuaded the Country Party, now led by a bluff and hearty former accountant, Arthur Fadden of Queensland, to return to the coalition. He renewed his invitation to Curtin to join a national government. Refusing these overtures, Curtin said: 'If there's one thing worse than a government of two parties, it would be a government of three parties.' Menzies, who understood Australian politics, never held Curtin's refusal against him, but it rankled with Churchill, who had a poor understanding of Australian politics and stubborn prejudices about them. His smouldering resentment was to have explosive results eighteen months later.

British Labour's accession to government at such a perilous time was a matter of pride for Labor in Australia. Older and more successful electorally, the Australian Labor Party had strong emotional and personal ties with the British Labour Party. Ideologically, both parties proclaimed that they owed more to Methodism than Marxism, and were deeply committed to the parliamentary system of government. The Australian union movement identified with its elder brother in Britain, and followed its structures, organisation, methods, and fortunes closely. Nor did Australian Labor forget that the British Labour Party had been decisive in making Churchill Prime Minister.

Curtin secured endorsement for his war policy by calling a special federal conference of the Australian Labor Party in Canberra at the end of June. 'Having regard to the gravity of the world situation and the immediate danger to the Commonwealth of Australia, the Empire and the Allies', the conference declared 'complete and indissoluble unity with the Allies in the war'. The key clause stated:

National training for defence in terms of the existing Defence Act to be maintained on the highest level of efficiency; complete participation in the Empire Air Force scheme; necessary provision for reinforcement of

the AIF division, the extent of European participation by a volunteer
army to be determined by circumstances as they arise, having regard to
the paramount necessity of Australia's defence.

The conference called on Australians 'to stand together in resisting
aggression from any source, to bear willingly any burden that may
be imposed in the interests of Australia's security, and to demonstrate to the Empire and its Allies that we shall not be found wanting
in the struggle for human liberty'. The stilted prose in parts of the
long resolution, and the mandatory denunciation of profiteering and
monopolies, could not disguise that Curtin had achieved a revolution in Labor's attitude to the war and the means of waging it.
Again, it must be emphasised that solidarity with Britain and the
Empire was central to Curtin's approach.

For Australia, the shape of things to come began to emerge in the
chaotic final days of fighting in France. As Churchill shuttled across
the English Channel in a desperate bid to shore up French morale,
then announced in the Commons the 'deliverance of Dunkirk', and
appealed in vain for American intervention, Japan served its
demands on the British Empire. Chief among them was the closure
of the Burma Road, China's supply route. Menzies urged compliance. In July Churchill acquiesced, a plain act of appeasement.
However he dressed it up to Roosevelt, nothing could demonstrate
more starkly Britain's impotence in the Far East, and the bankruptcy
of its Singapore strategy. On 29 June, the British Government officially advised Australia that the European situation meant that the
Royal Navy could no longer deter Japan. The British Combined
Chiefs asked for help in improving the land and air defence of
Malaya and Singapore: could Australia spare two RAAF squadrons
and a division for Malaya?

From London, High Commissioner Bruce cabled Menzies,
protesting against the lack of consultation and information about
this 'complete reversal' of policy. Bruce advised Menzies that 'the
wisest course for you would be masterly inactivity for two or three
days. If during that period I can get no satisfaction, I feel that it will
be necessary for you to send a strong cable to Prime Minister

Churchill, as it is essential that the United Kingdom Government should be stunned by someone into facing the great and fundamental issues that now confront us.' To placate Bruce and reassure Australia, Churchill had his personal military adviser, Major General Ismay, reaffirm the promises Churchill had made as First Lord of the Admiralty in November, 1939. Those undertakings rested on the safety of Singapore, Ismay said on Churchill's behalf, and it was to ensure that safety 'we have asked Australia to send a division and two squadrons of aircraft to Malaya'.

By asking Menzies to appeal to Churchill over the heads of his military advisers, Bruce ignored the crucial fact that the British Prime Minister had no intention of wasting men or materials reinforcing Malaya and Singapore, whatever the opinion of his Chiefs of Staff. Churchill confessed as much in his memoirs, where he wrote of the resistance he met from his own advisers in London and generals on-the-spot against his plans for concentration of all available forces for the defence of Egypt. He was determined 'to assemble the largest fighting force possible to face the Italian invaders. For this it was necessary to run risks in many other quarters.' He got his way 'only after a prolonged hard fight against the woolly theme of being safe everywhere. I did my utmost to draw upon Singapore and bring the Australian divisions which had arrived there, first to India for training and thence to the Western Desert.' In truth, Australia did even better to meet Churchill's wishes: its new 7th Division bypassed Singapore and India and sailed straight to Suez. But Churchill's false memory about a detail underlines the true purpose of his grand design – to get as many Australians as possible to the Middle East as quickly as possible. In the Australian War Cabinet he had found faithful adherents.

WHEN CHURCHILL AND AUSTRALIANS of the war generations spoke of the Middle East, they thought first of Egypt. The Suez Canal, the route to India and Australia flanked by Egypt and Palestine, was both the trophy of empire and its symbolic lifeline – even though the Cape of Good Hope route was as quick and easy for Australian shipping. Perceptions mattered. For all its prominence in imperial history, Egypt had never been formally incorporated into the British Empire. From 1885 to 1922, it was a British protectorate, run pretty much as a colony but never officially annexed. Churchill himself, as Colonial Secretary in 1921, had set up Egypt as a kingdom, and purported to recognise its sovereignty. But the British Ambassador and the British commander-in-chief, Middle East, effectively ran a parallel government, asserting full control over defence and diplomacy, the things that mattered most to the British.

Not surprisingly, Egypt became the home of Arab nationalism, and the cradle of the militant Muslim Brotherhood. These developments, like the occasional gesture of independence by the young King Farouk – a playboy and play-king already heading irretrievably to fat, futility, and exile – were mere nuisances to the British, as long as they were in full military control of Egyptian territory, its cosmopolitan capital of Cairo, its polyglot port of Alexandria, and the keys to the Canal – Port Said and Suez. The scores of thousands of Australian and British soldiers who fought in or from Egypt would have scoffed at the notion that they were guests or occupiers of a sovereign nation. In both world wars, the Anzacs were notorious for their rough treatment of the Egyptians. These facts did not prevent Churchill romantically, if pretentiously, dubbing the British and Australian forces that he cobbled together in Egypt, 'the Army of the Nile'.

Palestine filled another large part of Australia's imagining of the Middle East, made vivid through the exploits of the Light Horse in the lands of the Bible. It was vivid too for Churchill, through his heartfelt commitment to the 1917 Balfour Declaration that Palestine was the national Jewish home. His last stand against the Chamberlain Government after Munich had been his protest against its ban on further Jewish immigration; he supported Zionist claims that the restrictions amounted to the death warrant of European Jewry. The oil pipeline from Mosul to the port of Haifa gave Palestine additional strategic importance. Thus, the issues that define the Middle East in the twenty-first century – Arab nationalism, Islamic militancy, the Israeli–Palestinian conflict, and oil – were taking shape in the Eastern Mediterranean in 1940. For Churchill, the

Eastern Mediterranean was to be the launching pad for the Big Idea – the place where Britain would keep fighting until he could bring the United States into the war. It was improbable and desperate, but it worked.

In his authoritative survey of the North African and Mediterranean campaigns, *Hitler's Mediterranean Gamble*, the American historian Douglas Porch writes:

> In Churchill's mind, the Mediterranean became the epicenter of Britain's resurrection, the genesis of victory, the place where Chamberlain's appeasement strategy was buried and Britain's determination and valor were showcased to friend and foe alike. The failure of Churchill's Mediterranean strategy would have flattened British spirits, exhausted his political capital and breathed new life into Halifax and the appeasers.

For Churchill, holding Egypt now came second only to preventing a German invasion of Britain itself. The defence of Egypt ranked far above the defence of Singapore. These convictions, and the ruthlessness of purpose with which Churchill pursued them, are the key to his relations with Australia up to the Battle of El Alamein in 1942. Their most remarkable aspect was the extent to which he was able to make Australia's political and military leadership share his convictions and his priorities. When it all turned sour in 1942, Australia's compliance mocked its complaints about the consequences.

The Anzac tradition, with its emotional roots in the Middle East, ensured that when Churchill's grand strategy placed the British major effort in the Mediterranean and Middle East theatre, Australia would be there. The British leader strained every nerve, and used every device in his armoury of eloquence – the force of his personality, the power of his reputation, and his talent for marshalling undoubted facts and doubtful arguments – to make sure that he was able to put the Australians just where he wanted them. If this meant glossing over unpalatable realities such as the threat from Japan, or making impossible promises such as the safeguarding of Singapore, hard luck.

***

AS SOON AS the Second AIF began to assemble in the Middle East, Churchill took control of the details of its deployment. As Ronald Hyams wrote: 'With his mind on the total strategic picture, and the Empire as the buttress of British power, Churchill took the simple view that Dominion troops should be available for general deployment as seemed best as judged from the effective centre of gravity in London.' On 12 August 1940, Churchill complained to his Staff Military Adviser, General Ismay: 'I do not understand why the Australians and New Zealanders, who have been training in Palestine for at least six months, should be able to provide only one brigade for service in Egypt.' He demanded Ismay provide details of their number and state of training: 'These men were brought at great expense from Australia, having been selected as the first volunteers for service in Europe. How disgraceful it would be if, owing to our mishandling of this important force, only one brigade took part in the decisive operations for the defence of Egypt!' But as Britain prepared for Hitler's invasion, he instructed General Ismay to suspend the movement of Australian and New Zealand troops then in England to the Middle East via the Cape. He wrote: 'Would it not be better to keep the Australians back and delay the whole convoy until the third week in October? After all, none of these forces going round the Cape can possibly arrive in time to influence the impending battle in Egypt. But they may play a big part here.'

ON 11 AUGUST 1940, Churchill sent a 1200-word letter to both Menzies and the Labour Prime Minister of New Zealand, Peter Fraser. It was full of reassurance about Japan. 'I do not think myself that Japan will declare war unless Germany can make a successful invasion of Britain,' Churchill wrote. 'Once Japan sees that Germany has either failed or dares not try, I look for easier times in the Pacific.' He acknowledged that the United States had given no undertakings of support, 'but their main fleet in the Pacific must be a grave preoccupation to the Japanese Admiralty'. A Japanese attack on Singapore was unlikely, Churchill said, but in any case it would be able to withstand a long siege. A Japanese attempt to invade

Australia or New Zealand was even more unlikely. Churchill then repeated, in its most explicit form yet, the pledge he had given a year previously as First Lord of the Admiralty:

> If, however, contrary to prudence and self-interest, Japan set about invading Australia or New Zealand on a large scale, I have the explicit authority of the Cabinet to assure you that we should then cut our losses in the Mediterranean and sacrifice every interest, except only the defence and feeding of this Island, on which all depends, and would proceed in good time to your aid with a fleet able to give battle to any Japanese force which could be placed in Australian waters, and able to parry any invading force, or certainly cut its communications with Japan.

Churchill was increasingly confident that Hitler would never invade Britain. He told Menzies: 'If Hitler fails to invade and conquer Britain before the weather breaks, he has received his first and probably fatal check. We therefore feel a sober and growing conviction of our power to defend ourselves successfully, and to persevere through the year or two that may be necessary to gain victory.'

This letter to Menzies succeeded beyond its author's dearest hopes. It led directly to the most important strategic decision the Menzies War Cabinet ever made: the whole weight of the Second AIF would henceforth be thrown into the Middle East; as for Japan and its intentions in South Asia and the Pacific, Australia would take its chances. Australia's part in the defeat of the Axis in North Africa, and its vulnerability in its own region, were consequences of the Australian War Cabinet's decisions of August–September, 1940. Churchill had loaded the dice, but the Menzies Government made the gambler's throw.

Churchill had told Menzies that he was sending his letter as a 'brief foreword' in advance of the appraisal of the Pacific situation by the Combined Staffs. He glossed over or ignored outright the parts of the Staff paper most relevant and urgent for Australia. In particular, the Combined Chiefs dwelt on the need for land defence of Malaya and Singapore, 'in the absence of the Fleet'. They set out in some detail a plan for cooperation with the Dutch for the defence of Japan's ultimate target, the oil-rich Dutch East Indies (Indonesia). Holland was now German-occupied, but the administration in Batavia (Jakarta) maintained its allegiance to Queen Wilhelmina and her government in exile in London. The Chiefs feared that 'it was conceivable that Dutch cooperation would be withheld'. But, in the absence of full Dutch cooperation, they declared, 'we should concentrate on the defence of Malaya'.

The steps by which the Australian War Cabinet reached its decisions show that the dominant influence was Churchill's letter of 11 August 1940. The Australian Chiefs of Staff, more perceptive than their political masters, at first gave greater weight to the paper produced by their London counterparts; and on 23 August recommended that the 7th Division should be despatched to India or Malaya for training. On 28 August, the Australian Cabinet told the British Government that because lack of equipment and training precluded the division's immediate despatch to the Middle East, the 7th should go first to India, relieving an Indian division for service in Malaya, and then proceed to the Middle East. However, if the British Government still wanted the division in Malaya, the War Cabinet would agree. A week later, to make Australia's Middle Eastern preference clear, the British Chiefs were told: 'We cannot stress too strongly the importance we attach to the holding of this area [the Middle East] and urge that a maximum effort should be made there, compatible with the safety of the United Kingdom'. Churchill had, in fact, won out completely. With its eyes wide open, the Menzies Government had accepted his case that British priorities were paramount.

Menzies made it clear that he fully shared Churchill's Middle Eastern preoccupations and preferences. In the very telegram to London in which he said that the 7th Division would go to Malaya if the UK Government still desired it, he set out all the reasons why it should not go there:

We would prefer that the 7th Division should go to India to complete its training and equipment and to relieve for service in Malaya troops who are better equipped and more acclimatised [i.e. Indian Army]. This view is supported by our Service advisers, and the Government would add that the considerations of wider scope for training and greater occupation of interest, difference in climate, and a less circumscribed role than that of garrison duties at Singapore, would be more compatible with the psychology of the Australian soldier.

Further consideration was suspended during the campaign for the federal election on 21 September. Churchill, however, did not let constitutional niceties stand in his way. Three days before polling day, he notified the Australian Government that 'after balancing the risks between the Middle East and the Far East, we now consider the needs of the situation would best be met if the Seventh Australian Division were sent direct to the Middle East, where it could complete its training more quickly than in Malaya'. On 23 September, with the election results still coming in, the Australian War Cabinet finally decided to send the 7th Division directly to the Middle East. And it went one better than even Churchill had hoped. It decided to raise another division, specifically for service in the Middle East. The nucleus of this division would be the eight thousand troops already in Britain; the rest would be sent direct from Australia. Thus was born the 9th Australian Division of immortal fame.

Churchill had visited the Australians who were to form the nucleus of the 9th in their camp on Salisbury Plains, three weeks before the Australian Cabinet's decision. They had reached England via Cape Town three days before the fall of France. The official Australian war correspondent, Kenneth Slessor, wrote an account of Churchill's visit in his diary of 4 September:

The 'visitor' who arrived about 5.30 p.m. was Churchill, the Prime Minister, accompanied by a military secretary and a couple of detectives, and looking exactly like the caricature – pink, John Bullish, leaning on a stick, biting a cigar, and wearing a hat that seemed to be modelled on the lines of a small black gasometer.

Slessor, like Banjo Paterson, the war correspondent who had written about Churchill in South Africa forty years before, was a man of Sydney and one of Australia's finest poets. He wrote that 'the men cheered wildly, and his speeches, all impromptu, were stirring ones, though full of politicians' cliches'. Churchill's little addresses to the Australians on Salisbury Plains were a model of the genre:

> You have come a long way to see us in this island and at one time we thought we could have a party for you. Perhaps we still can have one . . . But things are very much more solid than they were when you first came. If that man you all know [Hitler] comes now he will have to come with a lot and that makes it all the easier for the Navy and the Air Force to look after him on the way. And anything that slips through we shall look to you to deal with.

Striking the perfect note for these sons of Anzac, Churchill said:

> I used to see the Anzacs in the last war, and I am certain that this new expeditionary force from Australia will revive and equal – it cannot excel – the glories of the famous Anzac Corps.

In the event, the Australians did not stay to defend Britain, but followed the first Anzacs to the Middle East. Slessor recalled that at the time of Churchill's visit, he had the impression 'that Churchill was powerfully distressed by the notion that he was saying goodbye to them on the eve of sending their army to a desperate adventure'. A poet's antennae perhaps – but could Churchill have known about the decision three weeks before the Australian Government had made it?

The victor of Corio, John Dedman, who was to be a senior minister in the Curtin and Chifley governments, would write of the decision of 23 September 1940 that 'the determination not to accede to the original British request to send a division to Singapore now stands out as the most far-reaching decision in the realm of higher strategy made by the Menzies Government'. We must recognise, however, that the pressures on the Menzies Government were immense. Churchill's demands were only part of it.

On the very day Cabinet was summoned to consider Churchill's letter, Menzies had to cope with the cruellest blow ever dealt an Australian ministry. On 13 August, an RAAF aircraft flying from Melbourne crashed into a hillside near the Canberra airfield: all ten occupants were incinerated. Three Cabinet ministers, Sir Henry Gullett (Vice President of the Executive Council), John Fairbairn (Civil Aviation), and Geoffrey Street (Defence), were among the dead; along with Sir Brudenell White, Australia's senior soldier, and after Monash the most distinguished officer of the First World War. He had been brought out of retirement at sixty-three to become Chief of the General Staff. 'In that terrible hour,' Menzies recorded, 'I felt that, for me, the end of the world had come.'

Since this terrific tragedy occurred only five weeks before the election, it had a huge political impact. In one of the most indecisive, yet momentous, elections in Australian history, the Coalition and Labor each won 36 seats (including five members from the break-away Labor group in New South Wales). There were two independents, both supporting the Government, one of them Arthur Coles, who won Sir Henry Gullett's Melbourne seat of Henty. The Government had polled much better than the result showed, improving its vote in every state except New South Wales, and retaining its majority in the Senate. Five of Labor's seven gains in the House of Representatives were in New South Wales, vindicating Curtin's long struggle to rebuild the party there. Curtin himself was nearly defeated in his Western Australian seat of Fremantle, and for a week after polling day, resigned himself to a defeat that never came. This Parliament, born of tragedy, division, and indecision, was to make John Curtin Prime Minister little more than a year later.

Churchill was given star billing in the Coalition's election campaign. Their advertisements featured his photograph, the Union Jack, and the Australian flag, with the caption, 'Back the Government That's Backing Churchill'. He was very much aware of his publicity value in Australia, and used it to rebuke Menzies for his impertinence in complaining about the Dakar fiasco in September, 1940. Their sharp exchange on the issue reveals much about Churchill's methods and his attitude to the

Australian polity; it is a case study in relations between Churchill and Australia.

The bungle at Dakar, capital of the French colony of Senegal in West Africa, was the first exercise of Churchill's 'fight anywhere' doctrine; he wanted a show of strength in the French Empire in Africa. In England, Brigadier General Charles de Gaulle had raised the standard of Free France against the servile French government installed by Hitler at Vichy, in the southern part of France. The Vichy Government was headed by the hero of Verdun of 1916, Marshal Philippe Pétain. Both Pétain and de Gaulle saw themselves as saviours of the soul of France; but Pétain was in defiant dotage, while de Gaulle cast himself as a latterday Joan of Arc, the incarnation of the unconquerable spirit of France. De Gaulle and Churchill concocted a plan to seize Dakar, and bring the French colonies into the Allied camp. Most of them, including the administration in Indochina, had transferred their allegiance to Vichy. Churchill agreed to transport and strengthen the expedition of 2500 Free French troops with over 6000 British troops, escorted by a naval squadron, of which HMAS *Australia* was part. He told the Australian Government nothing about it. By contrast, the Germans knew a great deal about it, as a result of a lack of security among the Free French in Britain. Alerted, the pro-Vichy administration in Dakar mounted an effective resistance with the aid of the French battleship *Richelieu*. Two of the British ships were badly damaged. The expedition withdrew in frustration and humiliation. To many, it looked like a Gallipoli in miniature, an amphibious operation adopted recklessly and planned haphazardly. But this time it was Gallipoli played out as farce.

Menzies cabled Churchill on 29 September, 'We are very disturbed in regard to the Dakar incident, which has had unfortunate effect in Australia.' It was difficult to understand why an attempt was made unless there were overwhelming chances of success, he wrote: 'To make what appears at this distance to be a half-hearted attack is to incur a damaging loss of prestige.' The Australian Prime Minister then delivered a lecture in terms Churchill had heard before from Deakin and Hughes:

> It is absolutely wrong that [the] Australian Government should know
> practically nothing of details of engagement and nothing at all of decision
> to abandon it until after newspaper publication. I have refrained from
> any public criticism, but privately can tell you that absence of real official
> information from Great Britain has frequently proved humiliating.'

He added: 'I must say frankly that [the] Australian Government
profoundly hopes difficulties have not been underestimated in the
Middle East, where clear-cut victory is essential.'

Churchill was not going to be taught how to suck eggs by a
colonial armchair strategist, even one who had just committed his
nation's army to Churchill's strategy, and whose flagship had been
involved in the fiasco. He replied: 'If it is to be laid down that no
attempt is to be made which has not "overwhelming chance of
success", you will find that a complete defensive would be imposed
on us. In dealing with unknown factors like the degree of French
resistance it is impossible to avoid uncertainty and hazard . . .' In
view of Britain's sacrifices, he expected 'a generous measure of
indulgence should any particular minor matter miscarry'.

Churchill's mix of touchiness and toughness contrasted with his
lack of sensitivity to Australian concerns:

> I cannot accept the reproach of making 'a half-hearted attack'. I hoped
> that you had not sustained the impression from these last five months
> of struggle which has excited the admiration of the whole world that
> we were 'a half-hearted Government' or that I am half-hearted in the
> endeavours it is my duty to make.

Menzies, of course, had said nothing of the sort; but this was to
become the characteristic Churchillian technique with Australian
prime ministers: to seize upon a particular word or phrase, rip it out
of context, take it as personal criticism, and turn his new gloss
against its poor, unsuspecting author, ending with a faintly menacing
punch line – in this case hinting at Menzies' ingratitude: 'I thought
indeed that from the way my name was used in the election quite a
good opinion was entertained in Australia of these efforts.'

'Every care will always be taken to keep you informed before news is published,' Churchill promised, 'but we could not prevent the German or Vichy wireless from proclaiming the course of events as they occurred at Dakar before we had received any confirmation from our commanders.' There was no mention of HMAS *Australia*. Churchill followed with a lengthy account of the arms build-up in the Mediterranean and Middle East:

> Still, my dear Prime Minister and friend, as you have allowed me to deem you, I cannot guarantee 'clear-cut victory' in the Middle East, or that Cairo, Khartoum, the Suez Canal and Palestine may not fall into Italian or German hands. We do not think they will, and we are trying our utmost to resist the attacks which are massing against us. But I can make no promises at all of victory, nor can I make any promises that regrettable and lamentable incidents will not occur, or that there will not be disappointments and blunders. On the contrary, I think the only certainty is that we have very bad times indeed to go through before we emerge from the mortal perils by which we are surrounded. I felt it due to your great position and the extremely severe tone of your message to reply with equal frankness.

Menzies rolled over. He was 'very disturbed', he replied, by some of the contents of Churchill's message. 'My telegram was somewhat crudely expressed,' he conceded, 'as I can see on perusing it again.' For someone as proud of his precision in the use of the English language as Menzies, this was the ultimate backdown. 'But I still cannot understand how it can be considered as containing even the faintest suggestion that you or the British Government are half-hearted in policy, spirit or achievement.' He put in his own plea for understanding: 'As the recent election here has left my own position extremely precarious and I may therefore soon go out of office, I would like to take the opportunity of saying to you that I have been very proud on behalf of Australia to be associated, even though at a distance, with the efforts of Winston Churchill and the British people.'

The Australian Prime Minister then spelt out for Churchill the political and military implications of the Cabinet decision of

23 September: 'I hope you do not entertain any idea that Australia is shirking her share. We have many thousands of men in the Middle East, as many as shipping has been able to take. We have in camp in Australia [a] further Expeditionary Force approximately 85-thousand men, many of whom will be shortly moving to the Middle East.' This had been achieved despite 'the parochial interests and issues which in the recent elections succeeded in defeating us in the all-important State of New South Wales', and also 'in spite of much public doubt caused by a real fear of what Japan may do'. Menzies concluded:

> Please, my dear Prime Minister, do not interpret anxieties arising from these facts as either fearful, selfish or unduly wrong-headed. And, above all, please understand that whatever interrogative or even critical telegrams I may send to you in secret, Australia knows courage when it sees it and will follow you to a finish, as to the best of my abilities I certainly shall.

Suitably soothed, Churchill purred in reply: 'I am deeply grateful for your generous message. Forgive me if I responded too controversially to what I thought was somewhat severe criticism.' He promised to send Menzies confidential information about the Dakar affair – the same kind of promise he had made to Hughes over the Chanak crisis. He was 'deeply grateful for all that Australia has done under your leadership in the Common Cause'. It had been a 'great comfort having some of the Australians here during these anxious months. I greatly admired their spirit and bearing when I inspected them.' They were now going to the Middle East and Churchill promised: 'We shall do everything in our power to equip them as they deserve.'

Bruce in London found himself the target of Churchill's resentment at Menzies' impertinence – the sharper perhaps because Churchill disliked and distrusted Bruce as the dominion archetype of the pro-Chamberlain appeasers. The Australian High Commissioner had called at 10 Downing Street to talk about a new secretary of state for the dominions – still the official channel between the

Australian and British governments. Churchill brushed this aside, asking Bruce testily: 'Are you under instructions from your Government to dictate to the British Government who should be appointed to the British Cabinet?' He then launched into a tirade about Menzies' complaint over Dakar, implying that Bruce himself had put the offensive words into Menzies' mouth. In a note on their row, Bruce recorded: 'The Prime Minister obviously took the telegram as an attack upon himself and said that he had replied fully to it, just as he would have if he had been attacked in the House of Commons.' Churchill again seized on the word 'half-hearted', and treated Bruce to 'a long recital' of all his actions since becoming prime minister. Bruce recorded: 'The Prime Minister then went on to say that Menzies had asked him for a guarantee as to what was going to happen in the Middle East and put the obvious question "how could anybody answer that?".' Bruce protested that Menzies 'had not asked for any such thing' but Churchill, 'with his usual habit of not quite replying to what was being said, then proceeded to make a statement as to the reinforcements which had been sent to the Middle East and said that when history came to be written it would be felt that risks had been taken that were dangerous beyond words'. With a certain self-satisfaction, Bruce wrote: 'There is no doubt that Winston regards me as the villain of the piece.' He concluded his record of conversation: 'The whole trouble with the Prime Minister is that he is surrounded by people who do not stand up to him.'

15

'For the sake of our kith and kin'
December, 1940–February, 1941

The Australians of the Second AIF wanted to be in the Middle East every bit as much as Churchill wanted them there. Like Churchill, they wanted to go where they could fight. Menzies had told Churchill that garrison duties in India or Malaya would 'not suit the psychology of the Australian soldier'. They had volunteered to fight and, like the first Anzacs, they expected the fighting to be somewhere in Europe, preferably France. With the fall of France, it looked for a time that they would have a chance to fight for Britain itself. But while they were being trained and equipped, the Middle East – by which they understood Egypt and Palestine – was the place to be. The idea of following in the footsteps of the first Anzacs impelled and inspired them.

More than eighty per cent of the fifty thousand Australian soldiers overseas by December 1940 were in Egypt and Palestine, in the British forces under the command of General Sir Archibald Wavell. Churchill's relationship with this proud and sensitive man was the most difficult he had with any of his generals in the entire war. Churchill never really knew what to make of Wavell. He met Churchill's steamy monologues with long and disconcerting silences;

with a Prime Minister who wanted to know everything about everything, he kept his plans closely guarded until they matured. Churchill suspected that he didn't have any. Son of a soldier, Wavell confessed to his friends that 'he was not really interested in war'. He was a man of duty to the Empire, in the high Victorian sense. After the French surrender, his order of the day, to the British and Australian troops under his command, read: 'Our gallant French Allies have been overwhelmed after a desperate struggle and have been compelled to ask for terms. The British Empire will, of course, continue the struggle until victory has been won. Dictators fade away. The British Empire never dies.'

The sawdust Caesar in Rome, Benito Mussolini, dreamed of another empire – a new Roman Empire that would stretch from the Italian colony of Libya, along the North African coast and desert, through to Egypt and the Sudan, linking up with his conquest of Abyssinia (Ethiopia), the Somalilands on the Horn of Africa, and down to British Kenya. Churchill welcomed Mussolini's challenge. Hitler cursed it. The man who said that all his decisions were made 'with the certainty of a sleepwalker' perhaps sensed how dearly the dreams of his ally might cost. Mussolini's opportunism was Churchill's opportunity. Egypt was the pivot on which the plans of both would turn. Mussolini's attempts to make his dream of empire a reality answered once and for all Churchill's basic question: Where to fight? The defence of Egypt and the Suez Canal justified itself – but, now, this was the place where Britain could take on the Axis and hope for a victory which would inspire the Empire and impress the United States. Mussolini's fantasies gave substance to Churchill's Big Idea.

The Italian commander in Libya, General Graziani, took his army of 300,000 men, strung out along the North African coast from Tripoli to Tobruk, at a leisurely pace towards Egypt. By October, 1940, he had occupied the coastal town of Sidi Barrani, fifty miles across the theoretical border between Libya and Egypt, mocked hourly by the winds and shifting sands of the desert. Churchill harassed Wavell unceasingly, demanding action from the 150,000 soldiers he had scraped together from all over the Empire to sweep the Italians from North Africa. The Anzacs of the 6th and 7th Divisions, with the New Zealand Division, comprised half Wavell's fighting force. Churchill made scant allowance for Wavell's huge problems – that his command stretched from Kenya to Iraq; that Egypt itself was a hotbed of Arab nationalism and pro-Axis intrigue; that he had to fight the Italians in Somaliland and liberate Ethiopia; that there was a big difference between his effective fighting strength and the numbers required to support and equip modern armoured forces. Nor did Churchill seem to make any allowance for the necessity of coordination with the Royal Navy and Air Force, crucial to such a vast operation.

When he was good and ready, Wavell went on the attack. He summoned the British and Australian war correspondents to his Cairo office on 8 December 1940, telling them: 'Gentlemen, I have asked you to come here this morning to let you know we have attacked in the Western Desert. This is not an offensive and I do not think you ought to describe it as an offensive as yet. You might call it an important raid. The attack was made early this morning and I had word an hour ago that the first of the Italian camps has fallen.'

The raid became a rout. As Wavell was speaking, Graziani's army was being cut off or down by British and Indian troops at Sidi Barrani; twenty thousand Italians were captured, with all their tanks and artillery, on 12 December. Over the next three weeks, the 6th Australian Division spearheaded the drive west to the Libyan port of Bardia. They took Bardia, and another thirty thousand prisoners, on 5 January. Next stop: Tobruk. Rome Radio told the Italian people that Churchill had 'turned loose the Australian barbarians'.

'The surprise was complete,' wrote Alan Moorehead, the famous Australian war correspondent. He was referring to the Cairo pressmen as well as the Italians, but he might almost have meant the Cabinet in Canberra. Two days after Wavell's press conference, Menzies read to the House of Representatives from a Dominions Office cable which claimed that the British forces were on the road to Buq Buq, between Sidi Barrani and Bardia. From London, Bruce immediately cabled Menzies about 'some trouble here' because 'there was disclosure of information sent in most confidential cable'.

More in anger than in sorrow, Menzies replied to Bruce: 'It had been announced by the B.B.C. and from other sources that Australian troops had been engaged in battle in the Western Desert. Government under pressure for statement and as usual in humiliating position of having to say "We have no official news".' As to secrecy and security, Menzies said: 'My colleagues and I are at complete loss to understand how Italy can fail to be aware of localities in which engagements are occurring.' Menzies concluded in terms familiar to Australian prime ministers in their dealings with London since 1914:

> I would like to add for your information that we at this end are never in a position to make any statement to Parliament or to the people about war events because the news we get from the Dominions Office is always a long way behind the Press and Radio and when cables to arrive they are invariably 'Most Secret'. The effect of this has been to discredit us very much. We are represented as a Government that knows less than the newspaper reporters.

Churchill lost no time in claiming vindication for his Middle East strategy. 'Remember,' he cabled Menzies on 13 December, 'that I could not guarantee a few months ago even a successful defence of the Delta and the Canal.' Emphasising Britain's dangers, and as usual minimising Australia's, he promised more of the same: 'We ran sharp risks here at home in sending troops, tanks and cannon all round the Cape while under threat of imminent invasion, and now there is a reward.' But success always demanded a greater effort, Churchill said. 'We are planning to gather a very large Army representing the whole Empire and ample sea power in the Middle East which will face a German lurch that way, and at the same time give us a move eastward in your direction if need be.'

Once the Australian Government committed the AIF to the Middle East, it locked Australia into Churchill's priorities. From then on, the AIF's safety and effectiveness demanded that resources and reinforcements be concentrated in the region where the Australians would be fighting. This was the inevitable consequence of the Australian decision. Australia's dependence on Britain for modern equipment, especially tanks and planes, always gave Churchill the upper hand in any argument about the use and supply of Australian forces overseas.

CHURCHILL FINISHED 1940 on a note of high confidence and reassurance to Australia. He wrote to Menzies in time for Christmas: 'The danger of Japan going to war with the British Empire is in my opinion definitely less than it was in June after the collapse of France . . . The naval and military successes in the Mediterranean and our growing advantage there by land, sea and air will not be lost upon Japan.' However, he said, it would not be possible to reinforce Singapore except 'by ruining the Mediterranean situation'. This, he was sure, Menzies and Australia 'would not wish us to do unless or until the Japanese danger becomes far more menacing than at present'. He asked Menzies to bear 'our Eastern anxieties patiently and doggedly'. Once again, Churchill gave his routine promise: 'If Australia is seriously threatened by invasion, we should not hesitate to compromise or sacrifice the Mediterranean position for the sake of our kith and kin.' Nevertheless, he wrote, 'I am also persuaded that if Japan should enter the war, the United States will come in on our side, which will put the naval boot very much on the other leg, and be a deliverance from many perils.'

Churchill's breezy optimism with Menzies contrasts with his urgent pleadings to Roosevelt. In mid-November, 1940, he began to prepare 'one of the most important letters I ever wrote'. The letter went through several drafts, crossing the Atlantic at least twice for vetting by the British Ambassador in Washington, Lord Lothian, until it was finally cabled to Roosevelt on 7 December, exactly a year before Pearl Harbor. In all its versions, Churchill dwelt on Britain's perils and sacrifices, its parlous financial position, the shortages of equipment and munitions, and the mortal dangers ahead. Its reference to Japan was brief and bleak. In its final form, Churchill's letter said:

A third sphere of danger is in the Far East. Here it seems clear that the Japanese are thrusting Southward through Indo-China to Saigon and other naval and air bases, thus bringing them within a comparatively short distance of Singapore and the Dutch East Indies. It is reported that the Japanese are preparing five good divisions for possible use as an overseas expeditionary force. We have today no forces in the Far East capable of dealing with this situation should it develop.

This Pacific section of the letter to Roosevelt had been cut from 135 words in the first draft to eighty. There were two main omissions. Churchill had originally said: 'We are almost entirely dependent on the deterrent effect of the American fleet and diplomacy.' This was cut out, presumably as too humiliating an admission for a great empire. Churchill had then suggested in his draft: 'If you were in a position to supply the intrepid airmen of Australia and New Zealand with modern machines, without taking them from more urgent theatres, an immense increase in our power to deter Japanese aggression southwards would immediately spring into being.' The editor of the *Complete Correspondence* between Roosevelt and Churchill, Warren Kimball, notes an annotation of Churchill's draft in an unknown hand: 'Omit. We want them all here.'

Churchill's justification for the contradictions between his letters to Menzies and Roosevelt would have been the different purposes he had in view; his vindication is the results he achieved. Recognising the urgency, Roosevelt announced his Lend-Lease project – 'getting rid of the silly old dollar sign' – on 17 December 1940. Lend-Lease would provide massive material support to Britain, and it was a huge step towards ending American neutrality. The United States, Roosevelt told the American people, would be the 'Arsenal of Democracy'.

As SOON AS the election results showed that he would have a parliamentary majority of one after providing a Speaker, Menzies renewed his invitation to the Labor Party to join a national coalition. When Curtin again refused, Menzies took up Curtin's idea of an Advisory War Council, consisting of four ministers and four Opposition members. For Menzies, it represented Labor involvement without sharing real power, and for Curtin, it meant sharing information and influence without accepting real responsibility. In practice, the Advisory War Council proved more useful to Curtin than to Menzies: it was no help in bringing stability to the Menzies Government but helped prepare Labor for government. And it was in the Advisory Council rather than in Cabinet that Churchill's Middle Eastern strategy, and its consequences for Australia, began to come under hard scrutiny. Pressure from the Council led to the decision to send the 8th Division to Malaya early in 1941.

Menzies chose the Advisory War Council to float the idea that he should go to London to meet Churchill personally. At its meeting on 25 November 1940, he particularly referred to the 'alarming position in regard to the defence of Singapore, as revealed by the recent Singapore Conference' [of British, Australian and New Zealand defence chiefs]. This required him to talk to Churchill face to face. Curtin supported the idea.

Menzies began to have second thoughts, however. Although Churchill welcomed the proposal when Bruce sounded him out in December, Menzies now worried about his 'precarious political position', and the 'inexperience of his principal lieutenants in Cabinet', presumably Arthur Fadden, the Country Party leader who would be acting Prime Minister in his absence. He cabled Bruce for advice on 3 January 1941: 'Would be glad if you could frankly give me idea of value of visit and also ascertain from Churchill whether this is a convenient time for him. In particular, I feel that clear definition where we stand in the Far East and reasonably long range policy of Middle East would enable me to plan Australian effort on manpower side more soundly.'

Bruce was less than enthusiastic. Consultation with British ministers apart from Churchill would be 'of limited value', Bruce told Menzies. 'Major policy is increasingly centred in [the] Prime Minister's hands and little influenced by other members of War Cabinet who frankly are not prepared to stand up to him.' Churchill would give Menzies a 'most cordial welcome – utmost courtesy – invitation to attend meeting of War Cabinet and apparently every opportunity for consultation'; but 'when you tried to pin him down to definite discussions of fundamental questions of major war policy, I am inclined to think you would find him discursive and elusive, necessitating your either (a) taking a line that would mean a considerable show-down between you or (b) leaving with a sense of frustration'.

In this self-important document, Bruce said, in effect, why risk a showdown with Churchill when there was nothing really worth discussing? A meeting might 'be imperative if there were any major lines of policy on which you felt [the] United Kingdom Government was going wrong and with regard to which you have to take a strong line'. But, Bruce wrote:

> While such a position has existed in the past, e.g. reinforcements for Middle East in August and September last, and maximum cooperation in regard to Far East with United States of America based on complete frankness, developments over past few months have removed all the major issues on which you would have had to take a strong line.

Everything was now governed by Hitler's next move, and therefore, Bruce concluded: 'I see no definite line we would want to press on the United Kingdom Government in the field of major policy.' There were, he conceded, important matters like farm products, shipping and trade. These, however, would be 'difficult politically for you to handle'. The High Commissioner as good as told the Prime Minister to stay at home and mend his fences. In his heart, Bruce really wanted and half-expected a call from the Australian conservatives to return home as Prime Minister himself. His frustration explains much about his tepid relations with Menzies and his torrid relations with Churchill.

One can hardly imagine a missive more calculated to spur on so proud and self-confident a man as Menzies. Even if Bruce really believed that there were no major policies to settle, then it was high time for some plain speaking with Churchill man to man. As to his political difficulties, he would have to do his duty by Australia and take his chances. Such must have been among Menzies' thoughts when he informed his Cabinet that he would leave for London via Singapore and the Middle East on 24 January 1941. Menzies' four-month absence would have huge consequences for him and for his nation. His stocks rose in Britain and sank in Australia. His tenuous hold on the loyalty of his party and Cabinet weakened, largely because Churchill used his presence in London to lock him personally into decisions that took the AIF to the brink of disaster.

Menzies was accompanied by the head of the Defence Department, Frederick Shedden, who had greater influence over defence policy-making during the war than any other Australian save the Prime Minister. Curtin later described Shedden as 'my right and left hand and my head, too'. Their stately Qantas Empire Airways flying boat took three days to reach Singapore, where Menzies and his senior officer were appalled by the air of colonial somnolence that seemed to have settled over the place. Menzies was unimpressed by the new commander in Malaya, Air Chief Marshal Sir Robert Brooke-Popham, who left Menzies with 'the vague feeling that his instincts favour some heroic but futile Rorke's Drift rather than clear cut planning, realism and science'. Menzies kept a diary of his journey, and wrote: 'Winston Churchill had lunched with him [Brooke-Popham] in London before he came out to this appointment and he was boyishly pleased that Winston's farewell exhortation to him had contained more than a hint of the forlorn hope.' A fine mimic with a sharp ear for the accents of Empire, the Australian Prime Minister imagined Churchill's parting words to Brooke-Popham: 'Hold out to the last, my boy, God bless you. If your grandfather had not broken his neck playing polo at Poona he would be proud of you this day!'

But it was no joking matter. 'This Far Eastern problem must be taken seriously and urgently,' Menzies confided to his diary after his two days in Singapore. If Menzies imagined, as his flying boat lumbered on towards the Middle East (via Bangkok, Rangoon, Calcutta, and Basra), that he might convey his new-found sense of urgency to Churchill, he was to be disappointed. Far from Churchill turning his urgent or serious attention to the Far East, he was about to take the most daring step so far in pursuit of his Big Idea: he would take the fight to Hitler on the mainland of Europe. The Greek tragedy was about to unfold, and the Second AIF would have a major but ill-starred role in it.

WHILE CHURCHILL AND MENZIES were cabling congratulations to each other on the British surge forward in Cyrenaica in December, 1940, Hitler had issued three directives which were to decide the course of the war. After stunning initial successes, they would lead to his total defeat at the hands of the Soviet Union, the United States, and Britain. To the extent that Hitler's directives were his response to British defiance, they constitute Churchill's ultimate vindication. But in 1941 the risks Churchill was running and the mistakes he was making seemed to spell disaster. On 10 December 1940, Hitler ordered his air force, the Luftwaffe, to break British air and sea control of the Mediterranean – his first move to retrieve the Italian rout in North Africa. On 13 December, Hitler directed the preparation of Operation Marita – his plan for the control of the Balkans and the invasion of Greece. The most fateful of Hitler's directives was made on 18 December – the order to prepare Operation Barbarossa, the invasion of the Soviet Union, confirming a decision he had made as early as July, soon after the fall of France. His generals were told to have the plan ready by May, 1941. The invasion of Britain was put on the shelf, never to be taken down. The chronology makes it clear that Hitler's invasion of Greece in April, 1941, was not merely an attempt to rescue Mussolini from the mess he had made for the Axis by his own disastrous invasion of Greece in November; it was an integral part of his strategy to gain control of the Balkans in order to guard the southern flank of his lunge eastwards to Russia.

Hitler had incensed Mussolini in September, 1940, by keeping him in the dark when he occupied Romania 'by invitation', in order to safeguard the Romanian oil fields, which were vital to the Axis. Mussolini told his Foreign Secretary and son-in-law, Count Galeazzo Ciano: 'Hitler always faces me with a *fait accompli*. This time I will pay him in his own coin. He will find out from the newspapers that I have occupied Greece.' Mussolini's pique led him to disaster, and again provided Churchill with an opportunity to pursue his Idea. Churchill, too, had his Balkan strategy – a dusted-off version of his Dardanelles schemes, but this time adding neutral Turkey to his vision of a Balkan combination against Germany. In his invincible optimism, he appeared not to have asked himself the question: Why, only twenty years after Smyrna and Chanak, would Turkey choose to ally itself with Greece and Britain against a victorious Germany?

For Churchill, the call of Greece was compelling. It had nothing to do with Greece as the cradle of democracy and all that. Indeed, the kingdom's Prime Minister, General Ioannis Metaxas, was a run-of-the-mill dictator of the 1930s 'strong man' type. When Western Europe had succumbed to Hitler, Greece had resisted Mussolini and by December had pushed the Italian army back to the coast of Albania, with huge losses on both sides. This gave Greece an irresistible claim on Churchill's instincts and imagination. Most of all, Greece was the only place in the world where he could fight the Germans and impress the Americans.

By early 1941, Churchill knew a good deal about Hitler's plans, through Ultra, the brilliant code-breaking operation whose intelligence was so vital to the Allied war effort that its secrets were not disclosed for thirty years. In his war memoirs, published in the late 1940s and early 1950s, Churchill could not reveal even its existence, much less its influence on his decisions. He usually attributed signals intelligence to 'daring agents' on the ground – 'humint' in the current jargon for spies. By March, 1941, he was able to piece together a rough picture of Hitler's plans for the Balkans and Russia.

Day by day, the dangers and possibilities in Greece began to loom larger and bolder in Churchill's imagination; the deserts of North Africa gave way to the mountains and valleys of Greece. In the same week that the 6th Australian Division took Bardia and drove towards Tobruk, he began to put pressure on Wavell to change priority from his careful and winning campaign to the hazards of a new, unplanned campaign. 'Destruction of Greece would eclipse victories you have gained in Libya,' he cabled Wavell on 10 January

1941, 'and may affect decisively Turkish attitude, especially if we have shown ourselves callous of fate of allies.' He told Wavell: 'You must now therefore conform your plans to larger interests at stake.' True, Churchill allowed, 'nothing must hamper capture of Tobruk'. But after that, 'all operations in Libya are subordinated to aiding Greece'. To make sure Wavell got the message, Churchill invoked the full authority of Cabinet: 'We expect and require prompt and active compliance with our decisions, for which we bear full responsibility.' This is the crucial message in everything that followed.

Obedient to Churchill, Wavell flew to Athens on 13 January to learn for himself what the Greeks wanted in the way of support. Far from welcoming his offer of two or three divisions, the Greeks rejected it on the grounds that such limited aid would only provoke a German attack. Relieved by the rejection, Wavell returned to Egypt to find his Operation Compass succeeding beyond all expectations. Supported by the British 1st Armoured Division, the 6th Australian Division broke through the Italian defences at Tobruk on 21 January, taking another twenty-five thousand prisoners. On 6 February, at least three weeks ahead of the most optimistic forecast, the 6th entered Benghazi. The British conquest of Cyrenaica – or at least the coastal strip to a depth of forty miles or so – was complete. In the seesaw of the Desert War, it was to change hands four more times. Menzies arrived in the Middle East in time to celebrate the Australian victories. He addressed the troops at Bardia, Tobruk, and Benghazi.

Churchill's congratulations to Wavell on his success came with a warning: 'This does not alter, indeed it rather confirms, our previous directive,' he cabled on 12 February. 'Your major effort must now be to aid Greece.' Churchill gave detailed instructions to his victorious general: 'no serious effort against Tripoli' – 'make yourself secure in Benghazi' – 'concentrate all available forces in the Nile Delta in preparation for movement to Europe' [i.e. Greece]. Churchill's instructions to Wavell were, in essence, to drop the pursuit of the Italian army, leave the enemy in possession of its headquarters at Tripoli, the main Libyan port, and divert his major effort to the opposite side of the Mediterranean Sea in Greece. Erwin Rommel, at this time Hitler's favourite general, arrived in Tripoli on the day he gave these orders. Between them, Hitler and Churchill were about to transform the war in North Africa, and the Australian role in it.

The distinguished British war historian Corelli Barnett asserts bluntly that Churchill's decision on Greece 'prolonged the war in Africa by two years'. Churchill was now shifting his Middle East/ Mediterranean strategy, not only geographically but conceptually, to a stratosphere where political objectives would override military objections. To make the new order of things clear to Wavell, Churchill told him in his message of 12 February that the Foreign Secretary, Anthony Eden, and the Chief of the General Staff, Sir John Dill, were on their way to Cairo 'to give the very best chance of concentrating all possible measures, both diplomatic and military, against the Germans in the Balkans'. Even if Greece failed in the end, Churchill said, 'there will always remain the support of Turkey'. Wavell replied immediately: 'We will do our best to frustrate the German plans in the Balkans, but Greek and Turkish hesitations and Yugoslav timidity have made our task very difficult. Owing to difficulties of shipping and ports, our arrival is bound to be somewhat piecemeal.' Churchill brushed such caution aside, but when everything went wrong, claimed that Wavell had advocated the Greek campaign from the start.

Anthony Eden now made the running. Churchill had just promoted him to be Foreign Secretary, having sent Halifax to Washington after the sudden death of Lord Lothian. The Greek affair was a major step for Eden towards positioning himself as Churchill's eventual successor; but he had to wait until 1955. In 1941, he became deeply committed to the Greeks, politically and emotionally. Churchill cabled Eden in Cairo on 20 February: 'Do not consider yourself obligated to a Greek enterprise if in your hearts you feel it will only be another Norway. If no good plan can be made please say so.' This was a loophole for the history books, because Churchill added immediately: 'But of course you know how valuable success would be.'

As he knew he would, Churchill had hit the right nerve with Eden, a vain, unstable, and ambitious man, who cabled to London;

'We are agreed we should do everything in our power to bring the fullest measure of help to Greeks at earliest possible moment. If the help we can offer is accepted by the Greeks, we believe that there is a fair chance of halting a German advance and preventing Greece from being overrun.' Churchill ever after claimed that this was the 'clear conviction of the men on the spot'. In all the messages back and forth between London, Cairo, and Athens, there is an ominous echo of Churchill's conduct over the Dardanelles, with its citing of 'high authorities' to pressure 'the man on the spot', mutually reinforcing each other in a circle of manipulation and misrepresentation.

Eden, Wavell, and Dill flew to Athens on 22 February. Metaxas had died of cancer in January. The new Prime Minister of Greece, Alexandros Koryzis, was more eager for British support than his predecessor had been. The pro-British King, George II, arranged for Eden to meet privately with Koryzis, without British or Greek generals present. Koryzis read out to Eden a statement which, he said, expressed the united view of the Greek Cabinet: 'Whatever the outcome and whether Greece has or has not any hope of repulsing the enemy in Macedonia, she will defend her national territory, even if she can only count on her own forces.' Churchill placed a special significance on this private meeting: 'The Greek Government wished us to understand that their decision had been taken before they knew whether we could give them any help or not. The King had wished Mr Eden to know this *before* the military conversations opened and this was the basis on which they took place.' For Churchill and Eden, this was the point of no return. From that moment, the British commitment to Greece became a political and personal commitment between Eden and Koryzis, and between the King of Greece and the Prime Minister of Britain, beyond all military considerations. In the days and weeks ahead, there might be wavering and questioning at both the political and military levels in London, Cairo, and Athens; but after 22 February, there could be no turning back.

Eden reported to Churchill. 'Agreement was reached today with the Greek Government on all points.' The extent to which everything had been predetermined is shown by the speed and concision of Churchill's response. Within hours, he was able to cable back to Eden, in a message dated 24 February:

> The Chiefs of Staff having endorsed action on lines proposed in your telegrams from Cairo and Athens, I brought the whole question before the War Cabinet this evening, Mr Menzies being present. Decision was unanimous in the sense you desire, but of course Mr Menzies must telegraph home. Presume, also, you have settled with New Zealand Government about their troops. No need anticipate difficulties in either quarter. Therefore, while being under no illusions, we all send you the order 'Full steam ahead'.

16

'A bold move into Greece'
February–May, 1941

Churchill trapped Menzies into endorsing his Greek adventure. He had welcomed Menzies to Britain with the ultimate seal of approval – an invitation to spend his first weekend at Chequers, the prime ministerial residence thirty miles from London. It was a traditional English country weekend, from the Friday evening to the following Monday morning, 24 February. Menzies found that the former 'idol with feet of clay' that he had met in the wilderness years was now 'a tempestuous creature, pacing up and down the room, oratorical even in conversation, the master of the mordant phrase and yet, I would think, almost without real humour. Enjoys hatred.' Menzies wrote in his diary that Churchill was 'completely certain of America's full help, of her participation in a Japanese war and of Roosevelt's passionate determination to stamp out the Nazi menace'. He asked himself: 'Is he right? I cannot say. If the P.M. were a better listener and less disposed to dispense with all expert or local opinion, I might feel easier about it. But there's no doubt about it, he's a holy terror.'

With Menzies aglow after a Sunday morning walk in the snow with Clementine and the Churchills' daughter Mary, the Holy Terror sprang his trap. 'Momentous discussion later with P.M. about defence of Greece, largely with Australian and New Zealand troops,' Menzies recorded. 'This kind of decision, which may mean thousands of lives, is not easy. Why does a peaceable man become a Prime Minister?' Churchill had shrewdly judged the moment and the man. His sense of timing, place, and drama proved an irresistible combination.

Menzies had known for several weeks that the British leader was contemplating some form of help to Greece. He had referred to the possibility of Australian units being used there in his complaint to Bruce the previous December about the lack of information from London. The first serious indication came when he met General Wavell in Cairo in February. In his war memoirs, Churchill gives a loaded account of the conversations between Wavell and Menzies: Wavell 'had already spoken to Mr Menzies, the Prime Minister of Australia, who was in Cairo on his way to London, about this, and found him very ready to agree to what he had suggested'. It is unlikely that Wavell, notoriously secretive and uncommunicative, even with Churchill himself, would have given much away to a visiting fireman from Australia. In fact, Wavell had vouchsafed to Menzies only 'the possibility of a Salonika (Greece) expedition' and asked for 'a certain latitude' in the future disposition of Australian forces under his command. Menzies says that he stressed Australia's strong desire to keep the Second AIF together and that it should not be split up without the approval of its commander, General Thomas Blamey. Blamey himself did not learn of the proposal to send the 6th and 7th Australian Divisions to Greece until 18 February. By that time, Menzies was somewhere between Cairo and London, via Khartoum in the Sudan and Lagos on the West Coast of Africa. He had left Cairo 'with a depressed feeling that Wavell didn't trust me, only to find, in London, that he had reported on me quite favourably'.

Churchill corralled Australian support for his Greek venture with consummate skill. Primed by him, Menzies recommended that the Australian Cabinet accept the British War Cabinet decision of 24 February, telling Fadden: 'The military arguments are fairly well balanced.' He added: 'You will of course have in mind that the enterprise is risky.' However, Menzies said: 'Politically, the argument is, I think, strongly in favour of the undertaking.' Menzies had taken Churchill's bait of a Balkan front. 'A bold move into Greece might possibly bring Yugoslavia and Turkey in, with the result that a strong Balkan front could be established.' In the event, Bulgaria joined the Axis on 1 March, clearing the German path to Yugoslavia and Greece, Bulgaria's neighbours. Making a nod in the direction of Australia's anxieties about Japan, Menzies told Fadden: 'I cannot think that an abandoned Greece should therefore do anything other than weaken our position in world opinion, scare Turkey and greatly hurry the Japanese.'

Menzies admitted that any diversion to Greece would 'deplete the efforts of our forces in North Africa', but insisted: 'If this proposal was only a forlorn hope I would not like it, and I so informed the War Cabinet. But the view of Dill and Wavell is that it is much more than a forlorn hope.' Having thus given the military view, such as it was, Menzies returned to the political question at the heart of the whole business: 'The effect on American opinion of our pursuing this bold course will unquestionably be great.' Menzies presented the clincher to Fadden and his colleagues in Canberra:

> It may help you in your discussion if I tell you most secretly that I spent the entire weekend with Churchill, that he has been in closest communication with Roosevelt through Hopkins [Roosevelt's closest adviser who had just visited Britain]. Churchill is emphatically optimistic about quite dramatic action by the President after the passage of the Lease and Lend Bill [then being considered by the US Congress]. He goes on to offer the positive view that if Japan goes to war against us, America will unquestionably come in and has reiterated to me that should Australia be attacked and America be not in, adequate naval support could at once be dispatched to Australian waters.

Menzies conceded that Churchill's view 'must be a little discounted' but insisted that 'the risk of American intervention should be sufficiently great to deter Japan'. But Menzies had linked the Greek venture directly and specifically to Churchill's Big Idea – to fight Hitler wherever the fighting was most likely to impress Roosevelt and American opinion and ultimately bring the United States into the war. Ironically, just when Churchill and Menzies decided to send the Australians to fight against the Germans in Greece, in order to impress Roosevelt and deter the Japanese in the Pacific, Hitler was sending Rommel and his Afrika Korps to fight the British and Australians in North Africa. Rommel's campaign would be the pivot on which the relations between Churchill and Australia were to turn for the next six months.

A few hours after receiving Menzies' cable, the Australian War Cabinet met in Canberra and accepted the proposal, with misgiving about the 'adequacy of the force for the task proposed'. 'Despite the risky nature of the adventure, we have been impressed with the necessity for an immediate decision,' Fadden told Menzies. Australian consent, however, 'must be regarded as conditional on plans having been completed beforehand to ensure that evacuation, if necessitated, will be successfully undertaken.' Defeatism permeated the Greek gamble before it even began.

Churchill had, in effect, challenged Menzies to veto not only the use of the AIF in Greece, but his whole war strategy; to set his doubts and reservations against the views of the men-on-the-spot, the opinion of the President of the United States, and, above all, the judgement and honour of Winston Churchill. Even Fadden's reservations about air support and transport for evacuation emphasised how little room the Australian Government had to manoeuvre. Its divisions in the Middle East depended on the capacity of the British Government to support them. In all these circumstances, it is inconceivable that Menzies could have brought himself to impose a veto on Churchill and his Greek proposal. Churchill left Menzies with no option and, in his turn, Menzies left his Canberra colleagues with no option but to go along. No wonder that Churchill, in his 'Full steam ahead' cable to Eden, had taken Australian and New Zealand agreement for granted.

The simmering anxieties in Canberra would have boiled over if they had known the opinion of their own man-on-the-spot, General

Sir Thomas Blamey, the highest profile soldier, and commander of the Second AIF in the Middle East. The first Blamey learnt of the major role in Greece to be borne by the men under his command was on 18 February, five days after Menzies had left Cairo. Wavell then told him that his 6th and 7th Divisions, together with the New Zealand Division and the British 1st Armoured Brigade, would form 'Lustre Force', the expedition to save Greece. 'I left the interview with great misgivings,' Blamey later wrote. When Blamey told Wavell that he would have to refer the proposal to his government, Wavell said airily that 'he had already discussed the possibility of such an operation with Menzies'. It was just not true. The Commander of the New Zealand Division, Major General Bernard Freyberg, VC, was given his riding instructions with similar abruptness. Freyberg recalled: 'Wavell had a secrecy mania. I was never in a position to make a well-informed and responsible judgement.'

Nor were these two commanders of two-thirds of Wavell's combat force asked their opinion of its impact on North African operations, now that Rommel and the first units of his Afrika Korps were moving into North Africa. Blamey, however, was slow to convey his concerns to the Australian Government. Indeed, his first complaint to them was that he had not been considered for the overall command. Wavell had given it to Sir Henry Maitland Wilson, known to his colleagues as 'Jumbo', described by one Australian general as 'that great façade' and by Freyberg as 'an amiable yes man'. Blamey's doubts did not reach the Australian Government or its advisers in Canberra until the expedition was well underway and the Australian advance units were already in Greece.

Thomas Albert Blamey, now fifty-seven, later became Australia's only field marshal. Starting out as a pupil-teacher at Wagga Wagga, New South Wales, he transferred his ambitions to the fledgling Australian army and won entry to the British Staff College at Quetta, India. In 1914 he was posted to Egypt and took part in the Gallipoli landing, and the evacuation in December, 1915. By war's end, he was Monash's Chief of Staff in France. In 1925, he left the regular army to become Victorian Police Commissioner. He resigned under a cloud of allegations, beginning with the discovery of his police badge in a Melbourne brothel, and ending in 1936 with a charge of issuing a perjured statement to protect a crony. He had incurred the hostility of the Labor Party for his ruthlessness in using his police against striking unionists, his brash lifestyle, and his suspected involvement with the proto-fascist White Guard.

The crises of command that bedevilled Australian military leadership make a sorry story of the rivalries and disloyalties which seethed around Blamey throughout the war. In 1939, his admirers, Menzies, Casey, and Shedden, procured his appointment to command the first Australian division raised for the new war, the 6th Division, and then put him in command of the whole Australian Army Corps in the Middle East. Menzies was to write in his memoirs: 'Although I had reason to know that he had a poor opinion of me, I had, and retained until the end of his life, a very high opinion of him.' Menzies found in Blamey 'the power of command, hard to define but impossible to mistake when you meet it'. Wavell said of him: 'Probably the best soldier we had in the Middle East. Not an easy man to deal with, but a very satisfactory man to deal with.' Churchill judged him to be 'a more ardent politician than soldier'. Blamey's ruling passion was to mould the AIF into a united fighting force, one national army under one national command – his – and to resist British attempts to use them up piecemeal. As he told Menzies in Cairo in 1941, 'If you give these British generals an inch, they'll take an ell'.

Too late to change anything, Blamey's report to Canberra made some shrewd points which might have punctured even Churchill's invincible optimism, if put earlier in the right quarters. He pointed out that the number of divisions Hitler could send would be limited only by the carrying capacity of the Balkan roads into Greece: 'In view of the Germans' much proclaimed intention to drive us off the continent wherever we appear, landing of this small British force would be most welcome to them, as it gives them good reason to attack.' The Greek dictator, General Metaxas, had voiced the same fear. As to the much-vaunted political effect on Turkey, Yugoslavia, and Greece, he asked simply: 'What about the effect of defeat and a second evacuation [another Dunkirk] on the same countries, and for that matter, Japan?' By the time his questions were circulating in the Canberra Cabinet and army headquarters at Victoria Barracks, Melbourne, Blamey himself was in Greece, commanding the Australian force. He had been successful with Wavell on one point – the battle-hardened 6th should go first, rather than the still under-trained and under-equipped 7th. The collapse of the campaign was so swift that – fortunately – the 7th never got there. It appears again later in this story, successful in Syria against the Vichy French, and then the intended victim of Churchill's impetuosity in 1942, saved by John Curtin's refusal to buckle under, living to fight another day in the crucial battles in New Guinea.

Nobody was prepared to stand up to Churchill over Greece in March, 1941, least of all Menzies, however much he grumbled in his diary about the docility of the British War Cabinet. He was delighted to find that in England, 'Australia is Dominion No. 1', and he was not about to endanger that gratifying position. In a message marked 'Most Secret and for personal information only', he told Fadden on 4 March: 'I have spent two weekends with Churchill whose qualities are much greater even than we thought. His experience since becoming Prime Minister has obviously ripened his judgement and he combines in a unique way the most remarkable fighting and driving qualities with an astonishing mastery of the details of both plans and equipment.' But, Menzies conceded, 'One thing that disturbs me a little is that his Cabinet is not disposed to entertain an independent view and there is therefore a shortage of criticism.'

Far from criticising Churchill in front of the British Cabinet in London, Menzies still seemed more concerned to shield Churchill from any criticism from his own Cabinet in Canberra. Messages passed almost daily between Menzies and Fadden, with Fadden ranging over Australian concerns, from the German moves in North Africa and their attack on Yugoslavia, and the disproportionate Australian and New Zealand burden in Greece, to Japan's likely reaction in the event of another defeat and evacuation, often using Blamey's exact words. To each message, Menzies countered with reassurance, often using Churchill's exact words. While acknowledging Fadden's concerns, Menzies adopted Churchill's political argument in its entirety. When all was said and done, he told Fadden on 8 March, the day after the British War Cabinet had given its final go-ahead:

> One is still left with the final conclusion that though the hazards are considerable, the proposal is by no means hopeless; and that under these circumstances, the overwhelming importance to our position in relation to the world at large and particularly America of not abandoning the Greeks, who have of all our allies fought the most gallantly, should be the decisive consideration.

Menzies made one protest in the British War Cabinet on 7 March. It was not good enough, he told Churchill, that the Australians should go to Greece merely because of Eden's promise to the Greeks; they needed assurance that the operation was based on the firm advice of the military men-on-the-spot. Thus prompted, Churchill cabled to Eden: 'We must be able to tell the New Zealand and Australian Governments faithfully that this hazard, from which they will not shrink, is undertaken not because of any commitment entered into by a British Cabinet Minister at Athens and signed by the Chief of the Imperial General Staff (Sir John Dill), but because Dill, Wavell and other commanders-in-chief are convinced that there is a reasonable fighting chance.' Churchill instructed Eden: 'A precise military appreciation is indispensable.' Eden never provided the indispensable military appreciation. The reason is obvious enough: it would have exposed the hopelessness of the venture in Greece and the new dangers in North Africa.

After the British Cabinet had given its final go-ahead, Menzies spent his third weekend at Chequers. General De Gaulle was among the dinner guests. Menzies needled both Churchill and De Gaulle by recalling the Dakar fiasco. Nevertheless, Churchill's young private secretary, John Colville, wrote that Churchill 'seemed relieved' that the 'irrevocable decision' had been taken, and spoke with new confidence about America's entry in the war. Churchill had told Colville that Menzies was 'an agreeable man with whom to dine'.

Churchill was a master of spin long before the term was invented. Even as late as 30 March 1941, six days before Hitler marched on Greece, the British Prime Minister spoke of political chaos in the Yugoslav capital, Belgrade, as ground for 'renewed hopes of forming a Balkan Front with Turkey', with seventy Allied divisions confronting Germany! In fact, the *coup d'etat* which deposed the pro-German Regent in Belgrade simply increased the speed and fury with which Hitler unleashed his army against Yugoslavia and Greece. The onslaught was preceded by a Luftwaffe bombing of Belgrade as savage as anything London endured. The awkward facts did not inhibit Churchill. In a personal message, Churchill told Fadden that these events put the Greek expedition 'in its true setting, not as an isolated military act, but as a prime mover in a large design'. The results were unknowable, he acknowledged, but 'the prize has increased and the risks somewhat lessened'. He assured Fadden: 'Am in closest touch with Menzies. Wish I could talk it over with you.'

To Canberra's concerns about inadequate air protection, the piecemeal arrival of the troops in Greece, and the new dangers in North Africa, Menzies answered Fadden on 7 April, the day after Hitler attacked with ten of the twenty-seven divisions he had earmarked for the conquest of Yugoslavia and Greece:

> I can assure you that the matters which are troubling you are constantly engaging my attention and discussions. Churchill is fully aware of the problem [of air cover] and is most helpful, but I do not doubt that whatever comes of it in the short term, the Greek campaign represents a sound and unavoidable decision which must have valuable results in more than one country.

The 'one country' that counted was the United States. When the mirage of a Balkan front vanished, when everything else fell apart, and the Greek campaign became the worst British disaster of the war until the next one, the impact on Roosevelt and American opinion remained Churchill's motivation and justification.

Yet even Churchill became nervous at the last minute. On the day Hitler gave the order to march, Churchill cabled Eden in Cairo:

'Grave imperial issues are raised by committing New Zealand and Australian troops to an enterprise which, as you say, has become even more hazardous.' Eden replied: 'In the existing situation we are all agreed that the course advocated should be followed and help given to Greece. We devoutly trust therefore that no difficulty will arise with regard to the dispatch of the Dominion Forces as arranged.'

The Greek debacle lasted barely three weeks. The Germans marched from Bulgaria into Yugoslavia and northern Greece on 6 April. Their divisions were superbly generalled, disciplined, and indoctrinated; their morale soaring since their triumph in the west. From the hour of contact with the might of German armour and air superiority, the Allied campaign became a series of withdrawals and retreats. General Papagos baulked at giving up Greek territory to form a shorter, stronger front with the British, Australian, and New Zealand forces. Seeping through all ranks was the knowledge that evacuation had been planned even before the fighting had begun. Yet, as one historian of the campaign, Lieutenant General John Coates, would write: 'The worst mistakes of the politicians and strategists were moderated by the bravery, fighting qualities and sheer dogged determination of the troops.'

Twenty-six years after Gallipoli, the Australians and New Zealanders were again fighting side by side on battlegrounds of the classical world, and once again they had been brought there by the driving force of Winston Churchill. Henceforth, Blamey informed his brigade commanders on 12 April, the Australian and New Zealand divisions were to be designated the Anzac Corps. 'The task ahead,' he declared, 'though difficult, is not nearly so desperate as that which faced our fathers 26 years ago. We go to it together with stout hearts and certainty of success.' The next day, the British commander-in-chief in Greece, Sir Henry Maitland Wilson, ordered the Anzacs to withdraw a hundred miles south, to hold the line at Thermopylae where, in 480 BC, Leonidas and his three hundred Spartans had stood against the invading Persians. In true laconic tradition, Brigadier George Vasey told his men of the 19th Brigade:

Here you bloody well are and here you bloody well stay. And if any
bloody German gets between your post and the next, turn your bloody
Bren around and shoot him up the arse.

Churchill's imagination, too, was fired by the name and fame of
Thermopylae. 'The intervening ages fell away,' he was to write.
'Why not one more undying feat of arms?' In April, 1941, however,
the purpose of holding on at the Thermopylae line was solely to
allow a more orderly and safer evacuation. The Greek campaign was
over. General Papagos demanded that the British leave to avert the
devastation. The Greek Government was falling apart. The Greek
army was seeking arrangements to surrender, as long as they could
negotiate with the Germans and not the Italians.

Churchill was still refusing to accept reality. As late as 20 April,
he told Eden: 'I am increasingly of the opinion that if the generals on
the spot think they can hold on to the Thermopylae position for a
fortnight or three weeks, and can keep the Greek army fighting, or
enough of it, we should certainly support them, if the Dominions
will agree.' It was a death-knock attempt to shift responsibility. How
on earth Churchill thought that the governments in Canberra or
Wellington, or even Menzies in London, could offer any useful
opinion at this stage, he never explained. Nevertheless, Churchill
continued: 'I am most reluctant to see us quit, and if the troops were
British only, and the matter could be decided on military grounds
alone, I would urge Wilson to fight on, if he thought it possible.
Anyhow, before we commit ourselves to evacuation the case must be
put squarely to the Dominions after tomorrow's Cabinet.'

It was all fantastically irrelevant. Neither the British nor
Australian War Cabinets now had any say in the matter, if they ever
had. Even as Churchill was presenting his new scenario of 'no
retreat, no surrender' to Anthony Eden, Wavell was making his last
flight to Athens to arrange capitulation. King George II of Greece,
his army surrendering, his government in collapse, his capital in
chaos, his Prime Minister dead by his own hand, apologised to
Wavell for letting everybody down and promised to do his best
to facilitate the evacuation before joining the escape to Crete.

Beginning on Anzac Eve, the Australians and New Zealanders were evacuated from ports and beaches in southern Greece, some bound for Alexandria in Egypt, others sent to the island of Crete, now designated by Churchill to be held at all costs. Under relentless air attack, the Royal Navy rescued fifty thousand British, Australian, and New Zealand troops. Like Gallipoli, the evacuation was the only successful part of the campaign. Unlike the Gallipoli evacuation, it was costly and chaotic.

At last Churchill accepted the inevitable. He wrote to Roosevelt on 24 April: 'The Anzacs have been fighting all day in the Pass of Thermopylae. But, Mr President, you will long ago have foreseen the conclusion of these particular Greek affairs. I wish we could have done more. I am sure we were bound to do our utmost.'

The Australians in Greece lost 320 killed, with 500 wounded, and 2030 taken prisoner, from a force of over 17,000. The New Zealanders lost 300 killed, 600 wounded, and 1600 prisoners from a force of nearly 17,000. The British casualties were 150 dead, 100 wounded, 6500 taken prisoner, from 22,000; the RAF lost 200 out of 2200. Palestinian and Cypriot units, used for labour and transport, lost 4000 out of 4700, almost all of them as prisoners of war because the British neglected to evacuate them. The Greeks, with 16,000 dead in battle, and their civilian dead uncounted, continued their resistance until British paratroops liberated Athens and the Germans were driven out in October and November, 1944.

On 27 April, Churchill made a broadcast to the world. It was a wonderful example of his power to make the best of a bad job. For half an hour, he drew on all his rhetorical skill, by turns eloquent, conversational, fierce, friendly, humorous, venomous, proud, humble, presenting a catalogue of disasters as the necessary prelude to the coming, inevitable victory, defiant of 'Hitler and his foul gang'; contemptuous of the 'whipped jackal Mussolini'; soothing the dominions and flattering the United States – the real target among his worldwide audience.

To have abandoned Greece, he said, would have been 'an act of shame'. It would have 'deprived us of the respect which we now enjoy throughout the world, and sapped the vitals of our strength'.

So, he said: 'We put the case to the Dominions of Australia and New Zealand, and their Governments, without in any way ignoring the hazards, told us they felt the same way as we did.' He acknowledged that more than half the force came from Australia and New Zealand. 'I see the German propaganda is trying to make bad blood between us and Australia by making out that we have used them to do what we would not have asked of the British Army. I shall leave it to Australia to deal with that taunt.'

But the key part of the broadcast was directed to the United States. With the Lend-Lease Bill through the Congress, tanks and munitions now beginning to flow, and with Roosevelt ordering his navy on armed patrols halfway across the Atlantic, Churchill felt more confident than ever that his Big Idea was working to bring the United States into combat. Comparing the passing disasters in the East with the prospects for ever-increasing American involvement, he finished with a poem by Arthur Hugh Clough:

> And not by eastern windows only,
> When daylight comes, comes in the light.
> In front the sun climbs slow, how slowly!
> But westward, look, the land is bright.

Without Churchill's prompting, Australia had already dealt with the German taunt. Fadden and Curtin issued press statements emphasising that there was 'no political disunity in Australia about the prosecution of the war'. Fadden took Dr Goebbels head on. The German propaganda drive was bound to fail because it was untrue, Fadden said, with a touching faith in the power of truth over Goebbels, the author of the dictum: 'The bigger the lie the more it is believed.' Curtin's statement, like Churchill's, was directed at America: 'I say to our enemies that the workers of this country are determined to give their all in the war that has been forced upon us. To the United States I say that the Labor Movement of Australia will be unflinching and unyielding to the end.'

At least one of Churchill's listeners was not impressed – Kenneth Slessor, the official Australian war correspondent. Slessor had been with the Australians in Greece from the landings to the evacuation, and he was still in a state of shock. He heard Churchill's broadcast in Alexandria, and he wrote in his diary: 'Churchill's deft evasion of the truth, his clever appeal to sentimentality and patriotic emotion, and his extraordinary mis-statements of the facts of the Greek campaign determined me to get the real story back to Australia.'

Slessor was convinced from what he had seen in Greece that 'either the British or Australian Government or both were prepared callously and cynically to sacrifice a comparatively small force of Australian fighting men for the sake of a political gesture – that is, to gamble with Australian lives on a wild chance, wilder than Gallipoli'. If his story was blocked by the censor in Egypt, as seemed certain after his experience in Greece itself, where his stories had been cut to pieces or just spiked, he would get it to Australia by some means, even if it meant going home himself:

> I decided also to consult Blamey and seek his assistance, which he may be prepared to give, since the campaign was apparently forced on him against his better judgement, and his reputation has suffered as much as anyone's. Also, if Menzies is implicated in the responsibility and tries to have the matter hushed, to bring the facts, by whatever means available, to Curtin.

Slessor got as far as Blamey in Cairo. Despite the damage to Blamey's reputation, or perhaps to spread the blame, Wavell had just promoted Blamey to be his deputy as Commander-in-Chief, Middle East. Blamey's reputation had indeed suffered in Greece, not least because he had given the last seat on the plane evacuating him to his son, a 28-year-old major. Blamey told Slessor that no story along the lines he was contemplating would get past the censor, but he gave him a long confidential interview. Slessor recorded it in his diary, where it remained unpublished for more than forty years. Blamey had made these points:

- We went in with our eyes open, and the 6th Division was thoroughly well-equipped. The guarantees were between Governments.

- We were told that the landing was tied up with the Lease and Lend Act in USA – if we didn't come to the aid of Greece, the Act would not be passed.
- The Greek strategic set up was impossible from the start.
- The Greek corps commanders asked the Greek Army Commander (Papagos) to ask the Germans for terms, rather than the Italians – this is where the crack started.
- The politicians, with encouraging words, continue fine argument, but I am thinking of the men I sent on the mountains of Greece. What is a gesture to the politicians is death to us.

ON 1 MAY 1941, Churchill received a message from Roosevelt which must have filled him with a sense of vindication beyond all expectations. It was a ringing endorsement, not only of the Greek campaign but everything Churchill was trying to do. Roosevelt said: 'You have done not only heroic, but very useful work in Greece and the territorial loss is more than compensated for by the necessity for enormous German concentration and resulting German losses in men and material.' This may have been the genesis of the unprovable theory that the Greek campaign delayed Hitler's invasion of Russia sufficiently to turn a quick and easy victory into stalemate and eventual defeat. Menzies was to embrace this notion as part of his self-justification for his part in the Greek fiasco. Roosevelt went beyond justifying disaster in Greece; he pointed the way for Churchill to justify the coming disasters in Crete and North Africa:

Having sent all men and equipment to Greece you could possibly spare, you have fought a wholly justified delaying action and will continue to do so in other parts of the Eastern Mediterranean, including North Africa and the Near East. Furthermore, if additional withdrawals become necessary, they will all be part of the plan which, at this stage of the war, shortens British lines, greatly extends the Axis lines and compels the enemy to expend great quantities of men and equipment.

It was almost as if Churchill had written Roosevelt's script and, in a sense, he had. Roosevelt concluded his Greek post-mortem: 'I am satisfied that both here and in Britain, public opinion is growing to realise that even if you have to withdraw further in the Eastern Mediterranean, you will not allow any great debacle or surrender, and that in the last analysis the Naval control of the Indian Ocean and the Atlantic Ocean will in time win the war.' Grateful for this shield against his critics, Churchill replied: 'Your friendly message assures me that no temporary reverses, however heavy, can shake your resolution to support us until we gain the final victory.' The part of Roosevelt's message that seemed to accept the eventual loss of Egypt worried Churchill. Drafting his reply, he had actually written the word 'depressed' but crossed it out. 'I adjure you, Mr President', he wrote, 'not to underrate the gravity of the consequences which may follow from a Middle Eastern collapse'. More bluntly than ever before, he urged the United States 'to range herself with us as a belligerent power'. He wrote: 'In this war, every post is a winning post, and how many more are we going to lose?' But Churchill's Big Idea was up and running, for all the crashing of hurdles behind and ahead.

17

'Winston is a dictator'
April–August, 1941

The disaster in Greece shook Menzies' faith in Churchill. 'W. is a great man,' he wrote in his diary the day after Churchill's broadcast, 'but he is more addicted to wishful thinking every day.' But Menzies was still determined to keep the lid on criticism from Australia. On a single day, when the Australian defence at Thermopylae was collapsing, he sent five messages to Fadden urging restraint and patience in Canberra. 'Our present duty,' he cabled Fadden on 22 April, 'is salvage and not recrimination.' In the first rumbling of a personal and political rivalry which defined the careers of both men over the next twenty years, Menzies singled out Herbert Vere Evatt, the former Australian High Court judge who had stood down to become a Labor MP in the 1940 election. London press reports, Menzies told Fadden, suggested that Evatt was 'endeavouring to make political capital out of our difficulties'. Churchill had telephoned him to complain. 'It would be a pity for a few politicians to impair our high reputation in Britain,' Menzies warned. 'Our losses are very small compared with those of, say, Scotland.' Confident that Fadden would 'handle this matter in your usual sensible way', he added: 'You may imagine how I feel, but we cannot make war without losses and the only means of victory is killing the Germans which our people are doing very notably.'

Unfortunately, the Germans were having the best of the killing. Rommel had taken full advantage of Churchill's Greek diversions. He ignored Hitler's orders to delay his North African offensive until the end of May. Even before Hitler invaded Greece, Rommel thrust eastwards into Cyrenaica, retaking Benghazi on 4 April. On 9 April he captured Bardia, four months after the AIF's victories over the Italians. But the Australians and British held on at Tobruk, which Wavell ordered be defended and reinforced by sea and air. By mid-April, the commander of the 9th Australian Division, Leslie Morshead, had thirty thousand Australian, British, and Indian troops within the thirty-mile perimeter around Tobruk; chiefly the 9th Australian Division and a brigade of the 7th Australian Division. Of the twenty-seven infantry, artillery and armoured units under Morshead's command, fifteen were Australian, eleven British (mainly artillery), and one Indian. Rommel encircled Tobruk on 13 April. The siege of Tobruk had begun. Broadcasting from Berlin, Lord Haw Haw, the renegade broadcaster William Joyce, warned the defenders that 'they would be dug out of their holes like rats'.

Meanwhile, on the northern shores of the Mediterranean, disaster in Greece was followed by disaster on Crete. Even as Menzies was sending his cables to Canberra, Hitler had given his directive for the occupation of the Greek island in the Aegean. Despite having scrapped earlier plans to fortify Crete, Churchill now instructed the New Zealand Division, with British, Australian, and Greek evacuees from Greece, to hold the island. He assigned the desperate task to the Commander of the New Zealand Division, General Bernard Freyberg, VC. Churchill dubbed him 'the Salamander' in tribute to his survival from twenty-seven wounds received at Gallipoli and France in the First World War. Through Ultra, Churchill had detailed intelligence about the German Operation Merkur (Mercury) and its plans for an airborne assault. By the end of May, however, after ten days of fierce fighting, Freyberg informed Wavell that his position was hopeless. There was nothing for it but another evacuation, despite Churchill's last-minute plea to

Wavell: 'Victory in Crete is essential at this turning point in the war. Keep hurling in all aid you can.' Three thousand Australians were among the fifteen thousand Allied troops left behind on Crete to be taken prisoner.

As the Greek and Crete campaigns collapsed and Tobruk held, Menzies felt increasingly frustrated and isolated. He had written in his diary on 14 April:

> W. C. speaks at length as the Master Strategist – 'Tobruk must be held as a bridgehead or rally post, from which to hit the enemy'. 'With what?' says I, and so the discussion goes on. Wavell and the Admiralty have failed us. The Cabinet is deplorable – dumb men most of whom disagree with Winston but none of whom dare to say so. This state of affairs is most dangerous. The Chiefs of Staff are without exception Yes men ... Winston is a dictator; he cannot be overruled ... The people have set him up as something little less than God, and his power is therefore terrific.

However, Churchill's was a very special kind of dictatorship. In one of his 'most secret' messages to Arthur Fadden, Menzies had paid tribute to Churchill's 'astonishing mastery of detail'. It was indeed phenomenal. The eagerness with which he added to his workload is breath-taking, when we contemplate, over the distance of seven decades of technological revolution, the immense output of a wartime Prime Minister writing and dictating, working in relays with two or three secretary-typists. In the anxious weeks of March/April 1941, with disaster looming in Greece and North Africa, he bombarded his generals and officials with memos and questions, often marked 'Action This Day', on a range of subjects including: balloon barrages over London; the decline in German air-raids; an 'egg-laying' device for bombers ('cut a hole in the floor of aeroplanes'); a proposal for raising a Jewish army (he wanted it put on hold); anti-submarine convoys; the localities of radar stations; converting cruisers to aircraft carriers; refrigerated meat ships for troops in the Middle East; the availability of cranes in British ship-yards and ports; the forms of government in Europe after Hitler ('being a strong monarchist myself'); the amount of food needed to feed Britain; communal feeding centres ('call them British Restaurants'). Decent food for Britain was always a high priority; earlier, he had written to the Food Minister: 'The way to lose the war is to try to force the British public into a diet of milk, oatmeal, potatoes, etc., washed down on gala occasions with a little lime juice.' He argued with his Information Minister over the orders given to the populace in the event of invasion. He objected to telling them to 'stay put'. That was American slang. 'What is the matter with "stand fast" or "stand firm".' At the same time, he told the Dominions Office to go easy on propaganda about the imminent invasion threat. 'I do not see the object of spouting all this stuff unless it is thought the Dominions require to be frightened into doing their duty.'

Menzies now spoke with at least five different voices about Churchill, in descending order from public adulation to private condemnation. In speeches and broadcasts, he was hyperbolic in his praise; in the British War Cabinet, he directed his concerns towards the competence and intelligence of the generals, rather than Churchill or his strategy; to his colleagues in Canberra, he complained of Churchill's highhandedness; in private conversations, usually over dinner with leading disaffected conservatives, press proprietors, and great has-beens like Lloyd George, still at seventy-seven vaguely hoping for a call to save the nation, Menzies fuelled their doubts about Churchill's fitness for leadership; and in his diary, he was often angry and derisive. Nevertheless, in his criticisms, Menzies sounded a consistent theme: that Churchill's real trouble was that nobody had the courage to stand up to him.

High Commissioner Bruce was unimpressed by his Prime Minister's public performance. 'Menzies had been very indiscreet in private,' he wrote to his old correspondent, Dick Casey, in Washington, 'criticising and ridiculing practically everyone here from Churchill downward.' He had left the impression, Bruce said, 'that he would not mind coming back here and leading the Conservative Party himself'. By the time Bruce gave Casey this assessment in

September, Menzies was no longer leader of the conservative party in Australia.

Two issues stand out in the deterioration of relations between Churchill and Menzies: Greece and Ireland. As the leader of a nation with a quarter of its population proudly Irish, Menzies was distressed by Churchill's bitterness towards Ireland (Eire) and its head of government, Eamon De Valera, who had declared his country's neutrality. In 1937, De Valera had forsworn Ireland's nominal allegiance to George VI under the 1921 Treaty which Churchill had helped Lloyd George write. Menzies saw himself as just the man to bring about some kind of reconciliation when he told Churchill that he proposed to visit Dublin at the end of March. Churchill said: 'Never with my approval will you visit that wicked man.' Menzies found 'Dev' charming but intransigent, especially on the use of Irish ports by the Royal Navy. 'On the whole, with all my prejudices, I liked him and occasionally succeeded in evoking from him a sort of wintry humour.' Menzies recommended to Churchill that he should invite the Irish leader to London. Churchill gave him short shrift. Ireland's neutrality, he told Menzies, was the product of '700 years of hatred and six months of pure funk'. He dismissed Menzies' report as 'very readable', as Menzies acknowledged, 'a most damning comment'. Plainly hurt by the rejection of his honest labours, Menzies wrote in his diary: 'Winston is *not* a receptive or reasoning animal'.

Menzies had found Belfast more congenial than Dublin; Ulstermen were like 'the best Australians – improved Scotsmen'. They also shared his view of Empire loyalty to the King: 'When that King makes war and makes it, as on the present occasion, most justly, then I have never felt inclined as a representative of my own country to sit down and engage in vague speculation as to whether or not I should declare war,' he said in a speech which the Prime Minister of Northern Ireland, J. M. Andrews, described as 'one of the greatest ever heard in the Belfast Ulster Club'.

There was a growing gap between Menzies' public triumphs in Britain and his failure to advance Australia's interests. His Canberra colleagues, bewildered by the disasters in Greece, and fearing worse to come in North Africa, were made even more uneasy when he sought an extension of his leave of absence. He told them: 'I appear to be the only minister around the Prime Minister who will question any of his views or insist on points being examined, and as Australia has so much at stake it would be unwise of me to leave here in the middle of a crisis.'

Menzies' visit had achieved little for Australia, whatever he had done for his own reputation in Britain. He had tried to get aircraft sent to Australia, and British help to build them in Australia. Churchill was uncooperative. Menzies' colleagues were exasperated by his failure to secure British guarantees for Australian exports, 'essential for our war strength'. All that Menzies seemed able to obtain from the British Government and Churchill was 'repeated expressions of sympathy'. They sent a long list of 'indispensable requirements' to which Menzies replied with a mixture of impatience, self-pity and homesickness: 'You may be assured that I am doing all I can in most difficult and trying circumstances. Canberra is more peaceful than having bombs dropping around you in London.' He added: 'I will be glad to see the homely countenances of my colleagues once more.' He repeated by now his constant theme: 'I confess I have no great confidence in the Chiefs of Staff who allow Churchill to determine their strategy for them.'

Far from turning Churchill's attention towards Australia's region in the Far East, Menzies had identified himself and Australia even more closely with Churchill's Mediterranean, Middle Eastern, and Atlantic priorities. Menzies' divided loyalties were tested when he learnt that America proposed to move the bulk of the US Pacific Fleet to the Atlantic. 'My first impression was unfavourable,' Menzies told Fadden on 2 May, 'on the view that Japan might be tempted to cash in to a temporary Pacific problem'. But on reflection, Menzies again became the Australian spokesman for Churchill's Big Idea. 'What takes America nearer to war will keep Japan further from it,' he cabled Fadden. The American decision would 'strengthen the belief in Japan that the United States is determined not to allow the British Empire to be defeated, and would come into war to prevent it'.

Bringing to bear all his barrister's skill in arguing to a brief, Menzies even went so far as to suggest that an American naval shift to the Atlantic would actually help Australia. By sending its fleet to the Atlantic, he said, America would 'enable a much quicker release of British battle strength for the Far East if Japan entered the war'. Such were Churchill's powers to persuade Menzies that black was white. Menzies did at least manage to mount his old hobby horse about lack of consultation. The British War Cabinet secretary, Sir Alexander Cadogan, noted that 'Menzies made a stink about it'. Menzies' own version in his diary has him making 'great argument in War Cabinet. I protest against W.C. deciding what advice to offer USA regarding moving Pacific fleet (or a real section of it) to the Atlantic *without* reference to Australia, though I was in London!' Yet to Canberra, Menzies urged compliance: 'I feel that the entry of the United States into the war as a belligerent transcends in importance every other present issue and we must therefore be very careful *not* to frustrate the present proposal.' In the event, the Americans dropped what Cadogan described as 'that insane proposal', the result of one of Churchill's 'midnight follies'.

Here, then, on the very highest level of war strategy, was the essential and inescapable dilemma which Australia and its leaders faced at this stage of the war. Menzies, Fadden, and Curtin each confronted different aspects of the dilemma: how to reconcile the overwhelming demands of worldwide, long-term strategic objectives, predetermined in London and Washington, with Australia's immediate problems and interests, as perceived in Canberra. When we consider the pressures faced by the Australian politicians accountable to their own people, who were reading the mournful catalogue of disasters in their daily newspapers, we may at least acknowledge their readiness to serve the common cause. Yet as early as January, 1942, one of Churchill's inner military circle, Colonel Sir Ian Jacob, was to write in his diary: 'The Australian Government have throughout the war taken a narrow, selfish and at times craven view of events, in contrast to New Zealand.'

* * *

IT WAS NOW time for Menzies to face his critics at home. His turmoil of spirit is revealed in an account of a bizarre episode on the eve of his departure, recorded by another indefatigable diarist, Maurice Hankey. At seventy-four, Hankey was now a lord, a member of the Cabinet of which he had been secretary for so long, a hangover from the Chamberlain era, and the confidant of a coterie of Chamberlainite grumblers who cultivated Menzies as a potential ally in their ineffectual efforts to clip Churchill's wings. Hankey attended a farewell lunch for Menzies at Grosvenor House on 1 May 1941. In his diary, he wrote: 'After lunch, we heard someone running down Park Lane and, lo and behold, it was Menzies himself. He burst out at once about Churchill and his dictatorship and his War Cabinet of Yes men. "There is only one thing to be done," he said, "and that is to summon an Imperial War Cabinet and keep one of them behind, like Smuts in the last war, not as a guest but as a full member".'

Hankey consulted with the arch-appeaser, Sir John Simon, now Lord Chancellor, who advised: 'Get Menzies to bell the cat [Churchill] before he leaves tomorrow; he has become a great Imperial figure, has attended the War Cabinet, has a big stake in the war, and is entitled to speak his mind.' Hankey then 'managed to get Menzies on the telephone and asked him to tackle Churchill when he went to say good-bye'. Menzies told Hankey that he had already decided to do it. Hankey claimed: 'I begged him to urge Churchill to drop his dictatorial methods and to use his military and political advisers properly.' The rest was predictable anti-climax. Menzies informed Hankey that he had 'got no change out of Churchill'. Churchill's parting words to the Australian had been: 'You see the people by whom I am surrounded. They have no ideas, so the only thing to be done is to formulate my own ideas.'

The conspiracy against Churchill, such as it was, was stillborn. Hankey claimed that he gave Menzies a letter to deliver in person to the British Ambassador in Washington, Lord Halifax. In it, Hankey expressed his anxieties about Churchill's conduct of the war, and his hopes that Menzies would return to London as a member of the War Cabinet. Menzies' acceptance of this mission as a go-between among disgruntled ex-appeasers, is an extraordinary commentary on how his sense of priorities and his political judgement had become distorted.

After his three months in Britain, Menzies spent three days in Washington, including an hour with Roosevelt, who offered vague assurances that America 'would not stand by and see Australia attacked'. In his diary, he wrote: 'Roosevelt and Hull [Cordell Hull, US Secretary of State] agreed that we all ought to tell Japan where she gets off, but each of them stops short of actually instructing the USA Ambassador to say so.' Menzies thought that Roosevelt was hoping for 'an incident' which would 'get the USA into war and R. out of his foolish election pledges that "I will keep you out of war".'

If Menzies had been in a proper frame of mind to take it in, he received excellent advice on dominion leadership from Mackenzie King, already Prime Minister of Canada for fifteen years, going back to 1921. King dictated a lengthy account of his conversation with Menzies during his stay in Ottawa on 7 and 8 May, full of shrewd, amused, and generous observations of his impressive guest. King thought that Menzies was clearly obsessed with Churchill – the grandeur of his vision, the power of his personality, his impatience to get his own way on matters large and small, his dictatorship of the Yes men in his Cabinet. 'The one thing that seemed mostly in his mind, and which Churchill evidently had told him to discuss with me was the desire for a conference of Prime Ministers – some kind of Imperial Cabinet.' If Churchill had indeed asked Menzies to raise this idea with Mackenzie King, it must only have been with the fore-knowledge of King's response – he wouldn't have a bar of it. King told Menzies that, as far as he was concerned, offering Churchill advice on strategy would be 'the act of an impostor'. He would stay where he was needed – in Canada. 'I could not say what division might arise in the Cabinet or in the country while I was away. I believed my real service was helping to keep all united. If we failed in that, nothing else would much matter.' Perhaps in the weeks ahead, Menzies may have reflected how much better he might have fared had he taken King's advice to heart. But, as Mackenzie King wrote: 'I sensed the feeling that he would rather be on the War Cabinet in London than Prime Minister of Australia.'

Like Julius Caesar in the second half of Shakespeare's play, Churchill dominated the drama of Menzies' downfall off stage. The central experiences of his London visit – his public success and the impact of Churchill – had made him unfit for his real job in Australia. The cheers of the embattled British had gone to his head, and his obsession with Churchill was eating at his heart. 'A sick feeling of repugnance and apprehension grows in me as I near Australia,' Menzies wrote in the last entry of his overseas journal on 23 May. 'If only I could creep in quietly into the bosom of the family, and rest there.' He had flown across the Tasman Sea from New Zealand through a fierce storm. When he stepped ashore at the flying-boat base at Rose Bay, Sydney, he looked, according to Arthur Fadden, 'about as happy as a sailor on a horse'.

Fadden was no sensitive flower, but he was 'surprised at the cold reception he gave me'. This most unpretentious and easy-going of all Australian Prime Ministers thought that he had done a fair job as Menzies' stand-in, especially in the cooperative relationship he had established with John Curtin and the Labor members of the Advisory War Council. 'Looking back now,' Fadden wrote in 1969, after he had led the Country Party for eighteen years and served as Treasurer in the Menzies-Fadden Government from 1949 to 1958, 'I believe that Menzies' attitude could have resulted only from the fact that while he was abroad, he was informed that some of his own party members were becoming dissatisfied with his leadership and were hoping to bring about his downfall.'

On his way home, Menzies had received a letter from his Army Minister, Percy Spender, telling him 'how his political grave was being dug'. After an oratorical triumph in Sydney Town Hall soon after his homecoming, Menzies, aglow at his reception, strode over to Spender and said, 'Well, Percy, where is this grave you wrote about?' Spender: 'It's been dug all right, Bob. It's only waiting for you to be pushed into it.' Menzies' obsession with Churchill diminished his ability to assert his authority over his supporters. It distorted his perspective about the kind of leadership Australia needed. It drove his determination to get back to London. It jaundiced his view of Australian party politics; he blamed the system for his own deficiencies.

'This correspondent's job is nothing to me,' Churchill told A.B.
'Banjo' Paterson in South Africa, reporting on the Boer War,
1900. © Singley/Corbis

Above: 'The great Winston Churchill' celebrates his escape from the Boers in the town square at Durban in South Africa, December, 1899.

Hulton Archive/Getty

'I do believe that I am a glow-worm', Churchill at thirty.

Ernest H. Mills/Getty

Alfred Deakin, the first Australian Prime Minister to tangle with Churchill, 1907.

NLA an23302062

Churchill and Kaiser Wilhelm II observe German army manoeuvres in January, 1909. Churchill warned in 1908 that 'destruction of the most appalling and idiotic character' would result from war with Germany.

Hulton Archive/Getty

A volatile pair harnessed together. Lord John 'Jacky' Fisher, First Sea Lord, and Winston Churchill, First Lord of the Admiralty, 1915.

Hulton Archive/Getty

Above: Discredited and depressed, Churchill left the Admiralty in May, 1915. 'I thought he would die of grief,' said his wife Clementine.

Topical Press Agency/Getty

When this photograph was taken in October, 1915, Lloyd George was on the way up and Churchill the way out.

Hulton Archive/Getty

Above: William 'Billy' Hughes and General Sir John Monash (centre and centre right) visited the Australians on the western front a month after the Battle of Amiens and two months before the Armistice.
AWM E03851

The peacemakers of the British Empire delegation in Paris, 1919. *Front row left to right*: Lord Balfour, Lloyd George, W.M. Hughes, Lord Birkenhead, and W.S. Churchill.

AWM A02616

Churchill returns to the Conservative Party in October, 1924,
and to his surprise is made Chancellor of the Exchequer.

'Will the bloody duck swim?' Churchill on his way to the House
of Commons to deliver his 1928 Budget, which contained
further tariff concessions for Australian produce.

Churchill and his daughter, Sarah, at Chartwell, September, 1928.
The bricklayers' union made Churchill an honorary member.
Davis/Topical Press Agency/Getty

Churchill addresses the Indian Empire Society in London,
December, 1930, and puts himself in the political wilderness.
Fox Photos/Getty

Churchill as author – correcting the proofs of *Life of the Duke of Marlborough* in 1936. Keystone/Hulton Archive/Getty

First meeting of the Australian War Cabinet in Melbourne, 27 September 1939. *Left to right*: Senator George McLeay (Commerce), Sir Henry Gullett (External Affairs), R.G. Casey (Trade), R.G. Menzies (Prime Minister and Treasurer), G.A. Street (Defence), and F.G. Shedden (Secretary of the Defence Department). W.M. Hughes (Attorney General) was absent. Gullett and Street were later killed in a Canberra air crash in 1940. AWM 042822

A month before he became Prime Minister, Churchill met members of the RAAF in Britain. They were among 'The Few' in the Battle of Britain, August–September, 1940. Keystone/Getty

Churchill became Prime Minister on 10 May 1940. With him are Air Minister Sir Kingsley Wood (left) and Foreign Secretary Anthony Eden. H. F. Davis/Topical Press Agency/Getty

General Thomas Blamey
welcomes his Prime Minister,
R.G. Menzies, to the desert
front in February, 1941.
AWM 006121

Prime Minister Menzies in Palestine,
February, 1941, between General Thomas
Blamey (left) and General Sir John Lavarack,
GOC 7th Australian Division. AWM 005797

Menzies found
Churchill 'a
tempestuous
creature' when they
met at 10 Downing
Street in February,
1941. AWM 006414

Churchill laid the foundation for the Great Alliance at this meeting with Franklin Roosevelt on board HMS *Prince of Wales*, August, 1941. Fox Photos/Getty

Against doctor's orders, John Curtin addressed a war loan rally in Martin Place, Sydney, 18 February 1942. Hughes and Fadden are at right. Singapore had surrendered three days earlier.
AWM 042769

First meeting between Curtin and General Douglas MacArthur, Canberra, 26 March 1942. 'We two will see this thing through together,' MacArthur told Curtin. AWM 042774

General MacArthur at the Advisory War Council, March, 1942. *Left to right*: MacArthur, Curtin, Fadden, Chifley, and J. Beasley. AWM 136225

'The man-on-the-spot', Churchill with General Leslie Morshead near El Alamein, August, 1942. AWM 024764

MacArthur and Blamey meet with Australian soldiers. Neither man fully acknowledged the Australian military's role in the Japanese defeat at Kokoda. AWM 013422

'I feel I have a new friend in Australia,' Churchill said after he met with Dr H.V. Evatt in London, May, 1942. NLA vn3663732

Churchill with his favourite Australian, Richard Gardiner Casey, just before appointing him Governor of Bengal. Cairo, January, 1943. NLA vn4319600

'Mr Churchill fires every shot and feels every wound,' Curtin said after their London meeting in May, 1944.

Five Premiers of the Empire. *Left to right*: Mackenzie King (Canada), Jan Smuts (South Africa), Winston Churchill (United Kingdom), Peter Fraser (New Zealand), and John Curtin (Australia) at 10 Downing Street, London, May, 1944.

Josef Stalin, Harry Truman and Churchill at the last wartime summit in Potsdam, July, 1945. Churchill spent the next ten years urging a new summit to settle with the Soviet Union. AFP/Getty

'These proceedings are closed.' MacArthur looks on as Blamey signs for Australia, on board USS *Missouri* in Tokyo Bay, 2 September 1945. AWM 040969

Menzies often quoted Churchill as saying, 'My Goodness, you Australians do seem to play your politics with a fine 18th century flair'. Whatever Churchill meant, it explained nothing about Menzies' difficulties in 1941. Almost his first public words on his return, at a brief press conference at the Rose Bay terminal, were: 'It is a diabolical thing that anybody should have to come back and play politics, however clean and however friendly at a time like this.' He repeated the thought, 'the clean and friendly', stressed with trademark sarcasm, in an otherwise impressive performance at Sydney Town Hall two days later and in his report to the House of Representatives on 28 May, provoking Opposition interjections and jeers in a speech they had heard hitherto with approval and respect.

Churchill watched the Australian political scene with a mixture of condescension, contempt, and ignorance. He saw the root cause of Menzies' trouble as 'an opposition thirsting for local power'. The real cause, however, was Menzies' inability to find a way out of the parliamentary impasse produced by the 1940 federal elections. He sought London and imperial solutions for a problem which lay in Canberra – mostly in his own Cabinet and party. The two paths he tried – forming a national government, and taking himself off to London again to be a member of an Imperial War Cabinet – both proved dead-ends. Curtin blocked one, and Churchill blocked the other.

Churchill damned Australia to eternity – quite literally, given the enduring authority which posterity has granted to his war memoirs – for its failure to create a wartime national government. His most severe censure was reserved for the Curtin Labor Government in 1942. He wrote in *The Hinge of Fate*, the fourth volume of his history: 'It will always be deemed remarkable that in this deadly crisis when, as it seemed to them and their professional advisers, destruction was at the very throat of the Australian Commonwealth, they did not all join together in a common effort. But such was their party phlegm and rigidity that local politics ruled unshaken.' While this refers to events post-Pearl Harbor, many earlier references make it clear that the political situation throughout 1941 incurred Churchill's grave displeasure and, more seriously, influenced his attitude to life-and-death decisions affecting Australian troops. Churchill did not attempt to show how Australia's war effort was adversely affected by Menzies' failure to form a national government, or by Curtin's refusal to join one.

Churchill's condemnation of the Australian political parties amounted to a condemnation of the Parliament itself and, by extension, the electors of 1940 who had created it. In truth, the Australian Parliament of 1940–43 was the greatest in Australian history. The seventy-three members of the House of Representatives include ten prime ministers, past, present, or future – Hughes, Scullin, Page, Menzies, Fadden, Curtin, Forde, Chifley, Holt, and McEwen, as well as two future Labor leaders, Evatt and Arthur Calwell. In that sense, it spanned the government and political life of Australia from 1901 to 1968. Despite the numerical instability, this Parliament produced an effective transition from peace to war under Menzies, a useful interim government under Fadden, and the Curtin Labor Government, whose performance in organising Australia's effort for total war was to be endorsed by the Australian people with a record majority in 1943. No 'national' government, however cobbled together, could have matched these achievements.

Menzies had renewed his offer of an all-party national government in a cable to Curtin from London on 22 April. Curtin replied: 'The mere political formula of a National Government would not add one scrap to our war effort. Far from that, it would be the signal for disturbances in our political, industrial and civil life that would be as dangerous as they would be inevitable.' Churchill never grasped this fact.

A national government would not have united the nation; it would have split the Australian Labor Party. All Curtin's painful endeavours since 1935 would have gone for nought. One of the oldest planks in the Labor Platform was a prohibition on alliances with other parties; it had been the source of its early strength; the betrayals that had led to anti-Labor national governments during the First World War and the Depression sanctified it. As recently as 1940, the Labor Federal Conference had reaffirmed the prohibition. Significantly for 1941, the trade union movement vehemently opposed the idea. Everything in its traditions and experience, so bitterly endured in the Depression, revolted against the idea of Labor's political wing being bought off by a handful of Cabinet seats. Menzies saw these facts and, however grudgingly, accepted them. Churchill never did. With the national government option barred by reality, Menzies then went down the track he hoped would lead him back to London. It took him over the precipice.

If Menzies had not been unbalanced by his London experiences, there would have been nothing new in the Australian political situation which he could not have managed successfully. There were challenges and opportunities for genuine national leadership in abundance. The war situation was changing dramatically. Rommel was again threatening Egypt, but Tobruk held. Churchill ordered the occupation of French-held Syria before the Vichy administration could hand it over to the Germans; once again, the Australians bore the major burden, this time the 7th Division, with brilliant success. For the second time in a quarter of a century, Australian forces captured Damascus.

Overriding every other consideration, Hitler invaded Russia on 22 June 1941. 'The world will hold its breath,' said Hitler. 'If Hitler were to invade Hell, I would at least make a favourable reference to the Devil in the House of Commons,' said Churchill. As a direct consequence, Japan made the fateful decision to 'go south', and by July the Japanese army was occupying French Indochina, in collusion with the pro-Vichy colonial administration. These tremendous developments were, of course, full of danger for Australia. But the point here is that if Menzies were the national war leader he aspired to be, they should have consolidated, not undermined, his authority and prestige. The only new factor since Menzies' absence overseas was, as Curtin repeatedly pointed out when rejecting Menzies' renewed overtures for a coalition, 'the dissension between your Government and certain of its nominal supporters'.

Menzies put his case for an Imperial War Cabinet in the form of personal letters to Mackenzie King of Canada and Field Marshal Smuts of South Africa. But Mackenzie King had already told Menzies in Ottawa that he was not interested; and Smuts had declared the previous March: 'A Dominion Prime Minister's business is in his dominion, and Churchill's business is in London.' Menzies' letter, dated 3 July 1941, began: 'We all have the greatest admiration for the genius, personality and work of Churchill, but I was greatly struck in London . . .', followed by a catalogue of complaints: 'Churchill carries far too great an individual burden . . . The War Cabinet members have too much departmental work, involving heavy preoccupation with detail . . . There is inadequate consideration of long-range policy in relation to the winning of the war . . . The Dominions Secretary is not a member of the War Cabinet and is therefore little more than a channel of communication . . . Churchill being absorbed for long hours every day in the supremely important tasks of strategy and the leading and stimulating of the public mind, financial and economic questions which are of vast importance, not only now but in the post-war period, tend to slip into the background and to have somewhat spasmodic attention.'

To meet all these vast problems, Menzies proffered his solution: 'an Imperial War Cabinet in a real sense, meeting daily, thinking out and discussing large matters, and in which Churchill would have constructively critical colleagues, able to give him the support and advice which even the greatest man must have if he is to reach his highest effectiveness'. In such a Cabinet, he said, 'I believe that a Dominions Prime Minister should, if one is available, have a place.' Menzies did not presume to say who should fill this interesting role, but suggested a short meeting of as many dominion prime ministers as possible, in order to 'jointly exercise a powerful influence in reshaping the machinery of central control, and to secure effective Dominion representation in a British War Cabinet'. None of this, he hastened to say, 'would be calculated to weaken the position of the Leader'. On the contrary, Menzies said, 'I feel that he is so outstanding and important to all of us that he must be given the greatest possible help in such a way as to secure the maximum united effort on the part of all British countries'. As for his own role, Menzies concluded, 'my own political difficulties are considerable since I have a practically non-existent majority, but I would be prepared to take any political risk at home if, by going to London for the suggested conference, I could contribute to what I feel is an essential change'.

Smuts and King pricked Menzies' fantasy. Smuts drily observed that the threat of war in the Far East, Australia's own region, rendered the concentration of Dominion war leadership in London inappropriate. Mackenzie King repeated the arguments he had made to Menzies personally in Ottawa barely six weeks previously. He added that, while the burden carried by Churchill might be too heavy, he could only be relieved of it by his own action, or by that of the British Parliament and people. It was a shrewd thrust at Menzies, reminding him of the fragile source of his own authority. Menzies must have known that his letters would meet this negative response. It is hard to resist the conclusion that his real purpose was to stake the ground for his return to London.

Churchill himself killed off Menzies' proposal. He cabled on 19 August: 'It would not be possible for a Dominion Minister other than a Prime Minister to sit in the War Cabinet, as this would entail representation of all four Dominions and would be too large a permanent addition to our own numbers.' Further, Churchill said that 'there seems no chance that the other Dominions would agree to being represented in the War Cabinet by a Minister from a single Dominion.' He grumbled privately that malcontents like Menzies just wanted to leave him to make the speeches.

Menzies' fatal instinct to return to London was sharpened by a Japanese threat to march into Thailand. He dropped his plan for a morale-boosting tour of the state capitals, and called an urgent Cabinet meeting, which agreed that he should go to London. Menzies was now acutely aware of his political peril. Once again, he sought advice from Bruce in London. On 13 August he cabled: 'There has been a clamouring here by a disgruntled and personally hostile section of the press that I should resign from the Premiership and be sent to London as an ordinary Minister. I have pointed out to my colleagues that such a course would in my opinion be fatal, for I could scarcely hope to carry real authority or weight in the British War Cabinet if I had in fact been just rejected in my own country.'

He blamed the press 'recalcitrance' on newsprint rationing which he had introduced as part of his 'Prospectus for All-Out War' in June. Press resentment had encouraged 'petty revolts among a few members and the whole atmosphere has become murky'. Menzies concluded his cable to Bruce with a statement which revealed the torn state of his mind at the root of his troubles: 'If you will allow a personal note, *I believe I am more effective in London than here*, where at present a hail-fellow well-met technique is preferred to either information or reason.'

'Get here as soon as it is physically possible to do so,' Bruce replied within hours. Bruce's answer reflected his own resentment of Churchill's dominance: 'Out of a considerable experience of these people and knowledge of the personalities in the United Kingdom Government, I say without hesitation that any Minister of lesser authority than the Prime Minister would be able to accomplish little; and even you, notwithstanding the remarkable impression you created during your recent visit, would find yourself frustrated without the status of a Prime Minister.' In other words, get to London while you are still Prime Minister, before they can drop you.

Far from 'thirsting for local power', as Churchill believed, Curtin angered some in the Labor Party by the cooperation he gave Menzies at this time. Evatt was restless and contradictory, criticising Curtin for his weakness, yet writing a letter to Menzies offering to serve in a national government. The root of the matter was Menzies' inability to command the loyalty of a significant number of his own party followers, in and out of Cabinet. Menzies claimed in his memoirs, *Afternoon Light*, that Curtin had told him: 'You know, old man, I was quite happy about you as Prime Minister. So were my fellows. Had you continued as you were going, we would have taken no steps to defeat you. But when your own people rejected you, my people decided to attack, and nothing could hold them.' 'Afternoon Light' itself is a cricketing term to describe the clarity that falls on the cricket ground in the last hour or so of play; and while Menzies' recollection is consistent enough with Curtin's character, it oversimplifies the political drama of August and September 1941.

In August, Menzies sought Curtin's approval for another London mission. In the Advisory War Council, Curtin tentatively agreed; but at a meeting of the Shadow Cabinet, the Parliamentary Labor Executive, on 21 August, his deputy, Frank Forde, whom Curtin had defeated by one vote for the Parliamentary leadership in 1935, warned him that the Caucus would never wear it. Evatt branded the whole idea as a stunt to get Menzies out of the firing line – not from his Labor opponents, but from his own followers. Caucus then adopted a recommendation from Shadow Cabinet: 'It is essential for Australia to have its Prime Minister here to direct the administration in the organization of a total war effort'.

Menzies had been shattered by the exposure of his vulnerability when he brought his proposal to return to London before the Parliament – first in a torrid secret session on 20 August, and in open session next day. Ominously, his main support came from Billy Hughes who, at the very time, was going around the corridors of Parliament House saying, not so privately, that 'Menzies couldn't lead a flock of homing pigeons'. Menzies may have allowed himself a wry smile as Hughes declaimed: 'He is a man who, apart from being Prime Minister, is eminently qualified to propound to such a conclave the views of Australia. He can hold his own with members of the British War Cabinet. Honourable members are able to judge of his qualifications. They know him.'

Barely three months before Pearl Harbor, Billy Hughes, the senior statesman of Australia and the Empire, saw Australia's situation in these terms:

MR HUGHES: At this time, London is the only place from which Australia can be guided . . . The British War Cabinet directs the fleet that has shielded us from the aggressor for 150 years. If we are to convince the War Cabinet that such naval forces as will be adequate to ensure our safety should be sent to the Pacific, the task calls for the services of the best representative that Australia can send . . . We are a garrison of a great outpost of Empire, which we hold for the white races. Australia is a vital strategic post of Empire. Pointing out those facts, the Prime Minister, clothed with the authority of the whole Parliament would put our case convincingly to the British War Cabinet.

MR CURTIN: Notwithstanding an equality with Great Britain in this struggle, the right honourable gentleman contends that Great Britain will not listen to our needs unless we send the Prime Minister himself to London.

This debate sealed Menzies' fate. Fadden moved to adjourn. To Opposition cries of 'No gag', the most public of Menzies' detractors on the government side, William McCall from New South Wales, shouted: 'I will not allow the gag to be applied in this debate.' Fadden was forced to withdraw his adjournment motion, and the debate went on, increasingly bitter against Menzies. The Government had lost control of the business of the House. From that moment, a defeat on a substantive matter, like the granting of supply or the forthcoming Budget itself, seemed inevitable. Menzies had been defeated and humiliated in parliament on an issue which involved, in almost all its facets, his relationship with Churchill.

The end came quickly. The day after the debate, Menzies made his last throw: he informed Curtin that he was willing to serve in an all-party Cabinet of ten, five from each side, under Curtin as Prime Minister. When the Labor Caucus rejected this offer on 26 August, Curtin replied that the offer itself was an admission that 'you are not able as Prime Minister to give stable government'. Menzies threw in the sponge. With no show of solidarity forthcoming from his Cabinet, where he met 'a chorus of silence', according to Percy Spender, or from a party meeting which Arthur Coles described as a lynching, Menzies advised the Governor-General, Lord Gowrie, to commission Arthur Fadden as his successor.

Churchill, oblivious to his own role in Menzies' downfall, sent his commiserations:

While I scrupulously abstain from all interference in Australian politics, I cannot resist telling you with what sorrow I have learned of your resignation. You have been at the helm during these two terrible years of storm, and you were with us during its most anxious time for Australia. We are all very grateful to you for the courage you showed and the help you gave. I am the gainer by our personal friendship. I went through a similar experience when I was removed from the Admiralty at a moment when I could have given the Anzacs a fair chance of victory at the Dardanelles. It is always a comfort in such circumstances to feel sure one has done one's duty and one's best.

The Gallipoli parallel, with its hint of a comeback, was not so far-fetched, as Menzies' subsequent career would show. For the present, however, Menzies told his secretary he would 'lay me down and bleed a while'. In a paradox worthy of Gilbert and Sullivan, Churchill helped keep Menzies in Australian politics by personally keeping him out of British politics. In October, when the Fadden Government had succumbed, Lord Gowrie wrote to Conservative friends in London, suggesting they find Menzies a seat in the House of Commons because his 'talents were being wasted in Australia'. They sounded out Churchill in his capacity as Conservative Party leader since Chamberlain's death in November 1940. Churchill didn't like the idea one bit. He told Menzies' Tory backers: 'It would be unwise of Menzies to leave Australia at the present time . . . he may play a far greater part in moulding the future there than would be possible for a newcomer to political life here.' Churchill succeeded in keeping Menzies in Australia. He was to be less successful at keeping the AIF in Tobruk.

18

'How different the Australians seem'

June–October, 1941

Churchill was as determined to keep the 9th Australian Division in Tobruk as Rommel was to get them out. From June to October 1941, Churchill waged a bruising battle against the governments of Menzies, Fadden, and then Curtin, to prevent its relief and replacement. It was the most serious dispute between Churchill and Australia until the fall of Singapore; and, for its long-lasting influence on Churchill's attitude towards Australia, one of the most significant of the war.

Tobruk had become the most powerful symbol of British resistance to Hitler since the Battle of Britain. By mid-1941, it was the only place on earth where British forces were not only standing against the Germans, but attacking and repulsing them. The Royal Navy and Air Force sustained the largely Australian defence. The Australian commander – 'Ali Baba Morshead and his 20,000 thieves' to Lord Haw Haw – believed in defence by attack. His standing order was the Churchillian 'No surrender, no retreat'. From behind their double defence lines around Tobruk the Australians kept the Germans off-balance, by attacking beyond the perimeter with nightly patrols in strength. Between 13 April and 4 May, the defenders repelled three fierce German assaults, not only saving Tobruk but blunting Rommel's thrust towards Egypt. Rommel himself, watching some Australian prisoners being marched off, noted: 'immensely big and powerful men, who without question, represented an elite formation of the British Empire'. Churchill signalled Morshead: 'The whole Empire is watching your steadfast and spirited defence of this important outpost of Egypt with gratitude and admiration.'

Churchill had good reason to be grateful. Tobruk was vital to the credibility of his strategy with Roosevelt, and he made the most of it. 'All questions of cutting the loss are ruled out,' he told the President. 'Tobruk must be held not as a defensive position, but as an invaluable bridgehead on the flank of any by-pass advance on Egypt.' In the same message to Roosevelt in which he had noted the Anzacs fighting all day at Thermopylae and forecast failure in Greece, he wrote: 'The magnet of Tobruk is exercising its powerful attractive influence and we are hoping both to reinforce our Army from the south and to harry, if not cut, hostile communications across the Mediterranean. In this theatre, we shall, I think, come through.'

Holding Tobruk became even more important to Churchill after Hitler's invasion of the Soviet Union. Churchill, recalling the fate of Napoleon, felt instinctively that Hitler had bitten off more than he could chew – if only the Russians could hold on until the winter. The experts around him predicted a rapid Soviet collapse, and the events of July and August seemed to prove them right. Their fear, shared by Churchill, was that the southernmost of the three massive German army groups could drive through to the Caucasus and threaten the whole British position in the Middle East. These fears must be borne in mind when judging Churchill's attitude to proposals for the relief of the Australians at Tobruk.

Even apart from Tobruk, the imperial importance of the Australian contribution to Churchill's strategy is demonstrated in his memoranda on the availability of troops to send to Wavell in March and June 1941. He told Wavell that it would be impossible to send more troops from Britain 'because we have to go round the Cape. The main accretion of this Army must come from India, Australasia and South Africa, with later on, munitions from the United States.' The most that Wavell could expect from Britain, where thirty-two divisions stood on guard against invasion, was 'three or four divisions'. Throughout this story, it must always be remembered that when Churchill was arguing the toss about this or that division for the Middle East or the Far East, he was always holding, with bulldog tenacity, his thirty or forty divisions in Britain, against a German invasion which had become highly doubtful by mid-1941. Australia and New Zealand were providing more than half of Wavell's infantry and a third of his total force. From these perspectives, it is easy to see why Churchill grasped as many Australian divisions as he could. Without them, his Big Idea might have fallen apart.

The British military historian Corelli Barnett wrote in 1960: 'Historically the Western Desert campaign constitutes the last act of the British Empire as a great independent, and united, power.' But in 1941, the imperial duty was unevenly spread. Of the dominions, only the Australian and New Zealand divisions had been in constant combat. Canada, completely secure as the neighbour of the United States, held its five divisions on guard in Britain. The forces of South Africa were legally prevented from service outside the continent of Africa despite the high profile and praise given by Churchill to its Prime Minister, General Jan Smuts. Churchill always made generous allowance for the racial and political constraints upon Canada and South Africa. New Zealand stood at the summit of Churchill's estimation, and enjoyed its reputation as 'more English than the English'. Only the Australians aroused Churchill's resentment, whenever they attempted to exercise a measure of independence. Churchill prejudiced even the King: 'How different the Australians seem to be to any of the other Dominions,' George wrote in his diary. 'In Australia, they are always being critical.'

CHURCHILL HAD NOW lost confidence in his chief commander in the Middle East. At this time, Wavell was juggling his resources between at least five different operations from North Africa to Persia (Iran). In Churchill's eyes, however, the progress of the 7th Australian

Division under Major General John Lavarack in Syria, Wavell's success in putting down a pro-German coup in Iraq, and restoring the Lion of Judah, the Emperor Haile Selassie, to his Ethiopian throne, were insufficient gains to set against the disasters of North Africa, Greece, and Crete – all the result of Churchill's own decisions. On 22 June, the day Hitler invaded Russia, Wavell received a message from Churchill: 'I have come to the conclusion that public interest will best be served by appointment of General Auchinleck to relieve you in command of armies of Middle East.' Wavell was shaving when brought the news. 'The P.M. is right. It needs a fresh eye and a new man,' he commented and continued his shave. It was to be a straight swap of commands – Sir Claude Auchinleck, the commander-in-chief in India, came to Cairo; Wavell went to India. Churchill refused Wavell's request for a short home leave; Wavell's deputy, General Thomas Blamey, who was now describing himself to the Australian Government as 'the fifth wheel in the Middle East command', was the only general to bother to go to the airfield to see Wavell off to Delhi.

During Wavell's last days in charge, Blamey had discussed with him his concerns about the dispersal and deterioration of the AIF forces in the Middle East. The 6th Division was recuperating from its ordeals in Greece and Crete. Most of the 7th Division was in Palestine and Syria, completing its campaign against the Vichy French. Another brigade of the 7th Division was in Tobruk, with the 9th Division. The 7th Australian Cavalry Regiment was garrisoning Cyprus. Eleven smaller units were scattered across the vast area of Wavell's Middle East command. Blamey argued that the comparative lull in North African fighting, following Operation Battle Axe, provided an opportunity for the concentration of the AIF into a more effective fighting force. Blamey reminded Wavell that he commanded the AIF under a charter which was a formal agreement between the British and Australian governments, as equal partners in the Empire. The basic principle of the agreement was that the AIF should operate as a single force under Australian command. Now was the time to fulfil the agreement. The first step, he argued, should be the relief and replacement of the AIF in Tobruk.

As the dispute over Tobruk developed, Churchill interpreted Australia's request for relief almost entirely in terms of Australian domestic politics. Yet the three Australian prime ministers involved in the dispute acted from June to October on the unanimous advice of their military advisers, in Tobruk, in Cairo, and at Victoria Barracks, Melbourne. Churchill never acknowledged this fundamental fact. In all his recriminations, at the time of the dispute and in his post-war accounts, Churchill insisted that politics, not tactics, lay at the root of Australia's conduct over the relief of Tobruk.

It was Menzies who first made the connection between the Australian electorate and the fate of the Australians in Tobruk. When Battle Axe petered out, Menzies cabled Blamey in Cairo: 'Are you satisfied that the garrison at Tobruk can hold out?' He told Blamey that the London authorities 'constantly underestimate the enemy'. Menzies said that 'a disaster at Tobruk, coming on top of those in Greece and Crete, might have far-reaching effects on public opinion in Australia'.

Blamey never visited Tobruk to see things for himself. This obviously weakened the force of his arguments. In fact, the first requests for the relief of Tobruk came from Morshead. When Auchinleck took over from Wavell, Morshead flew to Cairo for consultations. The first encounter between Auchinleck and his Australian commanders did not go well. Morshead expressed his concern at the garrison's diminishing ability to resist a sustained German assault. They had been fighting without let-up since March, subject to air and artillery attack day and night; morale was still excellent, but their health was declining, Morshead told the commander-in-chief. Auchinleck seemed sceptical about Morshead's views. Morshead's opinion of Auchinleck was that 'he suffered from an inferiority complex and was a terribly bad picker [of commanders in the field]'. Blamey's chief of staff, Brigadier Sydney Rowell, recorded that Auchinleck began with 'a crack at our indiscipline'. For his part, Auchinleck thought that 'old Blamey' derived his ideas about Army concentration from the western front in the First World War, 'quite inapplicable to modern mobile warfare in the desert'.

'Old Blamey' persisted. On 18 July, he put his request in writing to Auchinleck: 'The strain of continuous operations is showing signs of affecting the troops. The Commander of the Garrison [Morshead] informs me he considers the average loss of weight to be approximately a stone per man . . . Recovery from minor wounds and sicknesses is markedly slower recently. It may be anticipated that within the next few months, a German attack may be made on the garrison and by then at the present rate its capacity for resistance would be very greatly reduced.' The second half of Blamey's letter to Auchinleck stressed the principle that the Australian troops should operate as a single force. 'Because the needs of the moment made it necessary, the Australian Government has allowed this principle to be disregarded . . . during the present lull in active operations, action should be taken to implement this as far as possible.' By coupling his wider objective for AIF concentration with the immediate relief of Tobruk, Blamey gave Auchinleck and Churchill the opening they wanted to resist his demands. The Australians' mistake throughout the dispute was their failure to concentrate on their strongest point: the exhaustion of the 9th Division, and its reduced ability to maintain the siege.

Menzies compounded the mistake when he decided to go to Churchill over the heads of the British generals; he couched the case for AIF concentration in terms of Australian public opinion and Australia's national aspirations. He began by saying: 'We regard it as of first class importance that, now that the Syrian Campaign has concluded, Australian troops in the Middle East should be aggregated into one force.' Menzies told Churchill that this would 'give an opportunity for refreshment, restoration of discipline and re-equipment after strenuous campaigns'. Churchill could hardly be expected to be impressed by such an argument when making harsh choices about priorities amidst all his difficulties of mid-1941. Even less would Menzies' next point have impressed Churchill with any sense of urgency: 'It would also give immense satisfaction to the Australian people for whom there is great national value and significance in knowing that all Australian soldiers in any zone form one Australian unit.' Churchill never got it out of his head that the

Australian call for the relief of Tobruk was politically motivated. Menzies had put it there first.

At first, Auchinleck seemed to accept Australia's case. In his discussions with Blamey, he agreed as a first instalment to send a Polish brigade to replace the AIF's 18th Brigade, which would rejoin the 7th Division in Palestine. Auchinleck then flew off to London, to find that Churchill had other ideas altogether. As he told his emissary in Cairo, the British Minister, Oliver Lyttelton, 'I particularly stimulated Auchinleck not to prejudice the defence of Tobruk by making a needless relief.' Churchill stiffened Auchinleck's resistance, not only against any further relief at Tobruk but also to Blamey's idea of regrouping the AIF. Back in Cairo, Blamey found Auchinleck a changed man. He was under intense pressure from Churchill for a new desert offensive. There could be no further changes at Tobruk, he told Blamey; the 9th Division must stay where it was. On 16 August, Blamey wrote to Menzies: 'The British Staff in command do not like it and have never done. They like to juggle divisions as they wish to.' According to Blamey, getting an Australian unit back from the British was 'like prising open the jaws of a crocodile'. Blamey was unaware that Churchill was the real stumbling block. He was, however, well aware of Menzies' political difficulties and, thanking him for his 'solid backing', wrote 'I hope you will come out of it strengthened. There will always be some curs baying at the moon.'

In his war memoirs, Churchill slanted his account of the wrangle over Tobruk by beginning it with the downfall of Menzies. By this process of compression and selection, characteristic of his war memoirs whenever he wrote about Australia, he left Menzies out of it altogether, casting Fadden and Curtin as the villains of the piece. Yet Menzies had made the first request as early as 20 July, and had repeated it more urgently in a cable of 19 August, ten days before he handed over to Fadden. Churchill also ignored Blamey's arguments and agreements with Wavell and Auchinleck going back to the end of June. Thus Churchill portrays an Australian policy – initiated by its commander-in-chief, solidly backed for two months by Menzies and the Army Minister Percy Spender – as 'a sharp divergence harmful to our war effort', made by Fadden's new government 'under hard pressure from its opponents'.

'I am pretty sure the Australians will play the game if the facts are put before them squarely,' Churchill wrote to Auchinleck on 6 September. 'We do not want either your supply of Tobruk or your other combinations to be hampered. If meeting this demand would do this, let me have the facts to put to them. Australia would not tolerate anything shabby.' Auchinleck's game was to play Blamey's demands for the relief of Tobruk against Churchill's demands for a new desert offensive. In response to Churchill's message, Auchinleck said: 'I propose to abandon the idea of a further large-scale relief of Australian personnel in Tobruk.'

Blamey was furious. He told Spender: 'The Englishman is a born casuist. A plan was made for the relief. Everyone agreed . . . Then a crop of reasons were advanced and the C-in-C [Auchinleck] even went so far as to claim that the relief was not a feasible proposition . . . The real point at the back of the objections to the relief is that the Australians have great fighting capacity. They believe here that they would hang on in any event, but that if they come out, they must be thoroughly rested, and this will reduce the forces immediately available by a division.' Blamey then put the ball firmly in his Government's court:

> The matter is one for the Australian Government to decide, but I fervently hope our Government will take a strong stand on the question. If I lose this battle, I will have very little hope of being able to retain the Australian formations intact in the future, and I am convinced that they will make a force second to none if they can be placed so as to operate as an Australian force.

Blamey described himself as 'the most hated man in the Middle East'. His biographer John Hetherington, an Australian war correspondent on the scene, recorded this exchange:

BLAMEY: Gentlemen, I think you don't understand the position. If I were a French or an American commander making this demand, what would you say about it?

AUCHINLECK: But you're not.

BLAMEY: That is where you are wrong. Australia is an independent nation. She came into the war under certain definite agreements. Now, gentlemen, in the name of my Government, I demand the relief of these troops.

Blamey cabled Fadden on 4 September: 'The position causes me grave concern.' There were no difficulties about the relief of the garrison, he said, that 'cannot be overcome with the will to do so'. There were fresh British and South African formations available to replace the Australians. 'But if relief is not insisted on now, decline in the fighting value of the 9th Division will be considerable and recovery correspondingly long. Should the force be attacked with strength and determination after one or two months' further decline, it will not be fit to withstand such attack, and catastrophe is possible.'

Fadden immediately cabled Churchill. He recapitulated the Australian representations, made by Menzies on 20 July, 7 August and 19 August, and the undertakings given by Auchinleck. Further delay would move the withdrawal to a more dangerous time in late October. 'In view of decline of health resistance of troops and availability of fresher troops,' he said, 'I must reiterate request of my predecessor [Menzies] that directives be issued by you to Commander-in-Chief [Auchinleck] to give effect to our desires.' Fadden told Churchill:

Parliament is meeting at the middle of the month and it is my desire to make a statement when withdrawal has been completed and that reconcentration has been carried out. This is a vital question here and should any catastrophe occur to Tobruk garrison through further decline and inability to withstand a determined attack, there would be grave repercussions.

Fadden blundered by invoking Parliament. He gave Churchill two handles to his argument: security and politics. First, Churchill pointed out that the withdrawal and replacement could not possibly be completed in time for the meeting of the Australian Parliament in mid-September; any reference in Parliament, or anywhere else for that matter, 'might lead to heavy air attacks on Tobruk Harbour and along the coast at the time when your troops would be withdrawing'. Second, by putting the issue in the context of a parliamentary debate, Fadden confirmed Churchill's rooted belief that the whole business was political – and party-political at that. Churchill was never above a little moral blackmail to get his own way, and his message to Fadden of 11 September 1941 was a masterpiece of that particular art form. If Fadden still insisted that Australian troops must be relieved, he said, orders would be issued accordingly 'irrespective of the cost entailed and injury to future prospects'. But, Churchill thundered:

> I trust, however, that you will weigh very carefully the immense respon-
> sibility which you would assume before history by depriving Australia
> of the glory of holding Tobruk till victory was won, which otherwise, by
> God's help, will be theirs forever.

Fadden had not worked his way up from a fifteen-year-old billy-boy to a gang of canecutters in North Queensland to be overawed by 'Churchill's flowery phrases', as he put it euphemistically in his autobiography. He analysed and rejected Churchill's cable point by point, and restated all the arguments made to Churchill, Wavell, and Auchinleck since June, and even going back to the undertakings given about the use of the AIF in March 1940. He concluded:

> I am bound to request that the relief of the 9th Division and the recon-
> centration of the A.I.F. be proceeded with. Any reverse suffered by the
> garrison of Tobruk, in the light of reports and requests that have been
> made over an extended period, would have far-reaching effects. We do
> not consider that the military considerations put forward by the
> Commander-in-Chief outweigh the case for the relief of the garrison.

The curtness of Churchill's reply to Fadden on 15 September showed his anger: 'Orders will at once be given in accordance with your decision.' His message to Auchinleck on 17 September stated: 'I am grieved at Australian attitude, but I have long feared the dangerous reactions in Australian and world opinion of our seeming to fight all our battles in the Middle East only with Dominion troops.'

If Fadden or Blamey thought that ended the matter, they misjudged their man. Churchill kept silent until a brigade group of the 9th Division had been successfully withdrawn. Then, on 30 September, he unleashed what amounted to a threat to prosecute Fadden before the bar of history. He related how he had 'prevented only with difficulty' Auchinleck's resignation on the extraordinary ground that he had lost the confidence of the *Australian Government*! Nevertheless, Churchill said: 'I still hope that you will reconsider your decision that the last two Australian Brigades [of the 9th Division] must be pulled out of Tobruk without reference to the great impending operation by which we hope all will be relieved.' Although he himself had delayed the relief since July, Churchill now pleaded: 'Every day's delay in delivering the attack will make our task more formidable. Everything points to the first days of November, and the period during which the remaining Australian Brigades would be involved is very short. Australian troops have borne the burden of Tobruk and we should all deeply regret that they should be cut out of the honour.' Almost as if rehearsing the case he would make in his war history, Churchill told Fadden:

Believe me, everyone here realizes your political embarrassment, with a majority of only one. Nevertheless, Australia might think this is a time to do and dare. We have been greatly pained here by the suggestion, not made by you, but implied, that we have thrown an undue burden on the Australian troops. The debt to them is immense but the Imperial [i.e. British] forces have suffered more casualties actually and relatively . . . Therefore we feel we are entitled to count upon Australia to make every sacrifice necessary for the comradeship of the Empire. But please understand that at whatever cost your orders about your troops will be obeyed.

'I was astounded at the Australian Government's decision,' Churchill wrote to the British Minister in Cairo, Oliver Lyttelton, 'being sure it would be repudiated by Australia if the facts could be made known. Allowances must be made for a government with a majority of only one faced by a bitter Opposition, parts of which at least are isolationist in outlook.' This interpretation of the Australian position had become an obsession with Churchill, clouding his judgement; it was destined to distort his relations with Australia in the worst crisis of Australia's war.

Churchill carried his resentment through to his dealings with the new government about to be formed in Canberra. Whatever Churchill may have thought about the Australian way of conducting politics, everybody in Canberra, not least Fadden himself, realised that the Fadden Government was living on borrowed time from the day of its birth. Curtin's statement on 2 September was its death knell: 'If disintegration and dissension among our political opponents or the ill-conceived policies on their part result in a call being made to Labor, then we are ready to govern.' His worst fear during 1941 had been that some of his more eager or ambitious colleagues, such as Evatt, would wreck the Labor Party by grabbing minority government before Labor was ready to govern. When Curtin said at last that Labor was ready to govern, it was effectively a notice to quit – and Fadden knew it. He had 'reigned like Noah's Flood for 40 days and 40 nights'. On 3 October, after a debate on Fadden's Budget, the House of Representatives voted to put Labor into power. The crucial votes came from the two independent members, Arthur Coles and Alex Wilson. Whatever their private motives (and Coles was especially resentful of the UAP's treatment of his friend, Menzies) they both believed that all combinations short of a national government had been exhausted, and that it was time to give Labor its chance. If that too proved unworkable, then there was only one recourse left – dissolution of the Parliament and a general election. That option would have been open to Fadden, who rejected the idea of a divisive election campaign which was bound to end in his defeat anyway. The change of government effected by the House of Representatives in October 1941 was a supreme moment in the history of the Australian parliamentary system.

How far Churchill was astray in his assessment of Australian politics is shown by Fadden's own retrospect in his memoirs, writing as the man most entitled to feel aggrieved by the outcome:

> Looking back, although I did not see it so clearly at the time, the defeat of the Fadden Government after forty days and forty nights of office, may be said to have unforeseen advantages for Australia as well as for the Labor Party. With the outbreak of war in the Pacific, the most far-reaching measures had to be taken. Many of these would have been very difficult for a non-Labor Government in an evenly-divided Parliament to have undertaken without splitting the nation.

On the very night his government fell, Fadden framed a reply refusing yet another request from Churchill to delay further relief of Tobruk. Before sending it, he consulted with Curtin, who approved. Still, Churchill would not give up. A week after the Curtin Government had been sworn in on 7 October 1941, and after what he called 'a suitable interval', Churchill cabled Curtin:

> I feel it right to ask you to consider once again the issue raised in my telegram to your predecessor. I have heard again from General Auchinleck that he would be greatly helped and convenienced if the remaining Australians [two brigades of the 9th Division] could stay in Tobruk until the result of the approaching battle is decided. I will not repeat the arguments which I have already used, but I will only add that if you felt able to consent, it would not expose your troops to any undue or invidious risks, and would at the same time be taken very kindly as an act of comradeship in the present struggle.

It was, of course, an impossible ask, and Churchill must have known it, despite his message to Auchinleck on 14 October: 'It may be that the new Government will be willing to give you the easement you desire.' Churchill was asking Curtin, at the outset of his prime ministership, to repudiate Menzies as much as Fadden, and his own endorsement of the decision of the Prime Minister he had just replaced. It would have meant repudiating Blamey, the senior general in the field, as well as the Australian Chiefs of Staff, the permanent head of the Defence Department, and everyone else among the Government's military advisers, after four months of argument between London, Cairo, and Canberra. To the inevitable refusal, Churchill replied curtly on 26 October: 'Relief is being carried in accordance with your decision which I greatly regret.' Thereafter, Churchill would portray Curtin's reaffirmation as the crucial Australian refusal. He perhaps gave a hint of what was in store in his words to Auchinleck: 'I should be glad for the sake of Australia and history if they would do this.'

By the end of October, the 9th Division in Tobruk had been replaced by a British division. On the last night of the operation, the relief transports came under severe German air attack, and had to turn back before reaching Tobruk Harbour. The 2/13 Australian Battalion could not be taken away and remained in Tobruk. On 18 November, Auchinleck launched his long-awaited offensive (Operation Crusader) and, despite Rommel's counterattacks on Tobruk, drove the Afrika Korps out of Cyrenaica, back to the positions from which it had started nine months previously. Auchinleck announced to Churchill that the siege of Tobruk had ended on 7 December 1941 – the day of Pearl Harbor: 'I am as relieved as Tobruk.'

Churchill's intransigence over Tobruk undoubtedly reflected the immense pressures he was under. It was more than his rule of 'never give way in matters large or small'. For the whole duration of the dispute, from July to October 1941, Churchill was putting intense pressure on Auchinleck to take the offensive against Rommel. His urgency was increased by his knowledge, through Ultra intelligence, of a German build-up. He gives the key in the paragraph with which he introduces the episode in *The Grand Alliance,* the third volume of his war memoirs. There, Churchill connects his arguments with Auchinleck and Australia in this way: 'I have set out the military discussion about the delay in the offensive, and I must record my conviction that General Auchinleck's four and a half months' delay in engaging the enemy in the desert was alike a mistake and a

303

misfortune.' He immediately adds a bridge in his narrative: 'This Chapter must also include the account of differences with the Australian Government, whose brave troops played a vital part in the whole defence of Egypt.' By this device, Churchill implied that the relief of the Australians at Tobruk had delayed and weakened Auchinleck's offensive. He never admitted that Rommel's strength in North Africa was the result of the Greek diversion, for which he was completely responsible.

Given his preoccupations, Churchill must have seen Australian demands as a distraction and irritation. At this time, he was a man on the edge. At a meeting to discuss a mission to Moscow about to be undertaken by Lord Beaverbrook, he lashed out at all and sundry. A junior minister, Harold Balfour, who was present, reported to the inveterate gossip and diarist Henry 'Chips' Channon, MP, who recorded: 'Churchill began to abuse everybody and everything . . . He attacked the Army, said it always refused to fight . . . Always wants more divisions, more equipment.' Churchill, according to Channon, then said 'we were at war with almost every country, including Australia'.

Churchill had raised the Tobruk question from a rational military argument into a bruising emotional issue. Paul Hasluck, in his official history, put it this way: 'Churchill's appeal was now undoubtedly an appeal reaching above a question of military judgement. It was an appeal to the Australian Government to forgo independent judgement and to accept British leadership in the interests of Empire cooperation.'

Who was right about Tobruk in 1941? The official Australian war historian Barton Maughan wrote: 'Either Government might have been proved wrong: the British, if Crusader had failed; the Australian, if the German Air Force had fought a major battle to prevent the relief.' When Churchill came to justify himself in his war memoirs, he exaggerated 'dangers and losses to our cause'. None of the disasters feared, either by Blamey and Morshead on one side, or Churchill and Auchinleck on the other, eventuated. Both sides ignored the fact that changed circumstances rendered a reasonable request in July a risky one in October. But Churchill caused the delay.

It is quite likely that if Menzies had remained Prime Minister he would have finessed the dispute sufficiently to have allowed the 9th Division to remain until Auchinleck's Operation Crusader relieved Tobruk in December. Blamey's belief that the Australian 9th could not sustain another attack was never tested, although the prominent part that the remaining AIF battalion played in the final battle in November may suggest otherwise. We do know, however, that the 9th Division lived to fight another day. It may be, as Churchill said, that Fadden had 'deprived them of the glory of holding Tobruk till victory was won'. But, a year later, when Churchill found a winning general in Bernard Montgomery, the re-formed and revitalised 9th played a decisive part in the greatest desert victory of all – the Battle of El Alamein.

Churchill presented his case to posterity with his usual skill, adopting a stance of reluctant candour. 'It has given me pain to have to relate this incident,' he wrote in *The Grand Alliance*. It would have been impossible to suppress it, he wrote, with the implication that Australia had something to hide. But, he declared, 'The Australian people have a right to know what happened and why.' He conceded that 'apart from the limitations of their rigid party system', the Australian governments 'had little reason to feel confidence at this time in British direction of the war'. Then, with that true Churchillian touch which could disarm his severest critics, he wrote:

> We can never forget the noble impulse which had led Australia to send her only three complete divisions, the flower of her manhood, to fight in the Middle East, or the valiant part they played in all its battles.

The Tobruk dispute continued to rankle with Churchill, and set the tone for the rancour over the return of the AIF after the fall of Singapore. That is the real tragedy of the Tobruk affair of 1941 for Churchill and Australia.

19

'Sinister twilight'
June–December, 1941

Churchill's worst nightmare was that the United States might still stay out of the war if Japan limited its attacks to the British Empire in Asia. Almost as troubling was the second-worst case – America at war with Japan, but not Germany. He had stripped the Empire's Far Eastern defences to fight in the Middle East, and had kept fighting so many losing battles there to stiffen Roosevelt's resolve against Germany, not Japan. Churchill was not so much worried by Japan's military prowess, which he consistently under-estimated, or the losses Japan might inflict on the British Empire, including Australia. What concerned him most was the competition for American aid and resources which war with Japan might involve. Grateful as he was for American aid short of war, Churchill stuck resolutely to his main aim. He had repeatedly told Roosevelt 'that he had rather the United States came into the war now, and that we got no more supplies for six months, than that supplies from the U.S. should be doubled but the USA kept out of the war'. But he always meant the war against Hitler's Germany. Until Pearl Harbor, Churchill's Far Eastern strategy was to postpone war with Japan as long as possible, even if it meant the appearance of appeasement.

'I confess,' Churchill wrote in his war memoirs, 'that in my mind the whole Japanese menace lay in a sinister twilight.' He relied, he said, on his 'feeling that if Japan attacked us, the United States would come in'. It was always understood that, with or without America, 'if Japan invaded Australia or New Zealand, the Middle East should be sacrificed to the defence of our own kith and kin'. But he regarded this as 'remote and improbable, because of the vast abundance of easier and more attractive conquests offered to Japan by Malaya, Siam and above all the Dutch East Indies'. He was sure, he wrote, that 'nothing we could have spared at this time, even at the cost of wrecking the Middle Eastern theatre or cutting off supplies to the Soviet, would have changed the march of fate in Malaya'. On the other hand, 'the entry of the United States into the war would over-whelm all evils put together'. But for Churchill, the evil that really mattered was Hitler.

For all the risks Churchill was prepared to run in Australia's region, and despite his lack of candour and ambiguous assurances to Australia, nobody can deny the overarching consistency of his purpose. Throughout 1941, he rebuffed his own military chiefs and diplomats whenever their thoughts strayed towards reinforcement of the Far East, or warnings to Japan, or guarantees to the Chinese, the Siamese, the Dutch, or the Australians. He always brought them promptly to heel by reiterating his central doctrine. Cutting short an argument with the Admiralty, which wanted the United States Navy to reinforce the South-West Pacific, he had written to his First Lord back in February, 1941:

Our object is to get the Americans into the war, and the proper strategic dispositions will soon emerge when they are up against reality.

Two months before Hitler's invasion of Russia, Churchill had a sharp row with the Chief of the Imperial General Staff, Sir John Dill. In a long memorandum entitled 'The Relation of the Middle East to the Security of the United Kingdom', Dill questioned the entire basis of Churchill's strategy. His paper emphasised the contin-uing threat of invasion of Britain: 'Egypt is not even second in order of priority, for it has been an accepted principle in our strategy that in the last resort the security of Singapore comes before that of Egypt. Yet the defences of Singapore are still considerably below standard.'

'I was astonished to receive this document,' Churchill was to write. He promptly put Dill in his place: 'I gather you would be prepared to face the loss of Egypt and the Nile Valley, together with the surrender or ruin of the Army of half a million we have concentrated there, rather than lose Singapore.' The defence of Singapore, he informed the Chief of the General Staff, 'is an operation requiring only a very small fraction of the troops required to defend the Nile Valley against the Germans and the Italians'. In any case, the Prime Minister scolded the general, 'I have already given you the political data upon which the military arrangement for the defence of Singapore should be based: namely, that should Japan enter the war, the United States will in all probability come in on our side'. Furthermore, Churchill said, 'Japan would not be likely to besiege Singapore at the outset, as this operation would be an operation far more dangerous to her and less harmful to us than spreading her cruisers and battle-cruisers on the Eastern trade routes.'

Churchill could deal with Dill easily enough. Much more troublesome was an American mission to London in the last week in July, headed by Roosevelt's confidant, Harry Hopkins, on his second visit, this time accompanied by two generals and Roosevelt's envoy to Moscow, Averell Harriman. Accompanying Hopkins as 'a special observer' was Major General James Chaney, representing the US Chiefs of Staff. To Churchill's dismay, Chaney took Dill's line; he placed Singapore second only to defence of Britain, and the Middle East fourth and last in priority, after the Atlantic and Russia. 'This was indeed a tragic issue,' wrote Churchill, 'like having to choose whether your son or your daughter should be killed' – although, at best, Churchill never regarded Singapore as more than a stepdaughter of the Cinderella kind. He made his priorities clear to General Chaney and the Americans: 'I would not tolerate the idea of abandoning the struggle for Egypt and was resigned to pay whatever forfeits were exacted in Malaya.' This was an opening salvo in the long battle between Churchill and Roosevelt's top military advisers to win the President's heart for the 'Beat Hitler First' strategy.

Churchill now presented his case to Roosevelt in person. In the first week of August, 1941, he crossed the Atlantic in deepest secrecy aboard HMS *Prince of Wales*, still bearing scars from its part in the battle which sank the *Bismarck*. He arrived at Placentia Bay, Newfoundland, where Roosevelt awaited on board USS *Augusta*. At this meeting between 10 and 12 August, the limits that Congressional and public opinion placed on Roosevelt's freedom of action were made clear. Churchill reported to his Cabinet that the President was 'clearly skating on pretty thin ice in his relations with Congress'. Roosevelt had told him that 'he would wage war but not declare it and that he would become more and more provocative. If the Germans did not like it, they could attack American forces.' On the last day of their meeting, they heard the news that Congress had adopted Roosevelt's proposal to extend the army draft for another year – by one vote. This, in a House of Representatives where Roosevelt's Democrats had a solid majority. Nevertheless, Churchill informed his Cabinet, Roosevelt 'was obviously determined that they should come in'.

The public product of the shipboard meeting was the Atlantic Charter. It is a striking testimony to the priority Churchill gave to the destruction of Hitler above the preservation of the Empire. Its third clause was to become the trumpet-call for post-war anti-colonialism: 'They respect the right of all peoples to choose the form of government under which they live.' Churchill assured his Cabinet that this echo of Woodrow Wilson's 'self-determination' did not apply to the British Empire, including India. If he really believed this, he misjudged Roosevelt and the Americans. The fourth clause was essentially a free trade clause directed against imperial preference. Churchill successfully resisted Roosevelt's wish to add to the declaration that 'they will strive to bring about a fair and equitable distribution of essential produce', the words 'without discrimination and on equal terms' – a clear thrust against the Ottawa Empire Trade Agreement of 1932. Churchill stymied the Americans by saying that such words would have to be referred to Australia, New

Zealand, and Canada, who would reject them. He recorded with relish that he was able to present Britain as the traditional world champion of free trade, in much the same terms as he had used to Alfred Deakin thirty-four years previously. 'I could not help mentioning the British experience in adhering to Free Trade for eighty years in the face of ever-mounting American tariffs,' he wrote in his war memoirs. 'We had allowed the fullest importations into all our colonies . . . All we had got in reciprocation was successive doses of American Protection.' The Americans seemed 'a little taken aback'. Churchill felt entitled to boast in *The Grand Alliance*, with some poetic licence: 'Considering all the tales of my reactionary, Old World outlook, and the pain this is said to have caused the President, I am glad it should be on record that the substance and spirit of what came to be called the Atlantic Charter was in its first draft a British production cast in my own words.'

Churchill's last messages to Menzies before his resignation as Prime Minister dealt extensively with the Atlantic conference. On both Germany and Japan, Roosevelt's attitude had satisfied Churchill. It was greatly important, he told Menzies on 24 August, 'that the President should have agreed to a declaration [the Atlantic Charter] which refers to the final destruction of Nazi tyranny'. Moreover, Roosevelt had promised to issue a strong warning to Japan against further encroachments in South-East Asia, while in return Churchill would issue a matching warning 'that we will stand by the United States if they are attacked by Japan'. 'This, I know, represents your views,' Churchill told Menzies. 'I feel confident that Japan will lie quiet for a while.'

Japan had signed up to the Tripartite Pact with Germany and Italy in September, 1940. If Hitler hoped that his invasion of the Soviet Union would prompt Japan to attack Russia from the east, he was to be disappointed. That, at least, would have been the reaction of a rational military strategist. But Hitler's monomania to kill what he called 'the life force of the Slavs' was not subject to calculations of this kind. In any case, the Japanese failed to play their allotted role. They had been badly mauled in ferocious fighting with the Russians in Mongolia in 1939. They were still heavily embroiled in

China. Shortly before Hitler's attack on Russia, their volatile and voluble Foreign Minister, Matsuoka, had visited both Berlin and Moscow, and signed a mutual non-aggression pact with the Soviet Union. He had been kept completely in the dark about Hitler's intentions; and the consequent loss of face led to his dismissal. The Japanese Government, however, reassured Moscow that it would uphold Matsuoka's pact, enabling the Soviet to withdraw the best of its Siberian forces for the fight against Hitler. The dire consequence for Australia was Japan's crucial decision to 'go south', with Malayan rubber and the oil of the Dutch East Indies (Indonesia) among the prizes of its so-called Greater East Asian Co-prosperity Sphere. By the end of July, the Japanese army had occupied French Indochina, with the connivance of the pro-Vichy French Administration in Hanoi. Few in Washington, London, and Canberra now doubted that war with Japan was inevitable. The question then became: How long could and should open conflict be postponed? The answer for both Churchill and Australia was: 'As long as possible.'

Hitler's conquests in Western Europe had opened Japan's path to the rich pickings in South-East Asia. In particular, French Indochina and the Dutch East Indies now became ready for the taking. The French colonial administration took its orders from the Pétain regime installed at Vichy, in southern France. At Hitler's insistence in September, 1940, Vichy recognised that Japan should have 'preponderant interests in Indo-China'. The Dutch administration in Batavia (Jakarta) remained loyal to Queen Wilhelmina and the Dutch Government-in-exile in London. In the last months of 1941, the British Foreign Office tried to secure a declaration from Roosevelt that a Japanese attack on the Dutch East Indies would be an act of aggression and a cause for war. Dick Casey, the Australian Minister in Washington, diligently supported these efforts. Casey was well regarded by the Secretary of State, Cordell Hull, the Secretary for War, Henry Stimson, and by Roosevelt himself. While Roosevelt continued to plead the constraints imposed on him by Congress and public opinion, every step he took against Japan after July 1941 – a total oil embargo, the freezing of Japanese assets in the US and other economic sanctions – made war inevitable. The real cause of Roosevelt's hostility towards Japan was not its ambitions to replace the British Empire, but its aggression against China.

The war with China dominated every decision made by Japan. Japanese historians speak of a fifteen-year war, from Manchuria in 1931 to Hiroshima in 1945. Even at the height of the Pacific war, its main army was tied up on the Chinese mainland, fighting both Chiang Kaishek's Nationalists and Mao Zedong's communists, when they were not fighting one another. The 'China Incident' – as the Japanese called their war with China – entrenched the Imperial Army as the pre-eminent national institution, vying with Emperor Hirohito himself as the embodiment of the nation's soul. Japan's desperate need for raw materials and oil arose from the demands of the military in China. These problems were dominated by a single factor: the United States, then the world's leading oil producer, provided Japan with ninety per cent of its oil imports. Roosevelt did not need Congressional approval for his oil embargo, although no deadlier measure could be taken against Japan short of war. In all the negotiations between July and December 1941, Roosevelt insisted that he would ease or end his sanctions only if Japan agreed to get out of China. This was an impossible demand for the rulers of Japan, where the assassin's bullet and the fanatic's sword were always poised to strike against moderation and backsliding over China, even to the threshold of the Imperial Throne itself. Roosevelt knew that the best he could expect from his negotiations was a postponement of the inevitable.

When it came to dealing with Japan, Churchill was always reluctant to push Roosevelt further than he wanted to go. Churchill was entitled to claim vindication in the broad sweep of history: the United States did come in, Australia was not invaded, and Japan's defeat followed quickly the defeat of Hitler. Nor did the Australians, at that time, question the sincerity of Churchill's promise about dropping everything else to save the kith and kin, if Australia and New Zealand were invaded. In 1942, when everything had fallen apart, Churchill specifically defined what he meant by invasion: six to ten Japanese divisions on continental Australia. But British help in the extremity of actual invasion was neither the promise nor the premise on which Australia had planned and acted since 1940. The operative promise, as it had been for the previous twenty years, was the defence of Malaya and Singapore, to prevent the *threat* of invasion. It was because Australia relied on that promise that its government had despatched the bulk of the AIF to the Middle East. Churchill confided to his post-war readers in 1950: 'If the United States did not come in, we had no means of defending the Dutch East Indies, or indeed our own Empire in the East.' He never put that blunt proposition fairly and squarely to the Australian Government in 1941.

Churchill made his last gesture to meet Britain's longstanding promise to Australia in mid-October. Ironically, it cost him a hectic row with that same Admiralty with which he had fought over their 'Main Fleet to Singapore' doctrine sixteen years previously. Now the Admiralty begrudged sending any big ships anywhere except the Atlantic and the Mediterranean. But Churchill had his way. The squadron he sent east comprised the battleship HMS *Prince of Wales* and the battle cruiser HMS *Repulse*. Unfortunately, the aircraft carrier HMS *Indomitable* was unable to join this journey of deliverance; it had run aground in the Caribbean. This mishap, which was to seal the squadron's doom, did not prevent Churchill telling Roosevelt: 'This ought to serve as a deterrent on Japan. There is nothing like having something that can catch and kill anything.'

Churchill was less upbeat in his message to Curtin. He had chosen to convey this long-awaited answer to Australian pleas for naval reinforcement in the same cable in which he grudgingly accepted the Australian departure from Tobruk. As if to emphasise the contrast between Australian selfishness and British self-sacrifice, he told Curtin that 'in order further to deter Japan we are sending forthwith our newest battleship *Prince of Wales* to join *Repulse* in the Indian Ocean. This is done in spite of the protests of the Commander-in-Chief Home Fleet and is a serious risk for us to run.' He was 'still inclined to think that Japan will not run with the ABCD powers [America, Britain, China, Dutch] unless or until Russia is decisively broken. Perhaps even then they will wait for the promised invasion of the British Isles in the Spring. Russian resistance is still strong, especially in front of Moscow and Winter is now near.' Lest the Australians take too much for granted, Churchill concluded: 'I must, however, make it clear that the movements of the *Prince of Wales* must be reviewed when she is at Capetown because of the danger of *Tirpitz* breaking out and other operational possibilities.' In this grudging and partial fashion, Churchill purported to make good a promise which had been the foundation of imperial defence in the Far East for twenty years.

Churchill sent his trusted friend, Duff Cooper, to Canberra to assuage Australian anxieties. Cooper had been the only senior minister to resign from the Chamberlain Cabinet over Munich in 1938. In September 1941, Churchill had appointed him Resident Minister at Singapore to coordinate Britain's military and political position in the Far East. At a meeting of the Advisory War Council in Canberra on 7 November – exactly a month before Pearl Harbor – Duff Cooper reaffirmed that the British Government was 'prepared to abandon the Mediterranean altogether if this were necessary in order to hold Singapore'. Billy Hughes, jaunty as ever and now installed as leader of the United Australia Party, at the age of seventy-nine, was sceptical. He said that British public opinion would never stand for such a move. Menzies, who was still a member of the Advisory War Council, said that while Churchill had always told him of the importance he attached to Singapore, he doubted 'if he was fully seized with the significance'. Curtin maintained the faith in the conventional doctrine. He told Duff Cooper: 'Australia feels it is imperative that there should be a strong battleship force at Singapore. It's the core of the whole problem.'

Curtin's comment reflected the basic continuity of Australian war policy after Menzies and Fadden. There was still no question of the return of the AIF to Australia. In a statement to the House of Representatives of 5 November 1941, Curtin said that his Government had no intention of recalling the three divisions from the Middle East. In a press statement on the same day, the Minister for the Army and Deputy Prime Minister, Frank Forde, confirmed the previous government's decision to send Australia's only armoured division to the Middle East. When Curtin announced that Blamey was coming home for consultations, he insisted that the general would be returning to his Middle East Command. When Blamey himself discussed with the Cabinet the role of the 8th Division, now with two of its three brigades in Malaya, he still spoke about its eventual despatch to join the rest of the AIF in the Middle East. Curtin's War Cabinet did not disagree, although it did decide that 'no action should be taken at the present juncture for the transfer of the 8th Division from Malaya, in view of the present Far Eastern situation'. After telling the Australian people that they were 'like a lot of gazelles grazing in a dell on the edge of the jungle,' Blamey returned to Cairo a week before Pearl Harbor.

At first, Curtin, like Fadden and Menzies, accepted Churchill's official optimism that Japan would 'not run into war unless or until Russia was decisively broken'. John Dedman, charged with coordinating war production and manpower, explained the November decision to reinforce the AIF in the Middle East in these terms: 'So long as it thought that there was a possibility that Japan would not go to war, the Government was unwilling to weaken the British position in the Middle East, where the second Western Desert offensive was about to be launched.' Writing in 1967, Dedman still seemed unaware of the strength of the warnings about Japan's aggressive intentions, especially from US intelligence, which had cracked Japanese diplomatic codes. Their naval codes were not broken until after Pearl Harbor. Casey in Washington was well informed, and sent Canberra plenty of evidence about Japanese plans. Curtin and Evatt took false assurance from the Japanese Ambassador, Tatsuo Kawai, whom they liked and befriended, but who was well out of the Tokyo loop. It may be, as the authoritative Australian war historian David Horner suggests, that the Australian Government 'demonstrated a wishful optimism about events in the Far East'. Equally, they demonstrated their continuing faith in Churchill's judgement.

The continuity of Australian policy was personified by the presence of Sir Earle Page in London. When Menzies lost his battle to return to London, Fadden had appointed Page as minister representing

Australia. Curtin, as Opposition Leader, had approved the appointment, and immediately confirmed it as Prime Minister. Churchill welcomed it and undertook to receive the accredited representative of Australia 'with utmost consideration and honour'. He made it clear, however, that Page 'would not be and could not be a partner in the daily work of our Government'. Bruce, too, was happy to have his old partner in the Bruce-Page Government by his side in London. Bruce gave Page some good advice: 'Be brief and to the point, particularly with Winston.' Page ignored his advice. Sir Alan Brooke, who succeeded Sir John Dill as Chief of the Imperial Staff the week before Pearl Harbor, peppers his diaries with comments like: 'Sir Earle Page, Australian representative, as usual wasted most of our time!'.

Churchill gave Page the full treatment, whisking him off for a three-day tour of bombed areas in east and north England. Page chattered happily away, impressed, of course, with Churchill's 'inspired speeches and tireless energy', but finding that 'his shrewd political mind resisted my efforts to obtain firm decisions'. At the Lord Mayor's banquet on 9 November, Churchill 'virtually pledged the British Government to all the policies advocated by Australia respecting China and Singapore, and issued a definite warning, tantamount to a threat to Japan'.

Page presented a long strategic survey to his first meeting with the British War Cabinet, on 12 November 1941. He called for British and US warnings to Japan over Russia, China, the Philippines, Siam, Malaya, Singapore, and the Dutch East Indies. Churchill replied with his routine formula: 'To be safe everywhere is to be strong nowhere.' Beyond the warships now on their way to the Far East, there could be no further reinforcement in Malaya and Singapore. The Middle East remained the most useful place for our forces where 'a victory over the Germans and Italians would have a big effect in keeping Japan back'. We should endeavour to keep Japan out of the war as long as possible, Churchill said, 'but if we were unsuccessful, then we must secure the cooperation of the United States'. The longer the delay, the greater the chance of American participation. Churchill warned Australia against putting pressure on the United States. It was his experience, he remarked, that 'when

Roosevelt was pressed too hard, a sudden wall of silence would descend on proceedings for several weeks'.

Even more disturbing and revealing about British attitudes were Page's discussions with the Chiefs of Staff. The specific goal he had set himself was to secure more aircraft for the defence of Singapore. According to Page, the Chief of the Air Staff, Sir Charles Portal, 'produced some astonishing opinions'. He admitted that Singapore was inadequately defended, 'but regarded this as a political matter rather than a military question'. Page wrote: 'Portal expressed the incredible view that, if Singapore were lost, it could be picked up again later. Moreover, he thought it possible that Britain would not fight if Japan invaded the Netherlands East Indies, a course which would bring Japanese troops within four hundred miles of Darwin.' Page 'retorted warmly', telling Portal that if that was their attitude, Britain 'could split the Empire asunder'.

Portal was expressing the official British attitude far more accurately than Churchill would ever admit. For three months, when Menzies was still Prime Minister, Australia had been urging a mutual defence pact with the Dutch, with or without American support. Curtin urged it even more strongly, telling Churchill: 'Australia feels very strongly that we should give [the Dutch] an assurance of armed support irrespective of U.S. attitude.' Churchill baulked at making any move without Roosevelt's backing. As late as 3 December, four days before Pearl Harbor, he cabled Halifax in Washington that he would not immediately declare war if Japan attacked Dutch territory, unless Britain was assured of American support. Next day, Roosevelt at last agreed that if Japan attacked British or Dutch possessions, 'we should obviously be all in it together'. Only then did the British War Cabinet promise immediate 'aid to the Dutch if Japan attacked the East Indies.

Churchill had his reasons for resisting Australian urging for unilateral warnings to Japan. From his point of view, it was essential that the United States make the running. Roosevelt had to avoid at all costs any appearance of intervention in support of the British Empire in the Far East. The barriers against American entry into the war were coming down, not least because of his own long campaign with Roosevelt. Congress jumped the biggest hurdle in November, when it repealed most of the US Neutrality Acts. Yet even after two American destroyers had been attacked by German U-boats in the Atlantic, with the loss of one hundred and fifty American lives, opinion polls showed seventy per cent of Americans against going to war.

A generation that has seen American presidents wage a dozen wars, declared and undeclared, from Vietnam to Iraq, with or without congressional authorisation, may find it hard to realise the constitutional constraints accepted by the most powerful President in American history, now in the first year of an unprecedented third term amid the supreme crisis of the twentieth century. At a Cabinet meeting in London, Churchill delivered a constitutional lecture to Earle Page, in response to Page's statement of the Australian view that firm guarantees should be sought from America in advance of Japanese attacks. It would be 'a great error to press the President to act in advance of American opinion', Churchill said. While he, as Prime Minister of Britain, could go to the Mansion House and say publicly: 'Should the United States become involved in war with Japan, the British declaration will follow within an hour', the American President had no such power. The truth is, of course, that Roosevelt and Churchill both had their own reasons for emphasising, or even exaggerating, the constraints imposed by the US Constitution: Roosevelt to keep all his options open, and Churchill to emphasise the importance of his personal relations with Roosevelt. But Roosevelt was genuine and consistent in his belief that he could not take a united nation into war against, or even much ahead of, American public and congressional opinion.

Churchill cracked the whip at the first hint of Australian independence in international policy-making. The culprit was Bert Evatt, now Minister for External Affairs, and bursting to play a starring role on the world stage. Why was it, Evatt wanted to know, that Britain had not declared war on Finland, Hungary, and Romania although these countries had joined Hitler in declaring war on our great ally, the Soviet Union? In a wide-ranging statement in the House of Representatives on 27 November, Evatt included the

318

words: 'It is a strange feature of the present struggle that, while we are Allies of Russia in the fight against Germany, we are still at peace with these three eager satellites and accomplices of Germany.'

This brought forth a cry of pain and outrage from Churchill. In a cable to Curtin, ominously dated 1.00 a.m., he accused Evatt of 'criticising us in public'. Worse, Evatt was barging in 'upon a delicate and difficult question', ignorant of his correspondence with Stalin on the matter; and he was at that very moment awaiting a reply from Finland. 'It would be a great pity,' he wrote, 'if while these delicate and highly disputable matters are in the balance, your Ministers should start criticising our policy in public.' Then, with a bizarre mix of self-righteousness and self-pity, Churchill berated Curtin: 'We have never said a word in public about the Australian Government's insistence upon the withdrawal of all troops from Tobruk, which cost us life and ships, and added appreciably to General Auchinleck's difficulties in preparing his offensive; and no-one here or I presume in Australia outside the circles of government has the slightest inkling of the distress we felt.' To make sure Curtin understood the gravity of Evatt's offence, he reminded the Australian Prime Minister that he 'had sent the *Prince of Wales* into eastern waters in the face of the grave misgivings' of the Admiralty about the undoubted risks. 'Surely all this should convince you of our wish to act towards your Government in true comradeship and loyalty.' Churchill concluded with condolences to Curtin on the loss of HMAS *Sydney*, sunk with the loss of 645 crew off the Western Australian coast after an action on 19 November with the German raider *Kormoran*. More than a quarter of a century before, the first HMAS *Sydney* had sailed, under Churchill's orders, into the Indian Ocean, where it had destroyed the German raider *Emden*.

Curtin sent a soothing reply next day, at the businesslike time of 6.45 p.m. He greatly regretted Churchill's 'distress of mind from any attitude taken by this Government'. Nevertheless, he failed to see how Evatt's statement could be construed as criticism. 'We assume that your Government welcomes our independence of thought and advice.' But he undertook that 'we will be at great pains to see to it here that no criticism of your policy in respect of war and foreign affairs is given publicity'. The loss of the *Sydney* was a 'heavy blow which must be borne'. As to the despatch of the *Prince of Wales*, Curtin said: 'Finally, may I say that we do not need any concrete demonstration, such as you instance, to make us aware of your comradeship and goodwill towards us. We know that your great work is not only for Great Britain but for all of us, and we are doing and will continue to do everything in our power to give you practical assistance.'

For all this studied politeness, we can already sense a creeping hostility between Churchill and the new Labor Government. When we consider the essential continuity of Australian policy from Menzies to Curtin, Australia's unchanged support for Churchill's Middle Eastern strategy, and its acceptance of Britain's hardships in ordering Australia's own priorities, it is difficult to avoid the conclusion that Churchill's attitude reflected his visceral dislike of labour governments, if not a denial of their legitimacy.

THE JAPANESE MOMENTUM towards war with the United States had become irreversible. In October, a change of government saw the bellicose anti-American General Hideki Tojo replace the vacillating Prince Konoye as Prime Minister. In the presence of Emperor Hirohito, an imperial conference on 5 November ordered the finalisation of war plans and the termination of negotiations in Washington by 1 December (later extended by one week). That same afternoon, the chief of the Imperial Navy, Admiral Isoroku Yamamoto, issued his Order No. 1: 'To the east, the American fleet will be destroyed. The American lines of operation and supply to the Far East will be severed. Enemy forces will be intercepted and annihilated. Victories will be exploited to smash the enemy's will to fight.' Two days later, Yamamoto issued his Order No. 2: 'The Task Force will launch a surprise attack at the outset of the war upon the U.S. Pacific Fleet reported to be in Hawaiian waters and destroy it.'

The decisions and orders of November were the culmination of months of debate and planning. They reflected, to some extent, the rivalry between the Imperial Army and the Imperial Navy. This was much more than the usual interservice competition over resources and strategy. It was a struggle for the heart and mind of the Emperor. Hirohito was no puppet. His interventions were decisive. His word was final. And by November, 1941, the Emperor's word was for war.

The imperial debate in Tokyo was not about war or peace; it was about the choice of wars. As wars go, Japan's choice was relatively rational. Fundamentally, its plan was the rapid conquest of the vast area of South-East Asia from the Philippines, Malaya, and the Dutch East Indies to New Britain, and the isolation of Australia; all these conquests were to be strongly fortified, until the Americans and the British realised that re-conquest was impossible and agreed to negotiate a peace; Japan would hold so many bargaining chips that an advantageous settlement would be Japan's for the asking. Some of the Emperor's advisers believed that a devastating blow against the US navy in the Pacific would force a demoralised America to the negotiating table, like Russia after the Battle of Tsushima in 1905. A further key assumption, eminently credible in 1941, was that Germany would win the war in the West. Altogether, Japan's plan was not irrational, much less suicidal; and indeed, an immense amount of it was carried out with stunning success. In the same sense that Hitler reckoned without Winston Churchill's unreasonableness in 1940, the Japanese rulers reckoned without Franklin Roosevelt's unreasonableness in 1942.

After the basic decision to 'go south', the Japanese High Command considered various plans for the conquest of Malaya, the Philippines, and the Dutch East Indies. Since an attack on America's tutelary colony in the Philippines was common to each proposal, there was no question but that the United States would become involved. By mid-August, detailed planning began on operations against the Philippines and Malaya simultaneously, to be followed quickly by an assault on the oil-rich Dutch East Indies, by way of Borneo and Sumatra; they would seize Rabaul, New Britain (part of the Australian territory of New Guinea), from the sea. These plans envisaged the isolation of Australia, with the option of invasion left open. For so vast and ambitious a project, Japanese control of the central Pacific Ocean was crucial. Hence Pearl Harbor.

The prime mover for the attack on Pearl Harbor, the Pacific base of the United States Navy, was the commander-in-chief of the Combined Imperial Fleets, Admiral Yamamoto. He had spent several years in Washington as Japanese naval attaché, and had studied at Harvard University; he knew and admired the United States. Yamamoto understood clearly America's productive capacity, and warned his colleagues: 'Anyone who has seen the auto factories in Detroit and the oil fields in Texas knows that Japan lacks the national power for a naval race with America.' Within this insight into long-term reality, the 57-year-old admiral sought a short-term response: 'If I am told to fight regardless of the consequences, I shall run wild for the first six months or a year, but I have utterly no confidence for the second or third year.'

At the very hour of decision in Tokyo, urgent cables were crossing between London, Washington, and Canberra. Churchill informed Curtin on 5 November that he had written to Roosevelt a 'secret and personal message' acknowledging that the American policy of gaining time 'had been very successful so far, but our joint embargo is steadily forcing the Japanese to a decision for peace or war'. But what was needed now, Churchill said, was a 'deterrent to Japan of a most general and formidable character'. He had told Roosevelt: 'No independent action by ourselves will deter Japan, because we are so fully occupied elsewhere. But we will, of course, stand with the United States and do our utmost to back them in whatever course they choose.'

Churchill's worst nightmare was becoming Curtin's too. He was far less confident than Churchill about US intervention. He cabled Bruce on 29 November: 'There now seems grave danger of further armed aggression by Japan without any United States armed intervention.' While he agreed with Churchill's view that 'elasticity is desirable', it was essential, Curtin said, that 'we should know what is the understanding of action by Britain, in the absence of United States armed support'.

Reports on Japanese movements in South-East Asia accumulated, pointing to attacks on Thailand and Malaya. On 26 November, a convoy with fifty thousand troops was observed moving south past Formosa (Taiwan). In a lengthy cable to Churchill on 30 November, Curtin set out Australian concerns:

> It is urgent to impress U.S.A. with its obligations arising from the certification of Japanese aggression. We feel evidence warranting our taking precautions at least requires acceptance by U.S.A. of her responsibility for the course we thereby think inevitable. But if this is not practicable because of constitutional reasons, we hope preliminary understanding at least will be attained . . . Our latest advices from Washington [from Casey] are that in the event of Japanese attack on Thailand, no definite understandings of armed support from the United States can be anticipated. This may result in position which you regarded as worst possible from Empire point of view, namely war with Japan, United States neutral.

We may reasonably conjecture that Churchill would have dismissed with an irritable grunt Curtin's suggestion of an appeal to the US in terms of its obligations and responsibility. It was the last thing he wanted, as his long, patient efforts to coax America into the war neared their climax.

Bruce and Page went together to 10 Downing Street on the morning of Monday, 1 December. They found Churchill still determined not to push Roosevelt into open declarations against Japan. 'His reason for this,' Bruce reported to Curtin, 'is that he feels that American opinion will react favourably to a war which America has entered in defence of her own interests, but would be inclined to be antagonistic to the idea of entering a war into which we had already entered and America was coming to our assistance.' Churchill, Bruce said, was adamant against the British Empire taking action ahead of the United States. Bruce summed up the talks with Churchill in his usual patronising way: 'We think that the conversation has brought home to the Prime Minister . . . the danger of the policy which he was inclined to pursue of only taking his hurdles as he comes to them.'

Next day, Curtin cabled Churchill to urge 'greater concentration of naval strength, not necessarily all British'. Curtin told Churchill: 'I believe Japan's obstinacy is grounded in the belief that America would, at the best, be slow to come in.' He believed that naval concentration combined with a strong stance by Roosevelt 'would be a complete deterrent to Japan's entry in the war'. The pace of events was making nonsense of these exchanges. When Curtin sent his message to Churchill, the Japanese First Air Fleet of six aircraft carriers, protected by two battleships, three cruisers, and nine destroyers, had already been six days at sea, shrouded in the mists and storms of the North Pacific, awaiting its final order to attack the US naval base in Hawaii, Pearl Harbor. Almost at the hour when Churchill received Curtin's view about how best to deter Japan, Yamamoto sent his fleet the coded signal to attack Pearl Harbor: 'Climb Mount Niitaka'.

The paradox of these fateful days is that, despite all the knowledge about the massive operations Japan was mounting in East Asia, for all America's success in breaking the diplomatic codes, Roosevelt and his advisers were genuinely ignorant about the most important move of all – the attack on Pearl Harbor. For three reasons: the daring, brilliance and secrecy of the enterprise; the radio silence of the Japanese fleet, in contrast with the chatter of the diplomatic signals which the Americans were intercepting; and Western contempt for Japanese skills and initiative.

Afterwards, Roosevelt, Churchill, and Curtin exploited the notion of exceptional Japanese treachery, depicting the United States as the victim of unprovoked aggression at the very hour that the Secretary of State, Cordell Hull, was supposedly extending an olive branch. On the morning of Saturday, 6 December, Roosevelt sent a personal appeal to Emperor Hirohito. It was only for the record. He told Hopkins: 'This son of a man has just sent his last message to the son of a god.' That afternoon (Washington time), the Tokyo Government began sending its Washington embassy, in fourteen takes, its instruction to break off negotiations. The Magic intercepts received them simultaneously. As soon as they were deciphered and interpreted, they were taken to the White House. Roosevelt read the first thirteen takes around 9.00 p.m. on the Saturday night. 'This means war,' he said to Hopkins. The vital last take was received in Washington on the morning of 7 December at 10.00 a.m. The Japanese envoys, admirals Kurusu and Nomura, met Hull in his office at 1.00 p.m. to deliver what they regarded as an ultimatum. Japanese aircraft were already bombing Pearl Harbor. The two Imperial ambassadors knew nothing about the force heading for Hawaii, and probably were thinking in terms of war in a week or so. Hull had suggested to Roosevelt that the next Wednesday, 10 December, was the probable date.

'A date that will live in infamy', Roosevelt's description of Sunday, 7 December 1941, became the most enduring epithet from the Second World War, invoked with fearful resonance on 11 September 2001 as the supreme example of unmitigated treachery. Compared with the attack on the World Trade Center, Pearl Harbor was a traditional act of war. That the attack preceded a formal declaration of war did not make it unique in history. Ten days before, the Chief of Staff, General George Marshall, had sent a warning to all commanders in the Pacific, stating expressly: 'The U.S. desires that Japan commit the first overt act.' In its conception and execution, the Japanese attack on Pearl Harbor applied the first principle of military success – surprise. Pearl Harbor must be seen within the totality of Japanese operations not only on 7–8 December 1941, but in the days and weeks before. From the beginning of December at the latest, the world and his wife knew about the massive Japanese military movements in East Asia. Casey's last message to Curtin on the eve of Pearl Harbor stated: 'News is being published tonight (Saturday, 6 December) of two large heavily escorted convoys, totalling 35 ships escorted by 8 cruisers and numerous destroyers, having been *seen* this morning to south-east of Port Camau, the southern point of Indo-China, steaming westward towards the Gulf of Siam.' In the event, the attacks on the Malayan coast took place half an hour before the first attacks on Pearl Harbor; the attack on the Philippines nine hours after. Yet the unpreparedness and shock of surprise was everywhere the same. The real surprise is that the Japanese achieved so much surprise.

The Australian Cabinet had held a special meeting in Melbourne on the Thursday and Friday. Curtin cancelled his return to Canberra, to be close to army headquarters at Victoria Barracks. Signals from Singapore, Bangkok, Tokyo, London, and Washington all pointed to the inevitable. When he received the first news reports of Pearl Harbor (about 8.00 a.m., 8 December, Melbourne time), he commented to his press secretary and confidant, Don Rodgers: 'It has come.'

Churchill was at Chequers, dining with his guests, the American Ambassador, John Winant, and Averell Harriman, when they heard of a Japanese attack on Hawaii as a late item on the 9.00 p.m. BBC news. He telephoned Roosevelt. 'Mr President, what's this about Japan?' he asked. 'It's quite true,' Roosevelt replied. 'They have attacked us at Pearl Harbor. We are all in the same boat now.' Churchill saw the momentous consequences. As he wrote in his war memoirs: 'We had won the war. England would live; Britain would live; the Commonwealth of Nations and the Empire would live.' No doubt it would take a long time, he wrote, and he expected 'terrible forfeits in the East'. But he went to bed 'saturated and satiated with emotion and sensation', and slept 'the sleep of the saved and the thankful'.

Three days later, although not strictly bound to do so by the terms of the Tripartite Pact, Hitler went to the Reichstag and declared war on the United States. In the twisted world which Hitler inhabited, this was neither a mistake nor a gesture of honour to an ally; it was an act of contempt for a degenerate democracy, with its cripple for a President under the thumb of the international Jewish conspiracy. But, as Churchill told Roosevelt on the telephone: 'This certainly simplifies things.' Churchill's Big Idea, which had sustained him since May, 1940, had become against all the odds the defining reality, not only of the Second World War, but of the second half of the twentieth century.

20

'We look to the United States'
December, 1941

T his time, Australia declared war on its own. Curtin assembled his Cabinet in Melbourne within hours of the Japanese landings in Malaya and the attack on Pearl Harbor. As in 1914 and 1939, the first official verification came from the Admiralty in London, with the signal: 'Commence hostilities against Japan wherever possible.' Cabinet adopted the constitutional procedure devised by Evatt for an Australian declaration of war against Finland, Hungary, and Romania, during the episode that had caused Churchill so much anguish in November. Such was the certainty of war that the procedures had been finalised in cables between Curtin and Bruce over the weekend. Curtin despatched a telegram to Bruce to notify King George VI that, acting on the advice of his Australian Ministers, he was at war with Japan.

For the first time, Australia had declared war ahead and independently of the British Government. In a national broadcast that night, Curtin said:

Men and women of Australia, we are at war with Japan. That has happened because, in the first instance, Japanese naval and air forces launched an unprovoked attack on British and United States territory; because our vital interests are imperilled and because the rights of free people in the whole Pacific are assailed . . . We shall hold this country, and keep it as a citadel for the British-speaking race, and as a place where civilisation will persist.

Perhaps Curtin used the curious neologism 'British-speaking' for 'English-speaking' so as to include the Irish and the Scots; but it was clear enough as a call for national unity around the principle of White Australia. And, like Churchill's 'Never surrender' speech, it contained the outline of Curtin's own ruling idea for the war: that Australia would become the base from which Australia, Britain, and the United States would repel and then attack Japan.

Curtin stressed that this was a 'new war', not an extension of the old war. Close observers in Canberra saw in Curtin himself a new man. None were closer than the small corps of journalists in the Parliamentary Press Gallery. In the confines of the modest building now known as Old Parliament House, which stood isolated in a paddock in the 'bush capital', politicians and journalists lived and worked together in forced intimacy. Curtin's biographer, Lloyd Ross, a family friend who was, nevertheless, an occasional critic of the Prime Minister, wrote:

Canberra in December was in jitters. At the adjournment of Parliament on the 17th, Evatt moved among the press representatives, talking at great length but telling them little of the real situation and only adding to their fears. At 10.30 pm, Curtin leaned back into his chair wearily, 'Well, boys – anything further?' The pressmen asked whether on some occasion he would take them into his confidence and describe the strategic situation. 'No time like the present', he replied. Doors were shut, and the attendants excluded. Curtin talked till midnight. Most of the pressmen had been accustomed to hearing Menzies' polished phrases and were still disposed to dismiss Curtin as a woolly rhetorician, but as they listened to his remarkable description of the world situation, given without notes, without hesitation, without the promptings of an expert at his elbow, they felt his greatness. By midnight all of them were exhausted but the journalists felt that the Prime Minister had revealed sources of great strength.

For Churchill and Australia – and for the future of the British Empire – the 'world situation' which Curtin had surveyed was transformed in thirty minutes around midday on 10 December 1941. Hoping to intercept a rumoured Japanese landing on the Malayan coast, two hundred miles north of Singapore, Admiral Tom Phillips, RN, took his squadron into the South China Sea. Without air protection, *Prince of Wales* and *Repulse* were sitting ducks. Wave after wave of Japanese aircraft based in Saigon (Ho Chi Minh City) sank the two British warships in less than an hour. A thousand men, including Phillips, went down with their ships. Britain's entire Singapore strategy of twenty years, and its supposed guarantees to Australia, sank to the bottom of the South China Sea with the *Prince of Wales*.

Churchill was in bed when he was telephoned with the news of the loss of the ships he had sent to Singapore in the face of Admiralty protests. He wrote: 'In all the war I never received a more direct shock. As I turned over and twisted in bed, the full horror of the news sank in upon me. There were no British or American capital ships in the Indian Ocean or the Pacific except the American survivors of Pearl Harbor, who were hastening back to California. Over all this vast expanse of waters, Japan was supreme, and we everywhere were weak and naked.' His feelings towards Australia were not improved by the fact that he had managed to convince himself that he had acted under pressure from the Australians.

Curtin asked London for an urgent reassessment. Through the Dominions Secretary, Lord Cranborne, the British Government pleaded for patience: 'Things are moving so fast that a telegram drafted in the morning is often out of date by the evening.' Although there were anxious times ahead in the Pacific, 'we must not forget that Germany, who is still the main enemy, is in serious and increasing difficulties both in Russia and in Libya'. To make sure the Australians got things in perspective, Cranborne insisted: 'It is not considered that there is any immediate large scale threat to the territory of Australia, much less New Zealand.' As to possible raids on Australia by Japanese cruisers or seaborne aircraft, or the potential threat to Australia's sea routes, Lord Cranborne referred Curtin to the Far East Appreciation 'sent to the Australian Government on 12 August 1940'!

The two former Australian prime ministers in London, Bruce and Page, were beginning to realise how much they had been fobbed off with false assurances. Page scurried from meeting to meeting in Whitehall, from defence committees to the War Cabinet, reminding anyone who would listen about the complacency he had found in Singapore on his way to London, and urging again and again the need for air reinforcements in Malaya. His ceaseless flow of chatter, his habit of punctuating every second sentence with a 'You see, you see', his nervous giggle, grated on the brahmins of Whitehall. The head of the Foreign Office, Sir Alexander Cadogan, had written in his diary in November: 'He goes on in an endless cockney monotone. I asked Eden, who was sitting next to him, whether he couldn't find a handle or something that would switch off the talk.' At the British War Cabinet meeting on 10 December, Page urged that Russia should be asked to come in quickly against Japan, that the maximum number of aircraft possible should be transferred from the Middle East to the Far East, air manufacturing capacity be sent from Britain to Australia, and that the Pacific islands be reinforced to protect the American supply route to Australia. Page reported to Curtin: 'Churchill promised that this would be considered.'

Perhaps Churchill would have been less considerate if he had known that Page and Bruce were framing a cable to Curtin complaining about the lack of urgency, coordination and leadership in London. Bruce told Curtin: 'In our view, leadership on the highest plane is necessary on the Allies' side and that leadership must come from the British War Cabinet.' The British Cabinet, he said, 'must immediately lay down the line it considers should be followed with regard to our political and military strategy and try to get it accepted by Roosevelt'. To this end, Bruce suggested, Curtin should cable Churchill direct. 'This would be most effective in stimulating action or at all events in ensuring full consideration of the issues involved.'

By the time Curtin received this pompous message, Churchill was on board HMS *Duke of York*, sister ship of the *Prince of Wales*, steaming across the Atlantic to confer with Roosevelt in Washington. Their meeting was codenamed Arcadia.

After his sleep of 'the saved and the thankful', Churchill had woken to harsh reality. The spectacular way Japan had brought the United States into the war threatened his Big Idea. American public opinion had been the chief drag on Roosevelt's efforts to bring the United States into the war against Hitler. Now, Churchill feared, the same public opinion, inflamed by Pearl Harbor, would force Roosevelt to turn his main effort against Japan. Ominously, Roosevelt suspended new shipments of aid under the Lend-Lease program, pending a total review of American strategies and resources. It was therefore urgent to talk with Roosevelt face to face. He brushed aside Roosevelt's hints that they should wait until the picture became clearer in the New Year. Churchill knew that there would be tough talk ahead, and was already taking a new stance with Roosevelt. His new appointee as Chief of the Imperial General Staff, Sir Alan Brooke, noted that when a Cabinet Minister urged the need for a 'careful attitude' towards the United States, 'Winston turned to him and with a wicked leer in his eye, said: "Oh! That is the way we talked to her while we were wooing her. Now that she is in the harem we talk to her quite differently!"'

Churchill's objective was to confirm his 'Hitler First' strategy. The principle was easier to establish than the practice. Serious American action against Germany in Europe was purely hypothetical in December, 1941. The German army had been halted twenty miles from Moscow. Rommel had been driven back to Benghazi. But in Asia and the Pacific, the Allies faced immediately what Churchill called 'a cataract of disaster'. On 15 December, the British began withdrawals in Malaya and Burma. On 17 December, Japanese forces landed in North Borneo. In the Philippines, General Douglas MacArthur, who had been as badly surprised as the American commanders in Hawaii (with less excuse), was getting ready to declare the capital, Manila, an open city, and to begin his withdrawal to the Bataan Peninsula and the island of Corregidor in Manila Bay.

On Christmas Eve, the Japanese overran the US garrison on Wake Island; 'Remember Wake Island' joined 'Remember Pearl Harbor' in the litany of scores to be settled with Japan. In Hong Kong, four British and Canadian battalions surrendered on Christmas Day. Whatever their long-term priorities, Roosevelt and Churchill had no option but to turn urgently to the catastrophes in the Pacific.

Churchill knew that, to get acceptance of the 'Beat Hitler First' strategy, he had to prove to Roosevelt that Britain did not expect the United States to bail out the British Empire in the Far East. On the eve of his departure for Washington, he had decided that the 18th British Division, now at Cape Town on board the US transport *Mount Vernon*, a symbol of Anglo–American cooperation even before Pearl Harbor, should go to Bombay instead of Egypt, there to await a decision about its final destination. Churchill's thoughts then turned to the three Australian divisions in the Middle East. From the *Duke of York*, he signalled the Chiefs of Staff in London suggesting that at least one of those divisions should go to Singapore. 'Beware lest troops required for the ultimate defence of Singapore Island are not used up or cut off in Malayan Peninsula,' he minuted his Chiefs on 15 December. 'Nothing compares in importance with the fortress.' He asked his Chiefs: 'Are you sure that we shall have enough troops for prolonged defence?' His signal concluded: 'Consider with Auchinleck and Commonwealth Government moving Australian Division from Palestine to Singapore. Report action.'

It must be emphasised that his proposed redeployment of the Australian forces from the Middle East had nothing to do with the direct defence of Australia, or returning them to Australian control. It was entirely a matter of rejigging the forces available to him to meet the new emergency. Far from releasing the Australian divisions, Churchill was asserting British ownership and control. Nor, at this stage, had the Australian Government made any request for their redeployment, much less their repatriation. Thus it happened, contrary to legend, that it was Churchill, not Curtin, who made the first proposal to send an Australian division from the Middle East to fight Japan, barely a week after Pearl Harbor.

During his Atlantic crossing, Churchill dictated three strategic papers entitled 'The Atlantic Front', 'The Pacific Front' and '1943'. The first paper sketched possible moves against Germany, emphasising the need to send Russia the supplies promised 'without fail and punctually'. The memorandum on the Pacific war envisaged the Singapore 'Fortress' resisting Japanese attack for at least six months. The problem, Churchill conceded, was whether Singapore and the Philippines could hold out long enough for the United States and Britain to regain naval supremacy in the Pacific. In '1943', he set the northern summer of 1943 as the beginning of the liberation of Europe by three or four landings at various points on the continent, while American and British expeditions would be sent to recover 'places lost' to the Japanese. On the second-last day of his voyage, Churchill returned to the Pacific where, as he saw it, the real danger to the Allied cause would be 'if the United States assembled a vast army for the reconquest of the Pacific, absorbing all available American supplies and standing idle for two years defending the American continent'. If the Australians had known anything about Churchill's mid-Atlantic ruminations, they might have wondered whether he envisaged Australia among the 'places lost'.

Yet a layman reading his *Duke of York* papers must be struck by his insights. He anticipated the American naval chiefs, in seeing that Japan would be defeated ultimately by strangling its lines of communication and establishing island bases from which the Japanese homeland could be pulverised. He imagined, wrongly, that the British navy would make a major contribution to regaining naval supremacy; but he was spot-on in his prediction when he wrote on 20 December 1941:

> We may therefore look to the autumn of 1942 as the period when we shall have recovered superior naval control of the Pacific. From that moment on, the Japanese overseas expeditions will be in jeopardy, and offensive operations on the largest scale may be set on foot either against their country, their possessions or their new conquests.

Again, while his time frame was astray, in part because of his ignorant optimism about 'Fortress' Singapore, he predicted the eventual course of the war: 'Under the protection of the superior battle-fleet and seaborne air power, it should be possible to acquire or regain various island bases, enabling a definite approach to be made to the homeland of Japan. The burning of Japanese cities by incendiary bombs will bring home in a most effective way to the people of Japan the dangers of the course to which they have committed themselves.'

It might have saved a deal of heartburn in Canberra if Churchill had sent a copy of his 'Notes on the Pacific' to Curtin, or frankly shared his thinking with less bluster and bullying than he chose in January and February 1942. Two days before his arrival in Washington, the British Ambassador Lord Halifax had told Casey about the visit, in strictest confidence. Halifax insisted that Casey should not mention it in telegrams to his government, on the false assumption that Curtin would already have been informed. Casey immediately cabled Canberra, urging that Curtin send a 'strongly considered statement' for Roosevelt stressing the importance of holding Singapore. Casey said he was worried that 'while lip service is paid to Singapore, its importance is clearly subordinate to the Philippines in American minds'. He suggested that Curtin's message should 'include picture of situation that would exist in South-West Pacific, Australia and Indian Ocean if Singapore were to fall into Japanese hands'. Casey followed up this telegram by another on the day of Churchill's arrival and added a significant paragraph:

> I have reason to believe that the President will try very hard to have an American accepted as commander-in-chief in the Pacific and Far East theatre, and that General MacArthur (now in the Philippines) will probably be the individual nominated.

Casey added: 'I understand that, although not devoid of human frailties, MacArthur is a good man.'

Thus prepared, Curtin was able to send a long message addressed jointly to Roosevelt and Churchill and, as he instructed Casey, 'to be delivered immediately and if possible simultaneously'. This is a foundational document in Australian defence and foreign policy, and deserves to be quoted at length for a full understanding not only of Australia's position but of the subsequent relations between Curtin, Roosevelt, and Churchill. Dated Canberra, 23 December 1941, Curtin's message said:

At this time of great crisis I desire to address you both while you are conferring for the purpose of advancing our common cause.

I have already addressed a communication to Mr Churchill on the question of Russia which I regard of great importance in relation to the Japanese war . . .

I refer now to a matter of more pressing importance. From all reports, it is very evident that in North Malaya, the Japanese have assumed control of air and of sea. The small British army there includes one Australian division, and we have sent three air squadrons to Malaya and two to Netherlands East Indies. The Army must be provided with air support; otherwise there will be repetition of Greece and Crete, and Singapore will be grievously threatened.

The fall of Singapore would mean the isolation of Philippines, the fall of Netherlands East Indies and attempts to smother all other bases. This would also sever our communications between the Indian and Pacific Oceans in this region. The setback would be as serious to U.S.A. interests as to our own.

The reinforcements earmarked by United Kingdom Government for despatch seem to us to be utterly inadequate, especially in relation to aircraft, particularly fighters.

At this time, small reinforcements are of little avail. In truth the amount of resistance to Japan in Malaya will depend directly on the amount of assistance provided by Governments of United Kingdom and United States.

Our men have fought and will fight valiantly. But they must be adequately supported. We have three divisions in the Middle East. Our airmen are fighting in Britain, Middle East and training in Canada. We have sent great quantities of supplies to Britain, Middle East and India. Our resources here are very limited indeed.

It is in your power to meet the situation. Should the United States desire, we would gladly accept a United States commander in Pacific

area. The President has said Australia will be base of increasing importance, but in order that it shall remain a base, Singapore must be
reinforced. In spite of our great difficulties, we are sending further reinforcements to Malaya. Please consider this as a matter of greatest
urgency.

Subsequent events would show that Churchill deeply resented
Curtin's blunt assessment, not only for some of its contents, but
because it was addressed directly to Roosevelt. Raking over Greece
and Crete was bad enough. Much worse was telling the President of
the United States that Britain's reinforcements were 'utterly inadequate'. Just as unwelcome was Curtin's offer to place Australian
forces under American command. Perhaps Curtin's real mistake was
to send the same message to Roosevelt as to Churchill, and letting
Churchill know exactly what he had said to Roosevelt.

In his reply, written on Christmas Day, Churchill scarcely
bothered to conceal his impatience with Curtin's importunity. He
recounted at length the measures he had ordered to strengthen
Singapore, including his suggestion that one Australian division
should go from Palestine to the Far East, either to India or Singapore, and his dispatch of the 18th British Division. Further, he
informed Curtin, 'We have instructed the Commanders-in-Chief in
the Middle East to concert a plan for sending fighters and tanks to
Singapore immediately the situation in Libya permits.' Churchill as
good as told Curtin he needed no prompting from Canberra: 'I and
the Chiefs of Staff are in close consultation with the President
and his Advisers and we have made encouraging progress. Not only
are they impressed with the importance of maintaining Singapore
but they are anxious to move a continuous flow of troops through
Australia for the relief of the Philippines if that be possible.'
Speaking directly on behalf of Roosevelt, Churchill said: 'He is
also quite willing to send substantial United States forces to
Australia where the Americans are anxious to establish important
bases for the war against Japan. You may count on me doing
everything possible to strengthen the whole front from Rangoon to
Port Darwin.'

Back in London, Churchill had left Attlee at the helm, and the Chief of the Imperial Staff, Sir Alan Brooke, in charge of the war engine room. Brooke had replaced Sir John Dill who had fallen out of Churchill's favour after his unwelcome advice about Singapore and Far Eastern priorities in April. Brooke was the one general who could stand up to Churchill. His diaries give scathing accounts of their endless rows about tactics and strategy, right up to the closing stages of the war. Three days before Pearl Harbor, Brooke had summed up his attitude towards Churchill: 'God knows where we would be without him, but God knows where we shall go with him.'

General Brooke was by now even more impatient with the Australians than Churchill: 'We prepared a memorandum on our policy for the Far East,' he wrote in his diary on 19 December. 'Not an easy document . . . Attlee ran the meeting very well, which was not easy as Sir Earle Page, the Australian representative, with the mentality of a greengrocer, wasted a lot of our time.' On 24 December: 'Winston has arrived in Washington, far from the war, and is pushing for operation by USA and ourselves against North Africa and banking on further success of Middle East offensive towards Tripoli. On the other side Duff Cooper in Singapore, by his demands, is inspiring the Australians to ask for more and more in the Far East.' On 26 December: 'In afternoon rung up by Attlee to find out whether we were ready for a Defence Committee meeting to keep Australians quiet, as they were fretting about reinforcements to Singapore. Told him we had better wait until we had reply from prime minister. Later Mr Bruce asked to see me and I had to explain to him what we were doing for the Far East. He went away satisfied.' Next day: 'A long and wearying COS meeting with a series of difficult problems mainly connected with the prime minister and his Chiefs of Staff committee in USA brewing up a series of discrepancies with what we are preparing here. In the afternoon, a Cabinet Defence Committee meeting intended to satisfy Bruce and keep him quiet.'

On Christmas Eve, Curtin had received a cascade of cables from London, Singapore, and Washington, all telling a story of too little too late, and pointing to impending catastrophe. Attlee, standing in for Churchill, sent the War Cabinet's latest strategic assessment. In a covering note, Attlee warned Curtin against making complaints about British unpreparedness in the Far East. 'It would have been strategically unsound,' Attlee said, 'to deprive the theatre in which active operations against our principal foes were actually in progress in order to reinforce a theatre which was not at that time in the active war theatre.' The War Cabinet's assessment acknowledged that 'our position in Malaya is very serious'. The Japanese advance in Malaya would be disputed inch by inch, 'but should we be forced out of Malaya, we must make every effort to hold the other essential points in the East Indies, retention of which provides a barrier to the Indian Ocean and Australia'. There was no possibility of sending capital ships, or a balanced fleet of any kind, to Singapore or the Far East. As to air reinforcements (which Page and Bruce had consistently stressed as the most urgent need), the reinforcement program could not be completed for at least four months, because of the requirements of the Middle East. Despite all this, the British War Cabinet insisted: 'Nothing compares in importance with Singapore, which is to be held at all costs.'

Meanwhile, Casey sent Curtin an account of his first Washington meeting with Churchill on 23 December. Churchill had told the assembled dominion representatives: 'My principal task in coming here is to coordinate arrangements with the United States of America by which the control of the Pacific will be regained.' This, of course, was a gloss for Australian consumption only. In truth, the principal task Churchill had set himself was to confirm his 'Beat Hitler First' strategy. Casey reported that Churchill spoke of the 'drainage' on British and American tanks and aircraft by 'the necessity of diverting all possible supplies to help Russia' and the need 'to clean up Libya as soon as possible to release reinforcements to the Far East'.

The real situation was laid bare in a cable from Australia's man on the spot, Vivian Bowden, the Australian Government Representative in Singapore, a trade official with twenty-five years' experience in China and Japan. 'The deterioration of the air position in the Malayan defence is assuming landslide proportions,' he cabled Canberra, 'and I must emphasise my firm belief that it is likely to cause a collapse in the whole defence system.' The paltry air reinforcements being proposed could not save the position. 'The present measures for the reinforcement of Malayan defence can from a practical viewpoint be regarded as little more than gestures,' Bowden said. The urgent need was powerful reinforcements by air from the Middle East – large numbers of the latest fighter aircraft and troops, 'not in brigades but in divisions'. Anything less would be 'futility', Bowden wrote. 'As things stand at present, fall of Singapore is to my mind only a matter of weeks.'

Such was the bill of fare for Curtin's cheerless Christmas at the Lodge, the Prime Minister's official residence in Canberra; his wife, Elsie, and their children stayed home in Perth on the other side of the continent. Curtin discussed these documents with his two closest advisers, the Defence Department Secretary, Fred Shedden, and his press secretary, Don Rodgers. Their discussion produced one of the most memorable documents in Australian foreign policy, and an explosion of rage from Churchill. Shedden wrote a paper on Christmas Day and presented it to Curtin on Boxing Day. Pointing to the 'revolutionary effects of air power on warlike operations', he predicted that the 'lamentable failures' in Norway and Greece would be repeated in Malaya, despite Britain's pre-war promises to make Singapore impregnable. It was clear, Shedden wrote, that the main air strength would have to come from the United States, and that the Pacific would be the main theatre of the deployment of American forces. In the last resort, Australia might become the sole rallying point in the South-West Pacific, and would provide the largest forces in the region. Therefore, Australia's voice should be heard in the highest war councils. Nevertheless, Shedden concluded: 'Closer cooperation with the United States does not imply any lessening of Empire cooperation.' In Curtin's hands, these ideas would be transmuted into a rallying-call to the people of Australia.

Curtin's press secretary, Don Rodgers, was also writing busily. Formerly a journalist on the Sydney *Labor Daily*, he had been seconded 'for a few months' in 1937 as press secretary to the Leader of the Opposition. He served with Curtin and his successor, Ben Chifley, until 1951. Professor Clem Lloyd aptly described Rodgers in the *Australian Dictionary of Biography* as 'the most effective and influential' prime ministerial press secretary the nation had produced. Curtin's trust in him was complete, and never misplaced. In such rare relationships, the question 'who wrote what?' is immaterial. For the record, however, Rodgers acknowledged in an archival letter to be opened only after his death (in 1978) that he did indeed draft Curtin's famous and controversial New Year's message, which has become, for reasons which transcend its actual content, legendary in Australian annals. As one who had some forty years of this kind of collaboration with Australian Labor leaders, including the next two Labor prime ministers, Gough Whitlam and Bob Hawke, I can testify that the document is authentically Curtin's; and, in this particular case, the ideas and the best-remembered phrases are vintage Curtin. Neither the Prime Minister nor his press secretary foresaw the international coverage and notoriety their statement would achieve. In this miscalculation, they reckoned without Winston Churchill and – of all people – Keith Murdoch.

Just before Christmas, the Melbourne afternoon daily, *The Herald*, the flagship of the burgeoning Herald & Weekly Times network, headed by Murdoch, invited Curtin to contribute a New Year message to be published in its Saturday magazine of 27 December. Curtin took the opportunity to provide a long and considered review of Australia's situation, with the theme 'The Task Ahead'. It must be emphasised that his article of fifteen hundred words was not intended as a direct appeal to Roosevelt or the United States, although this is how it is generally portrayed. It was a message to the Australian people – an explanation, reassurance, and warning, about where they stood and what they could expect. According to Rodgers' posthumous testament, Curtin himself wrote at the top of the article a quotation from his favourite Australian poet, Bernard O'Dowd:

That reddish veil which o'er the face
Of night-hag East is drawn . . .
Flames new disaster for the race?
Or can it be the dawn?

'I see 1942 as a year in which we shall know the answer,' Curtin wrote. 'The Australian Government's policy has been grounded on two facts. One is that the war with Japan is not a phase of the struggle with the Axis Powers, but is a new war. The second is that Australia must go on to a war footing.'

The Australian Labor Government, he somewhat implausibly claimed, had a 'record of realism in foreign affairs', and instanced its efforts to encourage the Soviet Union to come in against Japan. He then wrote:

> We refuse to accept the dictum that the Pacific struggle must be treated as a subordinate segment of the general conflict. By that it is not meant that any one of the other theatres of war is of less importance than the Pacific, but that Australia asks for a concerted plan, evoking the greatest strength at the Democracies' disposal, determined upon hurling Japan back.

Then followed the four key paragraphs which came to be regarded as a turning point in Australia's relations with Britain and the United States, and the seminal statement in the creation of Australia's American Alliance:

> The Australian Government, therefore, regards the Pacific struggle as primarily one in which the United States and Australia must have the fullest say in the direction of the Democracies' fighting plan.
>
> Without any inhibitions of any kind, I make it quite clear that Australia looks to America, free of any pangs as to our traditional links or kinship with the United Kingdom.
>
> We know the problems that the United Kingdom faces. We know the constant threat of invasion. We know the dangers of dispersal of strength, but we know, too, that Australia can go and Britain can still hold on.
>
> We are, therefore, determined that Australia shall not go, and we shall exert all our energies towards the shaping of a plan, with the United States as its keystone, which will give to our country some confidence of being able to hold out until the tide of battle swings against the enemy.

Curtin summed up Australia's policy from then on: 'Our external policy will be shaped towards obtaining Russia's aid, and working out, with the United States, as the major factor, a plan of Pacific strategy, along with British, Chinese and Dutch forces.' The rest of the article sketched far-reaching measures on the home front to place Australia on a total war footing.

The response from Australia's conservatives was prompt and predictable. On Monday, 29 December, the newspapers led with the reaction of the Leader of the Opposition, Billy Hughes, who said that if Curtin meant that Australia should turn for aid to the United States to the exclusion of Britain, it would be 'suicidal and a false and dangerous policy'. Curtin called a press conference to deny that anything in his message meant a weakening of Empire ties. Hughes accepted that Curtin's clarification had removed 'the uneasy feeling in the minds of the people', and promised 'complete cooperation in the task ahead'.

Any chance that controversy over Curtin's article might be confined to Australia ended when Keith Murdoch realised that the *Herald* had a scoop on its hands. Now the maker and manager of Australia's first media empire, Murdoch had not lost his urge to be a mover and shaker in the other Empire. He happened to be in London when Curtin's message appeared in his Melbourne paper. Posthaste he wrote an article for the conservative mass-circulation *Daily Mail*, and a letter to *The Times*. In both he emphasised Curtin's demand for high-level consultation rather than the turning to the United States. *The Times* followed up with an editorial, saying that 'means should be speedily found for the inclusion of Australia to the fullest possible degree in the Allied war councils'. Murdoch's articles and letters, and the editorials he inspired, appearing on the last two days of 1941, lifted Curtin's message from the obscurity of the magazine pages of the Melbourne *Herald* to the limelight of the capital of the Empire. Australian conservatives raised the age-old question: What will they think in England?

The Greatest Living Englishman left no doubt about his own thinking: 'I hope there will be no pandering to this,' he cabled Attlee, 'while at the same time we do all in human power to come to their aid.' To Lord Cranborne, he categorised the article as 'misbehaviour'. He claimed in his memoirs that Curtin's article had been 'flaunted round the world by our enemies', but he gave no evidence for his assertion. He said that it had 'produced the worst impression in high American circles and in Canada', again without citing the evidence. Casey's wife, Maie, later alleged that Roosevelt thought Curtin's statements smacked of 'panic and disloyalty', presumably to Britain. It is reasonable to speculate that if Roosevelt ever expressed such a thought, it had been put in his head by Churchill himself. As to Canada, it is unlikely that Mackenzie King cared a fig about it one way or the other, except that Churchill himself 'spoke strongly' to the Canadian Cabinet during his two days in Ottawa. Churchill repeated his belief that Curtin, in his 'outpourings of anxiety', did not represent true Australian feeling. He recalled: 'I weighed promptly in my mind the idea of making a broadcast direct to the Australian people'.

In a conversation with Fred Shedden during the furore, Curtin acknowledged that it might have been better to have used Shedden's phrase 'without any lessening of the bonds with the United Kingdom' instead of his own 'free of any pangs'. But he made no apology for the thrust of his message. In turning to America, he was in 'quite good company', seeing that Churchill had suggested it 'as far back as 1916' – presumably a reference to Churchill's speech of March, 1914, when he had consigned Australia to the protection and goodwill of Japan. In any case, Curtin told Shedden, 'he was answerable for the security of this country, and had designedly expressed his feeling in the bluntest terms'.

Curtin's offence was compounded by its timing. Churchill saw it as an impertinent intervention by a colonial politician who did not truly represent his own country. In his eyes, everything was wrong about the message: a gift to German and Japanese propaganda; a challenge to his political position in Britain; yet another Australian attempt to seat itself in the British War Cabinet, and now a bid for the Anglo–American high table; an unwarranted assertion of Australian independence; a weakening of the unity of the Empire; an ill-timed exposure of the bankruptcy of three decades of British Far

Eastern strategy; an affront to his honour as the man who had given his pledged word about the rescue of the kith and kin; an insult to the efforts which even now he was making on their behalf; a competitive bid for American aid; a threat to the 'Beat Hitler First' strategy; and an infringement of his monopoly with Roosevelt as the voice of the Empire. Coming on the heels of Curtin's letter addressed jointly to Roosevelt, Churchill seems to have regarded the New Year message as an Australian attempt to gatecrash the White House Christmas party.

Roosevelt's real Christmas present to Churchill was to be a promise to produce 45,000 aircraft in 1942, and 100,000 in 1943, with 45,000 tanks in 1942 and 75,000 in 1943. Churchill, recorded his personal physician, Sir Charles Wilson, 'is drunk with the figures'. All this, of course, was hidden from the Australian Government. Curtin, Bruce, and Page were still pleading with Britain to bring the Singapore air defences up to the promised strength of three hundred first-rate aircraft.

On Boxing Day, Curtin had read another cable from Casey: 'I sought and obtained a discussion with Churchill at White House today (24 December). I emphasised the facts and point of view in your telegrams. British Chiefs of Staff Pound (Admiralty), Dill (Army) and Portal (Air Force) were called in. The President joined the discussion and subsequently called in Colonel Knox (Secretary of Navy).' When all these captains and kings had departed, Churchill and Casey were left alone. Casey later revealed that Churchill had turned on him and snarled: 'You can't kick me around the room. I'm not kickable.'

21

'Australasian anxieties'
January, 1942

Churchill's overheated reaction to Curtin's message to the Australian people distorted his relations with Australia for the rest of the war and beyond. His resentment bubbled up, and often over, at the slightest provocation. At the root of the trouble lay an irreconcilable difference of outlook. Curtin could never accept that Australia's fate must be completely subordinated to Churchill's grand strategy. On this level, the key part of Curtin's statement in the Melbourne *Herald* was not the idea of 'looking to America', but his cry of anguish: 'We know that Australia can go and Britain can still hold on.' What made Churchill so ungenerous towards Curtin was that he knew in his heart not only that this was true, but that his own policy had made it true.

Churchill began his post-war account of 1942 with a chapter entitled 'Australasian Anxieties'. He called this fourth volume *The Hinge of Fate*, and left his readers in no doubt that Australia was the creak in the hinge. As usual with Churchill when he dealt with Australia, he drew the distinction between its people and its political leaders:

Australia and New Zealand felt suddenly plunged into the forefront of the battle. They saw themselves exposed to the possibility of invasion. No longer did the war mean sending aid across the oceans to the Mother Country in her distress and peril. The new foe could strike straight at Australian homes. The enormous coastlines of their continent could never be defended. All their great cities were on the seaboard. Their only four well-trained divisions of volunteers, the New Zealand division, and all their best officers, were far away across the oceans. The naval command of the Pacific had passed in a flash and for an indefinite period to Japan. Australasian air-power hardly existed. Can we wonder that deep alarm swept Australia or that the thoughts of their Cabinet were centred on their own affairs?

Even in what seems a sympathetic picture, Churchill betrays his prejudice. There is, for example, an implied censure of Australian unpreparedness in his assertion: 'Australasian air power hardly existed.' To the extent that this was true, it was not for want of trying. The trouble with Australasian air power in 1942 was that it was dispersed around the world. As much as the AIF, the RAAF had been deployed to meet the demands of Churchill's grand strategy. Since April, 1940, Australia and New Zealand had contributed more than ten thousand pilots and aircrew through the Empire Air Training Scheme. They had served in the Battle of Britain, the Battle for the Atlantic, and the campaigns in the Mediterranean, North Africa, and the Middle East. Most of the survivors were retained in Britain for the air campaign against Germany. Even so, four RAAF squadrons were already based in Singapore when Japan struck. For eighteen months before Pearl Harbor, the British Air Ministry, unimpeded by Churchill, had obstructed the provision of first-class aircraft despite the urgings of Bruce, Page, Menzies, and Fadden, strongly supported by Curtin as Opposition Leader in the Advisory War Council. Churchill himself had seemed to acknowledge the problem when he had proposed to ask Roosevelt for 'modern machines for the intrepid airmen of Australia and New Zealand' (in the deleted passage of his December 1940 letter). Perhaps such considerations influenced the

Australian Cabinet as they became, according to Churchill, 'centred on their own affairs'.

Churchill linked his portrayal of Australia's plight with his standard criticism of the failure of the politicians to form an all-party government. 'Local politics ruled unshaken', he wrote. 'The Labour Government, with its majority of two, monopolised the whole executive power, and conscription even for home defence was banned.' It is simply wrong to say 'conscription even for home defence was banned'. To link the conscription issue with the failure to form a national government is profoundly misleading.

The Menzies Government had reactivated compulsory training for home service on 20 October 1939, in the first weeks of the war. The 'monopolisation' of the Executive power by the Curtin Government in October took the form of an order for the compulsory call-up of a further 114,000 men for the Citizen Military Force, to add to the 130,000 already on full-time duty. On 11 December, all single men between eighteen and forty-five, and all married men to thirty-five became liable for full-time service. It is true that Labor's 'ban' on conscription for overseas service, and the Menzies Government's acceptance of that fact for the sake of national unity, led to the development of 'two armies' – the all-volunteer AIF and the CMF; and that this invidious distinction led to serious military and manpower problems for the Australian defence forces, and political problems for Curtin. His efforts to solve these problems represented some of the most difficult and courageous achievements of his war leadership. In his first months as Prime Minister, he secured from the Labor Party Federal Conference a resolution extending the definition of 'home defence' to include the Australian Territories in Papua and New Guinea, and the adjacent islands. At its peak in 1943, the Australian army numbered 530,000, and over 900,000 men and women served in the armed forces during the war, from a total population of seven million. Two thirds of the army began as conscripts. Lack of recruits for the army, voluntary or compulsory, was never part of the army's problems, much less the result of a ban on 'conscription even for home defence'. Such a ban never existed – except in this sentence which Churchill permanently transmitted to posterity in the most widely read and believed account of the Second World War ever published.

'These partisan decisions,' Churchill wrote, 'did less than justice to the spirit of the Australian nation, and made more difficult our task in providing, so far as possible, for their security while observing a true sense of proportion in world strategy.' He conceded that the Australian Government had a duty to 'study their own position with concentrated attention'. On the other hand, Churchill wrote, 'we had to try to think for all'. Introducing his 1942 correspondence with Curtin in 'the sombre pages of this volume' Churchill reverted to Tobruk, to make it appear to his readers that Curtin had been the prime mover. 'Our discussions had not been agreeable.' However, Churchill acknowledged:

> Later in the war, in easier times, when he came over to England and we got to know him well, there was general respect and liking for this eminent and striking Australian personality, and I personally formed with him a friendship which, alas, was cut short by his untimely death. At this moment, however, when pressures from all sides were so fierce, I was too conscious of the depth and number of the differences in outlook that divided us.

A major 'difference in outlook' between Churchill and Curtin was about what constituted a threat to Australia. Despite all his promises before Pearl Harbor, Churchill now made it plain that only actual invasion would entitle Australia to special protection. Anything short of that – Japanese occupation of the rest of Australia's region, isolation by sea and air, the strangling of its trade routes, raids on its northern coasts by air or sea, bombardment of its cities or even occupation of some of its Northern Territory – all these, to Churchill, were dangers of a secondary kind, and should be accepted as part of the misfortunes of war. As he was to tell Curtin in January, 'we have had a good dose of all that in England without mortal result'. The Australian Government and people took a less philosophical view of their national danger.

Another 'difference in outlook' between Churchill and Curtin arose from Australia's demands for a greater say in the higher direction of the war. These demands, of course, went back to Menzies and his disillusion with Churchill's methods. Menzies, however, had always seen the problem in political and personal terms. He focused on the War Cabinet in London, seeing Australian representation, preferably by himself, as a means of curbing Churchill. Fadden had settled for Page, with his irritating, if not counterproductive, attendance at meetings of the War Cabinet and Imperial Defence Committees. With America's entry into the war and Japan's seemingly unstoppable drive south, the Curtin Government expanded Australia's demands to include the military as well as the political councils in both Washington and London. Evatt, more than Curtin, injected a nationalistic stridency into these demands. Within a week of Pearl Harbor, and before he knew that Churchill was on his way to Washington, Evatt cabled Casey: 'I want you to press and insist that in every conference between representatives of the associated powers, this Government must have the opportunity of separate representation . . . our point of view must be continuously stressed or our great needs will be overlooked.'

Curtin put his case directly to the people in an Australia Day broadcast on 26 January 1942:

> The whole philosophy of the way of life for which we are fighting means that in wartime, it is more important even than in peacetime that consultation as equals should mark the activities, firstly, of those charged with the Government of a democracy and, secondly, those jointly representing the several democracies. No single nation can afford to risk its future on the infallibility of one man, and no nation can afford to submerge its right of speaking for itself because of the assumed omniscience of another.

The Australian listeners, unaware of the cables streaming from Canberra, London, and Washington, probably did not realise that Curtin was taking a shot at Churchill.

The rift between Churchill and Curtin widened sharply on New Year's Day, 1942, not because of Curtin's *Herald* message to the

Australian people, but because of his stinging response to Churchill about the plans laid at the White House over Christmas. To Canberra, it seemed that the arrangements being hammered out between Churchill, Roosevelt, and their military chiefs left Australia out in the cold – in Curtin's words, 'isolated and left to defend our area without Allied assistance'. Curtin told Churchill that the Washington plans were 'made in a piecemeal fashion', 'were strategically unsound', and would 'frustrate the vitally important aim of making Australia "America's base against Japan"'. He wrote to the British Prime Minister: 'Our Chiefs of Staff are unable to see anything in these proposals except the endangering of our safety.'

The proposal which so alarmed the Australian Government was devised by the American Chiefs of Staff, led by General George Catlett Marshall. Marshall, the organiser of the Allied victory in Western Europe, exuded so much natural authority that he was even able to rebuke the President of the United States for calling him 'George'. His plan brought the South-East Asian theatre under a single unified command, to be known as ABDA – the American, British, Dutch, Australian area. The command comprised the area where all the actual fighting was, in a vast arc from Burma and Malaya through to the archipelago of the Dutch East Indies and the Philippines. Continental Australia was excluded from ABDA and consigned to a separate zone designated ANZAC. The United States took responsibility for the rest of the Pacific, east of the Philippines, but the US navy insisted that it could not undertake the defence of Australia's north-eastern approaches. In effect, the proposal made Australia responsible for the defence of the vast area covering Australia, New Guinea, New Britain, the Bismarck Archipelago, the Solomon Islands, the New Hebrides, and New Caledonia. In the words of the editor of *Documents on Australian Foreign Policy 1937–49*, W. J. Hudson, these arrangements meant that 'for a time in January 1942, with a powerful invader apparently at the gate, Australia was isolated and voiceless'.

Curtin's protest had been prompted by Casey, whom Churchill had invited to the White House for a briefing on his talks with Roosevelt and the American Chiefs. President Roosevelt himself,

Churchill told Casey, had suggested that the commander should be British – none other than General Wavell – and that he be designated as the Supreme Commander of ABDA. Churchill failed to mention that he had at first resisted the concept of a unified command; Roosevelt then took Churchill by surprise and nominated Wavell. The British Chiefs travelling with Churchill suspected a trap to saddle a British general with the odium of the coming disasters. Wavell himself, on learning of his appointment, commented sourly: 'I have heard of a man left holding the baby, but this is quadruplets.' Within two months, the entire ABDA command was in Japanese hands.

'Night and day I am labouring here to make the best arrangements possible in your interests,' Churchill assured Curtin on 3 January. The reason why Australia had been excluded from ABDA was because 'it is limited to the fighting zone where active operations are now proceeding'. He was trying his hardest to persuade the United States Navy to assume responsibility for the whole South-West Pacific and its vital lines of communication with Australia. As to Curtin's detailed critique of British plans for the defence of the Far East, it had 'been largely superseded by the appointment of General Wavell as Supreme Commander'. Nevertheless, he had laid it before the British Chiefs who were with him in Washington 'and I have no doubt that they will take to heart the various comments you have been good enough to make'. Churchill's justification for the exclusion of continental Australia from ABDA – that it was not in the actual fighting zone – really summed up his whole attitude to the defence of Australia. He had come to believe that his pledges to the 'kith and kin' stopped short at anything less than actual invasion.

In London, General Sir Alan Brooke did something unusual – he agreed with the Australians. He saw that it was 'a mistake' to exclude Australia from ABDA. 'I expect that we shall gradually be forced to change these back again,' he wrote in his diary on 12 January. A fortnight later he was writing: 'The show will never run properly until ABDA and ANZAC are amalgamated into one area.' By the end of January, they conceded that the Australians had been right all along, and the ABDA boundaries were extended to include northern Australia and New Guinea. It was a hollow victory. Within three weeks, with the fall of Singapore, Rangoon and Batavia, ABDA ceased to exist. New arrangements had to be made, and they were to be much closer to Curtin's ideas than Churchill's. In the meantime, however, Churchill professed to regard ABDA as 'a broadminded and selfless proposal, the merits of which as a war winner I have become convinced'.

Since Churchill's concepts of strategy were at the root of so much of the trouble between Churchill and Australia, it is fitting to give here the assessment of the man who knew most about Churchill as strategist. As Chief of the Imperial Staff from the eve of Pearl Harbor to the end of the war, Sir Alan Brooke met Churchill almost daily, and rowed with him at least weekly. After four years of it, Brooke wrote in his diary on 10 September 1944:

> The wonderful thing is that three-quarters of the world imagine that Winston Churchill is one of the Strategists of History, a second Marlborough, and the other quarter have no conception what a public menace he is and has been throughout the war . . . Without him, England was lost for a certainty; with him, England has been on the verge of disaster time and again.

Churchill had suffered a mild heart attack at the White House, known only to his travelling physician, Wilson, who did not vouchsafe his diagnosis even to Churchill himself. However, Churchill betook himself to Florida, where he vented his frustration with the 'bad stock' of Australia in the manner described at the beginning of this book. Yet, far from being the 'stiff message to Curtin' suggested in Wilson's diaries, Churchill's cable of 8 January 1942 went as far towards sweetness and light as a Churchill could go. Perhaps it was the influence of the Florida sun. The British Prime Minister told Curtin that he and Roosevelt contemplated three commands in the Asia-Pacific theatre: the South-West Pacific, under General Wavell, where all the fighting was now taking place; the South Pacific lines of communication, under American command; and the Defence of

Australia and its island territories, under Australian command. As to the 'defence of Australian soil', Churchill said: 'I thought you would prefer it to be in the hands of the Australian Commander-in-Chief.' 'Surely this is a reasonable layout,' he said, ignoring the substance of Curtin's case: that there was no plan for making Australia the main base against Japan. He then gave news which, he must have felt, would be music to Curtin's ears: 'The United States would be quite willing, I believe, to reinforce your home defence troops with 40 or 50 thousand Americans'. Churchill put the blunt question: 'Do you think you are in immediate danger of invasion in force?' But, anticipating the reply, he immediately added: 'It is quite true that you may have air attacks but we have had a good dose already in England without mortally harmful results.' Later Churchill was to specify what he meant by invasion: six to ten Japanese divisions on Australian soil.

Churchill then outlined the Washington proposals for strengthening the machinery for ministerial and staff consultation, with Australian participation, in London and Washington. 'However,' he said, 'it is not possible to promise that nothing will ever be said or done which has not previously received full approval of all five governments (American, British, Dutch, Australian and New Zealand). I may have to speak to the President on the telephone in matters of great urgency. These occasions should arise only rarely since the Supreme Commander (Wavell) will be doing the fighting, and there will probably be time to discuss the larger strategy and supply issues among ourselves before decisions are reached.' He begged for patience in matters of organisation 'where so many partners and factors take time to shape'. He asked for another week to present an entire scheme 'which you will be able to criticise or, if you will, reject'. He concluded: 'Believe me, I am thinking of your interests every moment.'

Before Curtin had time to digest Churchill's message, and perhaps before he had read it, he received the worst possible news about Malaya, and in the worst possible way. Just when Churchill was promising wider consultation, Curtin learnt that the battle for northern Malaya was lost, that the Japanese were thrusting forward to Johore at the southern end of the Malay Peninsula, and that the 8th Australian Division had been given 'the task of fighting the decisive battle' to prevent the Japanese crossing over to Singapore. It was all happening exactly as the Australians had predicted and feared – and they learnt about it only through a leaked copy of a message which Wavell had sent to the War Office in London. On 11 January, Curtin cabled Churchill:

> The Australian Government has no doubt that the 8th Division will acquit itself in accordance with the highest traditions of the A.I.F. However, I urge on you that nothing be left undone to reinforce Malaya to the greatest degree possible in accordance with my earlier representations and your intentions. I am particularly concerned in regard to the air strength, as a repetition of the Greek and Crete campaigns would evoke a violent public reaction and such a happening should be placed outside the bounds of possibility.

It was the wrong way to argue with Churchill. Curtin should have realised by now that complaints reviving Greece and Crete were like red rags to a bull. The Tobruk experience should have taught him enough about Churchill's technique of seizing on one sensitive point to distort an entire argument. By invoking public opinion to bolster his case, Curtin fell into the same trap as Menzies and Fadden over Tobruk.

'I do not accept any censure about Crete and Greece,' Churchill replied on 12 January, predictably seizing the opening Curtin had given him. He then rehearsed the British war effort since 1940, where 'we have sunk all party differences and have imposed universal compulsory service not only upon men but women'. He left unstated the implied contrast with Australia. Once more, he scratched the Tobruk scab: 'We have successfully disengaged Tobruk after the previous relief of all your men who gallantly held it for so long. I hope therefore that you will be considerate in the judgement which you pass upon those to whom Australian lives and fortunes are so dear.'

He added: 'I spent all last night with Mr Casey who explained to me very fully the views which your Government holds.' In fact,

Casey had travelled with Churchill on the special train taking him from Florida back to Washington on 10 January. This itself was a tribute to Casey's standing. During the four hours he spent in Churchill's private compartment, Casey canvassed 'all aspects of Australia's concern about representation and consultation'. Churchill floated the idea of a 'War Council of the Far East' in London, over which he himself would preside; such a Council would not supersede Page's right to address the War Cabinet on matters of immediate concern to Australia. Churchill may have been genuinely puzzled by the complaints about consultation from Canberra. As he saw it, he had given Page in London access to the Cabinet and it was not his fault if Page was ineffectual. He had been generous with his time and effort with Casey in Washington, and had facilitated Casey's access to Roosevelt. No other dominion representative had been given comparable treatment, and none had been as effective in putting his Government's views.

Churchill's exasperation would have turned to disbelief, had he known about the carping to which Casey was being subjected from Canberra, not from Curtin but from Evatt. The stream of instructions he issued to Casey were headmasterish, disapproving, ungenerous, even insulting. Far from being impressed by Casey's intimacy with both Churchill and Roosevelt, he was, if not jealous, certainly suspicious.

Suspiciousness close to paranoia was Evatt's fatal flaw. A man so distrustful of others was bound to engender mistrust in himself. 'Even I don't know what he will be getting up to next,' Curtin told his young friend and fellow journalist from Perth, Paul Hasluck, now working in Evatt's department. 'He needs watching, but even so, he can still do a lot of things for Australia and you have to help him do them.' Curtin valued Evatt's energy and intellect, admired his sacrifice of his High Court seat in 1940 to enter Parliament, had no illusions about his ambitions, but was too often swayed against his better judgement by Evatt's forceful advocacy of his views. Evatt especially prevailed whenever he could turn the argument into a legal question, as he did, for instance, over signing the Declaration of the United Nations issued by Roosevelt and

Churchill in Washington on 1 January 1942. This statement of Allied war aims, together with the Atlantic Charter, was designed to be the foundation of the post-war world order. Evatt urged that the twenty-seven nations committing themselves to the destruction of Hitlerism be listed in alphabetical order, thus putting Australia first, well ahead of the United States, the United Kingdom, and the Union of Soviet Socialist Republics. He queried the inclusion of India on the grounds that India was not a self-governing nation. Such pettifogging could only irritate Roosevelt and infuriate Churchill. In judging Evatt, one is reminded of a comment by the German Ambassador to London in 1912: 'A very vain man, bent, come what may, on playing a brilliant part.' The ambassador was speaking of Winston Churchill.

Casey was perfectly cast for the role of Evatt's prime suspect in 1942: Casey, twig of the Melbourne Establishment; Evatt, son of a feckless hotelkeeper who died when he was seven, brought up in hardship in Maitland and Sydney by his strong-willed mother, who sacrificed everything for her two brilliant sons. Casey, suave, well-groomed, with a passable Oxbridge accent, gliding smoothly through life, at ease in London society and Washington politics and diplomacy; Evatt, clumsy, dishevelled, with a harsh and grating voice, prodigiously hard-working, never fully at ease with himself or anyone else, save his accomplished and charming wife, Mary Alice. Casey flew his own plane around the United States; Evatt (like Curtin) hated flying. Three things in particular aroused Evatt's suspicions about Casey: he had been a senior minister in the Lyons and Menzies Governments; Menzies, Evatt's bête noire, had appointed him as Minister to Washington; and to Evatt, the ardent Australian nationalist, Casey epitomised the Australian conservative identification of Australian interests with British interests. In short, Evatt suspected Casey's loyalty to the Australian Labor Government and to Australia itself.

Evatt's suspicions were fuelled by Casey's contacts with Churchill. From the time Churchill arrived in Washington, Evatt bombarded his minister on the spot with orders and criticisms, coaching him on what he could say to Churchill, and what he was not to say, even instructing on the tactics he was to adopt. 'Please understand that the stage of gentle suggestion has now passed,' Evatt cabled Casey on Boxing Day. 'Much more is required. Please take immediate steps to inform Churchill that the requirements [for the air defence of Singapore] are only the very minimum, that anything less will be dangerous and that a definite timetable is required.' He accused Casey of giving too many press interviews, and making unauthorised statements of Australian policy. He complained that Casey was not answering his messages; and not 'reporting to us promptly on what action you have taken in relation to each point'. Casey's shortcomings, Evatt said, led 'to lack of coordination, to conflicting views and to frustration of this nation's war effort'.

Evatt could hardly have made a more serious charge, but Casey was remarkably temperate in his reply. He tried to put his position in perspective: 'Churchill lives and works in the White House and discusses military, air, naval and supply matters in connection with all theatres of war with the President at all hours of the day and night. The American and British Chiefs of Staff are in constant session day and night, broken only when they meet for discussion with the President and/or Churchill. I see the Chiefs of Staff as often as possible, usually early in the morning or late at night. I have good entrée to them all.' He told Evatt he was able to see Churchill himself and the American chiefs on every matter raised from Canberra. He concluded: 'I believe I am right in saying that these representations have not been without their influence on the volume and speed of U.S. air and other reinforcements that are on their way.'

Evatt was not impressed. He told Casey, 'we are much disturbed' by the proposals coming from Washington. 'We cannot allow the scheme for the South-West Pacific to go ahead without amendments designed to give us an equal voice in the final decisions.' He advised Casey to pay more attention to Roosevelt and less to Churchill. 'My general impression,' he cabled on 7 January, 'is that we are likely to get greater support from Roosevelt than from Churchill. In fact, I can hardly believe that President Roosevelt can know of the unfavourable reaction here to the scheme as agreed upon between himself and Churchill.'

The irony, of course, was that the 'scheme' had been sponsored by Roosevelt himself. By embracing it, Churchill had achieved in return his main objective: Roosevelt's strong reaffirmation of the Europe-first strategy. The Australian leaders failed to realise the strength of that commitment. They deceived themselves into believing that Roosevelt would be more sympathetic to Australia's plight than Churchill, if only they could put their case to him directly, unfiltered by Churchill's rhetoric and prejudices. In this, they mistook not only the Roosevelt–Churchill relationship, but Roosevelt's own situation and attitudes. They also mistook the complex nature of the decision-making processes in Washington and the competition for Roosevelt's ear between the chiefs of the US army and navy. They assumed that the importance of Australia as the main base against Japan would be as obvious in Washington as in Canberra. They failed to see that Australia's needs would never be given high priority until it became in America's interests to do so.

Curtin and Evatt's worst miscalculation in January 1942 lay in the way they dealt with Churchill. The prosecutorial tone of many of Curtin's cables – a fairly sure sign of Evatt's involvement – gave Churchill the cue for recriminations of his own. In that way, he was able to blunt the force of Curtin's arguments, or to sidestep them. Curtin and Evatt seemed to think that argumentative point-scoring would win him over. Unlike Roosevelt, Churchill genuinely worried about Australia or, at the very least, his standing with the Australian public. He was conscious of the promises he had made, and the obligations Britain had incurred. His touchiness and bad temper sometimes suggested a guilty conscience. He was deeply protective of his place in history. He was intensely sensitive to any criticism that impugned his honour. And, unlike Roosevelt, he was sentimental and warm-hearted. These well-known traits in Churchill's character could be treated in one of two ways: to get to his heart, or get under his skin. All too often, Curtin chose the second way. In writing his cables to Churchill in these disaster-filled weeks, he allowed Evatt too much say, and Evatt had a knack of getting under everybody's skin.

22

'Inexcusable betrayal'

January–February, 1942

'The only vital point is Singapore fortress,' Churchill had told Curtin in his cable of 12 January 1942. But 'Fortress Singapore' existed only in Churchill's imagination. It was a disastrous example of the power of a word over facts. Charles Bean's accusation that 'a Churchill's excess of imagination' caused disaster at Gallipoli in 1915 rings true for Singapore in 1942. The idea that the naval base at Singapore was an actual fortress, able to withstand a six-months siege, stirred his imagination and, perhaps, his ancestral memories of the great sieges laid by the Duke of Marlborough in the early eighteenth century. In twenty days, the Imperial Japanese Army brought Churchill down to earth, and shattered Australian illusions of twenty years.

While Churchill was still in Washington, he kept up a cheerful front about the Malayan campaign. In his cable of 12 January, he told Curtin: 'I have great confidence that your troops will acquit themselves in the highest fashion in the impending battles.' Taking white superiority for granted, he said: 'So far the Japanese have only had two white battalions and a few gunners against them.' So much for the sacrifices of the Indians. Now, the 18th British Division was about to arrive in Singapore, 'to take their stand with their Australian brothers'. There was justification, he said, 'for Wavell's hope that a counterstroke will be possible in the latter part of February'.

The Japanese forces in Malaya were outnumbered nearly three to one by the British, Indian, and Australian defenders. The Japanese General, Tomoyuki Yamashita, 'the Tiger of Malaya', used only three divisions, about thirty-five thousand soldiers, in a campaign which lasted only seventy days from the first landings, on the same day as Pearl Harbor. Japanese superiority lay not in numbers but in Yamashita's long and detailed planning, the morale and training of his forces, and, above all, supremacy in the air, all underwritten by Japanese control of the sea.

Even in the air, the Japanese advantage need not have been over-whelming. Yamashita had at his disposal about six hundred aircraft, including the unrivalled fighter Mitsubishi 6M2, known as the Zero. But instead of the three hundred to five hundred and fifty aircraft promised by Churchill at various times, the British scraped together about two hundred and fifty planes, including four RAAF squadrons. They were outclassed by the Zero and their pilots who, the British had taught themselves to believe, were incompetent and half-blind. When, barely a fortnight before the fall of Singapore, fifty Hurricane fighters arrived in crates, Churchill wrote them up as a splendid example of his willingness to sacrifice British interests in the Middle East.

Yet only three days after his confident message to Curtin, Churchill cabled Wavell: 'Please let me know your idea of what would happen in the event of your being forced to withdraw onto the island. How many troops would be needed to defend this area? What means are there of stopping landings.' Wavell replied immediately: 'Little or nothing has been done to construct defences on the north side of the island to prevent crossing the Johore Straits.' Churchill recalled in his war memoirs that he read this message 'with painful surprise'. 'So there were no permanent fortifications covering the landward side of the naval base and of the city!'

Now, at last, Churchill was being forced to face the even more astonishing truth: 'No measures worth speaking of had been taken by any of the commanders since the war began . . . to construct field defences.' The warnings Australia had passed on from its representative in Singapore, Bowden, had 'proved all too true', he wrote. 'I ought to have known. My advisers ought to have known and I ought to have been told, and I ought to have asked . . . The possibility of Singapore island having no landward defences no more entered into my mind than that of a battleship being launched without a bottom.' He chided General Ismay, his Chief of Staff: 'How is it that not one of you pointed this out to me? I warn you, this will be one of the greatest scandals that could possibly be exposed.' Churchill's rage over the lack of landward defences fed the enduring myth that Singapore was lost because its guns pointed the wrong way, out to sea.

In the grandest imperial style, Churchill sent out his orders to save the outpost of empire: 'The entire male population should be employed upon construction of defence works. The most rigorous compulsion is to be used, up to the limit where picks and shovels are available.' Churchill was unaware that the Singapore Government had declined to enlist the aid of the mainly Chinese population in order to avoid civilian panic. Nevertheless, Churchill ordered: 'The whole island must be fought for until every single unit and every single strong point has been separately destroyed. The city of Singapore must be converted into a citadel and defended to the death. No surrender can be contemplated.'

Wavell followed Churchill's new instructions. His first decision as Commander-in-Chief of ABDA was made over the head of the British army commander, General Arthur Ernest Percival. Percival, fifty-four, had been in command in Malaya since May, 1941; in his lack of drive and luck, he seemed a more tragic version of Sir Ian Hamilton. Wavell now ordered the abandonment of the campaign for Malaya in order to make a stand at Johore at the southern end of the Peninsula. To hold Johore, he placed the 8th Australian Division there, commanded by General Gordon Bennett, who in Wavell's opinion had shown a fighting spirit which distinguished him from the other officers, especially Percival. His confidence was not misplaced, in that three battalions of the 8th achieved the only noteworthy successes against the Japanese in the entire campaign. But by 31 January, the Australians were forced to retreat across the Causeway to the island of Singapore.

Churchill and Curtin seemed locked in a cycle of accusation and recrimination. When Curtin warned against a repetition of Greece, Churchill responded by revisiting Tobruk. But Curtin would not let it go: 'My observations on Crete and Greece imply no censure on you, but there is no denying the fact that air support was not on the scale promised.' Now, Curtin wrote on 17 January, the same kind of reports were being received about Malaya and Singapore. He traced the history of British assurances on Singapore going back to 1933. He claimed that the Australian Government, going back to Menzies, had correctly forecast the inadequacy of Malayan and Singapore defence as long ago as December, 1940.

Churchill was not going to let such a challenge pass, and his reach into history was as deep as Curtin's. He began his thousand-word reply on 19 January by recalling that in 1939 he had been out of office for eleven years, he was not to blame for Appeasement, and he had given 'ceaseless warnings for six years before the war began'. He then reviewed and defended his entire policy since becoming Prime Minister in May 1940. Exaggerating the temporary success in the Middle East ('the destruction of two-thirds of Rommel's army', he claimed) he had been able to send the 18th British Division and the 6th and 7th Australian Divisions to the Far East theatre, 'with all speed'. As well as the need to send aid to Russia, 'I am sure it would have been wrong to send forces needed to beat Rommel to reinforce the Malay Peninsula while Japan was still at peace'. No one could have foreseen the naval disasters in the Pacific and the China Sea. 'The blame for the frightful risks we have run and will have to run rests with all those who, in or out of office, failed to discern the Nazi menace and to crush it while it was weak.' Nevertheless, Britain was strengthening the Royal Navy in the Indian Ocean 'or to move to your protection as might be most helpful', and 'to enable large reduction in American strength in the Atlantic for the sake of the Pacific'. With this catalogue of old recriminations and new promises, Churchill concluded:

We must not be dismayed or get into recrimination but remain united in true comradeship. Do not doubt my loyalty to Australia and New Zealand. I cannot offer any guarantees for the future and I am sure that great ordeals lie before us, but I feel hopeful as never before that we shall emerge safely and also gloriously from the dark valley.

Churchill now prepared the ground for a breathtaking somersault. The immediate consequences for Anglo–Australian relations and, as will be seen in the next chapter, for the relations between Churchill and Curtin, were to be shattering. 'As a strategic object', he suddenly announced to his Chiefs of Staff on 21 January, 'I regard keeping the Burma Road open as more important than the retention of Singapore.' Would it not be better, he asked his Chiefs of Staff, to *evacuate* Singapore before the Japanese forced its *surrender*? Surely, he argued on 21 January, it would be better to concentrate on the defence of Burma, on which China and India depended, than lose everything in Singapore. It was an 'ugly decision', he acknowledged, but 'we may, by muddling things, lose *both* Singapore and the Burma Road'. It would not be worth losing men and aircraft by reinforcing Singapore for the sake of holding it for a few weeks. 'Moreover,' he said, 'one must consider that the fall of Singapore [as distinct from its deliberate evacuation], accompanied as it will be by the fall of Corregidor, will be a tremendous shock to India, which only the arrival of powerful forces and successful action on the Burma front can sustain.'

Any shock to Australia involved in such a stunning reversal was not among the considerations Churchill put to the British Chiefs of Staff. So far from warning the Australians of the impending revolution in his thinking, he tried to keep them in the dark. While the Chiefs of Staff and the Defence Committee were hesitating 'to commit us to so grave a step', Page got wind of the new game afoot. In his memoirs, Churchill puts it almost as a matter of grievance that 'by some means or other, Page was shown a copy of my minute to the Chiefs of Staff. He immediately telegraphed to his Government and on 24 January, we received a message from Mr Curtin, which contained a severe reproach.'

Churchill – or his researcher – erroneously asserted that he did not invite Page to the Defence Committee of 21 January. Whether invited or not, Page attended the meeting, and argued strongly that 'evacuation of Singapore would cause irreparable loss of prestige and irreparable damage to the Allied cause, quite apart from its military aspect'. It had been agreed 'after much argument to wait on events for a couple of days to see what happened'; Page telegraphed Canberra a full account of the proceedings. Churchill's error about Page's attendance at the meeting is quite unimportant in itself, except for the fact that he wove it into the fabric of his post-war case against Australia, in his attempt to depict the Australian Government's response as half-cocked and panic-stricken.

The 'severe reproach' in Curtin's message was an accusation of 'inexcusable betrayal'. Unknown to Churchill, Curtin was away from the capital when this response was sent under his signature. The Prime Minister had been persuaded by his Cabinet colleagues to take a break. Astonishingly, he chose to cross the continent by train to his home in Perth, a four-night journey, and was absent from Canberra for this critical fortnight. His absence seems so extraordinary that his first biographer, Lloyd Ross, was unaware of it or suppressed it. The editor of *Documents on Australian Foreign Policy* notes that Curtin 'took a holiday', and that unfavourable press comment on his absence led him to justify his journey by the implausible excuse that he was consulting the Premier of Western Australia on naval policy at the request of the British Admiralty. My personal speculation is that Curtin made the judgement that unless he could get away for a spell, he would break down completely.

Curtin's deputy and Minister for the Army, Frank Forde, had called an emergency meeting of the Australian Cabinet to consider a report from General Bennett saying that part of his force in Johore had been cut off 'without possibility of relief'. Bennett had also cast doubt on the Indian troops' will to fight. That morning Bowden, the Australian representative in Singapore, had reported that the British position was 'desperate and perhaps irretrievable'. These reports – not Page's bombshell about an evacuation of Singapore – were the first subjects discussed by the emergency Cabinet meeting and formed the first two paragraphs of its long message to Churchill. 'Whilst we have no intention of suggesting any criticism of the Indians who are fighting the common foe,' they said, 'we hope you are not placing too much reliance on the mere numerical strength of the land forces you are sending [to Singapore] without regard to their qualities.' With its collective mind still focused on reinforcements, encouraged to believe in 'Fortress Singapore' by every communication from Churchill for weeks, the Australian Cabinet's shock at Page's revelation is easy to imagine.

After stating that Page had reported that the Defence Committee had been considering evacuation of Malaya and Singapore, the third paragraph of the message sent in Curtin's name said:

> After all the assurances we have been given, the evacuation of Singapore would be regarded here and elsewhere as an inexcusable betrayal. Singapore is a central fortress of the system of Empire and local defence. We understood it was to be made impregnable; and, in any event, it was to be capable of holding out for a prolonged period until the arrival of the main fleet . . . On the faith of the proposed flow of reinforcements, we have acted and carried out our part of the bargain. We expect you not to frustrate the whole purpose by evacuation.

If the question arose of diverting further reinforcements destined for Singapore, they should go to the Dutch East Indies, not Burma. 'Anything else would be deeply resented and might force [the Dutch] to make a separate peace.'

It may be argued that, in an assessment of the desperate situation as of 23 January 1942, it was irrelevant to talk about Singapore and a 'system of Empire and local defence', when the whole system was collapsing – if indeed it had ever existed. But nobody had done more than Churchill to make the Australians believe in that system and plan accordingly, from November, 1940, to January, 1942. Who else but Churchill had told Curtin on 12 January that 'the only vital point is Singapore fortress'; or on 19 January that Singapore would be reinforced 'with all speed'? Now the Australians were suddenly confronted with a strategic revolution, without explanation, without consultation, and with notice of any kind deliberately withheld from their representative in London. Why shouldn't they feel that the *evacuation* of Singapore would be regarded as an inexcusable betrayal, and why shouldn't they tell Churchill so?

At the very hour of the Australia Cabinet meeting, Rabaul, the administrative centre of Australia's Mandate of New Guinea, was being attacked. Three Japanese battalions had landed after midnight on 23 January, supported by a naval force of battleships and two aircraft carriers. The Australian garrison of one battalion surrendered after a day's fierce fighting, four hundred managing to escape into the New Britain jungle and eight hundred taken prisoner. Rabaul was one of the best harbours in the South-West Pacific, and the Japanese built there a strong sea and air base which became a pivot of their operations for the next two years. The message to Churchill later that day referred to the attack on Rabaul 'as giving rise to a public feeling of grave uneasiness and Allied impotence to do anything to stem the Japanese advance'. The Australian people, 'having volunteered for service overseas in large numbers, find it difficult to understand why they must wait so long for an improvement in the situation, where irreparable damage may have been done to their power to resist, the prestige of the Empire and the solidarity of the Allied cause'.

A much more serious charge than offending Churchill is implicit in Churchill's post-war criticisms of Curtin and his Government. The basis of this charge is the tragedy of defeat and incarceration which befell the defenders of Singapore, including the 18th British Division and the 8th Australian Division. Churchill suggested that, except for Australian pressure, the 18th Division would not have been sent to Singapore. The plain fact is that Churchill himself made all the decisions which sent the British division to Singapore, starting in December when he diverted it from the Middle East in order to gain leverage with Roosevelt for the 'Beat Hitler First' strategy. The first brigade had reached Singapore and the rest were irreversibly committed, three days before the 'inexcusable betrayal' cable.

There is the further implication that if the Australian Government had embraced and supported Churchill's sudden proposal for evacuation, the 8th Division itself might have been saved. The 'What ifs?' of history are generally unrewarding; and there are few issues in which the 'What ifs?' are more numerous than the fall of Singapore. To indulge in just one: what if, in light of the doom-laden reports from its commander and its representative in Singapore, Curtin and the Australian Government had suddenly decided to demand the withdrawal of its division from Singapore, in the last fortnight of January, 1942? What would have been Churchill's reaction? The words that spring to mind sound remarkably like 'inexcusable betrayal'.

Churchill replied even-handedly, with mailed fist and velvet glove. He would not allow Australian discourtesy to cloud his judgement or lessen his efforts on Australia's behalf, he told Curtin. He warned: 'It would however make it very difficult for your representative to be present at our most intimate and secret councils if *ex parte* accounts of tentative discussions are to be reported to you and made the basis for the kind of telegrams you have sent me.' So much for Page and full consultation! Churchill then revealed his hurt over Curtin's New Year message: 'You have made it clear in public that you place your confidence in the United States . . . We are very glad you should consult with them and set up any arrangements necessary for that purpose. Pray continue to invoke our assistance in securing [American] attention to your views.' But, he warned, Australia would not find Washington receptive to its view that Singapore was more important than Burma: 'The great idea over there is China.' In other words, the price Australia would have to pay for US support was to accept the scrapping of the strategy which Britain had made the keystone of Empire defence for twenty years, and to embrace a policy cooked up in twenty days: Burma not Malaya, Rangoon not Singapore, were now to be Australia's front line. In London Page bore the brunt of Churchill's anger at the latest provocation from Canberra. 'Churchill went off the deep end about Australians generally,' Page wrote, 'and said if they were going to squeal he would send them all home again out of the various fighting zones.'

In the end, Churchill's fears about American opinion forced him to backtrack. 'It is not true to say that Mr Curtin's message decided the issue,' he wrote in his war memoirs. He was, however, conscious of a 'hardening of opinion' against abandoning Singapore – 'the renowned key post in the Far East', even though 'a purely military decision' should have resulted in evacuation. But, consistent with his whole policy since May, 1940, Churchill decided to fight on: 'The effect that would be produced all over the world, especially in the United States, of a British "scuttle" while the Americans fought on so stubbornly at Corregidor, was terrible to imagine.'

The reality was even more terrible. On 27 January, Wavell gave General Percival permission to withdraw all his forces to the island. The last units of the 18th British Division arrived with ten light tanks, the only armour Churchill ever sent to the Malaya–Singapore theatre. On 30 January, an entire Indian army brigade was cut off, and surrendered. By 31 January, the retreat to Singapore was completed, and the causeway, three quarters of a mile long, was blown up. All aircraft except one squadron were transferred to the 'safety' of the Dutch East Indies. The siege of Singapore began.

Meanwhile, the Japanese overran the Australian garrison guarding the Dutch naval base on the island of Ambon. From their base in the Celebes, they began bombing airfields in Java, destroying what remained of the Dutch air force. On 3 February, they began the bombardment of Port Moresby, capital of Australia's Papuan territory. In Singapore, in reply to Yamashita's demand for unconditional surrender on 4 February, General Percival issued his order to defend the island 'to the last man'. On 8 February, Japanese units landed on the north-west coast of the island, defended by the 8th Australian Division. By 10 February, fifteen thousand Japanese had crossed to the island in lighters and rubber boats. The 8th Division, with heavy losses, withdrew to a defensive position along the Jurong River. Wavell flew over from Java for two days. On 10 February, he issued his order-of-the-day, before returning:

It is certain that our troops on Singapore Island greatly outnumber any Japanese that have crossed the Straits. We must defeat them. Our whole fighting reputation is at stake and the honour of the British Empire . . . There must be no question or thought of surrender. Every unit must

fight it out to the end and in close contact with the enemy . . . I look to
you and your men to fight to the end to prove that the fighting spirit
that won our Empire still exists to enable us to defend it.

Churchill, too, sounded the bugle of Empire. To Wavell, he pointed
out that Percival had command over 100,000 men, 'of whom
33,000 are British and 17,000 Australian' (the rest were Indians).
'There must at this stage be no thought of saving the troops or
sparing the population,' Churchill declared. 'The battle must be
fought to the bitter end at all costs. The honour of the British Empire
and of the British Army is at stake. I rely on you to show no mercy
to weakness in any form. With the Russians fighting as they are, the
Americans so stubborn at Luzon [the Philippines], the whole reputation of our country and our race is involved.'

Despite their clarion calls to Empire, Wavell and Churchill
mutually acknowledged that the 'fight for Singapore was not going
well'. Even so, it was not until 12 February that the rulers of the
British Empire began to consider the fate of their fellow-subjects in
Singapore – the people, mainly Chinese, who had built this great
imperial city-port. The Governor, Sir Shenton Thomas, cabled
London: 'There are now one million people within a radius of
three miles. Water supplies very badly damaged and unlikely to last
more than 24 hours. Many dead lying in the streets and burial
impossible. We are faced with total deprivation of water, which must
result in pestilence. I have felt that it is my duty to bring this to the
notice of the General Officer Commanding (Percival).'

Churchill at last accepted the inevitable. Now, when Singapore's
doom was certain, he wrote, 'it would be wrong to enforce needless
slaughter, and without hope of victory to inflict the horrors of street
fighting on the vast city with its teeming, helpless and now panic-
stricken population'. As the official Australian war historian Lionel
Wigmore points out, the reference to a panic-stricken populace was
merely rhetorical; they had in fact remained steady, calm – and loyal
– throughout the ordeal which two conflicting empires had inflicted
upon them. Churchill released his commanders to make their own
decision. To Wavell, he cabled: 'You are of course sole judge of the

moment when no further result can be gained at Singapore and should instruct Percival accordingly.'

The moment came at 5.15 p.m. on 15 February 1942, when Percival, Union Jack on shoulder, marched into the Ford Motor Factory at Bukit Timah village on the outskirts of the city, to accept Yamashita's terms of unconditional surrender. Thereby, 130,000 British, Australian, and Indian soldiers became prisoners of war. The Australian commander, General Bennett, abandoned his men, escaped by sampan to Java and flew home. The Australian representative, Bowden, was not so fortunate. Evatt had refused him permission to leave his post by the last available ship, believing his diplomatic status would protect him. Bowden's last message to Canberra read: 'Our work completed. Will telegraph from another place at present unknown.' He escaped Singapore on a motor launch, was captured by a Japanese patrol boat, taken ashore and beaten, forced to dig his own grave, then shot and killed.

In the ten weeks of the Malayan campaign, the AIF, fourteen per cent of British combat strength, had suffered seventy-eight per cent of the deaths in battle. Fifteen thousand Australians were taken prisoner. The fall of Singapore was, as Churchill said, the greatest military disaster and largest capitulation in British history. Curtin broadcast to the nation: 'The Battle for Singapore is over. The Battle for Australia begins.'

In the final analysis, the fall of Singapore was part of the price the British Empire paid for Churchill's Big Idea. He had chosen the Middle East, North Africa, and Greece as the places where fighting offered the best prospects of bringing the United States into the war against Hitler. He gambled that Japan would not come into the war, and stripped the Far East of both the means and purpose of imperial defence. Serious reinforcement of the Far East would have cut across his Idea and might have undermined it. Hence his rows with his Chiefs of Staff in 1941, and his dismissive attitude towards Australian anxieties. Nevertheless, it is difficult to disagree with the Australian war historian, Dr Robert O'Neill:

It is scarcely to Australia's credit that it had preferred to take British reassurances at face value and to do so little of its own volition to exploit the defensive worth of the long approaches to its own shores. Australian recrimination over the British Government's tardiness in recognising the seriousness of the Japanese threat would have carried greater weight had Australian governments placed a little more faith in the warnings of their military advisers.

'I have been giving a good deal of thought during the last few days to the Far East,' Roosevelt cabled Churchill three days after Singapore surrendered. 'It seems to me that we must at all costs maintain our two flanks – the right based on Australia and New Zealand, and the left in Burma, India and China.' Churchill now made Roosevelt's message part of an astonishing proposition: that Australia's first duty to the common cause lay in the defence, not of Australia, but of Burma.

23

'Nothing else in the world . . .'
February–March, 1942

As Singapore fell, Churchill opened a new campaign to force the Australian Government to surrender its control over the AIF. On the outcome of this battle depended the fate of thousands of Australian soldiers crossing the Indian Ocean. His object was to prevent the return home of the 6th and 7th Australian Divisions, and to divert them to the battle for Burma. He was acting essentially on the same principle which had driven him since May, 1940 – to fight with whatever forces he could muster wherever he could most exert influence over President Roosevelt and the United States. To this end, having chewed up the 6th Australian Division in Greece and Crete, having resisted to the last the relief of the 9th Australian Division at Tobruk, and having lost the 8th Australian Division on Singapore, Churchill now demanded the sacrifice of the 7th Australian Division to his new concept of the needs of the Grand Alliance he had forged. The ensuing crisis in British–Australian relations was to find Churchill at his imperious and impetuous worst.

Churchill had discovered China – or, at any rate, its importance in getting Roosevelt to agree to beat Hitler first. The issue had disturbed the harmony of Arcadia; Churchill had been surprised and irritated by the priority Roosevelt had assigned to China and Chiang Kaishek's Nationalist regime during the Washington talks. He told Roosevelt that he 'over-estimated the contribution which China could make to the general war'. Roosevelt countered with sarcastic remarks about Churchill's attitude to India. Neither were issues on which Churchill was prepared to risk his relations with Roosevelt, particularly when he realised what he called 'the extraordinary influence of China on American minds'. What would happen in the future, Roosevelt had asked Churchill, if China's 'enormous population developed in the same way as Japan had done in the last century, and got hold of modern weapons?' Churchill replied: 'I'm speaking of the present war, and that's quite enough to go on for the time being.' To his son Elliott Roosevelt, the President spoke of China strictly in the present tense, as a constraint on Japan's otherwise unbridled military ambitions: 'If China goes under, how many divisions of Japanese troops do you think will be freed – to do what? Take Australia? Take India?'

Churchill decided that a show of concern for China was the price he would have to pay to maintain his influence over Roosevelt on the issue that really mattered to him – the Beat Hitler First strategy. The only place where Britain could make a show of helping China was Burma, with its vital supply road from Rangoon. There may have been some filial piety working on Churchill's emotions, because his father, Lord Randolph Churchill, had annexed Burma to the British Empire during his brief term as Secretary of State for India in 1886. But Churchill's need to keep Roosevelt on side was the key to his heavy-handed conduct towards Australia in February, 1942.

It will be recalled that Churchill had first suggested sending part of the AIF from the Middle East to the Far East in December, while he was in the mid-Atlantic on his way to Washington. There was no rush either in London or Canberra to act on his suggestion, despite the Japanese landings in Malaya. It was not until 3 January 1942 that the *British* Chiefs of Staff formally requested the dispatch of the 6th and 7th Divisions – not to Australia but to Java. Two days later, the Australian Government agreed 'to the transfer of the First

Australian Corps from the Middle East to the Netherlands East Indies'. In reply to Curtin's message of 12 January, expressing alarm at the collapse in Malaya and urging air reinforcements for Singapore, Churchill testily noted that the dispatch of the Australian divisions 'to the new theatre of so much interest to Australia' had been his idea, but grumbled that now 'we shall have to do our best to replace them from home'.

As we have seen, Churchill posed to his Chiefs the 'ugly decision' of saving Burma and losing Singapore, even before the Australians had embarked at Suez. The Australian Government was not consulted about this sudden switch in priorities. But now, Churchill pressed Burma's claims with all the zeal of a convert. In all the long and detailed messages of explanation, recrimination, and self-justification passing between Churchill and Curtin in January, 1942, there had been scarcely a mention of Burma, and nothing to suggest that the defence of Burma should involve Australian forces, or that it should have priority over Australia's immediate region, in Java, Timor, or New Guinea. Even as late as 7 February, when Churchill outlined to Curtin a new organisational structure for the ABDA and Pacific areas, with two Pacific Councils, one in London and one in Washington, there was no suggestion that Australian forces might be required for Burma.

It was not until February that the British Admiralty had assembled a convoy at Suez for the voyage east, via Aden and Bombay (Mumbai). A faster ship, the converted liner *Orcades*, went ahead with 3400 men, sailing direct to Batavia. The convoy was not tactically loaded – that is, the men sailed in different vessels from most of their equipment. Meanwhile, the GOC I Australian Corps, Sir John Lavarack, had flown ahead with his senior staff, to set up headquarters in Java. Other senior officers took seventeen days to reach Batavia by air, two days longer than the units which the *Orcades* took by sea. This separation of the men from both their commanders and their equipment is a fact of key importance in an extraordinary story.

Wavell conferred with Lavarack at Bandung, the Dutch military headquarters in Java, on 26 January. Fittingly for Australia Day, their meeting began with a rerun of the clash between Wavell and Blamey over the dispersal of Australian troops. Charged with defence of the so-called Malay Barrier, Wavell proposed to divide the I Australian Corps (comprising the 6th and 7th Divisions) between Sumatra, Java, and other parts of the archipelago. Lavarack protested at the 'extreme diversion' of his men, telling Wavell that their fighting quality would be 'at least doubled if the Divisions could fight side by side, or even back to back, if necessary, in one area'. From Cairo, Blamey cabled Curtin to warn that the British would attempt to 'scatter Lavarack's command in penny packets'. On 12 February, Curtin cabled Wavell, supporting the views of Lavarack and Blamey: 'The Government desires to emphasise that the concentration of the A.I.F. in one force under its own commander is a principle of cardinal national importance.'

It was an impossible attempt to impose order on chaos. Much of the I Australian Corps had not yet left Egypt. The leading brigade of the 7th was not due to arrive in Java until 1 March, and the division would not be complete until two weeks after that. The 6th Division, the other half of the Australian Corps, was scheduled to arrive in Java in April.

In any case, the Japanese army and navy were making the rules. Even before the fall of Singapore, they had gained footholds on the Malay Archipelago, in Sumatra, Borneo, the Celebes, Ambon, Bali, and Timor, using their air supremacy to bomb Java almost at will. There was now no 'Malay Barrier'; if anything, it had become the Malay Bridge to Australia. With the capture of Timor, where the Australian garrison retreated inland to begin one of the longest guer- rilla campaigns of the war, the Japanese were in easy striking distance of Australia. Four days after the surrender at Singapore, relays of enemy aircraft took off from Japanese carriers and bombed Darwin. Twelve ships, including the US destroyer *Peary*, were sunk. Two hundred and fifty people were killed. It was the first of more than sixty raids on Darwin.

With the fall of Singapore, Curtin for the first time specifically proposed that the AIF should be recalled home. Even then, their return became fixed Australian policy only when Wavell had informed

London and Canberra that Java could not be held. On 17 February, Curtin cabled Churchill: 'If possible, all Australian forces now under orders to transfer to the Far East from the Middle East [i.e. the 6th and 7th Divisions] should be diverted to Australia.' He asked Churchill that the recall of the 9th Division also be considered 'at an early date'. It must be emphasised that even at this stage, Curtin was not making a *demand* for the AIF's return to Australia, contrary to most written histories and popular versions. Nothing in his cables can be interpreted as an ultimatum to Churchill.

Curtin's cable to Churchill was based on the advice of the Chief of the General Staff, Sir Vernon Sturdee, who had seen his long-held convictions about the fallacy of the Singapore strategy borne out with devastating finality. Australia's object, he advised Curtin, should be 'to hold some area of the Australian continent from which we can eventually launch an offensive in the Pacific when American aid can be fully developed'. Australia's 100,000 men of the AIF were essential to such an effort. Their return home would double the numbers of fully-trained men available for the defence of Australia. Sturdee's advice was no routine recommendation. He made it clear to Curtin that he was prepared to stake his job on its acceptance.

Curtin's cable to Churchill reached London at the same time as one from Wavell in Java. With Singapore gone, Wavell said the Dutch East Indies could not be held. Accordingly, he said, the Australian Corps now moving from the Middle East should go either to Burma or Australia. He said that the Australian Corps commander, Lavarack, agreed with him, but did not mention that Lavarack had agreed to the Burma option 'only if the forces available for the defence of Australia were adequate'. This was to earn Lavarack a severe rebuke from Curtin, who reminded the general that he had been away from Australia for nearly two years, and that he was in no position to judge Australia's situation. The defence of Australia was far from adequate, Curtin told Lavarack. Wavell's cable was still enough to set Churchill on a collision course with Curtin, with almost irreparable damage to his relations with the Australian Government.

The first hint that Australia might be asked to send its troops to Burma came in a cable from Casey on 17 February. Casey said that he had been in close consultation with Roosevelt's righthand man, Harry Hopkins. Roosevelt was 'depressed at the continuous reverses' and now sought a place 'where a real stand could be made'. The top people in Washington, including the Chief of Staff, General Marshall, and Hopkins himself, were advancing the view that the 'mainland of Australia' was the only place which offered 'hope of eventually regaining areas already lost to Japan'. However, Casey continued, Hopkins had asked him 'if the United States undertook to send forces of considerable strength to Australia, whether Australia was likely to agree to two Australian divisions from the Middle East being diverted, say, to India or Burma'. Hopkins had mentioned '50,000 or 60,000 American troops with their equipment', had warned that shortage of shipping was a problem, but believed that 'by being ruthless it can probably be got together'. Casey asked Canberra for 'the earliest possible reply, as I believe this matter will be decided within a very few days'.

Then came a bolt from the blue. Page cabled Curtin on the same day (18 February in Australia) that the Pacific War Council in London had decided that 'there should be no attempt to land the Australian Corps in the N.E.I. [Netherlands East Indies]' and that 'Australia should be told that the Australian Government's policy of taking the whole of their forces back into the Pacific area and to Australia *would be accepted*'. So far, so good, but Page then dropped a bombshell. The War Council, Churchill presiding, had decided:

> The Australian Government should be asked to agree that the Seventh Australian Division already on the water should go to the most urgent spot at the moment, which is Burma.

Curtin asked Page for 'half a day to think about it'. Next morning, he replied: 'After most anxious consideration, Government has decided that it cannot agree to the proposal that the 7th AIF Division should be diverted to Burma'. He pointed out that the reason for sending the Australian Corps to the East Indies in the first place was 'to help stop the *southern* thrust of the enemy'. Now that the East Indies were to be abandoned, that objective could only be achieved from Australia, 'which is in imminent danger of attack, which is an essential Allied base and which is the nearest area of concentration south of the Netherlands East Indies'.

In the blitz of cables about to descend on Canberra from London and Washington, the 7th Australian Division is invariably referred to as if it were the splendid battle-hardened, cohesive force, well-led and well-equipped, which had won its laurels in North Africa and Syria. But by mid-February, 1942, the 7th Division simply did not exist at this level. It was stretched out in an array of vessels from the Red Sea to the East Indies. Lavarack, commander-in-chief of the Australian Corps, and his staff were in Java with Wavell. Advance units aboard the *Orcades* had been landed at Batavia, against Lavarack's wishes, but at Wavell's express insistence 'to avoid compromising British relations with the Dutch and lowering British prestige'. The divisional commander, Major General Arthur 'Tubby' Allen, was now sailing back to Colombo on the *Orcades*. The rest of the division was in three 'flights'. The leading brigade (the 21st) left Bombay on 13 February, still under orders for Java. The second brigade (the 18th) arrived in Bombay on 19 February, and was not ready to depart until 23 February. (Bombay is four thousand kilometres by sea from Rangoon, the capital of Burma.) The third brigade (the 16th) arrived at Colombo from Aden on 23 February. Such was the state of the division which Churchill now purported to believe could save Burma from the Japanese.

The Japanese thrust into Burma had been even faster than the conquest of Malaya. Their control of Thailand gave them airfields to bomb Rangoon whenever they chose. On 15 January, the Japanese 15th Army began land operations against Burma. The parallels with Malaya were appalling. The British defence was committed to two brave, but ill-trained, British–Indian divisions. The commander-in-chief, Sir Thomas Hutton, had arrived in Burma only a month before; the field commander, Major General J. V. Smyth, was a sick and exhausted man. By the second week of February, the Japanese had advanced to the Sittang River, about sixty miles from Rangoon. The Burmese capital was now almost useless as a port, incessantly bombed, and deserted by its mainly Indian labour force. This was the situation when Churchill asked the Australian Government to send its best division – or whatever parts of it were in sailing distance – to save Rangoon, four days after the 8th Division had been incarcerated in Singapore, three days after Wavell had declared the defence of the Dutch East Indies hopeless, two days after an Australian battalion bound for Timor had been turned back to Darwin by Japanese air attacks, and the very day the Japanese first bombed Darwin. Perhaps in the fog of war, Churchill did not know all this. But as he was to say in a not dissimilar context (about Singapore), 'I ought to have known. I ought to have been told and I ought to have asked.' In the space of forty-eight hours, the destination of an Australian force a few thousand strong, at sea somewhere in the Bay of Bengal, was being linked with the fate of the Anglo–American alliance, American aid to Australia, the entire Pacific strategy, and the destiny of China.

At first, the pressure on Curtin was not from Churchill directly. It came from Australia's own representatives in London. Throughout the dispute over the 7th Division, Bruce and Page were Churchill's strongest advocates. He lured them in with much the same skill with which he had locked Menzies into Greece. Bruce's message of 18 February set the tone. The decision of the Pacific War Council, he told Curtin, 'was the first encouraging indication of co-operative action based on well thought-out plans for the conduct of the war in the Pacific'. To exert moral pressure on his own government, Bruce noted that the Dutch Government had accepted the abandoning of Java – 'a most courageous action, showing great statesmanship in keeping with the character and toughness of the Dutch people'. Here Bruce is speaking about a government-in-exile in London, halfway round the world from its crumbling colonial empire, to his own government whose northern outposts were under immediate Japanese threat. For Bruce, this was insignificant compared with the results that might be achieved by sending the 7th Division to Burma. Its presence in Burma, said Bruce, 'offered the best hope of keeping open the Burma Road to China'. This was of paramount importance for the fight against Japan. Even if its presence did not achieve the purpose of keeping the Burma Road open, it would have a tremendous effect on China's morale and will to resist, 'which it is imperative to maintain if we are to avoid the incalculable disaster of her throwing up the sponge'.

Page chimed in, on the same note. He told Curtin on 19 February that 'Churchill expressed great anxiety of the effect on China of not reinforcing Burma, especially if troops so near the battle front and only troops available are not allocated at this critical moment'. Page said that both Churchill and Roosevelt now believed 'that China is the ultimate key of the whole Asian situation'. Page said that Churchill had promised to expedite the despatch of an American division to Australia in exchange for the 7th Australian Division. This idea of a trade-off was to be a constant refrain from both Churchill and Roosevelt for the rest of the year. Pending further advice from Canberra, Page said, 'no instruction had been sent to the convoy'. Curtin immediately cabled Page: 'If you have not done so, you should act at once to ensure that convoy should *not* (repeat not) be committed to Burma.'

Curtin now brought Blamey, who was still in Cairo, up to date about what was being proposed for his beloved AIF and his cherished dream of one great army under a unified command: 'With Singapore, the bastion of Empire defence gone, and with N.E.I., the outer screen to Australia indefensible, they propose to leave Australia bare.' Curtin ordered: 'Return here as speedily as possible.'

Curtin's messages to London and Cairo crossed Churchill's cable on 20 February. For its consummate skill in marshalling dubious arguments, for its presentation of contradictions as if they were consistent and axiomatic, the careful nuance of its promises and threats, and the subtle menace in every line, Churchill's cable to Curtin is unsurpassed. He began:

> I suppose you realise that your leading division, the head of which is sailing south of Colombo to N.E.I. at this moment in our scanty British and American shipping, is the only force that can reach Rangoon in time to prevent its loss and the severance of communication with China. It can begin to disembark at Rangoon about 26th or 27th. There is nothing else in the world that can fill the gap.

Churchill insisted that he was still 'in favour of all Australian troops returning home to defend their native soil'. But, he said, 'a vital war emergency could not be ignored and troops *en route* to other destinations must be ready to turn aside and take part in battle'. Every effort would be made to relieve this division at the earliest moment and send them on to Australia. He reminded Curtin that the Americans were floating a proposal to send the whole Australian army, including the 6th and 9th divisions, to Burma. Not on, said Churchill. 'They will return home as fast as possible but this one [the 7th] is needed now. It is the only one that can possibly save the situation.'

Churchill then revealed how deeply he had resented Australia's 'inexcusable betrayal' message. Because of it, Churchill now claimed, he had put the 18th British Division into Singapore instead of diverting it to Burma. They were lost in Singapore 'and did not save it, whereas they could almost certainly have saved Rangoon'. Churchill acknowledged that he took full responsibility for that decision, but to Curtin he said: 'You also bear a heavy share on account of your telegram.' (Quite apart from the incompatibility of chronology with this assertion, Churchill said in his war memoirs specifically that 'Mr Curtin's telegram did not decide the issue'.)

Churchill then brought the heaviest gun in the world to bear on Curtin: the President of the United States:

> Your greatest support in this hour of peril must be drawn from the United States. They alone can bring into Australia the necessary troops and air forces and they appear ready to do so. As you know, the President attaches supreme importance to keeping open the connection with China without which his bombing offensive against Japan cannot be started and also the most grievous results may follow in Asia if China is cut off from all Allied help.

Churchill's barrage concluded with naked blackmail:

> I am quite sure that if you refuse to allow your troops, who are actually passing, to stop the gap, and if in consequence the above evils affecting

the whole course of the war follow, a very grave effect will be produced upon the President and the Washington circles on whom you are so largely dependent.

Churchill demanded an 'immediate answer', as the 'leading ships of the convoy will soon be steaming in the opposite direction from Rangoon and every day is a day lost. I trust therefore that for the sake of all interests and, above all, your own interests, you will give most careful consideration to the case I have set before you.' The blackmail could hardly be clearer.

Churchill then enlisted Roosevelt direct, cabling in terms calculated to put Australia in the worst possible light. All he was asking the Australians for, he claimed, was a temporary diversion of the only troops who could reach Rangoon in time to stop the enemy. Even these 'we have promised to relieve at the earliest, and all other Australian troops are going home at the earliest'. But to this proposal, 'the Australian Government have refused point blank'. His offer of American troops to help defend Australia gave him the right to press for this 'movement of Allied forces', Churchill told Roosevelt. 'Please therefore send me a message which I can add to the very strong cable I have just sent off.'

Churchill's assertion to Roosevelt that the 'Australian Government had refused point blank' was itself misleading and prejudicial. Before Churchill's cables of 20 February, Curtin had replied only through Page. This first response 'after anxious consideration' addressed the general question raised by Wavell, as Supreme Commander of ABDA, of sending the Australian Corps to Burma instead of Java, not the specific issue of diverting one brigade to Rangoon. Even in his final rejection on 22 February, Curtin went so far as to say: 'If it were possible to divert our troops to Burma and India without imperilling our security in the judgement of our advisers, we should be pleased to agree to this diversion.'

Roosevelt obliged at once, replying to Churchill that day: 'I hope you can persuade Australian Government to allow proposed temporary diversion of their leading Australian Division to Burma. I think this is utmost importance. Tell them I am speeding additional troops as well as planes to Australia and that my estimate of the situation there is highly optimistic and by no means dark.' He added in his own handwriting: 'Harry [Hopkins] is seeing Casey at once.'

Churchill immediately passed Roosevelt's message on to Curtin. But Roosevelt went one better. Next day, he sent a personal message to Curtin, drafted by Hopkins, presumably after he had seen Casey. Australia could have every confidence, Roosevelt said, 'that we are going to reinforce your position with all possible speed'. But the Allied left flank against Japan – Burma, India and China – 'simply must be held'. If Burma went, 'it seems to me our whole position, including that of Australia, will be in extreme peril'. Apparently accepting without question Churchill's assessment of the miraculous power of a few thousand Australians, Roosevelt told Curtin: 'It would get into the fight at once, and would, I believe, have the strength to save what now seems to be a very dangerous situation.'

As to the threat to Australia, Roosevelt said, 'while I realise the Japs are moving rapidly, I cannot believe that, in view of your geographical position and the forces on their way to you or operating in your neighbourhood, your vital centres are in immediate danger'. He concluded:

> While I realise that your men have been fighting all over the world, and are still, and while I know full well of the great sacrifices which Australia has made, I nevertheless want to ask you in the interests of our whole war effort in the Far East if you will reconsider your decision and order the division now en route to Australia to move with all speed to support the British forces fighting in Burma.

In all this correspondence, a single word exposes Churchill's misrepresentations and Roosevelt's ignorance of the true nature of the demands Churchill was making on the Australian Government: the word 'temporary'. Roosevelt's phrase, 'proposed temporary diversion' conjures up a picture of this great Australian Division majestically sailing into Rangoon harbour, disembarking in full fighting trim, mopping up the Japanese 15th Army, and then, having saved Rangoon, the Burma Road, Burma, India, and China, and having been relieved by the victorious and grateful British, resuming its voyage to Australia.

The facts were that on the very days Churchill, Roosevelt, and Curtin were exchanging cables, the British–Indian force between Rangoon and the advancing Japanese army retreated across the Sittang River, the last line of natural defence, blowing up the bridge and leaving half its men to be slaughtered on the other side. 'This episode marked the beginning of the end of the campaign,' writes the British military historian Daniel Marston. Yet when this took place on 23 February, the leading ship of the Australian convoy was still four or five days' sailing from Rangoon harbour, on Churchill's own rosy estimate. 'By this stage, the situation in Rangoon was appalling,' writes another military historian, David Jordan. 'Many key units had fled their posts under bombing, many policemen had deserted, and the ethnic tensions between the native Burmese and Indians spiralled into violence.' Never at any time, right up to its fall, had the situation in Singapore been anything as bad as this. Into this maelstrom, Churchill proposed to send a few thousand Australians armed with their rifles, their armour and artillery inaccessible, the whereabouts of their own GOC unknown to them, into a wrecked and deserted port, subject to relentless and almost unopposed Japanese bombing.

Before replying to Churchill, Curtin placed the matter before the War Cabinet, the Advisory War Council, and even the Parliament itself, meeting in secret session. In the Advisory War Council, the non-government members, Menzies, Fadden, Hughes, and Spender, supported Churchill. This meeting of the Advisory War Council was held on 19 February in Sydney, a day after Curtin, in the presence of most of the Cabinet and the opposition leaders, had delivered one of his greatest wartime speeches at a rally in Martin Place. Percy Spender claimed in his memoirs that the council's heated discussion was interrupted by the Minister for Supply and Shipping, John Beasley, who burst in suddenly, and loudly proclaimed: 'The Japs have bombed Darwin. That settles it.'

Curtin, in severe pain from a gastric ulcer, had not attended the Advisory War Council meeting. He had spoken at the previous day's rally against his doctor's advice, and afterwards was rushed to Sydney's St Vincent's Hospital, where he spent two nights before going by train to Canberra for the secret session of Parliament on 20 February.

The factor that really settled the question was the steadying influence of Sturdee, the aptly named Chief of the General Staff. Sturdee's firm stance is a key fact often ignored. In their memoirs, Menzies, Bruce, Page, and Spender all justified Churchill's conduct on the grounds that he expressed the view of the British Chiefs of Staff in London; but they never mentioned the opposite view of the Australian Chiefs of Staff. Sturdee, now sixty-two, with his service in Gallipoli and France, and his military studies in Quetta, was Australia's senior general; in the 1930s, he had argued against Australia's reliance on the Singapore strategy. Now he told Curtin that if the AIF was not returned to Australia, he would resign.

'I have received your rather strongly worded request at this late stage', Curtin began his considered reply to Churchill on 22 February. He reminded the British Prime Minister that the release of Australia's troops from the Middle East had been announced to the House of Commons by Churchill himself on 27 January. In that speech, Churchill had claimed credit for initiating the move and had pledged: 'No obstacle would be placed in the way of the AIF returning to defend their homeland.' Curtin pointed out that although Churchill was now claiming that he only wanted a temporary diversion of the 7th, and only part of it at that, Wavell as Supreme Commander of ABDA and Dill, Churchill's military representative in Washington, were both requesting that the entire Australian Corps go to Burma. Without labouring the obvious contradictions, Curtin set out the advice he was receiving from his own Chiefs of Staff: 'Once one division became engaged, it could not be left unsupported. The indications are that the whole of the Corps might become committed to this region, or there might be a recurrence of the experiences of the Greek and Malayan campaigns.' In any case, Curtin told Churchill: 'In view of the superior Japanese sea power and air power, it would appear to be a matter of some doubt as to whether this division can be landed in Burma and a matter for greater doubt whether it can be brought out as promised.' Churchill never answered these fundamental points, either during their bitter dispute, or in his one-sided account in his memoirs ten years later.

Then came the most staggering episode of the whole affair. Churchill peremptorily instructed the British Admiralty to order the convoy to change course and sail to Rangoon. Churchill's excuse for this high-handed action was just as astonishing. He had done it, he told Curtin in a cable dated 22 February at 3.00 a.m. because 'we could not contemplate that you would refuse our request and that of the President of the United States'. So he had acted, he said, to save time and fuel. 'We knew that if our ships proceeded on their course to Australia while we were waiting for your formal approval, they would either arrive too late at Rangoon or even be without enough fuel to go there at all.' Even now, he said, it was not too late for the Australian Government to change its mind. If the ships did not go to Rangoon, he now claimed, they would have to go back to Colombo to refuel. 'These physical considerations give a few days for the situation to develop and for you to review the position should you wish to do so.'

For once, the Australians in London were as outraged as the Australians in Canberra. Bruce cabled: 'I am appalled . . . it is arrogant and offensive . . . any reaction on your part would be justified.' Nevertheless, Bruce counselled restraint: 'A crisis in the relations between Australia and the United Kingdom arising out of the action of one man must be avoided . . . at the moment, Churchill is so near the end of his tether owing to the strain of the war situation that allowance must be made for the tone of his telegram.' Page cabled in the same vein, his embarrassment sharpened by the exposure of his own incompetence and futility. He gave a rambling and unconvincing account of the convoy's fuel situation, which he laid at the door of the British Admiralty and 'inadvertence' due to 'the very disturbed position of the war'. Despite all this, both Bruce and Page called upon their own Government to accept the fait accompli and let the ships go on to Rangoon. At all costs, they both urged, Curtin should not allow this 'provocation' to damage the unity of the Empire – or, a cynic might suppose, expose them personally to the wrath of Winston Churchill.

Canberra had no need for the counsel of its representatives in London. In his reply of 23 February, Curtin briefly repeated the Australian arguments and concluded: 'In the circumstances, it is quite impossible to reverse a decision which we made with the utmost care and which we have affirmed and reaffirmed.' Churchill let it go at last. 'Your convoy is now proceeding to re-fuel at Colombo,' he replied that night. 'It will then proceed to Australia in accordance with your wishes.'

It should be remembered that Churchill had told Curtin (and Roosevelt) that the leading ships of the convoy might arrive in Rangoon on 26 or 27 February at the earliest. It should also be remembered that, when their destination was supposed to be Java, the commander of the Australian Corps, Sir John Lavarack, had told the Australian Government they could not be ready for combat for three weeks or a month after their arrival. This time-lag had been the decisive factor in changing their destination to Australia. But even if we accept the impossible, and assume that the leading battalions of the 7th Division would have been capable of fighting as soon as they landed at Rangoon, what would have been their situation?

We know how that situation looked from London, because we have the diaries of the Chief of the Imperial Staff, Sir Alan Brooke. Stiff-necked, cocksure, and censorious of everybody – Churchill included – Brooke approached life with an utter self-belief bred into his family by three hundred years of the Protestant Irish ascendancy. On 18 February (the day Page first informed Curtin of Churchill's request), Brooke wrote: 'Burma news now bad. If the Army cannot fight better than it is doing at present we shall deserve to lose our Empire!' On 19 February, Churchill decided to change the Burma command, replacing the hapless General Hutton with his favourite general, Sir Harold Alexander. Brooke wrote: 'Only hope Alexander arrives in time as situation in Burma is becoming very critical. Troops don't seem to be fighting well there either, which is most depressing.' This was the day Curtin replied to Churchill through Page that the Australian Government could not agree to the proposal to divert the 7th Division. 'Burma news getting worse,' Brooke wrote in his diary on 20 February. 'Very doubtful if we will succeed in holding Rangoon.' That was the very day that Churchill cabled Curtin: 'There is nothing else in the world that can fill the gap.' On 27 February, the day Churchill had envisaged that the first of the Australians might *begin* disembarking at Rangoon, Brooke wrote: 'I cannot see how we are to go on holding Rangoon much longer.'

On 2 March, Curtin received 'in utmost secrecy' the latest assessment by the British Chiefs of Staff which, by its length and detail, must have been some days in preparation; it forecast 'the probable loss of Rangoon'. The same day, Brooke reported a Cabinet meeting 'very gloomy' about Burma. Next day, Brooke met the Chinese Ambassador to London (Mr Wellington Koo) to 'discuss the Burma Road with him and the possible routes for Assam to join with it after the loss of Rangoon'. One wonders how much time General Brooke and Mr Koo spent discussing how different it all would have been if four thousand Australians had been in Rangoon for the previous three or four days, with their rifles. Or perhaps they discussed Wavell's rejection of an offer by Chiang Kaishek in December, to send three Chinese divisions to Burma, which had led Churchill to cable Wavell on 23 January: 'I am still puzzled about your reasons for refusing Chinese help in the defence of Burma and the Burma Road.' Wavell's explanation: 'I preferred that a country of the British Empire should be defended by Imperial troops rather than foreign.'

Meanwhile Wavell's ABDA command had been dissolved and he had sacked generals Hutton and Smyth, just when the Australian convoy had been turned towards Rangoon. 'I cannot send you an army but I send you a man,' Churchill now cabled Wavell, as General Sir Harold Alexander flew out to Burma 'over large stretches of enemy territory to save time'. Alexander reached 'the doomed capital' on 5 March. Wavell, now back in India, cabled Churchill on 7 March: 'Communication with Burma has been subject to long delays in last two days. Wireless seems to have broken down altogether, and I am without any message from Alexander.' In fact, as soon as Alexander arrived, he found Rangoon almost encircled by the Japanese and gave orders for an immediate withdrawal and 'for the whole force to cut its way out northwards'.

At best, then, the fate of the 7th Division, or so much of it as had been able to land at Rangoon, would have been to become part of the chaos of the desperate British retreat into the jungles and mountains of North Burma, finishing up in India – 'the longest retreat in British military history'.

Sir Alan Brooke's diary makes it clear that he and Churchill knew from the start that Rangoon was doomed and the Burma Road lost, with or without the Australians. Yet, in spite of everything, when Brooke came to tidy up his diaries in the 1950s, he still felt able to write a footnote: 'Looking back on the event, I still feel that the arrival of this division in Rangoon, at this time, might well have restored the situation and saved Burma.' Brooke's retrospective explanation of Australian 'obduracy' was that 'the outlook prevailing in Australia at that time was definitely parochial and centred solely on its own direct personal security'. Brooke did not think it worthwhile to record in his diary that the Japanese 15th Army entered Rangoon on 8 March. On the same day, the Australian, British, and Dutch forces remaining in Java, including three thousand from the advance units landed from the *Orcades*, surrendered.

Curtin had won his battle with Churchill; but his worst private ordeal was just beginning. He felt deeply that by defying Churchill he had made himself personally responsible for the lives of the Australians now moving through the submarine-infested waters of the Indian Ocean. His friend, Frank Green, Clerk of the House of Representatives from 1937 to 1955, recorded in his memoirs that Curtin's driver, Ray Tracey, worried 'that Curtin had not been to bed for some days and spent each night walking about the grounds of the Lodge'. One night in March, after the House arose after midnight, Green writes, 'I entered the grounds of the Lodge and walked around until I met Curtin face to face. I asked him what was the matter, but he did not answer me. We stood in silence in the darkness for some minutes, and then he said: "How can I sleep with our men in the Indian Ocean among enemy submarines?"' The convoys arrived safely in Adelaide between 23 and 27 March. Urged by Bruce and Page to make a conciliatory gesture to Churchill,

Curtin agreed to allow two brigades of the 6th Division to disembark at Colombo to defend Ceylon (Sri Lanka). When the need had passed, they re-embarked and returned to Australia in August. Barely six weeks later, they were fighting in New Guinea.

On the day Rangoon fell, the Japanese landed at Lae and Salamaua, villages in north-east New Guinea. In Paul Hasluck's words: 'The long and arduous campaign in New Guinea, which was to tie up the greater part of the Australian Army for much of the war and to cost the Japanese more than 100,000 dead, had begun.' The decisive battles, including Milne Bay, where the Japanese were defeated on land for the first time, and the protracted campaign on the Kokoda Track, which saved Port Moresby, were fought by forces drawn from the 7th Division who would have been swallowed up in Burma if Churchill had had his way. Yet Sir Alan Brooke could still write ten years later: 'They were certainly not needed for the safety of Australia.'

The blind obstinacy with which Churchill and Brooke continued to defend their conduct makes sense only upon the assumption that they had a hidden agenda – that the real intention of the diversion was to keep control of the whole AIF by preventing the 6th and 7th Divisions ever returning to Australia. Despite his assurances to the contrary, this seems to have been entrenched in Churchill's own mind and memory. John Dedman recalled that he had been introduced to Churchill at a garden party at Buckingham Palace in 1947. 'He shook his finger in my face,' Dedman recalled twenty years later, 'and said: "Ah, You are one of these blasted Australian Ministers who would not let me send the AIF to Burma when I wanted them to go there".'

24

'I shall return'
March, 1942

The noise over Burma was the sound of two Big Ideas clashing – Churchill's versus Curtin's. Churchill had achieved the first part of his, when America entered the war. Now he had to keep fighting to make sure that the Allied effort focused on beating Hitler – the whole point of the exercise since May, 1940. *Keep fighting* took on a new meaning: fighting to win Roosevelt over to his ideas of where the military effort against Hitler should be concentrated.

Curtin's Big Idea was that Australia should become the Allied base for victory over Japan. With the benefit of hindsight, this may seem obvious enough. In fact, Curtin's strategy was never fully embraced by the United States. The US Chief of Staff, General Marshall, was almost as grudging as Churchill about any departure from the Europe-first doctrine; but, unlike Churchill, he really meant Europe, first and soon, not sideshows in the Middle East or North Africa. The Chief of Naval Operations, Admiral Ernest King, who detested the British Empire almost as much as the Japanese empire, was determined to make the war in the Pacific a US navy show; Australia's role in King's naval strategy was marginal, and more symbolic than strategic. The catalyst for bringing American thinking closer to Curtin's was General Douglas MacArthur.

Churchill's opposition to Curtin's plan could be seen as automatic, because Curtin's ideas necessarily meant strong competition for American resources. He thought, mistakenly, that Curtin's sole reason for wanting to bring the AIF home was the defence of Australia. That was, of course, his immediate and urgent priority. But Curtin was also looking ahead, to the time when it would be possible to take the offensive against Japan. For Curtin, making Australia the main base meant not only protecting Australia, but attacking Japan. Making the Pacific War merely a holding operation would allow Japan to consolidate and prolong the war indefinitely. Curtin had set out his ideas in a long paper to Churchill on 4 March:

> The loss of Australia and New Zealand would mean the loss of the only basis for offering action by the Allied nations against the Japanese from the Anzac area. The defensive aspect is, of course, vital if these bases are to be held. The basis of our planning must be not only to ensure the security of Australia and New Zealand, but to use them as areas from which action will be launched.

The return of the AIF to Australia was as crucial to Curtin's objective in 1942 as the Dunkirk evacuation was to Churchill in 1940. Curtin did not intend simply to stand on the defensive on his continent any more than Churchill was prepared to stand still on his island after the Battle of Britain. Just as Churchill did not assess Lend-Lease merely in terms of saving Britain, nor did Curtin see American aid to Australia solely in terms of saving Australia from invasion. The proof lies in his conduct after the naval battles of the Coral Sea and Midway in May and June, 1942, turned the tide against the Japanese in the Pacific. If home defence had been Curtin's only concern, he could have relaxed Australia's war effort. On the contrary, it was then that he called upon the Australians, military and civilian, for a total effort to convert their country into the Allied base against Japan, and took the political risks involved in making his idea a reality. Without the central core of its battle-hardened divisions, the Australian army could not be developed into a strong attacking force, and Australia would become a bystander in the offensive against Japan.

'Our minds are set on attack,' Curtin said in a broadcast to the people of America on 13 March. 'We are not thinking only of the immediate security of Australia.' A month later, he told the people of Australia: 'With the growing assistance of the United States of America, we shall one day go out and drive the enemy from the positions from which he now menaces our security, challenges the life-lines of the British Empire, and endangers democracy in the Pacific and in all the world.'

Curtin had travelled far along an agonising path. He never converted a majority of the Labor Party to his attack policy or, in their hearts, probably not a majority of the Australian people. Memories of the First World War and the conscription debates were easily stirred. The limitation on the use of the CMF gave the Opposition a convenient handle to charge Curtin with inconsistency, and even hypocrisy. He himself was obliged to say during a House of Representatives debate on 1 May 1942 that 'in the absence of naval and aerial superiority, all talk about taking the offensive is meaningless'. Never far from Curtin's thoughts was the fate of the Australian prisoners of war. This was the great human factor in his desire to shorten the war by going on the attack against Japan. This is why the Roosevelt–Churchill strategy of a holding war until Germany's defeat was anathema: for Curtin, it meant prolonging the war and prolonging the POWs' ordeal. By now, there were nearly twenty thousand of them.

The first American troops to arrive in Australia had originally been destined for the Philippines. They left San Francisco in November, and were diverted to Australia when Pearl Harbor gave the Imperial Japanese Navy mastery of most of the north and west Pacific. Escorted by the cruiser USS *Pensacola*, the seven ships of the convoy, carrying 4500 troops, reached Brisbane on 22 December. My father took his two sons to witness, along with 100,000 other Queenslanders, this big moment in Australian history. The Yanks were coming! A week later, Air Force Major General George H. Brett was sent to Australia to take command of all American forces in the Australian region. At the same time, General MacArthur in Manila ordered Major General Lewis Brereton, commander of the US Far East Air Force, to go to Australia to organise operating bases to protect lines of communications with the Philippines, and to support MacArthur's defence. By February, it had become clear that the Philippines were doomed to the same fate as Malaya and Burma. It was only then that Roosevelt and his military chiefs, Marshall and his deputy, General Dwight Eisenhower, gave serious attention to creating a base against Japan in the only place left – Australia.

Despite Churchill's assurances to Curtin and Casey that he was 'labouring night and day' in Australia's interests, Roosevelt's aid to Australia in the first weeks after Pearl Harbor owed nothing to Churchill or, for that matter, Curtin. Roosevelt's decisions regarding Australia were governed by the situation in the Philippines. The withdrawal of the American Pacific Fleet to the Californian coast and the disarray of General MacArthur's forces in the Philippines in the weeks after Pearl Harbor had made that situation desperate. By February, 1942, Roosevelt's worry was not 'What to do for Australia?', but 'What to do with Douglas MacArthur?'.

Douglas Arthur MacArthur was now sixty-two. The most decorated American soldier of the First World War, he was US Army Chief of Staff from 1930 to 1935, when he went to Manila as military adviser to the semi-autonomous government. The Philippines, an American colony seized from Spain in 1898, had been given an interim American-style constitution, with independence scheduled for 1946. MacArthur, whose father had been military governor of the Philippines and had put down Filipino insurgencies with unrelenting violence, had a deep affection for its people and for the army he was building. As war with Japan loomed in July, 1941, he was given command of the US Army Forces in the Far East, based on the Philippines. Taken by surprise by Japanese attacks on Luzon, the main island, nine hours after Pearl Harbor, he had withdrawn his forces to the Bataan Peninsula, placing himself and his headquarters underground on the island of Corregidor in Manila Bay. On Bataan, he had eighty thousand troops, including thirty thousand Americans.

His defence of Bataan made him an American hero, and a problem for both Roosevelt and Churchill. As we have seen, MacArthur's example was a major influence in Churchill's decision to persevere with the defence of Singapore to the bitter end. Roosevelt's Republican opponents demanded the reinforcement of Bataan. On 20 February, the President of the Philippines, Manuel Quezon, left Corregidor by submarine, heading for Australia. MacArthur vowed to fight on or die.

General Marshall wanted MacArthur to follow Quezon. Roosevelt was reluctant to let him leave. 'It would mean that the whites would absolutely lose all face in the Far East,' he told Marshall. 'White men can go down fighting but they can't run away.' Three days later, however, white prestige had to give way to black reality. Roosevelt faced the facts and ordered MacArthur to leave Corregidor for Mindanao, southernmost of the larger islands of the Philippines; if the situation deteriorated beyond retrieval, he was to proceed to Australia and take command of all US forces there. MacArthur was granted permission to make his own decision on the timing of his departure. It was not until 9 March that he decided the time had come. The starving garrison on Bataan could not resist much beyond the end of the month. There was no hope of the relief repeatedly promised by Roosevelt. Handing over to his deputy, General Jonathan Wainwright, MacArthur said: 'If I get through, you know I'll come back as soon as I can with as much as I can.'

On the moonless night of 11 March, a US patrol boat slipped away from Corregidor, carrying MacArthur, his wife Jean, and his four-year-old son Arthur. Three other PTs carried his entourage of staff officers, who dubbed themselves 'the Bataan Gang'. After four days dodging Japanese patrols, MacArthur reached Mindanao to be taken to Darwin in one of the B17s ordered up from Australia. He set out for Darwin on 17 March. As he neared Darwin after a ten-hour flight, the port was being bombed; his plane put down at Batchelor Field forty miles south. Refusing to fly further than the railhead at Alice Springs, he boarded what was then the most primitive train in Australia, which is saying something. He held a news conference at Terowie, a rail-stop north of Adelaide: 'The President of the United States ordered me to break through the Japanese lines and proceed from Corregidor for the purpose, as I understand it, of organising the American offensive against Japan, a primary objective of which is the relief of the Philippines.' His mind and heart set on Bataan, he made his famous declaration: 'I came through and I shall return.'

On the train to Melbourne, MacArthur received what he later described as 'the greatest shock of the whole damn war'. He quizzed American officers sent to greet him on the number and make-up of the American forces already in Australia. The answer was twenty-five thousand, disorganised and ill trained, no tanks, no artillery, and only a handful of poorly maintained combat aircraft. His hopes of an early return to rescue the Philippines evaporated, as he said: 'God have mercy on us.'

MacArthur arrived at Melbourne's Spencer Street railway station on the morning of 21 March, after a journey of eleven days of danger and discomfort. He told the crowd of five thousand: 'No general can make something out of nothing. My success or failure will depend primarily on the resources which the respective governments place at my disposal.' Thus, MacArthur began his Australian career with an unabashed political statement, aimed directly at Roosevelt, Churchill, and Curtin. He had left Adelaide believing that his authority extended only to the scattered American units then in Australia. He had arrived in Melbourne to find that Roosevelt had appointed him Supreme Commander of all Allied forces in the Australian theatre. His appointment meant a major success for Curtin and his ideas.

MacArthur met Curtin for the first time in Canberra on 26 March. He wrote in his *Reminiscences*:

We promptly came to a sense of mutual trust, cooperation, and regard that we never once breached by word, thought, or deed. He was the kind of a man the Australians called 'fair dinkum'. As I rose to leave, I put my arm about his strong shoulder: 'Mr Prime Minister', I said, 'we two, you and I, will see this thing through together. We can do it and

we will do it. You take care of the rear and I will handle the front.'
He shook me by both hands and said: 'I know I was not wrong in select-
ing you as Supreme Commander'.

MacArthur's appointment had not been so clear-cut. On the
morning of 17 March, the day MacArthur put down at Batchelor
Field, the commander of the American forces in Australia, General
Brett, had informed Curtin of MacArthur's imminent arrival. He
also conveyed in writing Roosevelt's suggestion that the Australian
Government place its own forces under MacArthur's command.
Curtin immediately cabled Roosevelt:

> General Douglas MacArthur having arrived in Australia, the Common-
> wealth Government desires to nominate him as Supreme Commander of
> the Allied Forces in this theatre. His heroic defence in the Philippine
> Islands has evoked the admiration of the world and has been an
> example of the stubborn resistance with which the advance of the enemy
> should be opposed. The Australian Government feels that his leadership
> of the Allied forces in this theatre will be an inspiration to the Australian
> people and all the forces who will be privileged to serve under his
> command.

Curtin's message was conveyed to Roosevelt by his Under-Secretary
of State, Sumner Welles, who reported back to Casey that steps
would be 'immediately taken in accordance with the suggestion of
your Prime Minister'. Simultaneously, the US Secretary of State for
War, Henry Stimson, announced MacArthur's appointment 'at the
suggestion of the Australian Government'. This was a diplomatic
fiction. Roosevelt had made the decision himself. But it was to prove
of great value to Curtin in his relations with MacArthur, who always
gave Curtin the credit for his appointment. Curtin made himself
believe it. It suited MacArthur to believe that he was not beholden to
Roosevelt. It suited Roosevelt to maintain the fiction. He had no
desire to inflate MacArthur's ego or reputation by appearing to be
turning in desperation to the new American – and Republican –
hero. Roosevelt was happy enough for the Australians to hail

MacArthur as their saviour. The last thing he intended was to promote MacArthur as the saviour of the United States – or as the Republican candidate in the 1944 Presidential election. As it was, the *New York Times* headline of 18 March ran: MACARTHUR IN AUSTRALIA AS ALLIED COMMANDER. MOVE HAILED AS TURN OF TIDE.

CHURCHILL, TOO, REALISED that the tide was turning in his relations with Australia. His message to Curtin the day MacArthur arrived in Australia is an almost poignant mix of approval and regret, implied reproof mingled with resignation. He wanted 'here and now to make the following plain to you', he told Curtin:

> The fact that an American commander will be in charge of all the operations in the Pacific Area will not be regarded by His Majesty's Government as in any way absolving them from the determination and duty to stand to your aid to the best of their ability; and, if you are actually invaded in force, which has by no means come to pass and may never come to pass, we shall do our utmost to divert British troops and British ships rounding the Cape already in the Indian Ocean to your succour, albeit at the expense of India and the Middle East.

It would have been a noble message if it had not been so unrealistic. After all they had been through together since Pearl Harbor, here was Churchill repeating to Curtin all the old assurances and promises, as unkeepable as ever, still relying on the narrowest possible definition of Australia's danger, still proclaiming the duties and sacrifices of the Empire. Yet in a deeper sense, Churchill's touch was still sure; if he thought he could still tap the springs of Empire sentiment in Australia, he would prove correct, not least with Curtin. For much longer than is now commonly thought, Curtin 'looked to' Britain, as well as to the United States.

In a letter to Roosevelt on April Fool's Day, Churchill spelt out his definition of a threat to Australia: 'I have told Curtin that if he is seriously invaded – *by which I mean six or eight enemy divisions*

Britain will come to his aid.' Japan had conquered the whole of South-East Asia with that, and could not possibly have found, transported or supplied anything like six or eight divisions for the invasion of Australia. Churchill used his essentially meaningless promise to Australia in order to emphasise to Roosevelt the efforts he was making in the Middle East. Any British help for Australia 'could only be at the expense of the most urgent needs in the other theatres', he told Roosevelt. 'I hope you will continue to give Australia all possible reinforcement, and thus enable me to defend Egypt, the Levant and India successfully. It will be a hard task.'

While MacArthur's patrol boat had been making its escape through the islands of the Philippines, Roosevelt and Churchill were dividing up the world, or what was left to them. The row over Rangoon had surprised Roosevelt by its revelations of the divided counsels within the British Empire. It had also exposed the irrelevance of the ABDA arrangements. With all the ABDA area now in Japanese hands, and the ABDA command itself dissolved, Roosevelt proposed a division of responsibility into three areas: the United States would take over the whole Pacific Area; Britain would keep responsibility for the theatre from Burma and India to the Middle East and the Mediterranean; and the Atlantic should be a joint British and American theatre. The Pacific War Council in London would be replaced by a Pacific Council in Washington. Churchill accepted Roosevelt's proposals in principle, but wanted to retain the London Pacific War Council. Bruce weighed in to support strongly the removal of the Pacific War Council to Washington. He made clear to Curtin his belief that as long as Churchill dominated everything in London, he would be a drag on the 'utilisation of United States forces' in the Pacific.

MacArthur's arrival gave Roosevelt a convenient solution of his problems in balancing the competing demands of a worldwide war and the rivalry for resources between his army and navy. The Pacific Ocean Area, including New Zealand, was given to command of the US navy; the South-West Pacific area, including Australia and the Philippines, came under MacArthur as Supreme Commander. Australia was the link between the two commands. In the directives defining the purpose of their operations, the last of six objectives of the Pacific Ocean Area was stated: '(F) To prepare for the execution of major amphibious offensives to be launched from the South Pacific, and the South-West Pacific area.' The first objective of the South-West Pacific Area under MacArthur was to be: '(A) Hold the key military regions of Australia as bases for future offensive action against Japan, and strive to check Japanese aggression in the South-West Pacific Area.' MacArthur was instructed to 'check the enemy advance across Australia, and its essential lines of communications', to support naval and air operations in the entire Pacific Area.

AN APPOINTMENT OF a different kind caused another glitch in the relations between Churchill and Curtin. It involved the usual cast of characters – Churchill and Roosevelt, Curtin, Evatt, and Casey – and the same argument about priorities as between the Middle East and the Pacific. But a new element emerged – Herbert Vere Evatt in the novel role of peacemaker between Churchill and Curtin.

Two cables between Churchill and Curtin crossed one another on 13 March. In the first, Churchill said that he was thinking of appointing Casey as Minister of State in Cairo. 'Before going further,' Churchill said, 'I should like to learn what you think about it, and whether you could spare him from Washington.' The second cable, from Curtin, informed Churchill that he was sending Dr Evatt on a mission to the United States and Britain. While Evatt was in London, Curtin said, he would replace Page on the Cabinet and Pacific War Council.

Curtin jibbed at Casey for Cairo. He answered Churchill that 'at this stage it would be a matter of great difficulty' and 'all things considered, it would be in the interests of us all if approach were not made at this juncture'. But Churchill had already made up his mind. He now claimed that during their train journey from Florida to Washington in January, he had 'learned from Casey that he was very anxious for a change'. As to Casey's replacement, 'I venture to court your rebuke by asking whether Menzies, with his great distinction and success when passing through America might not fill the gap?'

In fact, Churchill had already offered the job to Casey, who cabled Curtin on 18 March that it had come as 'a complete surprise'. However, he said, he had already consulted Roosevelt, Hopkins, and Lord Halifax, all of whom 'expressed the firm view that I should accept'. The President, Casey told Curtin, 'whilst being good enough to say that he would be sorry for me to leave here, he rated extremely high the holding of the Middle East but he had most disturbing reports about the muddle that exists there'. If Curtin agreed, he would accept the appointment, but would stay in Washington until Evatt's arrival and 'make him fully conversant about the situation and personalities here'.

The irony is that Evatt's insulting treatment of Casey was a major factor in his desire to leave his post in Washington. Churchill's offer, hugely gratifying in itself, also meant escape from Evatt. It also suited Evatt to get rid of Casey, especially now that he was about to set foot on the great stage of the world. Washington was not big enough for the two of them. So it is no surprise that as soon as Evatt reached the United States on 19 March, he advised Casey to accept Churchill's offer. Casey reported to Curtin that, now that 'our Australian cause is now so bound up with the American cause, particularly with the appointment of MacArthur', Evatt believed that 'the matter of adequate representation in Washington presents no great difficulty'.

Before Curtin had heard from Casey or Evatt, Churchill announced the appointment in the House of Commons on 19 March. Although Curtin had told Casey that the matter 'was entirely one between yourself and Churchill', he had assumed that no final decision would be taken, much less announced publicly, without his concurrence. The first Curtin heard of it was on the 10.00 p.m. BBC news broadcast in Canberra. As he told Churchill next day: 'I learn what my Minister has done from the world at large.'

It was a classic Churchill manoeuvre: the unilateral decision already made before the request; the fait accompli locked in by the premature announcement; then the recrimination and the implied threat to expose the defaulter to the judgement of history. This time, Curtin expressed his anger to the British High Commissioner in

Canberra, Sir Ronald Cross, but publicly limited his annoyance to a midnight press statement saying that while the Australian Government would prefer Casey to stay in Washington, it would not instruct him to do so. Even this was too much for Churchill, who immediately staked the high ground by telling Curtin: 'I do not understand the tone of your public statement and I shall be forced to quote your telegram to me, unless some way or other you can clear up the situation.' One cannot but admire Churchill's audacity, the rhinoceros hide noted by Banjo Paterson in 1900, and his skill in shifting the onus of blame. What exactly was Curtin obliged to clear up? This time Curtin did not take the bait. He noted but let pass the gratuitous suggestion about Menzies. He challenged Churchill to publish all the telegrams, but added, neatly shifting the blame to Casey: 'I assure you that your personal part in this matter is above reproach and I have no complaint whatsoever. You said the matter was personal to Casey. I told Casey the wishes of the Australian Government to make no change but said that we would not press him to remain in the service of Australia. He has chosen, not you or us.'

The Casey affair disturbed Roosevelt. 'I realise it is but an incident,' he told Churchill on 22 March. 'The more important matter is the basic relationship of Great Britain and Australia.' He was worried about 'what appears publicly to be a rather strained relationship' at this critical time. 'I am simply wondering how something might be done in the immediate future to change all that to an atmosphere of good will which is so essential to the unity of our military efforts directed against the enemy. I confess at the moment that I have nothing to propose although I am going to direct my mind towards it and if I think of anything I will let you know.' He said that he felt himself 'greatly responsible for the turn of events' because he had told Casey 'quite frankly that I hoped he would take the job in the Middle East because he would be a person in the area who would know both the American and Australian angles as well as the British'.

An unrepentant Churchill continued to bad-mouth Australia with Roosevelt, adding partisan prejudice to his ill-informed understanding of Australian politics:

Former Naval Person to President, Personal and Secret, March 23, 1942

(1) You have no doubt seen the correspondence between me and Curtin, which speaks for itself. I accepted his agreement and waited five days before making the announcement.

(2) The matter is complicated by Australian party politics which proceed with much bitterness and jealousy regardless of national danger. The present Labour Government in Australia, with a majority of one, contains various personalities, particularly Evatt and Beasley, who have made their way in local politics by showing hostility to Great Britain. The failure of sea power to protect Australia from Japan brings this sentiment to a head. I am very glad you encouraged Casey to take up the appointment.

(3) I shall be interested to know your personal impressions of Evatt and how you get on with him.

Evatt may have realised that his own part in the affair had contributed to Curtin's embarrassment and anger. Anxious that the matter should not spoil his visit to Washington, or his forthcoming visit to London, he was uncharacteristically soothing and temperate. It is not hard to imagine how different his reaction might have been, had he been in Canberra. But in the glow of his first meeting with Roosevelt on 21 March, he wrote to Curtin that he had seen the President, Hopkins, and his friend US Supreme Court Justice Felix Frankfurter, like Hopkins a trusted adviser to the President: 'They are all most anxious to avoid further public argument with Churchill over Casey's appointment. Especially, they say, they are disturbed at local political embarrassment by disclosure of the fact that Casey privately consulted American leaders.' Evatt failed to mention his own advice to Casey. Urging Curtin to say nothing more about it, he added: 'I have suggested strongly that Churchill's method of dealing with Australia indicates party political bias.' Evatt was accurate enough in detecting Churchill's political bias, but was deceiving himself in thinking that American Democrats would turn out less judgemental than British Conservatives. But he had received the key message: Hopkins 'stressed the need of starting from scratch again with Churchill in order to re-establish the friendliest feelings and he will advise the President to approach Churchill on the same lines'.

Thrilled by his own performance in Washington, Evatt was convinced that he was just the man to deal with Churchill. 'The relations I have already established with the President and his special advisers are very close,' he told Curtin, 'and, I believe, unique for an Australian.' For the next three months, in Washington and London, Evatt was to succeed to a surprising degree in 're-establishing the friendliest feelings with Churchill'. Astonishingly, Evatt was about to invite, not Roosevelt or MacArthur, but Churchill, to become 'the saviour of Australia'.

25

'Starting from scratch'
March–June, 1942

Winston Churchill cast his spell over Herbert Evatt in May, 1942. Almost overnight, Evatt went from being Churchill's harshest critic in the Australian Cabinet to his stoutest champion. The transformation was a significant factor in shaping the new relationship between Australia, Britain, and America. The story of Evatt's conversion is almost an allegory of Australia's ambiguity towards its new relationship with America and Britain, and the ambivalence of the Australian Labor Government's relations with Churchill.

Evatt had begun his mission to Washington in March believing that he would find Roosevelt more sympathetic to Australia's needs than Churchill. This was true, to the extent that Roosevelt, unlike Churchill, was a good listener. He had to be, because so many conflicting voices competed for his ear. But he was a cool calculator of his own and America's interests. He had none of Churchill's impetuosity. When he was elected President in 1932, the great American jurist, Justice Oliver Wendell Holmes, then aged ninety-two, described Roosevelt as a 'second-class intellect but a first-class temperament'. He was a man of infinite charm; and only in his last declining months in 1945 did his power to charm fail to work its magic on Josef Stalin. Evatt got the full Roosevelt treatment in 1942 and lapped it up.

Evatt was a quick learner. He soon saw that Casey had been right about the complexity of policy-making in Washington. On his first full day in Washington, Evatt had two hours with Roosevelt, another two hours with Hopkins ('obviously the President's right hand man', he told Curtin, 'with whom I am on excellent terms') and conferences with General Marshall and Admiral King. He found Roosevelt eager to set up the Pacific War Council in Washington, with Australia fully represented. But in his discussions with Roosevelt, Evatt learnt another important lesson – that knocking Churchill was no way to please Roosevelt. Roosevelt took the view, Evatt told Curtin, that the Washington Council 'must be permitted to develop and that in the meantime the Council in London should not be disturbed'. It was Roosevelt's 'personal opinion that the centre of gravity in relation to the direction of the war generally is shifting to Washington but full recognition of the movement will be gradual and thus English susceptibility should not be upset'. By 'English susceptibility', both Roosevelt and Evatt meant Churchill's.

From that moment, Evatt realised the fundamental strength of the Roosevelt–Churchill partnership and its influence on Roosevelt's thinking. The Casey episode had been instructive. Evatt had been struck by American uneasiness over the affair. Roosevelt had raised it at their first meeting, and Evatt cabled Curtin: 'I believe the President is now wiring Churchill suggesting he should give no publicity to the matter', and advised Curtin likewise. Evatt said: 'The President is also anxious that if possible we should reach a general *modus vivendi* with Churchill'. Hopkins had made the same point with his 'starting from scratch' statement. From now on, Evatt took this up as his personal mission. It was an amazing reversal of form.

Evatt began to prepare the ground for his London visit during his first week in Washington. His first step was to cable Bruce. Fortunately for his plan, Page was out of action, exhausted and embittered by the treatment he had received from both Churchill and Curtin over Rangoon. His stint as Australia's representative on the British War Cabinet was about to end, and Bruce would replace him while retaining his post as High Commissioner.

'I wish we could do something to restore Churchill to favour in Australia,' Evatt cabled Bruce on 23 March, 'not because he is Churchill but because he is Prime Minister.' Evatt wrote: 'Every step taken recently suggests that the United Kingdom is throwing exclusive responsibility for the defence of Australia and New Zealand on to the shoulders of the United States.' The situation was bad everywhere, Evatt said, but 'our position in Australia for the next two months is a desperate one'. Evatt proposed a solution: 'Why could not Churchill agree to immediate deliveries to Australia of the entire United Kingdom allocation [of munitions and aircraft under Lend-Lease] for six weeks only? This would not take away from United Kingdom production, but it might make him the saviour of Australia.'

With a clinical detachment from his own conduct, Evatt added in his message to Bruce: 'The continuous rowing over unfortunate things and the attempt to hector over more important things gravely impair Empire solidarity. It is not for me to apportion blame, but I can assure you that the President is very disturbed and is anxious to effect conciliation, which, in my opinion, requires also some earnest from the United Kingdom Government.' Evatt asked Bruce to convey this message of goodwill to Churchill 'on the understanding that it is regarded as confidential and personal' – that is, don't tell Curtin. He suggested that Bruce should show Churchill an introductory letter from Billy Hughes, which he modestly quoted:

Dear Mr Churchill,

This will introduce my friend the Honourable H. V. Evatt. You know all about him – he was for ten years Justice of the High Court – a man of parts, and he comes to Britain to get help for Australia in the hour of supreme peril. He will tell you all about our position – Australia will fight, do not doubt for a moment – but the enemy is strong, fired by fanatical zeal and has complete local command of the sea – and great superiority in the air . . . We *must* hold Australia. We will fight as you bade the English do – on the beaches, on the roads, in every hamlet – but we want planes – and *now*. I ought to say I have known Dr Evatt for the last thirty years; he has, like all of us, an intense admiration for you; and he has great influence in Australia.

This intense admirer of Churchill was the same Dr Evatt who, barely a month before, had written a private letter to the British left-wing loner, the austere Sir Stafford Cripps, then being touted as not only a replacement for Attlee as leader of the British Labour Party, but for Churchill himself. Evatt had complained to Cripps about Churchill's broken promises over Singapore, his 'ungenerous and bitterly resented' statements about Australian troops, his 'preposterous side-tracking' over resources for the Pacific theatre, and his 'political ploy' of publicly praising Menzies to diminish Curtin. For good measure, he told Cripps that Menzies himself 'had privately described Churchill as suffering from a dictatorship complex which approaches megalomania'. Evatt concluded: 'The result of all this has been a growing conviction here that we cannot win this war without great and drastic changes in its higher direction.' Only three days later, Churchill brought the recipient of this letter, Sir Stafford Cripps, into his Cabinet. But in Washington, Evatt had discovered that the highest war director of all, Roosevelt, was very much on Churchill's side; if the Australians wanted his goodwill and cooperation, they had better get on side with Churchill too.

Bruce lost no time in acting on Evatt's message. His interview with Churchill on 31 March started badly. He was greeted, he recorded, with 'a tirade which was more or less down the lines that the Australian Government was impossible and quite unhelpful'. Churchill stormed that the Australians had 'pinned their hopes on the United States, but now having found in Washington that those hopes were not likely to be realised, they were falling back on the Old Country'. Churchill raked over Tobruk and Rangoon, and told Bruce he was 'not going to be scolded' over the Casey appointment. According to his own record of conversation, Bruce gave as good as he got. He claimed to have told Churchill that he ought to 'take a bigger attitude':

I urged on the Prime Minister that the very understandable resentment he might be feeling must not prejudice his attitude towards Australia as it would inevitably have unfortunate repercussions on the common cause. With this statement Winston became all high minded and respectable and even pompous by saying that his personal feelings would never prevent him doing his duty.

Bruce claimed that he replied that 'God might be able to take as exalted an attitude as that, but he, Winston, not being God, could not'. He stressed that Evatt's message showed 'an obvious desire to remove the present atmosphere of misunderstanding'. Churchill quietened down and then repeated his determination to carry out his undertakings to Australia. In his record, Bruce commented drily that Churchill was so emphatic about adhering to his pledges 'that I think he must be having some doubts as to the wisdom of what he has committed himself to'.

Whatever doubts Churchill may have had about his commitments, they were now irrelevant to Australia's situation. The really relevant decisions were being taken in Tokyo. In his talk with Bruce: 'Winston then stressed very strongly that the diversions which he was prepared to make from the Cape were dependent upon Australia's danger being a real one. He went on to elaborate his view that in fact Australia is not in danger of any serious attack. His view is that Japan will go on in Burma, trying to isolate China and eventually to knock China out altogether.'

Churchill was half-right about the Japanese and China. The Imperial Army's hopes of finishing off the war in China remained at the centre of its planning. A council of war between the army and navy chiefs had been held in Tokyo on 7 March, as Rangoon was about to fall. Their basic decision was that Japan should consolidate its gains by expanding them; this would enable Japan to 'establish a political and strategical structure capable of withstanding a protracted war'.

Rivalry between the Imperial Japanese Army and Navy determined Australia's fate. The army chiefs rejected a navy proposal for a full-scale invasion of Australia, on the grounds that it would need ten divisions and 1.5 million tons of shipping. Anxious about China, the army was prepared to leave only six divisions around the southern perimeter of the new Japanese Empire. As a compromise, the High Command agreed to concentrate on isolating Australia by occupying New Guinea, New Britain, the Solomons, New Caledonia, Fiji, and Samoa. By taking Port Moresby, they could control the Australian approaches by air and sea, dominate the Coral Sea, strike at the mainland at will, cut the American lines of communication with Australia and prevent the build-up of the Australian base against Japan. Meanwhile, Admiral Yamamoto drew up a plan to seize the island of Midway, north of Hawaii, expecting thereby to draw the US Pacific Fleet into a decisive battle. These decisions set the course of the war and ultimately sealed the fate of Japan.

There is a fascinating parallel between the assessments of the High Command in Tokyo and Churchill in London. The Japanese estimate of the number of divisions needed for the invasion of Australia matched exactly Churchill's new benchmark for the redemption of his pledges. He had kept on raising the bar, from six divisions to eight to ten. After his interview with Bruce, Churchill took pains to set the record straight. He wrote to Bruce on 3 April:

> You use the expression 'if Australia is in deadly peril', whereas what I said and mean is 'if Australia is being heavily invaded'. You use the expression 'a major threat to Australia'. I have never said anything about diverting troops to meet 'threats' . . . It is very important that there should be no misunderstanding about this, as Dr Evatt, from his telegrams, clearly holds that Australia is 'in deadly peril' and that a 'major threat' has developed.

In other words, mere 'deadly peril' or 'major threats' did not meet his test; his pledges would become operative only 'if Japan set about invading Australia or New Zealand on a large scale', which he now defined as ten Japanese divisions.

Far from moving reinforcements to Australia, Churchill was still trying hard to keep the 9th Australian Division in the Middle East. Since Churchill's speech in the House of Commons on 27 January, in which he had said 'that no obstacle would be placed in the way of the AIF returning to defend their homeland', the Australian Government had assumed that the 9th, the last of the three divisions in the Middle East, would be brought back to Australia as soon as shipping and safety permitted. Curtin made the formal request for their return on 17 February, two days after the fall of Singapore. The 18 February meeting of the Pacific War Council which had sparked the Rangoon row had 'accepted the Australian Government's policy of taking the whole of their forces back to Australia'. After the Rangoon fracas, Curtin's offer to allow two brigades of the 6th Division to garrison Ceylon had been made 'relying on the understanding that the 9th Division will return to Australia with proper escort as soon as possible'. Blamey, now nominally MacArthur's deputy, and commander-in-chief of Allied Land Forces in the SWPA, was as anxious as ever to bring the AIF together in one distinct army. MacArthur, still fuming over the paucity of American troops under his command and the tardiness of American reinforcements, strongly agreed with Blamey. But on 20 March, Churchill countered with a request of his own. After outlining American plans to send three more divisions to Australia and New Zealand, and the need to economise on shipping troops anywhere, Churchill said: 'I hope, in these circumstances, you will feel able to leave the 9th Australian Division in the Mid East where its presence is most sorely needed.'

This time there was no explosion from Canberra. Evatt doused the fuse. His cables to Curtin make it clear that Roosevelt not only knew of Churchill's request but was party to it. At the first Roosevelt–Evatt meeting on 22 March, the return of the 9th Division was only mentioned in passing, pending further discussion. 'Hopkins' view,' Evatt reported, 'is that it might be desirable to make a bargain over the matter.' It is unclear whether Hopkins and Evatt meant bargaining with Churchill over air reinforcements, or referred to Roosevelt's offer of American divisions in exchange for allowing the Australian division to stay in the Middle East. Either way, Roosevelt and Hopkins were anxious that Curtin avoid another confrontation with Churchill. 'In the meantime,' Evatt counselled Curtin, 'I should advise against a definite reply.'

Curtin followed Evatt's advice. Although neither he, Blamey nor MacArthur changed their view about the need for the 9th to come home, the Australian Government had obviously decided to subordinate its view to Roosevelt's. For his part, Roosevelt was anxious not to appear to be pressuring the Australians. In a cable on 26 March, he told Churchill that although he was in favour of leaving the 9th in the Middle East, he had advised Evatt that 'the decision as to whether the Australian division should be sent home or not must be made by Prime Minister Curtin and not by me'. On 2 April, Evatt cabled Curtin: 'Discussions here show that the President does not intend to depart from his non-committal attitude. General Marshall mentioned in conversation with me that he preferred the 9th Division to remain in the Middle East.'

Curtin waited a fortnight before announcing his decision. He told Churchill on 14 April that the delay had been caused by the need to consult with MacArthur and Blamey. MacArthur's view, he said, was that the 9th Division could be allowed to remain provided Australia received adequate air and naval reinforcements. While the Australian Government still believed that all Australian troops abroad should come home, 'it was prepared to agree to the postponement of the 9th's return until it can be replaced in the Middle East and the necessary shipping and escort can be made available for its transportation to Australia'.

Curtin ended his message with a shrewd swipe at Churchill's new promise that Australia could count on the diversion of an armoured division should invasion by, say, eight or ten Japanese divisions occur. The offer was gratefully acknowledged, said Curtin, 'but our advisers observe that, should Japan be able to launch an invasion on the scale mentioned by you, she would have such command of the sea that it would probably be impossible to reinforce Australia to any great extent by seaborne forces'.

Churchill ignored the implication that his promises were worthless and replied next day: 'I am very much obliged to you for your decision to allow the Australian 9th Division to remain in the Middle East for the present.' Shunning any notion that he might have been dealing with Roosevelt behind Curtin's back, Churchill wrote: 'It is fully understood and was certainly my wish that United States Forces should go to Australia unconditionally.' He concluded by living up to his motto, 'Magnanimity in victory', telling Curtin: 'You have always been and will be perfectly free to decide the movement of all your troops.'

For the time being, Churchill had had his way and the 9th stayed in the Middle East long enough to play a notable part in the British victory over Rommel at El Alamein in October and November. Curtin's reluctant decision proved advantageous to Australia. At a critical time, he had avoided a potentially disastrous row with Churchill and had given impressive evidence of Australia's willingness to sink its strong national view for the larger cause. He had maintained the principle of the return home of the AIF, without the old rancour and recrimination. Most importantly, he had not involved Roosevelt in what could have been a bruising brawl in which the President would certainly have come down on Churchill's side. MacArthur and Blamey continued to urge Curtin to press for the return. By linking MacArthur with both his desire for the return of the 9th and his acceptance of Churchill's request, he had cemented their partnership. Curtin's prudent course owed much to Evatt's counsel of delay and restraint and to his careful soundings of opinion in Washington. It was, for Evatt, the best possible introduction to the second part of his overseas mission – to London and Churchill.

Evatt's eagerness to meet Churchill turned into impatience with his Canberra colleagues when they ordered him to stay in Washington for more talks with Roosevelt and Marshall. To his dismay, Curtin and MacArthur were dissatisfied with the results of his mission so far. Curtin cabled Evatt on 28 April: 'MacArthur is bitterly disappointed with the meagre assistance promised for the Southwest Pacific Area'. In MacArthur's view, the promised ninety-five thousand air and ground troops, with five hundred planes, were 'entirely inadequate' for the defence of Australia, much less for offensive action against the Japanese. MacArthur's disappointment was deepened by grief: his army on Bataan had surrendered on 9 April and forty-five thousand Filipinos and thirteen thousand Americans began the Bataan Death March. The underground fortress on Corregidor held out for another month. MacArthur's intelligence sources indicated that Japan now intended 'to push southwards either in the islands north-east of Australia or to Australia', Curtin told Evatt. 'He does not hesitate to say that we may be left unsupported, as he was in the Philippines, or that any support may be too late, as in the case of Malaya and the N.E.I.' Unless the United States provided much greater support by way of men and materiel, MacArthur now believed that all talk about Australia as a base against Japan was becoming counterproductive and even dangerous, because it invited a pre-emptive attack.

Curtin sent MacArthur's grim assessment to Churchill, who replied with the standard assurances and qualifications, but added: 'Nevertheless, you may be sure that General MacArthur's recommendations will continue to be studied here, and I have also reported them to the President in case he may feel able to take any further action.' This was to earn MacArthur a rebuke from Marshall, who resented the impropriety of an American general's view being placed directly before a British Prime Minister by an Australian Prime Minister, even or especially if the American general was also an American hero. Churchill concluded: 'I am also looking forward to discussing the position with Dr Evatt, who will soon be here.'

Evatt insisted that his Washington mission was now complete. The proper course was to go to London for the full picture as it looked from both sides of the Atlantic and then return to Washington. This, he said, was also what the President wanted him to do. Roosevelt had repeatedly reminded him how important it was that he should proceed to London promptly. In language remarkably like Casey's explanations to Evatt himself, he told Canberra that 'people like Shedden, MacArthur and Blamey should know that supply quantities must be determined on a primarily military and strategic basis, and can seldom be affected by Government pressure'. In any case, it was too late to change his complicated and dangerous transport arrangements. Evatt, for whom flying of any kind was an ordeal and a flight across the Atlantic in wartime a nightmare, was on his way to Britain by May Day.

Over lunch in London with Evatt on 3 May, Bruce found him 'full of blood and thunder'. Evatt felt strongly, Bruce recorded, that Churchill and Roosevelt 'regarded the running of the war as a private and personal matter'. He was determined to have a show-down with Churchill. Bruce, who had heard it all before from Menzies, wryly noted: 'The future will show how far he does so.'

The 'blood and thunder' evaporated from the time of Evatt's first meeting with Churchill and the War Cabinet. In his first report to Curtin, he said that he had come to the 'broad conclusion' that Australia had very little share in British policy-making; so did the British Cabinet and the Pacific War Council; everything was decided by Churchill and his Service advisers. Nevertheless, Evatt said, Churchill had repeated in the presence of the Cabinet his promise to 'throw everything possible into the defence of Australia, preferring it to the defence of India' if Australia is 'heavily invaded'. Evatt presumably took this with the appropriate grain of salt. He now scaled down the objectives of his London mission. He told Curtin that he would concentrate on getting more British aircraft for Australia and persuading Churchill to give greater support in Washington for MacArthur's recommendations. Privately, Evatt told Bruce that Britain was now 'really a military dictatorship'.

Churchill gave Evatt the treatment that never failed – a conducted tour of Britain's bombed cities, this time Leeds, Hull, and Liverpool. As with Menzies and Page, Evatt was convinced not only of the fighting spirit of the people, but of Churchill's immense popularity. Bruce warned Evatt not to be 'too much influenced by these public demonstrations as the people's favour was notoriously a somewhat uncertain quantity'. Bruce was something of an expert, having lost both government and his own seat in parliament at the 1929 federal election – the only Australian Prime Minister to do so until Churchill's namesake, John Winston Howard, in 2007. Evatt stuck to his point, however, and told Bruce that 'Winston had complete control and he was the man who could give us what we wanted at the moment and it was not in our interests to antagonise him'.

Bruce saw what was coming. Only two weeks previously, Evatt had been heading for a showdown with Churchill to ensure that the

Australian representative on the War Cabinet (Bruce himself after Page's departure) would have his rights and position 'defined beyond all possibility of misunderstanding'. Now, said Bruce, Evatt's view seemed to be that 'he should get everything possible out of the cordial relations he has established with the Prime Minister, but that a show-down on the whole issue of our representation should be avoided'. Anyway, Evatt had said, if the British Cabinet was prepared to accept Churchill's dominance, it was not for us to upset things. 'It is clear,' Bruce noted, 'that Winston has exercised his charm and unquestionable astuteness upon Evatt.' Bruce could see how things would turn out. Churchill would promise Australia a couple of RAF squadrons, Evatt would bask in the glory, and the Australian representatives in London would be left with the same old frustrations they had been complaining about since Menzies. And that is more or less what happened.

In his final report to Curtin from London, Evatt claimed to have discovered a tremendous secret, and reported it almost as if he had uncovered a sinister plot. He had 'ascertained' that, in Washington over Christmas, Churchill and Roosevelt had agreed that 'notwithstanding the entrance of Japan into the war, Germany would still remain the primary enemy', and that Germany must be defeated before Japan. 'In a phrase,' Evatt told Curtin, 'it was "beat Hitler first".' Moreover, they had put it in writing. 'The existence of this written arrangement came as a great surprise to myself,' he told Curtin, 'and I have no doubt, to you.' In a fairly typical example of boosting himself while blaming others, Evatt said that neither Page nor Casey 'ever reported to us about it'. He said that he had seen another document which contained General Marshall's plan for American concentration against Germany in Western Europe. These revelations, he said, explained Washington's slow response to General MacArthur's requests for reinforcements. 'Their Pacific strategy was primarily defensive in character,' he wrote. 'The offensive was to take place in the future.'

If MacArthur and the Australians believed that they had been kept in the dark by Churchill and Roosevelt until May, 1942, they were being culpably blind or naive. Short of putting it up in lights in

Times Square, it is difficult to see how Roosevelt and Churchill could have made clearer that Hitler remained Public Enemy No. 1. At no stage did Churchill ever suggest that Japan's entry into the war had changed his Big Idea. On the contrary, he never disguised his jubilation that Japan had brought the United States into the war against Germany, despite the 'forfeits' he knew this would mean for the British Empire in the Far East. Churchill was under no obligation to tell Australia or anybody else that the goal he had pursued so relentlessly since May, 1940, remained unchanged. His fault lay in continuing to give the Australians undertakings and assurances about their security which he knew were impossible to keep. Australia's fault lay in continuing to accept them at face value.

Nothing more was heard of Evatt's outlandish proposal that Britain should give Australia six weeks' worth of Lend-Lease in order to make Churchill 'the saviour of Australia'. He reported to Curtin:

> Considering the difficulties created by the agreed grand strategy on which we were never consulted, the dramatic improvement in air fighting over the last three months in the Australian area, the fact that the United States accepted a primary responsibility for the Pacific and that a certain soreness had to be healed, I feel that the work of the mission here has been successful. We have greatly increased the personal concern of the Prime Minister and the Chiefs of Staff in our area. We certainly have made the British public and press more alive to our dangers and difficulties, and I think we are now assured of far greater support in Washington from the British representative there. The key is to retain the active interest and support of Churchill. He is supreme in the Cabinet and the country.

If Evatt's main purpose in London was personal reconciliation with Churchill, he had succeeded brilliantly. For the first time since the row over Tobruk nearly nine months previously, Churchill smiled on Australia. Indeed, it was smiles all round. Reporting to Curtin, Evatt glossed over the consultation issue, and hailed his own success in extracting from Churchill a promise of three RAF squadrons – two of them actually manned by Australians of the RAAF. In the most cordial exchange of messages they had ever had, Curtin told Churchill on 29 May:

> On behalf of the Government and people of Australia, I would express our warmest thanks for your assurances of support, for the instruction issued to your Chiefs of Staff to support the requisitions of General MacArthur and the representative of the Australian Government, and for the practical assistance you are giving in the matter of equipment.

In particular, said Curtin, 'we are most grateful for the provision of a wing of three Spitfire squadrons, which Dr Evatt has told me was your own conception'. This was a 'magnificent gesture' which was a great contribution to Australia's security and would have a 'demoralising effect' on the Japanese air force. This 'practical manifestation' of support would do much 'to encourage the Australian people in their inflexible determination to fight on until victory is won'.

Churchill replied next day: 'Evatt's visit here has been a great success and he has made many friends over here. I feel I shall have another friend in Australia. Evatt has also repeatedly assured me of your good will. This will be a great help in the many difficulties we have to face together.' This was more than window-dressing for Australian eyes. On the same day, Churchill cabled Roosevelt: 'Evatt is leaving quite soon for your side. He has shown himself most friendly especially to me personally, and I think you will find that he will help in every way.'

Not everyone was so friendly, the Chief of the Imperial General Staff, Sir Alan Brooke, for one. 'Evatt is a thoroughly unpleasant type of individual with no outlook beyond the shores of Australia,' Brooke wrote in his diary on 12 May. Evatt had 'refused to listen to a short statement of the global situation', Brooke wrote, 'and gave me the impression that he did not mind what happened to anybody else as long as Australian shores could be made safe'. Evatt failed to see that 'defeat in the Middle East, India and Indian Ocean must inevitably lead to the invasion of Australia, no matter what reinforcements were sent them now'. Brooke claimed that Evatt had produced 'strong blackmail cards' in urging more aircraft for Australia. 'If we did not ensure that MacArthur's requests were met,' Evatt had warned, 'we should probably be forced to part with the 9th Australian Division from the Middle East, or the Australian Squadron from England.'

Less jaundiced, but more to the point, was the judgement of General MacArthur himself. On 1 June, just after receiving Churchill's message, Curtin and MacArthur met in Melbourne for a session of the Prime Minister's War Conference, which Curtin had set up in April as the supreme council for the direction of the war. The conference comprised only Curtin and MacArthur, with ministers and military chiefs sometimes attending by special invitation. The minutes taken by Shedden, who always attended as secretary, record that MacArthur asked 'if he might speak with frankness'. Dr Evatt was undoubtedly a brilliant advocate, he said. He had aroused a lively interest in the English people about Australian security, and had been given a good press. He had no doubt evoked a sympathetic hearing from Mr Churchill. But from the practical military point of view, little had been achieved. MacArthur acknowledged that probably nobody could have done better than Evatt, because the agreement between Churchill and Roosevelt on the 'Beat Hitler First' strategy 'was a big hurdle to get over'. MacArthur told the War Conference: 'It is evident that Mr Churchill is determined that the seat of war shall *not* be in the Pacific Ocean. That's fine – as long as they agree to that in Tokyo.'

26

'A temporary deliverance'
May–June, 1942

Whether Tokyo agreed with Mr Churchill or not, the Japanese High Command was certainly determined that the Pacific Ocean should be the seat of war. While MacArthur in Melbourne was shaking his head over Evatt's self-delusion, the people of Sydney were shaking their heads in disbelief over a stunning event the night before. Three midget submarines, launched from mother submarines cruising eleven kilometres off Sydney Heads, had entered the harbour on the night of 31 May. Before all three were destroyed, one of them had torpedoed the depot ship HMAS *Kuttabul*, a converted ferry, with the loss of nineteen lives. It was a symbolic incident among what Churchill called 'the stirring events affecting the whole course of the war which now occurred in the Pacific Ocean'.

The plans sketched by the Japanese Imperial High Command in March had now taken shape under the driving force of Admiral Yamamoto. The Imperial Navy would make diversionary raids in the Aleutians, the chain of islands in the North-East Pacific, and seize the American base on the island of Midway; by threatening mainland America and Hawaii, Yamamoto expected to draw the

American fleet into a great battle, and settle the war at one victorious stroke, like the Battle of Tshushima against Russia in 1905, in
which he had participated. Southwards, the Imperial Army would
capture Port Moresby and the Australian-held island of Tulagi in
the Solomon Islands. As Churchill conceded in *The Hinge of Fate*:
'From New Guinea and from the Solomons, they could begin the
envelopment of Australia.' Australia, presumably, was expected to
be philosophical about this 'envelopment', like a sheep about to be
swallowed by a boa constrictor.

Yamamoto bears comparison with Rommel, in his risk-taking
and resilience – and in the legendary status accorded him by both his
compatriots and his adversaries. Churchill could well have extended
to the Japanese admiral his tribute to Rommel: 'Across the havoc of
war, may I say he is a great general.' In May and June, 1942,
Yamamoto's daring but complex plans were to founder on a crucial
Japanese failure, and a brilliant American success: the four aircraft
carriers of the US Pacific Fleet had been absent from Pearl Harbor
on 7 December and had thus escaped to fight another day; and
American intelligence had cracked the Japanese naval codes.

By mid-April, American code-breakers and Australian Coast
Watchers in New Guinea and the islands had pieced together the
Japanese plan for a concentration of troops and transports at their
new base in Rabaul. They knew that the destinations of these forces
were Port Moresby and Tulagi, and that Yamamoto had provided a
strong escort, including two aircraft carriers. From his headquarters
at Pearl Harbor, the Commander-in-Chief, Pacific, Admiral Chester
Nimitz, sent the carriers *Yorktown* and *Lexington* under Rear
Admiral Frank Fletcher to strengthen the Allied Task Force in the
Coral Sea, the north-east approach from the Solomons to northern
Queensland. This force included the cruisers HMAS *Australia* and
Hobart. But the novel feature of the Battle of the Coral Sea (5–8 May
1942) was that it was fought entirely by aircraft, operating from
carriers. It was the first naval battle in history in which the opposing
fleets never came into direct contact.

Each side lost one aircraft carrier, the Japanese *Shoku* and the
American *Lexington*, and about seventy aircraft each. The *Yorktown*

suffered some damage and, believing they had sunk it, the Japanese claimed Coral Sea as a victory. In truth, it was a critical Japanese reverse. The convoy heading for Port Moresby returned to Rabaul. What would have been an easy victory over the Australian garrison in Port Moresby from the sea became a ferocious land campaign from the eastern coast of New Guinea, across the mountains and jungle of the Owen Stanley range.

Undeterred, Yamamoto proceeded with his plan to seize the Midway Island and menace Hawaii. Japanese determination to risk everything on a decisive battle in the mid-Pacific had been sharpened by an American bombing raid on Tokyo masterminded by General James Doolittle, operating from the United States carrier *Hornet* on 18 and 19 April. The shame of endangering the Emperor's life had to be expunged. By a clever ruse, American intelligence was able to pinpoint the dates and places of Yamamoto's attack. Admiral Nimitz threw everything he had into Midway, including the *Yorktown*, which had been repaired at Pearl Harbor by three thousand men working night and day for three days. The result was a comprehensive American victory. Against American losses of *Yorktown*, fifty aircraft, and three hundred men, the Japanese lost four carriers, three hundred aircraft, and 3500 killed in action. In two days between 4 and 6 June, Japan had lost control of the Pacific. The historic significance of Midway matched its strategic importance. As Churchill saw it:

> The annals of war at sea present no more intense shock than these two battles [Coral Sea and Midway], in which the qualities of the United States Navy and Air Force and of the American race shone forth in splendour ... As the Japanese Fleet withdrew to their far-off home ports, their commanders knew not only that their aircraft carrier strength was irretrievably broken, but that they were confronted with a will-power and passion in the foe they had challenged, equal to the highest traditions of the Samurai ancestors, and backed with a development of power, numbers and science to which no limit could be set.

A twenty-first-century military historian, Robert Love, has spelt out the way in which Churchill's prophecy was to be fulfilled: 'The actions in the Coral Sea and Midway in 1942 set in train the replacement of Japanese with American power in the Pacific, a major military feature of the Cold War and the New World Order.'

THE CORAL SEA and Midway battles pushed Churchill and Curtin even further apart in pursuit of their ideas. Churchill grew even more dismissive about the threat to Australia. He saw the outcome as a vindication of his grand strategy. He had predicted it all in his paper on the Pacific war which he had written for Roosevelt on board the *Duke of York* in December. Moreover, in the weeks between Coral Sea and Midway, Rommel had launched his third offensive in North Africa, and Hitler had launched his summer offensive in Russia, thrusting hard towards the Black Sea and the Caucasus. As Churchill saw it, all the danger and urgency now lay in his own theatre of war.

It all looked very different to Curtin and MacArthur. General Wainwright had surrendered Corregidor and the Philippines on 9 May, the same day as the news of the Coral Sea battle. Far from removing the threat to Australia, the Coral Sea Battle had changed it into the form Australia dreaded most – a long and terrible struggle on Australian territory against the so-far invincible Japanese Imperial Army. The Port Moresby invasion force remained intact, readying itself at Rabaul for the overland assault on New Guinea. Japanese air and sea control in the South-West Pacific and the Indian Ocean seemed as strong as ever. The two American aircraft carriers which had decided the outcome in the Coral Sea were at the bottom of the ocean. If anything, American naval success at Midway fixed the focus of American attention on Admiral King's Central Pacific strategy away from MacArthur's South-West Pacific strategy, with Australia as his base for attack.

Churchill invited himself to Washington again. He found the mood there more testing. He was less sure of himself and beginning to sense the growing inequality of his relationship with Roosevelt.

The British Empire had already paid a huge price for his Big Idea, and now Egypt, the pivot of his 'Keep on Fighting' strategy, was once again under siege. The worst personal humiliation of the war came for Churchill on 21 June, when Roosevelt handed him a note with the news that Rommel had taken Tobruk at long last. 'What matters is that it should happen when I am here,' Churchill lamented to the ubiquitous Dr Wilson. 'I am ashamed. More than 30,000 of our men put their hands up.' Brooding, he asked Wilson, 'If they won't fight . . . ?' and left the question unfinished and unanswered.

Yet, in the perverse way of this war, the fall of Tobruk actually helped Churchill achieve his objective: to get Roosevelt to adopt the Mediterranean and North Africa, the 'soft underbelly' approach, as the first step along the road to Berlin. 'What can we do to help?' Roosevelt asked Churchill when they heard about Tobruk. 'Your men, tanks and planes to North Africa,' was Churchill's answer. From this point on, Roosevelt began to favour Churchill's view over General Marshall's, and North Africa over France, as the first place for America's major effort against Germany. Fifteen months earlier, when the Australians were holding Tobruk, Churchill had spoken to Roosevelt about its 'magnetic attraction'. Even in defeat, its symbolic power was still working to fulfil Churchill's Big Idea.

'Two men thousands of miles from here are inclined to think that Australia is in no great danger,' Curtin told representatives of the Canberra Press Gallery, at one of his secret briefings. Don Rodgers had persuaded Curtin to hold background briefings in strict confidentiality on a regular basis. They were recorded faithfully by the Australian United Press correspondent, Fred Smith, and their publication by the Australian National Library under the title *Backroom Briefings*, edited by Clem Lloyd and Richard Hall, is one of the richest sources we have of Curtin's wartime thinking and attitudes. At the briefing on 1 July 1942, Curtin said that he was bitterly disappointed by the outcome of the second round of talks in Washington. 'He was now looking to a harder and longer war. He would have to commence his fight for strength in the Pacific all over again.'

Curtin would have been even more disturbed if he had known the full extent of Churchill's sway over Roosevelt at this stage of the war. He would have been astonished to learn that the 'two men thousands of miles away' were making decisions in the face of bitter opposition and resentment from Roosevelt's military chiefs, General Marshall, Admiral King, and Henry Stimson, the War Secretary. He would have been delighted to know that the three advisers had tried to bluff Roosevelt out of following Churchill's line, and disappointed to discover that Roosevelt had called their bluff.

Churchill's Big Idea had become the big paradox. Determined since May 1940 to drag the United States into the war against Hitler, he was now determined to act as a drag on any direct assault on Hitler's Fortress Europe. All his experience from the First World War made him rebel against America's plan for an invasion of France in 1942, or even 1943. He was adamant that such an attempt would end in defeat – or even worse, a repetition of the stalemate and slaughter on the western front. He knew, too, that while the build-up of American strength in Britain (Operation Bolero) was the highest priority, a premature attack in France (Operation Sledgehammer) would have to be fought largely by British forces; and that they had more than enough on their hands fighting Rommel in North Africa. He knew too, that Roosevelt was anxious to get American troops into the German war as soon as possible, before the mid-term congressional elections due in November; otherwise, he might have to bow to the pressure of public opinion in America, and from General MacArthur in Australia, and concentrate American strength against Japan.

Churchill played the political card skilfully, and by the time he left Washington to face a censure motion in the House of Commons, sparked by the loss of Tobruk, he had persuaded Roosevelt to commit himself to Operation Gymnast, later called, at Churchill's insistence, the more inspiring Operation Torch. This would involve an Allied invasion of French North Africa. The US Joint Chiefs of Staff opposed the idea vehemently. On their behalf, General Marshall drew up a memorandum to Roosevelt on 10 July:

> If the United States is to engage in any other operation than forceful, unswerving adherence to *Bolero* plans, we are definitely of the opinion

that we should turn to the Pacific and strike decisively against Japan; in other words, assume a defensive attitude against Germany, except for air operations, and use all available means in the Pacific.

It was mostly bluff. Roosevelt immediately countered with a demand that his Chiefs provide the details of their plans for the Pacific. They had none. In any case, he told Marshall and Stimson, he was not going to leave Churchill in the lurch. Stimson produced a recently published book about the Dardanelles campaign, to remind Roosevelt that Churchill was 'addicted to half-baked schemes for expeditions that shifted the emphasis from the main front'. Roosevelt was unmoved – Operation Torch must go ahead. He promised his Chiefs his full support for the American build-up in Britain, and gave up any thought of combat troops for the British campaign in the Middle East; for the rest, however, the main American effort for 1942 would be in North Africa; the Pacific war would continue to take second place in Allied priorities, and it would remain a holding operation. Churchill had won again.

The first casualty was Churchill's vaunted promise of three Spitfire squadrons for Australia. When Churchill was still in Washington, the British Chiefs of Staff took their opportunity to reverse a proposal they disliked. They decided that the forty-two aircraft bound for Australia should be offloaded at the West African port of Freetown and flown to the Middle East. Their formal request reached Curtin on 20 June. Curtin refused consent. He pointed out that the promise had been made at 'the instance of Mr Churchill himself'. The Coral Sea battle, Curtin said, was only 'a temporary deliverance from the immediate threat of invasion and the enemy still possesses great strength and has the initiative'. Churchill, surviving the vote of censure in the House of Commons with only twenty-five members voting against him, backed his Chiefs in breaking his own promise. 'I can't see that the proposal involves any substantial departure from what was agreed with Evatt,' he asserted. Arrangements were being made for other aircraft to be sent to Australia and they would arrive only one month later than the original schedule. 'Please do not think that we have forgotten or under-estimate Australia's danger,' Churchill concluded. 'But it cannot be denied that the losses which the Japanese have sustained in the Midway action have had a material effect on the naval situation in the Pacific and on the imminence of the threat to Australia.' Curtin accepted the inevitable 'in view of your personal representaions'. So much for the 'magnificent gesture'.

The other part of Evatt's achievement in London was also unravelling. Bruce had found his situation as Australia's representative on the War Cabinet as frustrating and irrelevant as ever. The problem for Bruce, as always, was Winston Churchill, and his way of running everything. Being granted nominal status as a member of the British War Cabinet had made no difference to the Australian's status: there was no more information or consultation than before. In his frustration, Bruce approached Sir Stafford Cripps, now on the political ascendant. They agreed that ways had to be found to clip Churchill's wings. Cripps 'stressed the difficulty of handling Churchill who had such very definite preconceived notions'. Unless everybody in the Cabinet could agree to put a definite proposal to Churchill, such as an inner advisory group to supervise him, 'the Prime Minister would simply play one off against the other and demonstrate that the situation was as satisfactory as it could be'. To Curtin, Bruce said flatly that the situation was becoming 'unworkable'.

Despite Bruce's complaints, and the non-delivery of the Spitfires, Curtin made every effort to maintain less abrasive relations. Giving Bruce the brush-off, Curtin conceded Churchill's right to run his Cabinet and the war in his own way. 'There should be no problems,' he told Bruce, echoing Evatt, 'which could not be got over with goodwill.' Curtin was clear that nothing should be allowed to stand in the way of 'preserving the good relations between the United Kingdom and Australian Governments and, above all, my own personal friendly relations with Churchill which my Cabinet regard as of crucial importance to our joint effort.'

Nothing better demonstrated Curtin's new approach to handling Churchill than his renewed negotiations for the return of the 9th Division to Australia. This time he was able to secure definite acceptance of the troops' return in principle without an explosion of Churchillian wrath. Pressed by MacArthur and Blamey, Curtin wrote to Churchill on 16 July. He carefully avoided making a specific request or proposal, but set out his case in general terms. He wrote: 'I am putting the matter frankly to you in a personal manner. With the 9th Division in action, the subject must arise in the immediate future and I would like to have your views before it is considered by my War Cabinet.'

Curtin's renewed request followed receipt of the warmest message he had received from Churchill since Pearl Harbor. 'I am very glad that the 9th Australian Division is now in action in the Western Desert,' Churchill cabled on 11 July, 'and I am most thankful to you for making it available for this vital key point of the war.' Referring to the 'no-confidence' debate after the fall of Tobruk, he wrote: 'The House of Commons has proved a rock in these difficult days, as it did in the struggle against Napoleon, and I have also been greatly encouraged by the goodwill of your Government and people.' Churchill could have paid no higher compliment than to link the Australian Government and the House of Commons. He ended his long message of 11 July, devoted exclusively to the Middle East, bereft of even a mention of the Pacific war: 'I have never felt more sure that complete victory will be ours, but the struggle will be long and we must not relax for an instant.'

The 9th Division was now very much in action. Rommel continued his thrust from Libya into Egypt. Throughout July, the Afrika Korps, together with Italian divisions which now showed the difference that leadership made to their fighting calibre, fought a relentless desert duel against Auchinleck's British 8th Army. Mussolini flew his own plane to Libya, reputedly bringing with him a white horse on which he intended to enter Cairo in triumph. Churchill wrote to his new Minister in Cairo, Richard Casey, 'While Auchinleck fights at the front, you should insist upon the mobilisation of all the rearward services. Everybody in uniform must fight exactly as they would if Kent or Sussex were invaded, making every post a winning-post and every ditch a last ditch . . . Egypt must be held at all costs.'

The 9th Division had been brought to Egypt from its garrison duties in Syria, at the end of June. Auchinleck threw these welcome reinforcements into the battle at once, although not before another row with Morshead over the dispersal of his brigades. 'So you're being like Blamey,' Auchinleck fumed. 'You're wearing his mantle.' Auchinleck's army held the line at El Alamein, a rail stop near the coast about sixty miles from Alexandria. In this first battle of El Alamein, overshadowed in Australian military history by the second, decisive battle in October, the New Zealand division and the 9th Australian division played their part 'of high distinction', in Churchill's phrase. Thwarted, Mussolini, and presumably his horse, returned to Rome.

'Much depends upon the result of the battle now raging in Egypt,' Churchill replied to Curtin's 'personal inquiry' about the 9th's return home. Quoting an assessment from the Chiefs of the Imperial Staff, Churchill said: 'Even if General Auchinleck wins his battle, and all our reinforcements meet their destination, there will not be a man too many in the Middle East as a whole.' Churchill said that the withdrawal of the 9th at any time during 1942 must endanger the Abadan fields and refinery on which sixty per cent of Australia's oil supplies depended. There was also the matter of transportation, which would involve 'an unjustifiable and dangerous shipping commitment'. Churchill noted the difficulties Australia would have in reinforcing the 9th from Australia, but concluded: 'I very much hope that you will be able to overcome these difficulties and keep your fine division, now gaining fresh distinction, up to strength'.

Curtin replied in equally courteous terms: 'We know that we can count on an understanding by you of how vitally important the Pacific must loom before the Australian Government in reaching a decision on the disposition of its limited forces.' After reviewing the dangers, and repeating his view of Australia as the Allies' base for offensive action against Japan, Curtin told Churchill: 'It is impossible for us to do more than agree to an extension of the period for the temporary retention of the 9th Division in the Middle East.' Nevertheless, Australia would provide two thousand troops to reinforce the 9th, in order to maintain it at fighting strength for two more months, and to boost its morale. 'I much appreciate your decision', Churchill responded. Even though Australia had been placed in the American sphere of strategic responsibility, he said, 'we do not regard our obligation to do what we can to help Australia as being lessened in any way'.

The new and improved tone in the Churchill–Curtin correspondence reflected the new reality. Curtin still needed Churchill's goodwill, not because he could send aid from Britain, but because he could influence Roosevelt to send aid from America. Roosevelt was the key to everything. Curtin relied heavily on MacArthur to promote Australia's case, but MacArthur's clout in Washington could be weakened by Churchill's antagonism, if re-ignited. Curtin also had to manage Australian public opinion. The 1942 disasters had left Churchill undiminished in Australian regard. The Australians may have looked to America but they still belonged to the British Empire. The Union Jack remained the flag of choice for public commemorations on Anzac Day, Armistice Day, and Empire Day – and even Australia Day. Churchill and Curtin's rapprochement may have been brittle, but the bond of Empire was strong and real for both.

The uniqueness of the Australian war experience was made manifest in the second half of 1942: its homeland embattled, its outer territory invaded, its army split between two theatres divided by ten thousand miles of ocean, and much of its air force and navy on loan to the Empire. It was all very well for Churchill to talk to Casey about 'fighting for Egypt as if it were Kent or Sussex'. The Australians and the New Zealanders doing the actual fighting would have thought it ludicrous if they had known about it. So, for that matter, would the men of the British 8th Army. The Anzacs did, however, accept Churchill's Middle Eastern strategy as the pivot on which the defence of the Empire turned, and were still willing to make sacrifices for its success. But even Churchill's vast and vivid imagination could never quite grasp that the Australians might see their own territory in Papua New Guinea, albeit a colony, as vital to their security, to be defended by their own soldiers, sailors, and airmen as his Kent and Sussex on the Nile. He could not bring himself to acknowledge that Australia's situation was unique among the dominions, in having to balance its territorial, national, regional, and imperial priorities in a way Canada, South Africa and even New Zealand never did. These competing priorities stretched Australia's war effort to the limit. They form the background to Australia's role in the two great campaigns of late 1942 in the Middle East and the South-West Pacific, two turning points in the war in the West and the war in the East, enshrined in Australian memory by the names El Alamein and Kokoda.

27

'The end of the beginning'
August–November, 1942

Twenty-four years to the week after Churchill had visited Monash and his Australians in France, he visited Morshead and his Australians in Egypt. There is perhaps no more astonishing spectacle in the military history of the British Empire than the Winston Churchill of August, 1942: the 68-year-old Prime Minister flying 3500 miles (5500 kilometres) to Cairo, mostly in an unheated, unescorted American Liberator, disposing of the commanders of his armies in the field, appointing new ones, inspecting troops drawn from South Africa, New Zealand, and Australia, and then flying on via Teheran to Moscow for even more important and difficult work, to tell Stalin that there would be no Second Front in Europe that year. It would be the last time that Churchill was to be the driving heart, riding the whirlwind and directing the storm of the war. 'Now for a short spell I became the man on the spot,' Churchill wrote. 'Instead of sitting at home waiting for the news from the front, I could send it myself. This was exhilarating.'

The British leader had become gravely dissatisfied with the stand-off along the El Alamein line. He needed an emphatic win over Rommel to help Roosevelt get Marshall and his Chiefs to accept

North Africa and Operation Torch as the main Allied endeavour for 1942/43. Churchill had lost confidence in Auchinleck, just as a year before he had lost confidence in Wavell. Ironically, Wavell had been called over from India to join Churchill, the Chief of the Imperial General Staff, Sir Alan Brooke, the Prime Minister of South Africa, General Smuts, and the Minister of State in Cairo, Richard Casey, in the discussions to decide Auchinleck's fate. 'There was a lot of tension,' Casey wrote of their Cairo talks in his *Personal Reminiscences*. 'Although I do not think the description "agonising reappraisal" was then current, it might well have been used to describe this week in Cairo.'

Casey had made a seamless transition from serving the Australian Government in Washington to serving the British Government in Cairo. A couple of weeks before Churchill's arrival, Casey had taken Auchinleck to task for failing to describe the Australians as 'British'. He had asked Auchinleck for the overall totals of Allied forces in the Middle East. When Auchinleck gave the officers and men from the United Kingdom as being 'British' and then listed the Indians, South Africans, Australians, and New Zealanders separately, Casey protested. 'I said we all had the same right to be described as British, not the United Kingdom troops alone. He saw the point and will issue an order about it.' This was a curious reversal of the usual Australian complaint; from Gallipoli on, Australians had resented their exploits being reported as generically British. It is unlikely that Auchinleck got around to issuing his order. Churchill sacked him on 6 August. Churchill cabled Attlee in London: 'Minister of State Casey is in full agreement.' As Churchill had obviously made up his mind before he reached Cairo, Casey's opinion mattered not a jot. But Churchill always liked to claim the support of 'high authorities'. As his new Middle East commander-in-chief, he designated General Sir Harold Alexander, the 'man' he had sent instead of an army to save Rangoon.

Churchill visited sections of the 9th Australian Division at the Ruweisat Ridge on the northern flank of the Alamein line, 'where we were given breakfast in a wire-netted cube, full of flies and important military personages'. In their account, *Alamein – the Australian*

Story, Mark Johnston and Peter Stanley write that Churchill arrived 'dressed in a pale lilac suit and topee, sweating pinkly in the summer heat'. They record an Australian soldier, Bruce Sanders, writing in his diary: 'Churchill, Auchinleck and Morshead drive along the road – most of us too lazy to walk up.' They note, however, that the photographs of the event 'show crowds of cheering troops'. The military historian, Corelli Barnett, quotes another observer as saying: 'The last stage of Churchill's route along the Ridge was thinly lined with phlegmatic soldiers who seemed to be in two minds about the warmth of the reception they were going to give the Old War Horse.' Another account has an Australian gunner calling out 'to great amusement': 'When are you going to send us home, you fat old bastard?'

Churchill's main purpose in visiting the troops was to talk with Lieutenant General William 'Strafer' Gott in order to probe whether he was fit and eager enough to take field command of the 8th Army. 'By the same hour two days later,' Churchill wrote, 'he had been killed by the enemy in almost the very air space through which I now flew.' The command of the 8th Army fell instead to General Sir Bernard Montgomery, who had already been designated to lead the British share in Operation Torch against French North Africa. Resilient as ever, Churchill wrote to Clementine: 'In Montgomery we have a highly competent, daring and energetic soldier, well acquainted with desert warfare. If he is disagreeable to those about him, he is also disagreeable to the enemy.' Nor was Montgomery himself particularly worried about making himself agreeable, although he did go some of the way with Churchill, whom he at least allowed to smoke in his presence, a favour he refused to extend to the future Allied Supreme Commander, Dwight Eisenhower. This abstemious, egocentric, publicity-conscious son of a former Anglican Bishop of Tasmania, where he had spent a not very happy boyhood, once asserted: 'As God said, and I agree with Him . . .'

But Montgomery promised to go on the offensive against Rommel, and that was all that Churchill asked. No British general since Birdwood was so popular with the Australians. Montgomery's first message to them was:

We will stand and fight here. If we can't stay here alive, then let us stay here dead. If we have two weeks to prepare we will be sitting pretty. Rommel can attack as soon as he likes after that and I hope he does. It will be the beginning of a campaign which will hit Rommel for six right out of Africa.

Churchill loved this sort of stuff, although what the troops themselves thought of it is debatable. In the event, however, Montgomery was pretty much as cautious and painstaking as Wavell or Auchinleck. But Alexander and Montgomery had one advantage over Wavell and Auchinleck: Churchill's responsibility for their appointment was so complete that he had little choice but to back them.

As the story of the desert campaign which began in December, 1940, nears its tremendous climax at El Alamein, it may be useful to place in perspective the number of troops available to Alexander, Montgomery, and Churchill in the Middle East. The table which Auchinleck had provided to Casey, and which had so annoyed the independent Australian Briton, was as follows:

British	17,150 officers	268,000 other ranks
Indian	3,660 officers	111,600 other ranks
South African	3,260 officers	61,750 other ranks
Australian	1,485 officers	30,500 other ranks
New Zealand	1,970 officers	29,700 other ranks.

According to Casey, including colonial troops, Free French, Poles, Greeks, Czechs, and Yugoslavs, there was an overall total of 35,500 officers and 645,000 other ranks in the Middle East. The effective British combat strength against Rommel in Egypt was 200,000. Rommel had 110,000 men, about half of them in Italian divisions. Meanwhile, in Britain itself, there were now forty-five divisions, including five Canadian divisions – as Churchill put it, 'for two years eating their hearts out in Britain, awaiting the invader'.

Such were the 'proportions', to use a favoured expression of Churchill's, which Curtin had in mind when he once again approached Roosevelt for American assistance in September 1942. In long personal messages to Roosevelt on 31 August and 11 September, he set out Australia's situation – and its attitude – with urgency but without stridency. 'The Australian Government realises,' he said, 'that it is impossible to withdraw this division [the 9th] at the present time, although its need here is great.' Australia accepted that 'it would be better to allow this division to remain in the Middle East and meet the need for land forces in the South-West Pacific Area by additional forces from the USA.'

In fact, for all its matchless power and potential, the US war machine was mobilising its resources with excruciating slowness. Nine months after Pearl Harbor, and in the face of the Roosevelt–Churchill promise during the Rangoon row in February, there were still only two American divisions in Australia, training in Queensland. MacArthur had under his SWPA command a total of ninety-eight thousand American soldiers and airmen. By contrast, the Australian army had two infantry divisions in New Guinea and seven divisions in Australia, with two additional armoured divisions being organised. As Curtin told Roosevelt, over 600,000 men were enlisted in the Australian armed forces, from a male population between the ages of eighteen and forty-five of 1.5 million – which would have been even more remarkable if, as Churchill professed to believe, 'conscription was banned even for home service'.

Curtin emphasised to Roosevelt that his views were endorsed by MacArthur. MacArthur believed that if the Allies suffered further naval losses, 'the Japanese would probably bypass our isolated northern concentrations and attack nearer to the main centres of population in the south'. General MacArthur, Curtin told Roosevelt, 'considers our forces are too thinly spread to meet such a contingency, and places the minimum strength at three divisions more than we possess, including the two American divisions in Australia'. Curtin reiterated his idea of Australia as an attack base, setting it in the wider context:

> The additional requirements of the South-West Pacific Area to enable a decisive blow to be struck against Japan in this region are relatively small in relation to the resources of the United Nations, and do not

appear sufficient to have a vital influence in another theatre. We feel a real opportunity to gain a definite ascendancy over the enemy is being missed. If nothing is done, the Japanese will become more consolidated and the position will grow more difficult for offensive action on our part.

Pointedly, perhaps mischievously, Curtin recalled Churchill's threadbare pledge – to cut his losses in the Middle East if Australia were heavily invaded. 'The strengthening of the situation now,' he told Roosevelt, 'will act as a deterrent to invasion and preclude the possibility of [Churchill] having to fulfil this pledge.'

Curtin laid his case before Roosevelt against a background of events which were to determine the future course of the Pacific war. In the shorthand of history, these events are memorialised by the names of Kokoda and Guadalcanal; but the operations, of which these terrible ordeals were part, represented the first test of the priorities which had brought Churchill and Curtin into such bitter conflict since Pearl Harbor. Because the operations in Papua, New Guinea and the Solomon Islands ended in Japanese defeats, both sides to the strategic argument – Churchill versus Curtin, General MacArthur versus Admiral King – could claim vindication. For King and the US navy, Guadalcanal was the first step in the naval drive to Japan through the Central Pacific, the strategy envisaged by Churchill in the paper he had drawn up while crossing the Atlantic to rendezvous with Roosevelt in December, 1941. For MacArthur, the New Guinea campaign was the first step on the road back to the Philippines. For Curtin, the near-success of the Japanese thrust across the Owen Stanleys, coming almost within sight of Port Moresby, proved conclusively the power of Japan to isolate and invade Australia. Until the outcome of these long campaigns from August, 1942 to January, 1943, became clear, nobody could claim that Australia was out of danger, not even Churchill.

The strong base which the Japanese had built at Rabaul was their springboard for their drive across the mountains to Port Moresby. It was also the intended target of twin campaigns planned by General MacArthur in Brisbane and Admiral Nimitz in Honolulu.

Between 19 and 22 July, the Japanese forestalled MacArthur by landing an invasion force at Buna and Gona, coastal villages on the north-eastern side of New Guinea's 'tail'. On 7 August, US Marines attacked at Guadalcanal, at the southern end of the long island chain of the Solomons, eight hundred miles (thirteen hundred kilometres) from Rabaul. Next night, Japanese warships from Rabaul sank four cruisers, including HMAS *Canberra*, in the Battle of Savo Island – the worst Allied naval loss since Pearl Harbor.

Churchill himself summed up Japanese purposes with concision: 'With both Port Moresby and Guadalcanal in their possession, they hoped the Coral Sea would become a Japanese lake, bordering upon North-East Australia.' One would have thought that such a prospect would have amply justified 'Australasian anxieties', even in Churchill's eyes. He did not concede it, then or after. In recording the Japanese overland advance to Port Moresby, he noted blandly that it was 'guarded by two brigades of the 7th Australian Division back from the Middle East'. He refrained from mentioning that these were the very brigades which would have been pointlessly consumed in Burma, if he had had his way.

Heroically and tragically, the New Guinea campaign exposed all the problems caused by the 'two-army' system and the legacy of Hughes' handling of the conscription issue in the First World War. Because Papua New Guinea was Australian territory, units of the CMF (the militia) bore the first shock in its defence. Churchill paid tribute to their service, forgetting, apparently, their conscript origins. 'A single Australian militia battalion fought a stubborn delaying action,' he wrote in *Closing the Ring*. He meant the fighting withdrawals executed by the 39th Battalion along the Kokoda Track under the leadership of Lieutenant Colonel Ralph Honner, a Perth lawyer who, as an AIF officer had fought with the 6th Division in Libya, Greece, and Crete, and was a superb example of the citizen-soldier tradition. So were the men of the 39th; *conscripts* who had *volunteered* for service in Australia's tropical territories beyond Australian shores. But the backbone of the Australian forces was provided by the 7th Division. They had regrouped and retrained in south-eastern Queensland before being ordered to Port Moresby in August. MacArthur sent one of its three brigades to defend the airfield which American engineers were building at Milne Bay, on the south-eastern tip of the 'tail' of Papua Territory. These were the four thousand men whom Churchill had tried to divert for the hopeless defence of Rangoon.

Until the arrival of the 18th Brigade, the defence of Milne Bay had been assigned to a militia battalion. Unaware of its reinforcement, the Japanese landed a 3000-strong marine force at Milne Bay on 25 August, intending to provide a southern base for the overland drive towards Port Moresby. After a fortnight's heavy fighting, the Japanese took their survivors – less than half their force – off by sea. It was the first defeat of a Japanese amphibian force in the war. In the words of the Australian military historian Chris Coulthard-Clark, 'It was here at Milne Bay that the myth of Japanese invincibility was dispelled.'

The presence of the 7th Division was just as crucial to the outcome on the Kokoda Track itself. By November, the Japanese had been pushed back across the Owen Stanleys, and began their withdrawal to their Buna beachhead. For fifty years, Kokoda was denied its rightful place in Australian military annals as the supreme ordeal and achievement of the Australian citizen-soldier, volunteer, and conscript alike. A number of factors, including MacArthur's greed for glory, Curtin's reliance on MacArthur, and Blamey's disparagement of his subordinate officers, combined to diminish their achievement. It was not until Prime Minister Paul Keating visited Kokoda for the Anzac Day commemoration in 1992, and literally kissed the 'sacred ground', that the Kokoda campaign began to be restored to Australia's collective memory as the distinctive Australian experience of the Second World War.

During the critical weeks of September and October, when Kokoda and Guadalcanal hung in the balance, more than sixty cables passed between Churchill and Roosevelt. Not one of them mentioned the war in the South-West Pacific. Roosevelt referred to it only once in a handwritten letter which his wife, Eleanor, carried on her visit to London on 19 October:

Dear Winston, I confide my Missus to take care of you and Mrs Churchill. I know our better halves will hit it off beautifully.

All well here, though I am worried about the S.W. Pacific. Every day we are killing a number of Jap ships and planes, but there is no use blinking at the fact that we are greatly outnumbered.

Roosevelt and Churchill were preoccupied with the epic battle for Stalingrad, the huge losses which German U-boats were inflicting on the Arctic convoys taking tanks and planes to Russia, and the tug-of-war between the American and British Chiefs over Operation Torch in North Africa. Churchill had been able to extract from Stalin a grudging acceptance of Torch as a partial substitute for a second front in Europe, taking a slice of a loaf as better than none. Now the US Chiefs of Staff wanted to modify the agreed plan for the invasion of Tunisia and Algeria by confining the operation to the Atlantic side of North Africa, with Morocco and its capital of Casablanca as the objective. They still hankered after a direct and full-blooded assault in France, and resented the diversion of resources to North Africa, even after Eisenhower had been placed in command of the operation. Churchill saw that Stalin would be outraged by such a breach of faith, and such a puny effort, mocking the titanic struggle at Stalingrad.

To ensure that Roosevelt prevailed over his own Chiefs, Churchill urgently needed a Desert Victory. His old impatience with cautious generals reasserted itself. Alexander, the hand-picked successor to Wavell and Auchinleck as Commander-in-Chief Middle East, came under the same pressures for a final offensive against Rommel. Brooke tried to hose Churchill down. 'After lunch, P.M. sent for me to discuss a reply which he wanted to send to Alexander,' Brooke wrote in his diary on 23 September. 'I tried to stop him and told him he was only letting Alex see that he was losing confidence in him which was a most disconcerting thing before a battle. He then started all his worst arguments about generals only thinking of themselves and their reputations and never attacking unless matters were a certainty, and never prepared to take risks etc. etc. We had a hammer and tongs argument.' In his annotations for the published diaries, Brooke drew this portrait of Churchill on the eve of the Battle of El Alamein, the climax and consummation of Churchill's Big Idea:

> We then find him adopting the attitude that he was the only one trying to win the war, that he was the only one who produced any ideas, that he was quite alone in all his attempts, no one supported him. Indeed, instead of supporting him, all we did was to provide and plan difficulties etc. etc. Frequently in this oration he worked himself up into such a state from the woeful picture he had painted that tears streamed down his face! It was very difficult on those occasions not to be filled with sympathy for him when one realised the colossal burden he was bearing and the weight of responsibility he shouldered. On the other hand, if we had not checked some of his wild ideas, heaven knows where we should be now!

'Went to see Bruce who has received telegrams from Australia shouting for the 9th Australian Division from the Middle East,' Brooke wrote in his diary for 23 October – the day that Montgomery launched his attack along the Alamein line, heralded by the heaviest artillery barrage since the western front. 'A bad moment just as the attack is starting!' Brooke wrote.

'Australia shouting' took the form of a 1200-word message, based on new defence and manpower appreciations by the Australian Chiefs of Staff, supported by General MacArthur and Blamey. Curtin sent it to Churchill and Roosevelt on 17 October. His message began with a review of Australian manpower resources, which in itself should have shown Churchill how groundless were his later allegations that Australia had no conscription 'even for home defence'. The review emphasised the drain on the army by 'heavy wastage of personnel operating under extreme tropical conditions in New Guinea'. Curtin said: 'The Army resources of manpower will be taxed to the utmost to maintain the formation in New Guinea.' He then turned to the 9th Division 'now also engaged in active operations'. 'It follows that reinforcements for the 9th Division in the Middle East will not be available in the numbers required, and that unless the Division returns to Australia, it cannot be maintained. It will in a few months cease to be a fully effective fighting unit.'

Curtin risked the obloquy of history – and not only Churchill's version of it – not so much by the nature of his request, but its timing. It is important, however, to emphasise that this was no peremptory demand for the withdrawal of a division in the heat of battle, although this is how Brooke portrayed it and many military historians continue to misrepresent it. Nor was it a political demand. It was a closely reasoned military argument, provided by Shedden and the Australian Chiefs of Staff, urged ceaselessly by Australia's top general, Blamey, and supported emphatically by America's most famous general, MacArthur. 'The Government has consulted the Advisory War Council which as you are aware comprises the representatives of the Opposition Parties and Sir Earle Page as an additional co-opted member,' Curtin told Churchill. 'The unanimous conclusion was that the Government should request the early return of the 9th Division.' This is what Sir Alan Brooke called 'Australia shouting'.

Churchill's responses make it clear that he did not interpret Curtin's message as a demand for an immediate withdrawal from the battlefield, at least, not at that time. On 30 October, in reply to Curtin's request that General Alexander should be made aware of Australia's concerns about the return of the division 'in good shape', he replied: 'I understand your wishes and assure you of my personal interest in the matter.' The commander of the 9th Division, General Morshead, met Alexander at Montgomery's Field Headquarters on 27 October. Morshead reported that Alexander had said: 'Of all the formations in the Middle East, the 9th is the one I can least afford to lose. It would be quite impossible to lose their magnificent services until the present operations are brought to a successful conclusion.'

National pride must have jostled with Curtin's perception of Australia's national interest. It is at this point, however, that Curtin seems to have lost his sense of perspective and began to slip into the old querulousness. Instead of making the most of the 9th's great achievements in a battle still far from won, he complained to Bruce that they should never have been made, in Alexander's words to Morshead, 'the main pivot of operations without which the battle would collapse'. This was churlish and short-sighted, to say the least. They had been in position since the first Alamein; Australia had never sought any change during the weeks of Montgomery's preparations. Bruce, very properly, played for time in order to head off another row with Churchill, a row in which Churchill would have had every argument of military necessity, Australia's honour and reputation and, not least, the safety of the 9th Division itself, clearly on his side. Bruce replied to Curtin on 1 November:

> The position now is that the offensive has been launched with initial success in considerable measure due to the work of the 9th Division. Alexander in his conversation with Morshead has made it clear that the retention of the 9th Division in the operations is essential to their continued success. In view of this and the paramount importance of the present operations in the Middle East, I am presuming that you agree to the continued utilisation of the 9th Division until such time as the operational situation permits its withdrawal with a view to its return to Australia.

Bruce never rendered a greater service, not only to Australia's reputation but to Curtin's as well. It is fearful to contemplate what Churchill would have written in his war memoirs if Bruce had acted on Curtin's instruction 'to take the matter up with the United Kingdom authorities at once' – right in the middle of the greatest British battle of the war so far. As it was, Curtin replied to Bruce on 4 November: 'I agree with your interpretation of our attitude, in view of the situation with which we are now confronted.' Nevertheless, Curtin repented, 'it cannot be too strongly emphasised that the necessary reinforcements cannot be dispatched from Australia to maintain the Division abroad . . . We are relying on the 9th Division being returned in good shape and strength. Otherwise it will soon cease to be a fully effective fighting unit.'

In any case, it had all become irrelevant. By the time Curtin signalled his grudging concession, Rommel was in full retreat towards Tobruk. He had ignored Hitler's order to 'fight to the death'. Five days into the fighting, Churchill brought Curtin and the New Zealand Prime Minister, Peter Fraser, up to date. 'The great battle in Egypt has opened well, although one cannot yet forecast its result,' he told them. At the end of the report, Churchill wrote a personal note to each. The subtle nuances make a fascinating study of Churchill's style, and the care he took with his words, even under immense stress and excitement. To Fraser he wrote: 'You will have seen with pride and pleasure all that your valiant New Zealanders are doing and the part they are playing in what may well be a memorable event.' To Curtin: 'You will have observed with pride and pleasure the distinguished part which the 9th Australian Division are playing in what may be an event of first magnitude.' In his war memoirs, Churchill singled out the 9th Division for the highest praise: 'The magnificent forward drive of the Australians, achieved by ceaseless bitter fighting, had swung the whole battle in our favour.'

El Alamein was the last battle of the British Empire. The ranks of Montgomery's 8th Army were its grand last roll-call: the 9th Australian Division; the 2nd New Zealand Division; the 1st South African Division; the 4th Indian Division; the 5th Indian Brigade; the Baluchi Regiment; the 2nd Gurkha Regiment; the Rajputana Rifles, and regiments of the British army with traditions reaching back to Marlborough and Wellington. It was no coincidence that Churchill chose the victory luncheon at the Mansion House, London, on 10 November, to declare: 'We mean to hold our own. I have not become the King's First Minister in order to preside over the liquidation of the British Empire.'

Even as Churchill was speaking, at the western end of North Africa the United States Army was entering the war against Hitler by way of Operation Torch, with landings at Oran, Algiers, and Casablanca. It may be more or less true, as Churchill wrote in his war memoirs: 'Before Alamein we never had a victory. After Alamein we never had a defeat.' Increasingly the victories would be seen as American victories or, at least, the result of American preponderance. But for Churchill, Alamein represented a comprehensive vindication of everything he had worked for since May 1940.

'I have never promised anything but blood, tears, toil and sweat,' he said at the Lord Mayor of London's luncheon at the Mansion House. 'Now, however, we have a new experience – a remarkable and definite victory. The bright gleam has caught the helmets of our soldiers, and warmed and cheered all our hearts.' The British victory in the western desert and the American landings in North Africa, he said, constituted 'a new bond between the English-speaking peoples and a new hope for the whole world'. He ended with one of his most memorable flourishes:

> Now this is not the end. It is not even the beginning of the end. But it is, perhaps, the end of the beginning.

With the victory at El Alamein, something of the sort might also be said about the battles between Churchill and Australia.

28

'Hitler has nothing on Churchill'

November, 1942–September, 1943

As the church bells of England were set ringing to celebrate El Alamein, Curtin took up his unfinished business with Churchill concerning the return of the 9th Division. The last act of this drawn-out drama reflected the changing roles of the main players, with Roosevelt now moving into the lead. After Alamein, Churchill was no more willing to let go of the division than before. But he had run out of plausible lines. For example, when he got around to replying to Curtin's renewed request at the end of November, the best he could come up with was that it might be needed for 'large scale action in the *Eastern* Mediterranean' come spring. 'The position of Turkey,' he told Curtin, 'is of peculiar interest'.

Rather closer to Australian concerns than Turkey, the Papuan campaign hung in the balance. November–December 1942 saw the critical month. Driven back over the Kokoda Track, the Japanese entrenched themselves in strongholds in the Buna 'Triangle', around the coastal villages of Buna, Gona, and Sanananda. In the stinking swamplands of the Triangle, malaria, fever, and dysentery devastated both sides. The 25th Brigade of the 7th Division, for example, had been reduced by the Kokoda fighting and disease to an effective fighting strength of 850, down from four thousand. Paul Ham in *Kokoda* writes: 'The Australian 7th Division lost 5905 men in the month between 25 November and 23 December: killed, wounded, missing, or too sick to fight.' At Buna and Gona, 850 Australians were killed, compared with 620 at the second battle of El Alamein. These were the harsh statistics behind Curtin's demand, if the renewal of a request of nearly a year's standing can at last be styled 'a demand'.

Scraping the barrel of argument, Churchill came up with an astounding proposal – or threat. 'It might be most economical to move one of the American divisions in Australia or destined for the Pacific direct to Suez,' he suggested. Their transports could then pick up the 9th and bring them back to Australia! Churchill told Curtin:

> The object should be to bring the greatest number of the United Nations divisions into contact with the enemy, and certainly it would appear more helpful for the common cause if fresh troops were moved from the United States into the Pacific and into action against Japan than that troops already engaged with the enemy in another part of the world should be withdrawn.

Churchill concluded with his routine swipe: 'As I know the great importance which you have always attached to American opinion and how much you value the substantial aid they have given to the defence of Australia, I feel bound to put these points to you.'

Curtin replied 'with frank disappointment'. Of course, he wrote, Australia was deeply grateful for American and British assistance, although 'quite candidly, it has not been as much as we had reason to expect'. Although Australia had 'surrendered part of our sovereignty' by placing its forces under American command, the Allied Forces in the South-West Pacific Area were still predominantly Australian, with ten Australian divisions and two American divisions. Churchill's extraordinary suggestion that an American division earmarked for Australia might replace the 9th Division 'fills me with the gravest misgiving'. Curtin replied to Churchill's hints about American public opinion with a hint of his own:

I should be surprised to learn that the return of the 9th Division would have any adverse reaction on the opinion of the American people, as to the degree of assistance that should be afforded Australia to defend itself, as a base of operations against Japan, particularly in view of the co-operation we have given in other theatres. On the other hand there is a body of American opinion which thinks that too little has been sent to this area. I have, however, resolutely refused to be drawn into any controversy.

But the 'disposition of our own troops,' Curtin told Churchill, 'is a different question.' He returned to the matters of the morale and reinforcement of the 9th, and noted that even General Smuts was demanding home leave for his South Africans now that Egypt was safe. Curtin 'strongly requested' Churchill to exert his influence with President Roosevelt to 'give effect to the original decision'.

Churchill had, of course, exerted his influence with Roosevelt altogether the other way. Roosevelt had already intervened to urge the retention of the 9th Division while the battle of El Alamein was still in progress. Now, on 3 December 1942, he made a last-minute appeal as Churchill's proxy. He began with 'heartiest congratulations on the heroic part' the 9th had played 'in the recent victory in the Middle East'. He acknowledged that 'in view of its strenuous combat service' it should be returned to Australia 'at the earliest date practicable'. The timing, however, depended on two factors: the pursuit of Rommel's forces across North Africa to 'a final and decisive victory', and 'the drain on available shipping'. But Roosevelt did not ask specifically that Curtin change his decision. He spoke vaguely about the 9th Division 'arriving home as soon as possible after 1 January 1943'. With the imminent arrival of a third American division, he told Curtin, 'you can be reassured as to the adequacy of troops available to drive the Japanese away from Australia to such a distance as to make invasion impossible'.

After outlining how Operation Torch and the defeat of Rommel would open the sea-lanes of the Mediterranean and the Suez Canal, Roosevelt said: 'The benefits thus derived will be felt in the South-West Pacific, just as they will be in all other theatres in which troops of the United States are engaged. I feel that by contributing to our success in the Mediterranean, the 9th Division has added to the security of Australia more than it would have, had it remained at home.' Perhaps Roosevelt here was making a veiled reference to Curtin's early opposition to sending Australian divisions overseas, although Churchill himself never resorted to such an argument. The plain fact is that, by 1943, Roosevelt and Churchill could give no better reason for keeping the 9th Division in the Middle East than that it suited their convenience.

Curtin's reply – exactly a year after Pearl Harbor – was masterly. Without worrying about the openings for argument Roosevelt had given, he seized on the points that mattered and narrowed the room for disagreement: 'I am very glad that you are agreeable to the return of the 9th Division to Australia at the earliest date practicable.' He linked the 9th directly to MacArthur's New Guinea campaign. 'The 6th and 7th Australian divisions after the Buna operations are completed must have a prolonged rest out of action. They both have a very large number of reinforcements to absorb and a great number of sick to return. There is therefore a pressing need for the services of the 9th Division in this area. It is also required for the subsequent phases of the campaign to drive the Japanese from New Guinea and the adjacent islands.' Ignoring Roosevelt's point about the pursuit of Rommel, he said: 'I wish you to know that we shall cooperate in the plan you have outlined which, as we see it, does not envisage the utilisation of the 9th Division for any further operations in the Middle East or adjacent areas.' Taking the gamble that Roosevelt would not challenge his interpretation, Curtin concluded: 'We look forward, therefore, to the fulfilment of the understanding that the 9th Division shall be returned to Australia as early as possible in the New Year.'

Churchill let it go at last, eleven months after he had told the House of Commons that no obstacle would be placed against the return of the AIF. Contenting himself with just one barb ('The fact that the New Zealand Division is to remain in the Middle East makes it easier for us to meet your wishes'), he brought the long dispute to an end on 10 December, with the true Churchillian touch:

'The 9th Australian Division will carry with them from the African Desert a splendid reputation, and the honour of having played a leading part in a memorable victory for the Empire and the common cause.'

In his final request for the return of the division, Curtin had linked the issue with the hardest political decision of his career. He told Churchill and Roosevelt on 23 November 1942: 'The question is also arising indirectly in connection with my proposed amendment of the Defence Act to enable members of the Militia Forces, as distinct from the AIF, to serve outside Australia in the South-West Pacific.' By this he meant, without spelling it out, that the absence of the 9th Division made it all the harder for him to convince the Labor Party to modify its stand against conscription for service overseas. The main pressure on Curtin to change the law was coming from MacArthur. Curtin told a press backgrounder on 20 November that MacArthur 'was asking for all handicaps to be removed which would prevent his disposition of troops wherever they were needed'. But it was more than a matter of military logic or logistics. 'There was a barrage of criticism in the United States,' Curtin said, 'that we want the Americans to defend Darwin but will not fight for the Philippines.' In this sense, Curtin, like Hughes in 1916, was responding to external pressures. Unlike Hughes, he went to extraordinary lengths to adapt his response to the will of the Labor Party and, above all, keep it united. Throughout the party debate, at two national conferences in November, 1942 and January, 1943, in the Cabinet and the Caucus, he insisted that he was not seeking a new policy on conscription, but merely a redefinition of 'the defence of Australia'.

The new definition of where conscripts could be sent was so limited that it did not include the whole of SWPA; the new defence area extended only as far north as the Equator, thus excluding the Philippines and even Singapore. Yet even so modest a change aroused fierce opposition. Curtin's colleague and implacable enemy, Eddie Ward, led the attack and sneered: 'You are putting young men into the slaughterhouse. Thirty years ago, you wouldn't go yourself.' In a later Caucus debate after a Special Conference had given Curtin the go-ahead, the Member for Melbourne, Arthur Calwell, told Curtin: 'The way you're going, you'll finish up on the other side leading a national government.' Curtin hurried from the meeting and dictated a letter of resignation: 'I invite the Party to dissociate itself from the accusations or appoint another leader. Obviously if the charge has a semblance of justification, the Party is in an invidious position in entrusting its leadership to a political traitor.' Calwell apologised and Curtin was unanimously confirmed. The military historian, John Robertson, writes: 'Curtin gave a significant portion of his time and skills to achieving a result which was virtually meaningless in ultimate military terms.' MacArthur was disappointed, Roosevelt puzzled, and Churchill, no doubt, confirmed in his opinion of the obduracy of Australian party politics.

THE HOME VOYAGE of the 9th Division in February, 1943, symbolised the sea change in the relations between Churchill and Australia. With every mile they sailed nearer to Australia, destined for a punishing campaign in New Guinea, the 9th carried Australia's part in the war away from Churchill's orbit, into a theatre in which all the major decisions were made in Washington. Now that the specific cause of irritation between Churchill and Curtin had been removed, their relations calmed and matured. In a sense, each lost leverage over the other. Henceforth, Australia's most significant contribution to the war against Hitler was the participation of fifteen thousand RAAF aircrew in bombing raids over Germany. The bombing campaign was touted by Churchill as a substitute for a second front, and a way to bring Germany to its knees. It probably distorted the British war effort as much as it damaged German industry or morale. A year before, Wavell had complained about the lack of aircraft in his command: 'It certainly gives us furiously to think, when we see that over 200 heavy bombers attacked one town in Germany.' With all its troops now withdrawn from the Western theatre, Australia could no longer claim special consideration from Britain, distinct from the other dominions. Curtin stopped urging Churchill to redeem his pledges and Churchill stopped pretending to stand by them.

The change in relations between Churchill and Australia prompted Bruce to write a 3000-word personal letter to Curtin, summing up his experiences in the nine months since he had become a member of the British War Cabinet. Most of the letter was designed to prove Bruce's indispensability, but he wanted Curtin to have the benefit of his thoughts 'in the event of my being wiped out by a bomb'. Bruce had come to the conclusion that Australia's representation on the War Cabinet would never work in the way that Curtin had intended and Churchill had promised. There were two main reasons for this, Bruce said: '(a) The personality of Mr Churchill; and (b) The fact that the War Cabinet is not a War Cabinet except in name.'

'Mr Churchill in his own person combines the most remarkable qualities of drive, initiative and leadership together with an intense individualism which makes him impossible to work with,' Bruce declared. The result was that his relations with his War Cabinet were 'almost unconstitutional'. His Cabinet colleagues, however, recognised that it 'was impossible to expect a heavily burdened man of 68 to make fundamental changes in his methods'. In war, said Bruce, 'the great thing is to get on with the job', and Churchill was certainly doing that. Contradicting his own unceasing complaints, Bruce now denied that Cabinet's acquiescence in Churchill's methods meant 'a purely one-man direction of the war'. Churchill made full use of the Chiefs of Staff and the joint planners. 'While he uses his great personality to influence their recommendations and appreciations in the direction in which his own mind is working, he does not dominate them to the extent that many people believe.' The product of this team work was 'a blend of the Chiefs' hard realism with Churchill's imaginative genius'.

Bruce said that he had come to the conclusion that, instead of seeking new undertakings about consultation and information, his best course was to pursue his contacts with influential individuals in and outside the Cabinet. He mentioned his close association with Eden, Cripps, and the economist John Maynard Keynes. Bruce concluded: 'Although I do not pretend I find my own position a pleasant one, my considered judgement is that we should continue to work on the present lines which, on the whole, I think are yielding reasonably satisfactory results.' Even Mr Bruce had succumbed at last to Mr Churchill's personality.

It was only a truce. Within weeks, Bruce revived all his old complaints. But his surrender to Churchill, or at least to the realities of his power, had been as sudden as Evatt's. As recently as mid-January, he had startled the unflappable Deputy Prime Minister, Clement Attlee, with an outburst against Churchill. 'Hitler has nothing on Churchill as a dictator,' Bruce raged. He later recorded: 'I am somewhat ashamed of being so rough with Attlee as it is extraordinarily like hitting a child, but he is really so hopeless that one is almost forced to be offensive.' The encounter says more about Bruce than Attlee. The cause of his anger, however, was that he had been kept in the dark about another meeting between Churchill and Roosevelt. Churchill 'went off on his present adventure', he told Curtin, 'without any prior discussion with the War Cabinet. This must appear astounding to you and even somewhat startling to me, familiar as I am with the Prime Minister's methods and the way he treats the War Cabinet.' Churchill's 'present adventure' had taken him to a venue which was about as exotic and exciting as any place in the world in January 1943 – Casablanca, the newly liberated capital of French Morocco.

Casablanca, the 1942 film, ends with 'the beginning of a beautiful friendship'. Casablanca, the 1943 conference, was the full flowering of the friendship between Churchill and Roosevelt. Surrounded by their military chiefs and field commanders, they settled on the invasion of Italy via Sicily as the next step to Berlin. For the last time, Britain was the predominant fighting partner in the Grand Alliance. For the last time, Churchill got his way with Roosevelt in setting the war strategy. When they were still at Casablanca, enjoying each other's company immensely, the German 6th Army was on the verge of surrender at Stalingrad, the real turning point of the war. From then on, Roosevelt began to modify his relations with Churchill in order to cultivate his relations with Stalin. His unilateral declaration of Allied war aims as 'unconditional surrender', dropped at a press conference in Casablanca, was the first sign of the new approach. It was meant to reassure Stalin that his Western Allies would never make a separate peace with Hitler. It had the unintended consequence of giving Hitler a propaganda weapon for making the extermination of the European Jews his own fundamental war aim.

Churchill had long foreseen the shift in power to America; and, indeed, it was the inevitable result of the working out of his Big Idea since 1940. His approach now was to nurse British resources, influence, and prestige as much as possible. He was in no hurry to bring the war to an end by needless risk-taking, such as a premature invasion of France. This was not a new Churchill, but rather the Churchill of old, with his obsessions about 'the soft underbelly of Europe', the ideas that had produced Gallipoli and Greece. Now, at Casablanca, he could claim success. The Germans were being cleared out of North Africa, although the campaign in French North Africa was proving harder than anticipated. Next stop: Sicily. Then on to Rome. And who knows? Turkey might come into the war on our side; perhaps the Americans could be inveigled into the Balkans; the possibilities were endless.

Casablanca confirmed that the war in the Pacific would be treated as a holding operation until Germany's defeat. On the day he had ordered the bells of the churches of England be rung to celebrate Alamein, Churchill had outlined his approach to his luncheon guests at 10 Downing Street: 'The war will still be long. When we have beaten Germany it will take us two more years to beat Japan.' Nor was that a bad thing, he said. 'It will keep America and ourselves together while we are making peace in Europe.' To this scenario, he added brightly: 'If I am still alive, I shall fling all we have into the Pacific.'

Roosevelt and Churchill put it less dramatically in their communiqué at the end of the Casablanca Conference: 'After Germany is defeated, Great Britain will pursue the war against Japan with her maximum available resources by sea, land and air.' But, for the time being, the Pacific War was still to be a holding operation. The operations in the Pacific theatre, they agreed, 'will be kept within such limits as not to prejudice the capacity of the United Nations [at this point, a term for the Allied forces] to take advantage of any favourable opportunity for an endeavour to defeat Germany in 1943'.

Curtin was disappointed but not surprised. MacArthur was livid. They had collaborated on a new appeal for a Pacific offensive, addressed jointly to Roosevelt and Churchill at their conference. Curtin enclosed MacArthur's assessment of the Buna and Guadalcanal campaigns. 'The outstanding military lesson', MacArthur said, 'was the continuous calculated application of air power.' MacArthur claimed: 'For hundreds of miles, bombing provided all-around reconnaissance, protected the coast from hostile naval intervention and blasted the way for the infantry as it drove forward.' This, said MacArthur, was 'a new form of campaign which points the way to the ultimate defeat of the enemy'. Curtin said MacArthur's analysis was of 'transcending importance', and went on to tell Roosevelt and Churchill: 'These operations have been an extraordinary demonstration of the manner in which air power, closely integrated with ground forces and under the control of one Commander, can enable effective blows to be struck at Japan's sprawling holds on the archipelagos in the Pacific.' Accordingly, Curtin asked for fifteen hundred additional fighters and bombers and five hundred more transports for the South-West Pacific Area as soon as possible. Given proper air and naval support, Curtin said, 'it is not improbable that a mortal blow might be dealt Japan while she is still so extended and vulnerable'. Curtin concluded: 'Such a step will allay the growing anxiety that the Japanese are to be left indefinitely to their own devices with the consequence that the war in the Pacific, even after the defeat of Germany, will be of the most prolonged duration.' In a paragraph addressed to Churchill personally, Curtin hoped that his proposal would make a special appeal 'in view of your great knowledge of the history and methods of war'.

It didn't. Two months went by, until on 17 March, MacArthur sent Curtin a teleprinter message from his headquarters in Brisbane calling 'the failure to receive any reply an astonishing development'. He himself had heard nothing from Washington. MacArthur urged Curtin to try again with Churchill. 'If Churchill could be persuaded that America could do much more here than at present, without in any way jeopardising direct assistance to the British islands,' MacArthur said, 'he might be willing to add his pressure to our appeal.' Curtin did as MacArthur suggested next day, however sceptical he must have been by now about the efficacy of such appeals. The Advisory War Council had agreed in February that 'it would not be profitable to send cablegrams challenging the decisions of the Casablanca Conference'.

Churchill's reply was predictable. The Curtin–MacArthur proposal had been water off the duck's back. It is not clear whether Churchill's copy had ever reached him. 'I remember the President showing it to me at Casablanca,' he wrote on 27 March. The gist of Churchill's reply was that the Japanese air force was a waning force, and that there were enough American and RAAF air forces in the region to meet any threat. He said nothing about the Curtin–MacArthur proposal for a new strategy to defeat Japan, and repeated: 'The agreed strategy puts the defeat of Germany as the first charge on the forces of the United Nations, after which every man who can be carried and every suitable ship and aircraft will be concentrated on Japan.'

Yet, just as they had found at the Arcadia Conference in Washington after Pearl Harbor, Roosevelt and Churchill could not avoid the military and political realities. Because of the bloody drama of Guadalcanal, American public opinion still focused on the war against Japan. MacArthur's political clout was greater than ever; leading Republican senators publicly discussed drafting him as the Republican nominee for President in the 1944 election. Admiral King and the US navy were determined to push on with their Central Pacific strategy. Until late 1943, American personnel serving in the Pacific outnumbered those in the North Atlantic theatre. By September 1943, the American force in Australia had grown from twenty-five thousand when MacArthur arrived, to 250,000.

Curtin and MacArthur now accepted that Churchill's chief value to Australia was his influence with Roosevelt. Evatt was about to make his second visit to London and Washington. His brief was to obtain enough aircraft for seventy-two RAAF squadrons by 1944, up from the 1943 program of forty-five squadrons. MacArthur had suggested, Curtin instructed Evatt, that these should come from the allotment the United States had made to Britain and 'urges that you should press this point of view with Mr Churchill'.

Roosevelt pre-empted Evatt. Ahead of welcoming 'his old friend' to Washington, Roosevelt gave Sir Owen Dixon, Casey's successor as Australian Minister in Washington, an important message for Curtin. Within the last few days, Roosevelt told Curtin on 29 March, the American Chiefs had made 'an upward revision' of aircraft numbers for the South-West Pacific Area and, as a result, there would be 'a very considerable increase over what had previously been thought possible'. MacArthur would receive more than seven hundred additional bombers, fighters, and transports – in all, about a third of the Curtin–MacArthur proposal, and a doubling of MacArthur's existing air force. Roosevelt told Curtin: 'The strategical importance of the gallant battle the forces of our two countries are waging in the South-West Pacific is fully appreciated by me and every effort will be made to provide the necessary aircraft'. There had been many forceful advocates for this change of attitude, not least MacArthur's air force commander, General George Kenney, whom MacArthur had sent to Washington to press the case. It had been Kenney who convinced MacArthur of the importance of air power in combined operations as the key to defeating Japan. The new decisions had already been made when Evatt set out for Washington and London. Yet, in his reports back to Curtin, from April to July, he portrayed himself as the prime mover in extracting big new concessions from both Roosevelt and Churchill.

The latter part of Evatt's stay in Washington coincided with yet another Roosevelt–Churchill conference codenamed Trident, in May 1943. Evatt found Churchill 'radiating confidence' after the Allied victory in Tunisia. 'Although he undoubtedly sticks to his plan of primary concentration against Germany,' Evatt reported to Curtin on 22 May, 'he does not talk in old slogans and he is really anxious to join with Roosevelt and push against Japan as soon as practicable.' While 'nothing could exceed the cordiality and friendliness' of both Roosevelt and Churchill, Evatt cautioned Curtin: 'For the time being, I would strongly counsel your striking a note of restrained optimism in relation to the Pacific War.'

As usual, Evatt ignored his own advice when it came to lesser mortals. Bruce, despite all his complaints about lack of information on high policy decisions, was abreast of all the gossip in London, and reported that Evatt had had a first class brawl with Admiral Sir James Somerville during the Washington talks. Somerville, who was Commander-in-Chief of the Royal Navy in the Indian Ocean theatre, had dropped a casual remark to the effect that the men of the 9th Australian Division must be feeling unhappy at being cut out of the fighting after El Alamein. Bruce wrote: 'Evatt got all worked up and proceeded to say that this was the dirtiest crack he had ever heard.' According to Bruce, Churchill acted as peace maker at a White House garden party. 'Churchill brought Evatt over to Somerville and proceeded to put their two hands together, with his own over the top, and said that they had all got to be friends in Washington.' The charming scene is rather spoilt for posterity by Sir Alan Brooke, who wrote in his diary for 20 May 1943: '5 to 5.45 Garden Party at the White House with Marine band; 5.45 to 7.30 Meeting of Dominion representatives under prime minister, including Mackenzie King (Canadian prime minister) and Dr Evatt (Australian nuisance!).'

After six weeks of 'almost unbearable strain', Evatt wrote a breathless account claiming 'complete success' in obtaining more planes for Australia. 'The difficulty was almost insuperable,' he told Curtin. 'What I was asked to do was the practically impossible task of the reversal of very recent decisions by the American and British Chiefs of Staff.' The US advisers, he said, had already drafted a letter for Roosevelt rejecting the Australian application.

'Then Mr Churchill arrived . . . I had always been hopeful that we would obtain some support from Mr Churchill.' Without cabling 'the ups and downs of this difficult matter,' he told Curtin, 'it is sufficient to say that without obtaining an absolute promise from Mr Churchill, I did obtain substantial support from him . . . After dozens of encouragements and set-backs, this afternoon, practically on the eve of my departure for Britain, the President finally approved the allocation to Australia of approximately 475 planes for the purpose of expanding the RAAF during this year and the next'. In a separate cable, Evatt instructed his departmental head in Canberra, W. R. Hodgson, to get the word out to selected Cabinet colleagues, Opposition leaders, and newspaper proprietors that: 'Whatever befalls us, something big has been done for Australia and the Empire.'

It all turned sour within weeks. By July, Evatt was complaining that the US Chiefs were ignoring or misinterpreting Roosevelt's 'special contribution'. The Commander-in-Chief of the US Army Air Force, General 'Hap' Arnold, explained that military strategy had to come first and no more bombers could be spared for the South-West Pacific. Evatt returned to Washington from London, and wrote to Roosevelt that his 'generous gift to Australia' was not being carried out in the spirit of 'your noble intention'. Roosevelt replied with half an apology and a fraction of his original promise. 'I hope to make some heavy bombers available in 1944 [sic],' he said, 'but I cannot promise this definitely now'. Australia would have to wait until aircraft losses in battle and American production schedules were known more definitely. In the event, the sum total of Evatt's bluster, Churchill's 'cordiality', and Roosevelt's 'noble intention' was the delivery to Australia of 132 aircraft of a model already in the course of being superseded.

Evatt remained in thrall to Churchill, at least whenever they met face to face. His second mission to London had the same practical purpose as his first – to get more aircraft for Australia. It had the same kind of result – a token promise of three squadrons, only one of which ever materialised. Churchill had to work overtime getting his military chiefs to appease his visitor. To the objections voiced by his Air Minister, Sir Archibald Sinclair, that Evatt's requests were 'quite indefensible', Churchill declared: 'It is my duty to preserve goodwill between the Mother Country and this vast continent of Australia, inhabited by six million of our race and tongue.' Britain must 'try to make a good showing in Australia,' he said. To Evatt, however, the gesture was infinitely more important than the substance. His relations with Churchill and his reputation at home required that he exaggerate his achievement. He cabled Curtin urging him to announce 'the complete success of my mission as soon as possible'. It suited Curtin to go along with the charade. Replying to a no-confidence motion moved by Fadden in the House of Representatives on 22 June, Curtin praised Churchill's generosity and Evatt's tenacity.

Curtin let Evatt enjoy his illusions but knew where the real credit lay for any improvement in Washington's attitude. He specifically singled out General Kenney's mission in press briefings at the end of May. 'Things had happened in the last three months since Kenney and Sutherland [MacArthur's Chief of Staff] went and changed the attitude of the US High Command towards Australia,' he said. There would still be huge deficiencies, he cautioned, 'but for the first time we have a global strategy'. Curtin told the pressmen: 'For the first time it is possible to see daylight in the ultimate result – if our own mistakes do not beat us, and I do not think too many will be made.'

Curtin took the opportunity to tackle the Melbourne *Herald* over an article written by Keith Murdoch, who had criticised his relations with Churchill and Roosevelt. Murdoch had accused Curtin of 'squealing' with his demands for reinforcements. According to Fred Smith's record, Curtin said that his relations with Churchill 'had always been on the highest plane of cordiality and responsibility'. 'Representations have to be made of course,' said Curtin. 'They will, of course, be another squeal.'

Churchill himself gives the clearest account of the results of Curtin's 'squealing'. 'By the latter half of 1943,' he wrote in *Closing the Ring*, 'the Japanese had lost the eastern end of New Guinea.' Before General MacArthur could attack the Philippines, he wrote, 'he had first to reoccupy all its northern shore. As the 41st US Division worked their way to Salamaua at the end of June, they were joined by the 3rd Australian Division from Wau . . . The attack on Lae began on 4 September 1943, when the 9th Australian Division, of Alamein fame, landed on the coast ten miles east of the town'. Churchill continued:

Next day American parachutists dropped on Nadzap in the Markham Valley, and with the help of Australian pioneers, rapidly made an airfield. The 7th Australian Division flew in, and immediately advanced. Attacked from two sides, Lae was taken on 16 September . . . the 7th Australian Division, swift to exploit success, occupied the length [of the Markham Valley] in a series of airborne assaults . . . by mid-November, the 5th Australian Division was moving forward through the mountains of the Huon Peninsula, while the 9th Australian Division was clearing the heights overlooking the Markham Valley.

The two-year New Guinea campaign, Churchill wrote, was 'as arduous as any in history'. Australians may be permitted a certain grim satisfaction. Of the Australian divisions mentioned by Churchill, the 3rd and 5th were militia divisions, the 5th being the first new CMF division formed when Menzies reintroduced compulsory national service in 1940 – the conscription which Churchill informed the world in these same war memoirs 'was banned even for home defence'. The 7th and 9th Divisions would have been somewhere in Burma or India or Africa, except for Curtin's 'squealing'.

29

'For the Empire's future'
June–October, 1943

John Curtin lagged more than a year behind Winston Churchill in declaring that Australia was out of danger – if, indeed, Churchill ever thought it was in danger. After a Sydney meeting with MacArthur on 10 June 1943, Curtin announced that the chief risk now was 'marauding raids which from time to time will cause heavy losses'. Just as Churchill had insisted that Britain might still be invaded long after Hitler's failure in Russia had made it impossible, Curtin had continued to stress the direct threat well after the Japanese failure at Kokoda and Buna had removed it. The politics of war ruled. MacArthur had encouraged Curtin to maintain pressure on Roosevelt to divert more resources to the South-West Pacific. Curtin wanted to retain public support for the stringent demands the war effort was making on the Australian people and economy. He also needed moral leverage against the revival of industrial militancy, particularly on the New South Wales coalfields. Moreover, as recently as mid-March, 1943, MacArthur had advised Curtin that a Japanese build-up in troops and airfield construction in the East Indies presaged a new threat to north-west Australia. Heavy bombing raids on Darwin on 15 March appeared to confirm what

MacArthur called 'a menacing move which must be met'. Menacing moves did not, of course, meet Churchill's exacting standards of a threat to Australia.

By June, however, Curtin stated that the Pacific War was entering a 'second phase'. 'We have established that the enemy cannot occupy this country or any appreciable part of it,' he told the Canberra press. 'We can definitely hold it as a base for future action.' This second phase, he said, would involve 'certain limited offensive action'. Eighteen months of wrangling with Churchill and pleading with Roosevelt had shrunk the dimensions of Curtin's big idea. He warned that the second phase was going to be fairly long, because 'we are not going to make a bloody business of it'. The strategy would be 'to detain the enemy in certain places or perhaps immobilise them, shut them off and batter them from the air, rather than throwing masses of infantry against them'. This was a fair description, in layman's language, of the leap-frogging strategy MacArthur was about to adopt on his way to the Philippines. 'I feel sure that by the end of the year, if these things go as planned, the extent of the sacrifice demanded of the public may be lessened,' Curtin said. 'The punishment which war is imposing on the community should be diminished.' Recording it all, Fred Smith commented: 'Curtin seems to have become suddenly election conscious.'

The people of Australia gave Churchill a convincing answer to his objections against Curtin's rule 'with a parliamentary majority of one'. 'While I should never wish to intrude upon domestic party issues in Australia,' Churchill told Curtin grandly four days after the federal elections on 21 August 1943, 'I hope I may send my private and personal congratulations on the return of your Government, with so large and stable a working majority.' In fact, it was a rout. Labor won forty-nine of the seventy-three seats in the House of Representatives, and a majority in the Senate. The United Australia Party disintegrated. Menzies returned to the leadership of the Opposition, and began the work of regrouping the conservative forces under the revived title of the Liberal Party of Australia.

Churchill knew more about the transforming power of elections than anyone else in parliamentary history. He had been their beneficiary in 1905, twice in 1910, and in 1924. He had been their victim in 1922, 1929, and, through Baldwin's success, in 1935. He yearned for a people's mandate of his own; and when the British electorate rejected him in 1945, he jeopardised his place in history as the peerless statesman above party by his determination to obtain the vindication that only elections can give a party leader, as he did at last, too little and too late, in 1951. Now, in August 1943, Churchill saw Curtin in a new light, if not with positive benevolence, at least with the respect due to a fellow politician who was the undoubted master of his own house.

Churchill's low opinion of Australian party politics was not improved by the election campaign. In July, he had complained that his name was being invoked in campaign controversies. 'I am concerned,' Churchill told Curtin, 'at the possibility that these controversies may lead to disclosures of secret information.' Curtin said that he agreed totally with Churchill that wartime decisions should be kept out of domestic politics. But, he said, there were interests who sought to use Churchill 'as an umbrella for their party slogans. Neither you nor myself can avoid this, as it happened in the elections of 1940.'

Later in the campaign, Curtin sought Churchill's permission to publish part of a 1941 cablegram in order to rebut an allegation made by Fadden. Fadden claimed that in September, 1941, Curtin, as the Opposition leader on the Advisory War Council, had urged a reduction of numbers in the compulsory call-up. Curtin should have contented himself with charging Fadden with breach of faith in referring to the secret proceedings of the Advisory War Council. Instead, he wanted to go further and place his remarks in the context of a cable from Churchill, who had said on 31 August 1941, barely three months before Pearl Harbor: 'Events about Japan have taken a favourable turn in the past month.' Properly and peremptorily, Churchill refused: 'I cannot give my sanction to the partial publication of most secret and personal telegrams,' he told Curtin. 'Once publication starts, the full correspondence may be dragged out.' Furthermore, his cable had referred to United States negotiations with Japan, and 'might give grave offence there'. The President,

Churchill said, 'would also consider that a breach of confidence had been committed. My relations with him might be prejudicially affected and serious injury done due to the common cause.'

Curtin's victory vindicated not only his wartime leadership but his long struggle for the unity of the Australian Labor Party. Both had involved soul-searing struggles with himself. Churchill loved making war, and revelled in the exercise of the power he had gathered into his own hands, from the direction of the highest strategy with Roosevelt, to the minutiae of every military decision, ordering his generals and admirals about with gusto and ignorance. Curtin was no war lord like Churchill, and never pretended to be. He hated the whole business, and came to it every day with a sense of dread, deepened by his self-knowledge of his own limitations.

Curtin's reliance on MacArthur reflected that self-knowledge. Australian war historians focus on Curtin's acquiescence in the sidelining of the Australian army chiefs, including Blamey, and MacArthur's downgrading of Australia's fighting role after 1943. There is evidence that Curtin himself came to regret the free rein he had given the all-powerful American general. Curtin's attitude to MacArthur, however, was not governed only or even mainly by the Prime Minister's sense of inadequacy as a military strategist. In 1942 they shared fully the same ruling idea – Australia as the base for attack. The overwhelming point for Curtin was that MacArthur represented not so much the United States, but the vital link between Australia and Roosevelt. It is arguable, as Professor David Horner asserts, that 'in practice, Curtin surrendered civilian control of grand strategy to MacArthur'. In fact, he surrendered more than that. In Curtin's own words to Churchill, he 'surrendered part of Australia's sovereignty' by placing all Australian forces under MacArthur's supreme command. In the final analysis, Curtin's wartime leadership must be judged not by his personal success or failure as a military strategist, but by the degree to which that sacrifice of sovereignty was justified by the outcome. The distinguished American war historian, Richard B. Frank, describes the Curtin–MacArthur relationship as 'perhaps the most exemplary bond as existed in the West between senior political and military leaders'.

If the issue is one of constitutional propriety in a democracy, Churchill's relations with his military chiefs could hardly be described as exemplary.

On occasion, when he used his secret press briefings to wind down or get things off his chest, Curtin compared his job with Churchill's. 'Look at Churchill,' he complained. 'Even though Chifley [his Treasurer] spares me as much as possible, he has to tell me the details of taxes and the financial position, so I can speak about them. Churchill knows and cares nothing about the economic position – he leaves all that to the Chancellor of the Exchequer.' The comparison may verge on the ludicrous, but it is a reminder of Curtin's real achievement as Australia's wartime leader – the mobilisation of Australia's manpower, industry, and resources for a total war effort. The basis for his success was the political unity he achieved for his party and his nation.

At the same briefing, he alluded indirectly to his problems with Churchill: 'It sometimes happens that I should have given more consideration to a phrase in a cable. It is necessary to think of temperaments. Now and again, I talk too bluntly perhaps.' Some blunt talking with MacArthur might have redressed one failure definitely within Curtin's competence as a journalist and his responsibility as Prime Minister. As Frank writes in his short biography *MacArthur*:

> Eventually, seven Australian divisions would serve under MacArthur. New Zealand contributed a two-brigade division that served in the Solomons. What lingers as a source of great anger is that in his wartime communiqués MacArthur masked the huge contribution of Australia and New Zealand to his campaigns by usually referring to their units as 'allied troops' while he customarily was explicit about according credit to American units.

IN THEIR DIFFERENT SPHERES, Roosevelt, Churchill, and Curtin began planning for the post-war world. On the very day that Churchill banned the publication of old secrets, Bruce sent Curtin a message about the biggest new secret of them all – the Manhattan Project to build the atomic bomb. At their Trident Conference in May, Roosevelt and Churchill formally agreed to develop the bomb as a joint US–British project codenamed Tube Alloys. Remarkable for its knowledge and prescience, Bruce's cable to Curtin on 16 August – five days before the election – said that 'these developments are of so secret a character that I cannot telegraph you about them', but were of 'profound importance' not only for the war, but for the post-war economy. Bruce said: 'The main deposits of the raw material required are in Canada and the Belgian Congo, over both of which the Americans have obtained control, and Australia.' Bruce meant, of course, uranium, and continued: 'It is imperative that the Australian deposits should be safe-guarded and that we should be brought into the picture, and kept in touch with all future developments.' He urged that Curtin should ask Churchill that Professor Marcus Oliphant [an Australian nuclear physicist, then professor of physics at Birmingham University, and a member of the Tube Alloys Committee] 'be allowed to make a flying visit, in all senses of the term, to Australia for consultation with you and your advisers'. Curtin failed to follow up. Churchill would probably have been flabbergasted to learn how much Bruce, and through him, Curtin, knew about the secret that was to end the war and cast a fearful shadow over the whole future of civilisation.

Curtin was much more interested in the post-war role of the British Empire, and Australia's place in it. It is perhaps the strangest paradox of the relations between Churchill and Curtin that the Empire re-emerged as a dominant theme in their thinking, drawing them together after 1943, as much as it had pushed them apart in 1942. Sixty years of Australian political rhetoric about which party founded the American alliance has obscured the truth that there was no sudden turning to America after Pearl Harbor, and no abrupt turning away from Britain after the fall of Singapore. Military necessity had decided everything. Even for Curtin, Roosevelt remained a remote figure, smiling and friendly, but inaccessible and almost inscrutable. Churchill was still the man to do business with, and Australia was still very much in the business of the British Empire.

In 1943, John Curtin donned the imperial mantle which Winston Churchill had stripped from Alfred Deakin in 1907. During the election campaign, Curtin refloated Deakin's idea of a supreme council of Empire. He used almost exactly the same language and ideas as Deakin. Although he referred to the 'British Commonwealth of Nations', his statements after the election were headed 'Empire Government'. His messages to Churchill called specifically for an 'Empire Council'. This, he said, would be a permanent body, meeting regularly, sometimes in Canberra, Ottawa, Pretoria, and Wellington as well as London, with a permanent secretariat. Like Deakin, Curtin sought the mirage of a single Empire policy and the old dream of an equal voice for Australia. Like Hughes, he thought the experience of war made a single Empire policy achievable and necessary. He spelt it out in a statement on 6 September 1943:

> The place Australia will occupy in the Pacific after the war can never be the same as it was up to 1939 and she must have available the advantage of a concerted Empire policy if she is to be a Power to stand for democracy in the South Pacific. Similarly, the power of Britain as a force for peace in the future will be strengthened in the world if the firm voice against potential aggressors comes from the Empire, and not merely London.

The Empire Council, he said, would mean 'the association of the best minds of Britain and the Dominions', with Australia's voice 'heard equally in peace as it is now in war'. Curtin prepared to put his case direct to Churchill in London. No doubt he hoped to get a better reception than Deakin had.

Churchill, too, was rethinking his attitude to Australia and the Empire. 'It is of the highest importance for the future of the British Commonwealth and Empire', he wrote to his Air Minister on 12 July 1943, 'that we should be represented in the defence of Australia and the war in the Pacific.' Churchill was now seeing the Pacific theatre in a new light – the light of American success and power. The Trident Conference in Washington had given the war against Japan a new and higher priority. This did not mean any lessening of the main effort against Germany. On the contrary, the successful invasion of Sicily, followed by Allied landings in Italy and the collapse of Mussolini and the Fascist regime, created a new enthusiasm, even in a hitherto reluctant and cautious Churchill, for Operation Overlord, the invasion of Northern France, now set for May 1944. The higher priority for the Pacific war reflected growing American strength, and Roosevelt's confidence that America now had the resources and capacity to fight as hard in the Pacific as in Europe. This was why Curtin had felt able to tell the Canberra press: 'At last we have a global strategy.'

Churchill now had to confront the unintended consequences of his own handiwork. 'Beating Hitler First' had meant leaving the United States and Australia to deal with Japan in the Pacific after the fall of Singapore. If he had chosen to give due weight to Australia's role, and had treated Australia as Britain's fighting proxy in the Pacific, he could at least have kept up the appearances of an Empire partnership. Instead, he had chosen confrontation with Curtin, insisting for as long as possible that Australia's imperial duty lay in the Middle East. He had continued to sneer at Australia's turning to the United States, yet his own conduct had ensured that Australia would take the very course he professed to deplore. The surprising thing is how much Australia, not least its Labor Government, still thought, and was willing to act, in terms of its relationship with Britain and the Empire, of which Churchill himself remained the embodiment.

With success in both the Mediterranean and the Pacific, Churchill felt able to give serious thought to the future of the British Empire in the Far East. In December, 1941, as he had crossed the Atlantic for his first war meeting with Roosevelt, he had written about the 'terrible forfeits' he was willing to pay for bringing the United States into the war. Now, in August, 1943, he was crossing the Atlantic once again to meet Roosevelt at Quebec, Canada. His thoughts turned to winning back 'the lost places' of Empire and, just as important, its lost prestige.

On board the *Queen Mary*, he produced a paper for the Chiefs of Staff travelling with him. In the Far East, he acknowledged 'we have none too good a tale to tell'. Before meeting the Americans, he wrote, 'we must settle upon positive proposals for attacking the enemy and proving our zeal in this theatre of war'. British 'failures and sluggishness' merited 'reasonable reproach'. The issue at Quebec, Churchill claimed, was really about Britain's demand for a 'full and fair place in the war against Japan from the moment when Germany was beaten'. His greatest fear, he wrote in his memoirs, was that American critics would say 'England, having taken all she could from us to help her beat Hitler, stands out of the war against Japan and will leave us in the lurch'. But his proposals for Quebec made it clear that he also had other aims: to devise strategies to restore the 'lost places' of the British Empire in the Far East. This time, however, his ideas were to run him into conflict with both the American military chiefs and his own – and with Roosevelt himself.

The venue itself spurred Churchill's imperial imagination. Roosevelt and Churchill met in the Citadel of Quebec, captured from the French in 1759 during the Seven Years War, sometimes called the first world war, under the helmsmanship of Pitt the Elder, the greatest war leader of England until Churchill himself. In agreeing to a Canadian venue, Roosevelt had been worried that Prime Minister Mackenzie King might want to attend as a member of the Conference. If this happened, Roosevelt feared 'similar demands by Brazil and other American partners'! 'We also had to think of the claims of Australia and the other Dominions,' Churchill wrote. However, 'the delicate question was solved and surmounted by the broadminded outlook of the Canadian Prime Minister and Government. I for my part was determined that we and the United States should have the Conference to ourselves.'

The first Quebec Conference in August, 1943, was different from its predecessors because for the first time the war in the Pacific had high, if not yet equal, billing. It was also distinguished by open bickering within the British delegation. The American Chiefs urged three plans: an assault through northern Burma into China; Admiral King's plan for an attack across the Central Pacific; and MacArthur's thrust to the Philippines, from the bases the Americans and

Australians were establishing in New Guinea and the Dutch East Indies. Churchill strongly supported the King and MacArthur plans. 'The bold sweep of this concept was the more attractive in that it rested squarely on the might of American sea power,' he was to write. 'Very large naval forces would be needed, but only in the final phase would great armies be required, and by then Hitler would be overthrown and the main strength of Britain and the United States could be hurled against Japan.' But Churchill baulked at Burma.

All the arguments Churchill had used in his attempt to put Australian troops into Burma in 1942 were now forgotten or turned on their heads. Then, he had urged that the supreme importance the Americans gave to China justified the sacrifice of the 7th Australian Division. Now, he argued, the American plan to aid China 'ignored the impossibility of deploying large armies, most of which would have to be found by Britain, in the jungles of Burma'. In 1942, he had said that holding Burma to aid China was more important than holding Singapore. Now he concocted a scheme to bypass Burma and make an amphibious attack on Sumatra, as a springboard for the recapture of Singapore.

Such ideas were bound to bring Churchill into conflict with Roosevelt. A campaign in North Burma would mesh with two of Roosevelt's key ideas for the post-war world. He wanted to see China going up in the world and the British Empire going down. He named China as one of his 'four policemen' who, with the United States, the Soviet Union, and Britain, would keep the peace of the world. There was no place in his vision of a United Nations Organization for a restored and powerful British Empire. As he had told his son, Elliot, 'When we win the war, I will work with all my might and main to see to it that we will not be wheedled into a position to aid or abet the British Empire and its imperial ambitions.'

Churchill realised that a hard campaign in the jungles of northern Burma, borne mainly by British forces from India in collaboration with the American forces in China under General Joseph Stillwell, would do nothing to restore British prestige in the Far East. The only beneficiaries would be Chiang Kaishek, whom he despised, and his Chinese communist rivals for power, whom he detested. Churchill had been enthusiastic about the ideas of the daring English maverick, General Orde Wingate, for guerilla raids against the Japanese. But he was repelled by any large-scale operations that would exhaust British resources in a futile campaign to shore up Chiang Kaishek. Yet this was what his great ally was now pressing upon him.

Churchill unveiled his alternative with a flourish. An attack on Sumatra, he told Roosevelt and the assembled military chiefs, would be a 'great strategic blow'. Operation Culverin, as he called his scheme, would be the Torch of the Indian Ocean. How much better and easier, he said, would be an amphibious landing on the tip of Sumatra, within striking distance of Malaya and Singapore, than 'toiling through the swamps and jungles of Burma'. Then came the Churchillian punch line: his Sumatra project 'promised decisive consequences' – just like the Dardanelles! There would not have been another person in that room in the Quebec Citadel who would have regarded the Dardanelles and Gallipoli as anything but an unmitigated disaster. One can almost hear the gasps from the American Chiefs, the groans from the British Chiefs, and the chuckle from Roosevelt.

Like Gallipoli long ago, Sumatra became his obsession, and it became the cause of the war's worst split between Churchill and his Chiefs – or, as Churchill himself put it blandly, 'the only considerable difference which I and the War Cabinet had with our trusted military colleagues'. This disguises the real cause of a dispute which simmered away for nine months: Churchill's motives were highly political – nothing short of the restoration of the lost places of Empire and the prestige of reclaiming Singapore and Malaya; but the Chiefs regarded his Sumatra project as militarily irrelevant and potentially disastrous. The Chief of the Imperial General Staff, Sir Alan Brooke, wrote in his diary on the last day of the Quebec Conference ('Thank God for it'), that the trouble was 'a peevish, temperamental prima donna of a Prime Minister, suspicious to the very limits of imagination, always fearing a military combination against political dominance'. Churchill had been more unreasonable and trying than ever, Brooke wrote. 'He had during the sea voyage in a few idle moments become married to the idea that success against Japan can only be secured through the capture of the north tip of Sumatra! He has been like a peeved child asking for a forbidden toy.'

At Quebec, Churchill had thrown away the tactical advantage the British had always had in getting their way with Roosevelt against the advice of the American Chiefs; they had always agreed among themselves before presenting a united front against the Americans, often divided on strategy between the pro-Europe General Marshall and the pro-Pacific Admiral King. Now Churchill had broken ranks and gone off on his Sumatra frolic alone. The issue could not be settled at Quebec. They agreed to 'further study'; and Churchill comforted himself by reporting back to Attlee and the British Cabinet: 'There is no doubt that the United States Chiefs-of-Staff are gratified at the constructive interest which we have shown in war plans against Japan in 1944.' There was more substance to the claim than might appear from Roosevelt's scepticism over Sumatra and the arguments over Burma. The Quebec Conference established a new South-East Asia Command based in India. Churchill nominated the 43-year-old Lord Louis Mountbatten as Supreme Commander. Debonair, publicity-seeking, and considered by his military peers as a lightweight, Mountbatten was the son of Lord Louis Battenberg, and uncle to Philip, future husband of Princess Elizabeth, the heir to the British throne. He was the hero of Noel Coward's film, *In Which We Serve*, dealing with the loss of his ship, HMS *Kelly*, in the Mediterranean, and was the architect of the Dieppe fiasco. The appointment delighted the patrician Roosevelt who, for all his democratic instincts, loved a lord.

Churchill underlined his new interest in the Pacific war by getting General Marshall's consent for a British general to join MacArthur's staff. When Marshall agreed, he telegraphed Curtin 'pointing out that this will bring us more closely into touch with the war in the Pacific'. His choice for the liaison job was General Herbert Lumsden, 'one of our most distinguished and accomplished officers, who at the very beginning of the war, in the first contact with the enemy, had brought the armoured car back into popularity'. By now, MacArthur had excluded Australian officers from his 'court', and had sidelined Blamey. So Churchill probably learnt more about MacArthur's plans than Curtin.

To give further emphasis to his renewed interest in the future of the Empire, Churchill ended his Quebec sojourn with a broadcast to the people of Canada. Paying tribute to the Canadian contribution, he added: 'I only wish indeed that my other duties, which are exacting, allowed me to travel still farther afield and tell Australians, New Zealanders and South Africans to their faces how we in Britain feel towards them for all they have done, and are resolved to do.'

Churchill's dispute with his Chiefs intensified when they all returned to London. Brooke even accused Churchill of abandoning the 'Beat Hitler First' strategy! He recorded in his diary on 1 October 1943 'an hour's pitched battle' with Churchill who, he said, wanted to withdraw troops from the Mediterranean to the South-East Asian theatre. 'I was refusing to impair our amphibious potential power in the Mediterranean in order to equip Mountbatten for adventures in Sumatra,' Brooke wrote. 'He on the other hand was prepared to scrap our basic policy and put Japan before Germany.' It took Brooke an hour to make the heretic recant: 'However, I defeated most of his evil intentions in the end!'

The significance for Australia is that the long wrangle over Churchill's obsession with Sumatra delayed and distorted British planning for the Pacific war before and after Germany's defeat. This in turn hindered Blamey and the Australian Chiefs in making their own plans for cooperation with Britain in a distinctive Commonwealth and Empire contribution. As late as May, 1944, when Blamey was in London with Curtin, he was being told by Brooke, who had given him a statement about Australia's role as a base for British sea, air, and army allocations if Germany was defeated by the end of 1944: 'It should be clearly understood that the statement does not imply any commitment or the adoption of any specific policy or plan of operation in the Pacific.' America's overwhelming power and the suddenness of Japan's surrender are the two main reasons why Britain's contribution in 1944–45 was relatively limited except, ironically, for its remarkable campaign in Burma – General William

Slim's 'defeat into victory'. By then, however, the distractions and ructions caused by Churchill's obsessions had already undermined his ability to carry through his post-Alamein boast: 'If I'm alive, I'll fling all we have into the Pacific.'

30

'Winston's dislike for Curtin . . .'
November, 1943–May, 1944

Curtin was in no hurry to meet Churchill. The British leader wanted to hold a Dominion Prime Ministers Conference in London before the end of 1943 as a show of Empire solidarity ahead of the first meeting of the Big Three. Curtin insisted he could not leave Australia until April, 1944, at the earliest. The British High Commissioner in Canberra, Sir Ronald Cross, whose patronising disdain for Australians, high and low, coloured all his reporting to London, thought he knew the reason for Curtin's reluctance: he was 'apprehensive' about facing Churchill, Cross wrote, fearing 'he might prove inadequate'. Curtin may have feared many things, flying for one, but meeting Churchill was not one of them. What Curtin feared was being forced to act a false part, to be made to appear what he was not. 'I was not trained to be a war-lord,' he once said. 'Yet fate pushed on to me at least the appearance of being one.'

Churchill had originally suggested November, 1943, for the prime ministers' conclave. He had to drop this idea when Roosevelt and Stalin agreed to meet in Teheran for the first summit at the end of November. The Teheran Conference was to be preceded by a Roosevelt–Churchill meeting in Cairo. So November was out.

Churchill now proposed December. 'All manner of issues are coming up for decision which vitally affect the members of the British Commonwealth, as well as their relations to the outside world in the post-war set-up,' he told Curtin, 'and the most practicable way of reaching agreement is to get round a table together'. Curtin replied: 'It is essential I remain here for a few months.' A radical review of Australian manpower was underway, he explained, the food problem had become 'very acute', and 'if we are to play our part in providing food in increasing quantities to Great Britain and our Allies, it will require constant watching over the next few months'. The coal situation was 'now more delicate' than ever before. Unwilling to say outright that strikes were hampering the war effort, Curtin told Churchill: 'I am fearful of a serious breakdown in our own industries and primary production systems unless I give it my personal attention until a better position has been reached.' Churchill, preoccupied with the business of Cairo, Teheran, the furious German counterattack in Italy, the planning for Overlord, disputes with the Americans over Operation Anvil (their plan for invading Southern France) and his continuing row with his own Chiefs over Far Eastern strategy, may have accepted all this, however grumpily, but must have snorted in disbelief at Curtin's final reason: there was to be a national conference of the Australian Labor Party on 7 December!

It must have been incomprehensible to Churchill that a Prime Minister should put a party conference before a conference of his dominion peers. Yet it reflected Curtin's sense of the source of his authority and his entitlement to power, even with the great mandate he had just received from the people – the inner conviction that he was nothing without the Australian Labor Party. 'My efforts during the Conference period will be directed to pointing the way to the great tasks which we have to face and bring all to a realisation of the duties and obligations which we owe to the Empire and Allies,' he told Churchill. 'I put it to you quite frankly that my work around and during this Conference will be, I hope, the greatest contribution I am able to make to the strength and efforts of the British Commonwealth.'

Curtin's work at the ALP Conference did, in fact, show how Empire-minded he remained. He ensured that Labor's official policy expressed his views. Every bit as much as Churchill, Curtin was explicit in stating that the war in the Pacific should not be left to the United States alone. He had spelt it out in a 3000-word message to Churchill on 8 October 1943. He explained the need for a revision of Australian manpower, pointing out that 71.5 per cent of males between fourteen and sixty-four were engaged in war work and essential services, comparable with the British figure of 73 per cent. The Australian military contribution in the South-West Pacific Area still exceeded the American: MacArthur's forces comprised nearly 500,000 in the Australian army, compared with just under 200,000 Americans, and 136,000 in the RAAF, compared with 55,000 American airmen. Only in operational squadrons did the United States component exceed Australia's – fifty-nine to forty-eight; and for them, the feeding and maintenance fell largely upon Australia. Curtin raised with Churchill the eventual return of the twenty thousand RAAF personnel serving in Britain, the Mediterranean, India, and Canada. But this time, Curtin was not asking for British help, but establishing Australia's credentials for the next phase of the war – the attack upon Japan. 'The interests at stake in this paramount question are not those of Australia alone,' Curtin told Churchill. 'They also include those of the British Empire in the Pacific.' It was essential, he said, that the governments of the United Kingdom, Canada, and New Zealand should understand the vital importance of 'maintaining the military effort in the Pacific by Australia alone, or in association with other parts of the Empire'. 'If the defeat of Japan is to await the end of the war in Europe, the struggle in the Pacific will be more prolonged and it is imperative that a certain minimum effort should be maintained by or on behalf of the British Empire in the Pacific.'

As things turned out, the 'retardation', as Curtin called his veto on 1943 for a dominion conference, saved a great deal of wasted time, travel, and embarrassment. On his way back from Teheran via Cairo and Tunis, Churchill contracted pneumonia, and convalesced in Morocco. He was unable to return to London until 19 January.

As soon as he got home, he became further embroiled with his Chiefs of Staff in the brawl over Pacific strategy. The role of Australia as a base for future British operations was central to this dispute. If Curtin had been in London while it was raging, Churchill would undoubtedly have tried to bring him into the thick of the domestic row with the military chiefs.

During his convalescence in Morocco, Churchill had hardly allowed himself a day out of touch or action. Back in London, he amazed his colleagues with his resilience and charmed them with the optimism and wit of his reports on Teheran. 'Trying to maintain good relations with [Stalin] is like wooing a crocodile,' he told the Cabinet. 'You do not know whether to tickle it under the chin or to beat it on the head. When it opens its mouth, you cannot tell whether it is trying to smile, or preparing to eat you up.'

On his visits to Cairo before and after Teheran, Churchill had stayed with Dick Casey at his villa near the Pyramids. He was soon to reward Casey's hospitality with the offer of the governorship of Bengal, now devastated by famine, the result of war, cyclones and Britain's refusal to provide shipping for so unmilitary a task as carrying grain to Calcutta. Patrick French, in his *Liberty or Death*, writes: 'Churchill's decision to restrict grain imports to India in order to save ships for the war effort was deliberate, and to that extent the famine was man-made.' Three million Bengalis died of starvation. Casey, however, answered this latest call to duty for the British Empire.

In appointing Casey to Bengal, Churchill may have hoped that this new 'man-on-the-spot' would help him promote his pet Sumatra scheme, against the advice of almost everybody else, up to and including Roosevelt. Roosevelt had insisted on inviting Chiang Kaishek to the Cairo Conference and, at Teheran, was anxious to extract from Stalin a pledge to enter the war against Japan as soon as possible after the defeat of Germany. This remained a high priority for the United States until the atomic bomb made Soviet support redundant in 1945. In December, 1943, however, the presence of Chiang Kaishek in Cairo, unpalatable as it was to both Churchill and Australia, and the need to impress Stalin at Teheran, placed aid to China at the top of Roosevelt's Far Eastern agenda. From the conferences at Cairo and Teheran, there emerged three proposals for British involvement before and after Germany's defeat: an all-out drive through northern Burma into China; the despatch of a British fleet to the Pacific Ocean based in Australia and New Zealand; and a build-up of British forces in Australia for a thrust through the Dutch East Indies and Borneo to support MacArthur's drive to the Philippines. The Australian-based option was the preferred choice of the British Chiefs. Churchill didn't care for that idea. What he wanted was to use 'the very large air and military forces we have standing in India and around the Bay of Bengal for an advance eastwards to the Malay peninsula and the Dutch Islands'. Specifically, he wanted amphibious landings on the northern tip of Sumatra. This, he was convinced, was the only way to restore the prestige of the British Empire.

As soon as he came home, Churchill lined up his Cabinet against the soldiers. 'All my Ministerial colleagues have spoken in a strongly adverse sense against these plans', he informed the Chiefs of Staff on 24 January 1944. 'I had long and difficult arguments with the prime minister', Sir Alan Brooke was complaining by February. 'He was again set on carrying out an attack on north tip of Sumatra and refusing to look at any long term projects or concrete plans for the defeat of Japan.' Churchill, Brooke alleged, was siding with the American generals in opposing the British operation in the East Indies 'working via Australia'. Churchill, Brooke wrote, was again 'showing his terrible failing of lack of width or depth in his strategic vision'. The Chief of the Imperial General Staff recorded his considered opinion of the Prime Minister of the United Kingdom thus: 'Now that I know him well, episodes such as Antwerp and the Dardanelles no longer puzzle me. But meanwhile I often doubt whether I am going mad or whether he is really sane.'

As Brooke saw it, there were two rational choices of grand strategy for Britain's part in the defeat of Japan, boiling down to a decision about India or Australia as the best base for British operations against Japan. Brooke and his military colleagues favoured operations based in Australia, to be carried out by naval, land, and air forces cooperating closely with American and Australian forces in the Pacific. Their second choice was for operations based on India, to be carried out by Mountbatten's South-East Asia Command, 'with the object of liberating Burma, Malaya, Singapore and possibly Java, Sumatra or Borneo'. The British Chiefs argued that India-based operations could not begin until six months after Hitler's defeat, while Australia-based operations 'could be begun much sooner'. Ironically, Brooke himself favoured the Australian option for a political as much as a strategic reason: 'I felt at this stage of the war, it was vital that the British should partake in direct action against Japan in the Pacific . . . to prove to Australia our willingness and desire to fight with them for the defence of Australia as soon as possible after the defeat of Germany'. According to Brooke, the only thing that prevented rational discussion about these options, leading, he thought, to a sound and practical combination of both, was that 'Winston had now got all his desires centred onto the north tip of Sumatra'. Churchill, Brooke claimed, 'refused to look at any strategy or operation that did not contemplate the tip of Sumatra as its first stage, or indeed its only stage, as I never got out of him what his subsequent stages would be'.

Brooke claimed that there was another reason for Churchill's failure to engage in a rational strategic debate: his attitude to Australia. In yet another discussion on Pacific strategy on 25 February – or, as Brooke put it, 'spending seven and a half hours with Winston, most of it engaged in heavy argument' – Churchill claimed that the Chiefs were ganging up against 'his pet Sumatra operation and almost took it up as a personal matter'. Brooke described the meeting, which included Attlee and Eden, as 'desperate with no opportunity of discussing strategy on its merits'. Brooke added: 'Furthermore, his dislike for Curtin and the Australians at once affected any discussion for cooperation with Australian forces through New Guinea towards the Philippines.'

The Imperial Japanese Navy now intervened in the London debate, dramatically and decisively. They suddenly moved a powerful fleet, including seven battleships, from their base at Truk in the west Pacific to Singapore. It was the first and only fleet ever to use the Singapore Naval Base. The Japanese wanted to protect the fleet from American air attack, and to protect Japan's oil supply in the Dutch East Indies. But the immediate effect, as Churchill admitted, was to arouse fears in London and Canberra that 'they might break into the Bay of Bengal' or even menace western Australia. This possibility, Churchill wrote, 'put a stop for the time being to *Culverin* [his Sumatra project] or other amphibious adventures in Indian waters'. For the only time in its existence, the Singapore Naval Base acted as a deterrent – by the Japanese against Churchill.

THE DISPUTE WAS no nearer solution when Churchill announced that the dominion prime ministers would assemble in London on 1 May 1944. They would be meeting four years after he had gambled everything on his Big Idea, and one month before it reached its fulfilment with the Allied invasion of France. Now the leaders of the Empire and Commonwealth which had fought 'until the New World stepped forth to liberate the old world', would come to its capital and citadel for a grand council of the Empire at war. Curtin himself felt moved by the symbolism. When seeking to postpone the conference, he had told Shedden, 'If I have to go, it's only to avoid being a defaulter.' Now he told a parliamentary farewell: 'It seems like a dream that the lad who once ran only the streets of Creswick, Ballarat and Brunswick is about to represent his country overseas.'

Curtin's mode of travel matched and perhaps partly explained his reluctance to leave Australia. Accompanied by his wife, Elsie, and by Blamey, Shedden, and Rodgers, he embarked at Sydney on the USS *Lurline* on 5 April. He had declined to fly by US aircraft and MacArthur had arranged for this converted liner to take the party to San Francisco, along with four hundred American wounded and fifty Australian wives of American servicemen. Blamey annoyed his now teetotal Prime Minister by taking a case of whisky on board ship in the 'dry' US navy. They crossed America by train, arriving in Washington on 23 April. On Anzac Day, Curtin lunched with Roosevelt in South Carolina, where the President was resting under doctor's orders at a friend's estate. During hours of talking, Curtin made no requests and Roosevelt no offers, except to invite Curtin to have treatment at the Washington Naval Hospital for the condition which caused the cast in his eye. Curtin no doubt kept in mind the warning he had received from MacArthur before he left Australia: 'Roosevelt is quite unscrupulous in getting away from his own expressions of agreement and repudiating his word if it suits him.' Next day, Curtin fell ill himself and cancelled meetings with Marshall and Stimson. He made a broadcast to the people of America that night. Screwing himself up for the trans-Atlantic crossing, on 28 April he boarded the Boeing flying boat which Churchill had found so luxurious and enjoyable on his way home from the Arcadia Conference in January, 1942. Curtin had effectively spent three working days in Washington, compared with the month he was to spend in London; and he would return for another three days on his way back to Australia. The distribution of time between North America and Britain was roughly the same as Menzies in 1941, before Pearl Harbor, Singapore, and the 'looking to America'.

'I speak for seven million Britishers,' Curtin told the reporters at London's Croydon Airport. He repeated it when he received the Freedom of the City of London a fortnight later: 'Australia is a British people, Australia is a British land, and seven million Australians are seven million Britishers.' No doubt Curtin intended these effusions to reassure the British British, not least Churchill, but the fact is that he knew that he spoke for Australians. There were more of them willing and proud to call themselves British at that moment than at any other time in Australia's history, and Churchill had done more to create and articulate that pride than anyone in Britain's history.

In his biography of Curtin, David Day corrects the impression given by Lloyd Ross that, except for his official appearances, Curtin holed up in the Savoy Hotel, disconsolate and lonely without Elsie, whom he had left back in Washington. It is probably true that on one occasion he said in exasperation to Don Rodgers: 'Let us go out and meet some bloody Australians.' But David Day makes it clear that, although the tourism bit was limited, (including a visit to the churchyard at Stoke Poges, the inspiration for Gray's *Elegy in a Country Churchyard*), Curtin's itinerary was typical for a visiting Prime Minister, with the Royal Family sharing top billing with Churchill. One member of the Royal Family he was particularly keen to meet was the King's brother, Prince Henry, Duke of Gloucester, whom he was to appoint Governor-General of Australia, in violation of Labor policy. Churchill's candidate had been Wavell, but Curtin outplayed Churchill on this one – a Royal Duke trumped a field marshal. The Australian leader did get out of one invitation to a tête à tête with Churchill at Chequers, telling Shedden: 'I don't care to sit in an armchair and listen to one man.' On another of his three or four visits to Chequers, Churchill had promised him 'afternoon tea with my daughters'; but he found Churchill surrounded by ministers and military chiefs discussing Pacific strategy. So instead of the anticipated tea party, 'I had to go into bat,' Curtin told Shedden.

At the conference opening on 1 May, Curtin had an early win over Churchill, who wanted the prime ministers to meet without their official advisers. His idea was that the conference should be just like a Cabinet meeting, which no doubt he would dominate as he did his own. Curtin insisted that Blamey and Shedden should sit beside him, to 'keep me on the rails', as he frankly admitted. Curtin explained that as Churchill had not allowed him to bring along a minister, he was 'more dependent than ever on his two officials'. Churchill gave way, insisting, however, that 'in some circumstances, the advisers would have to leave the meeting'. It was typical of Curtin's self-honesty that he was prepared to expose his own limitations in front of men like Churchill, Smuts, and Mackenzie King (who recorded it all in his diary), when he felt his duty to Australia was at stake.

'Curtin did not spare anyone's feelings in the way he spoke out,' Mackenzie King wrote in his diary about Curtin's first address to the conference on 3 May. 'I confess I admired his straightforward direct statements. I equally admire Churchill's restraint in listening to the presentation as Curtin made it.' Curtin tackled Churchill at his most vulnerable point: the lack of policy direction on Britain's role in the

Pacific War. This in turn, he said, prevented Australia from making proper decisions about its own role, especially about the use of its manpower. 'We must know just what is expected, what is needed and without delay,' he said, 'and if Australia is expected to furnish supplies to British forces fighting the Japanese, we cannot continue as we are. We will have to withdraw some of our men from active service.' Blamey backed up Curtin with an account of Australia's 'narrow shave', and Mackenzie King found it all 'very deeply moving'.

Curtin said that he welcomed the prospect of British forces in Australia, despite the added strains they would place on Australian resources. He made the crucial point that Australia was in the sphere of American strategic responsibility, and that any changes in command arrangements would have to be approved in Washington. He was signalling to Churchill that British forces in the South-West Pacific would have to come under MacArthur's command.

Churchill's unresolved dispute with his Chiefs meant that he was able to bring to the conference only the broadest of outlines for Britain's role in the Pacific. This was the so-called 'middle strategy' which, Churchill told the prime ministers, would 'advance northwards from Australia, help General MacArthur to liberate Borneo, and then strike either at Singapore and Malaya or at Hong Kong and the China Coast'. A military mission would be sent to 'report promptly on existing facilities in Australia and on the recaptured islands to the north of it' for military and naval action. Churchill now supported the idea of a joint British–Australian force under an Australian commander. This naturally got Blamey onside. Curtin again emphasised that such a force would be operating in the United States area of responsibility (which Churchill himself had arranged with Roosevelt in 1942) and therefore must be answerable to MacArthur. This earned the comment from Brooke: 'Curtin, who is entirely in MacArthur's pocket, was afraid we were trying to oust MacArthur.' Brooke claimed that Curtin 'showed very little desire for British forces to operate from Australia'. But Churchill conceded Curtin's point and acknowledged that the proposed British–Australian force would be subordinate to MacArthur. Curtin obtained Churchill's agreement to Australia's manpower reorganisation which set army strength at six divisions and the RAAF at fifty-three squadrons. Even Brooke was satisfied with the results of the conference deliberations, or, rather, their effect on Churchill: 'I think we have at last got him swung to an Australia-based strategy as opposed to his old love of the "Sumatra tip".'

Churchill was much less interested and even less forthcoming when Curtin broached the subject of Empire governance after the war. There are uncanny parallels with Deakin in 1907. Like Deakin, Curtin had previously canvassed ambitious proposals, including some form of Imperial Council of Ministers. Like Deakin, he scaled them down to a proposal for a permanent secretariat. Curtin, too, hoped to enlist the support of the Canadian Prime Minister, but found King as contented with the status quo as Laurier had been. In all, he found Prime Minister Churchill as frosty as Under-Secretary Churchill.

Churchill was absent when the prime ministers reached Curtin's motion for imperial governance on 15 May, two weeks into their conference. Lord Hankey, now in full retirement but still keenly observing the affairs of Empire, wrote in his diary that Curtin, who had visited him, was 'so hurt that he did not develop his full case on his proposals, and the discussion degenerated into a barging match between him and Mackenzie King'. Attlee chaired the session in Churchill's absence and ended the debate with an undertaking that the Government would study the matter further. Hankey commented: 'That is as good as shelving the proposals. That is how the present Government fosters the loyalty of the Empire!'

Churchill half-apologised for his absence, explaining to Curtin on 20 May that he had been 'prevented at the last minute' from attending. He accepted Curtin's proposal that the British Prime Minister should hold monthly meetings with the dominion high commissioners. 'This arrangement,' said Churchill, 'would make it unnecessary for Mr Bruce to attend meetings of the War Cabinet regularly.' That was the sole outcome of Curtin's grand scheme. It actually left Australia worse off than before, as far as top-level consultation was concerned. As Deakin had said in

1907, the mountain had laboured; this time it had not brought forth even a mouse.

Churchill had the best reason in the world for his absence on 15 May: his attendance, with George VI by his side, at the final briefing by Eisenhower and Montgomery on their plans for the Normandy invasion. Churchill had overcome his doubts and fears of the last two years, to the extent that he was now able to say: 'Gentlemen, I am hardening on this operation.' Which was just as well, seeing that the greatest amphibious operation in military history was scheduled to take place in the first week of June, two weeks away. Nevertheless, Curtin had a valid complaint. If Churchill had been remotely interested, he could easily have rescheduled the debate. For all his grandiloquence about the Commonwealth and Empire of the future, he had not fundamentally changed from the Churchill of 1907, who had told his friend Leo Amery that consultation with the dominions would be worthwhile only when they were military powers who could be of value to Britain. Now that they had indeed reached that stage, their military usefulness was the only aspect of imperial affairs in which he was really interested, never more so than at this culminating moment.

Churchill must have been irked by Curtin's failure to enter fully into the spirit of this great moment. Curtin did not join his fellow prime ministers in a visit to Eisenhower's Headquarters, perhaps inhibited by the absence of any Australian component, although he made a point of visiting airfields in Lincolnshire to thank the RAAF squadrons engaged in the bombing of Germany. To Churchill's surprise, and Blamey's disappointment, he decided to leave London for his return visit to Washington, a week before the Normandy invasion on 6 June 1944.

In all his public speeches, Curtin emphasised the British and imperial connection. He told a gathering of the Empire Parliamentary Association at the House of Commons that Australians regarded themselves as 'the trustee for the British way of life'. He assured them that 'Britain would have in the Antipodes a people and a territory corresponding in purpose and in outlook and in race to the Motherland itself'. Churchill chaired a luncheon at the Australia

Club in which he 'joined the right hand of friendship to that most commanding, competent, whole-hearted leader of the Australian people'. Curtin replied that just because Australia was located within an American sphere of responsibility, 'that did not involve any reallocation of relationships'.

Curtin took the opportunity to answer two of Churchill's complaints against Australia – the failure to form a national government in wartime, and the 'turning to America'. Receiving the Freedom of the City of London, Curtin claimed that 'the very foundation on which this great Empire has evolved [is] the right of the people to quarrel with their own government, to criticise it and defeat it'. In a spirited defence of the party system as the mainstay of democracy, Curtin said:

> With all our diversities of political parties and practices, nonetheless out of that discussion, that distinctiveness, that variation in the point of view, a unity emerges as a result of all that . . . It is a unity born of the supremacy of persuasion. It is a unity that emerges to give triumph to conviction rather than either cowardice or weakness. It is the strength of the triumph of reason.

This is the credo by which he tried to live.

After a dinner at Chequers four days before Curtin's departure, Churchill tackled him on his New Year's message of 1941, as 'contrary to imperial principles'. Shedden recorded:

> CURTIN: If the British Commonwealth had been at war with Japan, and war with Germany arose later, what would you have done? Would you have appealed to the United States?
> CHURCHILL: Yes, most certainly.
> CURTIN: Well, that was just what I did when you were at war with Germany and Japan came in.

31

'Recovering our lost property'
June, 1944–September, 1945

Churchill's conversion to the importance of Australia as a base against Japan came three years too late. For the rest of the war, until the people of Britain dismissed him in July 1945, Churchill's relations with Australia were dominated by his erratic efforts to return Britain in strength to the Pacific. However reluctantly and belatedly, he was forced to admit that Australian bases, resources, and men were part of the answer to the question which he now asked himself: 'How, when, and where could we strike at Japan, and assume for Britain an honourable share in the final victory there?'

'For nearly three years, we had persisted in the strategy of "Germany First",' Churchill wrote in his war memoirs. 'The time had now come for the liberation of Asia, and I was determined that we should play a full and equal part in it. What I feared most at this stage of the war was that the United States would say in after years "We came to your help in Europe and you left us alone to finish off Japan".' Churchill was to find that, far from welcoming British aid, the Americans, from Roosevelt down, would put obstacles in his way. They not only saw British help as redundant; they recognised and resisted Churchill's motives. He confessed them himself in his war memoirs: 'We had to regain on the field of battle our rightful possessions in the Far East, and not have them handed back to us at the peace table.'

Churchill and Curtin's ideas now converged along remarkably traditional lines – the Empire and role of the Royal Navy. At his first press briefing after the London and Washington visits, Curtin scoffed at reports that Churchill would send 'a million men' to Australia to fight Japan after Germany's defeat. That was 'poppy-cock', he said. The big British presence in the Pacific would be naval and air power, although there would be some British infantry oper-ating from Australia. 'The British flag will fly.' In any case, he said, the advance in Normandy had slowed down. He held to his view that the defeat of Germany would be longer, and Japan's shorter, than expected. Churchill had thought this view 'too sanguine'. Churchill, he said, 'seemed to have a great tiredness about him'. He put this down to anxieties about the second front in Europe. 'Mr Churchill fires every shot and suffers every wound,' Curtin said.

Curtin was now as proprietorial as Churchill himself in his language about the British Empire. Where Churchill spoke of 'regaining our rightful possessions', Curtin used the words 'recover-ing our lost property'. In messages to Churchill in July and August, Curtin reminded him – not that he needed any reminder – of 'the importance to the British Commonwealth of "flying the Union Jack" in the Pacific'. On 12 August, Curtin cabled Churchill: 'I am deeply concerned at the position that would arise in our Far East Empire if any considerable American opinion were to hold that America fought a war on principle in the Far East and won it rela-tively unaided, while the other Allies, including ourselves, did very little towards recovering our lost property.'

Curtin had conferred with MacArthur as soon as he returned home, and had written to Churchill on 4 July: 'Without wishing to appear importunate, I would like to reiterate what I said in London about the time factor being the governing consideration in relation to the United Kingdom contribution.' He said that, because British land and air forces would not become available until the fighting in Europe was over, he had 'come to the conclusion that the best manner of ensuring the earliest and most effective association of British forces with those of the United States and Australia in the war against Japan would be to assign to the Commander-in-Chief, South-West Pacific Area [MacArthur] the naval forces becoming available this year'. This would be, he wrote, 'the most effective means of placing the Union Jack in the Pacific alongside the Australian and American flags' and would 'evoke great public enthusiasm in Australia and contribute greatly to the restoration of Empire prestige in the Far East'.

In his enthusiasm for a Royal Navy presence, Curtin echoed MacArthur, who was suspicious of any British attempt to dilute his command. MacArthur was opposed to the idea of a British–Australian army based in Australia, because it would weaken his control over Australian deployment. On the other hand, he was quite happy to have a British fleet in the Pacific, and even said that 'it would be a great thing that an American general should sail into Manila under the British flag'. MacArthur made this remark to the British High Commissioner, Sir Ronald Cross, who reported it to Churchill. Cross offered his own interpretation: 'The question that surrounds MacArthur is centred upon his absorption with the business of being a great man,' he told his Prime Minister, who was hardly a novice in that line of business. As to the questions which Curtin and Blamey were now raising about the proposed Empire force, Cross said: 'General Blamey tends to hang on to every vestige of authority'. This explained Blamey's attitude, because he wanted to command the task force himself. As to Curtin, Cross said, 'Mr Curtin is much influenced by General MacArthur and is inclined to support any Australian authority in upholding anything that may touch Australian nationhood. This triumvirate is hypersensitive on command questions, and tends to smell a rat where none exists.'

MacArthur welcomed British naval strength anywhere in the Pacific, as a counterweight to the US navy's Central Pacific strategy designed to finish the war the navy way. At the end of July, 1944, MacArthur had beaten off a challenge from Admiral King to take complete control of the Pacific war, scrap MacArthur's Philippines strategy, and place MacArthur's American forces under US navy command. By MacArthur's account, it was a close run thing. President Roosevelt himself had summoned MacArthur to meet him at Pearl Harbor. Before MacArthur arrived from Australia, on 26 July, Admiral Nimitz put King's plan to bypass the Philippines, and thrust into the Western Pacific to Formosa (Taiwan), which would then become the main American base from which to bomb and invade Japan. MacArthur, not surprisingly, was 'in total disagreement'. Securing the Philippines would 'enable us to clamp an air and naval blockade from the south of Japan, paralysing her industries and forcing her to an early capitulation'. The navy plan, he argued, would mean 'heavy losses in a frontal assault on strongly held islands like Iwo Jima and Okinawa'. These, he said, 'were not essential to the enemy's defeat' and 'could be isolated and neutralised with negligible loss'. Even more strongly, MacArthur urged his personal view of America's moral obligations. 'To sacrifice the Philippines a second time could not be condoned or forgiven,' he told Roosevelt.

Unlike Churchill, the obsessive interventionist, Roosevelt preferred the role of umpire of grand strategy. He made the rules and knew how he wanted the game to end. At Pearl Harbor in July, 1944, he was dealing with a clash of personal rivalries as much as a clash of strategies. Admiral King, in General MacArthur's judgement, 'claimed the Pacific as the rightful domain of the Navy; he seemed to regard the operations there as almost his own private war; he felt that the only way to remove the blot on the Navy disaster at Pearl Harbor was to have the Navy command a great victory over Japan'. General MacArthur also took the war as personal; his entire strategy, including his use of Australian forces as long as he needed them, and his sidelining of them when they became redundant to his goals, expressed his pledge: 'I shall return.'

Although Roosevelt had been delighted to hear from Curtin on his return to Washington after London in June that 'General MacArthur has told me a dozen times that he has no more idea of running against you for the Presidency than I have', there was no way he was going to give the Republicans an election slogan by abandoning the Philippines for a second time. Nor was he going to upset admirals King, Nimitz, and Halsey and the whole US navy by interfering in their plan for victory. So Roosevelt did exactly what he had come to Pearl Harbor intending to do. He gave King and MacArthur his blessing and support, with the promise of massive resources for both their strategies, on a scale inconceivable two years previously. With two nods of his massive head, he settled American strategy in the Pacific in a day, in a way Churchill had been unable to achieve by warring with his Chiefs in a year. The overwhelming difference between them was, of course, that Roosevelt was commander-in-chief of the greatest military power in the world and Churchill, a mere Prime Minister, had to make do with whatever he had.

When they were done, MacArthur asked Roosevelt: 'What chance do you think Dewey has?' Thomas Dewey, a New York lawyer, was the Republican candidate in the Presidential election due in November. 'I don't know,' Roosevelt replied. 'I've been too busy to think about politics.' They both burst out laughing. Roosevelt then added earnestly: 'If the war with Germany ends before the election, I will not be re-elected.' The shadow of death was already upon Roosevelt. MacArthur noted that 'he was a shell of his former self'. But Roosevelt's comment eerily foreshadowed Churchill's electoral fate, a year on, exactly to the day.

Churchill now crossed the Atlantic once more for a second conference at Quebec. For eighteen months from May 1940, Churchill had been the 'ardent suitor' wooing Roosevelt to bring the United States into the war against Germany. Now, as his Big Idea was reaching its terrific climax in Europe, he found he had to woo Roosevelt to be allowed to send to the Pacific the British fleet that had been promised and denied for so long. 'I asked for a definite undertaking about employing the British Fleet in the main operations against Japan,' he wrote. 'I should like,' said the President, 'to see the British Fleet wherever and whenever possible.' Admiral King said the 'question was being actively studied' – and promptly set about undermining Roosevelt's airy assurances to 'those blasted Limeys', as King habitually referred to Churchill and the British. Actually, King was being at his most polite with Churchill. His own daughter once said that King was the most even-tempered man she ever knew – 'he was always angry with everybody'.

'This conference has been a blaze of friendship and unity,' Churchill cabled Curtin. 'The only difficulty here,' he said, 'has been to persuade the Americans to give us the space and facilities to deploy in the Pacific. Some of them wanted to keep it all to themselves.' Nevertheless, he said, he was 'greatly relieved at the reception all our ideas have met'. Brooke, too, was relieved; Churchill was 'gradually coming round to sane strategy, now accepts a naval contingent to the Pacific, a Dominion Task Force under MacArthur etc. etc.' It was to be the last time Roosevelt and Churchill met as the 'Big Two' to discuss Pacific strategy. They would next meet briefly at Malta on the way to Yalta, the most controversial of the wartime summits.

Curtin was also relieved. After receiving Churchill's 'complete account', he told a press briefing: 'The decisions of the Conference brought down to a definite shape Allied participation in the defeat of Japan.' Fred Smith recorded that Curtin said: 'A target date had been set for the defeat of Japan.' He had refused to say what the date was but 'said jokingly that it ought to be a month before the next election'. Curtin had then added seriously: 'It could easily be that too.' (The next federal election was due in mid-1946.) Curtin ended his briefing by saying: 'I go home tonight more relieved than I have been since the war commenced.'

The two conferences – Roosevelt with MacArthur at Pearl Harbor, and Roosevelt with Churchill, for the second time at Quebec – laid out Allied strategy in the Pacific for the rest of the war. Churchill's persistence paid off. He broadly achieved his political aims: in the Pacific Ocean, showing the Union Jack alongside the Stars and Stripes, and an Indian Ocean strategy that ultimately saw the Union Jack flying again over Rangoon, Kuala Lumpur, and Singapore. He had always set his face against being 'bogged down in the jungles of North Burma', despite Roosevelt's pressure. As he had wanted all along, the British campaign from India into Burma went southwards towards the Irrawaddy and Rangoon, not north to China. Mountbatten's combined operations from the Bay of Bengal led at least to the appearance of British 'recovery of the lost possessions' of Malaya and Singapore. The Royal Navy reappeared in fighting strength in the Pacific, although the idea of a joint British–Australian force, which he never much liked in any case, never materialised. Yet to achieve his aims, Churchill had been obliged to face the fact that he was now very much the junior partner in the Grand Alliance.

If it all fell far short of Churchill's post-Alamein war cry that he would 'fling all we have against Japan', it was more than the Americans wanted, and as much as Britain could spare from the main show in Europe. Even there, Churchill was finding it hard to adjust to the role of junior partner in the Alliance he had created. In fact, he never would accept it; the next ten years of his political life, in Opposition and in his second prime ministership, would be a defiant assertion of Britain's equal status as a world power, with or without its Empire.

Curtin and Australia were also making adjustments appropriate to a junior partner. Churchill and Roosevelt had accepted Australia's need to reorder its over-stretched manpower resources. The new plan envisaged a release of twenty thousand troops for other war work, and a reduction of the army from ten to six divisions, two to be allocated to MacArthur for the liberation of the Philippines, and three for the final assault on Japan. Curtin and Blamey now recognised that the role of the Australian army would increasingly be taken over by the Americans. As the Australian military historian Jeffrey Grey puts it: 'The problem for Australia in the last eighteen months of the Pacific War was not only that MacArthur's ego would not permit him to share the glory of the final defeat with others – and this included the US navy as well as the British, Australians and Dutch – but that the enormous military might which had been mobilised by the United States made the contribution of small allies largely superfluous.'

THE WORLDWIDE REACH of the responsibilities that Churchill took upon himself may be illustrated by just one day in his life: 20 October 1944. He was in Cairo again, after a week in Moscow with Stalin. Between the two of them, they had carved out the spheres of influence that the Soviet and British would exercise in Eastern Europe and the Balkans; 50–50 in Romania, 5–2 in Yugoslavia, and 1–9 in Greece. Churchill had written the figures on a piece of paper which he called 'the naughty document'. Stalin ticked it with a blue pencil. Churchill suggested they burn it. 'No, you keep it,' Stalin replied. The Realpolitik of Moscow set the tone for Yalta in February. Now in Cairo, Churchill had summoned Mountbatten from India to discuss British strategy in the war against Japan. Brooke recorded: 'Conference went well and we got PM to agree to Dickie's plan connected with freeing Arakan [Burma] of Japs.' At another conference with Lord Moyne, Casey's successor as Minister in Cairo, the discussion was about the 'undesirability' of letting France back into Syria, which the 7th Australian Division had taken from the Vichy French in 1940. Churchill found time to prepare his Moscow reports for Roosevelt and the House of Commons. 'Towards the end of dinner', Brooke recorded, 'PM was in great form and produced several gems'. He was a month short of his seventieth birthday.

Late that night, Churchill composed a signal to General MacArthur: 'Hearty congratulations on your brilliant stroke in the Philippines.' Half a world away, on the same day, 20 October, MacArthur waded ashore, in a carefully choreographed and photographed landing, near Tacloban, chief town of Leyte, one of the largest islands of the Philippine archipelago, between Mindanao and Luzon. He commanded an invasion force of 120,000 Americans, under General Walter Kreuger, escorted by the US Seventh Fleet under Vice-Admiral Thomas Kincaid. From a mobile broadcasting unit set up near the beach, MacArthur announced: 'People of the Philippines – I have returned.'

The Japanese High Command had ordered their army to fight to the death of the last man. But they staked their main hopes on a huge and decisive sea battle which, by attacking the US escort fleet, would draw in the US Third Fleet under Admiral William Halsey. The result, known as the Battle of Leyte Gulf, was the largest naval engagement in history, although it was, as Churchill was to write, 'at the time almost unknown to the harassed European world'. It lasted for five days from 22 October 1944, and was notorious for the first appearance of the kamikaze, the 'divine wind', the pilots of bomb-laden aircraft diving on ships to commit suicide in the service of the Emperor. The Australian cruiser, HMAS *Australia*, attached to Admiral Kincaid's escort, was damaged and its captain killed in one kamikaze attack. After Leyte, as Churchill wrote, 'the suicide bomber was the only effective naval weapon left to the foe, an instrument of despair with no hope of victory'. The RAN force commanded by Commodore John Collins was the only Australian component in MacArthur's Leyte operation. Churchill made the most of their representative presence on behalf of the British Empire in his telegram of congratulations to Roosevelt: 'We are very glad to know that one of His Majesty's Australian cruiser squadrons had the honour of sharing in this memorable event.'

As late as September, Curtin and Blamey had believed that MacArthur intended to use the Australian army in the liberation of the Philippines. Curtin had told the Advisory War Council on 7 September that 'we would have two divisions in the Philippines operations, and this would ensure the Australian flag going forward with the United States'. Blamey told the Council the same on 27 September. But by 30 September, MacArthur was telling Curtin a different story. After explaining his invasion plans, MacArthur said that the role of the Australian divisions would be 'to capture British Borneo and Java'. His objective, MacArthur said, was 'gradually to withdraw all American forces north from Australia' with the Australians taking over. Curtin made no comment. Although it must have been obvious that MacArthur intended to cut the Australians out of the main action, Curtin failed to raise any query about the participation of Australian ground or air forces in the operation which had been the great goal of their partnership since April 1942 – MacArthur's return to the Philippines. This conference was the last time Curtin and MacArthur ever met.

Australian military historians largely agree that Curtin's silence or acquiescence on 30 September led to the relegation of Australian forces to roles which, although costly and successful in themselves, were redundant in terms of the final defeat of Japan. 'It is difficult to know,' writes David Horner, 'whether Curtin was blinded by his loyalty to MacArthur, or whether in his heart, he was happy for Australian lives to be spared.' Horner, however, makes a crucial point about the choices open to a nation in Australia's position. In *High Command, Australia and Allied Strategy 1939–45*, he writes:

> Whatever Curtin's private views, the non-use of Australians in the Philippines was another example of the fact that in an alliance between unequal allies, the lesser ally can say where her forces may not fight; but, especially when the greater ally has the ships and planes, the lesser ally has little capacity to direct where her forces might be employed. Curtin showed a keen awareness of this reality in international relations.

Curtin had confronted this reality in his battles with Churchill. Now, with the determination of the United States that the rest of the Pacific War would be emphatically an American show, Churchill himself, as much as Curtin, had to live with the reality of being a 'lesser ally'.

'THE EAGLE SHOULD permit the small birds to sing', Churchill told Roosevelt and Stalin at Yalta in February, 1945, 'and care not wherefore they sang'. They enjoyed his poetic flight of fancy all the more because it neatly expressed their ideas for the post-war world. The other nations could have their say in the United Nations Organization, due to be launched in San Francisco in April, 1945; but the Big Three would continue to make the real decisions. Bruce had made his usual protest at Churchill's failure to consult Australia before the Yalta meeting. 'It is clearly intolerable that we should be faced with a series of *faits accomplis*,' he cabled to Curtin, fittingly on Australia Day, 1945, 'but this would appear to be what is again going to happen.' A telegram to Churchill 'reminding him of Australia's vital concerns in the questions to be discussed would be most valuable,' Bruce told Curtin. The Prime Minister replied that there was little point in repeating views already expressed, 'the more so when repetition might cause misunderstandings with Churchill'.

Beating Hitler was taking longer than had been expected after the Liberation of Paris in August 1944. The Führer, whose survival of an assassination attempt in July 1944 only fuelled his lust for vengeance, sustained himself with fantasies that the United States and the Soviet Union would turn on each other. At the Big Three Conference at Yalta, on the Crimean Peninsula on the Black Sea, Roosevelt exerted all his fading energies to placate Stalin, even if it meant sometimes siding against Churchill and making little jokes at his expense. Basically, Yalta ratified what the Red Army had won, effectively placing Eastern Europe, from the Baltic to the Balkans, under Soviet domination and, by 1947, under communist rule. 'Nations, comrades in arms, have in the past drifted apart within five or ten years of war,' Churchill warned. 'We now have a chance of avoiding the errors of previous generations and of making a sure peace.'

Churchill and Roosevelt pressed on Stalin the need for an effective world organisation. Roosevelt, whose frail appearance was a shock to everybody and a grief to Churchill, was determined to make this his crowning legacy, and to achieve what his hero, Woodrow Wilson, had been unable to do when his country had rejected the League of Nations. Stalin was sceptical but prepared to go along. One of his objections was about the equal representation of nations in the proposed general assembly. All these little nations – about forty had now declared war on Germany and Japan – would have the same voting power as the Soviet Union and the United States – the power of one each. At first Stalin demanded sixteen votes, one for each Soviet republic, but then agreed to four – Russia, the Ukraine, White Russia (Belarus), and Lithuania. Churchill saw Stalin's point. 'It is not too much to ask,' he cabled Attlee. After all, he said, Britain itself was asking 'a great deal' in having Canada, Australia, South Africa, and New Zealand as members of the proposed assembly. 'We will be in a strong position, in my judgement, because we shall then not be the only multiple-voter in the field.' Churchill's assumption, of course, was that all the dominions would always vote with Britain. Those little birds, at least, were expected to sing in harmony.

Yalta produced another zoological metaphor from Churchill. Back in London at a luncheon for Beneš, the President-in-exile of Czechoslovakia, he said: 'A small lion is walking between a huge Russian bear and a great American elephant, but perhaps it may prove to be the lion who knows the way.' Czechoslovakia, like Poland, would turn out to be a casualty of the arrangements made with the Bear at Yalta. For the moment, however, the Lion and the Elephant had other priorities. 'A speedy termination of the Japanese war,' Churchill had written to his Foreign Secretary Anthony Eden on the eve of Yalta, 'such as might be procured by the mere fact of a Russian declaration against Japan, would undoubtedly save us many thousands of millions of pounds.' Stalin repeated – and was to keep precisely to the day – his promise that he would declare war against Japan three months after Germany's defeat.

After Yalta, Churchill had taken himself by sea to Sebastopol to inspect battle sites – not where the Soviet army had recently sacrificed a million men and women fighting the Germans, but of the Crimean War, in which Britain and France fought Russia. He was particularly keen to see Balaklava, where the six hundred rode through the 'Valley of Death' in the Charge of the Light Brigade in 1854. It must have seemed self-indulgent and insensitive to his Russian hosts. Yet this was the same Churchill who said to his daughter Sarah, who had accompanied him to Yalta and whom he had no need to impress with statements contrived for posterity: 'I do not suppose that at any moment in history has the agony of the world been so great or widespread. Tonight the sun goes down on more suffering than ever before in the World.'

Churchill's benevolent view of the singing of the small birds may explain his apparent indifference towards Evatt's efforts on behalf of small nations like Australia, when the United Nations Organization was launched at San Francisco on 25 April 1945. Evatt took his stand on the principle of the equality of nations. Over the next two months he waged an epic battle with the representatives of the Big Three on the 'veto' question – the great powers' right to overrule any resolution of the proposed Security Council. Evatt deeply believed and strongly argued that the veto would be used to paralyse the United Nations Organization, whenever there was a conflict of interest among the Big Three. The British delegation, led by Lord Halifax, proved to be Evatt's strongest opponent and detractor. Evatt failed, but on a range of matters, especially in making colonial trusteeships answerable to the UNO, he secured valuable amendments to the UN Charter. As usual, his style and methods aroused antagonism. Sir Frederic Eggleston, now Australian Minister in Washington and a member of the delegation at San Francisco, wrote that Evatt had performed 'a great intellectual *tour de force*' and 'played a very constructive part, and conducted a very fine campaign'. But then came the reservation: 'As you know, Evatt is not very tactful, his manners are none of the best, he can be exceedingly rude and he did not restrain himself', Eggleston told Bruce after it was all over in June. 'We had right on our side and must not be penalised because Evatt got a bad name.' Nevertheless, the campaign for a more independent Australian foreign policy which Evatt began on Anzac Day, 1945, was as much a milestone on the road to Australian nationhood as Anzac Day, 1915.

Roosevelt did not live to see his grand design taking shape at San Francisco. He died suddenly at his retreat in Warm Springs, Georgia, of a brain haemorrhage on 12 April 1945. 'I have a terrific headache', were his last words. 'What an enviable death was his,' Churchill said in his tribute in the House of Commons. 'He died in harness and we may well say in battle harness.' In Berlin, Goebbels greeted Hitler: 'My Führer, the Tsarina is dead.' Hitler knew exactly what he meant: the death of the Empress Elisabeth of Russia had broken the coalition against Prussia in 1762, and had saved Frederick the Great from what had seemed certain defeat. But on 30 April, Goebbels sent his last piece of propaganda to German Radio: 'The Führer is dead, fighting with his last breath against Bolshevism.' When he heard of it, Churchill commented: 'I must say I think he was perfectly right to die like that.' Churchill's magnanimity was misplaced. Hitler had shot himself amid the squalor of the Berlin bunker as the Red Army closed in, raging to the last not only against the Jews, but against the German people who had proved themselves unworthy of him.

'In all our long history,' Churchill told the vast crowd milling along Whitehall on 8 May 1945, 'we have never seen a greater day than this one. This is your victory.' The crowd roared back: 'No – it's yours'. In the many speeches Churchill made that day, even to the rapturous Londoners who, as late as March, had been on the receiving end of Hitler's secret weapons – flying bombs and pilotless rockets – he emphasised that the war was still going on: 'I rejoice we can all take a night off today and another day tomorrow, but there is another foe who occupies large portions of the British Empire, a foe stained with cruelty and greed.' Churchill sent a cable to Curtin:

> Today, we celebrate the final defeat of the first of our two chief enemies. On this occasion on behalf of the Government and people of the United Kingdom, I convey to our brothers in Australia our cordial congratulations on their part in this great achievement.
>
> The people of these Islands now, after five years and eight months relieved from imminent danger, remember with gratitude the steadfast support which throughout their ordeal has come from Australia and are resolved to persevere to the end in all measures needed to destroy our second enemy. We do not forget the contributions which the armed forces of Australia have made nor the immense exertions with which, despite the close approach of the war to their shores, the people of Australia have continued to produce the supplies of munitions and food necessary to maintain our joint effort.
>
> We can look forward with confidence to the day not far distant when once again we can turn all our energies to the arts of peace and to the building of a new prosperity founded on freedom and security.

This was the last message from Churchill which Curtin was ever to read. He had never fully recovered from a heart attack in November, 1944. He had spent two months in a Melbourne hospital, returning to Canberra for the installation of the Duke of Gloucester as Governor-General in January. His last major speech to Parliament was on 28 February. Faced by a now reviving and critical Opposition, he defended his record against Menzies' charge that Australia had turned away from Britain:

> I say to the country that no decision reached by the Australian Government was incompatible with the decisions reached by the President of the United States and the Prime Minister of Great Britain. This country has never been sufficiently strong or sufficiently sure of itself to be able to defend itself with its own strength. We have had to depend upon not only the strength of Great Britain, but also the strength of the United States of America ... An assignment of Australian forces to General Douglas MacArthur was made by this Government, because, in order to ensure the minimum strength that General MacArthur needed to carry out the directive given to him by five governments, including the Government of Great Britain as well as the Government of Australia, it was necessary that the Australian land forces as a whole should be assigned to him. Otherwise, he would not have been able in 1942, and in the greater part of 1943, to carry out the directive given to him.

In a passage somewhat reminiscent of Churchill's line about the impossibility of being strong everywhere, Curtin said: 'This is a collective war, a global war in which you cannot dispose strength in one place unless you take it from somewhere else.' Aware of press criticisms that his ill health was impairing his capacity to lead, Curtin concluded: 'I am responsible to the Parliament. The Parliament can dismiss me if I fail to do the right thing. Until it does so, I propose to carry out the functions of government as I see them.'

In fact, Curtin was, characteristically, willing enough to leave office. 'Why shouldn't a Prime Minister be outed,' he asked a close friend in April. 'I'm not fit and I should be outed.' But Chifley, who assumed the full burden of leadership in the absence of Forde and Evatt in San Francisco, had persuaded Curtin to stay on, hoping that he would recover sufficiently to see the Pacific war through. Curtin was in hospital again when he received Churchill's VE Day message. On 22 May, he went home to the Lodge, never to return to active duty. Shortly after midnight on 5 July 1945, he told Elsie Curtin, 'I'm ready now', and died peacefully just before dawn.

On the day Curtin died, MacArthur announced that the liberation of the Philippines was complete. In 1943, just before Curtin's election victory, MacArthur had said: 'When I stand at the gates of Manila, I want the President of the Commonwealth of the Philippines at my right hand, and the Prime Minister of the Commonwealth of Australia at my left.' According to MacArthur, Curtin had replied: 'I can't pledge that the Prime Minister of Australia will be there. That depends on the people of Australia. But I can pledge that John Curtin will be there.' As Curtin died, men of the Australian 9th Division were making more landings in Borneo, in operations that might not have been undertaken had MacArthur made good his own assurances to Curtin about Australia's role in the liberation of the Philippines.

Almost at the hour of Curtin's death, Churchill had despatched his last cable addressed to Prime Minister Curtin. Appropriately, the message contained Churchill's proposal for a British Commonwealth Force to take part in the invasion of Japan. 'I am sure you will agree with me,' Churchill wrote, 'that a joint Commonwealth Force of British, Australian, New Zealand, British-Indian and possibly Canadian divisions would form a striking demonstration of Commonwealth solidarity'. It was important, Churchill said, 'that we should share with the Americans the burden of the assault on Japan'.

This was also to be Churchill's second-last message to Australia as wartime Prime Minister. As soon as the war in Europe ended, Churchill had asked Attlee and the Labour Party to continue the coalition until the end of the war in the Pacific. Instead, Attlee offered to continue only until October, 1945. Churchill rejected this idea. He was under pressure from the Conservative Party to cash in on the victory and hold another khaki election. He himself became increasingly attracted to the notion, and the Labour Party was also having second thoughts. Attlee, after consulting with his colleagues, telephoned Churchill to say: 'We do not believe that it would be possible to lay aside political controversy now that the expectation of an election has engaged the attention of the country.' On 23 May, the King commissioned Churchill to form a Conservative Government.

Polling day was set for 5 July; but to allow the votes of servicemen overseas, from Berlin to Burma, to be counted, the result would not be announced until three weeks later, 26 July. At the last meeting of the old Cabinet on 28 May, Churchill, 'with tears visibly running down his cheeks', saluted his wartime comrades: 'The light will shine on every helmet.'

This remarkable demonstration of British parliamentary democracy enabled Churchill to attend the last of the Big Three conferences – at Potsdam, near Berlin – as Prime Minister, taking Attlee with him as Leader of the Opposition. They both returned to London for the declaration of the polls on 26 July. Churchill went to bed, he wrote, 'confident in the belief that the British people would wish me to continue my work'. But just before dawn, he wrote in his memoirs: 'I woke suddenly with a sharp stab of almost physical pain. A hitherto subconscious conviction that we were beaten broke forth and dominated my mind . . . the power to shape the future would be denied me . . . I was discontented at the prospect, and turned over at once to sleep again.' It was a landslide for Labour, with 393 seats to 213 for Churchill's Conservatives. At breakfast next morning, Clementine comforted him: 'It may well be a blessing in disguise.' He replied: 'At the moment, it seems quite effectively disguised.' As almost his last official act as Prime Minister of Britain, Churchill sent a cable to Australia, in the afternoon of 26 July, informing Ben Chifley, now Prime Minister of Australia, that the American and British Chiefs of Staff had agreed that a British Commonwealth Force should take part in the final assault against Japan.

These plans were overtaken by events at and after Potsdam. Harry Truman, who had made the transition from Vice-President to President of the United States with a combination of humility and breezy self-confidence, had revealed to Stalin that testing 'in the desert of New Mexico had proved the power of a new type of bomb'. Stalin's calm reaction suggested to Truman and Churchill that Stalin 'had no idea of the significance of what he was being told'. This exchange took place on Churchill's last night in Potsdam. On the day the British election results were declared, the Big Three issued the Potsdam Declaration, calling for Japan's unconditional surrender. However, Truman had taken Churchill's advice to give the peace party in Tokyo, which they hoped by now might include the Japanese Emperor himself, some grounds for believing that unconditional surrender did not mean the destruction of the Japanese nation or even its monarchy. So the Potsdam Declaration spoke of 'the return of Japanese military forces to their homes after being completely disarmed', and the withdrawal of the occupying forces from Japan 'as soon as there has been established in accordance with the freely expressed will of the Japanese people, a peacefully inclined and responsible government'. Without, of course, referring to the atomic bomb, the Potsdam Declaration said: 'The alternative for Japan is prompt and utter destruction.'

Despite the warning, 'We shall brook no delay', Japan's Imperial Government temporised, still hoping against deluded hope that the Soviet Union would mediate an armistice. Tojo had been ousted in July, 1944, but his successor as Prime Minister, Kantaro Suzuki, dismissed the Potsdam Declaration as 'a rehash' of previous calls for surrender. One minister is reported to have said: 'Churchill has fallen. America is beginning to be isolated. This Government will ignore it. There is no need to rush.'

In making his decision to use the atomic bomb, Truman was heavily influenced by his military advisers, who estimated an American casualty rate of one million men in an invasion which would be contested to the bitter end by a Japanese army of five million. And not only by the army. Tens of thousands of civilians had been involved in the fight-to-the-death defence of the Japanese island of Okinawa, which had lasted from April to June. Furthermore, American power to destroy with conventional bombs every city in Japan and millions of its people, was limited only by the time it would take. 'The historic fact remains,' Churchill wrote in his war memoirs, 'that the decision whether or not to use the atomic bomb to compel the surrender of Japan was never even an issue. There was unanimous, automatic, unquestioned agreement around our table; nor did I even hear the slightest suggestion that we should do otherwise.'

At 8.00 a.m. on 6 August, a lone American B-29 bomber dropped a single bomb on the city of Hiroshima, killing eighty thousand people in the blast, and leaving another 100,000 to die from wounds and radiation over the next five years. The tail-gunner on the *Enola Gay* cried: 'My God, what have we done?' On 8 August, the Soviet Union declared war on Japan. On 9 August, the second, and last available, atomic bomb was dropped on Nagasaki. At midnight, Hirohito called the Imperial Council together to ask his military chiefs whether they were ready yet to order a surrender. He had decided that Japan could not continue the war and gave his decision to an evenly divided Council, on the understanding that the Potsdam Declaration 'did not prejudice the prerogative of the Supreme Ruler'. Truman, the failed haberdasher but wily senator from Independence, Missouri, realised that he would be able to interpret this as he wished, making only the proviso that the Emperor would be 'subordinate to the Supreme Allied Commander'. In his turn, Hirohito accepted this as a guarantee of the survival of his Throne. In one of the great understatements of history, he broadcast to his people on 15 August that 'the war has proceeded not necessarily to the advantage of Japan'. He called upon them 'to think the unthinkable and bear the unbearable'. He spoke in archaic and stilted language hardly intelligible to his subjects, who were hearing their Emperor's voice for the first time; but they understood enough to know what he meant. On 2 September, on board USS *Missouri* in Tokyo Bay, General MacArthur received the instrument of surrender, in the presence of General Wainwright, who had surrendered at Corregidor, and General Percival, who had surrendered at Singapore in 1942. Blamey signed for Australia. MacArthur ended a brief speech by saying: 'These proceedings are closed.'

32

'In command of history'
1945–1965

Churchill did not waste time resting on the laurels of victory or repining over his electoral defeat. He now mobilised history – or his version of it – for new battles, not only to vindicate himself but to reverse the British people's verdict. Nor was being 'in command of history' limited to the past; his war memoirs, his role as Leader of the British Opposition – or Prime Minister-in-waiting – and his unique status as world leader were all directed towards developing a grand new theme: that British prestige and influence with the United States should be used to keep the Big Three talking instead of fighting. As he was to put it, inelegantly but succinctly, 'Jaw-jaw is better than war-war.' His variations on this theme would lead to charges of warmongering, racism and imperialism. Sometimes the striking Churchillian phrase – 'Iron Curtain' for example – got in the way of his real message, giving a new twist to Menzies' observation in 1941: 'His tyrant is the glittering phrase.' But the theme of a new summit meeting for a settlement with the Soviet Union was to give a purpose and consistency to the last ten years of his active political career. Without it, those years might seem merely the chronicle of an old man in a hurry to get back to 10 Downing Street and in no hurry to leave it. Unfortunately, his zestful and often spiteful partisanship dented his credibility as the champion of peace in our time. Otherwise, we might now be able to see more clearly how much Churchill contributed to the single most important fact of the second half of the twentiety century: that the Cold War did not become the Third World War, inevitably a nuclear war.

This other Churchill – the advocate of summit meetings, 'settlements', and 'understandings' with the Soviet Union – never made much of a mark in Australia, partly because of the exigencies of its domestic politics which he had so often disparaged. Menzies appointed himself as custodian of the Churchill legend as soon as the war was over. When the House of Representatives celebrated the Pacific victory on 29 August 1945, he reminded Chifley that, while the House had paid special tribute to the dead Roosevelt and Curtin, it had not yet done so for Churchill, very much alive. Menzies conceded that Churchill had taken on a new persona: 'Recent political events in Great Britain may have tended to obscure our view of Winston Churchill, the great war leader,' Menzies said. 'But the truth is that, were we to select one man in the world as the chief architect of victory, we would select Churchill.' Rowley James, the rough-diamond coalminer from Newcastle, interjected: 'The right honourable gentleman is now introducing party politics.' Menzies: 'There is nothing of party politics about my remarks. They far transcend such considerations.' Menzies said he was addressing himself to the 'real depths of every human mind and imagination in this matter'. He concluded:

> If ever in human history one man, by undaunted courage, matchless moral force, and unsurpassed eloquence, altered the whole course of history, it was Churchill. I believe that he has, and will continue to have, the love and gratitude of every good Australian now living in this country, or to live in it in centuries to come.

Fadden, never one to bear grudges, leapt to his feet to demand a debate on a motion for 'a proud, grateful and perpetual record of admiration for the outstanding leadership, inspired courage and dogged tenacity by which the Right Honourable Winston Spencer Churchill brought the peoples of the British Commonwealth of Nations out of the abyss of 1940, through the perils and tribulations of 1941 and 1942, to the victories of 1943 and 1944 and the complete and glorious European triumph of 1945'. Chifley's honesty or dislike of humbug led him into a political mis-step. It would have been simple and easy to have allowed the debate and let everyone deliver themselves of their praise or their platitudes. But he had been the man closest to Curtin throughout the war, particularly during the ordeals of February and March 1942. He knew that the rows with Churchill had taken an immense toll on Curtin and believed, rightly or wrongly, that they had hastened his death. For his part, he told Menzies and Fadden: 'At this moment, my thoughts turn to another great man who gave everything he had, Australia's own leader, the late John Curtin.' By refusing a debate which would have disappeared into the unread pages of Hansard, Chifley invited, and almost ensured, that the Churchill name and fame would become weapons in the partisan contest. But it is in the nature of parliamentary proceedings that a row becomes the story, just as these days the cover-up becomes more damaging than the crime. Fadden revived his motion from time to time until Chifley lost office in December, 1949, evoking the same refusal and the same reproach.

Chifley was similarly maladroit in handling the long-running issue of an invitation to Churchill to visit Australia. Menzies raised the question several times between 1946 and 1949. Sometimes he said he was passing on requests from the Returned Servicemen's League or unnamed 'sporting bodies'. At first, Chifley contented himself by referring to the standing invitation first issued by Curtin in London in 1944. When, however, he invited Prime Minister Attlee to Australia in 1947, he wrote a separate invitation to Churchill, assuring him of a warm welcome. But the public was left with the impression that there was some deep personal resentment or political reluctance on the part of Chifley and the Labor Government to have Churchill in Australia.

The fact is that Churchill never intended or wanted to visit Australia. His invariable response was 'I'd love to go', but perfectly valid reasons of time, pressure of work, political and international crises, his health and his age always intervened. It was sometimes suggested, before the war, that he was uncertain of his reception because of Gallipoli; and, in the first years after the war, that he would not venture to Australia as long as Labor was in government. But when Menzies became Prime Minister for the second time in December 1949, he was no more successful with his invitations than Curtin or Chifley; and when Churchill became Prime Minister for the second time in October 1951, all his reasons for not coming applied with growing force. The plain fact is that there was never a dividend or advantage to Churchill in making a visit to the Antipodes, the longest voyage by sea or air in the world, sufficient to overcome his ancient ambivalence towards Australia.

We may assume, however, that no such calculations entered Churchill's head when serious illness forced King George VI to cancel a tour of Australia and New Zealand in 1949. 'They would have killed you by kindness,' he wrote to the King on 22 November 1948. 'The distances are enormous and everywhere there would have been delighted and loyal crowds.' He added: 'I ever hope in spite of my age to stand at Your Majesty's side once again.' To the King's private secretary, Sir Alan Lascelles, Churchill wrote: 'I always dreaded this Australian visit.' He added: 'Few human beings could undergo such an ordeal without an immense loss of vitality.'

Churchill's defeat – or rather the coming of a British Labour Government – had confirmed Britain in its pre-war place at the heart of Australia's political, economic, cultural, and even defence thinking. The Australian Labor Party held a celebration in Sydney Town Hall. The Australian conservatives grumbled about the ingratitude of the British people. But the identification with Britain, and with the people of Britain in their post-war hardships, was bipartisan, deepened by the memory of the Finest Hours.

Chifley's speeches between 1946, the year of the re-election of the Labor Government, and 1949, the year of its defeat, are notable for their consistent emphasis on support for Britain and the British Commonwealth. 'I know that I can speak for my fellow-Prime Ministers when I say that the Dominions are standing shoulder to shoulder with Britain,' Chifley, in London for the first post-war Imperial Conference, said on the BBC in May, 1946. 'In Australia, we are following a policy that will ensure our being able to give every possible assistance to Britain.' He described Australia as 'the strongest bastion for the English-speaking race south of the Equator'. He would return home, he said, 'greatly confirmed in my belief of the future greatness of the British people'. Speaking at the New South Wales Labor Party Conference in June, soon after his return, Chifley told the delegates at Sydney Town Hall: 'I believe that only by close co-operation with the people of Great Britain and the people of America – indeed, with the English-speaking peoples of the world – can we keep world peace in the future.'

'You know the almost intolerable burden which rests on Britain today', he told the Labor Conference. 'She cannot meet the same expenditure for the defence of the British Commonwealth as previously. Therefore, the Australian people have to face up to doing more than they did in the pre-war years.' At the same conference a year later, Chifley said: 'The economic problems which beset Britain today have left her in a position in which she must look to the Dominions to play a great part in maintaining stability and security.'

Only four months before, Churchill had made the idea of cooperation between the English-speaking peoples the theme of his most famous post-war speech. This was to become known as the 'Iron Curtain' speech, delivered on 5 March 1946 at Westminster College, Fulton, Missouri, in Truman's home state, at Truman's invitation and in Truman's presence. Because of its timing and the reaction to it, notably from Stalin, Churchill has been praised for, or accused of, firing the opening shot in the Cold War. But the Fulton speech actually first expressed Churchill's post-war theme, that a third world war could only be averted by talking. 'This can only be achieved,' Churchill said, 'by reaching now, in 1946, a good understanding on all points with Russia under the general authority of the United Nations Organization; and by the maintenance of that good understanding through many peaceful years, by the world instrument, supported by the whole strength of the English-speaking world and all its connections.'

Churchill's purpose at Fulton was to stake Britain's claim at the summit of world affairs. That was where Australia and the other dominions came into Churchill's scenario. 'Let no man under-rate the abiding power of the British Empire and Commonwealth,' he told his American audience, in a national radio broadcast. 'Do not suppose that we shall not come through these dark days of privation, as we have come through the glorious years of agony; or that, half a century from now, you will not see 70 or 80 millions of Britons spread about the world, and united in defence of our traditions, our way of life, and of the world causes which you and we espouse.'

Churchill asserted the need for an 'overall strategic concept' in order to 'guard the homes of the common people from the horrors and miseries of another war'. The first element was the United Nations Organization, making sure that 'it is a reality and not a sham, a force for action and not merely a frothing of words, not merely a cockpit in a Tower of Babel'. He proposed that, as a first step, the United Nations should create an international air force, provided by each member state and directed by the UNO. He hastened to add that the United States and Britain should not entrust the atom bomb to the UN 'while it is still in its infancy'. Possession of the bomb 'in largely American hands' gave the world 'a breathing space to set our house in order'. If the dangers of war and tyranny were averted, Churchill said, science and international cooperation could bring the world, in the next four decades, to a level of well-being beyond anything that had yet occurred in human experience. But a 'shadow had fallen upon the scenes so lately lighted' by the Allied victory.

Churchill did not invent the phrase 'Iron Curtain', nor was Fulton the first time he had used it. But he made it his own by his vivid imagery: 'From Stettin in the Baltic to Trieste in the Adriatic, an iron curtain has descended across the Continent. Behind that line lie all the capitals of the ancient states of Central and Eastern Europe.' Churchill expressed his admiration for 'the valiant Russian people and for my wartime comrade, Marshal Stalin'. 'We understand the Russian need to be secure on her western frontiers by the removal of all possibility of German aggression. We welcome Russia to her rightful place among the leading nations of the world.' But the Russian-dominated Polish Government was making 'enormous and wrongful inroads upon Germany' and 'mass expulsion of millions of Germans on a scale grievous and undreamed of'; Communist regimes were being imposed in all the countries occupied by the victorious Russian army. 'This is certainly not the liberated Europe we fought to build up. Nor is it one which contains the essentials of permanent peace.' Confident that the Soviet Union did not want war, Churchill said: 'What we have to consider here today, while time remains, is the permanent prevention of war and the establishment of conditions of freedom and democracy as rapidly as possible in all countries.' Disclaiming any thought of appeasement, Churchill came to his main proposition: 'What is needed is a settlement, and the longer this is delayed, the more difficult it will be and the greater our dangers will become.'

Churchill then made a point which must have seemed to him, his listeners and his readers, even now, entirely appropriate and relevant to his argument, yet which left him open to serious misinterpretation. He said:

> Up till the year 1933 or even 1935, Germany might have been saved from the awful fate which has overtaken her and we might all have been spared the miseries Hitler let loose upon mankind. There never was a war in all history easier to prevent by timely action than the one which has just desolated such great areas of the globe. It could have been prevented in my belief without the firing of a single shot.
>
> Last time, I saw it all coming and cried aloud to my own fellow-countrymen and to the world, but no one paid any attention . . . No one would listen and one by one we were all sucked into the awful whirlpool.

What made the Fulton Speech so shocking to so many, in the United States as well as Britain and Australia, was the implication that there was a new common cause – against the Soviet Union. Talk of preparedness so soon after the war could not but revive memories of 1919 and Churchill's anti-Bolshevik crusade.

Churchill's other purpose at Fulton was to warn against an American withdrawal from Europe. That is why he placed such emphasis on the partnership between Britain and America. 'Neither the sure prevention of war, nor the continuous rise of world organization will be gained without what I have called the fraternal association of the English-speaking peoples,' Churchill said. 'This means a special relationship between the British Commonwealth and Empire and the United States.' This was the origin of a term, and a policy, which was to become the ruling principle for successive British Governments, not least Labour Governments, into the twenty-first century and into Iraq. Churchill, being Churchill, took the idea of a 'special relationship' into visionary realms: 'Eventually there may come – I feel eventually will come – the principle of common citizenship, but that we may be content to leave to destiny.' Nevertheless, we may recall, with fascination or surprise, that in 1946, Churchill and Chifley were saying the same things about cooperation between the 'English-speaking' democracies.

Although Churchill had shown his speech to Truman on the train to Missouri, and although he was to make selective use of it when the Cold War erupted in full force with the Berlin Blockade in 1948, Truman withheld public endorsement until its impact became clearer. Stalin showed no such reticence. In a carefully prepared response through the device of an interview in *Pravda* on 14 March, he called Churchill's speech 'a dangerous act, calculated to sow the seeds of discord'. Mr Churchill, Stalin said, 'is now in the position of a warmonger. But in this Mr Churchill is not alone – he has friends not only in England but the USA.'

Coming less than a year after the Great Patriotic War, which had left thirty million Soviet soldiers and civilians dead, Churchill's parallel with Hitler's Germany was easily portrayed as a gross affront to Stalin and the Russian people. Stalin showed his anger – and the brutal political skill which he used to dispose of his enemies and comrades alike – with a savage attack on Churchill's vision of an English-speaking union, turning the knife in what would always be, and remains, the most vulnerable and repellent part of the whole idea.

'Mr Churchill and his friends are strikingly reminiscent of Hitler and his friends,' Stalin told the fearless reporter from *Pravda*. 'Hitler began the process of unleashing war by pronouncing his racial theories, declaring that only those people whose mother tongue was German could be considered a full-blooded nation.' He continued:

> Now Mr Churchill is starting his process of unleashing war also with a racial theory, declaring that only those people who speak English are full-blooded nations, whose vocation it is to control the fate of the whole world. In point of fact, Mr Churchill and his friends in England and in America are presenting those nations who do not speak English with a kind of ultimatum: recognise our supremacy over you, voluntarily, and all will be well – otherwise war is inevitable.

It may have been crude, but its resonance in the colonial world was instant and immense. Stalin's use of the word 'warmonger' caught on, applied to Churchill by the obedient communist parties around the world. In the West, his criticism of the Soviet drowned out his basic message – the appeal for a settlement through talking and negotiation. At this level, at least, it may be said that, against Churchill's intentions, the Fulton speech led to the first shots in the Cold War.

Australian reaction to the Fulton Speech was mixed. Chifley and Menzies both endorsed the call for British–American cooperation, and Chifley explicitly adapted the idea for his own speeches. Evatt welcomed Churchill's support for the United Nations Organization. None of the Australian leaders, including Menzies, was ready to support anything that might hint at provocation of the Soviet Union, only nine months after war's end. Over the next three years, Chifley and Evatt deplored the sharpening polarisation of the world between the Western and communist blocs. In this, they found themselves at odds not so much with Churchill as with the Attlee Government and its Foreign Secretary, Ernest Bevin, much more the Cold Warrior than Churchill.

Churchill reinforced the more hostile responses to his Fulton speech by his grudging attitude towards Indian independence. He still spoke as if India was the key to Britain's greatness. As the Attlee Government moved to ratify the inevitable, he recalled his speeches against dominion status for India in the 1930s as if they entitled him to the same claims to foresight and wisdom as his speeches against Hitler. Now, he watched 'with grief the clattering down of the British Empire with all its glories'. He still counselled delay 'to mitigate the ruin and disaster that will follow the disappearance of Britain from the East'. Let us not add, he said, 'by shameful flight, by a premature hurried scuttle, the taint and smear of shame'.

In the end, Churchill had nothing to offer except a quibble. By 1947, he had accepted the plans of the last Viceroy, Lord Louis Mountbatten, for the partition of the sub-continent into the predominantly Hindu India and the predominantly Muslim West Pakistan and East Pakistan (now Bangladesh). But when Attlee sent him the draft bill which ended British responsibility for any part of British India after 15 August 1947, under the title *Indian Indepen-dence Bill*, he protested: 'The only reason I gave support to the Mountbatten proposals is because they establish the phase of Dominion status.' Turning on its head his 1930s argument, he told Attlee: 'Dominion status is not the same thing as Independence, although it may be freely used to establish Independence.' He would support the bill if it were entitled 'Indian Self-Government Bill'. It was all reminiscent of the word-play with Alfred Deakin at the 1907 Colonial Conference. Attlee brushed his quibbles aside. 'Dominion Prime Ministers constantly stress the point,' he patiently explained to Churchill, 'that they are independent States within the British Commonwealth.' The formula for India and Pakistan, Attlee said, was 'a most valuable counter to the demand for independence outside the Commonwealth, as it shows that this demand can be satisfied within it'. In future years, the formula would be extended to allow dominions like India which became republics to remain in the Commonwealth of Nations, accepting the Queen simply as its Head.

Around this time, 'on a foggy afternoon in November 1947', Churchill claimed to have had a dream, in which his father, Lord Randolph Churchill, appeared and asked to be brought up to date about the current state of the world. It was amazingly coherent for a dream and Churchill wrote it all down. Churchill told his father that the United States was now the world's leading power, adding: 'I have always worked for friendship with the United States and, indeed, throughout the English-speaking world'. The Dream continued:

> 'English-speaking world,' he repeated, weighing the phrase.
> 'You mean, with Canada, Australia and New Zealand, and all that.'
> 'Yes, all that.'
> 'Are they still loyal?'
> 'They are our brothers.'
> 'And India, is that all right? And Burma?'
> 'Alas! They have all gone down the drain.'

To that, Lord Randolph 'gave a groan'. Churchill, however, had lost none of his old ability to make the best of a bad job. Publicly, 'down the drain' became the hope that the 'many nations and states of India may find their unity within the mysterious circle of the British Crown'.

Churchill's major impact in his relations with Australia in the early post-war years came through the publication of his war memoirs. David Reynolds' *In Command of History*, with the subtitle *Churchill Fighting and Writing the Second World War*, is one of the most important books ever written about Churchill. It is a masterful survey and analysis of the financing, production, research, writing, and publication of the six volumes between 1946 and 1954. They won for Churchill the Nobel Prize for Literature in 1953, although he would have preferred the Nobel Peace Prize for his continuing efforts to bring about summit talks and a settlement with the Soviet Union. Reynolds shows how careful Churchill was to slant his account so as not to offend or embarrass the United States, particularly in the last volume, *Triumph and Tragedy*, especially now that Eisenhower was President, and Churchill was Prime Minister for the second time. Churchill showed no such sensitivity towards Australia.

The first volume, *The Gathering Storm* (1948), leads up to *The Finest Hour* (1949), the story of 1940, on which Churchill could speak with unrivalled authority and prestige. These volumes established public attitudes to the entire series. Assumptions about its accuracy only began to be whittled away when other leading actors began to have their say. Probably the first such work was the aptly named *The Turn of the Tide,* by the British historian Sir Arthur Bryant. Published in 1957, it was based on the diaries of Sir Alan Brooke (now Field Marshal Lord Alanbrooke), carefully pruned and edited. Even this mild revisionism aroused Churchill's wrath. But it was too late for Australia. Churchill's versions of events took hold. Contemporary rebuttals sank without trace, until Dr David Day's comprehensive studies began the retrieval of Australia's reputation in the 1980s.

It must have tickled Churchill's impish humour to find that he could use Australian party politics to his advantage. By 1948, Menzies had reinvented himself and was on the ascendant as leader of a resurgent coalition. When Menzies visited Britain in August, 1948, Churchill charmed him with a guided tour of Chartwell, much as he had done at Chequers in 1941. This confirmed Menzies as Churchill's booster-in-chief. Despite the concerns of the British Cabinet Secretary, Norman Brook, over the way Churchill was using official papers (Churchill of course made his own rules, as Banjo Paterson had noted in 1900), Churchill took the opportunity to get Menzies' permission to publish their correspondence over the Dakar affair in 1940. Menzies, in fact, gave Churchill a blank cheque. He told him: 'To save you from having to make special requests in future, I can tell you at once that you may publish all or any of them, but on one condition – if I ever had the nerve to send a reply, you must agree to include it in the record.' Menzies wrote in *Afternoon Light* that 'he chuckled appreciably, agreed, and acted on it!'

Churchill returned the favour when, in 1949, he came to write about Tobruk. David Reynolds writes: 'Churchill's account of the story, originally a separate chapter entitled 'The Relief of the Australians in Tobruk' throws the onus firmly on Fadden and Curtin. Deletions he made in a copy of one of Menzies' telegrams suggest that this was not accidental.' Reynolds notes the change in their relations after the Chartwell visit, and how Churchill built up

Menzies, in successive drafts of the Tobruk saga, into the ablest figure in the Australian Government. When Cabinet Secretary Brook saw the draft on Tobruk, he pressed Churchill to modify it, fearing that 'the Australians would ask for their side of the story to be printed as well'. Brook was worried that this volume would appear about the time of the Dominions Prime Ministers' Conference, scheduled for January, 1950, and that Chifley might still be one of them. According to Reynolds, Brook's 'discreet persistence paid off', and Churchill 'moved the most contentious telegrams to an appendix, cut some of his aspersions on Australian politics and added a summary, composed by Brook, of why Canberra wanted to pull out its troops'.

At Brook's suggestion, Attlee then asked Chifley for the Australian Government's approval for publication of the correspondence. On 26 November 1949, Chifley told Attlee that he would not agree unless all the Australian replies to Churchill were also published. This was a fortnight before the federal elections. The Chifley Government lost office on 10 December. Menzies as the new Prime Minister and Fadden as Deputy Prime Minister – the same posts they had held in 1941 – agreed to allow Churchill to publish the correspondence. They made no effort to ensure that Churchill put the Australian case fully or fairly. As Reynolds writes, they 'did not push [Chifley's] request for more on Australia's position'.

By the time Churchill was finishing off his fourth volume, *The Hinge of Fate*, the political situation in both Australia and Britain was readymade for Churchill, in David Reynolds' words, 'to turn some of his most savage fire in all six volumes on the Australian Labor Government of John Curtin'. Another British election was imminent, with the Attlee Labour Government in deep trouble; Menzies would condone posthumous attacks on Curtin. Norman Brook, solicitous as ever of good Commonwealth relations, persuaded Churchill to remove 'some sniping', says Reynolds – for instance, a passage which read: 'The usual stream of complaint and reproach came from Mr Curtin.' Again, Churchill took advantage of a visit from Menzies, then in London for the Prime Ministers' Conference in July, 1950, to obtain Menzies' acquiescence in his attack on Australia. Of the draft chapter dealing with the fall of Singapore and the Rangoon episode, Menzies wrote to Churchill: 'I have no objection to the reproduction of the messages you mention.'

According to another account by the official biographer, Martin Gilbert, Churchill made an amendment to his description of Australian anxieties after Pearl Harbor, not at the request of Australian ministers but in deference to Attlee. Churchill had written of Australia's 'deep fears'. Attlee said that this implied 'cold fear', and suggested Churchill substitute the word 'apprehensions'; Churchill then wrote 'deep alarm'. The sentence became: 'Can we wonder that deep alarm swept Australia or that the thoughts of their Cabinet were centred upon their own affairs.'

Under the baleful influence of the Cold War, Australian politics were entering their most bitter decade, when extracts from *The Hinge of Fate* were published by the Sydney *Telegraph* and Melbourne *Herald* in October, 1950, several months ahead of the book. Chifley left it to Evatt to take up the cudgels in defence of Curtin. The great Menzies–Evatt duel was approaching its most acrimonious stage. Evatt would become leader of the Labor Party after Chifley's death in June, 1951. He would render his greatest service to Australia and its democracy by his almost singlehanded battle to defeat Menzies' draconian legislation to outlaw the Australian Communist Party, first through the High Court and then, against all the odds, at a referendum in September, 1951. But even as early as 1950, the poisonous atmosphere which, by 1955, was to envelop the Labor Party, leading to its most disastrous and long-lasting split, weakened Evatt's efforts to mount a defence against Churchill, now almost untouchable in Australia as the champion against totalitarianism, old and new.

Paying tribute to Churchill as 'a greater war leader than Lloyd George, greater even than Pitt', Evatt defended Curtin's Rangoon refusal by saying that Churchill would have done exactly the same thing, only much tougher and much rougher. But this tit-for-tat missed the real point, that the diversion would have been futile, and left unchallenged Churchill's claim that a brigade of the 7th Australian Division could have saved Burma. Evatt challenged outright and irrefutably Churchill's claim that 'conscription even for home defence was banned'. David Reynolds reveals that, in fact, the Tory Research Department, part of the Conservative Party's secretariat in London, had given Churchill the specific details about the various conscription measures taken between 1939 and 1943. The efforts of the Tory office and Dr Evatt notwithstanding, the libel stood uncorrected through the multitude of editions, and so stands to this day. But even if Evatt was able to refute specific errors, it was impossible for him or anybody else to withstand the overwhelming effect of Churchill's majestic prose, written and accepted as the word of an unimpeachable authority.

Above all, Churchill had protected himself from Australian criticism by the care he took to distinguish between the Australian Government and the Australian soldier. Australian readers were never likely to be unduly troubled by attacks on their politicians. It hardly counted as a blemish on the record, set against the gratifying praise Churchill gave to the AIF, and the high place he assigned them in the history of the war.

The Second World War, however, was receding into history in another sense. A new war now dominated the headlines. North Korea invaded South Korea, on 25 June 1950. The division of Korea at the 38th parallel between a Russian-backed communist regime in Pyongyang and an American-backed regime in Seoul was the pay-off for Russia's last-minute entry into the war against Japan, so ardently desired by Roosevelt at Yalta, and still sought by Truman at Potsdam. Taking advantage of the fortuitous absence of the Soviet member of the UN Security Council (in protest against the refusal of the US to admit the People's Republic of China to represent China in the United Nations) and thus unable to use its power of veto, President Truman procured United Nations authority for the defence of South Korea. Despite the Labor Party's firm support for the United Nations resolutions and for Australia's participation in the United Nations forces, the Korean War provided a sharp focus for the anti-communism which now pervaded the political debate. When China intervened with massive force to save the North Korean regime, the Cold War came to Asia in a very hot form.

In this climate, Australia's new treaty with the United States took on a far-reaching significance. The ANZUS Treaty between Australia, New Zealand, and the United States had been originally conceived as a measure of reassurance to Australia to accept a 'soft' peace treaty with Japan. Under the 'shogunate' of General MacArthur, Japan had begun its transformation into a modern democracy and economy. Since the 1949 victory of Mao Zedong's Communists over Chiang Kaishek's Nationalists, now under siege on Taiwan, it became the major aim of American policy in the Pacific to enlist as many allies as possible against the People's Republic of China, especially Japan. But Australian fears of Japan died hard; hence ANZUS. The treaty contained no binding military guarantees. It merely provided that the parties would 'act to meet the common danger in accordance with their constitutional procedures', in the event of 'armed attack'. It was a small price for the United States to pay to encourage Japan and placate Australia and New Zealand. But on this slender foundation, Australia has built the elaborate structure of the American Alliance over the last 50 years.

Churchill resented ANZUS. There was more to his resentment than Britain's exclusion, although he saw in that fact unmistakable signs that Australia was now 'turning to the United States' in earnest. The root cause of his resentment was the same as in 1942: even more than the Curtin Government, the Menzies Government was dealing direct with Washington, and bypassing London. This was not what he had meant by the 'fraternal association of the English-speaking peoples'.

In Opposition, Churchill had been critical of the Attlee Government's failure to press for Britain's inclusion in ANZUS. The Attlee Government had been disappointed, but in the words of the Australian war historian Peter Edwards, in his *Crises and Commitments*, had 'kept its chagrin to itself'. Churchill failed to understand the reason for the American refusal. Their concern was with Asian opinion in a region where nationalism and communism were competing for the leadership in the struggle against European colonialism. As Edwards points out, 'the Americans did not wish to strengthen the feeling in Asia that ANZUS was a "white man's pact"'. John Foster Dulles, Truman's negotiator for the Japanese and ANZUS treaties, and soon to become Eisenhower's Secretary of State, had unsuccessfully tried to persuade Australia and New Zealand to include the Philippines, now fully independent. The Americans were not inclined to reward them by bringing the head of the British Empire into a treaty arrangement which, in any case, was peripheral to their objectives in Asia. All this was a closed book to Churchill.

When Churchill became Prime Minister again in October 1951, he pressured Menzies to reopen the question with Washington. Even if there had been any desire in Canberra, Wellington, or Washington to do so, it was too late. The treaty had been signed at San Francisco in September, 1951. The Australian Parliament approved it in February, 1952, with bipartisan support. The all-important passage through the US Congress did not occur until April, and the ANZUS Treaty duly came into force on 29 April 1952.

It was the blow to British prestige which hurt Churchill most. 'What impudence to suggest,' he wrote to Anthony Eden, once again Foreign Secretary, in June, 1952, 'that France and I suppose Portugal (who has interests in these waters) are on the same terms with Australia and New Zealand as Britain.' Now even Menzies and his conservative colleagues were threatened with the old device of drawing a distinction between the government and people of Australia. He told Eden: 'If this point became public in either of those countries, I am sure there would be a violent reaction.' The old lion growled: 'This is not a thing to let slip. We should bite hard.'

Churchill tried his persuasive charms on his old friend Dick Casey who, he must have thought, would understand his viewpoint if anyone did. Casey was now Menzies' foreign minister. Although his immediate predecessor, Percy Spender, had been the architect of ANZUS, Casey was now its custodian. He was not about to tamper with the treaty, even to please Churchill. In London for a foreign ministers' meeting, he recorded in his diary on 8 October 1952: 'Winston has sent a pretty direct cable to R.G.M. on ANZUS in the last 48 hours. What the U.K. people fail to understand is that the ANZUS treaty is of great *political* importance to us.' The emphasis on the word 'political' is Casey's, but one must credit him with meaning the politics of international relations, and not the domestic political contest in which ANZUS has been enlisted for the past fifty years. Casey continued: 'The U.K. people keep on saying that they would declare war and spring to our aid if we were attacked, but they have very small resources with which to do this.' Casey concluded his diary entry: 'The fact is that the Americans are the only people who can in fact help us in South-East Asia or the Pacific.'

If it were possible to set a date, place, and occasion at which Churchill confronted the realities of the new world he had done so much to shape, it could well be fixed at 12 December 1952, at 10 Downing Street. The dominion prime ministers were in London for a Commonwealth economic conference. Churchill summoned Menzies and the New Zealand Prime Minister, Sidney Holland, to the official residence. 'I am anxious to find a solution to the problem caused by the exclusion of the United Kingdom from ANZUS,' he told them. Churchill complained that the ANZUS military planners seemed to be seeking to extend the scope of ANZUS throughout the Pacific and South-East Asia. 'It is unreasonable,' he said, 'that this planning should go ahead without Britain, now facing a communist insurgency in Malaya.' Churchill thought he had a new string to his bow: his friend Dwight Eisenhower had just won the Presidential elections in November and would take over from Truman in January 1953. 'I will go to Eisenhower,' Churchill said.

Menzies shrugged. He reminded Churchill about the origins of ANZUS as a reassurance against Japanese resurgence. He recalled that originally the Americans had wanted to include the Philippines in the treaty, but that Australia had 'regarded the Philippines as a mere liability'. Australia had attempted to persuade the United States to include Britain, but the Americans had opposed it, 'fearing that if any concession were made to Britain, then France, the Philippines and others would be clamouring for the same right'. That would have meant, said Menzies, 'the end of any effective planning and a grave danger to security of information'. Holland complained that some British criticism of ANZUS 'seemed to imply that New

Zealand had done something disloyal to Great Britain' in signing the treaty. 'Nothing surely could be further from the truth', Holland protested. The three prime ministers agreed that there should be close consideration of new and wider defence arrangements for South-East Asia and the Pacific. In the meantime, Churchill said, he would continue to press the Americans for inclusion of Britain in ANZUS with the new United States administration.

Just eleven years before, Churchill had crossed the Atlantic to set the terms of the Grand Alliance after Pearl Harbor. Six years before, he had to argue hard with the Americans to allow the British Fleet to take part in the final attack on Japan. Now he was reduced to pleading that the United States, Australia, and New Zealand let him join their new treaty. His supposed influence with Eisenhower proved useless against the opposition of the new Secretary of State, John Foster Dulles – that 'great slab of a face', as Churchill called him.

Churchill still would not let it drop. Six months later, the prime ministers gathered in London again, this time for the coronation of Queen Elizabeth II. On 12 June 1953, the Sydney *Daily Mirror* published a story claiming that Churchill and Menzies had had a shouting match over ANZUS. Menzies issued a denial to the press: 'This story is a monstrous invention. All our discussions have been on the most friendly terms.' A few months later, the issue was still gnawing at Churchill. On another visit to London, Casey called at 10 Downing Street. 'Almost at the end,' Casey wrote in his diary on 6 October 1953, 'he raised the question of ANZUS, after looking rather slyly at me.' Churchill said that he welcomed our close association with the Americans 'but that he would have hoped that we would all have been in it together'. Casey wrote: 'He looked rather menacingly at me and said that he hoped it was realised that Great Britain and the Philippines were countries of quite different standing in the world. I knew what he meant – but did not pursue the subject.'

Churchill was no more successful with Eisenhower in pursuit of his idea for a grand summit of the Big Three. By 1953, he was the sole survivor in office from the days of Yalta and Potsdam. He saw

himself as the bridge between the two eras, but for the successor of
Roosevelt and Truman, and for Stalin's heirs, he was an obstacle.
Eisenhower and Dulles on one side, and the rivals for Stalin's power,
Malenkov, Molotov, Beria and Khrushchev in the Kremlin, were
united in their suspicions of Churchill's motives. So was his own
heir-in-waiting, Anthony Eden. It seemed to Eden, and many of
his conservative colleagues, that Churchill's repeated calls for a
new summit were merely excuses for delaying his departure from
Downing Street.

Whatever his contemporaries thought, his speeches urging talks
and agreements with Russia can be read today as models of foresight
and commonsense; and, for a man nearing his eighties, of freshness.
It is now difficult to convey how deeply a sense of the inevitability of
a world war took hold in the West in the fifties. Churchill's was the
most powerful voice against that view, but his record and reputation
and, all too often, his descent into partisan spite, muffled it. In all his
glowing tributes, Menzies brushed over this aspect of Churchill's
later career. It did not fit into his picture. More surprising, in view
of the turmoil into which the Australian Labor Party was being
plunged by Cold War issues, is the failure of Evatt and his supporters to make more of Churchill's advocacy of positions so close to
their own.

Churchill's special insight was to see that the Soviet Union itself
might change. He saw Stalin's death in March, 1953, as a unique
opportunity. In a major speech in the House of Commons on
11 May 1953, he said that it would be a shame if impatience
'were to impede any spontaneous and healthy evolution which may
be taking place inside Russia'. This speech is remarkable for the
number of 'firsts'. He was the first Western leader to assert that
Russia's security interests and anxieties were valid. 'Russia has a
right to feel assured,' he said, 'that as far as human arrangements
can run, the terrible events of the Hitler invasion will never be
repeated, and that Poland will remain a friendly Power and a buffer,
though not, I trust, a puppet State.' He was the first to propose a
security guarantee for the Soviet Union against any renewed German
threat. At the same time, he was the first to urge rapprochement

between France and Germany, envisaging for the first time the reunification of Germany. Again, he urged a summit, 'confined to the smallest number of Powers and persons possible'. 'At the worst the participants in the meeting would have established more intimate contacts,' Churchill told the House. 'At the best we might have a generation of peace.' Late in 1953, at Bermuda with Eisenhower, he proposed 'infiltrating the Soviet Union by trade and other contacts'. 'We should have a two-fold policy of strength, and readiness to look for any hope of an improved state of mind . . .' In his comprehensive survey, *Churchill's Cold War*, Klaus Larres argues persuasively: 'To some extent he was proposing the policy which was to be at the centre of Richard Nixon's and Henry Kissinger's *detente* policy and Willy Brandt's *Ostpolitik* of the 1970s.'

Churchill had given Eden a broad hint, well short of a promise, that he might retire in May 1954, when Queen Elizabeth and Prince Philip returned from their long tour of Australia and New Zealand. Part of the trouble was that Eden's health was sometimes as bad as Churchill's. Churchill had bounced back from a severe stroke in June, 1953, while Eden was still dogged by the effect of a badly botched operation for gallstones. 'I feel like an aeroplane at the end of its flight, in the dusk, with the petrol running out, in search of a safe landing,' Churchill told his Chancellor of the Exchequer, Rab Butler, on 12 March 1954. 'The only political interest I have left is in talking to the Russians.' The Queen came home in triumph. Moving the Address of Welcome on 17 May, Churchill said: 'I assign no limits to the reinforcement which this Royal journey may have brought to the health, the wisdom, the sanity and hopefulness of mankind.'

Churchill's celebration of the 1954 Royal Tour underlines the essential point that Australia never made any sudden lurch away from Britain towards America. Churchill was as wrong about Australia's motivation in 1952–54 as he had been in 1942–44. The outstanding feature of Australian policy over the decade is not the 'turning to America' but the priority given to cooperation with Britain and the Commonwealth in defence and trade, by Curtin and Chifley as much as Menzies. As late as 1956, Australian defence planners worked on the basis that, in the event of a world war, Australian forces would be deployed with British forces in their traditional theatre, the Middle East.

Until the war in Vietnam changed everything, Australia's major deployment overseas was with the British forces engaged in the Malayan Emergency, which may be seen either as the last military effort of the British Empire in the Far East, or the most successful operation in the transition from empire to independence. Rebuffed over ANZUS, Churchill remained Prime Minister long enough to see Britain included in the South-East Asia Treaty Organization (SEATO), devised by Dulles as a Pacific counterpart of the North Atlantic Treaty Organization (NATO), along with France, the Philippines, Pakistan, Thailand, Australia, and New Zealand. Its lopsided membership made it expensive and ineffective from its start in 1954. It was never invoked for Vietnam, the one conflict that might have seemed relevant to the purposes for which Dulles contrived it. Churchill warned Eisenhower and Dulles against taking over from France in Indochina after the French catastrophe at Dien Bien Phu in 1954. Eisenhower's successors ignored his advice, but Churchill's successors accepted it. Thus Britain, unlike Australia, escaped the trauma of Vietnam.

'Merely try to imagine in outline the first few weeks of a war,' Churchill said in one of his last significant interventions in the House of Commons on 27 July 1954. He had been appalled by the implications of the testing of the hydrogen bomb at the Bikini Atoll in the Pacific Ocean and, indeed, of his own decision in June to build a British H-bomb. He knew that these events would unleash the arms race which he so feared and deplored. So when the British Parliament debated a new Anglo–Egyptian Agreement by which Britain agreed to withdraw its troops from the Suez Canal Zone, Churchill was in the throes of an 'agonising reappraisal' about British prestige and the future of mankind. 'Fancy ending my career with clearing out of Egypt,' he groaned. A rebel Tory hit one of the most sensitive nerves in Churchill's political body, when he waved a copy of the Agreement and said to Churchill: 'In this piece of paper, we have got all that is left of eighty years of British endeavour, thought and forethought.' In a four-minute reply, as passionate and effective as any in his career, Churchill said: 'How utterly out of proportion to the Suez Canal and the position we hold in Egypt are the appalling developments and the appalling spectacle which imagination raises before us.'

'If I never speak again in the House of Commons,' Churchill told Lord Moran next day, 'I can say I have done nothing better.' If Anthony Eden, and for that matter, Robert Menzies, had been guided by this 'sense of proportion', the last chapter in the long story of the British Empire and Egypt might have been very different from the farce of 1956. The world did not end with the bang Churchill feared; but Churchill's Empire, in which Egypt had played so large a role from Omdurman to Alamein, was to end at Suez with something very like a whimper.

'I don't believe Anthony can do it,' Churchill said to his private secretary, John Colville, on his last night in 10 Downing Street, sitting on the edge of his bed, still wearing his Blue Ribbon of the Order of the Garter. That day, 5 April 1955, he had refused Queen Elizabeth's offer of a dukedom. 'And do you know,' he told Colville, 'it's an odd thing but she seemed almost relieved.' Presumably not as relieved as Eden. Even as late as March, Churchill was poring over an ambiguous message from Eisenhower in the hope that it meant support for a 'Four-Power meeting with the Russians', perhaps in June. According to Colville, 'W. began to form a cold hatred of Eden who, he repeatedly said, had done more to thwart him and prevent him from pursuing the policy he thought right than anybody else.' Colville then adds: 'But he also admitted to me on several occasions that the prospect of giving everything up, after nearly sixty years of public life, was a terrible wrench. He saw no reason why he should go; he was only doing it for Anthony. He sought to persuade his intimate friends, and himself, that he was being hounded out of office.'

Churchill's career ended with another paradox. Eden reacted to Churchill's last-minute dickering over the prospects of a summit with all the emotion and rage he had bottled up for a decade. He left Churchill no choice but to confirm 5 April as the day of his resignation. Thus, their mutual frustration over the summit issue ended Churchill's career. Barely a month later, Eisenhower, Eden, and the French Prime Minister, Edgar Faure, jointly invited the Soviet leadership to attend a summit conference as soon as possible. On 21 May, Nikita Khrushchev, the victor of the Kremlin power struggle since Stalin's death, accepted. The first summit since Potsdam met at Geneva in July, 1955, almost as soon as its main advocate for a decade was unable to attend it.

'I have tried very hard to set in motion this process of a conference at the top level and to bring about actual results,' Churchill had said in his last major speech as Prime Minister in February, at a time when he believed that his efforts since Fulton in 1946 had failed. 'I still believe,' he said, almost the last words he uttered in the House of Commons, 'that vast and fearsome as the human scene has become, personal contacts of the right people in the right place, at the right time, may yet have a potent and valuable part to play in the cause of peace which is in our hearts.'

EIGHTEEN MONTHS AFTER he left office, Churchill made a brief appearance on the shrinking stage of Empire – not in person, but with Menzies literally mouthing his words. This bizarre scene was laid in Cairo in September, 1956, appropriately enough in view of the pivotal role Egypt had played in the relations between Churchill and Australia. In July, 1956, the Egyptian President, Gamal Abdul Nasser, nationalised the Suez Canal, six weeks after the withdrawal of the last British troops from Egypt. Eden, who had urged the withdrawal upon a reluctant Churchill in the first place, now became obsessed with Nasser, whom he began to liken to Hitler. In September, Eden tempted Menzies into heading a mission to Cairo to persuade Nasser to hand over the running of the canal to an international body; it was taken for granted that the Egyptians were too incompetent to run it themselves. Menzies' mission was foredoomed, not least because he approached a question involving the deepest emotions of Egyptian pride and Arab nationalism as if he were arguing a case before the Privy Council. Nasser's confidant, the newspaper editor Mohamed Heikal, described their first meeting over a convivial dinner at the Presidential Palace:

> Menzies asked Nasser: 'Have you ever met Churchill?' Nasser replied: 'No, but I admired him.' 'Have you ever heard him talking?' asked Menzies, and again Nasser said, 'No.' 'Do you know,' said Menzies, 'I have the reputation for being the best imitator of Churchill.' And throughout the dinner, Menzies kept whispering in Nasser's ear and everyone thought that they were talking important business about Suez when, in fact, Menzies was imitating Churchill's speech.

It is hard to think of a single Churchill story which would not have jarred with an Egyptian dictator who was also the champion of pan-Arab nationalism. Nevertheless, Nasser found Menzies 'very likable' according to Heikal; but the mission became an 'abject failure' when Menzies adopted a Churchillian pose in earnest. At their third session on 6 September, Heikal wrote:

> Menzies leaned forward over the desk, his thick eye-brows bristling, and growled: 'Mr President, your refusal of an international administration will be the beginning of trouble.' Nasser immediately closed the files on the desk in front of him and said: 'You are threatening me. Very well, I am finished. There will be no more discussion. It is all over.'

It was not quite over. Eden continued his military preparations to force the regime change he was determined to make. In secret collusion with France and Israel, he concocted a plan for an Israeli invasion of Egypt across Sinai, whereupon the British and French would also invade, on the pretence of separating the combatants in order to safeguard the Suez Canal. The conspirators reckoned without Eisenhower who, facing his re-election in November, had ruled out the use of force against Egypt. They reckoned, too, without the Soviet Union which, taking advantage of Western disarray over Suez, invaded Hungary to suppress the people's uprising there in October – a brutal success, but one which contained the seeds of the ultimate collapse of European communism in 1989, and the even more incredible collapse of the Soviet Union in 1991. In the face of American hostility, a double-cross by Dulles, condemnation in the United Nations, a divided Commonwealth with Canada and India taking the lead against Britain, a catastrophic run on the pound sterling, and unprecedented demonstrations in Trafalgar Square, Eden retreated from Egypt in confusion, and from his prime ministership in humiliation. Churchill never forgave his successor for ignoring his parting injunction to his Cabinet in 1955: 'Never be separated from the United States.' He offered lukewarm support in public; but in private he said: 'I would never have dared go in, but if I had dared, I would certainly never have dared stop.'

On one of Menzies' post-war visits, Churchill had drawn for him a diagram showing Britain at the centre of three interlocking circles, connecting with North America, Europe, and the wider Commonwealth. These, Churchill explained, represented Britain's unique position in the world. Suez broke each of Churchill's circles. Eden's successor, Harold Macmillan, made it his priority to mend the relationship with the United States, but any idea of equality had vanished: the special relationship became at best a very junior partnership. As a result of Suez, the United States replaced Britain as the imperial power in the Middle East. When Macmillan sought to take Britain into the European Common Market in 1962, Britain's loss of prestige was such that de Gaulle was able to veto his application, recalling perhaps Churchill's wartime warning: 'If I have to choose between the United States and France, I shall always choose the United States'. In the event, the choice which Britain had to make was not between America and France, but between Europe and the Commonwealth. In his 'Wind of Change' speech in 1960, Macmillan accepted and hastened the inevitability of independence for the remaining British colonies in Africa and Asia. All these things, no doubt, would have happened without Suez. Nonetheless, it is certain that from the time of Suez, and because of Suez, neither the old nor new members of the Commonwealth, whether they remained constitutional monarchies or became republics, ever again accepted Britain's political primacy or looked for its leadership. It brought no joy to Churchill to realise that he would be the last Prime Minister of

Britain to be acknowledged as leader of the British Empire and Commonwealth.

Macmillan's earnest efforts to maintain Britain's leadership proved counterproductive. There were too many centrifugal forces at work: South Africa's apartheid policy; India's leadership of the Non-Aligned nations as a third force in the Cold War; the sensitivity of the new members to any signs of condescension from the old 'club' members; the extreme sensitivity of Menzies and his generation to any hint of criticism of White Australia; and, above all, Britain's push at the door of the European Common Market.

Menzies sought aid and comfort from Churchill. 'My dear Winston,' he wrote in October, 1961, 'You must feel just as puzzled as I am about some of the modern developments in the Commonwealth.' Menzies questioned whether 'we are paying too great a price for the doubtful advantage of retaining some countries as nominal members of what used to be a splendid Crown Commonwealth'. Menzies told Churchill: 'The fact that I am terribly concerned about the strange products of the new Commonwealth relationship is one of the many reasons why I look forward to seeing you, who have always been able to concentrate on the essentials without being distracted by the form.' It was the last correspondence on high policy between Menzies and Churchill. Churchill was as puzzled as Menzies, but he was past concentrating on anything less essential than his final fading efforts to prevent nuclear war. However, he passed Menzies' letter on to Macmillan, who replied: 'It seems to me that we must now concentrate on the opportunities rather than regret the changes which the New Commonwealth has made inevitable.'

Anthony Montague Browne, who sacrificed his diplomatic career to serve Churchill to the end of his days, wrote in his moving memoir, *Long Sunset*, that, in the last years, 'WSC's opinion of Menzies was sky-high.' As evidence, he recalled: 'I was present at a later dinner where WSC set out with apparent seriousness to persuade Menzies to leave Australia, enter the House of Commons immediately, and soon succeed the incumbent as Prime Minister.' Browne does not specify the year or the incumbent, but the story says more about Churchill's sense of mischief and skills at flattery than about any sincere admiration for Menzies, who might have reflected ruefully that the offer came a couple of decades too late.

Churchill certainly enjoyed Menzies' company. On the same occasion, according to Montague Browne, the pair recited alternate lines of an 'Australian ditty' which largely consisted of repetition of what used to be called the great Australian adjective, ending:

> The bloody horse was bloody drowned
> The stockman reached the bloody ground
> Ejaculating 'Bloody, bloody, bloody, bloody.'

'Then WSC drank some brandy,' wrote Browne, 'and said: "And that seems to me to be a most adequate summary of the world situation."'

The last Australian to record a brief encounter with Churchill was Paul Hasluck, who had first met him as an official with Evatt in 1945, and saw him as a minister with Menzies during the Prime Ministers' Conference of 1963. Macmillan gave an evening reception at 10 Downing Street. 'Churchill, looking old and weary, was sitting by himself on a couch against a wall,' Hasluck recorded in his book *Diplomatic Witness*. 'He was besieged by an African Ambassador who stood squarely in front of him and with wagging forefinger seemed to be admonishing him about something.' Hasluck wrote that 'the old man was turning his glance rather vaguely from side to side as though hoping to escape'. Hasluck 'distracted the Ambassador from his harangue and took his place'.

> He moved away and I recalled myself by name to Churchill and said I hoped he did not mind my butting in to pay my respects. The old style revived. 'I observed how adroitly you managed the relief operation,' he growled. 'These Africans can be very tedious.' Then after the exchange of another two or three sentences, he seemed to fall asleep, a weary old man thankfully alone at the edge of a noisy and crowded room.

'I have had a long life and have done many things,' Churchill told his daughter Mary Soames not long before his death on 24 January 1965, 'but in the end I have achieved nothing.' Yet, perhaps more than any other great historical figure, Churchill had fulfilled most of his earliest ambitions – and not only the ones he had confided to Banjo Paterson in 1900. When he was sixteen and still at Harrow, Churchill is supposed to have said to a school friend:

> I have a wonderful idea of where I shall be eventually. I have dreams about it. I can see vast changes coming over a now peaceful world, great upheavals, terrible struggles, wars such as we cannot imagine, and I tell you, London will be in danger – London will be attacked and I shall be very prominent in the defence of London. I repeat: London will be in danger and in the high position I shall occupy, it will fall to me to save the Capital and save the Empire.

If one could believe that any sixteen-year-old boy ever talked like that, one can believe it of Churchill. He was only half right, of course. If he saved London, or rather, all that London stood for in 1940, it cost the capital its Empire, or everything that Churchill understood the Empire to mean. Hence the frequent observation in January, 1965, that his funeral ceremonies were the delayed obsequies of the British Empire.

In his broadcast from St Paul's Cathedral, Menzies placed the London of 1940 at the emotional heart of his eulogy of Churchill and his voice broke briefly when he referred to 'his London', paused and added '*our* London'. The Anglocentric theme was echoed at memorial services around Australia, in Catholic as well as Anglican cathedrals. That something deeper than mere nostalgia was at work, however, was shown when Menzies launched a national appeal for the Winston Churchill Memorial Trust just a month after the funeral. The trust was established 'to perpetuate and honour the memory of Sir Winston Churchill by the award of travelling fellowships'. Its success was phenomenal. Menzies had matured his plans long before Churchill's death, secured the services of superb organisers and fund-raisers, and ensured bipartisan support. His target of a million pounds was more than doubled, most of it raised in a door-knock campaign on a single day in February, 1965. The Australian response was much the most impressive among similar appeals in Britain, Canada, and New Zealand. John Ramsden, in two acutely observed essays on Churchill and Australia in his book, *Man of the Century – The Legend Since 1945*, notes significant factors in the timing of the appeal: Britain moving closer to Europe with the election of the Wilson Labour Government in October, 1964, and Australia on the brink of joining the United States in combat in Vietnam, the first war Australia fought in without Britain alongside. Ramsden writes: 'The appeal's success may well have owed at least something to Australians' awareness that this would be "one last rally" for all that Churchill had stood for in the Anglo-Australian identity.' Menzies made his Vietnam announcement four days after the fiftieth anniversary of the landings at Gallipoli.

Incomparably, Winston Churchill thought more about Australia and more about what Australia thought of him than any world leader before or since, or ever will again. Which foreign President or Prime Minister will ever write about 'my solemn responsibility to the Australian people' with half so good a will as Churchill did? And why should Australians want or expect it to be otherwise? In the disputes with Curtin in 1942, the essential difference between Churchill and Roosevelt was this: that Churchill genuinely believed that Australia's interests, however waywardly he interpreted them, counted for something in the common cause, and Roosevelt did not. In this, as in so much else, Churchill was the Grand Exception. It is no doubt a good thing to have great and powerful friends, as Menzies never tired of saying; and, for all his ambivalence and contradictions, none was as great and powerful a friend as Churchill. In every sense, we shall not look upon his like again. That being so, the best lesson to be drawn from the long story of Churchill and Australia is how much, in the final analysis, we must rely upon ourselves. And, of course, the lesson of his whole life: 'Never despair.'

Notes and sources

Prologue

Page

1. 'bad stock': Lord Moran, *Winston Churchill – The Struggle for Survival*, Heron Books, London, 1966, p. 21.
2. 'I did not worry about the Australians': Moran, p. 21.
3. 'My faith in our race . . .': Randolph Churchill, *Winston S. Churchill – Youth 1874–1900*, William Heinemann, London, 1966, p. 418.
3. In his will, Cecil Rhodes . . .: See Niall Ferguson, *Empire – How Britain Made the Modern World*, Penguin, 2004, p. 238.
3. 'I do not admit . . .': quoted in Martin Gilbert, *Churchill and the Jews*, Simon & Schuster, London, 2007, p. 120.
4. 'When you learn . . .': Moran, p. 395.
4. '. . . made of sugar candy': Speech by Churchill addressing the Canadian Parliament, Ottawa, 30 December 1941, quoted by Martin Gilbert, *The Road to Victory*, William Heinemann, London, 1966, p. 34.
4. 'Your birthstain . . .': *Sydney Morning Herald*, 11 May 1899, quoted in Crowley, *Colonial Australia – A Documentary History*, Vol. 3, Thomas Nelson Australia, Melbourne, 1980, p. 563.
5. 'The mettle that a race': AB Paterson, 'We're All Australians Now', *Complete Poems*, A & R Classics, Sydney, 2001, p. 308.

6. '. . . the Empire was a possession': Extract from *A Study in Failure 1900–1939* by Robert Rhodes James, Copyright © 1970 Robert Rhodes James, is reproduced by permission of Sheil Land Associates Ltd., Weidenfeld & Nicolson, London, 1970, p. 199.

7. 'Winston is incurably colonial-minded': Alan Lascelles, *King's Counsellor – Abdication and War; the Diaries of Sir Alan Lascelles*, Duff Hart-Davis (ed.), Weidenfeld & Nicolson, London, 2006, entry for 6 October 1943; and Note, p. 168.

Chapter 1: 'Our account with the Boers'
Page

8. 'The great Winston Churchill': AB Paterson, *From the Front – Despatches from the Boer War*, Pan Macmillan, Sydney, 2000, p. 364.

9. 'This correspondent job': AB Paterson, *Happy Despatches*, Angus & Robertson, Sydney, 1935, p. 22.

10. 'Our account with the Boers': See Randolph Churchill, *Youth*, p. 449. Randolph Churchill says that the article was not published.

10. Paterson's interview with Olive Schreiner: Paterson, *From the Front*, pp. 125–128.

11. Edmund Barton on 'England's quarrels': *Sydney Morning Herald*, 21 February 1885, quoted in Frank Crowley (ed.), *A Documentary History of Australia*, Vol. 3, Thomas Nelson Australia Pty Ltd, 1980, pp. 172–173.

12. 'Methods of barbarism': In a letter to *The Times* (15 June 1901), Sir Henry Campbell-Bannerman wrote: 'When is war not a war? When it is carried on by methods of barbarism in South Africa.'

12. 'I am loyal to the Empire': New South Wales Legislative Assembly, 10 January 1899. For Holman's speech and Barton's interjection, see *H.V. Evatt – Australian Labor Leader*, Angus & Robertson, Sydney, 1940, pp. 89–90. 'Mr Cook' is Joseph Cook (1860–1947) later Prime Minister of Australia (1913–1914).

13. 'Kipling speaks very humorously . . .': Paterson, *From the Front*, p. 248.

13. *With French to Kimberley*: Paterson, *Complete Poems*, A & R Classics, Sydney, 2001, p. 104.

13. 'Long-legged young fellows': Paterson's despatch, *Sydney Morning Herald*, 9 May 1900, reporting the capture of Bloemfontein.

14. Churchill's first despatch: Winston Churchill, *The Boer War*, Pimlico Edition, London, 2002, pp. 3–4.

14. 'Thank God you have come here': For Churchill's escape, see Randolph Churchill, *Youth*, p. 483 and pp. 491–492.
15. 'Colonel de L'Isle's Corps ...': Churchill, *The Boer War*, pp. 352–353.
15. Paterson wrote a long pen-portrait ...: Paterson, *Happy Despatches*, pp. 20–22.
17. 'All the colonials did well': Lord Roberts quoted in *Australian Encyclopaedia*, Vol. II, p. 483.
17. 'Churchill had such a strong personality ...': Paterson, *Happy Despatches*, p. 24.
18. 'A ... forgiving policy ...': See Roy Jenkins, *Churchill*, p. 63.
18. 'They came to prove to all the earth': Paterson, *Complete Poems*, p. 104.

Chapter 2: 'I am a glow-worm'
Page
19. Churchill's maiden speech: House of Commons, 18 February 1901, see Randolph Churchill, *Young Statesman*, William Heinemann, London, 1967, pp. 9–10.
20. 'a lickspittle reverence for the Empire ...': *Documents on Australian International Affairs, 1901–1918*, Gordon Greenwood and Charles Grimshaw (eds.), Thomas Nelson Australia, for the Australian Institute of International Affairs, 1977, p. 54.
21. '... prigs, prudes and faddists': James, *Churchill – A Study in Failure*, p. 21.
21. 'Australian allegiance at a penny a pound of wool': Churchill in the House of Commons, 8 March 1905, see Randolph Churchill, *Young Statesman*, pp. 100–108.
22. 'their vicious policy of protection ...': Randolph Churchill, *Young Statesman*, p. 57.
23. 'Churchill at the Colonial Office ...': Ronald Hyams, *Elgin and Churchill at the Colonial Office*, Macmillan, London, 1968, p. 497.
24. 'hooliganism' in Natal: see Ronald Hyams in Robert Blake and W. Roger Louis (eds.), *Churchill*, Oxford University Press, Oxford, 1993, p. 169.
24. 'I am a glow-worm': recorded by Violet Bonham Carter in *Winston Churchill as I Knew Him*, Eyre & Spottiswoode, London, 1965, p. 16.
24. 'a bumptious youth ...': quoted in Graham Stewart, *Burying Caesar: Churchill, Chamberlain and the Battle for the Tory Party*, Weidenfeld & Nicholson, London, 1999, p. 40.

26. Churchill bombarded Lord Elgin . . .: For Churchill's efforts and statements on behalf of the Australian States, see Hyams, *Elgin and Churchill*, pp. 324–325.

29. Lord Elgin confided . . .: Hyams, *Elgin and Churchill*, p. 318.

29. 'Our robust young Colonials . . .': Morley's statement quoted by Hyams, *Elgin and Churchill*, p. 318. Morley referred to Deakin and his colleague, Sir William Lyne, as 'the kangaroo breed'.

29. 'an hour and a half of hammer and tongs . . .': quoted by Randolph Churchill, *Young Statesman*, p. 211.

30. 'The Australians for the most part . . .': Sir Wilfred Laurier's views on Australian leaders in Oscar Douglas Shelton, *Life and Letters of Sir Wilfred Laurier*, Oxford University Press, London, 1922, Vol. II, Note on p. 342.

30. 'Kidnapping Laurier . . .': Deakin's letter to Jebb, see JA La Nauze, *Alfred Deakin – A Biography*, Vol. II, Melbourne University Press, Melbourne, 1965, pp. 500–501.

30. 'Life has ended . . .': Deakin's diary quoted in La Nauze, *Deakin*, Vol. II, p. 636.

31. 'Are they all Dominions?': For the exchange between Churchill and Deakin, *Proceedings of the Colonial Conference 1907*, H.M. Stationery Office, London, 1907, pp. 79–80.

32. 'We will have a White Australia': *Proceedings*, p. 176.

32. 'The right of the white colonies . . .': Winston Churchill, *My African Journey*, Heron Books, London, 1962, pp. 36–37.

32. 'There was once a fetish of Protection . . .': *Proceedings*, p. 317.

33. Churchill then rose . . .: *Proceedings*, 7 May 1907, pp. 400–407.

34. Churchill declared his own victory: Churchill's Edinburgh speech quoted in Randolph Churchill, *Young Statesman*, p. 216.

35. Deakin and Churchill had a parting spat: *Proceedings*, pp.. 555–559.

Chapter 3: 'Commence hostilities . . .'

Page

37. Cox was especially contemptuous: Bertram Cox's minutes to Churchill, his opinions about Australians and Deakin, with Churchill's instruction to Marsh in La Nauze, *Deakin*, Vol. II, p. 489.

38. 'It ought to be discouraged . . .': La Nauze, *Deakin*, Vol. II, p. 490.

38. 'I hardly understand your want of sympathy . . .': Deakin's letter to Leo Amery, La Nauze, *Deakin*, Vol. II, pp. 490–491.

39. 'But for the British Navy . . .': Deakin's speech of welcome quoted by AW Jose, *The Royal Australian Navy: Official History of Australia in the War of 1914–18*, Vol IX, Angus & Robertson, Sydney, 1928, Introduction, p. xxvii.

39. 'one sea, . . . one Empire, . . . one Navy': *Proceedings*, p. 129.

40. 'Our tutelary stages are past': *Commonwealth Parliamentary Debates* (House of Representatives), 24 November 1909, Vol. 54, pp. 6251–6252.

40. 'The alarmists have no ground . . .': Churchill's Swansea speech quoted in Randolph Churchill, *Young Statesman*, pp. 511–513.

43. 'We compromised on eight . . .': Winston Churchill, *The World Crisis*, Australasian Publishing Company, Sydney, 1923, p. 37.

43. 'Rum, sodomy and the lash': Sir Martin Gilbert, the ultimate authority, has frequently denied that Churchill ever said this.

43. 'The British Empire would dissolve': Winston Churchill, *The World Crisis*, Vol. I, p. 119.

44. 'First born of the Commonwealth Navy . . .': London *Times* report of 10 February 1910, given in Frank Crowley (ed.), *Modern Australia – A Documentary History*, Vol. 4, Thomas Nelson Australia, Melbourne, 1980, p. 151.

45. 'Strip it of its bombast': Keith Murdoch's article in *Lone Hand*, 1 September 1913 in *Documents on Australian International Affairs*, pp. 215–216.

46. '. . . if Australia isn't ready to fight': Sydney *Bulletin*, 31 October 1912, in *Documents on Australian International Affairs*, p. 212.

46. Churchill's attitude to Japan . . .: Extracts from Churchill's House of Commons speech, 17 March 1914, in *Documents on Australian International Affairs*, pp. 208–210.

48. 'the first dignitary of the Imperial shipping department . . .': Melbourne *Punch* article of 2 April 1914, in Crowley, *Modern Australia*, Vol. 4, p. 212.

49. 'The pages of history are strewn . . .': Senator ED Millen, reported in *The Age*, 13 April 1914, in Crowley, *Modern Australia*, Vol. 4, pp. 212–213; also in Commonwealth Parliamentary Proceedings (Senate), Vol. II, p. 208, 13 April 1914, *Documents on Australian International Affairs*, p. 210.

51. 'We cannot possibly hold the Mediterranean': Churchill's letter to Haldane quoted in Robert K Massie, *Dreadnought*, Ballantine Books and Random House, London, 1991, p. 283. Lord Kitchener's protest, *Dreadnought*, p. 285.

52. 'we could not stand aside': Sir Edward Grey's speech and the reaction in the House of Commons from Massie, *Dreadnought*, p. 905.

55. 'Winston is all for this way of escape . . .': Michael and Eleanor Brock (eds.), *H.H. Asquith's Letters to Venetia Stanley*, Oxford University Press, London, 1982, Letter No. 107, p. 129. Also see William Jannen, *The Lions of July – Prelude to War 1914*, Presidio Press, California, 1997, p. 197.

55. 'Winston dashed into the room radiant . . .': Asquith's letter quoted in AN Wilson, *After the Victorians 1901–1953*, Hutchinson, London, 2005, p. 183.

55. 'Is it not horrible to be built like that?': Churchill to Clementine, Martin Gilbert, *Winston Churchill*, Vol. III, p. 31; Churchill to Violet Asquith, in Violet Bonham Carter, *Winston Churchill As I Knew Him*, p. 361.

55. 'It was 11 o'clock': Churchill's description of the outbreak of war is in his *The World Crisis 1911–1914*, the first volume of his account of the First World War, published in 1923, p. 229.

Chapter 4: 'Australia will be there'
Page

58. Australia was in the middle of a Federal election: The reports of Cook's speech (*Argus*, Melbourne, 3 August 1914) and Fisher's speech (*Argus*, Melbourne, 1 August 1914) are in Crowley, *Modern Australia*, Vol. 4, pp. 214–215.

58. Labor's little dynamo . . .: Hughes' manoeuvres to cancel the election and Fisher's refusal to be panicked are dealt with by LF Fitzhardinge, *William Morris Hughes: The Little Digger, 1914–1952*, (Vol. II of his full-scale biography), Angus & Robertson, Sydney, 1979, pp. 4–6.

59. 'The immensely significant and important thing . . .': *The Age* report of 26 September 1914 is in Crowley, *Modern Australia*, Vol. 4, pp. 222–223.

60. 'If your Ministers desire . . .': See Jose, *The Royal Australian Navy*, p. 47. As Jose wrote: 'It is now known that this proposal emanated from a sub-committee constituted on 4 August by the Committee of Imperial Defence'. Churchill ran this sub-committee through his representative, Admiral Sir Henry Jackson.

60. 'willingly render the required service . . .': Jose, p. 49.

61. The Australian sailors were not happy . . .: Jose, p. 111. Jose also complains that 'somebody in London was pressing the Pacific Dominions to send off little expeditions into unsearched and dangerous waters . . .', p. 149.

62. 'The Australian Squadron was by now scattered . . .': Jose, p. 149.

62. 'Fisher . . . a man of extreme caution . . .': Jose, p. 153.

62. Churchill responded sympathetically . . .: Admiralty cable to Australia and New Zealand in Jose, p. 155.
63. Churchill's hands-on approach . . .: For Churchill's instruction to the Admiralty, 1 October 1914, see Churchill, *The World Crisis*, Vol. I, pp. 300–301.
63. 'This shot went home': See Churchill, *The World Crisis*, p. 301.
64. an unwelcome proposal . . .: see Churchill, *The World Crisis*, p. 303.
64. 'The 26 Australian transports formed up . . .': CEW Bean, *Anzac to Amiens – A Shorter History*, Australian War Memorial, Canberra, 1946, p. 48.
65. 'The reader will remember . . .': Churchill's account of the *Emden* sinking in *The World Crisis*, Vol. I, p. 433.
65. *Australia will be there* . . .: Crowley, *Modern Australia*, pp. 223–224, provides an account of 'Skipper Francis, a crippled Welsh vocalist' and his tours to promote his patriotic songwriting. 'Its success was electrical.'
66. 'not a ship was sunk': Churchill, *The World Crisis*, pp. 304–305.

Chapter 5: 'An excess of imagination'
Page
68. 'So, through a Churchill's excess . . .': CEW Bean, *The Story of Anzac, The Official History of Australia in the War of 1914–1918*, Vol. I, Angus & Robertson, Sydney, 1921, p. 201.
68. Churchill saw at once: Churchill's response to Bean in his *The World Crisis*, Vol. II, p. 122.
69. 'We have dropped the Churchill way . . .': AK Macdougall (ed.), *War Letters of General Monash*, Duffy & Snellgrove, Sydney, 2002, pp. 69–70.
69. 'The Dardanelles failure was due . . .': David Lloyd George, *War Memoirs*, Vol. I, Odhams Press, London, 1933, p. 139.
71. 'the two pillars of the British Government . . .': Bean, *The Story of Anzac*, Vol. I, p. 175.
71. 'He won his way to the Premiership . . .': Lloyd George, *War Memoirs*, Vol. I, p. 56.
71. 'Winston, whom most people would call ugly . . .': Note on p. 176 of Gilbert, *Winston Churchill*, Vol. III, Letter to Venetia Stanley, 2 November 1914.
72. '. . . one of the most extraordinary communications . . .': Michael Howard in his chapter, 'Churchill and the First World War' in Robert Blake and William Roger Louis (eds.), *Churchill*, Oxford University Press, Oxford, 1993, p. 133.

73. 'Homeric laughter': Brock, p. 263.
73. '. . . glittering commands': quoted by Michael Howard in Blake and Louis, *Churchill*, p. 134.
73. 'Mr Churchill, having seen the German heavy howitzers . . .': Churchill, *The World Crisis*, Vol. II, p. 105.
73. 'Churchill's alluring vision . . .': Bean, *The Story of Anzac*, Vol. I, p. 200. It is worth noting that when Bean published an abridged version, *Anzac to Amiens*, in 1946, he dropped most of his criticisms of Churchill.
74. 'Who is co-ordinating and directing . . .?': quoted in Les Carlyon, *Gallipoli*, Pan Macmillan Australia, Sydney, 2001, p. 58.
74. 'Are there not other alternatives . . .': Churchill's letter to Asquith, 29 December 1914, Churchill, *The World Crisis*, Vol. II, p. 44.
75. '. . . the three salient facts . . .': Churchill, *The World Crisis*, Vol. II, p. 29.
75. 'Mr Churchill suggested . . .': The War Council minutes were recorded by Sir Maurice Hankey, the long-serving Cabinet Secretary. See Gilbert, *Winston Churchill*, Vol. III of the Official Biography, p. 220.
76. 'These ships are vital . . .': See Churchill's account in *The World Crisis*, Vol. I, pp. 208–209.
77. . . . the Grand Duke asked . . .: See Churchill, *The World Crisis*, Vol. II, p. 93.
78. 'Nobody would expose a modern fleet . . .': See Robert Rhodes James, *Gallipoli* (Australian edition), Angus & Robertson, Sydney, 1965, p. 4.
78. 'The British . . . persisted . . .': James, *Gallipoli*, p. 16.
79. 'Catch-22 . . .': Carlyon, *Gallipoli*, p. 34.
79. 'Please assure the Grand Duke . . .': See Churchill, *The World Crisis*, Vol. II, pp. 94–95.
79. 'The only place . . .': Kitchener to Churchill, 2 January 1915, Churchill, *The World Crisis*, Vol. II, p. 94.
79. 'Do you consider . . .': Churchill's telegram to Admiral Carden, 3 January 1915, Churchill, *The World Crisis*, Vol. II, pp. 97–98.
79. 'With reference to your telegram . . .': Carden's reply to Churchill, 5 January 1915, Churchill, *The World Crisis*, Vol. II, pp. 98–99.
80. 'heard with extreme interest . . .': Churchill in *The World Crisis*, Vol. II, p. 99.
80. 'Your view is agreed . . .': Churchill to Carden, 6 January 1915, Churchill, *The World Crisis*, Vol. II, p. 99.
80. '. . . it *might* be done . . .': In his evidence before the Dardanelles Commission, Carden further qualified his qualified

reply to Churchill. 'I did not mean distinctly that the Straits could be forced', he said. See *The Dardanelles Commission 1914–1916*, London, The Stationery Office, 2000, Uncovered Edition, p. 38.

81. Acting in the belief . . .: Carden made it clear to the Commission that he assumed that the Board of Admiralty and Lord Fisher in particular supported Churchill. Fisher himself told the Commission: 'Naturally, Carden would think I was in it, would he not?' *The Dardanelles Commission Report*, p. 39.

81. '. . . events took a dramatic turn . . .': Hankey's diary entry for 13 January 1915 quoted from James, *Gallipoli*, p. 32.

81. 'He was beautiful . . .': Fisher's evidence to Dardanelles Commission quoted in James, *Gallipoli*, p. 32.

82. 'would probably result in indiscriminate massacres': Sir Henry Jackson's memo to Churchill dated 5 January 1915 is given in *Dardanelles Commission Report*, pp. 39–40.

82. 'Asquith was seen to be writing . . .': James, *Gallipoli*, p. 32.

83. 'Your scheme was laid . . .': Churchill's telegram to Carden, 15 January 1915, Churchill, *The War Crisis*, p. 111.

83. Churchill took it upon himself . . .: Churchill writes in *The World Crisis*, p. 118: 'I now proceeded to open the matter to the French Government.'

83. 'by urgent political considerations . . .': Churchill's letter to the Admiralty, 20 January 1915, in Churchill, *The World Crisis*, p. 120.

84. 'It would be inexcusable to waste [AE2] . . .': see Gilbert, *Winston Churchill*, Vol. III, p. 259.

84. Lord Fisher's anxieties . . .: Martin Gilbert, *Winston Churchill*, Vol III, has a very full account of Fisher's attempt to resign, the meeting with Asquith and Churchill and the confrontation with Kitchener on pp. 268–272. Gilbert gives Fisher's letters to Asquith and Churchill on 28 January in full on pp. 268–269. Churchill in *The World Crisis*, Vol. II, pp. 164–165, quotes the minutes of the War Council meeting of 28 January 1915, with a commentary by Fisher himself, in which Fisher writes: 'After further talk, Lord Fisher reluctantly gave in to Lord Kitchener', and added 'silence or resignation was the right course'.

86. 'Damn the Dardanelles': In *The World Crisis*, Vol. II, Churchill gives a selection of Fisher's changing views, including this outburst on 5 April 1915. (See pp. 302–303.)

86. 'He out-argues me': Violet Bonham Carter, *Winston Churchill As I Knew Him*, p. 355.

86. 'Surely in your position . . .': Gilbert, *Winston Churchill*, Vol. II, p. 278, gives Churchill's letter to Asquith of 8 February 1915, including the unsent portion.

86. 'If the First Sea Lord had not approved . . .': Author's emphasis. Churchill's resignation speech, House of Commons, 15 November 1915, is given very fully by Martin Gilbert, *Winston Churchill*, Vol. III, pp. 566–568.

Chapter 6: 'Only dig, dig, dig'

Page
87. 'Are the Australians good enough?': quoted by Gilbert in 'Churchill and Gallipoli', Chapter 11, in *The Straits of War – Gallipoli Remembered*, Sutton Publishing, London, 2000, p. 132.

88. 'the arrival of the Anzacs . . .': Churchill, *The World Crisis*, Vol. I, pp. 499–500.

88. 'the Australian battalions trampled . . .': Churchill, *The World Crisis*, Vol I, p. 500.

88. 'crammed Cairo full every night . . .': Godley's comments on the Anzacs quoted by Jeffrey Grey, 'The Australian Army', *The Australian Centenary History of Defence*, Vol. I, Oxford University Press, Australia, 2001, p. 42.

88. 'My principal impression . . .': quoted by Geoffrey Serle, *Monash*, Melbourne University Press, Melbourne, 1982, p. 211.

88. 'The Day of Resolve': Churchill's account of the War Council of 16 February 1915 is at pp. 180–181, *The World Crisis*, Vol. II. Also see Gilbert, *Winston Churchill*, Vol. III, pp. 287–288.

89. 'You get through . . .': Kitchener to Churchill, Gilbert, *Winston Churchill*, Vol. III, p. 288.

89. Kitchener reneged: Churchill's protests to Kitchener and Asquith, and his intense foreboding, at pp. 184–189 of *The World Crisis*, Vol. II. Asquith's refusal to overrule Kitchener is at pp. 184–185.

89. 'Should we get through . . .': Churchill's letter to Sir Edward Grey is quoted in full in Gilbert, *Winston Churchill*, Vol. III, p. 315.

90. 'I was sitting with Clemmie . . .': For Violet Asquith's account of Churchill's euphoria on 1 March 1915, see Violet Bonham Carter, *Winston Churchill As I Knew Him*, pp. 368–369.

90. 'I must now put on record . . .': Churchill, *The World Crisis*, Vol. II, p. 186.

91. 'We are all agreed . . .': Asquith's letter to Venetia Stanley quoted in Gilbert, *Winston Churchill*, Vol. II, p. 304.

91. 'Winston was at his worst . . .': Gilbert, *Winston Churchill*, Vol. III, p. 310.
92. Kitchener ordered Birdwood . . .: Bean, *The Story of Anzac*, Vol. I, p. 193.
92. 'I am very doubtful . . .': Bean, *The Story of Anzac*, Vol. I, p. 193.
92. 'We are sending a military force . . .': Kitchener to Sir Ian Hamilton, 10 March 1915, Churchill, *The World Crisis*, Vol. II, p. 208.
92. 'If the Fleet gets through . . .': Kitchener quoted in Alan Moorehead, *Gallipoli*, Hamish Hamilton, London, 1956, p. 83.
93. Another decisive factor . . .: Sir Henry Jackson's memorandum to Churchill, 11 March 1915, is given in *The Dardanelles Commission Report*, p. 117. His assertion that 'it would be a very mad thing' is given at p. 93.
93. a keen insight into the character of the Australians . . .: Sir Ian Hamilton's *Report of An Inspection of the Military Forces of the Commonwealth of Australia, 24 April 1914*. See Greenwood and Grimshaw, *Documents on Australian International Affairs*, pp. 256 ff.
94. Churchill cabled Carden on 15 March . . .: Churchill, *The World Crisis*, Vol. II, p. 218.
95. 'We suggest for your consideration . . .': Churchill to Carden, 11 March 1915, Churchill, *The World Crisis*, Vol. II, p. 218; Churchill to Carden, 14 March 1915, Churchill, *The World Crisis*, Vol. II, p. 218.
95. 'By God, I'll go through tomorrow . . .': Quoted in Martin Gilbert, *A History of the 20th Century*, Vol. I, 1900–1933, HarperCollins, London, 1997, p. 365.
96. 'The mighty ships wheeling . . .': Churchill, *The World Crisis*, Vol. II, p. 225.
97. 'What more could we want?': Churchill, *The World Crisis*, Vol. II, p. 234.
97. 'Looking back . . .': Churchill, *The World Crisis*, Vol. II, p. 235.
98. 'a masterly paper': Hamilton on Churchill, Gilbert, *Winston Churchill*, Vol. III, p. 64; Churchill on Hamilton in Churchill, *The Boer War*, p. 284.
98. 'The sailors say special craft . . .': Hamilton's complaint about 'beetles' is quoted in Carlyon, *Gallipoli*, p. 80.
98. Hamilton's concept . . .: This interpretation follows Simon Foster, *Hit The Beach – Landings Under Fire*, Rigel, London, 2004, Chapter 2.
99. Churchill's cry of despair . . .: Churchill, *The World Crisis*, Vol. II, pp. 252–253.

100. 'It had been intended . . .': Churchill's description of the Anzac landings, *The World Crisis,* Vol. II, pp. 321–322.
101. 'to hold the ridges . . .': Lord Kinross, *Ataturk – The Rebirth of a Nation,* Weidenfeld & Nicolson, London, 1964, p. 73.
101. 'I order you to die': Kinross, *Ataturk,* p. 76. Kemal's Order continued: 'In the time it takes us to die, other troops and commanders can come and take our places.'
102. 'The long-limbed athletic Anzacs . . .': Churchill, *The World Crisis,* Vol. II, p. 323.
102. '. . . all the way from the Southern Cross . . .': Hamilton's description quoted in Carlyon, *Gallipoli,* p. 151.
102. 'Both my divisional generals . . .': Birdwood's message to Hamilton is given in Bean, *The Story of Anzac,* Vol. I, p. 458.
102. 'Your news is indeed serious': Bean, *The Story of Anzac,* Vol. I, p. 460. The postscript, 'Dig, dig, dig', p. 461.
103. Ashmead-Bartlett's account: A full version from *The Argus,* Melbourne, 8 May 1915 is given in Crowley, *Modern Australia,* Vol. 4, pp. 234–236.
104. 'first mad rush ashore': Letter from Monash dated Anzac, 18 July 1915 in Tony Macdougall (ed.), *War Letters of General Monash,* Duffy & Snellgrove, Sydney, 2002, p. 66.
105. 'I am off to Scotland . . .': Fisher's letter to Churchill, 15 May 1915, Churchill, *The World Crisis,* Vol. II, p. 359. Fisher's anger was increased by the fact that Churchill had marked his Order to the Admiralty 'First Sea Lord to see *after* action'.
106. 'What are we to do for you?': Churchill, *The World Crisis,* Vol. II, p. 366.
107. 'The paralysis of the Executive . . .': Churchill, *The World Crisis,* Vol. II, p. 516.

Chapter 7: 'The last and finest crusade'
Page

109. 'Asquith lacks initiative . . .': Quoted in John Grigg, *Lloyd George – From Peace to War 1912–1916,* HarperCollins edition, London, 1997, p. 246.
110. 'The Dardanelles haunted him . . .': Gilbert, *Winston Churchill,* Vol. III, p. 429.
110. 'Beyond those few miles . . .': Churchill's Dundee speech, Gilbert, *Winston Churchill,* Vol. III, pp. 488–491.
111. 'A very hot discussion . . .': Churchill, *The World Crisis,* Vol. II, p. 393.

111. 'The long and varied annals of the British Army . . .': Churchill, *The World Crisis*, Vol. II, p. 432.

112. 'The Anzac Corps fought . . .': Ashmead-Bartlett's report of the August offensive in *The Times*, 3 September 1915, is reproduced in facsimile in Harvey Broadbent, *Gallipoli – The Fatal Shore*, Viking, Australia, 2004, p. 221.

113. 'the most ghastly and costly fiasco . . .': Ashmead-Bartlett's letter to Asquith. See Fred and Elizabeth Brenchley, *Myth Maker – Ellis Ashmead-Bartlett, the Englishman Who Sparked Australia's Gallipoli Legend*, John Wiley & Sons, Australia, 2005, pp. 165–166.

113. 'the perfect picture of a fallen minister...': Brenchley, *Myth Maker*, p. 108.

114. 'a wheedling letter...': Brenchley, *Myth Maker*, p. 163.

114. 'begged me to write a letter . . .': RM Younger, *Keith Murdoch – Founder of a Media Empire*, HarperCollins, Australia, 2003, p. 64.

114. 'Your fears have been justified . . .': Murdoch's letter to Andrew Fisher, Younger, *Keith Murdoch*, pp. 66–68.

116. 'throwing up the sponge . . .': See Gilbert, *Winston Churchill*, Vol. III, pp. 538–539.

116. Churchill played the Australia card: Churchill's memorandum, 15 October 1915, Churchill, *The World Crisis*, Vol. II, pp. 485–487.

116. 'British gas should be sent out without delay . . .': Churchill, *The World Crisis*, Vol. II, pp. 487–488.

117. 'What is your estimate...': Kitchener to Hamilton, 11 October 1915, Churchill, *The World Crisis*, Vol. II, p. 488.

117. 'It would not be wise . . .': Hamilton's reply, Churchill, *The World Crisis*, Vol. II, p. 488.

117. 'He came, he saw . . .': Churchill, *The World Crisis*, Vol. II, p. 489.

117. 'like a thunderbolt': Kitchener to Birdwood, Churchill, *The World Crisis*, Vol. II, p. 490.

118. 'I have a clear conscience . . .': Churchill's letter of resignation, 11 November 1918, Gilbert, *Winston Churchill*, Vol. III, p. 564. Churchill's resignation speech in House of Commons, 15 November 1915, Gilbert, *Winston Churchill*, Vol. III, p. 567.

Chapter 8: 'True to the Empire'
Page

120. 'They're all Australians now . . .': Paterson, *Complete Poems*, p. 308.

120. Australia's oldest Catholic newspaper: *Freeman's Journal* quoted in Crowley, *Modern Australia*, Vol. 4, p. 255; the RSL view at p. 264.

122. 'I am in the unhappy position . . .': Quoted in John Robertson, *Anzac and Empire*, Hamlyn Australia 1990, p. 239; Andrew Fisher's Minute of Dissent, *The Dardanelles Commission Report*, pp. 84–85.

123. 'Like a new Joshua . . .': Australian press opinion in Robertson, *Anzac and Empire*, p. 235.

123. 'It will then be understood . . .': Churchill's submission to the Dardanelles Commission quoted in Gilbert, *Winston Churchill*, Vol. IV, pp. 10–11.

126. 'I am sorry you have put that question . . .': Carlyon, *Gallipoli*, p. 501 (House of Representatives, 29 October 1915).

126. 'The Call to Arms': Hughes' letter, 15 December 1915, quoted in Crowley, *Modern Australia*, Vol. 4, pp. 249–250.

127. 'the whole fate of the world': Hughes' Melbourne speech, 13 January 1916 in Crowley, *Modern Australia*, Vol. 4, pp. 250–251.

128. 'does not look like a Labour Premier . . .': Lord Stamfordham quoted in Fitzhardinge, *The Little Digger*, p. 91.

129. *The Times* report: See John Williams, *Anzacs, the Media and the Great War*, UNSW Press, Sydney, 1999, p. 110.

130. A banquet at the Ritz Hotel: Speeches by Hughes and Churchill quoted in W. Farmer Whyte, *William Morris Hughes – His Life and Times*, Angus & Robertson, Sydney, 1956, pp. 260–263.

134. 'The great enemy of Australia . . .': Crowley, *Modern Australia*, Vol. 4, pp. 267–269.

136. 'You curs . . .': See Graham Freudenberg, *Cause for Power – The Official History of the New South Wales Labor Party*, Pluto Press, Sydney, 1991, p. 110.

136. 'The Black Day of the German Army . . .': Sir John Monash, *The Australian Victories in France in 1918*, Hutchinson, London, 1920, pp. 130–131. Monash used Ludendorff's *Memoirs* published in the London *Times* on 27 August 1919.

137. 'my whole interests and sympathies are British': Monash's letter to his American cousin in Macdougall, *War Letters*, pp. 13–14.

137. 'The Australian armoured cars . . .': Churchill's letter to Clementine, 10 August 1918, Gilbert, *Winston Churchill*, Vol. IV, p. 133.

138. 'A hole had been driven . . .': Monash, *Australian Victories in France*, p. 131.

139. 'I am so glad . . .': Letter to Clementine, Gilbert, *Winston Churchill*, Vol. IV, p. 133.

140. 'much interrupted' by visitors . . .: Monash's account of his meeting with Churchill and other visitors in a letter to his wife, dated 11 August 1918, Macdougall, *War Letters*, p. 198.
140. 'The war must be ended . . .': SLA Marshall, *World War I*, Mariner Books, New York, 2001, p. 418.

Chapter 9: 'Mr Churchill backslides'
Page
144. 'And do you mean, Mr Hughes . . .': Winston Churchill, *The Aftermath: A Sequel to the World Crisis*, Macmillan, London, 1929, p.152.
144. 'in early life you were a cannibal . . .': Churchill, *The Aftermath*, pp. 152–153.
145. 'the least creditable of Churchill's career': Roy Jenkins, *Churchill*, Pan Macmillan, London, 2001, p. 345.
145. 'Do, my darling, use your influence': Clementine Churchill's letter of 18 February 1921 quoted in Jenkins, *Churchill*, p. 362.
146. 'Kill the Bolshies . . .': Quoted in Gilbert, *Winston Churchill*, Vol. IV, p. 278.
148. He didn't trust Churchill: Page in House of Representatives, 13 April 1921, quoted in Sir Earle Page, *Truant Surgeon*, Angus & Robertson, Sydney, 1963, p. 66.
149. 'Getting Japan to protect you . . .': Churchill on Japan, Gilbert, *Winston Churchill*, Vol. IV, p. 607.
150. 'Would I prefer . . .': Hughes' speech on the Anglo–Japanese Treaty quoted in Fitzhardinge, *The Little Digger*, p. 472.
151. The notes shot around the table: Notes between Curzon, Lloyd George, A. Chamberlain and Churchill, Gilbert, *Winston Churchill*, Vol. IV, p. 607.
152. 'The unity of the Empire . . .': WM Hughes, *The Splendid Adventure*, Ernest Benn, London, 1929, pp. 133–134.
152. 'Mr Churchill Backslides . . .': Hughes, *The Splendid Adventure*, pp. 134–136.
153. 'impossible to shift him by argument': Hughes, *The Splendid Adventure*, p. 138.

Chapter 10: 'All was to end in shame'
Page
157. 'a rebel to a warrior prince . . .': Churchill, *The Aftermath*, Macmillan, 1941 Australian edition, pp. 368.
157. Lloyd George on the Greeks: Churchill, *The Aftermath*, p. 391.

157. 'preference for the Turk': Fitzhardinge, *The Little Digger*, p. 485.
157. 'died of this monkey's bite': Churchill, *The Aftermath*, p. 386.
157. 'on this world so torn . . .': Churchill, *The Aftermath*, p. 378.
158. 'If the Greeks go off . . .': Churchill, *The Aftermath*, p. 396.
158. 'The re-entry of the Turks . . .': Churchill, *The Aftermath*, p. 419.
159. 'immediately push a bayonet . . .': Lord Beaverbrook, *Decline and Fall of Lloyd George*, Collins, London, 1963, p. 166.
159. Telegram to the Dominions: Churchill, *The Aftermath*, pp. 424–425; also Fitzhardinge, *The Little Digger*, pp. 486–487; for Churchill's press release, see Churchill, *The Aftermath*, pp. 426–427.
160. 'None of the British Ministers . . .': Churchill, *The Aftermath*, p. 428.
161. Hughes . . . did his Imperial duty: Fitzhardinge, *The Little Digger*, pp. 487–488.
161. 'Your telegram came as a bolt from the blue': Hughes' protest to Lloyd George, Fitzhardinge, *The Little Digger*, pp. 487–491.
163. 'Prepared at all times . . .': Speeches by Hughes, Charlton and Page, House of Representatives, 19 September 1922, *Commonwealth Parliamentary Debates*, p. 2351 ff.
164. 'To say that this savoured of sharp practice . . .': Hughes, *The Splendid Adventure*, p. 243.
165. '"Chastened" is an unlikely word . . .': Churchill's messages to Dominion Prime Ministers, Gilbert, *Winston Churchill*, Vol. IV, pp. 842–847.
166. 'You are indeed right . . .': Churchill to Harington quoted in Gilbert, *Winston Churchill*, Vol. IV, p. 851.
168. 'Situation is now greatly relieved . . .': Document in the National Archives of Australia, Barcode 353292, dated London, 11 October 1922.

Chapter 11: 'Winston has gone mad'
Page
171. "That extraordinary fellow Winston . . .': Quoted in James, *Study in Failure*, p. 168.
172. 'I found myself . . .': James, *Study in Failure*, p. 149.
172. 'Will the bloody duck swim?': Gilbert, *Winston Churchill*, Vol. V, p. 59.
172. 'Ten years is a long time . . .': Churchill, *The Gathering Storm* (Vol. I of his war memoirs), p. 43.

173. 'The long continuance of this rule . . .': Quoted in James, *Study in Failure*, p. 166.

173. 'We converted ourselves to military impotence': James, *Study in Failure*, p. 166.

173. 'How large should Australia's navy be?': Jellicoe's Report in James Neidpath, *The Singapore Naval Base and the Defence of Britain's Eastern Empire 1919–1941*, Clarendon Press, Oxford, 1981, p. 22.

173. 'the key to the Far East': Neidpath, *Singapore Naval Base*, p. 30.

174. 'that we had a Naval Policy': British Cabinet Minute 16/6/21 in Neidpath, *Singapore Naval Base*, p. 56.

174. '. . . our finger on the trigger . . .': Quoted in Gilbert, *Winston Churchill*, Vol. V, p. 85.

175. 'A war with Japan!': Quoted by Robert O'Neill, Chapter 28, 'Japan and British Security in the Pacific' in Blake and Louis (eds.), *Churchill*, p. 279.

175. 'Great as are the injuries . . .': Gilbert, *Winston Churchill*, Vol. V, p. 85.

176. 'The number of our capital ships . . .': Quoted in AN Wilson, *After the Victorians: 1901–1953*, Hutchinson, London, 2005, p. 325.

177. 'We do not wish to put ourselves . . .': Martin Gilbert (ed.), *Churchill: Companion Volume to the Years 1922–39*, William Heinemann, London, 2005, p. 1033.

177. Casey told Bruce in May . . .: WJ Hudson and June North (eds.), *My Dear P.M. – R. G. Casey's Letters to S.M. Bruce 1924–1929*, Australian Government Publishing Service, Canberra, 1980, Letter No. 20, 7 May 1925, pp. 39–40.

177. 'I saw Admiral Field . . .': Hudson and North, *Dear P.M.*, Letter No. 27, 23 July 1925, p. 63.

179. Churchill 'very civil': WJ Hudson, *Casey*, Oxford University Press, Melbourne, 1986, p. 38.

179. 'Churchill finds himself in some difficulty . . .': Hudson and North, *Dear P.M.*, Letter No. 26, 6 July 1925, p. 61.

180. 'Churchill is the snag': WJ Hudson and Wendy May (eds.), *Letters From a 'Secret Service Agent' – F.L. McDougall to S.M. Bruce 1924–1929*, Australian Department of Foreign Affairs, 1986, Letter No. 36, 22 October 1925, p. 103.

180. 'There is a general feeling . . .': Hudson and May, *McDougall to Bruce*, Letter No. 83, 5 August 1926, p. 274.

181 'So long as the bulk of the Tory Party . . .': Hudson and May, *McDougall to Bruce*, Letter No. 188, 3 October 1928, p. 655.

181. Casey's view on Churchill's prospects: See Hudson and North, *Dear P.M.*, p. 186.

181. 'They are great diners out . . .': Hudson and North, *Dear P.M.*, pp. 43–44.
183. 'We must hold our own . . .': Article in London *Daily Mail*, 27 May 1934.
183. '. . . a seditious Middle Temple lawyer . . .': Churchill's speech to West Essex Conservative Association, 23 February 1931, quoted in Gilbert, *Winston Churchill*, Vol. V, p. 390.
183. 'a crazy dream with a terrible awakening': Gilbert, *Winston Churchill*, Vol. V, p. 399.

Chapter 12: 'The gathering storm'
Page
186. 'Hitler's lies and untimely truculence . . .': AW Martin, *Robert Menzies – A Life*, Vol. I, Melbourne University Press, 1993, p. 155.
186. 'It is very dangerous to underrate . . .': Gilbert, *Winston Churchill*, Volume V, p. 644.
186. 'His theme is a constant repetition . . .': Martin, *Menzies*, Vol. I, p. 155.
186. 'My impression . . .': Martin, *Menzies*, Vol. I, p. 153.
187. 'May I add . . .': Menzies to Hughes quoted in Martin, *Menzies*, Vol. I, p. 140.
187. 'A red letter day': Martin, *Menzies*, Vol. I, pp. 161–162; 'Mr Menzies is Australian-born', quoted in Martin, *Menzies*, Vol. I, p. 160.
188. 'Baldwin flourishes . . .': Gilbert, *Winston Churchill*, Vol. V, note on p. 833.
189. 'It is our duty . . .': Lyons' speech quoted in JM McCarthy, 'Australia and Imperial Defence 1918–1939', *Australian Journal of Politics and History*, Vol. 17, No. 1, April 1971.
189. 'A trade-off for good behaviour . . .': See Gough Whitlam, *The Whitlam Government*, p. 116.
191. Menzies' main criticism . . .: See Martin, *Menzies*, Vol. I, pp. 234–235; 'a dreamer, a man of ideas', p. 235; 'an irresponsible backbencher', p. 234.
192. 'There appears to be a gloomy feeling . . .': Menzies to Lyons, 6 August 1938, *Documents on Australian Foreign Policy (DAFP)*, Department of Foreign Affairs, Australian Government Publishing Service, 1975, Vol. 1, Document No. 237, p. 401.
193. '. . . A total and unmitigated defeat . . .': Churchill's speech, and Lady Astor's interjection, is given in Gilbert, *Winston Churchill*, Vol. V, p. 997.
195. A more convincing counterfactual: See John Lukacs, *The Hitler of History*, Phoenix Press, London, 2002, pp. 144–145.

195. 'The overwhelming majority of ordinary people . . .': AJP Taylor, *English History 1914–1945*, Oxford University Press, 1965, p. 430.
195. 'It is the end of the British Empire . . .': Harold Nicolson, *The Harold Nicolson Diaries 1907–1964*, Phoenix edition, 2005, 22 September 1938, p. 196; for Lyons and White, see Martin, *Menzies*, Vol. I, p. 237.
196. 'At the best . . .': *Sydney Morning Herald* quoted in EM Andrews, *Isolationism and Appeasement in Australia – Reaction to the European Crises 1935–1939*, ANU Press, Canberra, 1970, p. 144.
198. Curtin's secret binges: David Day, *John Curtin – A Life*, Harper-Collins, Sydney, 1999, pp. 365–366.
198. 'Socialism is the only way . . .': See Geoffrey Serle in Vol. 13, John Ritchie (ed.), *Australian Dictionary of Biography*, Melbourne University Press, Melbourne, 1993.
199. 'our business is to keep Australia . . .': Quoted in Andrews, *Isolationism and Appeasement*, p. 27.
199. 'as one who knew the man': Paul Hasluck, *The Government and the People 1939–1941*, Vol. II, *Australia in the War of 1939–45*, Australian War Memorial, Canberra, 1952, p 75.
200. 'Sadly we must put aside . . .': *Australian Worker*. 9 November 1938.
200. 'If an Eastern first-class power . . .': Quoted in Hasluck, *Government and People*, Vol. I, p. 83.
201. 'We stand for the maintenance...': Federal ALP Conference decisions, May 1939, see Hasluck, *Government and People*, p. 91.
201. '. . . the theme is emerging . . .': Gilbert, *Winston Churchill*, Vol. V, p. 1063.
202. 'Danzig . . . is the danger spot . . .': Gilbert, *Winston Churchill*, Vol. V, p. 1087.
202. 'two sides to the Polish question': Andrews, *Isolationism and Appeasement*, p. 178.
203. 'Bruce came to see me': Gilbert, *Winston Churchill*, Vol. V, p. 1086.

Chapter 13: 'Australia is also at war'
Page
204. 'my melancholy duty . . .': Quoted in Hasluck, *Government and People*, Vol. I, p. 152.
207. 'I feel like one . . .': Winston Churchill, *The Second World War*, Vol. I, London, 1948, pp. 339–340.
209. 'It may be that . . .': Menzies quoted by Gavin Long, 'To Benghazi', Official History, *Australia in the War of 1939–45*, Australian War Memorial, Canberra, 1952, p. 39.

209. 'if Japan adopted . . .': David Horner, *Crisis of Command*, ANU Press, Canberra, 1978, p. 10.
210. 'If the choice . . .': *Documents in Australian Foreign Policy 1937–1949*, Vol. III, 17 November 1939.
210. 'It was my recorded conviction . . .': Churchill, *The Second World War*, Vol. II, p. 12. The emphasis is Churchill's.
210. 'Mr Churchill never hesitated': Neidpath, *The Singapore Base*, p. 179.
211. 'Am bound to tell you . . .': *DAFP*, Vol III, p. 441.
211. 'An accident would be a disaster': Gavin Long, *The Six Years War – Australia in the 1939–45 War*, Australian War Memorial, Canberra, 1973, p. 24.
212. Menzies weighed in: See Martin Gilbert, *Finest Hour – Winston S. Churchill 1939–1941*, Heinemann, London, 1983, p. 130.
213. '. . . this timid gang': Nicolson, *Diaries*, 8 May 1940, p. 243.
213. 'It was a marvel . . .': David Reynolds, *In Command of History*, Allen Lane, London, 2004, p. 126,
214. 'This is not the decisive point . . .': *The Memoirs of Lord Ismay*, Heinemann, London, 1960, p. 140.

Chapter 14: 'I can see my way through'
Page

217. 'It almost causes me pain . . .': See Oscar Pincus, *The War Aims and Strategies of Adolf Hitler*, MacFarland and Company, North Carolina & London, 2005, p. 119.
218. 'Shoot Gandhi': see Niall Ferguson, *The War of the World – History's Age of Hatred*, Penguin, London, 2007, p. 414.
219. '. . . like a stinker . . .': see AN Wilson, *After the Victorians*, p. 370.
219. 'I trust you realise . . .': Warren F Kimball (ed.), *Churchill and Roosevelt – The Complete Correspondence*, Vol. I, Collins, London, 1984, p. 38.
220. In reply, Roosevelt promised: Kimball, *Complete Correspondence*, Vol. I, pp. 38–39.
220. 'I shall drag in . . .': Gilbert, *The Finest Hour*, p. 358.
223. 'The people . . . were deciding . . .': Long, *Six Years War*, p. 31.
223. 'all–round sacrifice . . .': Long, *Six Years War*, p. 30.
225. 'Could Australia spare . . .': See David Horner, *Defence Supremo – Sir Frederick Shedden and the Making of Australian Defence Policy*, Allen & Unwin, Sydney, 2000, pp. 85–86.
225. Bruce cabled Menzies: 3 July 1940, *DAFP*, Vol. IV, Document No. 7.

226. Ismay said on Churchill's behalf: 4 July 1940, *DAFP*, Vol. IV, Document No. 9.

226. Churchill confessed . . .: Churchill, *The Second World War*, Vol. II, pp. 372–373.

228. 'In Churchill's mind . . .': Douglas Porch, *Hitler's Mediterranean Gamble*, Cassell, London, 2004, p. 26.

229. 'With his mind on the total strategic picture': Blake and Louis, *Churchill*, p. 180.

229. 'I do not understand . . .': Churchill, *Second World War*, Vol. II, p. 377.

229. 'Would it not be better . . .': Churchill, *Second World War*, Vol. II, p. 410.

229. 'I do not think myself . . .': Churchill to Menzies, 11 August 1940, *DAFP*, Vol. IV, Document No. 64.

230. 'If contrary to prudence . . .': 11 August 1940, *DAFP*, Vol. IV, Document No. 66.

231. 'We cannot stress . . .': Quoted in Hasluck, *The Government and the People*, Vol. I, p. 225.

231. 'We would prefer . . .': 29 August 1940, *DAFP*, Vol. IV, Document No. 84.

232. Further consideration was suspended: See *DAFP*, Vol. IV, Document Nos. 123 (18 September 1940), 134, (24 September 1940), 135 (24 September 1940).

232. Churchill's visit: Clement Semmler (ed.) *The War Diaries of Kenneth Slessor*, University of Queensland Press, 1985, p. 105.

233. Churchill's speech: Long, *To Benghazi*, p. 309.

233. 'powerfully distressed': Slessor, *War Diaries*, p. 124.

233. Dedman's assessment: See Horner, *Defence Supremo*, p. 88.

234. 'In that terrible hour . . .': Menzies, *Afternoon Light*, p. 18.

236. 'It is absolutely wrong . . .': 29 September 1940, *DAFP*, Vol. IV, Document No. 144.

236. 'If it is to be laid down . . .': 2 October 1940, *DAFP*, Vol. IV, Document No. 152.

237. 'My telegram was somewhat crudely expressed': 4 October 1940, *DAFP*, Vol. IV, No. 158.

238. Churchill purred in reply: 6 October 1940, *DAFP*, Vol. IV, Document No. 160.

238. Bruce . . . found himself: 2 October 1940, *DAFP*, Vol. IV, Document No. 153.

Chapter 15: 'For the sake of our kith and kin'

Page

241. 'not really interested in war . . .': Quoted in Porch, *Hitler's Mediterranean Gamble*, p. 110.
241. 'Our gallant French Allies . . .': Victoria Schofield, *Wavell: Soldier and Statesman*, John Murray, London, 2006, p. 145.
242. 'Gentlemen, I have asked you . . .': Quoted in Alan Moorehead, *African Trilogy*, Hamish Hamilton, London, 1944, p. 60.
242. 'some trouble here . . .': Bruce to Menzies, 10 December 1940, *DAFP*, Vol. IV, Document No. 220; 'it had been announced . . .': Menzies to Bruce, 12 December 1940, *DAFP*, Vol. IV, No. 222.
243. 'Remember that I could not guarantee . . .': Churchill to Menzies, 13 December 1940, *DAFP*, Vol. IV, Document No. 225.
244. 'The danger of Japan . . .': Churchill to Menzies, 23 December 1940, *DAFP*, Vol. IV, Document No. 236.
244. 'A third sphere of danger . . .': Two drafts of Churchill's famous letter of 7 December 1940 are in Kimball, *Complete Correspondence*, Vol. I, pp. 89–102. The letter as sent is C-43, pp. 102–109.
245. 'Omit. We want . . .': Kimball, *Complete Correspondence*, Vol. I, p. 91.
246. 'alarming position in regard to the defence of Singapore . . .': Advisory War Council Minute, 25 November 1940, *DAFP*, Vol. IV, Document No. 208.
246. 'Would be glad . . .': Menzies to Bruce, 3 January 1941, *DAFP*, Vol. IV, Document No. 243.
246. 'Major policy is increasingly centred . . .': Bruce to Menzies, 5 January 1941, *DAFP*, Vol. IV, Document No. 246.
248. 'my right hand . . .': For the high opinion of Menzies and Curtin of Shedden, see especially David Horner, *Defence Supremo*.
248. 'Churchill had lunched with him . . .': AW Martin and Patsy Hardy (eds.), *Dark and Hurrying Days – Menzies' 1941 Diary*, National Library of Australia, Canberra, 1993, p. 23.
248. 'This Far Eastern problem . . .': *Menzies 1941 Diary*, p. 24.
249. 'Hitler always faces me . . .': Mussolini quoted in Ian Kershaw, *Fateful Choices*, Allen Lane, London, 2007, p. 169.
250. 'Destruction of Greece . . .': Churchill to Wavell, 10 January 1941, Churchill, *Grand Alliance* (Vol. III of War Memoirs), p. 17.
251. 'This does not alter . . .': Churchill to Wavell, 12 February 1941, Churchill, *Grand Alliance*, pp. 58–59.
252. 'prolonged the war in Africa by two years . . .': Corelli Barnett, *The Desert Generals*, George Allen & Unwin, London, 1960, p. 46.

252. 'We will do our best . . .': Wavell to Churchill, Churchill, *Grand Alliance*, p. 59.
252. Do not consider . . .': Churchill to Eden, *Grand Alliance*, p. 63.
253. 'Whatever the outcome . . .': Churchill's account of Eden's visit to Athens and Eden's cables are in Churchill, *Grand Alliance*, pp. 66–68.
254. 'The Chiefs of Staff having endorsed . . .': Churchill to Eden, 24 February 1941, *Grand Alliance*, pp. 68–69.

Chapter 16: 'A bold move into Greece'
Page
255. 'a tempestuous creature': Martin and Hardy, *Menzies' 1941 Diary*, Saturday 22 February 1941, p. 63.
256. 'Momentous discussion . . .': Martin and Hardy, *Menzies' 1941 Diary*, p. 64.
256. 'had already spoken to Mr Menzies . . .': Churchill, *Grand Alliance*, p. 59.
256. 'a certain latitude . . .': For Menzies' discussion with Wavell, see Horner, *Defence Supremo*, pp. 100–101, and Sir Robert Menzies, *Afternoon Light – Some Memories of Men and Events*, Cassell, Australia, 1967, p. 27.
256. 'The military arguments': Menzies to Fadden, 25 February 1941, *DAFP*, Vol. IV, Document No. 321.
258. 'Despite the risky nature . . .': Fadden to Menzies, 26 February 1941, *DAFP*, Vol. IV, Document No. 322.
259. 'I left the interview . . .': For Blamey's 'great misgivings' and Freyberg's opinion of Wavell, see David Horner, *Blamey – The Commander in Chief*, Allen & Unwin, Sydney, 1998, pp. 168–169.
260. 'Although I had reason to know . . .': Menzies on Blamey, see *Afternoon Light*, p. 27.
260. 'Probably the best soldier . . .': Wavell on Blamey, see David Horner, *Australian Dictionary of Biography*, Vol. 13, p. 198.
260. 'more ardent politician . . .': Churchill on Blamey quoted in Horner, *Blamey*, p. 264.
260. 'In view of the Germans' . . .': Blamey's report, see David Horner, *High Command – Australia's Allied Strategy 1939–1945*, Australian War Memorial, Canberra, 1982, p. 73.
261. 'Australia is Dominion No. 1': Menzies to Fadden, 4 March 1941, *DAFP*, Vol. IV, Document No. 330.
262. 'One is still left . . .': Menzies to Fadden, 8 March 1941, *DAFP*, Vol. IV, Document No. 344.

262. 'We must be able to tell . . .': Churchill to Eden, 7 March 1941, Churchill, *Grand Alliance*, pp. 92–93.

262. 'seemed relieved': John Colville, *The Fringes of Power – 10 Downing Street Diaries 1939–55*, Norton, London, 1985, 7 and 8 March 1941, p. 362; 'agreeable man': quoted in Martin, *Menzies*, Vol. I, p. 329.

263. 'in its true setting . . .': Churchill to Fadden, Churchill, *Grand Alliance*, p. 152.

263. 'I can assure you . . .': Menzies to Fadden, 7 April 1941, *DAFP*, Vol. IV, Document No. 389.

264. 'Grave imperial issues . . .': Churchill to Eden, 6 April 1941, and Eden's reply quoted in Alan Clark, *The Fall of Crete*, Cassell Military Paperbacks, London, 2001, p. 17.

264. 'The worst mistakes . . .': John Coates in Peter Dennis, Jeffrey Grey, Ewan Morris, Robin Prior, John Connor (eds.), *Oxford Companion to Australian Military History*, Oxford University Press, Melbourne, 1995, p. 275.

265. 'Here you bloody well are . . .': Vasey's order in Gavin Long, *Greece, Crete and Syria*, Australian War Memorial, Canberra, 1953, p. 70.

265. 'The intervening ages . . .': Churchill, *Grand Alliance*, p. 202.

265. 'I am increasingly of the opinion . . .': Churchill to Eden, 20 April 1941, Churchill, *Grand Alliance*, p. 202.

266. 'The Anzacs have been fighting . . .': Churchill to Roosevelt, 24 April 1941, Kimball, *Complete Correspondence*, Vol. I, C-82, p. 175.

266. The Australians in Greece lost . . .: Casualty figures from Long, *Greece, Crete and Syria*, p. 182, and Martin Gilbert, *Second World War*, Phoenix Press, London, New Edition, 2000, p. 178.

266. Churchill made a broadcast to the world: Churchill's speech in *Collected Speeches*, edited by his grandson, Winston Churchill, Pimlico, London, 2006, pp. 266–274. The poem is by Arthur Hugh Clough (1849).

267. 'no political disunity . . .': Statements by Fadden and Curtin, *DAFP*, Vol. IV, Documents No. 433 (26 April 1941) and No. 434 (27 April 1941).

268. 'Churchill's deft evasion . . .': Kenneth Slessor, *War Diaries*, p. 267.

268. 'We went in with our eyes open . . .': Slessor's interview with Blamey, *War Diaries*, p. 271.

269. 'You have done not only heroic . . .': Roosevelt to Churchill, 1 May 1941, Kimball, *Complete Correspondence*, R-38, pp. 178–180.

270. 'Your friendly message . . .': Churchill's reply, Kimball, *Complete Correspondence*, C-84, p. 181.

Chapter 17: 'Winston is a dictator'

Page

271. 'W. is a great man . . .': Martin and Hardy, *Menzies' 1941 Diary*, p. 120.

271. 'Our present duty . . .': Menzies to Fadden, 22 April 1941, *DAFP*, Vol. IV, Document No. 421.

271. London press reports . . .: 22 April 1941, *DAFP*, Vol. IV, Document No. 418.

271. 'our losses are very small . . .': 22 April 1941, *DAFP*, Vol. IV, Document No. 422, Martin and Hardy, *Menzies' 1941 Diary*, p. 116.

271. 'You may imagine . . .': 22 April 1941, *DAFP*, Vol. IV, Document No. 421.

273. 'W.C. speaks . . .': Martin and Hardy, *Menzies' 1941 Diary*, p. 112.

273. Special kind of dictatorship . . .: For Churchill's memoranda, see Churchill, *Grand Alliance*, Appendix C, pp. 665–668.

274. '. . . leading the Conservative Party . . .': Bruce quoted in Horner, *Defence Supremo*, p. 109.

275. '. . . that wicked man': Menzies, *Afternoon Light*, p. 37.

275. Menzies on de Valera: See Martin, *Menzies*, Vol. I, pp. 342–343.

275. 'When that King . . .': Martin, *Menzies*, Vol. I, p. 339.

276. 'I appear to be the only minister . . .': 15 April 1941, *DAFP*, Vol. IV, Document No. 404.

276. 'You may be assured . . .': 18 April 1941, *DAFP*, Vol. IV, Document No. 418, dated London.

276. 'My first impression . . .': 2 May 1941, *DAFP*, Vol. IV, Document No. 443.

277. 'Menzies made a stink . . .': Martin, *Menzies*, Vol. I, pp. 350–351.

277. Menzies urged compliance . . .: 2 May 1941, *DAFP*, Vol. IV, Document No. 443.

277. Churchill's 'midnight follies . . .': David Dilks (ed.), *The Diaries of Sir Alexander Cadogan 1938–1945*, Putnam, New York, 1972, p. 375.

278. 'After lunch, we heard . . .': For Lord Hankey's account of Menzies' mission, see Cameron Hazlehurst, *Menzies Observed*, Allen & Unwin, Sydney, 1979, pp. 222–223.

279. 'Roosevelt and Hull agreed . . .': Martin, *Menzies*, Vol. I, pp. 360–361.

279. King dictated a lengthy account: For Menzies' talks with King, see Hazlehurst, *Menzies Observed*, pp. 226–227.
280. 'A sick feeling of repugnance': Martin and Hardy, *Menzies' 1941 Diary*, 23 May 1941, p. 134.
280. '. . . cold reception . . .': AW Fadden, *They Call Me Artie*, Jacaranda Press, Brisbane, 1969, p. 60.
280. 'Looking back now . . .': Fadden, *They Call Me Artie*, p. 62.
280. 'It's been dug . . .': Percy Spender, *Politics and a Man*, William Collins (Australia), 1972, p. 158.
281. 'It will always be deemed . . .': Churchill, *Hinge of Fate*, p. 4.
282. 'The mere political formula . . .': For the correspondence between Menzies and Curtin, see Patrick Weller (ed.), *Caucus Minutes 1901–1949*, Vol. 3, Melbourne University Press, Melbourne, 1975, pp. 258–266.
284. 'We all have the greatest admiration . . .': Menzies to King and Smuts, 3 July 1941, *DAFP*, Vol. V, Document No. 1.
285. . . . a shrewd thrust: For King's reply, see *DAFP*, Vol. V, Document No. 1, Note 4 at p. 5.
285. Churchill himself killed off: Martin, *Menzies*, Vol. I, p. 380.
285. 'There has been a clamouring . . .': Canberra, 13 August 1941, *DAFP*, Vol. V, Document No. 41. Author's emphasis.
286. 'Get here as soon as . . .': 13 August 1941, *DAFP*, Vol. V, Document No. 43.
286. 'You know, old man': Menzies, *Afternoon Light*, p. 126.
287. 'It is essential . . .': Weller, *Caucus Minutes*, p. 275. Also see Graham Freudenberg, 'Victory to Defeat' in John Faulkner (ed.) *True Believers*, Allen & Unwin, Sydney, 2001, pp. 76–77.
287. 'London is the only place . . .': Hughes' speech in House of Representatives, 21 August 1941.
288. 'While I scrupulously . . .': Churchill, *Grand Alliance*, p. 366.
289. 'It would be unwise . . .': Martin, *Menzies*, Vol. I, p. 391.

Chapter 18: 'How different the Australians seem'

Page
290. 'No surrender, no retreat': David Coombes, *Morshead*, The Australian Army History Series, Oxford University Press, Melbourne, 2001, p. 106.
291. 'immensely big and powerful men . . .': Rommel, see Peter Fitzsimons, *Tobruk*, HarperCollins, Australia, 2006, p. 383.
291. 'The whole Empire . . .': Churchill quoted in Fitzsimons, *Tobruk*, p. 382.

291. 'All questions of cutting the loss . . .': Churchill to Roosevelt, 13 April 1941, Kimball, *Complete Correspondence*, Vol. I, C-79, p. 169.

291. 'The magnet of Tobruk . . .': Churchill to Roosevelt, 24 April 1941, Kimball, *Complete Correspondence*, C-82, p. 175.

291. Even apart from Tobruk . . .: Churchill's message to Wavell on available troops in Churchill, *Grand Alliance*, Appendix F, pp. 705–706.

292. 'Historically the Western Desert . . .': Corelli Barnett, *The Desert Generals*, George Allen & Unwin, London, 1960, Author's Preface to First Edition, p. 10 of Phoenix Paperback Edition, Cassell, 1999.

292. 'How different the Australians seem . . .': David Day, *The Politics of War – Australia at War 1939–45*, HarperCollins, Australia, 2003, p. 162.

293. 'I have come to the conclusion . . .': Wavell's dismissal, Schofield, *Wavell*, p. 208.

293. 'the fifth wheel . . .': Blamey to Spender, 27 June 1941, Horner, *Blamey*, Allen & Unwin, Sydney, 1998, p. 228.

293. 'time to fulfil the agreement': Horner, *Blamey*, pp. 232–233.

294. 'Are you satisfied . . .': Menzies to Blamey, Horner, *Blamey*, p. 227.

294. The first encounter did not go well: Coombes, *Morshead*, p. 119; Horner, *High Command*, p. 114; 'Old Blamey', Horner, *High Command*, p. 114; Blamey's letter to Auchinleck, Horner, *High Command*, p. 115.

295. 'We regard it as of first class importance . . .': Menzies to Churchill, 20 July 1941, *DAFP*, Vol. V, Document No. 10.

296. 'I particularly stimulated . . .': Churchill quoted in Horner, *Blamey*, p. 235.

296. 'The British Staff in command . . .': Blamey to Menzies, 16 August 1941, quoted in Horner, *Blamey*, pp. 235–236.

297. 'I am pretty sure the Australians . . .': Churchill to Auchinleck, 6 September 1941, Churchill, *Grand Alliance*, p. 367.

297. 'I propose to abandon . . .': Auchinleck to Churchill, Churchill, *Grand Alliance*, p. 367.

297. 'The Englishman is a born casuist . . .': Blamey to Spender, Horner, *Blamey*, pp. 237–238.

297. 'Gentlemen, I think you don't understand . . .': quoted in John Hetherington, *Blamey*, FW Cheshire, Melbourne, 1954, p. 123.

298. 'The position causes me . . .': Blamey to Fadden, 4 September 1941, *DAFP*, Vol. V, Document No. 58.

298. 'I must reiterate request . . .': Fadden to Churchill, 5 September 1941, *DAFP*, Vol. V, Document No. 59.

299. 'irrespective of the cost entailed . . .': Churchill to Fadden, 11 September 1941, *DAFP*, Vol. V, Document No. 64.
299. 'I am bound to request . . .': Fadden to Churchill, 11 September 1941, *DAFP*, Vol. V, Document No. 68.
299. 'Orders will at once': Fadden, *They Call Me Artie*, p. 77; 'I am grieved . . .': Churchill to Auchinleck, *Grand Alliance*, p. 368.
300. 'prevented only with difficulty . . .': Churchill to Fadden, 30 September 1941, *DAFP*, Vol. V, Document No. 73.
301. 'I was astounded . . .': Churchill to Lyttelton, 18 September 1941, *Grand Alliance*, p. 369.
301. 'If disintegration and dissension . . .': Day, *Curtin: A Life*, p. 413.
302. 'Looking back . . .': Fadden, *They Call Me Artie*, p. 65.
302. 'I feel it right . . .': Churchill to Curtin, 14 October 1941, Churchill, *Grand Alliance*, pp. 370–371.
302. 'the easement you desire . . .': Churchill to Auchinleck, 14 October 1941, Churchill, *Grand Alliance*, p. 371.
303. 'if they would do this': Churchill, *Grand Alliance*, p. 371.
303. 'I have set out the military discussion . . .': Churchill, *Grand Alliance*, p. 364.
304. 'Churchill began to abuse . . .': Sir Henry Channon, *Diaries*, entry for 17 September 1941.
304. 'Churchill's appeal was now . . .': Hasluck, *Civil Government*, Vol. I, p. 622.
305. 'It has given me pain . . .': Churchill, *Grand Alliance*, p. 372.

Chapter 19: 'Sinister twilight'
Page

306. 'rather the United States came into the war now . . .': Gilbert, *Finest Hour*, p. 1173.
307. 'I confess . . .': Churchill, *Grand Alliance*, pp. 522–523.
307. 'Our object is to get the Americans . . .': Quoted in Neidpath, *Singapore Naval Base*, p. 189.
307. 'Egypt is not even second . . .': Dill's Memorandum 6 May 1941, Churchill, *Grand Alliance*, p. 375.
308. 'I was astonished . . .': Churchill, *Grand Alliance*, p. 376.
308. 'This was indeed a tragic issue . . .': Churchill, *Grand Alliance*, p. 379.
309. 'clearly skating on pretty thin ice . . .': Churchill to War Cabinet, 19 August 1941, Gilbert, *Finest Hour*, pp. 1167–1168.
309. 'They respect the right . . .': Churchill on Atlantic Charter, Churchill, *Grand Alliance*, pp. 385–388.

310. Churchill's last messages to Menzies . . .: Churchill to Menzies, 24 August 1941, *DAFP*, Vol. V, Document No. 50; the words 'I feel confident that Japan will lie quiet for a while' were in a message on 15 August 1941, see Churchill, *Grand Alliance*, p. 399.

313. 'If the United States did not come in . . .': Churchill, *Grand Alliance*, p. 522.

313. 'This ought to serve . . .': Churchill to Roosevelt, 2 November 1941, Kimball, *Complete Correspondence*, Vol. I, C-125, p. 265.

313. Churchill was less upbeat . . .: Churchill to Curtin, 26 October 1941, *DAFP*, Vol. V, Document No. 91.

314. 'prepared to abandon the Mediterranean altogether . . .': Advisory War Council Minute 60, 7 November 1941, *DAFP*, Vol. V, Document No. 104; also for views of Hughes and Curtin.

314. Curtin's comment reflected . . .: For statements by Curtin, Forde and Blamey, see Hasluck, Vol. I, pp. 544–545.

315. 'like a lot of gazelles . . .': For Blamey's conduct and statements in Australia, see Horner, *Blamey*, pp. 252–3.

315. 'not run into war . . .': quoted in Horner, *High Command*, p. 138; John Dedman, 'Defence Policy Decisions before Pearl Harbour', *Australian Journal of Politics and History*, Vol. 13, No. 3, December 1967 (quoted in Horner, *High Command*, p. 133).

316. '. . . would not be and could not be a partner . . .': Horner, *High Command*, p. 131; 'Sir Earle Page, Australian representative . . .': See Field Marshal Lord Alanbrooke (edited by Alex Danchev and Daniel Todman), *War Diaries 1939–45*, Weidenfeld & Nicolson, London, 2001, entry for 19 January 1942, p. 221.

316. 'inspired speeches and tireless energy . . .': Page on Churchill in *Truant Surgeon*, p. 313.

316. Page presented a long strategic survey . . .: Page, *Truant Surgeon*, p. 314.

317. Portal 'produced some astonishing opinions . . .': Page, *Truant Surgeon*, pp. 315–316.

317. 'Australia feels very strongly . . .': 2 December 1941, *DAFP*, Vol. V, Document No. 153; for Churchill to Halifax, and Roosevelt's 'all in it together', see Neidpath, *Singapore Naval Base*, p 183.

318. 'a great error to press the President . . .': Churchill's 'constitutional lecture' and his Mansion House statement, 16 November 1941, Page to Curtin, *DAFP*, Vol. V, Document No. 113.

319. 'It is a strange feature . . .': Evatt's statement on Russia given by Curtin, 29 November 1941, *DAFP*, Vol. V, Document No. 134, in reply to Churchill's complaint, 26 November 1941, *DAFP*, Volume V, Document No. 131.

320. 'To the east . . .': Yamamoto's signals in Alan Schom, *The Eagle and the Rising Sun*, WW Norton, New York, 2004, p. 117.

321. After the basic decision to 'go south' . . .: Japanese plans analysed in Lionel Wigmore, *The Japanese Thrust: The Official War History, Australia in the War of 1939–1945*, Vol. IV, Australian War Memorial, Canberra, 1957, pp. 109–112.

322. 'Anyone who has seen the auto factories . . .': Yamamoto quoted in Winton Groom, *1942 – The Year That Tried Men's Souls*, Grove Press, New York, 2005, p. 46.

322. Churchill informed Curtin . . .: Churchill to Curtin, 5 November 1941, *DAFP*, Vol. V, Document No. 102.

322. 'There now seems grave danger . . .': Curtin to Bruce, 29 November 1941, *DAFP*, Vol. V, Document No. 135.

323 'It is urgent to impress...': Curtin to Churchill, 30 November 1941, *DAFP*, Vol. V, Document No. 142.

323. 'His reason for this . . .': Bruce to Curtin, 1 December 1941, *DAFP*, Vol. V, Document No. 147.

324 'I believe Japan's obstinacy . . .': Curtin to Churchill, 2 December 1941, *DAFP*, Vol. V, Document No. 149.

324. 'This son of a man . . .': Schom, *Eagle and Rising Sun*, p. 129.

325. 'This means war . . .': Groom, *1942*, p. 66.

325. 'The U.S. desires': Schom, *Eagle and Rising Sun*, p. 126.

325. 'News is being published tonight . . .': Casey to Curtin, 6 December 1941, *DAFP*, Vol. V, Document No. 169.

326. 'It has come': Day, *John Curtin*, p. 430.

326. Churchill was at Chequers . . .: Churchill, *Grand Alliance*, p. 540.

Chapter 20: 'We look to the United States'
Page
327. 'Commence hostilities . . .': Lloyd Ross, *John Curtin – A Biography*, Macmillan, Melbourne, 1977, p. 240.

327. Cabinet adopted the constitutional procedure . . .: *DAFP*, Vol. V, Documents No. 165 (6 December 1941), 166 (7 December 1941) and 172 (8 December 1941).

327. 'Men and women of Australia . . .': Ross, *Curtin*, p. 241.

328. 'Canberra in December was in jitters . . .': Ross, *Curtin*, p. 243.

329. 'In all the war . . .': Churchill, *Grand Alliance*, p. 551.

329. 'Things are moving so fast . . .': Cranbourne to Curtin, 11 December 1941, *DAFP*, Vol. V, Document No. 185.

330. 'He goes on . . .': Quoted from Cadogan Papers, Peter Thompson, *The Battle for Singapore*, Portrait, London, 2005, p. 80.

330. 'Churchill promised . . .': Page to Curtin, 11 December 1941, *DAFP*, Vol. V, Document No. 183.

330. 'In our view, leadership . . .': Bruce to Curtin, 13 December 1941, *DAFP*, Vol. V, Document No. 189.

331. 'Winston turned to him . . .': Alanbrooke, *War Diaries*, p. 209.

332. 'Beware lest troops . . .': Churchill's Minute to CIGS, 15 December 1941, Churchill, *Grand Alliance*, p. 565.

333. Churchill dictated three strategic papers . . .: The *Duke of York* papers in full in Kimball, *Complete Correspondence*, Vol. I, C-145, pp. 294–308; summarised in Gilbert, *Road to Victory*, pp. 9–13.

334. 'a strongly considered statement . . .': Casey to Department of External Affairs, 20 December 1941, *DAFP*, Vol. V, Document No. 210.

334. 'I have reason to believe . . .': Casey to Curtin, 22 December 1941, *DAFP*, Vol. V, Document No. 213.

335. 'At this time of great crisis . . .,': Curtin to Casey, for Roosevelt and Churchill, 23 December 1941, *DAFP*, Vol. V, Document No. 214.

336. In his reply, written on Christmas Day . . .: Churchill to Curtin, 25 December 1941, *DAFP*, Vol. V, Document No. 231.

337. 'God knows where . . .': Alanbrooke, *War Diaries*, 4 December 1941, p. 207.

337. 'We prepared a memorandum . . .': Alanbrooke, *War Diaries*, 19 December 1941, p. 212; 'Winston has arrived . . .': pp. 213–214; 'In the afternoon . . .': pp. 214–215; 'A long and wearying . . .': p. 215.

338. 'It would have been strategically unsound . . .': Attlee to Curtin, 23 December 1941, *DAFP*, Vol. V, Document No. 216.

338. 'our position in Malaya is very serious . . .': Cranbourne to Curtin, 27 December 1941, *DAFP*, Vol. V, Document No. 215.

338. 'my principal task in coming here': Casey to Canberra, 23 December 1941, *DAFP*, Vol. V, Document No. 218.

338. 'The deterioration of the air position . . .': Bowden from Singapore, 23 December 1941, *DAFP*, Vol. V, Document No. 217.

339. Shedden wrote a paper . . .: Horner, *Defence Supremo*, pp. 130–131.

340. 'That reddish veil . . .': Curtin's *New Year Message* (Melbourne *Herald*, 27 December 1941) quoted in full in Crowley, *Modern Australia*, Vol. 5, pp. 49–52.

342. 'suicidal and a false and dangerous policy . . .': Hughes' statements in Fitzhardinge, *The Little Digger*, p. 655.

342. Murdoch's articles and letters . . .: see Younger, *Keith Murdoch*, pp. 252–253.

342. 'I hope there will be no pandering . . .': Churchill's statements, 'I weighed promptly . . .': Churchill, *The Hinge of Fate* (War Memoirs, Vol. IV), pp. 7–8; Maie Casey's claim, see David Day, *The Great Betrayal*, WW Norton & Co., New York, 1989, p. 223.

343. In a conversation with Fred Shedden . . .: See Horner, *Defence Supremo*, pp. 131–132.

344. 'drunk with the figures...': Moran, *Diaries*, p. 22.

344. 'I sought and obtained . . .': Casey to Canberra, 24 December 1941, *DAFP*, Vol. V, Document Nos. 222 and 223.

344. 'You can't kick me . . .': Casey, *Personal Experience 1939–46*, Constable, London, 1962, p. 81.

Chapter 21: 'Australasian anxieties'

Page
346. 'Australia and New Zealand felt suddenly plunged . . .': Churchill, *The Hinge of Fate* (War Memoirs, Vol. IV), p. 4.

346. 'Australasian air-power . . .': See Alan Stephens, *The Royal Australian Air Force – A History*, Oxford University Press, Melbourne, 2001, pp. 59–75.

347. 'Local politics ruled . . .': Churchill, *Hinge of Fate*, p. 4.

348. 'These partisan decisions . . .': Churchill, *Hinge of Fate*, pp. 4–5.

349. 'I want you to press . . .': Evatt to Casey, 16 December 1941, *DAFP*, Vol. V, Document No. 196.

349. 'The whole philosophy . . .': Curtin's broadcast in Hasluck, *Government and People*, Vol. II, p. 55.

350. '. . . isolated and left to defend . . .': Curtin to Churchill, 1 January 1942, *DAFP*, Vol. V, Document No. 247.

350. '. . . for a time in January 1942 . . .': *DAFP*, Vol. V, Introduction p. xiii.

351. 'this is quadruplets . . .': Schofield, *Wavell*, p. 231.

351. 'Night and day . . .': Churchill to Curtin, 3 January 1942, *DAFP*, Vol. V, Document No. 254.

351. 'I expect that we shall . . .': Alanbrooke, *War Diaries*, 12 January 1942, p. 219.

352. 'The wonderful thing . . .': Alanbrooke, *War Diaries*, 10 September 1944, p. 590.

353. 'Surely this is a reasonable layout . . .': Churchill to Curtin, 8 January 1942, *DAFP*, Vol. V, Document No. 262.

354. 'The Australian Government has no doubt . . .': Curtin to Churchill, 11 January 1942, *DAFP*, Vol. V, Document No. 266.

354. 'I do not accept any censure . . .': Churchill to Curtin, 12 January 1942, *DAFP*, Vol. V, Document No. 271.
355. 'all aspects of Australia's concern . . .': Casey to Canberra, 13 January 1942, *DAFP*, Vol. V, Document No. 274.
355. 'Even I don't know . . .': Curtin on Evatt, Paul Hasluck, *Diplomatic Witness*, Melbourne University Press, Melbourne, 1980, p. 126.
356. 'A very vain man . . .': Prince Lichnowski (German Ambassador) quoted in Klaus Larres, *Churchill's Cold War – The Politics of Diplomacy*, Yale University Press, New Haven and London, 2002, p. 19.
357. 'Please understand . . .': Evatt's cables to Casey, 26 December 1941, *DAFP*, Vol. V, Document No. 226; 3 January 1942, *DAFP*, Vol. V, Document No. 250.
357. 'Churchill lives and works . . .': Casey to Evatt, 4 January 1942, *DAFP*, Vol. V, Document No. 256.
357. 'We cannot allow . . .': Evatt to Casey, 7 January 1942, *DAFP*, Vol. V, Document No. 260.

Chapter 22: 'Inexcusable betrayal'
Page
359. 'The only vital point . . .': Churchill to Curtin, 12 January 1942, *DAFP*, Vol. V, Document No. 271.
360. 'Please let me know . . .': Churchill to Wavell, 15 January 1942; 'Little or nothing . . .': Wavell to Churchill, 16 January 1942; 'with painful surprise', Churchill, *Hinge of Fate*, pp. 42–43.
361. 'I ought to have known . . .': Churchill, *Hinge of Fate*, p. 43.
361. 'How is it . . .?': Churchill to Ismay, 19 January 1942, Churchill, *Hinge of Fate*, p. 44.
361. 'The entire male population . . .': Churchill, *Hinge of Fate*, p. 45.
362. 'My observations on Crete': Curtin to Churchill, 17 January 1942, *DAFP*, Vol. V, Document No. 278.
362. He began his thousand-word reply . . .': Churchill to Curtin, 19 January 1942, *DAFP*, Vol. V, Document No. 281.
363. 'As a strategic object . . .': Churchill to COS, Churchill, *Hinge of Fate*, pp. 49–50.
363. 'by some means or other . . .': Churchill, *Hinge of Fate*, p. 50.
364. 'evacuation of Singapore would cause irreparable loss . . .': Page to Curtin, 22 January 1942, *DAFP*, Vol. V, Document No. 292.
364. 'took a holiday . . .': *DAFP*, Vol. V, Editor's Note, p. 463.

364. 'without possibility of relief . . .': For reports by Bennett and Bowden, 23 January 1942, see *DAFP*, Vol. V, Document No. 293.
365. 'Whilst we have no intention . . .': The 'inexcusable betrayal' cable, 23 January 1942, *DAFP*, Vol. V, Document No. 294.
367. not allow Australia's discourtesy . . .: Churchill's reply quoted in Horner, *High Command*, p. 152.
367. 'Churchill went off the deep end': Page quoted in Horner, *High Command*, p. 152.
367. 'It is not true to say . . .': Churchill, *Hinge of Fate*, p. 51; 'the effect . . . all over the world', p. 52.
368. 'It is certain that our troops . . .': Wavell's Order, quoted in Wigmore, *Japanese Thrust*, p. 342.
369. 'There must . . . be no thought . . .': Churchill to Wavell, 10 February 1942, Churchill, *Hinge of Fate*, pp. 87–88.
369. 'There are now one million people . . .': Shenton Thomas quoted in Wigmore, *Japanese Thrust*, p. 375.
369. 'it would be wrong . . .': Churchill, *Hinge of Fate*, p. 92; 'You are of course sole judge . . .': Churchill to Wavell, 14 February 1942, Churchill, *Hinge of Fate*, p. 92.
370. 'Our work completed': Bowden to Canberra, 14 February 1942, *DAFP*, Vol. V, Document No. 333.
371. 'It is scarcely to Australia's credit . . .': O'Neill in Blake and Louis, *Churchill*, p. 286.
371. 'I have been giving a good deal . . .': Roosevelt to Churchill, 18 February 1942, Kimball, *Complete Correspondence*, Vol. I, R-106 p. 363

Chapter 23: 'Nothing else in the world . . .'
Page
373. 'the extraordinary influence of China on American minds . . .': Churchill and Roosevelt quoted in John Costello, *The Pacific War*, Perennial, 2002, p. 181; 'if China goes under . . .': Roosevelt quoted in Barbara Tuchman, *Stillwell and the American Experience 1911–1945*, Macmillan, New York, 1970, p. 238.
373. 'the transfer of the First Australian Corps . . .': Australian Government to Dominions Office, 6 January 1942, *DAFP*, Vol. V, Document No. 257.
374. 'the new theatre of so much interest . . .': Churchill to Curtin, 12 January 1942, *DAFP*, Vol. V, Document No. 271.
374. It was not until February . . .: See Wigmore, *Japanese Thrust*, pp. 444–445.

375. 'extreme diversion . . .': Lavarack's protest to Wavell, Brett Lodge, *Lavarack: Rival General*, Australian Military History Series, Allen & Unwin, Sydney, 1998, p. 204; 'penny packets': Lodge, *Lavarack*, p. 207; Curtin to Wavell, 12 February 1942, *DAFP*, Vol. V, Document No. 329; 7th Division schedule, see Lodge, *Lavarack*, pp. 205–206.

376. 'If possible, all Australian forces . . .': Curtin to Churchill, 17 February 1942, *DAFP*, Vol. V, Document No. 336.

376. 'to hold some area of the Australian continent . . .': Sturdee's advice, see Long, *Six Years War*, p. 161.

377. Roosevelt 'depressed . . .': Casey to Canberra, 17 February 1942, *DAFP*, Vol. V, Document No. 340.

377. A bolt from the blue . . .: Page to Curtin, 18 February 1942, *DAFP*, Vol. V, Document No. 341; 'half a day': Curtin to Page, *DAFP*, Vol. V, Document No. 343; 'After most anxious considera-tion . . .': Curtin to Page, 19 February 1942, *DAFP*, Vol. V, Document No. 345.

378. 'to avoid compromising British relations . . .': Wavell quoted in Long, *Six Years War*, p. 161.

379. 'the first encouraging indication . . .': Bruce to Curtin, 18 Feb-ruary 1942, *DAFP*, Vol. V, Document No. 344.

380. 'Churchill expressed great anxiety . . .': Page to Curtin, 19 Feb-ruary 1942, *DAFP*, Vol. V, Document No. 347; 'If you have not done so . . .': Curtin to Page, 20 February 1942, *DAFP*, Vol. V, Document No. 348.

380. 'Return here . . .': Curtin to Blamey, 20 February 1942, *DAFP*, Vol. V, Document No. 349.

380. 'I suppose you realise . . .': Churchill to Curtin, 20 February 1942, *DAFP*, Vol. V, Document No. 352.

382. Churchill then enlisted Roosevelt . . .: Churchill to Roosevelt, 20 February 1942, Kimball, *Complete Correspondence*, Vol. I, C-31, p. 365.

382. 'If it were possible . . .': Curtin to Churchill, 22 February 1942, *DAFP*, Vol. V, Document No. 357.

382. 'I hope you can persuade . . .': Roosevelt to Churchill, 20 February 1942, Kimball, *Complete Correspondence*, Vol. I, R-107, p. 365.

383. 'we are going to reinforce . . .': Roosevelt's message to Curtin copied to Churchill, Kimball, *Complete Correspondence*, Vol. I, R-108, p. 366.

384. 'This episode marked . . .': Daniel Marston in *Pacific War Companion*, Osprey Publishing, Oxford, 2005, p. 108; 'At this stage . . .': David Jordan, *A Chronology of World War II*, p. 169.

384. 'The Japs have bombed Darwin . . .': Spender, *Politics and a Man*, pp. 148–149.
385. 'Your rather strongly worded request . . .': Curtin to Churchill, 22 February 1942, *DAFP*, Vol. V, Document No. 357.
386. 'We could not contemplate . . .': Churchill to Curtin, 22 February 1942, *DAFP*, Vol. V, Document No. 362.
386. 'I am appalled . . .': Bruce to Curtin, 23 February 1942, *DAFP*, Vol. V, Document No. 364; Page to Curtin, Document No. 365.
387. '. . . it is quite impossible to reverse . . .': Curtin to Churchill, 23 February 1942, *DAFP*, Vol. V, Document No. 366; Churchill to Curtin, 23 February 1943, Document No. 367.
387. 'Burma news now bad . . .': Sir Alan Brooke's diary entries 18 February–3 March 1942, Alanbrooke, *War Diaries*, pp. 232–236.
388. 'in utmost secrecy . . .': Imperial Chiefs of Staff assessment, 2 March 1942, *DAFP*, Vol. V, Document No. 380; 'I am still puzzled . . .': Schofield, *Wavell*, p. 239; 'I preferred . . .': Long, *Six Years War*, p. 163.
388. 'I cannot send you an army . . .': Churchill to Wavell, Churchill, *Hinge of Fate*, p. 146; 'communication with Burma . . .': Wavell to Churchill, *Hinge of Fate*, p. 147; 'the longest retreat . . .': Marston, *Pacific War Companion*, p. 106.
389. 'Looking back . . .': Alanbrooke, *War Diaries*, p. 232.
389. 'I entered the grounds of the Lodge . . .': Frank Green, *Servant of the House*, Heinemann, Melbourne, 1967, p. 128.
390. 'The long and arduous campaign . . .': Hasluck, *The Government and the People*, p. 136.
390. 'He shook his finger . . .': John Dedman, 'The Return of the A.I.F. from the Middle East', *Australian Outlook*, Vol. 21, No. 2 (August 1967), p. 151.

Chapter 24: 'I shall return'

Page
392. 'The loss of Australia . . .': Curtin to Churchill, 4 March 1942, *DAFP*, Vol. V, Document No. 388.
393. 'Our minds are set on attack . . .': Curtin's broadcasts, Hasluck, *The Government and the People*, p. 157.
393. 'in the absence of naval and aerial superiority': Curtin, *Commonwealth Parliamentary Debates*, Vol. 170, pp. 797–802.
393. The Yanks were coming!: The author's memory as a seven-year-

old has possibly fused with the visit of the US Pacific Fleet earlier in 1941.

395. 'It would mean that the whites . . .': Roosevelt quoted in Geoffrey Perret, *Old Soldiers Never Die*, Andre Deutsch, London, 1996, p. 272; 'If I get through . . .': Perret, p. 274.

396. 'I came through . . .': MacArthur's statements in Adelaide and Melbourne quoted in Perret, pp. 283–284.

396. 'We promptly came . . .': Douglas MacArthur, *Reminiscences,* McGraw-Hill, New York, 1964, p. 283.

397. 'General Douglas MacArthur having arrived . . .': Curtin to Roosevelt, 17 March 1942, *DAFP*, Vol. V, Document No. 415.

397. 'at the suggestion of the Australian Government . . .': Stimson quoted in *DAFP*, Vol. V, Document No. 419; 'MacArthur in Australia', *New York Times* headline quoted in Stanley Weintraub, *Fifteen Stars – Eisenhower, MacArthur, Marshall*, Free Press, New York, 2007, p. 55.

398. 'The fact that an American commander . . .': Churchill to Curtin, 17 March 1942, *DAFP*, Vol. V, Document No. 417.

398. 'I have told Curtin . . .': Churchill to Roosevelt, 1 April 1942, Kimball, *Complete Correspondence*, Vol. I, C-62, p. 438. Author's emphasis.

399. 'utilisation of United States forces . . .': Bruce to Curtin, 9 March 1942, *DAFP*, Vol. V, Document No. 401.

399. MacArthur's arrival gave Roosevelt . . .: For command directives, see Hasluck, *The Government and the People*, Vol. II, p. 112.

400. 'Before going further . . .': Churchill to Curtin, 12 March 1942, *DAFP*, Vol. V, Document No. 406; Curtin to Churchill, Documents No. 408 and 409; 'Casey . . . anxious for change': Document No. 412; Casey to Curtin, 15 March 1942, Document No. 414; Curtin to Casey, 17 March 1942, Document No. 416; Casey to Curtin, 18 March 1942, Document No. 423.

401. 'I learn . . . from the world at large . . .': Curtin to Churchill, 20 March 1942, *DAFP*, Vol. V, Document No. 427; 'Curtin expressed his anger . . .': Explanatory Note, *DAFP*, Vol. V, p. 658; 'I do not understand the tone . . .': Churchill to Curtin, 19 March 1942, *DAFP*, Vol. V, Document No. 426; 'I assure you that your personal part . . .': Curtin to Churchill, 20 March 1942, Document No. 427.

402. 'I realise it is but an incident . . .': Roosevelt to Churchill, 22 March 1942, Kimball, *Complete Correspondence*, Vol. I, R-127, p. 428.

403. 'Former Naval Person to President . . .': Churchill to Roosevelt, 23 March 1942, Kimball, *Complete Correspondence*, Vol. I, C-56, p. 429.
403. 'They are all most anxious . . .': Evatt to Curtin, 26 March 1942, *DAFP*, Vol. V, Document No. 433.

Chapter 25: 'Starting from scratch'
Page

406. Evatt was a quick learner: Evatt to Curtin, 21 March 1942, *DAFP*, Vol. V, Document No. 433; 22 March 1942, Documents No. 435 and 437.
406. 'English susceptibility . . .': Evatt to Curtin, 29 March 1942; *DAFP*, Vol. V, Document No. 446.
407. 'I wish we could do something . . .': Evatt to Bruce, 23 March 1942, *DAFP*, Vol. V, Document No. 438.
408. 'The result of all this . . .': Evatt to Cripps, 16 February 1942, *DAFP*, Vol. V, Document No. 335.
408. greeted with 'a tirade . . .': Bruce's Note of Conversation with Churchill, 31 March 1942, *DAFP*, Vol. V, Document No. 449.
409. Churchill was half-right . . .: For Japanese decisions, see Long, *Six Years War*, p. 175 and David Horner, 'The Anzac Contribution' in *Pacific War Companion*, p. 143.
410. 'You use the expression . . .': Churchill to Bruce, 3 April 1942, *DAFP*, Vol. V, Document No. 455.
411. 'no obstacle would be placed . . .': Churchill, House of Commons, Parliamentary Debate Series V, Vol. 177, column 614.
411. 'relying on the understanding . . .': Curtin to Evatt, 20 March 1942, *DAFP*, Vol. V, Document No. 428; 'I hope in these circumstances . . .': quoted by Curtin to Evatt, *DAFP*, Vol. V, Document No. 428.
411. 'In the meantime . . .': Evatt to Curtin, 22 March 1942, *DAFP*, Vol. V, Document No. 435.
412. 'the decision . . . must be made by Curtin . . .': Roosevelt to Churchill, 26 March 1942, Kimball, *Complete Correspondence*, Vol. I, R-128, p. 433.
412. 'Discussions here show . . .': Evatt to Curtin, 2 April 1942, *DAFP*, Vol. V, Document No. 454.
412. 'prepared to agree to the postponement . . .': Curtin to Churchill, 14 April 1942, *DAFP*, Vol. V, Document No. 465.
412. 'I am very much obliged . . .': Churchill to Curtin, 15 April 1942, *DAFP*, Vol V, Document No. 466.

413. 'MacArthur is bitterly disappointed . . .': Curtin to Evatt, 21 April 1942, *DAFP*, Vol. V, Document No. 475.
414. 'Nevertheless, you may be sure . . .': Churchill to Curtin, 30 April 1942, *DAFP*, Vol. V, Document No. 477.
414. Evatt insisted . . .: Evatt to Canberra, 23 April 1942, *DAFP*, Vol. V, Document No. 474.
415. 'full of blood and thunder . . .': Bruce's Note of Conversation, 3 May 1942, *DAFP*, Vol. V, Document No. 504.
415. from Evatt's first meeting . . .: See *DAFP*, Vol. V, Document No. 484; 'really a military dictatorship'; *DAFP*, Vol. V, Document No. 504.
415. 'a somewhat uncertain quantity . . .': Bruce's Note of Conversation with Evatt, 18 May 1942, *DAFP*, Vol. V, Document No. 491.
416. In his final report to Curtin . . .: Evatt to Curtin, 28 May 1942, *DAFP*, Vol. V, Document No. 500.
417. 'Considering the difficulties . . .': Evatt to Curtin, 28 May 1942, *DAFP*, Vol. V, Document No. 500.
418. 'On behalf of the Government . . .': Curtin to Churchill, 29 May 1942, *DAFP*, Vol. V, Document No. 505.
418. 'Evatt's visit here . . .': Churchill to Curtin, *DAFP*, Vol. V, Note on p. 806.
418. 'Evatt is a thoroughly unpleasant type . . .': Alanbrooke, *War Diaries*, 12 May 1942, p. 257.
419. 'speak with frankness . . .': MacArthur at the Prime Minister's War Conference, 1 June 1942, *DAFP*, Vol. V, Document No. 510.

Chapter 26: 'A temporary deliverance'
Page
420. 'the stirring events . . .': Churchill, *Hinge of Fate*, p. 215; 'the envelopment of Australia': p. 215.
421. 'Across the havoc of war': Churchill on Rommel, House of Commons, 27 January 1942.
422. 'The annals of war at sea . . .': Churchill, *Hinge of Fate*, pp. 226–227; 'the actions in the Coral Sea . . .': Robert Love in *Pacific War Companion* (ed. Marston), p. 105.
424. 'I am ashamed . . .': Moran, *Diaries*, 21 June 1942, pp. 37–38.
424. 'Two men thousands of miles from here . . .': Clem Lloyd and Richard Hall (eds.), *Backroom Briefings*, National Library of Australia, Canberra, p. 51.
425. 'If the United States is to engage': See Forrest C. Pogue, *George C. Marshall – Ordeal and Hope 1939–42*, Macgibbon & Kee, London, 1966, pp. 340–342.

426. 'a temporary deliverance . . .': Curtin to Attlee, 25 June 1942, *DAFP*, Vol. V, Document No. 530; Churchill to Curtin, 27 June 1942, *DAFP*, Vol. V, Document No. 534; 'in view of your personal representations': Curtin to Churchill, 30 June 1942, *DAFP*, Vol. V, Document No. 536.

427. Cripps 'stressed the difficulty of handling Churchill . . .': Bruce/Cripps exchange, 13 July 1942, *DAFP*, Vol. VI (July–December 1942), Document No. 5.

427. 'There should be no problems . . .': Curtin to Bruce, 7 August 1942, *DAFP*, Vol. VI, Document No. 17.

428. 'I am putting the matter frankly . . .': Curtin to Churchill, 16 July 1942, *DAFP*, Vol. VI, Document No. 7.

428. 'I am very glad . . .': Churchill to Curtin, 11 July 1942, *DAFP*, Vol. VI, Document No. 4.

428. 'While Auchinleck fights . . .': Churchill to Casey, 30 June 1942, Churchill, *Hinge of Fate*, p. 383.

429. 'So you're being like Blamey . . .': Quoted in Mark Johnston and Peter Stanley, *Alamein – The Australian Story*, Oxford University Press, Australia, 2006, p. 50.

429. 'Much depends upon the result . . .': Churchill to Curtin, 24 July 1942, *DAFP*, Vol. VI, Document No. 10.

429. 'We know that we can count . . .': Curtin to Churchill, 30 July 1942, *DAFP*, Vol. VI, Document No. 12; 'I much appreciate your decision . . .': Churchill to Curtin, 6 April 1942, *DAFP*, Vol. VI, Document No. 18.

Chapter 27: 'The end of the beginning'

Page

432. 'Now for a short spell . . .': Churchill, *Hinge of Fate*, p. 412.

433. 'There was a lot of tension . . .': Casey, *Personal Experience*, p. 125.

433. 'I said we all had the same right . . .': Casey, *Personal Experience*, p. 122; 'Casey in full agreement': *Personal Experience*, p. 126.

433. 'where we were given breakfast . . .': Churchill, *Hinge of Fate*, p. 414.

434. 'dressed in a pale lilac suit . . .': Johnston and Stanley, *Alamein – The Australian Story*, p. 123; 'The last stage of Churchill's route . . .': Barnett, *Desert Generals*, Cassell, London, 1999, p. 233; 'you fat old bastard': Mark Johnston, *The Magnificent 9th*, Allen & Unwin, Sydney, 2002, p. 97.

434. 'By the same hour . . .': Churchill, *Hinge of Fate*, p. 414;

'In Montgomery we have . . .': Letter to Clementine, 9 August 1942, Gilbert, *Road to Victory*, p. 168.

435. 'We will stand and fight here': Montgomery's Order quoted in John Bierman and Colin Smith, *War Without Hate*, Penguin, London, 2002, p. 232.

435. The table which Auchinleck had provided . . .: Casey, *Personal Experience*, p. 122.

435. 'eating their hearts out . . .': Churchill, *Hinge of Fate*, p. 393.

436. In long personal messages to Roosevelt: Curtin to Roosevelt, 31 August 1942, *DAFP*, Vol. VI, Document No. 31; 11 September 1942, *DAFP*, Vol. VI, Document No. 43.

438. 'With both Port Moresby and Guadalcanal . . .': Churchill, *Closing the Ring*, p. 16.

438. 'A single Australian militia battalion . . .': Churchill, *Closing the Ring*, p. 21.

439. 'It was here at Milne Bay . . .': Chris Coulthard-Clark, *Where Australians Fought: The Encyclopedia of Australia's Battles*, Allen & Unwin, Sydney, 1998, p. 229.

440. 'Dear Winston, I confide my missus . . .': Roosevelt to Churchill, 19 October 1942, Kimball, *Complete Correspondence*, Vol. I, R-196/1, p. 633.

440. 'After lunch, P.M. sent . . .': Alanbrooke, *War Diaries*, 23 September 1942, pp. 323–324.

441. 'We then find him . . .': Alanbrooke, *War Diaries*, p. 324.

441. 'Went to see Bruce . . .': Alanbrooke, *War Diaries*, 23 October 1942, pp. 332–333.

441. 'Australia shouting' took the form . . .: Curtin to Churchill and Roosevelt, 17 October 1942, *DAFP*, Vol. VI, Document No. 62.

442. 'I understand your wishes . . .': Churchill to Curtin, 30 October 1942, *DAFP*, Vol. VI, Note on p. 139.

442. 'Of all the formations in the Middle East . . .': Alexander quoted in Curtin to Bruce, 31 October 1942, *DAFP*, Vol. VI, Document No. 67.

443. 'The position now is . . .': Bruce to Curtin, 1 November 1942, *DAFP*, Vol. VI, Document No. 69.

443. 'I agree with your interpretation . . .': Curtin to Bruce, 4 November 1942, *DAFP*, Vol. VI, Document No. 70.

444. 'The great battle in Egypt . . .': Churchill to Curtin and Fraser, *Hinge of Fate*, pp. 534–536.

444. 'We mean to hold our own . . .': Churchill's Mansion House speech, Gilbert, *Road to Victory*, p. 254; 'before Alamein . . .': Churchill, *Hinge of Fate*, p. 541.

Chapter 28: 'Hitler has nothing on Churchill'

Page

446. 'The position of Turkey . . .': Churchill to Curtin, 24 November 1942, *DAFP*, Vol. VI, Document No. 79.

447. 'The Australian 7th Division lost . . .': Paul Ham, *Kokoda* HarperCollins, Australia, 2004, p. 518.

447. 'The object should be . . .': *DAFP*, Vol. VI, Document No. 79.

447. 'frank disappointment': Curtin to Churchill, 30 November 1942, *DAFP*, Vol. VI, Document No. 83.

448. 'heartiest congratulations': Roosevelt to Curtin, 3 December 1942, *DAFP*, Vol. VI, Document No. 85.

449. 'I am very glad that you are agreeable': Curtin to Roosevelt, 8 December 1942, *DAFP*, Vol. VI, Document No. 87.

449. 'The fact that the New Zealand division . . .': Churchill to Curtin, 10 December 1942, *DAFP*, Vol. VI, Document No. 89.

450. MacArthur 'was asking for all handicaps . . .': Curtin on conscription, see Lloyd and Hall, *Backroom Briefings*, 20 November 1942, pp. 105–106.

450. 'You are putting young men . . .': For Ward, Calwell and Curtin, see Freudenberg, 'Victory to Defeat' in *True Believers*, pp. 79–81.

452. 'The personality of Mr Churchill . . .': Bruce to Curtin, 5 March 1943, *DAFP*, Vol. VI, Document No. 132.

453. 'Hitler has nothing on Churchill . . .': Bruce Note of Conversation with Attlee, 13 January 1943, *DAFP*, Vol. VI, Document No. 100; 'went off on his present adventure . . .': Bruce to Curtin, 21 January 1943, *DAFP*, Vol. VI, Document No. 108.

454. 'The war will still be long . . .': Churchill quoted in Gilbert, *Road to Victory*, p. 251.

454. 'After Germany is defeated . . .': Curtin to MacArthur, 8 February 1942, *DAFP*, Vol. VI, Document No. 117.

455. 'The outstanding military lesson . . .': Curtin to Roosevelt and Churchill, 19 January 1942, *DAFP*, Vol. VI, Document No. 105.

455. 'the failure to receive any reply . . .': MacArthur to Curtin, 17 March 1943, *DAFP*, Vol. VI, Document No. 138.

456. 'I remember the President . . .': Churchill to Curtin, 27 March 1943, *DAFP*, Vol. VI, Document No. 145.

457. 'an upward revision . . .': Roosevelt to Curtin, 29 March 1943, *DAFP*, Vol. VI, Document No. 147.

457. Churchill 'radiating confidence . . .': Evatt to Curtin, 22 May 1943, *DAFP*, Vol. VI, Document No. 197.

458. 'Evatt got all worked up . . .': Bruce, Note of Conversation with Admiral Somerville, *DAFP*, Vol. VI, Document No. 207; 'Evatt –

Australian nuisance': Alanbrooke, *War Diaries*, 20 May 1943, p. 408.

458. 'almost unbearable strain . . .': Evatt to Curtin, 12 June 1943, *DAFP*, Vol. VI, Document No. 222.

459. 'Whatever befalls us . . .': Evatt to Canberra, 12 June 1943, *DAFP*, Vol. VI, Document No. 223.

459. It all turned sour . . .: Evatt to Roosevelt, 13 July 1943, *DAFP*, Vol. VI, Document No. 244; Roosevelt to Evatt, 31 July 1943, *DAFP*, Vol. VI, Document No. 251; '132 aircraft': see Horner, *High Command*, p. 261.

459. 'It is my duty to preserve . . .': Churchill to Sinclair, 12 July 1943, Churchill, *Closing the Ring*, Appendix C, pp. 572–573; 'complete success': Evatt to Curtin, 19 June 1943, *DAFP*, Vol. VI, Document No. 226.

460. 'Things had happened . . .': Lloyd and Hall, *Backroom Briefings*, 28 May and 1 June 1943, pp. 150–152.

460. 'By the latter half of 1943 . . .': Churchill, *Closing the Ring*, pp. 489–490.

Chapter 29: 'For the Empire's future'

Page

462. 'marauding raids': See Day, *Curtin*, p. 505; 'menacing move': Hasluck, Vol. II, pp. 207–208.

463. 'We have established that the enemy . . .': See Lloyd and Hall, *Backroom Briefings*, 1 June and 9 June 1943, pp. 152–157.

463. 'While I should never wish to intrude . . .': Churchill to Curtin, 25 August 1943, *DAFP*, Vol. VI, Document No. 264.

464. 'I am concerned . . .': Churchill to Curtin, 17 July 1943, *DAFP*, Vol. VI, Document No. 245; 'as an umbrella': Curtin to Churchill, 19 July 1943, *DAFP*, Vol. VI, Document No. 246.

464. Later in the campaign: Curtin–Churchill exchange, 13–16 August 1943, *DAFP*, Vol. VI, Documents No. 255, 256, 257.

465. 'Curtin surrendered civilian control . . .': Horner, *High Command*, p. 438.

466. 'Look at Churchill . . .': Lloyd and Hall, *Backroom Briefings*, 2 February 1943, p. 134.

466. 'Eventually seven Australian divisions . . .': Richard B Frank, *MacArthur*, Palgrave Macmillan, New York, 2007, p. 69.

467. 'developments . . . of so secret a character . . .': Bruce to Curtin, 16 August 1943, *DAFP*, Vol. VI, Document No. 258.

468. 'The place Australia will occupy . . .': Curtin's statement, 'Empire Government', 6 September 1943, *DAFP*, Vol. VI, Document No. 272.

468. 'It is of the highest importance . . .': Churchill to Sinclair, 12 July 1943, Churchill, *Closing the Ring*, Appendix C, p. 572.

470. 'none too good a tale . . .': Churchill on board *Queen Mary*, 7 August 1943, Churchill, *Closing the Ring*, p. 82.

470. a 'full and fair place': Churchill, *Closing the Ring*, p. 82.

470. 'the delicate question': Churchill, *Closing the Ring*, p. 61.

471. 'The bold sweep of this concept . . .': Churchill, *Closing the Ring*, p. 78 ff.

471. 'When we win the war . . .': Roosevelt to Elliott Roosevelt, quoted in Larres, *Churchill's Cold War*, p. 54.

472. Churchill unveiled his alternative . . .: See Churchill, *Closing the Ring*, pp. 78–79.

472. 'peevish, temperamental prima donna . . .': Alanbrooke, *War Diaries*, 27 August 1943, p. 447.

473. 'There is no doubt . . .': Churchill to Attlee, 22 August 1943, Churchill, *Closing the Ring*, pp. 79–80.

473. 'one of our most distinguished . . . officers . . .': Churchill, *Closing the Ring*, p. 84.

474. 'I only wish . . . my other duties . . .': Churchill, *Closing the Ring*, p. 108.

474. 'an hour's pitched battle . . .': Alanbrooke, *War Diaries*, 1 October 1943, p. 457.

474. 'It should be clearly understood . . .': Brooke quoted in Horner, *High Command*, p. 318.

Chapter 30: 'Winston's dislike for Curtin'
Page

476. 'he might prove inadequate . . .': Day, *Curtin*, pp. 533–535; 'I was not trained . . .': Day, *Curtin*, p. 625.

477. 'All manner of issues . . .': Churchill to Curtin, 21 October 1943, *DAFP*, Vol. VI, Document No. 307; 'It is essential . . .': Curtin to Churchill, 23 October, *DAFP*, Vol. VI, Document No. 310.

478. He had spelt it out . . .: Curtin to Churchill, 8 October 1943, *DAFP*, Vol. VI, Document No. 293.

479. 'Churchill's decision to restrict grain imports . . .': Patrick French, *Liberty or Death – India's Journey to Independence and Division*, HarperCollins, London, 1997, p. 18.

480. 'All my Ministerial colleagues . . .': Churchill to Chiefs of Staff, 24 January 1944, Churchill, *Closing the Ring*, p. 505; 'I had long and difficult arguments . . .': Alanbrooke, *War Diaries*, 24 February 1944, p. 521.

481. 'could be begun much sooner . . .': Churchill, *Closing the Ring*,

pp. 504–505; 'I felt at this stage of the war . . .': Alanbrooke, *War Diaries*, 25 February 1944, pp. 525–526; 'his dislike for Curtin . . .': p. 525.

482. 'put a stop for the time being . . .': Churchill, *Closing the Ring*, p. 508.

482. 'If I have to go . . .': Curtin to Shedden, in Horner, *Defence Supremo*, p. 189; 'It seems like a dream . . .': Day, *Curtin*, p. 532.

483. Curtin made no request . . . for Curtin in Washington, see Day, *Curtin*, pp. 537–58 ff and Horner, *Defence Supremo*, p. 243 ff.

483. 'Roosevelt is quite unscrupulous . . .': Note of Conversation, Curtin, MacArthur, Shedden, 17 March 1944, *DAFP*, Vol. VII, Document No. 82 (p. 175)

483. 'I speak for seven million Britishers . . .': Day, *Curtin*, p. 540.

483. 'Let us go out . . .': Day, *Curtin*, p. 542.

484. 'I don't care to sit in an armchair . . .': Horner, *Defence Supremo*, p. 197.

484. 'keep me on the rails . . .': Horner, *Defence Supremo*, p. 196.

484. 'Curtin did not spare . . .': Mackenzie King on Curtin, Horner, *Defence Supremo*, p. 196.

485. This . . . 'middle strategy' . . .: Churchill, *Closing the Ring*, pp.512–513; 'entirely in MacArthur's pocket . . .': Alanbrooke, *War Diaries*, 26 May 1944, p. 550; 'I think we have at last . . .': Alanbrooke, *War Diaries*, 24 May 1944, p. 550.

486. 'so hurt . . .': Hankey quoted in Horner, *Defence Supremo*, p. 201.

486. 'prevented at the last minute . . .': Churchill to Curtin, 20 May 1944, *DAFP*, Vol. VII, Document No. 160.

487. 'Gentlemen, I am hardening . . .': Churchill, *Closing the Ring*, p. 542–543.

487. 'trustee for the British way . . .': Curtin's speech, Day, *Curtin*, pp. 542–543.

488. 'With all our diversities . . .': Ross, *John Curtin – A Biography*, Macmillan, Australia, 1977, p. 359.

488. 'contrary to imperial principles . . .': Churchill-Curtin exchange, Horner, *Defence Supremo*, p. 199.

Chapter 31: 'Recovering our lost property'
Page

489. 'How, when and where . . .': Churchill, *Triumph and Tragedy*, p. 129.

489. 'For nearly three years . . .': Churchill, *Triumph and Tragedy*, p. 129.

490. 'The British flag will fly . . .': Lloyd and Hall, *Backroom Briefings*, 3 July 1944, pp. 208–210.
490. 'I am deeply concerned . . .': Curtin to Churchill, 12 August 1944, *DAFP*, Vol. VII, Document No. 248.
490. 'Without wishing to appear importunate . . .': Curtin to Churchill, 4 July 1944, *DAFP*, Vol. VII, Document No. 212.
491. 'it would be a great thing . . .': MacArthur to Cross quoted in Horner, *High Command*, pp. 339–340.
492. MacArthur in 'total disagreement': MacArthur with Roosevelt, MacArthur, *Reminiscences*, pp. 196–199; 'King claimed the Pacific as the rightful domain': *Reminiscences*, p. 183.
492. 'General MacArthur has told me . . .': Curtin to Roosevelt, MacArthur, *Reminiscences*, p. 185.
493. 'What chance do you think Dewey has?': Perret, *Old Soldiers Never Die*, pp. 406–407.
493. 'I asked for a definite undertaking . . .': See Churchill, *Triumph and Tragedy*, pp. 134–137, where he details his difficulties in overcoming American reluctance over British participation in the Pacific.
494. 'a blaze of friendship and unity': Churchill to Curtin, 18 September 1944, *DAFP*, Vol. VII, Document No. 288; 'gradually coming round to a sane strategy . . .': Alanbrooke, *War Diaries*, 12 September 1944, p. 591.
494. Churchill's 'complete account . . .': Lloyd and Hall, *Backroom Briefings*, 20 September 1944, p. 230.
495. 'The problem for Australia . . .': Jeffrey Grey, *A Military History of Australia*, Cambridge University Press, 1990, p. 182.
496. 'the naughty document . . .': Churchill, *Triumph and Tragedy*, p. 198; 'Conference went well . . .': Alanbrooke, *War Diaries*, 20 October 1944, pp. 611–2.
496. 'I have returned . . .': MacArthur, *Reminiscences*, p. 218.
496. 'unknown to the harassed European world': Churchill, *Triumph and Tragedy*, p. 153.
497. 'We are very glad to know . . .': Kimball, *Complete Correspondence*, Vol. III, C-813, p. 376.
497. 'we would have two divisions . . .': Curtin at Advisory War Council, Horner, *High Command*, p. 345; 'to capture British Borneo': Horner, *High Command*, p. 346.
497. 'It is difficult to know . . .': Horner, *High Command*, pp. 348–349.
498. 'The eagle should permit . . .': Churchill quoted in Christopher Waters, *The Empire Fractures: Anglo–Australian Conflict in the 1940s*, Australian Scholarly Publishing, Melbourne, 1995, p. 31;

'It is clearly intolerable . . .': Bruce to Curtin, 26 January 1945, *DAFP*, Vol. VIII, Document No. 16; Curtin's reply, *DAFP*, Vol. VIII, Note at p. 25.

499. 'Nations, comrades in arms . . .': Churchill quoted in Gilbert, *Road to Victory*, pp. 1194–1195.

499. 'It is not too much to ask . . .': Churchill quoted in Gilbert, *Road to Victory*, pp. 1187–1188.

500. 'A small lion . . .': Churchill quoted in Gilbert, *Road to Victory*, p. 1233; 'A speedy termination of the Japanese war . . .': Churchill quoted in David Reynolds, *Summits – Six Meetings that Shaped the Twentieth Century*, Allen Lane, London, 2007, p. 119.

500. 'more suffering than ever before . . .': Churchill quoted in Gilbert, *Road to Victory*, p. 1182.

501. 'a great intellectual *tour de force*': FW Eggleton to Bruce, 9 July 1945, *DAFP*, Vol. VIII, Document No. 130.

502. 'In all our long history . . .': Churchill, 8 May 1945, see Gilbert, *Road to Victory*, pp. 1344–1349; 'today we celebrate the final defeat': Churchill to Curtin, 8 May 1945, *DAFP*, Vol. VIII, Document No. 85.

503. 'I say to the country . . .': Curtin, House of Representatives, 28 February 1945, Ross, *Curtin*, p. 376.

503. 'I'm not fit . . .': Curtin quoted in Day, *Curtin*, p. 568; 'I'm ready': Day, *Curtin*, p. 575.

504. 'When I stand at the gates of Manila': MacArthur, *Reminiscences*, p. 160.

504. 'I'm sure you will agree . . .': Churchill to Curtin, 4 July 1945, *DAFP*, Vol. VIII, Document No. 126.

505. 'The light will shine . . .': Gilbert, *Never Despair*, p. 27.

505. 'I woke suddenly . . .': Churchill, *Triumph and Tragedy*, p. 583.

506. 'The alternative for Japan . . .': For Potsdam Declaration, see Herbert Bix, *Hirohito and the Making of Modern Japan*, Harper-Collins, New York, p. 500 ff.

506. 'Churchill has fallen . . .': See Bix, *Hirohito*, p. 501.

506. 'The historic fact remains . . .': Churchill, *Triumph and Tragedy*, p. 553.

507. Japan could not continue: See Gerhard L Weinberg, *A World at Arms*, p. 871 ff.

Chapter 32: 'In command of history'
Page

509. 'Recent political events . . .': *Commonwealth Parliamentary Debates* (House of Representatives), 29 August 1945, pp. 4960–4961.

511. 'They would have killed you . . .': Churchill to George VI, 22 November 1948, Gilbert, *Never Despair*, p. 446; 'I always dreaded': p. 447.

511. Chifley's speeches between 1946 and 1949: See JB Chifley, *Things Worth Fighting For*, edited by AW Stargardt, Melbourne University Press, Melbourne, 1952, pp. 19, 23, 26.

512. 'Iron Curtain' speech: Gilbert, *Never Despair*, pp. 181–206; Stalin's response: p. 209.

517. 'with grief, the clattering down . . .': Churchill on India, Gilbert, *Never Despair*, pp. 301–302.

517. 'The only reason I gave support . . .': Gilbert, *Never Despair*, p. 334.

517. 'on a foggy afternoon . . .': Churchill's dream, see Gilbert, *Never Despair*, pp. 364–372.

518. 'the mysterious circle of the British Crown . . .': Quoted in Norman Rose, *Churchill – An Unruly Life*, Simon & Schuster, London, 1994, p. 330.

519. 'To save you from having . . .': Menzies to Churchill, Menzies, *Afternoon Light*, p. 91.

519. 'Churchill's account of the story . . .': Reynolds, *In Command of History*, p. 257; 'discreet persistence': p. 258. For Reynolds' comprehensive analysis, see *In Command of History*, pp. 256–259 and pp. 294–300.

521. 'Can we wonder . . .': Attlee amendment, see Gilbert, *Never Despair*, p. 494.

521. 'a greater war leader than Lloyd George . . .': Evatt's reply, in Reynolds, *In Command of History*, p. 355.

523. 'kept its chagrin . . .': Peter Edwards, *Crises and Commitments*, Allen & Unwin and Australian War Memorial, Sydney and Canberra, 1992, p. 109.

524. 'Winston has sent . . .': Casey's diary, 8 October 1952, Casey, *Australian Foreign Minister – The Diaries of R. G. Casey 1951–60*, Collins, London, 1972, p. 90.

525. 'I am anxious to find . . .': Minutes of meeting, Churchill, Menzies, Holland, 12 December 1952, National Archives of Australia 201788, Series A1209.

526. 'This story is a monstrous invention . . .': Martin, *Menzies*, Vol. II, p. 234 (Note).

526. 'Almost at the end...': Casey, 6 October 1953, *Australian Foreign Minister*, p. 110.

527. Churchill's special insight: Churchill's speeches quoted in Larres, *Churchill's Cold War*, pp. 222–223.

528. 'To some extent he was proposing...': Larres, *Churchill's Cold War*, p. 309.

528. 'I feel like an aeroplane...': Gilbert, *Never Despair*, p. 958; 'I assign no limits...': p. 976.

529. 'Merely try to imagine...': Churchill quoted in Gilbert, *Never Despair*, pp. 1036–1037; 'Fancy ending...': Moran, *Diaries*, 28 July 1954, p. 582.

530. 'If I never speak again...': Moran, *Diaries*, 30 July 1954, p. 585.

530. 'I don't believe Anthony...': Colville, *Fringes of Power*, p. 708; 'she seemed almost relieved...': Gilbert, *Never Despair*, p. 1124; 'a cold hatred of Eden': Colville, p. 706.

531. 'I have tried very hard...': Churchill quoted in Larres, *Churchill's Cold War*, p. 370.

532. 'Menzies asked Nasser...': Heikal's account quoted in Hazlehurst, *Menzies Observed*, pp. 348–351.

533. 'I would never have dared...': Jenkins, *Churchill*, p. 902. The best recent account is Alesandr Fursenko and Timothy Naftali, *Khrushchev's Cold War*, WW Norton and Company, New York, 2006. Drawing on Soviet archives, the authors provide remarkable insights into the complex connection between the 'twin crises' of Suez and Hungary, concluding that their combined result 'served to give Khrushchev an inflated sense of what he could do abroad'.

534. 'My dear Winston...': Menzies and Macmillan, Stuart Ward, *Australia and the British Embrace*, Melbourne University Press, Melbourne, 2001, pp. 146–147.

534. 'WSC's opinion of Menzies...': For Menzies and Churchill together, see Anthony Montague Browne, *Long Sunset*, Cassell, London, 1995, p. 168 ff.

535. 'looking old and weary...': Hasluck, *Diplomatic Witness*, p. 175.

536. 'I have a wonderful idea...': Martin Gilbert, *In Search of Churchill*, p. 216.

537. 'The appeal's success...': John Ramsden, *Man of the Century—Winston Churchill and his Legend Since 1945*, HarperCollins, London, 2002, p. 523.

Select bibliography

The Churchill literature is immense – not to mention the War. This selection lists books quoted or drawn upon directly in the text. Any book on Churchill must rest on his own writings and the monumental work of Sir Martin Gilbert. I am particularly indebted to the pioneering work of Dr David Day, and among Australian war historians, Dr David Horner. However, the indispensable core of the second half of this book is provided by the volumes of *Documents on Australian Foreign Policy*, edited by WJ Hudson and others, and published by the Australian Department of Foreign Affairs and Trade in the 1980s.

Addison, Paul, *Churchill – The Unexpected Hero*, Oxford University Press, Oxford, 2005.

Alanbrooke, Lord, *War Diaries 1939–1945* (edited by Alex Danchev and Daniel Todman), Orion Books, London, 2002.

Andrews, EM, *Isolationalism and Appeasement in Australia – Reaction to the European Crises 1935–1939*, Australian National University Press, Canberra, 1970.

Barnett, Corelli, *The Desert Generals*, George Allen & Unwin, London, 1960; Phoenix Paperback, Cassell, London, 1999.

Bean, CEW, *Official History of Australia in the War of 1914–1918*, Vols. I and II, *The Story of Anzac*, Angus & Robertson, Sydney, 1924.

Anzac to Amiens, Angus & Robertson, Sydney, 1944.

Beaverbrook, Lord, *Decline and Fall of Lloyd George*, Collins, London, 1963.

Best, Geoffrey, *Churchill and War*, Hambledon ad Continuum, London, 2005.

——*Churchill – A Study in Greatness*, Hambledon, London, 2001.

Bix, Herbert, *Hirohito and the Making of Modern Japan*, Harper-Collins, New York, 2000.

Blake, Robert and W Roger Louis (eds.), *Churchill – A Major New Assessment of his Life in Peace and War*, Oxford University Press, 1993.

Bonham Carter, Violet, *Winston Churchill as I Knew Him*, Eyre & Spottiswood, London, 1965.

Brenchley, Fred and Elizabeth, *Myth-maker – Ellis Ashmead Bartlett, the Englishman Who Sparked Australia's Gallipoli Legend*, John Wiley and Sons, Australia, 2005.

Broadbent, Harvey, *Gallipoli – The Fatal Shore*, Viking, Australia, 2004.

Brock, Michael and Eleanor (eds.), *H. H. Asquith's Letters to Venetia Stanley*, Oxford University Press, 1982. Material reproduced by permission of Oxford University Press.

Brune, Peter, *Ralph Honner – Kokoda Hero*, Allen & Unwin, Sydney, 2007.

Bryant, Arthur, *The Turn of the Tide – based on the War Diaries of Field Marshal Viscount Alanbrooke*, Collins, London, 1957.

Carlyon, Les, *Gallipoli*, Pan Macmillan, Australia, 2001.

Casey, Richard Gardiner, *Personal Experience 1939–46*, Constable, London, 1962.

——*Australian Foreign Minister – The Diaries of R.G. Casey 1951–60*, Collins, London, 1972.

Churchill, Randolph, *Winston S. Churchill – Youth 1874–1900*, (Vol. I of the Official Biography), Heinemann, London, 1966.

——*Winston S. Churchill – Young Statesman 1901–1914*, (Vol. II), Heinemann, London, 1967.

Churchill, Winston, *The Boer War* (London to Ladysmith via Pretoria; Ian Hamilton's March), Pimlico, London, 2002 (first published 1900).

——*My African Journey*, London, 1908.

——*The World Crisis 1911–1914*, Australasian Publishing Company, Sydney and Melbourne, 1923.

——*The World Crisis 1915*, Australasian Publishing Company, Sydney and Melbourne, 1923.

——*The Aftermath*, Macmillan, London, 1941 (first published 1929).

Churchill, Winston, *The Second World War* in six volumes, first published by Cassell, London, between 1948 and 1954:
Vol I *The Gathering Storm* (1948)
Vol II *Their Finest Hour* (1949)
Vol III *The Grand Alliance* (1950)
Vol IV *The Hinge of Fate* (1951)
Vol V *Closing the Ring* (1952)
Vol VI *Triumph and Tragedy* (1954).
Clark, Alan, *The Fall of Crete*, Cassell, London, 1962.
Clarke, Peter, *The Last Thousand Days of the British Empire*, Allen Lane, London, 2007.
Coates, John, *Bravery Above Blunder – The 9th Division in New Guinea*, Oxford University Press, Australia, 1999.
Coates, Tim (ed.), *The Dardanelles Commission*, The Stationery Office, London, 2001.
Colville, John, *Fringes of Power – 10 Downing Street Diaries 1939-1955*, Hodder & Stoughton, London, 1985.
Coombes, David, *Morshead – Hero of Tobruk and El Alamein*, Oxford University Press, Australia, 2001 (The Australian Army History Series).
Costello, John, *The Pacific War*, Perennial, New York, 2002.
Coulthard-Clark, Chris, *Where Australians Fought: The Encyclopaedia of Australia's Battles*, Allen & Unwin, Sydney, 1998.
Crowley, Frank, *A Documentary History of Australia*, Vol. 3, *Colonial Australia 1875–1900*, Thomas Nelson, Australia, 1973.
——Vol. 4, *Modern Australia – 1901–1939*, Nelson, 1973.
——Vol. 5, *Modern Australia – 1939–1970*, Nelson, 1973.
Day, David, *Menzies and Churchill at War*, Angus & Robertson, Sydney, 1986.
——*The Great Betrayal – Britain, Australia and the Onset of the Pacific War 1939–42*, WW Norton & Company, New York, 1989.
——*Reluctant Nation: Australia and the Allied Defeat of Japan 1942–45*, Oxford University Press, Melbourne, 1992.
——*John Curtin – A Life*, HarperCollins, Australia, 1999.
——*Chifley*, HarperCollins, Australia, 2001.
——*The Politics of War – Australia at War 1939–45: From Churchill to MacArthur*, HarperCollins, Australia, 2003.
Dilks, David (ed.), *The Diaries of Sir Alexander Cadogan 1938–1945*, CP Putnam and Sons, New York, 1972.
Dixon, Norman, *On the Psychology of Military Incompetence*, Pimlico, London, 1994.

Edwards, Peter (with Gregory Pemberton), *Crises and Commitments – The Politics and Diplomacy of Australia's Involvement in South-East Asian Conflicts 1948–1965*, Allen & Unwin, for the Australian War Memorial, Sydney & Canberra, 1992.

Evatt, Herbert Vere, *Australian Labor Leader*, Angus & Robertson, Sydney, 1940.

Ewer, Peter, *Forgotten Anzacs – The Campaign in Greece, 1941*, Scribe, Melbourne, 2008.

Fadden, Arthur, *They Call Me Artie*, Jacaranda Press, Brisbane, 1969.

Faulkner, John and Macintyre, Stuart (eds.), *True Believers – The Story of the Federal Parliamentary Labor Party*, Allen & Unwin, Sydney, 2001.

Fenby, Jonathan, *Alliance – The Inside Story of How Roosevelt, Stalin and Churchill Won One War and Began Another*, Simon & Schuster, London, 2006.

Ferguson, Niall, *Empire – How Britain Made the Modern World*, Penguin, London, 2004.

——*The War of the World – History's Age of Hatred*, Penguin, London, 2007.

Field, LM, *The Forgotten War – Australian Involvement in the South African Conflict of 1899–1902*, Melbourne University Press, 1979.

Fitzhardinge, LF, *William Morris Hughes – A Political Biography*, in two volumes, Angus & Robertson, Sydney, 1979.

Fitzsimons, Peter, *Tobruk*, HarperCollins, Australia, 2006.

Foster, Simon, *Hit the Beach – Landings under Fire*, Rigel, London, 2004.

Frank, Richard, B, *MacArthur*, Palgrave Macmillan, New York, 2007.

French, Patrick, *Liberty or Death – India's Journey to Independence and Division*, HarperCollins, London, 1997.

Freudenberg, Graham, *Cause for Power – The Official History of the New South Wales Labor Party*, Pluto Press, Sydney, 1991.

Fromkin, David, *A Peace to End All Peace – The Fall of the Ottoman Empire and the Creation of the Middle East*, Andre Deutsch, London, 1989.

Gilbert, Martin, *Winston S. Churchill 1914–1916*, (Vol. III of the Official Biography), Heinemann, London, 1971.

——*Winston S. Churchill 1917–1922* (Vol. IV), Heinemann, London, 1975.

——*Winston S. Churchill 1922–1939* (Vol. V), Heinemann, London, 1976.

——*Finest Hour – Winston S. Churchill 1939–1941*, (Vol. VI), Heinemann, London, 1983.

——*Road to Victory – Winston S. Churchill 1941–1945*, (Vol. VII), Heinemann, London, 1986.

——*Never Despair – Winston S. Churchill 1945–1965*, (Vol. VIII), Heinemann London, 1988.

——*In Search of Churchill*, HarperCollins, London, 1994.

——*History of the 20th Century*, Vol. I, 1900–1933, HarperCollins, London, 1997.

——*The Second World War*, Phoenix Press, London, 2000.

——*Churchill and the Jews*, Simon & Schuster, London, 2007.

Green, Frank, *Servant of the House*, Heinemann, Melbourne, 1969.

Greenwood, Gordon and Grimshaw, Charles (eds.), *Documents on Australian International Affairs 1901–1918*, Thomas Nelson Australia for the Australian Institute of International Affairs, 1977.

Grey, Jeffrey, *A Military History of Australia*, Cambridge University Press, 1990.

——*The Australian Army*, the Australian Centenary History of Defence, Oxford University Press, 2001.

Grigg, John, *Lloyd George – From Peace to War 1912–1916*, Harper-Collins, London, 1997.

Groom, Winton, *1942 – The Year That Tried Men's Souls*, Grove Press, New York, 2005.

Ham, Paul, *Kokoda*, HarperCollins, Australia, 2004.

Harvey, Robert, *American Shogun – MacArthur, Hirohito and the American Duel with Japan*, John Murray, London, 2006.

Hasluck, Paul, *The Government and the People 1939–1941*, Vol. I, Official War History, Australian War Memorial, Canberra, 1952.

——*The Government and the People 1941–1945*, Vol. II, 1970.

——*Diplomatic Witness*, Melbourne University Press, 1980.

Hazlehurst, Cameron, *Menzies Observed*, George Allen & Unwin, Sydney, 1979.

Hetherington, John, *Blamey*, FW Cheshire, Melbourne, 1954.

Hitchens, Christopher, *Blood, Class and Nostalgia – Anglo-American Ironies*, Chatto & Windus, London, 1990.

Horner, David, *Crisis of Command – Australian Generalship and the Japanese Threat 1941–1943*, Australian National University Press, Canberra, 1978.

——*High Command – Australia and Allied Strategy 1939–45*, Australian War Memorial, Canberra, 1982.

——*Blamey – The Commander-in-Chief*, Allen & Unwin, Sydney, 1998.

——*Defence Supremo – Sir Frederick Shedden and the Making of Australian Defence Policy*, Allen & Unwin, Sydney, 2000.

Horner, David (ed.), *The Commanders – Australian Military Leadership in the 20th Century*, Allen & Unwin, Australia, 1984.

Hudson, WJ, *Casey*, Oxford University Press, Melbourne, 1986.

Hudson, WJ and North, June (eds.), *My Dear P.M. – R. G. Casey's Letters to S. M. Bruce 1924–1929*, Australian Government Publishing Service, Canberra, 1980.

Hudson, WJ and May, Wendy (eds.), *Letters From a 'Secret Service Agent' – F.L. McDougall to S.M. Bruce 1924–1929*, Australian Department of Foreign Affairs, Canberra, 1986.

Hudson, WJ and Stokes, HJW (eds.), *Documents on Australian Foreign Policy*, Vol. IV (July 1940–June 1941), Department of Foreign Affairs and Trade, Canberra, 1980.

——*Documents on Australian Foreign Policy*, Vol. V (July 1941–June 1942), Department of Foreign Affairs and Trade, Canberra, 1982.

——*Documents on Australian Foreign Policy*, Vol. VI (July 1942–December 1943), Department of Foreign Affairs and Trade, Canberra, 1983.

Hudson, WJ (ed.), *Documents on Australian Foreign Policy*, Vol. VII (1944), Department of Foreign Affairs and Trade, Canberra, 1988.

Hudson, WJ and Way, W (eds.), *Documents on Australian Foreign Policy*, Vol. VIII (1945), Department of Foreign Affairs and Trade, Canberra, 1989.

Hughes, WM, *The Splendid Adventure*, Ernest Benn, London, 1929.

Hyams, Ronald, *Elgin and Churchill at the Colonial Office*, Pan Macmillan, London, 1968. Copyright © Ronald Hyams, 1968.

Ismay, Lord, *The Memoirs of Lord Ismay*, Heinemann, London, 1960.

James, Robert Rhodes, *Churchill – A Study in Failure 1900–1939*, Weidenfeld & Nicolson, London, 1970.

——*Gallipoli* (Australian edition), Angus & Robertson, Sydney, 1965.

Jannen, William, *The Lions of July – Prelude to War 1914*, Presidio Press, California, 1997.

Jenkins, The Rt Hon Lord, *Churchill*, Pan Macmillan, London, 2001. Copyright © The Rt Hon Lord Jenkins, 2001.

Johnston, Mark and Stanley, Peter, *Alamein – The Australian Story*, Oxford University Press, Australia, 2006.

Johnston, Mark, *The Magnificent 9th*, Allen & Unwin, Sydney, 2002.

Jose, Arthur W (ed.), *The Australian Encyclopaedia*, Angus & Robertson, Sydney, 1927.

——*Official History of Australia in the War of 1914–18*, Vol. IV, *The Royal Australian Navy*, Angus & Robertson, Sydney, 1928.

Keegan, John (ed.), *Churchill's Generals*, Cassell, London, 1991.

Kershaw, Ian, *The Hitler Myth – Image and Reality in the Third Reich*, Oxford University Press, 2001.

——*Fateful Choices – Ten Decisions that Changed the World*, Allen Lane, London, 2007.

Kimball, Warren F (ed.), *Churchill & Roosevelt – The Complete Correspondence*; Vol. I, *Alliance Emerging*, Vol. II, *Alliance Forged*, Vol. III, *Alliance Declining*, Collins, London, 1984.

Kinross, Lord, *Ataturk – The Rebirth of a Nation*, Weidenfeld & Nicolson, London, 1964.

Lamb, Richard, *Churchill as War Leader – Right or Wrong*, Bloomsbury Publishing, London, 1993.

La Nauze, JA, *Alfred Deakin – A Biography* (in two volumes), Melbourne University Press, 1965.

Larres, Klaus, *Churchill's Cold War – The Politics of Diplomacy*, Yale University Press, New Haven and London, 2002.

Lascelles, Alan, *King's Counsellor – Abdication and War; The Diaries of Sir Alan Lascelles*, edited by Duff Hart-Davis, Weidenfeld & Nicolson, London, 2006.

Lloyd, Clem and Hall, Richard (eds.), *Backroom Briefings – John Curtin's War,* (based on notes by Frederick T. Smith), National Library of Australia, Canberra, 1997.

Lloyd George, David, *War Memoirs*, in two volumes, Odhams Press, London, 1933.

Lodge, Brett, *Lavarack: Rival General*, Australian Military Series, Allen & Unwin, Sydney, 1998.

Long, Gavin, *To Benghazi*, Vol. I, Official War History, Australian War Memorial, Canberra, 1952.

——*Greece, Crete and Syria*, Australian War Memorial, Canberra, 1953.

——*The Six Years War – Australia in the 1939–45 War*, Australian War Memorial, Canberra 1973.

Lowe, David, *Menzies and the 'Great World Struggle' – Australia's Cold War 1948–1954*, UNSW Press, Sydney, 1999.

Lukacs, John, *The Hitler of History* , Phoenix Press, London, 2002.

——*Five Days in London – May 1940*, Yale University Press, New Haven, 1999.

MacArthur, General Douglas, *Reminiscences*, McGraw Hill, New York, 1964.

McCarthy, Dudley, *South-West Pacific – First Year*, Vol. V, Official War History, Australian War Memorial, Canberra, 1959.

Macdougall, AK (ed.), *War Letters of General Monash*, Duffy & Snellgrove, Sydney, 2002.

Mansell, Philip, *Constantinople – City of the World's Desire 1453–1924*, Penguin, London, 1997.

Marston, Daniel (ed.), *The Pacific War Companion – From Pearl Harbor to Hiroshima*, Osprey Publishing, Oxford, 2005.

Martin, AW, *Robert Menzies – A Life*, Volume 1, 1894–1943; Volume 2, 1944–1978; Melbourne University Press, 1993 and 1999.

Martin, AW and Hardy, Patsy (eds.), *Dark and Hurrying Days – Menzies' 1941 Diary*, National Library of Australia, Canberra, 1993.

Massie, Robert, K, *Dreadnought*, Ballantine Books, London, 1991.

Maughan, Barton, *Tobruk and El Alamein*, Vol. III, Official War History, Australian War Memorial, Canberra, 1966.

Menzies, Sir Robert, *Afternoon Light – Some Memoirs of Men and Events*, Cassell, Australia, 1967.

——*Dark and Hurrying Days – Menzies' 1941 Diary* – see Martin.

Monash, Sir John, *The Australian Victories in France in 1918*, Hutchinson, London, 1920.

Montague Browne, Anthony, *Long Sunset*, Cassell, London, 1995.

Moorehead, Alan, *African Trilogy*, Hamish Hamilton, London, 1944; republished, Text Publishing, Melbourne, 1997.

Moran, Lord (Sir Charles Wilson), *Winston Churchill – The Struggle for Survival*, Heron Books, London, 1966.

Neidpath, James, *The Singapore Naval Base and the Defence of Britain's Eastern Empire 1919–1941*, Clarendon Press, Oxford, 1981. Material reproduced by permission of Oxford University Press.

Nicolson, Harold, *The Harold Nicolson Diaries 1907–1964*, Phoenix edition, London, 2005.

O'Neill, Robert, *Australia in the Korean War 1950–53*, Vol. I: *Strategy and Diplomacy*, Australian War Memorial, Canberra, 1981.

Page, Sir Earle, *Truant Surgeon – The Inside Story of Forty Years of Australian Political Life*, Angus & Robertson, Sydney, 1963.

Pakenham, Thomas, *The Boer War*, Weidenfeld & Nicolson, UK, 1979.

Parker, RAC, *Churchill and Appeasement*, Macmillan, London, 2000.

Paterson, Andrew Barton, 'Banjo', *Complete Poems*, A & R Classics, Sydney, 2001.

——*From the Front – Despatches from the Boer War*, Pan Macmillan, Sydney, 2000.

——*Happy Despatches*, Angus & Robertson, Sydney, 1935.

Perret, Geoffrey, *Old Soldiers Never Die – The Life of Douglas MacArthur*, Andre Deutsch, London, 1996.

Pincus, Oscar, *The War Aims and Strategies of Adolf Hitler*, MacFarland and Company, North Carolina and London, 2000.

Pogue, Forrest C, *George C. Marshall – Ordeal and Hope 1939–42*, Macgibbon and Kee, London, 1966.

Porch, Douglas, *Hitler's Mediterranean Gamble*, Cassell, London, 2004.

Potts, E Daniel and Annette, *Yanks Down Under 1941–45 – The American Impact on Australia*, Oxford University Press, Melbourne, 1985.

Ramsden, John, *Winston Churchill – Man of the Century – and his Legend since 1945*, HarperCollins, London, 2002.

Reynolds, David, *In Command of History – Churchill Fighting and Writing the Second World War*, Allen Lane, London, 2004. Copyright © David Reynolds, 2004. Reproduced by permission of Penguin Books Ltd.

——*Summits – Six Meetings that Shaped the Twentieth Century*, Allen Lane, London, 2007.

Roberts, Andrew, *Hitler and Churchill – Secrets of Leadership*, Phoenix, London, 2004.

Robertson, John, *Anzac and Empire*, Hamlyn Australia, 1990.

——*Australia at War 1939–1945*, Heinemann, Melbourne, 1981.

Rose, Norman, *Churchill – An Unruly Life*, Simon & Schuster, London, 1994.

Roskill, SW, *The Navy at War 1939–1945*, Collins, London, 1960.

Ross, Lloyd, *John Curtin – A Biography*, Macmillan, Australia, 1977.

Schofield, Victoria, *Wavell: Soldier and Statesman*, John Murray, London, 2006.

Schom, Alan, *The Eagle and the Rising Sun*, WW Norton, NY, 2004.

Semmler, Clement (ed.), *The War Diaries of Kenneth Slessor*, University of Queensland Press, 1985.

Serle, Geoffrey, *Monash*, Melbourne University Press, 1982.

Slessor, Kenneth – see Semmler.

Smith, Colin, *Singapore Burning – Heroism and Surrender in World War II*, Penguin, London, 2006.

Shelton, Douglas, *Life and Letters of Sir Wilfred Laurier*, Oxford University Press, London, 1922.

Spector, Ronald H, *Eagle Against the Sun – The American War with Japan*, Random House, New York, 1985.

Spender, Percy, *Politics and a Man*, Collins, Sydney, 1972.

Stanley, Peter, *Quinn's Post – Anzac, Gallipoli*, Allen & Unwin, Sydney, 2005.

Stargardt, AW (ed.), *Things Worth Fighting For: Speeches of J.B. Chifley*, Melbourne University Press, 1952.

Stephens, Alan, *The Royal Australian Air Force – A History*, Oxford University Press, Melbourne, 2001.

Stevens, David (ed.), *The Royal Australian Navy in World War II*, Allen & Unwin, Sydney, 2005.

Sublet, Frank, *Kokoda to the Sea – A History of the 1942 Campaign in Papua*, Slouch Hat Publishing, Melbourne, 2000.

Swinson, Arthur, *Defeat in Malaya: The Fall of Singapore*, Purnell, London 1970.

Taylor, AJP, *English History 1914–1945*, Oxford University Press, Oxford, 1965.

Thompson, Peter, *The Battle for Singapore*, Portrait Press, London, 2005.

Thorne, Christopher, *Allies of a Kind – The United States, Britain and the War Against Japan*, Hamish Hamilton, London, 1978.

Tuchman, Barbara, *Stillwell and the American Experience 1911–1945*, Macmillan, New York, 1970.

Ward, Stuart, *Australia and the British Embrace – The Demise of the Imperial Ideal*, Melbourne University Press, 2001.

Waters, Christopher, *The Empire Fractures – Anglo-Australian Conflict in the 1940s*, Australian Scholarly Publishing, Melbourne, 1995.

Watt, Alan, *Australian Diplomat – The Memoirs of Sir Alan Watt*, Angus and Robertson, Sydney, 1972.

Weinberg, Gerhard L, *A World at Arms – A Global History of World War II,* Cambridge University Press, New York, 1994.

Weintraub, Stanley, *Fifteen Stars – Eisenhower, MacArthur, Marshall*, Free Press, New York, 2007.

Weller, Patrick (ed.), *Caucus Minutes 1901–1949*, Volume 3, 1932–1949, Melbourne University Press, 1975.

Whitlam, Gough, *The Whitlam Government 1972–1975*, Penguin Books Australia, 1985.

Whyte, W Farmer, *William Morris Hughes – His Life and Times*, Angus and Robertson, Sydney, 1957.

Wigmore, Lionel, *The Japanese Thrust*, Vol. IV, Official War History, Australian War Memorial, Canberra, 1957.

Williams, John, *Anzacs, the Media and the Great War*, UNSW Press, Sydney, 1999.

Wilmot, Chester, *Tobruk 1941*, Penguin Books, Australia, 2007.

Wilson, AN, *After the Victorians 1901–1953*, Hutchinson, London, 2005.

Wurth, Bob, *Saving Australia – Curtin's Secret Peace with Japan*, Lothian Books, Melbourne, 2006.

Younger, RM, *Keith Murdoch – Founder of a Media Empire*, Harper-Collins, Australia, 2003.

Index